The British Army and the First World War

This is a major new history of the British Army during the Great War written by three leading military historians. Ian Beckett, Timothy Bowman and Mark Connelly survey operations on the Western Front and throughout the rest of the world as well as the army's social history, pre-war and wartime planning and strategy, maintenance of discipline and morale and the lasting legacy of the First World War on the army's development. They assess the strengths and weaknesses of the army between 1914 and 1918, engaging with key debates around the adequacy of British generalship and whether or not there was a significant 'learning curve' in terms of the development of operational art during the course of the war. Their findings show how, despite limitations of initiative and innovation among the high command, the British Army did succeed in developing the effective combined arms warfare necessary for victory in 1918.

Ian Beckett retired as Professor of Military History at the University of Kent in 2015 and is now Honorary Professor there. He is a past Chairman of the Army Records Society and is secretary of the Buckinghamshire Military Museum Trust.

Timothy Bowman is Senior Lecturer in Modern British Military History at the University of Kent. He is Secretary of the Army Records Society.

Mark Connelly is Professor of Modern British History at the University of Kent, where he runs the interdisciplinary master's programme in First World War studies.

The British Army and the First World War

Ian Beckett
University of Kent, Canterbury

Timothy Bowman
University of Kent, Canterbury

Mark Connelly
University of Kent, Canterbury

CAMBRIDGE
UNIVERSITY PRESS

University Printing House, Cambridge CB2 8BS, United Kingdom

Cambridge University Press is part of the University of Cambridge.

It furthers the University's mission by disseminating knowledge in the pursuit of education, learning and research at the highest international levels of excellence.

www.cambridge.org
Information on this title: www.cambridge.org/9781107005778

First published 2017

Printed in the United Kingdom by Clays, St Ives plc

A catalogue record for this publication is available from the British Library.

Library of Congress Cataloging-in-Publication Data
Beckett, I. F. W. (Ian Frederick William), author. | Bowman, Timothy, author. | Connelly, Mark, author.
The British Army and the First World War / Ian Beckett, University of Kent, Canterbury; Timothy Bowman, University of Kent, Canterbury; Mark Connelly, University of Kent, Canterbury.
New York : Cambridge University Press, 2017. | Series: Armies of the great war | Includes bibliographical references and index.
LCCN 2016047809 | ISBN 9781107005778 (hardback)
LCSH: Great Britain. Army. British Expeditionary Force – History – World War, 1914–1918 – Historiography. | Great Britain. Army – History – World War, 1914–1918 – Historiography. | World War, 1914–1918 – Historiography.
LCC D546 .B43 2017 | DDC 940.4/1241–dc23
LC record available at https://lccn.loc.gov/2016047809

ISBN 978-1-107-00577-8 Hardback
ISBN 978-0-521-18374-1 Paperback

Contents

Figures

Maps

Introduction

Studies of the British Army's role in the Great War started long before the Armistice as instant histories were produced of the great battles, but as might be expected, these were driven by largely propagandist aims and so provided little in the way of analytical insight. During the 1920s, the role of the British Expeditionary Force (BEF) was covered in various works but was mostly dominated by the view from the top, which occasionally took the form of overt point-scoring, as was most famously seen in the memoirs of Lord French and David Lloyd George. A significant contribution was made by Basil Liddell Hart. A former officer who had experienced the war on the Western Front, albeit very briefly, he largely condemned the British war effort as unimaginative and ill conceived in his influential 1930 work, *The Real War*.

These works competed against the exhaustive official histories of the war, which provided an overview of the army's global military operations in a project that was not completed until the 1940s. Often condemned as rather dry and anodyne accounts, recently the Official Histories have been rehabilitated by Andrew Green, who has argued that they contain a wealth of critical insights deliberately designed to be accessible to those who study the texts closely.[1] A welter of divisional and regimental histories was also produced providing robust narratives of their subjects. As most served the dual function of celebratory record and memorial, few of these took highly analytical approaches, although the ability of the writers to access ephemeral materials that have long since disappeared from the archive means they retain value and should never be dismissed lightly.

At the other end of the spectrum were the memoirs of individuals and fictionalised accounts based on actual experience. Although these rarely sought to examine the army and its performance, they nonetheless gave a flavour of life at the sharp end and provided important support for

[1] Andrew Green, *Writing the Great War: Sir James Edmonds and the Official Histories, 1915–1948* (London: Routledge, 2004).

Liddell Hart's thesis. During the 1960s, literary scholars and critics helped to solidify a canon from these works, which often tended to obscure the sheer diversity and complexity of the army's demographic, attitude and roles.

The arrival of the fiftieth anniversary cycle in 1964 combined with a less deferential attitude towards class and rank saw the emergence of a different approach which privileged the voices of the ordinary man in the army. Demography assisted this development, for by the 1960s the great players were largely dead, and the only available form of direct testimony came from those who were junior officers or rank and file during the conflict. At the same time, there was also the growing realisation that the recollections of these men had to be captured before it was too late. The BBC's 1964 television series, *The Great War*, then pioneered the large-scale application of oral history techniques to veterans. By the 1970s, these processes had matured and resulted in studies that made a deep impact on the wider interested public, with the works of Martin Middlebrook and Lyn Macdonald being particularly successful. The highly valuable work of the oral history–based studies made obvious the immense diversity of the army's personnel in terms of socio-economic rank, regional background and identity. These added a further insight into the army and society approach that had developed since the 1950s and matured with Arthur Marwick's influential book, *The Deluge: British Society and the First World War* (1965). Using similar research methods and questions, historians such as Ian Beckett and Keith Simpson in their edited collection, *A Nation in Arms: A Social Study of the British Army in the First World War* (1985), and Peter Simkins in his *Kitchener's Army: The Raising of the New Armies, 1914–1916* (1988) analysed the demographic of the army closely and led the way to further examinations of discipline and morale.[2]

From the late 1980s and 1990s, cultural history emerged as a new way of looking at the huge mechanism that was the British Army and took the questions of social historians in a new direction. Although intimately concerned with the internal structures and dynamics of the army and its roles, this approach is largely unconcerned with the issues of overall performance and effectiveness foregrounded by many military historians. Instead, cultural historians have sought to understand how concepts such as masculinity and gender affected the way soldiers viewed their tasks and positions within the army, the wider conflict and post-war

[2] For examples, see Timothy Bowman, *Irish Regiments in the Great War: Discipline and Morale* (Manchester University Press, 2003); and Helen McCartney, *Citizen Soldiers: The Liverpool Territorials in the First World War* (Cambridge University Press, 2005).

identity.[3] Such methodologies have seen studies of ex-servicemen move from investigations of their internal organisation and degree of political activism towards issues such as coping with disability and the extent to which it caused marginalisation within society.[4] A further development stemming from cultural history is the greater attention paid to the cultural construction of technology and its use for military purposes. Popular military history of the British Army has often been fixated on the identification of 'war-winning weapons', with tanks and aircraft often given starring roles. By contrast, academic military history has tended to contextualise weapons development far more closely and is highly suspicious of identifying any particular piece of hardware as the key to success.

In fact, the modern military history of the British Army in the conflict is often a blend of many different approaches and has challenged many of the myths that accumulated around the army partly as a result of the over-emphasis placed on a narrow range of literary works. The development of the contemporary historiography really commenced in the early 1960s *before* the main archival collections of state papers were fully accessible. John Terraine's *Mons: The Retreat to Victory* (1960) remains a very fine study based upon a close comparison of the sources available at the time. Indeed, from this initial study, Terraine went on to become a leading proponent of what can be labelled the 'revisionist school'. Determined to place the experience of the Western Front in context, Terraine's subsequent studies emphasised the imbalance between weaponry, transport and communications technologies experienced during the conflict. By arguing that few armies foresaw the awful potential for stalemate created by these inequalities, Terraine sought to reveal that the performance of the BEF and its high command was by no means as incompetent and unimaginative as was popularly believed, an opinion he expressed strongly in his 1963 work, *Douglas Haig: The Educated Soldier*. In pursuing this thesis, Terraine clashed with Liddell Hart particularly over the scripts for the BBC's monumental twenty-six episode series, *The Great War*. Commissioned to mark the fiftieth anniversary of the conflict's outbreak, *The Great War*'s narrative thrust was driven by the team of Terraine and Correlli Barnett. Although their treatment of the war was indeed a departure from the

[3] For examples, see Joanna Bourke, *Dismembering the Male: Men's Bodies, Britain and the Great War* (London: Reaktion, 1996); Jessica Meyer, *Men of War: Masculinity and the First World War in Britain* (Basingstoke: Palgrave-Macmillan, 2012).

[4] For examples of the two different approaches, see Niall Barr, *The Lion and the Poppy: British Veterans, Politics and Society, 1921–1939* (Westport, CT: Praeger, 2005); J. P. Anderson, *War, Disability and Rehabilitation in Britain: Soul of a Nation* (Manchester University Press, 2011); Fiona Reid, *Broken Men: Shellshock, Treatment and Recovery in Britain 1914–1930* (London: Continuum, 2011).

popular view of the British Army's prosecution of the war, viewers often failed to detect it, and ironically, most came to conclusions very similar to those of Liddell Hart.

Nonetheless, Terraine's influence was pervasive and influenced a whole new generation of popular historians who took a similar line arguing that Haig's insight into the realities of war on the Western Front and his commitment to the protracted attritional central phase of the conflict were vital prerequisites of victory.[5] Since the mid-1960s, there has been a profusion of macro and micro operational and strategic histories dedicated to this core theme. The vast majority of these studies were sympathetic to elements of Terraine's interpretation as they stressed the difficulty of expanding the army's entire infrastructure during the course of a conflict against a well-organised enemy. In effect, these works explored the meaning behind Lord Kitchener's comment, '[W]e must make war as we must and not as we would like.'[6] Others have been less convinced; while historians such as Tim Travers, Robin Prior and Trevor Wilson accepted that the performance of the British Army had to be judged against a whole range of factors, they highlighted weaknesses in the culture of the army and its understandings of modern warfare.[7] Nonetheless, by the mid-1990s, the dominant orthodoxy emphasised the immense improvement made by the British Army during the course of the war, particularly in its conduct of operations on the Western Front, and deemed it the deciding force in 1918. More recently, an element of post-revisionism has set in, questioning the idea of progressive, improving steps towards military effectiveness. Instead, the patchiness of the British Army has been identified, revealing its inconsistencies as a force containing a strange mixture of excellent and indifferent elements, many of which were reflections of its pre-war strengths and weaknesses.[8]

[5] For examples, see Gordon Corrigan, *Mud, Blood and Poppycock: Britain and the First World War* (London: Cassell, 2003); and Charles Messenger, *Call to Arms: The British Army, 1914–1918* (London: Weidenfeld & Nicolson, 2005).

[6] For examples, see Stephen Badsey, *Doctrine and Reform in the British Cavalry, 1880–1918* (Aldershot: Ashgate, 2008); Gary Sheffield, *Forgotten Victory: The First World War Myths and Realities* (London: Headline, 2001).

[7] For examples, see Robin Prior and Trevor Wilson, *Command on the Western Front: The Military Career of Sir Henry Rawlinson, 1914–18* (Oxford: Blackwell, 1992); Robin Prior and Trevor Wilson, *Passchendaele, The Untold Story* (New Haven, CT: Yale University Press, 1996); Tim Travers, *The Killing Ground: The British Army, the Western Front and the Emergence of Modern Warfare* (London: Unwin, Hyman, 1987); Tim Travers, *How the War Was Won: Command and Technology in the British Army on the Western Front, 1917–1918* (London: Routledge, 1992).

[8] For examples, see Jonathan Boff, *Winning and Losing on the Western Front: The British Third Army and the Defeat of Germany in 1918* (Cambridge University Press, 2012); Timothy Bowman and Mark Connelly, *The Edwardian Army: Recruiting, Training and*

Despite the outpouring of popular and academic investigations, certain aspects remain under-researched. New work is furthering our understanding of the general staff and military administration, command below the army level is likewise coming under great scrutiny and there is still much to be done on the impact of conscripts on the British Army and the influence it may have had on combat effectiveness.[9]

This study examines the British Army in the First World War drawing upon the full breadth of the historiography and intimate knowledge of the primary sources. Its central focus is the pursuit of the conflict on the Western Front, which was the army's overwhelming priority throughout the war. Despite commitments to other fronts, most notably in 1915 and 1917, the army's high command and many of the most influential politicians never wavered from the centrality of France and Belgium as the determining theatre of war. Where the Germans attempted to distract the British with the intention of drawing resources from the Western Front to other theatres, most notably Africa, they failed entirely as locally raised colonial and Indian forces shouldered the burden. This is not to diminish the arduous nature of these campaigns, nor to ignore a key British strategic concern – the overall security of the Empire – but the extent to which that aim was pursued in France and Belgium.

The imperial commitment to the war provided Britain with immense support in terms of money, raw and manufactured materials and human resources.[10] Over the last thirty years, studies of the imperial contribution have proliferated. Of particular importance to this work are the military histories of the Dominion and Indian forces. Popular histories have tended to play up concepts of invincible Australian, Canadian and New Zealand units, with the secret of their success identified in their peculiar national atmospheres. Much recent academic research in the former Dominions has tended to revise such simplistic concepts, stressing the importance of continuing intimate links with British forces, particularly staff officers, and common lines of development and thinking despite the

Deploying the British Army, 1902–1914 (Oxford University Press, 2012); J. P. Harris, *Douglas Haig and the First World War* (Cambridge University Press, 2008).

9 For examples of these approaches, see Ilana Bet-El, *Conscripts: The Lost Legion of the Great War* (Stroud, UK: Sutton, 1999); Aimée Fox-Godden, '"Putting Knowledge in Power": Perspectives on Learning and Knowledge Sharing in the British Army of the First World War', unpublished PhD thesis, University of Birmingham, 2015; Peter Hodgkinson, *British Infantry Battalion Commanders in the First World War* (Farnham: Ashgate, 2015); Andy Simpson, *Directing Operations: British Corps Command on the Western Front 1914–1918* (Stroud: Spellmount, 2006).

10 For a summary of the imperial war effort, see Robert Holland, 'The British Empire in the Great War 1914–1918', in Judith M. Brown and William Roger Louis (eds.), *The Oxford History of the British Empire*, Vol. IV (Oxford University Press, 1999), 114–37.

growing isolation of Australian and Canadian forces in their own corps.[11] Studies of Indian forces have also expanded significantly and in the process have escaped many of the old clichés about the strengths and weaknesses of the Indian Army.[12] In terms of this work, the role of imperial troops is commented upon, but only in the wider context of the British Army and, in particular, the BEF on the Western Front, as detailed examinations of their particular attributes would significantly expand the scope of this study. For the same reason, detailed examinations of the roles of female service in the Women's Auxiliary Army Corps and colonial peoples in labour units have been excluded. Both played vital roles, but without both deploying a distinctly different methodology and exploring distinctly different questions, it is impossible to accord them the depth they deserve.[13]

This exploration of the British Army in the Great War places the fighting on the Western Front at its core, but it is contextualised by examinations of the social history of the army, the wider strategic framework and a survey of the war it pursued in other theatres. When taken together, it demonstrates that the British Army was the single most important component of the British Empire's immense war effort between 1914 and 1918.

[11] For examples, see Geoffrey Hayes, Andrew Iarocci and Mike Bechthold (eds.), *Vimy Ridge: A Canadian Reassessment* (Waterloo, Ontario: Wilfrid Laurier University Press, 2007); Robert Stevenson, *The Centenary History of Australia and the Great War: The War with Germany* (Sydney, NSW: Oxford University Press, 2015).

[12] Most important for this study is George Morton-Jack's, *The Indian Army on the Western Front* (Cambridge University Press, 2014).

[13] For good examples of these kinds of studies, see Janet S. K. Watson, *Fighting Different Wars: Experience, Memory and the First World War in Britain* (Cambridge University Press, 2004); Tim Winegaard, *Indigenous Peoples of the British Dominions and the First World War* (Cambridge University Press, 2014).

1 The Pre-War Army

During the period between the end of the South African War in 1902 and the outbreak of the First World War, no government made a clear statement of what they saw the priorities of the British Army to be in terms of a focus on home defence, imperial policing or a continental commitment.[1] Contemporaries still referred to the memorandum compiled by Edward Stanhope, then Secretary of State for War, in December 1888. Stanhope had listed the priorities of the British Army as being, in order, maintaining civil order at home, providing soldiers for India and the Imperial garrisons, home defence and an ability to send a sizeable number of troops overseas in the event of war. Stanhope noted the low priority given to an expeditionary capacity and explained that any European war was highly improbable, which accounted for this assessment.[2] R. B. Haldane introduced a sweeping range of reforms while Secretary of State for War between 1906 and 1912, but despite the generally positive reception these reforms received from contemporaries and the generally favourable treatment of Haldane by historians, his reforms did little to resolve this fundamental issue of what the British Army actually existed to do.

In brief, Haldane's reforms sought to reorganise the elements of the British Army that were in the United Kingdom into the British Expeditionary Force (BEF) of six infantry and one cavalry divisions. He

[1] For a wider discussion of the topics discussed in this chapter, see Timothy Bowman and Mark Connelly, *The Edwardian Army: Recruiting, Training and Deploying the British Army, 1902–14* (Oxford University Press, 2012).

[2] The Stanhope memorandum is reproduced in full in E. M. Spiers, *The Late Victorian Army, 1868–1902* (Manchester University Press, 1992), 337. See also I. F. W. Beckett, 'Edward Stanhope at the War Office, 1887–92', *Journal of Strategic Studies*, 5, 2 (1982); and I. F. W. Beckett, 'The Stanhope Memorandum of 1888: A Reinterpretation', *Bulletin of the Institute of Historical Research*, LVII, 136 (1984). See also John Gooch, *The Plans of War: The General Staff and British Military Strategy, c.1900–1916* (London: Routledge and Kegan Paul, 1974); Michael Howard, *The Continental Commitment: The Dilemma of British Defence Policy in Two World Wars* (Harmondsworth: Penguin, 1972); and Hew Strachan, 'The British Army, Its General Staff and the Continental Commitment, 1904–1914', in D. French and B. Bond (eds.), *The British General Staff: Reform and Innovation, 1890–1939* (London: Frank Cass, 2002), 75–94.

further sought to organise the auxiliary forces into a Territorial Force (TF) of fourteen infantry divisions and fourteen cavalry brigades, with the supporting logistical and medical services, all enlisted for home defence only. Haldane also formed the Officer Training Corps (OTC), which brought together a number of Volunteer units at, mainly, public schools and universities and was meant to provide a trained officer corps for the new TF.[3] While many of the Haldane reforms were to endure, the celebration of Haldane as one of the most intellectual Secretaries of State for War rather ignores two uncomfortable facts. Firstly, the post of Secretary of State for War was not regarded as one of the leading offices of state, and most of its holders brought little intellectual dynamism to the post, so Haldane's reputation is being measured against a rather low bar. Indeed, it is worth reflecting that H. O. Arnold-Forster, Haldane's immediate predecessor, was, supposedly, the sixth or seventh choice for this post.[4] Secondly, the driver behind the Haldane reforms was financial, to bring in the army estimates below £28 million per annum. To this end, it is often forgotten that the Haldane reforms actually saw cuts in the regular army, with nine infantry battalions and some elements of the Royal Field Artillery and Royal Garrison Artillery disbanded.[5]

Nevertheless, Haldane's appointment as Secretary of State for War received widespread support from contemporaries. The warmest reception came, predictably, from the liberal press. In the *Manchester Guardian*, an editorial welcomed Haldane to the post, referring to his 'aptitude for thinking out a problem from first principles' which was much needed as the chief cause of the difficulties with army reform 'has been want of clearness' exacerbated by H. O. Arnold-Forster, 'the least successful

[3] I. F. W. Beckett, *Rifleman Form: A Study of the Rifle Volunteer Movement 1859–1908* (Aldershot: Ogilby Trust, 1982); Hugh Cunningham, *The Volunteer Force: A Social and Political History 1859–1908* (Hamden: Archon Books, 1975); John Gooch, 'Mr. Haldane's Army', in John Gooch (ed.), *The Prospect of War* (London: Frank Cass, 1981); John Gooch, 'Haldane and the "National Army"', in I. F. W. Beckett and John Gooch (eds.), *Politicians and Defence: Studies in the Formulation of British Defence Policy 1845–1970* (Manchester University Press, 1981); Michael Howard, 'Lord Haldane and the Territorial Army', in Michael Howard (ed.), *Studies in War and Peace* (London: Temple Smith, 1970); A. J. A. Morris, 'Haldane's Army Reforms, 1906–1908: The Deception of the Radicals', *History*, 56, 181 (1971); and E. M. Spiers, *Haldane: An Army Reformer* (Edinburgh University Press, 1980).

[4] Ian Beckett, 'H. O. Arnold-Forster and the Volunteers', in Ian Beckett and John Gooch (eds.), *Politicians and Defence: Studies in the Formulation of British Defence Policy 1845–1970* (Manchester University Press, 1981), 50; and A. Tucker, 'The Issue of Army Reform in the Unionist Government, 1903–5', *Historical Journal*, 9, 1 (1966), 92–3. For a different view, see Rhodri Williams, *Defending the Empire: The Conservative Party and British Defence Policy 1899–1915* (New Haven, CT: Yale University Press, 1991), 42–3.

[5] 1908 (Cd. 3798), *The General Annual Report on the British Army for the Year Ending 30th September, 1907*, 2–3; and H. C. Wylly, *History of the Manchester Regiment (Late the 63rd and 96th Foot)* (London: Forster Groom, 1925), 63–4.

Secretary of War that this country has ever had'.[6] The *Westminster Gazette* and the *Daily News* rejoiced that the War Office and army had finally gained a calm, reflective and intelligent political head.[7] The *Observer* took a similar line, condemning the haste with which Brodrick and Arnold-Forster had commenced their poorly judged army reforms.[8] The *Pall Mall Gazette, Illustrated London News, Daily Express* and the *Times* all stated that Haldane's desire to keep the question of army reform free from political partisanship and in the best interests of the nation was an impressive commitment, and the *Times* added that his position among his colleagues was much higher than that commanded by Arnold-Forster.[9]

Critical comment appeared on the Haldane reforms fairly quickly, and it was reform of the auxiliary forces which proved the most divisive issue. This was a subject which polarised the press, but it did not occur instantly, with some papers moving their positions only gradually. The *Pall Mall Gazette* was one of the few papers unconvinced from the start, and it referred to Haldane's Territorial Force scheme as 'playing at soldiers'.[10] By contrast, the firmly Conservative *Morning Post* remained remarkably impartial.[11] The *Times* was the main heavyweight paper to shift its position. Initially it supported Haldane's scheme, and its editorial line persisted in this even after Charles Repington, the paper's military correspondent, had declared his scepticism. Geoffrey Buckle, editor of the *Times*, was prepared to allow this division of thought as part of the newspaper's dialogue with its readers.[12] An editorial on the 22 March 1907 reported on Haldane's plans to reform the Militia and gave him wholehearted support in this endeavour. Repington, however, pursued a different line and, while never wishing to undermine Haldane nor his plans for the new Territorial Force, expressed his doubts that it would prove an effective answer to Britain's military problems.[13] A year later the editorial line was still at variance from Repington's, with a leading article reporting enthusiastically on the quality of Territorial Force training and preparation.[14] Gradually, however, the two approaches came

6 *Manchester Guardian*, 7 March 1906.

7 *Westminster Gazette*, 17 February 1906; *Daily News*, 5 January 1906.

8 *Observer*, 11 March 1906.

9 *The Times*, 5 January 1906; *Pall Mall Gazette*, 16 June 1906; *Illustrated London News*,. 130, 3541 (2 March 1907), 322; *Daily Express*, 9 March 1906.

10 *Pall Mall Gazette*, 26 February 1907.

11 *Morning Post*, 24 January 1906, 24 February 1907, 1, 2 April 1908, 13 February 1913.

12 See Morris, *Repington*, 16–17.

13 See, for example, *The Times*, 26 June 1907. See also W. Michael Ryan, 'The Invasion Controversy of 1906–1908: Lieutenant-Colonel Charles à Court Repington and British Perceptions of the German Menace', *Military Affairs*, 44, 1 (February 1980), 8–12.

14 *The Times*, 4 August 1908.

closer together, and by 1912, under the new editor, Geoffrey Robinson, the editorial line switched to an outright support for compulsory service in a home defence force.[15]

Supporting the idea that Britain needed a large home defence force, the *Manchester Guardian* was suspicious of the Imperial Service Obligation (ISO), which it believed revealed that Haldane's real plan was not to create a sustainable home defence force but a pool of personnel for the regular army. Such allegations of militarism and imperialist ambitions levelled against Haldane were not allayed by creation of the Special Reserve.[16] More broadly, the radical left in British politics feared that Haldane was endorsing the views of Lord Robert's National Service League and that the TF set the basis for universal and compulsory military service.[17]

Much of the unionist press moved towards opposition and outright hostility to the TF. The *Daily Express* condemned creation of the TF unreservedly, believing it to be an ill-thought-out solution dictated by Liberal Party pressure for a quick, cheap solution. This paper went on to accuse Haldane of introducing a class element into the officer corps by reserving commissions for the gentry, who would essentially serve without pay or allowances, rather than offering them to the more motivated urban middle class.[18] Among the unionist press, the *Observer* under Garvin's firm editorial hand moved rapidly from an initial welcome of the Haldane reforms to implacable opposition. As soon as Haldane announced his scheme for reform of the auxiliary forces, the *Observer* vented scepticism. The entire structure was condemned as unworkable, particularly the county associations, which were meant to introduce a local and democratic element into the TF. A fortnight before the TF came formally into existence, the paper's editorial strongly supported Lord Robert's call for conscription.[19]

The most vocal opposition to the Haldane reforms came from the National Service League (NLS), which was formed in 1902 and claimed to have 270,000 members by the summer of 1914. The League proposed a very mild form of conscription compared to that in use in most of continental Europe. In their plan, conscripts would serve for two to four months of full-time training, followed by a further fifteen days in each of

15 *The Times*, 10 December 1912.

16 *Manchester Guardian*, 15 September, 26 November 1906, 15 January, 26 February, 10 April, 20 June, and 30 November 1907.

17 Matthew Johnson, *Militarism and the British Left 1902–1914* (Basingstoke: Palgrave Macmillan, 2013), 134–43.

18 *Daily Express*, 13 July 1906, 26 February 1907, 1 April 1908.

19 *Observer*, 15 July 1906, 15 March 1908.

the subsequent three years. The League did gain some significant support, with something like eighty Members of Parliament (MPs) as members of the organisation at its height. However, neither of the major parties committed themselves to the scheme advocated by the League, and each of the five bills which the League introduced into Parliament between 1908 and 1914 were heavily defeated.[20] Initially, the NSL was wary of attacking the TF as denigrating those who were patriotically giving of their time to join auxiliary units would have done little to help their cause. However, from 1911, the acrimony between the NSL and supporters of the TF and voluntary principle more broadly became increasingly bitter.[21] It is worth noting that had the views of the NSL prevailed, it is unclear how their moderate conscription system would have done anything to help with imperial defence, and at best, large numbers of poorly trained conscripts would have been able to take the field in August 1914.

Critics of the Haldane scheme with regard to the TF did have a lot of evidence to support their case, though this was not always obvious to contemporaries. The TF did not actually prove much more successful than the old Rifle Volunteer movement in terms of recruitment and retention. In 1906, the Rifle Volunteers had an establishment of 338,452 all ranks but an actual strength of just 255,854. Indeed, between 1903 and 1907, this force was never less than 80,000 men under establishment.[22] With the creation of the TF, the overall establishment, which also included the Yeomanry, was 11,202 officers and 302,473 other ranks. Haldane had therefore set a less ambitious target for the size of the auxiliary forces, and this seems to have been based on what it was thought could be raised rather than on any strategic assessment of the number of troops needed for home defence. However, while initially recruitment to the new force seemed to be developing well, 1909 actually proved to be the high point of TF strength, with 9,652 officers and 260,389 other ranks. The strength of the force declined subsequently, until the outbreak of the First World

[20] R. J. Q. Adams and P. P. Poirier, *The Conscription Controversy in Great Britain 1900–1918* (Basingstoke: Macmillan, 1987), 16–32; Ian Hamilton, *Compulsory Service: A Study of the Question in the Light of Experience* (London: John Murray, 1910); A. J. A. Morris, *The Scaremongers: The Advocacy of War and Rearmament 1896–1914* (London: Routledge and Kegan Paul, 1984), 224–50; Lord Roberts, *Fallacies and Facts: An Answer to 'Compulsory Service'* (London: John Murray, 1911); Hew Strachan, 'Liberalism and Conscription, 1789–1919', in Hew Strachan (ed.), *The British Army: Manpower and Society into the Twenty-First Century* (London: Frank Cass, 2000), 3–15; and Williams, *Defending the Empire*, 143–8, 184–9.

[21] *Daily Express*, 10 February, 18 April 1913; *Daily Mail*, 11 February 1913; *Pall Mall Gazette*, 10 February 1913; *Observer*, 2, 9 February 1913.

[22] Abstracted from 1907 (Cd. 3367), *The Annual Return of the Volunteer Corps of Great Britain for the Year 1906*, 63; and 1908 (Cd. 3801), *The Annual Return of the Volunteer Corps of Great Britain for the Year*, 63.

War, reaching a nadir of 9,390 officers and 236,389 other ranks in 1913. The problem of recruitment was compounded by the fact that many members of the Territorials did not attend their annual training camp, and many of those who did merely attended for one week rather than the planned two. Thus, even in 1909 when recruitment appeared promising, 20,333 other ranks of the TF did not attend camp at all.[23]

Plans for the TF to have an expeditionary element also quickly collapsed. While, in the South African War, large numbers of Militiamen, Rifle Volunteers and Yeomanry had served overseas, this enthusiasm did not easily translate into the TF. The Imperial Service Obligation (ISO), to serve overseas in the event of war, was taken up by very few TF members before the outbreak of the Great War and by even fewer complete units. In September 1913, only 1,090 officers and 17,788 other ranks were noted as having entered into the ISO. When units did sign up, it seems to have been entirely on regimental initiative. The Commanding Officer (CO) of the 7th Middlesex Regiment tried to persuade all existing members to sign up for the ISO and ordered that, from 1910, no officer or man should be accepted as a member of the unit unless he was willing to serve overseas. Only the Northumberland Hussars, 8th Middlesex Regiment and 6th East Surrey Regiment adopted a similar policy. This additional commitment does not appear to have affected the ability of the 7th Middlesex Regiment to recruit. In 1909 it had 816 men; this increased to 890 in 1910, 892 in 1911 and 902 in 1912 before dipping slightly to 865 in 1913. However, it does not seem to have done much to help its re-engagement rate as in 1913, 350 men were listed as 'recruits'.[24] This is the context in which Lord Kitchener's decision to expand the army through his New Armies rather than the TF must be understood.

The Militia, which since its re-establishment in 1852, had provided large numbers of recruits to the regular army and had sent complete units abroad during both the Crimean and South African Wars, was used as the basis for the Special Reserve set up under the Haldane reforms. Militia reform had proved a major problem for Haldane's predecessor, H. O. Arnold-Forster, who had come up against a large Militia lobby in Parliament when he attempted to disband the most inefficient Militia units and convert the sixty most efficient battalions into short-service regular battalions for home service only. The Militia had then been

[23] Cd. 7254 (1914), *The Annual Return of the Territorial Force for the Year 1913*, 124.

[24] 1914 (Cd. 7254), *The Annual Return of the Territorial Force for the Year 1913*, 129; King, *History of the 7th Battalion Middlesex Regiment*, viii–x, 150–4; Army Lists, 1910–1914; and Howard Pease, *The History of the Northumberland (Hussars) Yeomanry 1819–1919 with Supplement to 1923* (London: Constable, 1924), 64.

reprieved over arguments of tradition and cost.[25] Negotiations by Haldane with Militia colonels over formation of the Special Reserve led to a situation in which Special Reservists enlisted with an automatic duty to serve overseas in time of war. But the Militia colonels, most of whom transferred to the Special Reserve, seem to have accepted this only on the condition that, in time of war, their units would serve overseas as complete units rather than simply serving as draft-finding units for the regulars.[26] In trying to impose this condition, Militia officers were ignoring the peacetime practice of large numbers of Militiamen enlisting in the regular army. In 1907, 12,113 Militiamen enlisted as regulars, and in 1913, 9,235 Special Reservists did likewise. This was when the Special Reserve as a whole had 55,606 other ranks.[27] The agreement regarding unit integrity, known as the 'pledge' in the TF, was cast aside on the outbreak of war, for the Special Reserve and the North and South Irish Horse were to be the only Special Reserve units which served overseas during the Great War. Other Special Reserve units became draft-finding units for regular battalions and also provided a proportion of non-commissioned officers (NCOs) to the New Armies. As early as 6 August 1914, the 3rd Manchester Regiment had already sent 615 other ranks and two officers to the 2nd Manchester Regiment to bring it up to its wartime establishment.[28] Cyril Falls noted that, during the entire war, the 3rd Royal Irish Rifles sent 8,069 men overseas; the 4th Royal Irish Rifles, 2,188; and the 5th Royal Irish Rifles, 1,934.[29]

Just as recruitment and retention were problems for the Rifle Volunteers and the TF, so the same problems were evident for the Special Reserve. In 1903, the Militia was 25,619 short of an establishment of 131,583, and even at this, 33,111 Militia officers and men had not attended their annual camp. In 1907, the figure was little better, with the Militia 37,397 short of its establishment of 130,737, albeit with only 9,948 Militia all ranks absent from camp. Under the Special Reserve system, this situation deteriorated further. In 1911, the Special Reserve had an establishment of 91,219, but

[25] Beckett, 'H. O. Arnold-Forster and the Volunteers', 53; and Williams, *Defending the Empire*, 41–58.

[26] Cd. 3513, 1907, 'Report of the War Office Committee Appointed to Discuss Certain Militia Questions with Representative Officers of Militia'; and PRONI, D.1889/4/1/1, R. H. Wallace papers, out letter book, letter Wallace to James Craig, 11/7/06.

[27] 1908 (Cd. 3798), *The General Annual Report on the British Army for the Year Ending 30th September, 1907*; and 1914 (Cd. 7252), *The General Annual Report on the British Army for the Year Ending 30th September, 1913*.

[28] Tameside Record Office, MR1/3/1/25, C. M. Thorneycroft, 'The 3rd Battalion (Militia) The Manchester Regiments: Its Origins and Services with Special Reference to its Work during the Great War 1914–18', unpublished manuscript, 29.

[29] C. Falls, *The History of the First Seven Battalions, Royal Irish Rifles (Now the Royal Ulster Rifles) in the Great War* (Aldershot: Gale and Polden, 1925), 186.

its strength was a mere 60,931.[30] At the regimental level, these recruitment problems are clear. The 3rd North Staffordshire Regiment had 662 other ranks present at its annual camp in June 1904, 698 in 1905 and 625 in 1906. The position declined with establishment of the Special Reserve, with just 464 present in 1909 and 364 in 1913.[31]

Training for the auxiliary forces remained very limited, even for those who did attend annual camp for the full two-week training period each summer. One of the compromises made by Haldane in his TF scheme was that TF units would train full time for six months on mobilisation before being asked to serve overseas. This, of course, was another element of the TF scheme which was set aside on the outbreak of the First World War, with TF units serving on the Western Front from October 1914. Field Marshal Lord Roberts seized on the impossibility of training TF artillery units in any proper manner as one of his major criticisms of the TF as a whole. Speaking in a debate in the House of Lords in May 1908, he stated

> Then the annual training is to be for fifteen days only; and even for this short time, under recent instructions, it would appear that no one who has anything else to do need attend; and I would ask you please to remember that this might be all the training the Territorial Artillery would get before an enemy lands on these shores. For, however much it may be desired, no one, not even the most sanguine of Mr. Haldane's supporters, would, I imagine, take upon himself to guarantee that we shall have sufficient warning to ensure the artillery being given the six months much-needed training ... From the fifteen days two must be deducted for Sundays, two for coming and going into camp, and one day for inspection, paying the men, survey boards, etc. Thus the fifteen days have dwindled down to ten days for actual training, two of which are to be devoted to artillery tactics and gun practice. Now, even if the ranges happen to be close at hand, this would allow a ridiculously short time for carrying out such essential duties.[32]

Elsewhere, training was compromised for recruitment purposes among the auxiliary forces. The commanding officers of many units believed that holding a camp at a prominent place in their recruiting area was vital to secure recruits, even though the training facilities would be poor and the opportunity for training with other regular or reserve units very limited.

30 Figures calculated from 1904 (Cd. 1903), *Return Showing the Establishment of Each Unit of Militia in the United Kingdom and the Numbers Present, Absent and Wanting to Compete at the Training of 1906*, 14–15; 1908 (Cd. 3932), *Return Showing the Establishment of Each Unit of Militia in the United Kingdom and the Numbers Present, Absent and Wanting to Compete at the Training of 1907*, 13–14; and 1912–1913 (Cd. 6065), *The General Annual Report on the British Army for the Year Ending 30th September 1911, with Which Is Incorporated the Annual Report on Recruiting*, 26.

31 Staffordshire Regimental Museum, 'Digest of Service 3rd North Staffordshire Regiment 1853–1914', 50–65; and 'Digest of Service 4th North Staffordshire Regiment 1853–1914', 12.

32 HL Deb 18 May 1908, vol. 188, chap. 1548.

Figure 1. East Kent Yeomanry, Lewes, 1911.
Source: From authors' collections

Thus, the 4th Leinster Regiment mobilised local opinion to ensure that it continued to hold its annual camp at the Great Heath, Maryborough, when the military authorities had sought to send it to the Curragh Camp.[33] By 1913, the rather desperate situation in TF recruitment, retention and attendance at camp meant that a holiday atmosphere was definitely promoted at some camps, which were held in seaside resorts. The 5th Cameronians (Scottish Rifles) camp near Troon in 1913, for example, left the men free from about 2 PM 'nearly every day'. As Lieutenant-General Sir John Keir reflected, 'Everything in reason, and some things out of reason were resorted to to tempt men to enlist and to make the Force popular, even at the expense of discipline, training, and efficiency. The sites for summer camps, for instance, were chosen more with a view to the enjoyment of the men than for the benefit of their training.'[34]

The equipment available to the TF was obsolete on the outbreak of war. The 5th Cameronians (Scottish Rifles), despite being one of the first TF units selected for overseas service in 1914, was still armed with the

[33] PRONI, D. 618/178, 'Manuscript History of the 4th Leinster Regiment (Old Queen's Co. Militia)', 45.
[34] *Fifth Battalion, Scottish Rifles Gazette*, II, 1 (January 1914), 24; and John Keir, *A Soldier's Eye-View of Our Armies* (London: John Murray, 1919), 35.

Lee-Metford rifle in August 1914, a rifle phased out of the regular army in the mid-1890s.[35] When the 1/14th London Regiment (London Scottish) first went into action at Messines on 31 October 1914, they were armed with defective rifles, which had only been issued when they left England, leaving no time for training or testing. These were Lee-Enfield Mark I rifles, converted to take Mark VII ammunition but with too weak a spring, with the result that the breach mechanism kept jamming.[36]

Another major problem for the TF was the supply of horses. By 1912, it was clear that London units were going to have particular problems as the last of the Omnibus companies which used horses, and upon which the Territorial Association relied for 750 draught horses on mobilisation, had decided to motorise. The three London-based Yeomanry regiments were also facing serious problems in sourcing horses. This led Lord Esher to state 'that the sooner the Military Authorities realised the fact that within a measurable distance of time mounted troops for Home Defence could not be provided with horses, the sooner they might be brought to realise the importance of reconsidering the Strategical and Tactical aspects of Home Defence.'[37] Elsewhere, the problems of horse supply were equally acute. Orders issued to the Staffordshire TF infantry brigade in 1909 for an exercise noted that they would have no cavalry support 'as the Yeomanry horses are required for another regiment'.[38]

While the Haldane scheme is often seen as important in bringing in a uniform system of organisation for the auxiliary forces, some curious anomalies remained. The constitutional peculiarities of the Channel Islands and the Isle of Man meant that the Militia survived in the former and the Rifle Volunteers in the latter. The TF, with the exception of eight OTC units, was not extended to Ireland, which meant that Yeomanry units there were formed as units of the Special Reserve, whereas in Great Britain they would have been part of the TF. Two of the oldest and most socially exclusive regiments of the auxiliary forces – the Honourable Artillery Company and the Inns of Court Regiment – secured special treatment from the War Office. Following guarantees from Haldane and the War Office and the passing of a special Act of Parliament to protect their property interests, the Honourable Artillery Company continued

[35] Regimental Publications Committee, *The Fifth Battalion, The Cameronians (Scottish Rifles) 1914–1919* (Glasgow: Jackson and Son, 1936), 7.

[36] J. H. Lindsay, *The London Scottish in the Great War* (London: Regimental HQ, 1925), 37–8.

[37] LMA, A/TA/1, Minutes of T. F. Association of the County of London, Minutes for 24/11/10, 28/11/12 and 22/7/13; and A. S. Hamilton, *The City of London Yeomanry (Roughriders)* (London: Hamilton Press, 1936), 4.

[38] Staffs RO, D.5528/2, 'Staffordshire Territorial Force in 1909', report on 'The Staffordshire Territorial Brigade Encampment at Towyn', 14/8/09.

with its traditions and premises intact, and members were still elected and paid a membership fee of two guineas per annum. The Honourable Artillery Company now formed two artillery batteries and an infantry battalion in the TF, recruiting 553 new members in 1908–1909 to reach this establishment.[39] The Inns of Court Regiment, of course, drew on the legal profession for the bulk of its members and thus found itself in a good position to lobby Haldane, a fellow lawyer. The Inns of Court Regiment was incorporated into the TF as an OTC contingent, which allowed it to keep a cavalry squadron. This was despite concerns raised by some civil servants at the War Office, who felt that the men joining this 'class corps' would be of more value to the TF as a whole if they accepted commissions elsewhere.[40]

One of the major elements of the Haldane reforms was to establish the OTC, which was meant to provide large numbers of officers to both the auxiliary forces and the regulars. The concept behind this scheme was that men could qualify for 'Certificate A' (which many did at public school), which qualified them for a commission in the TF or Special Reserve, or the more demanding 'Certificate B', which would qualify them for a regular commission, without the necessity to attend a course at Sandhurst or Woolwich. Qualification for 'Certificate B' included a four-week attachment to a regular battalion and passing the relevant promotion examinations, which a regular officer undertook to qualify for captain.[41]

The training for OTC units was not dissimilar to that of TF units as a whole, a number of weekly, evening drills throughout the year and a two-week annual camp. Absenteeism, which was such a problem in TF camps as a whole, was also evident in the OTC. In the University of London OTC, only 402 cadets attended the annual summer camp for the full two weeks in 1909, out of a total of 596.[42] Most training was carried

[39] HAC Archive, 'HAC Act Papers 1907–1908'; and Court Minutes for 3/2/08 and 4/2/08; G. Goold Walker, *The Honourable Artillery Company 1537–1987* (London: Honourable Artillery Company, revised edition, 1986), 262–3; and Justine Taylor, 'Preserving Property and Privilege: The Formation of the Territorial Army and the HAC Act of 1908', in *Honourable Artillery Company Journal*, 85, 474 (2008).

[40] TNA, WO32/18557, 'Application to Form the 27th Bn into a Mixed Unit or Division of Cavy. and Infy. of the Officers Training Corps'; and LMA, A/TA/1, Minutes of T. F. Association of the County of London, Minutes for 28/2/08.

[41] J. K. Dunlop, *The Development of the British Army, 1899–1914* (London: Methuen, 1938), pp. 294–5; E. M. Spiers, 'University Officers' Training Corps and the First World War' (COMEC Occasional Paper No. 4, Reading, 2014); E. M. Teagarden, 'Lord Haldane and the Origins of Officer Training Corps', *Journal of the Society for Army Historical Research*, XLV, 182 (1967); and Ian Worthington, 'Socialization, Militarization and Officer Recruiting: The Development of the Officers Training Corps', *Military Affairs*, 43, 2 (1979).

[42] University of London Special Collections, ME1/1/1, 'Report of Military Education Committee to the Senate', 1910.

out by schoolmasters and academics who were given commissions, often on the basis of very thin military experience. Of the initial five academics commissioned into the University of London OTC, only two had any military experience. Captain A. R. Richardson, an assistant in the Department of Pure Mathematics at University College London, had served for three years as a private in the 4th West Kent Regiment and in the South African War with the Imperial Yeomanry for two years. Major D. S. Capper, Professor of Engineering at King's College London, had served for three years as a private in the University Company of the Queen's Edinburgh Rifle Volunteer Brigade, Royal Scots. Interestingly, while Richardson had more military experience, these men's relative academic positions seem to have decided who was given the higher rank.[43]

While, as discussed later in this book, the OTC was to prove important in providing officers for the New Armies and Territorials during the war itself, pre-war the scheme seemed to be failing spectacularly. While large numbers of school pupils and university students enrolled in the OTC, as many as 18,000 having passed through it as early as February 1912, the numbers who took up commissions seem to have been as low as 694 by February 1914. The University of London OTC, which could claim to have 734 cadets in 1913, had only 146 commissioned between 1909 and 1913 as a whole. Even this figure compared well with the experience at Bangor University College, which had provided just four officers over the same period.[44] Lieutenant-General Sir Neville Lyttleton, then General Officer Commanding (GOC), Ireland, predicted this poor conversion rate when inspecting the Queen's University of Belfast OTC at their annual camp in August 1909. He wrote: '[A] very fine lot of young fellows quite up to standard ... A very large percentage of them are going to be doctors, in which case this corps will hardly justify its existence.' Indeed, in 1913 when Cardiff University College offered to raise an OTC contingent, it was turned down as conversion rates had been so poor at other University of Wales institutions, and the university authorities could make no guarantees to the War Office about the likelihood of cadets taking up commissions.[45]

[43] University of London Special Collections, ME1/1/1, Military Education Committee Minutes, 8/1/09; and *Hart's Army List*, 1908–1910.

[44] Spiers, 'University Officers' Training Corps and the First World War', 16–17; and University of London Special Collections, ME1/1/2, 'Report of Military Education Committee to Senate', 1913.

[45] LHCMA, NGL/KL/825a, Lyttleton Papers, Letter, Lyttleton to his Wife, 10/8/09; and Spiers, 'University Officers' Training Corps and the First World War', 17.

Figure 2. Cambridge University Officer Training Corps, 1912.
Source: From authors' collections

The fact that so few university graduates were prepared to consider a career as officers in the regular or auxiliary forces is a testament to the fact that the regular army officer corps in the Edwardian period was still drawn from a fairly small section of society. Officers needed a private income to supplement their pay, which only partly covered the costs of uniforms, mess bills, servants' wages, horses and personal weapons. As a result, Edward Spiers suggests that among senior officers in 1914, 7 per cent were drawn from the peerage and baronetage, 26 per cent from the gentry, 23 per cent from the armed forces, 12 per cent from the clergy and 12 per cent from other professions. This saw a slight decline in the numbers from the peerage and baronetage and a slight increase in clergy and professionals over 1899.[46] A sample of 418 officers drawn from the Sandhurst cadet registers between 1910 and the outbreak of the Great War suggests that this picture was not very different for that of junior officers in the Edwardian period. Of these cadets, 155 had fathers who were serving or retired army officers, 128 described their fathers as 'gentleman', 12 were sons of peers, 21 were sons of clergymen, 20 had fathers who were members of the legal profession, 16 had fathers who worked in the Home or Indian Civil Service and 12 had fathers who were civil engineers. Only four had fathers who could be considered 'captains

[46] Spiers, *Late Victorian Army*, 94, 338–9.

of industry'. Reinforcing the class consciousness of the Edwardian officer corps was the small number of schools from which cadets came. Bedford Grammar School, Cheltenham College, Clifton, Eton, Harrow, Marlborough and Wellington provided the majority of cadets to the Royal Military College (RMC) between 1902 and 1914.[47] Therefore, the regular officer corps drew on the 'leisured class' who were prepared to commit to the part-time, part-paid nature of peacetime soldiering at least for a few years. Some men certainly became officers to establish their families in polite society, their families having made their fortunes in industry. Family tradition saw many sons of professional soldiers join the army, even when their family finances appear to have been severely stretched. Another group were the sons of solid middle-class families who were deemed to be incapable of qualifying for any other profession.

Those going into the army as officers certainly needed a private income, but this could vary enormously and depended on a number of factors. At the entry level, fees at the Royal Military Academy (RMA) and RMC were placed on a sliding scale. A gentleman cadet whose father was classed as a 'private gentleman' would have to find £150 per annum in fees. At the other end of the scale, a cadet whose father had been an army officer who had died, leaving his family in genteel poverty, could qualify for a special £20 per annum fee. A King's cadet or King's India cadet would be educated free; these cadets were drawn from the category which would otherwise have had to pay £20 per annum on the basis of entrance examination results or school examination grades.[48]

Major-General H. R. Abadie believed that expenses for cavalry officers were much too high, requiring a private income in excess of £300 per annum.[49] S. C. M. Archibald reflected that in 1910 any young Royal Artillery officer who was not guaranteed a private income of at least £100 per annum would have to enter the despised ranks of the Royal Garrison Artillery (RGA), although even in the RGA an absolute minimum of £12 per annum was required.[50] The future Field Marshal Bernard Montgomery, son of an impecunious colonial bishop, who had hoped to qualify for the Indian Army, where pay and allowances were

[47] RMAS, WO151/8, RMC Cadet Register 1910–14; and Thomas, *The Story of Sandhurst*, 141.

[48] *Report of the Committee Appointed to Consider the Education and Training of Officers of the Army* (Cd. 982), 1902 (Akers-Douglas Report), 86, 112. IWM, PP/MCR/136, *Memoirs of Brigadier G. S. Brunskill, Who Was a King's India Cadet, entering RMC in 1911.*

[49] *Report of the Committee Appointed to Consider the Education and Training of Officers of the Army* (Cd. 982), 1902 (Akers-Douglas Report), app. XLII, 134–5.

[50] IWM, PP/MCR/11, *Memoirs of Major-General S. C. M. Archibald*, 43–4; and IWM, 87/41/1, Major-General L. A. Hawes, 'The Memories and Dreams of an Ordinary Soldier' (unpublished manuscript), 28.

much higher, noted candidly, 'Army life was expensive and it was not possible to live on one's pay. It was generally considered that a private income or allowance of at least £100 a year was necessary.'[51]

Prior to the Great War, there were a number of ways in which a man could secure a commission. Complete figures survive only for 1913, and this is problematic as before the expansion of Sandhurst with the completion of New College in 1912, more candidates came from the so-called Militia (post-1908 Special Reserve) back door. In 1913, the main route to a commission was through the RMC, Sandhurst, which prepared cadets for the Guards, cavalry, infantry and Indian Army, and this accounted for 371 commissions. The other British cadet college, the RMA, Woolwich, which prepared cadets for the Royal Artillery and Royal Engineers accounted for just 130 commissions. The Canadian equivalent of Sandhurst, the Royal Military College, Kingston, Ontario, also provided a small number of commissioned officers to the British Army proper, five in 1913, though its main role was to provide officers for the permanently embodied elements of the Canadian Militia. What is surprising in the pre-1914 period is the large number of commissions granted to those who had never been cadets at any military college or had any previous military training. In 1913, seventy-nine regular commissions were granted to those who had been officers in Special Reserve or Territorial units. Seventy-four university candidates were directly commissioned in 1913 through the OTC. A handful of colonial candidates also received commissions in regular forces (a mere three), and the Guards had their own probationary officer scheme which provided nine officers. A mere seven men were promoted from the ranks (or 1 per cent of the total commissioned), and these presumably were either long-service NCOs who were given the 'dead end' appointment of lieutenant and quarter master or 'gentlemen rankers' who had the private income needed to maintain their commissioned status.[52]

This variety of commissioning routes reflected serious confusion on the part of the military authorities over the extent to which the army was viewed as a profession. The cadet entry route, through the RMA and RMC via competitive examinations, suggested a modern, meritocratic profession. However, commissions awarded to Special Reserve and TF officers and, to some degree, men from the ranks suggested that an apprenticeship route was deemed most effective, as these men would have gained experience of military command. The university entrance

[51] B. L. Montgomery, *The Memoirs of Field Marshal Montgomery* (London: Collins, 1958), 23.

[52] Figures taken from *Report of the Committee on the Education and Training of Officers* (Cmd. 2031), 1924, 30.

route suggested that the army wanted intelligent young men who, with limited OTC experience, could be trained as officers when they were actually posted to regular regiments. Of course, in large part these various routes had survived due to the problem of recruiting sufficient numbers of officers. Nevertheless, this variety of routes to commissioning in peacetime goes some way to explain the ad hoc commissioning process which developed during the First World War itself.

The standard of instruction at the two cadet colleges was variable. RMA, Woolwich, impressed the Akers-Douglas Committee, which was set up to consider officer education and training in 1902. The standards of technical education in science and engineering were seen to be high, and the prized Royal Engineer commissions, which were only available to the best-performing gentlemen cadets, were clearly an incentive for hard work. However, instruction in French and German was felt to be superfluous, as cadets had to perform well in the entrance examination in these subjects in any case. The lack of a course in military history, poor classroom and living accommodation and the fact that the guns provided for instruction were obsolete were all seen to be issues which needed to be addressed. The Akers-Douglas Committee was much more critical of RMC, Sandhurst. There was heavy criticism of the standard of education, and it was noted that gentlemen cadets had 'absolutely no inducement to work' as those who failed to reach the 'low qualifying standard demanded' were commissioned anyway. The committee found the standard of instructors at the RMC to be poor, as few inducements were offered to promising officers, and the pay was inadequate. As a result, there were few applicants for posts at Sandhurst and no obvious replacements for officers who were found to be unsuitable. It was also felt that too much of the instruction, especially in drill, riding practice and gymnastics, was left to staff sergeants.[53]

Incredibly, the almost purely military instruction at Sandhurst was found to be wanting. Cadets, whether destined for the cavalry or for other arms, only received thirty-nine hours of riding practice per year and were also not instructed in revolver shooting or musketry, despite the availability of facilities nearby. Indeed, cadets who wanted to practice their shooting had to join a club which cost £1 per term. This was seen as a particular anomaly as gentlemen cadets at Woolwich were trained in revolver shooting. Cadets were also not instructed in drilling a squad or company in their time at Sandhurst. The cleaning requirements of 'bull' also confused the committee, as while gentlemen cadets had their rifles

[53] *Report of the Committee Appointed to Consider the Education and Training of Officers of the Army* (Cd. 982), 1902 (Akers-Douglas Report), 15–19.

(which they never fired) cleaned and maintained by their servants, they had to pipe-clay their own waist belts. 'This is remarkable, for while a cadet might acquire a familiarity with the mechanism of the rifle from being required to clean it, the educational value of pipe-claying a belt is extremely slight.'[54]

It is clear that some of the criticisms of the Akers-Douglas Committee's report on the RMC were acted on. From 1904, cadets were sent on an annual musketry course to Hythe, and by 1907, the practice of going into camp in July had been established.[55] The accommodation at the RMC was also expanded and improved, with new buildings being constructed between 1908 and 1912, allowing for accommodation for an additional 424 gentlemen cadets and 12 company officers.[56]

Surviving records make it clear that the courses at RMA and RMC were not particularly rigorous, with failure uncommon. Of the September 1903 entry to RMC, for example, only one cadet failed all components of the course and failed to receive a commission.[57] The Commandant of the RMC, Colonel Kitson, stated that he wanted to raise standards in November 1903, noting that '[t]he difficulties of removing undesirable officers from their regiments are so far greater than those incurred in getting rid of inefficient Cadets here.'[58] The Commandant returned to the standards expected at the RMC in more detail the following year. With the introduction of new examinations at the RMC, he was concerned that forty to fifty cadets would fail their examinations that year. Voicing his concerns to the Army Council, Kitson stated: 'As such a large number of failures has never been the custom at Sandhurst, it is probable that parents will be indignant and a considerable storm will be raised, and questions may be asked in the House of Commons . . . The fault lies in the fact that if so many as 180 Cadets are accepted at any one entrance examination, the standard of intelligence of the last 60 is lamentably low. The Company Officers are constantly complaining to me of the crass stupidity of so many of their Cadets . . . Further in this same class of 180 Cadets, there are no less than 22, who as King's Cadets & c., had

[54] *Report of the Committee Appointed to Consider the Education and Training of Officers of the Army* (Cd. 982), 1902 (Akers-Douglas Report), 19–28; and Appendices XXXII, XLII and XLIV, 119–23, 134–5, 144–5.

[55] WO152/73, RMC correspondence, 1903–1906; Annual Report by Commandant, 21/12/04 and WO152/74, box 142; RMC correspondence, 1907–1909; letter, Commandant to B. G. G. S., Southern Command, 8/2/07.

[56] Shepperd, *Sandhurst*, 107, 112–13; and Thomas, *Story of Sandhurst*, 166.

[57] RMAS, WO151/6, RMC Cadet Register, September 1903–January 1907, entry for Hon. I. J. L. Hay.

[58] RMAS, WO152/73, RMC correspondence, 1903–1906, circular from Commandant to Company Officers, 11/11/03.

only to pass a qualifying examination. These Gentlemen are, almost always, of a low standard of intelligence.'[59] After much moralising about the Army Council having 'no desire or intention' to lower standards, they then proceeded to do exactly that. Kitson was ordered to add term marks to the examination marks so that average marks would be artificially raised, allowing almost all cadets to pass.[60]

Discipline at the cadet colleges was poor, hampered by the fact that as gentlemen cadets, students were not serving members of the military and so not under military discipline. Indeed, the term 'gentleman cadet' was almost as heavily lampooned as the First World War 'temporary gentleman', its subjects being described as 'almost an officer and not quite a gentleman'.[61] Bernard Montgomery's near expulsion from Sandhurst, on the eve of his commissioning in December 1907, for setting fire to a fellow cadet's shirt tails and causing serious skin burns, itself the culmination in a series of what appear to have been gang fights, is infamous.[62] As at public schools of the period, a fair amount of bullying still occurred. Any cadet seen to have misbehaved could be 'court martialled' by his peers and sentenced to an ink bath.[63] At the RMA at least one cadet was stripped naked and brought around the grounds in a handcart as he 'was not showing sufficient signs of masculinity'.[64]

Strangely, given the supposedly formative nature of the time spent at Sandhurst and Woolwich, many officers, at least in their published memoirs, had little to say of their time there. Christopher Lynch-Robinson reflected that he had 'a most enjoyable time there [Sandhurst] where I greatly appreciated the freedom after public school life'.[65] General Sir Richard O'Connor's biographer recounted that 'he never spoke about his time at Sandhurst in later life.'[66] Those who did reflect on their time there were rarely complimentary. G. S. Brunshill, who attended the RMC from 1910 to 1911, reflected, 'My recollection is that there was some academic military instruction, chiefly in history, but most of the training was as a young private soldier with no introduction to the duties of an officer.'[67] Frederick Pile reflected on his time as a cadet at the RMA between 1903 and 1904, noting that '[t]he education at "the Shop" ... was a general

[59] WO152/73, RMC correspondence, 1903–1906, letter Colonel G. C. Kitson, to Secretary, Army Council, 3/5/04.
[60] WO152/73, RMC correspondence, 1903–1906, letter Major E. M. Percival, D.A.A.G. for D[irector].S[taff]. D[uties]., War Office to Commandant, 21/5/04.
[61] John Smyth, *Milestones: A Memoir* (London: Sidgwick & Jackson, 1979), 24.
[62] Hamilton, *Monty*, 48–9 and Montgomery, *Memoirs*, 24–5.
[63] Thomas, *The Story of Sandhurst*, 169–71.
[64] IWM, PP/MCR/11, *Memoirs of Major-General S. C. M. Archibald*, 47.
[65] Lynch-Robinson, *Last of the Irish R.M.s*, 59–60. [66] Baynes, *Forgotten Victor*, 4.
[67] IWM, PP/MCR/136, *Memoirs of Brigadier G. S. Brunskill*, unpaginated.

education with a leaning towards military affairs. The one thing they did not teach you was anything about your job as an officer. One learned quite a lot about field engineering. One great military campaign was studied, and no doubt the cadet could have won that campaign pretty easily. One learned to dress smartly and to sit a horse with reasonable security, but what happened to one when one took a battery on parade was never revealed.'[68] The most damning criticism of either of the cadet colleges came from Frederick Morgan, who attended the RMA from 1912 to 1913. He reflected, '[N]othing nowadays can approach the standard of futile absurdity set out for our delectation ... The usefulness of much of what we did can never have been thought of.'[69]

Those gaining commissions from the ranks were a small group among the Edwardian officer corps. Most were in the 'dead end' job of quartermaster, which tended to be given to long service NCOs and was largely clerical in nature. William Kelly, who was commissioned into the 1st Leinster Regiment as a lieutenant and quartermaster in 1909, had seventeen years and three months service in the ranks, ultimately as a regimental sergeant major, but had never been on active service, showing that bravery in the field was not an essential requirement for a long-service NCO to be promoted to commissioned rank.[70] Some of those promoted from the ranks were given the normal duties of an officer and the opportunity for further promotion; the best example of this is the case of Field Marshal William Robertson, the only man in the history of the British Army to have risen from private soldier to field marshal. Robertson came from an impoverished background and enlisted as a trooper in the 16th Lancers in 1877, gaining his commission in the 3rd Dragoon Guards in 1888. The outbreak of the First World War found him a major-general and director of military training at the War Office.[71]

Of course, Robertson's case was exceptional; most men promoted from the ranks found themselves rising no further than major before the age limits forced them to retire. This is neatly demonstrated in the case of Captain J. E. I. Masterson, 2nd Devonshire Regiment, who had risen from the ranks after winning a Victoria Cross at Wagon Hill, Ladysmith, during the South African War. On his confidential report for 1911, his CO stated, 'Has capacity for command and leadership. Is self reliant and

[68] Frederick Pile, *Ack-Ack: Britain's Defence against Air Attack during the Second World War* (London: George G. Harrap, 1949), 13.
[69] Morgan, *Peace and War: A Soldier's Life*, 24.
[70] TNA, WO76/24, 'Record of Officers service, 1 Leinster Regiment'.
[71] D. R. Woodward (ed.), *The Military Correspondence of Field-Marshal Sir William Robertson, Chief of the Imperial General Staff, December 1915–February 1918* (London: Bodley Head for the Army Records Society, 1989), 1–16.

possesses tact. Is a v. g. officer and looks after the welfare of his men. I have not recommended this officer for accelerated promotion yet I think it would be a gracious act to promote him to substantive Major, so as to allow him to draw an increased pension. He will be compulsorily retired in 14 months time, and there does not seem much chance of his getting promotion in his own regiment.' These comments were acted on, and Masterson was promoted to major in the Lancaster Regiment before retirement.[72]

Those promoted from the ranks faced financial problems in trying to maintain themselves in their commissioned status, and this probably explains why so many of them served with unfashionable colonial units. For example, Captain J. F. MacKay, who, like Masterson, was awarded a Victoria Cross for heroism in the South African War and then was commissioned into the Argyll and Sutherland Highlanders, served in the West African Frontier Force from 1903 to 1908. Even when he returned to Britain, he was seconded from his regiment to serve as the adjutant of the 7th Royal Scots, a TF battalion. Similarly, Major M. N. Turner, commissioned from the ranks in July 1890 into the 1st Duke of Cornwall's Light Infantry, spent much more than his fair share of service overseas. Between July 1890 and April 1906 he spent just forty-one months in the United Kingdom, and from 1897 to 1902 he was the adjutant of the Upper Burma Volunteer Rifles. All these postings brought special allowances and reduced living costs.[73]

Financial problems could also be a problem for the group known as 'gentlemen rankers', men who were from middle-class backgrounds but who enlisted in the ranks for a variety of reasons: failure to pass the entrance examinations to the cadet colleges or lack of family support, moral or financial, for their choice of career. A good example of this group is C. H. Bacon, who had been educated on the army side of St. Paul's School and then enlisted in the King's Royal Rifle Corps. After two and a half years of service he was commissioned as an officer in the 1st Oxfordshire and Buckinghamshire Light Infantry in July 1909. However, in August 1913 it was noted that '[a]fter making every effort to live upon his pay and the small allowance which is all that his father can afford to give him, Mr. Bacon feels compelled to give up the struggle to make both ends meet.' Bacon had applied for secondment to the Canadian Militia, which seems to have brought his case to the attention of the

[72] LHCMA, Hamilton, 5/2/6, Ian Hamilton Papers, 'Confidential Report on Captain J. E. I. Masterson', May 1911.

[73] TNA, WO76/460, 'Record of Service of Officers', 1 Argyll and Sutherland Highlanders and DCLI Museum; Bodmin, 'Record of Service of Officers', 1 Duke of Cornwall's Light Infantry.

authorities at the War Office, and after personal intervention by J. E. B. Seeley, the Secretary of State for War, the solution to his case seems to have been to promote him to the rank of full lieutenant in the less expensive Northamptonshire Regiment.[74]

While a snob like General Sir William Nicholson could voice concern about those risen from the ranks, commenting on William Robertson's 'want of breeding' when he was being considered for the post of Commandant of the Staff College, other senior officers were concerned at the narrow social basis of the officer corps.[75] Lieutenant-General Sir Ian Hamilton raised the possibility of, as he put it, 'slipping, here and there, a Field Marshal's baton into the knapsack of Thomas Atkins' in a memorandum of August 1912. Hamilton felt that those opposed to more widespread commissioning from the ranks would base their arguments on four main points. Firstly, ranker officers had not proved to be a success with officers or men. Secondly, more 'ranker' officers would destroy 'the social life of the regiment'. Thirdly, the increase in officers' pay required to allow rankers to remain in their new posts would make it difficult to get officers to serve in India or Africa as the differentials for overseas service would largely be removed. Fourthly, the army needed to tap more educated men for the officer corps than were to be found in the ranks. Hamilton himself was concerned that, if handled badly, more widespread commissioning from the ranks would merely benefit the 'orderly room clerk class' and 'crammers failures', neither of which he felt would produce effective leaders. Hamilton himself advocated a scheme, which was implemented in 1914, whereby selected NCOs would be commissioned on the outbreak of war. He also proposed a number of special scholarships aimed at pupils in grammar schools, free education for all cadets at Sandhurst and the reform of the cavalry to make the cost of living in a cavalry mess much less, but these plans came to nought.[76]

After commissioning, very limited professional development was open to officers. Almost all went through a practical course in musketry at Hythe, and there were also practical courses in machine guns, signalling and mounted infantry work. Officers did have to pass promotion exams which covered drill, interior economy and disciplinary powers if they were to advance. However, the Akers-Douglas Committee felt that these were

[74] LHCMA, Hamilton 5/1/62, Ian Hamilton Papers, 'Letter J. S. King, War Office to Hamilton', 5/8/13; and *Army List*, August 1914, c.1334.

[75] Keith Jeffery, *Field Marshal Sir Henry Wilson: A Political Soldier* (Oxford University Press, 2006), 78.

[76] LHCMA, Hamilton 5/1/7, Hamilton Papers, 'Letter Hamilton to J. E. B. Seeley', 27/8/12; and Hamilton 5/1/11, 'Letter Hamilton to R. B. Haldane', 6/4/14.

not very rigorous as they were conducted by examining officers from the candidate's own battalion, who knew the candidate too well.[77] Nevertheless, Christopher Lynch-Robinson, who seems to have had an easy time passing the Sandhurst entrance exam and to have done well there, found his 'D' examination for promotion to captain 'very hard'.[78] By 1910, the promotion examinations to lieutenant and captain included a military history component concerning either the American Civil War or the Russo-Turkish War of 1877–8.[79] In 1906, the Inspector General of the Forces was critical of the promotion examination from major to lieutenant-colonel. He noted that officers had to pass the entrance examination for the Staff College – that is to say, they had to pass the minimum amount of marks to qualify, not enough to actually secure a place. As noted later, the Inspector General, and others, felt that a distinction should be made between 'command' and 'staff' posts, the former not requiring the officer to have attended Staff College.[80]

Other professional development after commissioning was rare. The Staff College at Camberley underwent something of a 'golden age' in the period just before the Great War with an impressive succession of commandants: Brigadier-General Henry Rawlinson, Brigadier-General Henry Wilson, Major-General W. R. Robertson and Brigadier-General Launcelot Kiggell. The creation of a General Staff in 1906 and establishment of a Staff College at Quetta, India, in 1911 can also be seen as signs of increasing professionalism.[81] However, the British General Staff was, in many instances, simply a redefinition of existing administrative posts, and the Staff College at Quetta was, not surprisingly, designed to professionalise the Indian Army, not the British Army proper. In both Staff Colleges there was too much emphasis on sport and games and too little emphasis on the basic administrative functions of staff officers. In any case, the numbers of officers attending Staff Colleges were very small: 103 officers were listed as students at the Staff College at Camberley and 51 as students at the Staff College at Quetta on the outbreak of war. Of the students at Quetta, only fifteen were from the British Army.[82] Apart from the two Staff Colleges, the only formal staff training was in a course established at the London School of Economics which commenced in

77 *Report of the Committee Appointed to Consider the Education and Training of Officers of the Army* (Cd. 982), 1902 ('Akers-Douglas Report'), 31–2.
78 Lynch-Robinson, *Last of the Irish R.M.s*, 68.
79 RMAS, WO152/74, Box 143, RMC Correspondence 1910, 'Letter Director Military Training to Commandant', 15/7/10.
80 TNA, WO27/491, 'Annual Report for 1906 of the Inspector-General of the Forces', 13.
81 Gooch, *The Plans of War.*
82 Bond, *The Victorian Army and the Staff College*, 181–298; Jeffery, *Field Marshal Sir Henry Wilson*, 64–84; and *The Army List*, August 1914, c.2480–1.

1906. This course covered law, economics, statistics and geography and was designed to prepare officers for staff duties. Up to the outbreak of the First World War, 241 officers had qualified in this course. This whole scheme was viewed with suspicion by Henry Wilson, who was concerned that it would develop as a rival to the Staff Colleges.[83]

Given the small number of officers who attended Staff College and the lack of other systematic professional development after commissioning, the question then arises over how the promotion system worked in the Edwardian army. Unfortunately, it is impossible to reconstruct the decision-making process as it existed between 1902 and 1914 as a number of key War Office records have either been destroyed or withheld and a number of officers, who were either at, or to rise to, the height of their profession either did not keep or, in a surprising number of cases, destroyed their personal papers. Tim Travers has considered the promotion system and has developed the concept of the 'personalised' army. In Travers's view, the years 1902–18 saw a conflict between a traditional and professional promotions system, with patronage remaining important. There are, of course, some examples which Travers can use to support this argument. Douglas Haig clearly benefitted from being a protégé of John French and in turn acted as a patron for a number of officers, perhaps most notably Hubert Gough. However, Travers failed to appreciate the limits of patronage in the years before the First World War, and too much of his evidence is based on the unreliable memoirs of J. E. Edmonds.[84] The simple fact of the matter seems to be that in the long-established tradition of British public service; the principle of 'buggin's turn' was all important. Officers might jump the queue a little by passing Staff College, performing an act of bravery or calling upon the support of patrons, but in a small army, with few senior vacancies, and in the years 1902–14 very limited opportunities for active service, it was seniority which became the guiding principle. As a result, promotion was glacial before the Great War, and in 1914, to use two random examples, the senior captain in the Grenadier Guards had been promoted to that

[83] Bond, *The Victorian Army and the Staff College*, 252; R. Dahrendorf, *A History of the London School of Economics and Political Science 1895 to 1995* (Oxford University Press, 1995), 89; Peter Grant, 'Edward Ward, Halford Mackinder and the Army Administration Course at the London School of Economics, 1907–14', in Michael Locicero, Ross Mahoney and Stuart Mitchell (eds.), *A Military Transformed? Adaption and Innovation in the British Military, 1792–1945* (Solihull: Hellion, 2014), 97–109; Command Papers: 1907 (Cd. 6285), 1908 (Cd.4052), 1909 (Cd. 4610), 1910 (Cd. 5213), 1911 (Cd. 5597), 1912–13 (Cd. 6285) and 1913 (Cd. 669).

[84] Tim Travers, *The Killing Ground: The British Army, the Western Front and the Emergence of Modern Warfare 1900–1918* (London: Routledge, 1987), 3–36; and T. H. E. Travers, 'The Hidden Army: Structural Problems in the British Officer Corps, 1900–1918', *Journal of Contemporary History*, 17, 3 (1982).

rank as long ago as 1905 and had sixteen years of service in total, and his counterpart in the Connaught Rangers had been promoted to captain in 1901.[85]

The only significant collection of papers relating to the promotion system of this period are those of General Sir Ian Hamilton. Hamilton, as Inspector of Overseas Forces (1910–14), was responsible for completing confidential reports on a number of officers of the rank of major and above and commenting on their suitability for promotion. He also, as a senior officer and member of the War Office selection board, received a number of letters asking for his help in securing promotion. These papers suggest that the system of confidential reports was taken seriously and, despite the fact that officers had to be shown and had the right of appeal to the Army Council over any adverse report, that honest appraisals were made. Thus, a patron could do very little to promote the interests of an officer who received an adverse report or who had failed his promotion examination.

The nature of the Edwardian army also set limits. Promotions were to fill set vacancies, so however brilliant an officer was judged to be and however great the patronage behind him, he could not receive significantly accelerated promotion. Thus, Hubert Gough, coming from a well-established military family, wealthy, experiencing a 'good war' in South Africa and with the patronage of Douglas Haig behind him, still had to wait until he was thirty-six years old to become a regimental commanding officer.[86] Linked to this was the operation of the regimental system. The army was loath to cross post officers from one regiment to become majors or lieutenant-colonels in another as this struck at the whole concept of regimental seniority. When Henry Beauvoir De Lisle, a future general and corps commander during the First World War, was promoted from the Durham Light Infantry into the 5th Dragoon Guards as a major and brevet lieutenant-colonel in 1903, this was done at the express wish of Field Marshal Lord Roberts, who realised that De Lisle and he had similar views on the future employment of cavalry as mounted infantry. De Lisle's transfer meant that in 1905 he became the commanding officer of the 5th Dragoon Guards. De Lisle reflected that his position was 'at times a little difficult'.[87]

This did, of course, then result in a bizarre situation in which some battalions were judged to have a wealth of talent, most of which would not

[85] *Hart's Army List*, 1914, c.284 and 499.

[86] Gary Sheffield and Helen McCartney, 'Hubert Gough', in I. F. W. Beckett and S. J. Corvi (eds.), *Haig's Generals* (Barnsley: Pen & Sword, 2006).

[87] Beauvoir De Lisle, *Reminiscences of Sport and War* (London: Eyre & Spottiswoode, 1939), 121–3.

Figure 3. 'Old Soldiers' 1st Royal West Kent Regiment, 1910.
Source: From authors' collections

be fully recognised by promotion, whereas others were deemed to have very little. Thus, Lieutenant-General Sir J. G. Maxwell, as GOC Egypt, commented on Major W. B. Wallace of the 1st Suffolk Regiment, 'It seems a pity that an officer who has specialised in S.A. [Small Arms] and has the experience of Maj. Wallace cannot be made more use of. I was most favourably impressed with this officer. With so many high qualified officers recommended by their C.O. for accel. prom. [accelerated promotion] it is a pity that prom. [promotion] should be blocked in this particular battalion.'[88] It says much for the pre-war promotion system that an officer of the calibre of H. H. Tudor, later to become a major-general and highly effective divisional commander during the Great War, was not selected for accelerated promotion while a major despite enthusiastic support from Lieutenant-General Julian Byng, then GOC Egypt.[89]

The lack of promotion prospects for other ranks, the likelihood of postings to uncomfortable imperial garrisons, harsh discipline and poor

[88] LHCMA, 5/1/11, General Sir Ian Hamilton Papers, 'Confidential Report on Major W. B. Wallace', 13/4/11.
[89] LHCMA, 5/1/11, General Sir Ian Hamilton Papers, 'Confidential Report on Major H. H. Tudor', 14/4/13.

pay all meant that service in the ranks of the British regular army before the war was unpopular. From 1903, when the situation returned to normal after the South African War, up to the outbreak of the First World War, the effective strength of the British Army consistently fell below its establishment. In 1912–13, the establishment of the rank and file of the regular army was 256,839, but the strength was just 241,709. Allied to problems in initial recruiting was a relatively high desertion rate, with 2,934 men deserting in 1912–13 alone, and a poor retention rate, with only 8,543 men opting to extend their periods of service.[90] While St John Brodrick and H. O. Arnold-Forster had experimented with very short periods of service, of just three years of colour service, followed by nine in the reserve, Haldane restored the late Victorian system for most soldiers, with enlistment for seven years of colour service, followed by five with the reserve. The experiment with very short service had not been successful, with just 43 per cent of men enlisted under this scheme agreeing to extend their service.[91]

Ex-servicemen were also not particularly favoured in the civilian jobs market when they had completed their active service. While a number of bodies, such as the National Association for the Employment of Ex-Soldiers, Incorporated Soldiers' and Sailors' Help Society, the Army and Navy Pensioners' and Time-Expired Men's Employment Society and the Guards' Employment Society, existed to help ex-servicemen secure work, the jobs into which they were likely to place men were relatively low status. Ex-servicemen were favoured in the more menial civil service posts as messengers, postmen, watchers, warders, park-keepers, attendants and porters. By September 1913, about 19,500 ex-servicemen were employed in these positions. Otherwise, the post office and police forces were keen to employ ex-servicemen, employing 2,644 and 1,098, respectively, between October 1912 and September 1913. In private firms, the railway companies were most notable for their desire to employ ex-soldiers. By September 1913, 23,724 ex-soldiers were employed by them.[92] These are quite impressive figures, but given the high turnover of soldiers in the regular army, they are not that impressive. We should also reflect that the rationale for employing soldiers in many of these positions was not one of altruism; in many the

90 1914 (Cd. 7252), *The General Annual Report on the British Army for the Year Ending 30th September 1913*, 33–6.

91 L. T. Satre, 'St. John Brodrick and Army Reform, 1901–1903', *Journal of British Studies*, 15, 2 (1976); and Albert Tucker, 'The Issue of Army Reform in the Unionist Government, 1903–5', *Historical Journal*, 9, 1 (1966); Williams, *Defending the Empire*, 41–83; and 1908 (Cd. 3798), *The General Annual Report on the British Army for the Year Ending 30th September, 1907*, 4 and 8.

92 1914 (Cd. 7252), *The General Annual Report on the British Army for the Year Ending 30th September 1913*, 16–23.

soldier's small pension would enable him to eke out a living, whereas the small wages offered were otherwise inadequate. The Army Reports for the Edwardian period, in common with their Victorian predecessors, attempted to disguise just how reliant the army was on the unemployed and unskilled workforce for its recruits. It seems likely that a large number of the 19,433 men who enlisted in 1913 and were categorised as 'unskilled labour' were actually unemployed at the time of their attestation, but there was no category for 'unemployed' in the official statistics, merely 'previous occupation'.[93] Senior military figures were quite clear about the class upon which the regular army relied for its recruits. In a telling phrase, General Sir William Nicholson, the Quartermaster General, referred to the army's dependence on the 'compulsion of destitution' to fill its ranks. The Inspector General of the Forces, writing in 1904, offered a similarly bleak analysis, concluding that 'the Army only gets the "wasters" of the civil population.'[94] Civil servants felt that a combination of the establishment of labour exchanges and the falling costs of emigration were having a detrimental impact upon regular army recruiting by 1913. Somewhat surprisingly, given its non-combatant nature and the skills which a man would learn while serving in it, recruitment for the Royal Army Medical Corps (RAMC) was particularly poor, with the height requirement being lowered to just five feet, three inches in December 1912.[95] A telling statistic on the poor nutrition of many of those who attempted to join the regular army is that in 1912–13, 21 per cent of men presenting for enlistment failed the rather rudimentary medical examination.[96]

There were other reasons why men enlisted in the army beyond sheer poverty. Certainly some men did enlist to maintain a family tradition. William Magee, who had risen to the rank of company sergeant-major by the time of his death at Gallipoli in 1915, is a good example of this. He had sixteen years of service and was the third generation of his family to have served in the Royal Inniskilling Fusiliers. Similarly, when F. O. Mason enlisted in the Royal Garrison Artillery as a bugler on his fourteenth

[93] *Ibid.*, 60.

[94] TNA, WO105/41, 'Letter Nicholson to Lord Roberts', 10/11/06, cited in I. F. W. Beckett, 'The Compulsion of Destitution: The British Army and the Dilemma of Imperial Defence, 1868–1914', in Peter Dennis and Jeffery Grey (eds.), *Raise, Train and Sustain: Delivering Land Combat Power* (Canberra: Australian Military History Publications, 2010), 31; and TNA, WO27/491, *Annual Report for 1904 of the Inspector-General of the Forces with Remarks by the Army Council*, 61.

[95] TNA, WO27/491, *Annual Report for 1904 of the Inspector-General of the Forces with Remarks by the Army Council*, 7–8.

[96] 1908 (Cd. 3798), *The General Annual Report on the British Army for the Year Ending 30th September, 1907*; and 1914 (Cd. 7252), *The General Annual Report on the British Army for the Year Ending 30th September 1913*.

birthday, he was following his father and older brother into the army.[97] E. G. White, born and raised in London and apprenticed as a boot-maker, decided to join the army as he thought he would prefer an outdoor life. T. H. Painting, who had worked for W. H. Smith at Lichfield Trent Valley Station since he had left school aged eleven, had read about the army in India in the magazines and books he sold and felt that he would 'like to join the army and see the world'. A similar rationale informed E. S. Humphries' decision to enlist as he worked in a hotel with a former soldier who told him about his army career in India. Percy Snelling was a poor farmer's son who wanted to work with horses, so decided to enlist in the cavalry.[98]

The Cardwell-Childers regimental system developed between 1868 and 1881 meant that most infantry regiments in the British Army, with the notable exceptions of the Guards, King's Royal Rifle Corps and Rifle Brigade, were allocated a specific recruiting area from which, in theory, they were meant to draw the vast majority of their recruits. However, the experience of local recruitment varied enormously. Partly this was due to the fact that the regimental areas allocated under the 1868–81 reforms had been allocated for historical as much as demographic reasons. Thus, the regimental districts in the Highlands of Scotland and rural Ireland could not provide the manpower to support their local regiments due to the depopulation of these areas over the previous century. The 27th Regimental District, designed to feed the Royal Inniskilling Fusiliers, provided just fifty-eight regular recruits and the 72nd Regimental District, designed to feed the Seaforth Highlanders, provided just fifty-three regular recruits between October 1912 and September 1913, whereas the average number of recruits per regimental district in the Eastern Command was 147. Where regiments could not gain their recruits locally, they relied on those recruited in other areas, notably in the major cities, which were left outside the territorial scheme. For example in 1912–13, 832 men enlisted in the regular army in Dublin and 558 in Glasgow. The other problem apparent with local recruitment was that some regiments had been much less successful than others at building up local identities and loyalty. At one extreme, 100 per cent of those who enlisted into the infantry in the 72nd Regimental District in 1912–13 joined the Seaforth Highlanders; at the other extreme, only 33 per cent of those who enlisted into the infantry in the 83rd

[97] *The Sprig of Shillelagh*, IX, 105, July 1915, 1; and IWMSA, 49/8, interview with F. O. Mason.

[98] IWMSA, 188/7, interview with E. G. White; 212/4, interview with T. H. Painting; 314/12, interview with Percy Snelling; and 4935/5, interview with E. S. Humphries.

Regimental District joined the Royal Irish Rifles.[99] This variety of regimental identity partially explains why the 'Pals' system, based largely on industrial cities, rather than the pre-war regimental identification with rural counties, was so popular.

Between 1902 and 1914, the British Army was largely English in composition; the 1913 returns noted that 179,237 regular soldiers were English, 3,124 Welsh, 17,282 Scottish and 20,780 Irish. The pattern of recruitment in Ireland appears to have been little affected by politics. Despite anti-recruitment campaigns over the 1902–14 period by the Irish Transvaal Committee, Dungannon Clubs, Sinn Fein, Ancient Order of Hibernians, Irish National Foresters and the *United Irishman*, Irish recruitment to the British Army remained buoyant and roughly in line with its population share of the United Kingdom, which was not the situation in Scotland, where enlistment rates had fallen below the Scottish proportion of the UK population. A fair proportion of recruits to the British Army were born in India (7,574 in 1913), and the assumption is that most of these men were the sons of soldiers who were serving in India.[100] In terms of age, the vast majority of recruits to the regular army were between eighteen and twenty-five years old when they enlisted. In 1905–6, 34,848 of a total of 37,099 recruits were from this age group.[101]

The Victorian period had seen general improvements in barracking in systematic attempts to alleviate the appalling conditions in which many men were housed. However, this programme of building and rebuilding had by no means cured the problem.[102] Many men, and their families, were still housed in poorly constructed and occasionally unsanitary conditions. In 1901, a Committee on Barrack Accommodation reported and made a number of recommendations designed to rationalise and improve barracks across the United Kingdom.[103] Although it was accepted in the main, work was not carried out on a uniform basis, largely due to government parsimony, and it took a long time for all soldiers to feel the benefit. Facilities in Ireland were often thought to be the worst, with men housed in dilapidated buildings often located in the worst districts of towns and cities. In response to a 1906 questionnaire,

99 1914 (Cd. 7252), *The General Annual Report on the British Army for the Year Ending 30th September 1913*, 42–7.

100 1914 (Cd. 7252), *The General Annual Report on the British Army for the Year Ending 30th September 1913*, 92; and Terence Denman, 'The Red Livery of Shame: The Campaign against Army Recruitment in Ireland, 1899–1914', *Irish Historical Studies*, XXIX (1994), 114.

101 1914 (Cd. 7252), *The General Annual Report on the British Army for the Year Ending 30th September 1913*, 57.

102 Spiers, *Late Victorian Army*, 138–43.

103 TNA WO 33/178, 'Report of the Committee on Barrack Accommodation', 1901.

Major-General L. W. Parsons, commanding the Cork district, complained bitterly about the state of the barracks in his district and urged immediate action.[104]

Intimately connected to the availability of basic amenities was the provision of good food. Although most soldiers were fed regularly, and for the recruits from the most impoverished elements of British society, this was something of a novelty, there were continual complaints that the portions were too meagre, particularly from young soldiers. Soon after arrival at Curragh Camp, the new (or rather re-enlisted) recruit Horace Wyndham realised that he was continually hungry.[105] John Lucy experienced the same sensation along with his fellow new recruits and noted that the 'work was too hard for growing youths, and we devoured everything edible we could lay our hands on.'[106] Percy Snelling, a cavalryman who enlisted in 1906, remembered: 'From the time I was a trooper till I was a sergeant in the sergeants' mess, I never got up from a meal that I couldn't have eaten as much again, except when I was on furlough, at home.'[107]

Alcohol certainly caused disciplinary problems and in some cases required hospital and medical treatment. In 1908, 192 men were hospitalised with alcohol-related issues in the United Kingdom, India and the colonies; by 1913, the figures had not changed much, with 113 admissions. However, the 1913 figures excluded India, so the final total was probably not too dissimilar.[108] Intimately connected with alcohol abuse, at least in the minds of many senior officers, was sexual health and morality. The British Army had a poor record in terms of sexually transmitted diseases (STDs). In 1908 it had the second-highest rate among the armies of the major powers at 68.4 admissions per 1,000 men, with Germany at the bottom with 19.3. By 1912 the figure was down to 55.5 per 1,000, with a steep decline in the number of infantrymen infected and an equally steep decline in invaliding rates.[109] As might be expected, rates were highest among men serving overseas, especially in India. Despite these generally high figures, most commanding officers were quick to dismiss alcohol abuse and STDs as minor problems, at least

[104] TNA WO 33/2979, Advisory Committee on the Spiritual and Moral Welfare of the Army, *Reports from Commands on the Conditions of Soldiers' Life at Home and Abroad, 1907*, 68 (hereafter known as *Report on Welfare*).

[105] Wyndham, *Following*, 36–46. [106] Lucy, *Devil in the Drum*, 27.

[107] Quoted in David French, *Military Identities: The Regimental System, the British Army, and the British People, c.1870–2000* (Oxford University Press, 2005), 122

[108] *Army Medical Department Report*, 1908 Cmd. 4933, 123, 135, 144, 153, 166; *Report on the Health for the Army*, 1912 Cmd. 7201, 139.

[109] *Army Medical Department Report*, 1908 Cmd. 4933, vi, xiii, 93–5, 123, 135, 144, 153, 166; *Report on the Health for the Army*, 1912 Cmd. 7201, 46–7.

in the home-based army, and pointed out the noticeable rate of decline in their own units.[110]

Chaplains were seen as useful in encouraging men away from various temptations. Colonel E. Herbert, commanding officer of the Rifle Brigade Depot, was certainly convinced about the influence of a chaplain and wrote, 'A wonderful influence is here exercised among the men, especially among the recruits, who form the bulk of the garrison, by the Reverend E. G. F. Macpherson, Church of England Chaplain to the Forces. He so gets hold of the lads when they arrive, that there is hardly any intemperance, sexual immorality, or gambling among them during the 3 months they are here.'[111] The army was extremely solicitous about religion and tried to ensure that each man had an opportunity to follow his own particular denomination.[112] However, as the army concentrated more and more attention on the facilities around Salisbury Plain, the lack of places of worship became increasingly apparent. In 1906, Major-General E. O. Hay, on behalf of Southern Command, complained that there were now nearly 6,000 soldiers in and around Salisbury Plain, and yet there were no religious spaces reserved for their use.[113] Sectarianism, particularly in Ireland, also caused friction. Major-General L. W. Parsons echoed the sentiments of the Reverend F. B. D. Bickerstaffe-Drew, a senior Chaplain to the Forces, when he noted that soldiers' institutes and homes had to be ecumenical if they were to be truly effective.[114]

Soldiers' institutes and homes tried to offer men a friendly welcome and provided them with games, newspapers and books. Reading was certainly an extremely important pastime, and many men were voracious readers. Wyndham stated that the men in his battalion had broad reading tastes, enjoying Conan Doyle, Kipling, romances by Mrs Henry Wood and Miss Braddon and histories, travel books and biographies.[115] Official reports on library usage were equally enthusiastic. 'The books are largely read, especially novels, and every encouragement is given for the men to read as much as possible' was the judgement on the Western Heights, Dover, garrison library, while that at Curragh Camp was 'extensively and intelligently used by the troops', and the library at Cork was 'very largely used and appreciated by all ranks'.[116] Live entertainments were often performed in the institute, while men based in the larger garrison towns and cities had the opportunity of visiting local theatres and cinemas.[117] By far the biggest diversion, regardless of season and weather, was sport.

[110] TNA WO 33/2979, *Report on Welfare'* 7, 9, 31, 77, 93, 163, 183. [111] *Ibid.*, 205.
[112] *Ibid.*, 4–5; Wyndham, *Following*, 67.
[113] TNA WO 33/2979, *Report on Welfare'* 136, 169. [114] *Ibid.*, 68, 169.
[115] Wyndham, *Following*, 52. [116] TNA WO 33/2979, *Report on Welfare*, 11, 63, 75.
[117] *Ibid.*, 4, 9, 11, 17, 42; Wyndham, *Following*, 121.

The army indulged in sport to an almost fanatical degree, buttressed by a passionate belief in its moral and physical benefits.

Most sports were heavily subsidised from regimental subscriptions and were not given much direct government funding. This situation was remarked upon by Colonel W. H. Lindsay of the Royal Artillery, who complained that far too much of the expense fell on officers' purses.[118] In addition, playing fields were often at a premium. Most officers noted the desperate lack of quality space for sports.[119] Even at Aldershot, the leading garrison of the British Army, facilities were lacking. Lieutenant-General Sir Horace Smith-Dorrien saw the provision of additional sporting facilities as a crucial part of his work in the command.[120]

These morale-building activities seem to have made some impact as across the period 1902–14 the total number of courts martial cases convened declined year by year. In 1902, a year which included a period of active operations in the field and thus conditions in which transgressions of discipline were more likely, saw 15,009 cases brought before courts martial.[121] By 1913, the figure had shrunk to 4,854, an average of 2.11 per cent of the army's strength compared with 4.25 per cent in 1902.[122] A further continuance of the late-nineteenth-century pattern was the much higher instance of courts martial in the United Kingdom compared with soldiers stationed in India and the colonies. In 1913, 3,090 men were brought before the courts martial compared with 1,764 abroad.[123] As with the Victorian army, the explanation for this phenomenon most probably can be found in the very different complexions of the UK and overseas elements of the army. The UK-based army very largely consisted of young, new recruits who had not yet reached either the age or degree of basic training suitable for deployment abroad. For example, in 1913, just short of half the home-based army consisted of men under the age of twenty-two.[124] These young, inexperienced men were far more likely to fall foul of the army's disciplinary system than older men acclimatised to army life. This factor also helps to explain the story behind the single biggest problem dealt with by courts martial: desertion. In 1902, 2,830 men were *charged* with this offence. On the surface this more than halved by 1913, as a glance at the figures reveals 1,325 cases.[125] However, these statistics have to be treated carefully and do

[118] TNA WO 33/2979, *Report on Welfare*, 137. [119] *Ibid.*, 8, 17, 36, 76.

[120] General Sir Horace Smith-Dorrien, *Memories of Forty-Eight Years' Service* (London: John Murray, 1925), 356.

[121] *Report on Discipline*, 1902, Cmd. 1775, 1–22.

[122] *Report on Discipline*, 1913, Cmd. 7331, 1–7. [123] *Report on Discipline*, 1913, 4.

[124] *Annual General Report on the British Army, 1913*, Cmd. 7252, 88–9.

[125] *Annual General Report on the British Army, 1911*, Cmd. 5481, 70; and *Annual General Report on the British Army*, Cmd. 7252, 1913, 74–5.

not perhaps reveal the true underlying trend, for the army's figures from 1907 onwards record only those *convicted* of desertion. Whatever the actual pattern, it is clear from the statistics that many young men must have found their immersion in army life a profoundly shocking experience which drove them to desperate measures. In 1913, the desertion rate was highest among those who had served for between one and two years, closely followed by those with fewer than three months' service and those with between six months' and a year's service. A second major problem was that of violence and disobedience to superiors, which appears to have shown a pronounced increase on the situation in the late Victorian army.[126] Simple use and presentation of army statistics gave the impression that the problem was a minor one, especially when combined with the effect of recording convictions only, for the two elements of the charge, violence and disobedience, were disentangled and treated as separate offences after 1909. When these nuances are taken out, the supposed decline from 1902 onwards appears far less convincing.

The reasons behind the rise in violence and disobedience are difficult to fathom set against the wider context of a generally improving discipline. It is made all the harder to explain given the decline in drunkenness as a problem. In 1902, 16,292 men were fined by commanding officers for drunkenness. Many men appeared to learn their lesson, for 9,756 received one fine only, but there were 6,536 men who were fined at least once more (one soldier received no fewer than ten fines).[127] By 1913, the numbers had dropped to 9,230 in total, consisting of 6,464 single offenders and 2,766 multiple offenders (two men were fined on ten separate occasions. The record in this period was set in 1913 when one man collected thirteen fines).[128] Once again, however, care has to be taken with statistics, for they have to be combined with those brought before courts martial. In 1902, a total of 2,765 were dealt with in this manner, and in 1913, 426 men were *convicted* for the offence. These figures reveal drunkenness to be a continuing issue for the army but one that was being slowly brought under control. On the whole, fewer soldiers were being fined and court-martialled for drunkenness than in the 1870s and 1880s, thus continuing the trend established in the 1890s.

The British Army, given its varied responsibilities in terms of home defence, imperial policing and a continental commitment, failed to define

[126] *Annual General Report on the British Army*, Cmd. 7252, 1913, 74. See also French, *Military Identities*, 182.
[127] *Annual General Report on the British Army, 1911*, Cmd. 5481, 70, 74.
[128] *Annual General Report on the British Army,* Cmd. 7252, 1913, 74, 78.

a solid doctrine before the First World War.[129] This was further complicated by the fact that in the British Army the battalion remained the key unit of organisation, not the brigade or division, as on the continent, which left each CO with considerable latitude over how he conducted training. A belief in Jominian 'general principles' of war and an unwillingness to create set solutions to problems at Staff College and on manoeuvres contributed to this. This is not to state that the British Army was an 'unthinking army'. For example, in 1907, Major-General Sir James Grierson, commander of 1st Division at Aldershot, chaired a debate on the fire fight led by Lieutenant-Colonel N. R. McMahon of the School of Musketry at Hythe. Grierson remarked at the end of the lecture his belief that given the increases in firepower, soldiers required more guidance in order to stop what he called the 'go as you please' approach often witnessed in exercises and manoeuvres.[130] The following year the Inspector-General's report asked whether a sufficient knowledge of the principles of war and some familiarity with the workings of others arms had permeated the entire army.[131] Matters seemed to improve after these warnings, which may reflect the ever-increasing levels of debate about firepower. Haig attempted to impose a centralised approach on Aldershot Command, and in 1913 he noted the good progress 'towards establishing a uniform doctrine throughout the staffs of the command'.[132] Tellingly, Haig's phrase concerns only staff, not regimental officers.

The General Staff, as created in 1906, did not take a lead in the creation of doctrine, as one might have expected. Important training manuals were produced, which drew on the British Army's experience of the South African War and which were amended and revised to incorporate observations from the Russo-Japanese War. The list includes *Cavalry Training, 1904* and its replacements *Cavalry Training, 1907* and *1912; Combined Training, 1905; Infantry Training, 1905* (with amendments in 1908) and *1914* and the summation of overarching principles contained in the *Field Service Regulations, Parts I and II* in 1909. Precise authorship of these manuals can be hard to determine. Certainly *Cavalry Training, 1904* was commenced by Haig while he was preparing to travel to India to take up

[129] For alternative interpretations, see Stephen Badsey, *Doctrine and Reform in the British Cavalry 1880–1918* (Aldershot: Ashgate, 2008), 143–238; and Spencer Jones, *From Boer War to World War: Tactical Reform of the British Army, 1902–14* (Norman: Oklahoma University Press, 2012).

[130] Lieutenant-Colonel N. R. McMahon, *Fire Fighting* (London: Hugh Rees/Aldershot Military Society, 1907), 17. Grierson was considered by many to be one of the ablest generals in the army. He went to France in August 1914 as commander of II Corps but died of a heart attack before seeing action.

[131] TNA WO 27/508, *Inspector-General's Report for 1908*, 35.

[132] TNA WO 279/53 'Aldershot Command, Comments on the Training Season, 1913', 11.

the role of Inspector-General of Cavalry and was notoriously altered by Field Marshal Sir Frederick Roberts in order to reflect his own particular views.[133] From 1905 on, the various directors of military training, assisted by other specialists, played the leading role in the production of manuals, and in 1909, Haig oversaw the writing of the *Field Service Regulations* in his role as Director of Staff Duties at the War Office. Central to all these instructions was an acceptance of the great impact of modern firepower on both defence and offence. Contrary to much popular belief about the British Army before the Great War, firepower was not ignored but accepted and debated fiercely. The problem, as the British Army's training regimes revealed, was determining the best way of dealing with this issue.

Training in the British regular army was complicated by the fact that recruits could be accepted at any time of the year, which created a great disadvantage compared to the conscript system used in most of Europe. Brigadier-General Ivor Maxse made this point most forcefully in an address to the Royal United Service Institution in 1911. He noted that most company commanders 'begin to realise that the new comers are raw recruits totally ignorant of field work, and with a large proportion of these he proceeds to army manoeuvres'. 'What company officer in a foreign army, where all recruits join the same day, has such a difficult task?' he asked his audience.[134] The need to find drafts to reinforce units overseas also eroded training efficiency. Major-General S. C. M. Archibald recalled his early service in the Royal Artillery and noted that '[w]inter always began with the annual nightmare of having to find a draft for India. Most of one's best NCOs and men seemed to be taken away from one every year and replaced by a lot of untrained recruits from whom one was expected to build the battery again by the spring into a first class show.'[135]

Intimately connected with this problem was the lack of numbers, both officers and men, available for training duties. Maxse identified fifteen different tasks which often demanded the detachment of officers and men for other duties during the training season. According to his knowledge, this led to company strengths averaging about forty men, when there were eight companies per battalion.[136] Sir John French recognised this problem while GOC in Aldershot Command and urged his battalion commanders to resist the temptation to spread themselves too thinly by

[133] Badsey, *Doctrine and Reform in the British Cavalry, 1880–1918*, 175–82.
[134] Brigadier-General F. I. Maxse, 'Battalion Organization', *Royal United Service Institution Journal*, 56, 1 (January–June 1912), 52–86.
[135] Imperial War Museum Department of Documents (hereafter known as IWM D) PP/MCR/11, Major-General S. C. M. Archibald handwritten memoir.
[136] Maxse, 'Battalion Organization', 59.

continually shuttling between their companies to oversee mundane tasks.[137] Southern Command reported an extreme shortage of men for exercises in 1905, while the 1908 Inspector-General's report noted the weaknesses in company training due to lack of numbers and subalterns and urged that no subaltern be allowed to take a course while company training was underway.[138] Exercises were undermined in 1907 by lack of numbers, as was made clear at the General Staff conference in January 1908 when it was noted that 'they found hardly any regulars, but a miscellaneous collection of units of the auxiliary forces'.[139]

It was disturbing to the General Staff to note continuing problems with the quality and approach of officers leading training. Colonel J. T. Johnson, GSO1 4th Division, told the 1908 General Staff conference that '[o]fficers had not always a clear idea of what they wanted to teach, nor, when they wanted to test officers, what was a really sound solution of the problem.'[140] The surviving personal papers from battalion officers do not imply a particularly rigorous attitude towards training. A young lieutenant's diary reveals that the battalion training period lasting from the 16 July to 1 August 1906, consisted of mornings only.[141] Captain J. H. Brocklehurst of the Coldstream Guards recorded a similar pattern in his diary, and he was clearly shocked when he was ordered 'to conduct Company in musketry for five hours!'[142] During company training in 1912, one of Brocklehurst's fellow captains recorded that he went 'to barracks to look in on company training', which implies that he did not rigorously supervise it himself.[143] While at Aldershot Command, French attempted to impose more rigour and condemned much training as 'manifestly wrong'.[144]

There is a tendency to portray the British Army before the First World War as a colonial gendarmerie. However, from 1867, in a process accelerated by the Haldane reforms, efforts had been made to devolve responsibilities for Imperial defence to locally raised dominion or colonial forces, removing British regular troops from various far-flung garrisons. In terms of the dominions, Canada became responsible for its own defence in

[137] TNA WO 27/504 'Memorandum on Military Training, 1905', Aldershot Command.
[138] TNA WO 27/508, *Reports by the Inspector-General of Forces* – submitted to the Army Council, 1903–13. *Inspector-General's Report for 1905*, 51; *Inspector-General's Report for 1908*, 13–14.
[139] Defence College Library, Shrivenham, 'Report on a Conference of General Staff Officers at the Staff College, 7–10 January, 1908', 16.
[140] 'Report on a Conference of General Staff Officers, 1908', 9.
[141] NAM 9605-11, General Sir Walter Venning Diary, 16 July–1 August 1906.
[142] Coldstream Guards' Archive, Wellington Barracks (hereafter known as CGA); diary of Captain J. H. Brocklehurst, 2 January 1912.
[143] CGA, Captain C.M. Perreira diary, 9 December 1912.
[144] TNA WO 27/504, 'Memorandum on Military Training, 1905', Aldershot Command.

1867, Australia in 1901 and New Zealand in 1909. South Africa developed its own permanent defence forces in 1910, but a sizeable British garrison was retained there, with the South African War of 1899–1902 an all too recent memory. The presence of the British regular army in Canada, Australia and New Zealand was absolutely minimal by 1914, amounting to a handful of senior officers. However, a similar process of devolving Imperial defence to the colonies was rather more difficult and saw a significant number of British regular army officers and NCOs serving with locally raised colonial forces. This was most obvious with the creation of the King's African Rifles (KAR) and West African Frontier Force (WAFF), which evolved from a number of ad hoc local units, some raised by private business interests rather than the British government. 1901 saw the formation of the WAFF, which consisted of the Gold Coast Regiment, Sierra Leone Battalion and attached Gambia Company and the Northern and Southern Nigeria Regiments. 1902 saw the creation of the six-battalion-strong KAR formed from the former Central African Rifles, East African Rifles and Uganda Rifles. By 1913, the WAFF had an establishment of 231 British officers and the KAR 75.[145]

The organisation of the KAR and WAFF remained complicated throughout the Edwardian period. The Colonial Office remained in overall charge of these units, and army officers serving in them were, technically, seconded to the Colonial Office. Periods of secondment were for three years, with a possible extension of no more than seven additional years, which, of course, meant that, unlike in the British-officered Indian Army, officers could not forge an entire career in the KAR and WAFF and had little motivation to develop an in-depth knowledge of the languages or cultures of the men under their command. Related to this, service in Africa was unpopular, as sickness was a constant problem for Europeans, which meant that the Colonial Office only wanted officers aged between twenty-two and thirty-five. Officers were awarded generous pay and allowances, with a minimum of £300 per annum additional pay and, of course, negligible expenses while serving in Africa. But this had a limited impact on solving the recruiting shortage of British regular officers, and a number of posts were filled by Militia and Special Reserve officers, much against the wishes of the Colonial Office.[146] Indeed, while these

[145] For the development of these forces, see Colonial Office Annual Reports, No 260: *Niger, West African Frontier Force, Reports for 1897–8* (London: HMSO, 1899); Lieutenant-Colonel H. Moyse-Bartlett, *The King's African Rifles: A Study in the Military History of East and Central Africa, 1890–1945*, Vol. I (Aldershot: Gale & Polden, 1956), 3–131; Colonel A. Haywood and Brigadier F. A. S. Clarke, *The History of the Royal West African Frontier Force* (Aldershot: Gale & Polden, 1964), 5–36; and *Army List*, January 1914.

[146] TNA CO 445/21, *WAFF Reports, 1905*, Vol III: correspondence 20 April 1905; and CO445/34 *WAFF Reports, 1914*, correspondence 2 February 1914.

forces did obtain the services of some very capable officers, they seem to have received more than their fair share of problem cases, with alcoholism a major problem.

Despite these problems, the WAFF and KAR were effective in the colonial small wars they were required to carry out in protection of British Imperial interests. Between 1902 and 1914, the WAFF took part in forty-five expeditions, the KAR, thirty-eight, and at the same time an almost continual low-level campaign was being pursued in Somaliland, which was not brought to a conclusion until 1920.[147] Some historians have branded the WAFF and KAR as poorly trained militias capable of little more than armed police work. This sentiment was not accepted at the time. Inspector-General G. H. Thesiger declared in 1910 that certain units of the KAR were 'not only suited for so-called savage warfare, but one that could hold its own in any form of fighting'.[148] Indeed, the KAR was to be a victim of its own success, as having dealt effectively with its responsibilities, it was reduced from six to four battalions between 1910 and 1914 due to financial restrictions imposed by the Colonial Office, which left a small cadre on which to expand during the First World War.[149]

For soldiers of the British regular army, with the exception of those serving in Guards regiments, frequent postings throughout the Empire were normal, with India still seen as the natural home of the British Army. In 1914, just before the outbreak of war, eighty-three infantry battalions were based on home service, with fifty-two in India, five in Egypt, five in Malta, two in Gibraltar, four in South Africa, three in Hong Kong and one each in Mauritius, the West Indies and Malaya. The fact that units on home service were usually considerably under-strength and composed largely of recruits undergoing training must also be factored into this balance sheet of home and Imperial service.

The experience of serving in overseas colonies was far from uniform. While Egypt was thought to be an interesting posting, with a low cost of living, Aden had a reputation as a furnace, with few leisure pursuits available.[150] Opinions of India, where soldiers were most likely to serve

[147] See Haywood and Clarke, *Royal West African Frontier Force*, 38–96; Moyse-Bartlett, *King's African Rifles*, Vol. I, 132–256, Vol. II, 419–433; General Staff, War Office, *Official History of Operations in the Somaliland 1901–1904*, Vols. I and II (London: HMSO, 1907); Damian O'Connor, 'The Lion and the Swallow. The Somaliland Field Force, 1901–1920', *Royal United Services Institute Journal*, 151, 5 (October 2006), 68–73.

[148] See Parsons, *African Rank and File*, 2; TNA CO 534/10, *KAR Reports, 1910; Inspector-General's Report*, 12 December 1910.

[149] Moyse-Bartlett, *The King's African Rifles*, 50–9.

[150] W. F. Stirling, *Safety Last* (London: Hollis & Carter, 1953), 28; IWM 77/3/1, 'The Army Life of J. W. Riddell, an NCO in the Rifle Brigade, 1907–1933', handwritten manuscript, 31; and *Hampshire Regimental Journal*, 1, 1 (October 1903), 2.

on an overseas posting, varied considerably depending on the location to which units were directed. Few men relished the hot season in Bombay. G. L. Boys-Stones was shocked by the heat of Bombay on his first arrival in India and was pleased that he was directed to the hills, finding Kasauli particularly agreeable.[151] In December 1908, the 2nd Cheshire Regiment left Madras in a tropical downpour. Once at their new barracks in Secunderabad, spirits rose, for 'the arid climate of Secunderabad is a welcome change to those of us who have been used to the humidity of Madras, and it is safe to say that very few regrets at leaving the latter place have been expressed.'[152] The winter weather then proved a pleasant reminder of home, as Christmas was spent in chilly, frosty conditions. The next destination of the 2nd Cheshire Regiment was Jubbulpore, and it made an immediately favourable impression: 'The climate, on the whole, appears to be good; a trifle hotter than Secunderabad in the hot weather; pleasant in the rains, with a real genuine cold weather . . . we may consider ourselves to be extremely lucky.'[153] While various attempts were made to provide activities, particularly sports, for soldiers serving in Imperial outposts, STD rates remained high in India, although the numbers of men suffering from them declined over the years, albeit slightly. In 1908, 4,786 men were admitted to hospital with STDs; by 1912, the figure had fallen to 3,913. Fortunately for the army, improvements in treatment brought the invaliding figure down markedly.[154]

In the spring of 1914, it appeared that the most likely warlike scenario for which the British Army would have to prepare was to suppress, or at least contain, a civil war in Ireland. While the Liberal government remained determined to introduce home rule, a moderate form of devolved government into Ireland, Ulster Unionists remained implacably opposed to this measure. Ulster Unionists had formed the 100,000-strong Ulster Volunteer Force (UVF) and were determined, if home rule was passed, to establish a Provisional Government of their own which would govern the nine historic counties of Ulster, in defiance of the new home-rule parliament in Dublin. In March, Lieutenant-General Sir Arthur Paget, the GOC in Ireland, held a series of meetings with officers in the Irish Command and seems to have made a number of very ill-thought-out statements, essentially telling officers that if they had relations in Ulster, they would not be expected to serve against the UVF but otherwise would be expected to do their duty.

151 IWM D 03/21/1, Boys-Stones Letters, 4 March 1910, 19 January 1911.

152 *The Acorn: Monthly Magazine of the 2nd Battalion Cheshire Regiment*, 3, 1 (January 1909), 7–8.

153 *The Acorn*, 4, 11 (November 1910), 199.

154 *Report on the Health of the Army, 1908*, 93–95, 153; *Report on the Health of the Army, 1912*, 46, 142.

Brigadier-General Hubert Gough and most of the officers in the 3rd Cavalry Brigade made it clear that they would rather resign their commissions than serve against the UVF. Incredibly, the Secretary of State for War, J. E. B. Seely, and Field Marshal Sir John French, CIGS, then issued a guarantee to Gough and his officers, stating that they would not be expected to act against Ulster. This event saw a major breakdown in civil–military relations as the Prime Minister, H. H. Asquith, insisted that both Seely and French resign for exceeding their authority, and many other army officers made it clear that they were quite prepared to follow Gough's lead if disciplinary action was taken against him. The Irish home-rule crisis appeared to worsen after the Curragh, when the UVF landed 20,000 rifles, purchased in Germany, at Larne, Bangor and Donaghadee, with no interference by police or troops. The Irish Volunteers, formed by Irish Nationalists to support home rule, grew considerably in numbers throughout 1914, perhaps reaching a total of 180,000 by the outbreak of war. They also brought in rifles, on a much smaller scale, in July 1914 in an action which saw the 1st King's Own Scottish Borderers called out in aid of the civil power and firing into a crowd, killing three people and wounding a further thirty-two in central Dublin at Bachelor's Walk on 26 July 1914. It was only the outbreak of the First World War, when Sir Edward Carson, leader of the Irish Unionists, and John Redmond, the Irish Nationalist leader, pledged their support to the British war effort which diffused this situation.[155]

Therefore, whatever the debates about the role of the British Army as a colonial police force, continental force or home defence force, it should be remembered that the primary duty of the army, as outlined under the Stanhope memorandum, of maintaining the civil power at home, was the key focus of senior officers in the weeks before the outbreak of the First World War. The tight financial ceiling under which the army operated and the fact that neither the regular army nor auxiliary forces were recruited to full strength further hampered the war planning of the British Army. Unlike the great continental armies, which relied on conscription, the volunteer British Army entered the Great War with no planned way to expand beyond the one cavalry and six regular divisions of the BEF and fourteen infantry divisions and fourteen yeomanry brigades of the TF, whatever R. B. Haldane's post-war statements to the contrary.

[155] I. F. W. Beckett (ed.), *The Army and the Curragh Incident, 1914* (London: Bodley Head for the Army Records Society, 1986), 1–32; Timothy Bowman, *Carson's Army: The Ulster Volunteer Force, 1910–22* (Manchester University Press, 2007), 45–162; and F. X. Martin (ed.), *The Irish Volunteers 1913–1915* (Dublin: James Duffy, 1963), 3–144.

2 The Officer Corps

The image of the British Army officer corps in the Great War is not a particularly flattering one. The work of self-proclaimed 'revisionist historians' of the war has done little to shake the popular view of the senior officer corps as bunglers, if not exactly butchers; the middle-ranking officer corps as elderly 'dug outs' and the junior officer corps as naive public school boys who led men to their deaths unquestioningly. In reality, the British officer corps faced remarkably similar problems to those faced by other combatant armies and struggled, rather more successfully than some, to overcome these problems. The heavy losses of officers throughout the war and the massive expansion of the officer corps, from 28,060 to over 229,300, meant that vast numbers of officers were needed at all levels. Officer casualties in the British Army totalled 116,781 killed, wounded and missing (including POWs) between 1914 and 1919, with 29,889 killed on the Western Front alone.[1] To meet these demands, large numbers of civilians had to be commissioned after very cursory training; a number of senior and middle-ranking officers had to be recalled from retirement; a large staff had to be assembled, few of whose members had the luxury of attending the Staff College; officers had to be found for new, technologically driven corps; and officer training courses had to be improvised.

In the first chaotic months of the war, as the New Armies were formed and the Special Reserve and Territorial Force (TF) massively expanded, the view was taken that men of appropriate education and background, though often with little or no military experience, could be posted directly to units and would learn their professional duties while actually serving as army officers. The high financial outlay expected of a pre-war officer was almost entirely removed, leading to the portrayal of many wartime officers as 'temporary gentlemen'. It is not clear quite how many temporary

[1] War Office, *General Annual Reports of the British Army for the Period 1 October 1913 to 30 September 1919* (London: HMSO, 1921), 71–2, cited in Keith Simpson, 'The Officers', in I. F. W. Beckett and Keith Simpson (eds.), *A Nation in Arms: A Social Study of the British Army in the First World War* (Manchester University Press, 1985), 82, 88.

commissions were granted to those gazetted to the New Armies between August 1914 and February 1916, but it seems to have been just over 80,000. In addition, 30,376 Special Reserve commissions were granted over the course of the war, as opposed to a mere eighty-one in 1913, and 60,044 commissions were granted in the Territorial Force (TF), whereas the entire officer corps of the TF on 4th August 1914 was a mere 9,563. As the war continued, a more formalised system of officer training developed, originally based on university Officer Training Corps (OTC) units and later on officer cadet battalions. From February 1916, commissions were meant to be granted only to products of officer cadet battalions, and these thirty-eight training units provided 107,929 officers.

Most of those granted commissions in the Great War received only temporary commissions, which would not convert into permanent commissions in peacetime and gave no pension entitlement. A mere 1,109 temporary commissions, 1,008 Special Reserve commissions and 335 Territorial Force commissions were converted to permanent commissions during the war. Unlike in peacetime, many officers were promoted from the ranks. Indeed, the ranks provided 6,713 permanent commissions during the war, almost as many as the Royal Military Academy (RMA) and Royal Military College (RMC) combined. Between 5 August 1914 and 1 December 1918, the RMA commissioned just 1,928 officers and the RMC 5,013.[2]

As discussed in Chapter 1, before the war, the British regular army did not quite have an officer caste, on the model of the Prussian Junkers. However, the officer corps of the regular army was drawn from a very narrow section of British society, and the unpopularity of service in the officer corps, reliant as it was on the possession of a private income, meant that in peacetime there was a shortfall in the number of officers. The Army Council in 1910, with very optimistic calculations of likely casualty rates, recognised that 3,201 officers would be needed for the British Expeditionary Force (BEF) on mobilisation alone. They recommended that large numbers of non-commissioned officers (NCOs) should be commissioned to make up the shortfall.[3]

Assessments of British generalship of the First World War started, shortly after the war itself, with the so-called battle of the memoirs.[4]

[2] All figures taken from War Office, *Statistics of the Military Effort of the British Empire during the Great War* (London: HMSO, 1922), 234–5.

[3] TNA, WO163/15, 'Minutes of the Army Council, 1910', précis number 453; 'Supply of Officers', 19–20.

[4] A useful summary of these debates can be found in Ian Beckett, 'Frocks and Brasshats', in Brian Bond (ed.), *The First World War and British Military History* (Oxford: Clarendon Press, 1991), 89–112.

Richard Holmes' thoughtful biography of Sir John French, the first commander of the BEF, did something to rescue his reputation. While French was not a success on the Western Front and was removed in 1915 after the disastrous Battle of Loos, he had proved himself a very capable soldier during the South African War and had been effective as General Officer Commanding (GOC) Aldershot and as Inspector General of the Forces. Even French's critics allowed that he was very effective in holding the BEF together in the retreat from Mons. As Holmes concluded, '[T]he problems faced by French were far harder that those which confronted his successor: it was French who sustained the first onslaught, in new and strange conditions, when the BEF was at its weakest and the enemy at his strongest.'[5] Keith Jeffery has similarly done much to rehabilitate the reputation of Field Marshal Sir Henry Wilson from the damage done to it by his first biographer, Sir Charles Callwell. Wilson's career remains an unusual one, as most of his war was spent in Staff positions rather than in command (IV Corps from December 1915 to November 1916 being the exception), and he clearly did not have a particularly good relationship with Haig. Wilson's military capabilities were shown in the retreat from Mons, when as sub Chief of Staff he essentially had to take over from General Sir Archibald Murray, the Chief of Staff, when he suffered a breakdown on 24 August. Wilson's advice meant that the BEF continued to retreat south rather than making for the Channel Ports, and his careful liaison work with Joffre was important in ensuring co-operation between the BEF and French forces during the retreat. Later in the war, Wilson played an important role in coalition warfare, developing a close working relationship with Foch, and he also proved effective in dealing with British political leaders, essentially offering David Lloyd George a change of personality, rather than a change in strategy, when Lloyd George tired of General William Robertson as Chief of the Imperial General Staff (CIGS).[6]

Controversy over the abilities, or lack thereof, of French's successor, Field Marshal Sir Douglas Haig, have continued ever since the 1920s, with consensus remaining elusive. J. P. Harris's important recent work on Haig, based on painstaking research, paints a nuanced picture of a commander who was originally cautious and hesitant, but developed grandiose strategic visions and seemed rather more reckless with the lives of his troops as the war progressed. Haig, in Harris's view, was not very reflective or self-critical and cannot be regarded as a 'great captain'

[5] Richard Holmes, *The Little Field Marshal: Sir John French* (London: Jonathan Cape, 1981), 367.

[6] Keith Jeffery, *Field Marshal Sir Henry Wilson: A Political Soldier* (Oxford University Press, 2006).

because of his lack of strategic vision. Often over-optimistic, he believed the German army to be close to collapse in mid-1917, though by early 1918 he believed that a negotiated peace might be the best option for the British forces. Gary Sheffield's more recent work is much more complimentary regarding Haig's abilities. In Sheffield's view, Haig was a reflective and innovative commander, and his capabilities were fairly shown by the campaigns of 1918.[7]

However, the destruction of the Military Secretary's records for 1914–18 during the Second World War and the decision of a number of senior officers, or their families, to destroy their own personal papers mean that important questions regarding appointments, promotion and removal for the officer corps as a whole remain difficult, if not impossible, to answer. Henry Horne, who was to become GOC First Army in September 1916, has been the subject of two recent biographies. However, Horne still appears as a decidedly uncharismatic figure, and while he emerged as a protégé of Haig in August 1914 when commanding the artillery of I Corps, it remains unclear how a career of standard regimental duty led him to this post in the first place. Richard Haking, who was temporary commander of First Army in August 1916, remains an even more elusive figure, despite Michael Senior's biography, which makes a determined attempt to restore Haking's reputation, a task severely complicated by the lack of any surviving private papers.[8]

Compared to their counterparts in the continental European armies, British generals were much more likely to have held combat command, particularly in the South African War (1899–1902), but much less likely to have commanded large formations. To put this in context, it is worth noting that Hubert Gough was, on the outbreak of war, commanding the 3rd Cavalry Brigade at the Curragh, which is about 1,600 men on mobilisation, whereas in January 1917, when promoted to lieutenant general, he was commanding the Fifth Army, over 250,000 strong. At least for Gough, it is possible to discern the reasons for his promotion. He had a number of natural advantages; he was from an old military family and was independently wealthy. On top of this, he had a 'good war' in South Africa, managing to escape from the Boers when taken prisoner, and was

[7] J. P. Harris, *Douglas Haig and the First World War* (Cambridge University Press, 2008), esp. 531–46; and G. D. Sheffield, *The Chief: Douglas Haig and the British Army* (London: Aurum Press, 2011).

[8] Don Farr, *The Silent General: Horne of the First Army* (Solihull: Helion, 2007); Simon Robbins (ed.), *The First World War Letters of General Lord Horne* (Stroud: History Press for the Army Records Society, 2009); Simon Robbins, *British Generalship during the Great War: The Military Career of Sir Henry Horne (1861–1929)* (Farnham: Ashgate, 2010); and Michael Senior, *Lieutenant General Sir Richard Haking, XI Corps Commander 1915–18: A Study in Corps Command* (Barnsley: Pen & Sword Military, 2012).

a protégé of Haig. Similarly, the reason for Gough's dismissal in April 1918 is clear, given the failure of the Fifth Army to hold its positions against the German Spring Offensive, though Gough had some justification for feeling that he was the scapegoat for poor staff work at GHQ, limited Anglo-French co-operation and the Lloyd George government's manpower policy.[9]

When considering what was, then, the lowest general rank in the army, John Bourne has shown the problems of securing officers with sufficient training and seniority. Of the fifty-one infantry brigade commanders whose formations were part of the order of battle at the start of the Battle of the Somme on 1 July 1916, four had begun the war as infantry battalion commanders, twenty-two more had been infantry battalion officers (eighteen of them majors) and sixteen had been staff officers. Five of these officers were dugouts who had been brought back from retirement; the oldest was J. D. Crosbie, commanding the 12th Brigade, 4th Division, who had retired as long ago as 1893. Two of these officers were Royal Engineers: H. Bruce-Williams, 137th Brigade, 46th Division, and G. C. Kemp, 138th Brigade, 46th Division. Only one, J. B. Jardine, 97th Brigade, 32nd Division, was a cavalryman. The youngest of these brigadier generals was Frank Burnell-Nugent of 167th Brigade, 56th Division, who was just thirty-five. By 29 September 1918, the 189 brigadier generals of the BEF were still predominantly men who had been regular officers in August 1914. Only six were TF officers, including Arthur Maxwell of the 174th Brigade, who was a banker by profession, and W. F. Mildren of the 141st Brigade, who pre-war was a company director. By September 1918, the average age of brigadier generals had fallen to just over forty-two, and twenty-eight officers under the age of thirty-five had been promoted to brigade command during the war. The youngest British brigadier general of the Great War was Roland Boys-Bradford VC, who on 10 November 1917 was promoted to command the 186th Brigade when he was only twenty-five. Bradford was killed twenty days later during the Battle of Cambrai.[10]

9 Hubert Gough, *Soldiering On* (London: Arthur Barker, 1954), 145–80; Gary Sheffield and Helen McCartney, 'Hubert Gough', in I. F. W. Beckett and S. J. Corvi (eds.), *Haig's Generals* (Barnsley: Pen & Sword Military, 2006), 75–96; and D. R. Woodward, *Lloyd George and the Generals* (Newark: University of Delaware Press, 1983), 291–3.

10 Peter Simkins, '"Building Blocks": Aspects of Command and Control at Brigade Level in the BEF's Offensive Operations, 1916 and 1918', in Gary Sheffield and Dan Todman (eds.), *Command and Control on the Western Front: The British Army's Experience 1914 to 1918* (Staplehurst: Spellmount, 2004), 152–4, citing J. M. Bourne, 'The BEF on the Somme: Some Career Aspects, Part 1, July 1916', *Gun Fire: A Journal of First World War History*, 35, 11–14; J. M. Bourne, 'The BEF on the Somme: Some Career Aspects, Part 2, July to November 1916', *Gun Fire: A Journal of First World War History*, 39, 18–25; and J. M. Bourne, 'The BEF's Generals on 29 September 1918: An Empirical Portrait with

The massive expansion of the British Army meant that a large number of staff officers had to be found. GHQ of the BEF alone expanded considerably during the Great War. In November 1918, it was thirteen times bigger than in August 1914, and GHQ in August 1914 had consisted of only about thirty staff officers. This was irrespective of the large numbers of staff officers who had to be found for other theatres and new formations, the Home Commands and at the often hastily improvised Army level in France and Belgium.[11] As noted in Chapter 1, the General Staff was a very recent creation in Britain, and the Staff College had produced very few graduates pre-war. Matters were further confused by the desire of staff officers based in the War Office to return to a combat role with their own regiments and the decision made at the start of the war to close the Staff College. In closing the Staff College the government was demonstrating both its belief in a short war and an acknowledgement of the fact that, without the immediate appointment of instructing staff and students from the Staff College to staff posts, the BEF could not be properly organised or despatched.

Writing shortly after the end of the war, one senior staff officer wrote a description of work at GHQ which suggested that the army had been very good at promoting pre-war civilians with useful relevant skills into staff posts: 'Put to the test of getting a post at G.H.Q., which was supposed to be the crowning test of efficiency, the New Army Officers did not do badly. I made a rough poll one night at the club dinner. More than half the officers present were "New Army" men. In what may be called "specialist" branches New Army men predominated.'[12] However, in his important work, *British Generalship on the Western Front*, Simon Robbins constructed a sample of 700 British Army officers, of the rank of lieutenant colonel and above, who held senior command and staff posts in the British Army between 1914 and 1918 which provides a very different view. Robbins work is important in demonstrating what a 'closed shop' these higher ranks remained, dominated by pre-war regulars, who made up 82 per cent of the sample. Those who were civilians at the outbreak of war accounted for just 0.6 per cent, and serving TF officers accounted for exactly the same percentage.[13] Cuthbert Headlam, a pre-war officer in the Bedfordshire Yeomanry, certainly felt that he was lucky to be promoted to temporary lieutenant colonel and GSO1 in July 1918, having

Some British and Australian Comparisons', in Peter Dennis and Jeffery Grey (eds.), *1918: Defining Victory* (Canberra, 1999), 100–5.

[11] Sheffield and Todman, *Command and Control on the Western Front*, 39–46.

[12] 'G.S.O.', in *G. H. Q. (Montreuil-sur-mer)* (London: Philip Allan, 1920), 177.

[13] Simon Robbins, *British Generalship on the Western Front 1914–18: Defeat into Victory* (London: Frank Cass, 2005), 188–204.

previously been told, indirectly, that as a 'civilian' he should regard himself as fortunate to be a temporary major and GSO2.[14] The highest rank at which a civilian was commissioned into the British Army during the Great War occurred in December 1916 when Sir Eric Geddes, a leading businessman who had worked closely with David Lloyd George at the Ministry of Munitions and was then holding the post of Director-General of Military Railways at the War Office, was directly commissioned as a major general and posted to GHQ in France as Director General of Transport for the BEF.[15]

It is clear that as the war progressed, pre-war professional soldiers were much more likely than temporary officers to find themselves in Staff posts, often far removed from danger. This situation may explain why there was often such ill-feeling between front-line combat officers and Staff officers. The Earl of Winterton, who served as an officer in the Sussex Yeomanry and Imperial Camel Corps during the Great War, remembered that in one of his few conversations with Field Marshal Sir Henry Wilson, he asked Wilson if he understood why regimental officers had held Staff officers in such 'contempt'.[16] Just as revisionists have sought to rehabilitate British generals of the Great War, so Aimée Fox-Godden has suggested that Staff officers at brigade level have been unfairly found guilty of incompetence. The small number of Passed Staff College (PSC) officers available for brigades was, not surprisingly, quickly exhausted. While, of the 105 infantry brigades on the Western Front in November 1915, twenty-seven (26 per cent) of brigade majors were graduates of the Staff College, by July 1916 this had fallen to just seven (or 4 per cent) of the then 163 infantry brigades. But, to counter this, a number of Staff courses were established within the BEF, 1st Division taking the lead in mid-1915 with a four-week course which included attachments to brigade and divisional HQ. In April 1916, a centralised system was established, with Staff courses held back in the United Kingdom which lasted for ten weeks. A Junior Staff School was established at Hesdin in late 1916 which concentrated on preparing officers for second-grade appointments, and in October 1917, this transferred to Cambridge University.[17] Jim Beach's careful study of the Intelligence Corps, a vital section of the Staff which was established on

[14] Jim Beach (ed.), *The Military Papers of Lieutenant Colonel Sir Cuthbert Headlam 1910–1942* (Stroud: History Press for the Army Records Society, 2010), 207, 210.

[15] Keith Grieves, 'Sir Eric Geddes', in *Oxford Dictionary of National Biography*, available at: www.oxforddnb.com.chain.kent.ac.uk/view/article/33360?docPos=5.

[16] Sixth Earl of Winterton, *Orders of the Day: Memories of Nearly Fifty Years in the House of Commons* (London: Cassell, 1953), 110.

[17] Aimée Fox-Godden, '"Hopeless Inefficiency"? The Transformation and Operational Performance of Brigade Staff, 1916–18', in Michael Locicero, Ross Mahoney and

the outbreak of war, shows that '[i]n early 1915 the Intelligence Corps' officer cadre was a loosely controlled and rather egalitarian pool of around 100 inexperienced amateur soldiers engaged mainly as odd-job men for GHQ. By 1918 this had evolved into a well-regulated group of over 300 intelligence specialists, many with previous operational experience, clad in a distinctive uniform and integrated formally into every headquarters in the BEF down to divisional level.'[18]

While the Staff College closed at the outbreak of war, one of the curiosities of Britain's wartime mobilisation between 1914 and 1918 was that the work of the RMA, Woolwich and RMC, Sandhurst continued on essentially a pre-war pattern: a very odd example of 'business as usual'. While New Army and TF battalions had to make do with hastily commissioned civilians, regular units continued to receive a proportion of their commissioned officers from the cadet colleges, who never had less than three months training and for most of the war nine months training. In May 1918, with victory expected in 1919–20, it was decided by the Army Council that the course of instruction at the RMA and RMC would be extended to eighteen months starting with the next intake of cadets in February 1919.[19]

With the outbreak of war, confusion over whether a potential officer should learn his trade through a cadet course or actually serving with a unit continued from the Edwardian period. Initially, RMA and RMC courses were truncated. Indeed, those who were serving as gentlemen cadets in the senior classes in the military academies, on the outbreak of war, were immediately commissioned, with 156 RMC cadets and 62 RMA cadets receiving their commissions on the 4 August 1914. The future Lieutenant General Sir Brian Horrocks thought himself fortunate to have been so commissioned as, having travelled back to Sandhurst from Gatwick races by train without purchasing a ticket, he was facing expulsion from the RMC for ungentlemanly behaviour.[20] The junior cadet classes at the RMA were commissioned in September and November 1914, respectively. The first intakes of wartime cadets went through truncated courses at the RMC which lasted for as few as three months and the RMA which lasted for as few as six months as a desperate attempt was made to provide cadets, passing through the regular

Stuart Mitchell (eds.), *A Military Transformed? Adaptation and Innovation in the British Military, 1792–1945* (Solihull: Helion, 2014), 139–56.

18 Jim Beach, *Haig's Intelligence: GHQ and the German Army, 1916–1918* (Cambridge University Press, 2013), 73.

19 *The Times*, 10 May 1918.

20 *The Times*, 4 August 1914 and 5 August 1914; and Brian Horrocks, *A Full Life* (London: Collins, 1960), 14.

commissioning route, to replace officer casualties in regular units. Holidays were abolished and games cut to a minimum. At the RMA, strictly military instruction was provided, with classes in languages, mathematics and science suspended. The RMA expanded its intake slightly; the new class which joined on 14 August 1914 consisted of 125 cadets, an increase of 50 on the previous year's intake. However, quickly it was realised that trying to provide replacements, even to just regular units, was an impossible task, and there also seem to have been some concerns about the professional abilities of the post-war officer corps. At the RMA, courses were extended to nine months in June 1916 and twelve months in June 1917. Indeed, of the 247,061 commissions given out during the Great War, only 1,928 went to products of the RMA and 5,013 to products of the RMC.[21] This was in sharp contrast to the Second World War, when those cadets who were training at the RMC found themselves commissioned en masse into the Royal Signals Corps, and the two cadet colleges closed down for the duration of the war. In the Second World War, as a result of the experiences of the Great War, all commissions granted were 'emergency commissions', and the Officer Cadet Training Units, which were the logical successors of the Officer Cadet Battalions, discussed later in this chapter, became responsible for officer training.[22]

There were a few important changes to the fees and entry requirements at the RMA and RMC. A major one dated from November 1914 when the Army Council decided to suspend the fees paid by parents for cadets, though it was made clear that parents would still have to contribute £35 towards the cost of uniforms and books. At the same time it was decreed that Indian Army commissions would not be open to RMC products on a competitive basis, as pre-war. Cadets could be up to twenty-five years of age when joining a cadet college, which was an increase in age of two years, though cadets could be as young as sixteen and a half when joining the RMA or seventeen when joining the RMC.[23]

Francis Law, who as a callow seventeen-year-old entered the RMC in September 1914 and completed his truncated course in March 1915, remembered

> We were worked very hard as was only to be expected, for casualties in France had been heavy and a steady flow of trained young officers was required ... Our

[21] *Statistics of the Military Effort of the British Empire during the Great War*, 234–5; and K. W. Maurice-Jones, *The Shop Story 1900–1939* (Woolwich: Royal Artillery Institution, 1954), 29–39.

[22] J. A. Crang, *The British Army and the People's War 1939–1945* (Manchester University Press, 2000), 21–44; and David French, *Raising Churchill's Army: The British Army and the War against Germany 1919–1945* (Oxford University Press, 2000), 48–80.

[23] *The Times*, 4 November 1914.

training, apart from the drill was simple but strenuous and severely practical. The aim was to teach us speedily all that was thought necessary for a young platoon commander to know, that he might lead and inspire men in battle, and look to their welfare at all times. We took part in simple tactical exercises, map-reading, compass work by night, patrolling and shooting on the range.[24]

When posted to the 2nd Irish Guards, Law recalled further training of a decidedly pre-war nature: 'Soon after joining all "young officers" were required to pass a simple written exam – covering subjects as diverse as the histories of the Household Brigade and of the regiment, correct modes of dress, and how when in plain clothes to wear a Brigade tie!'[25]

The social composition of both the RMA and RMC remained largely unchanged throughout the war. Bedford Grammar School, Cheltenham College, Clifton, Eton, Harrow, Marlborough and Wellington provided the majority of cadets to the RMC between 1902 and 1914. During the war, products of these schools were still over-represented among RMC intakes, though as the war continued their dominance was far from absolute. It was stated that between 29 December 1914 and 29 October 1915, of the 2,223 cadets at both the RMA and RMC, 60 were educated at Bedford Grammar School, 104 at Cheltenham College, 42 at Clifton, 114 at Eton, 70 at Harrow, 68 at Marlborough and 105 at Wellington. During these early months of the war, a number of other leading public schools, which pre-war did not have a tradition of acting as feeders to the cadet colleges, provided large numbers of former pupils. Thus, Charterhouse provided fifty-six cadets, Dulwich thirty-three, Haileybury fifty-one, Oundle thirty and Rugby sixty-four. Some cadets came from schools which were not normally included in the *Public Schools Yearbook*, but these were in single figures and still from minor public schools or grammar schools where parents would have paid significant fees. Products of Burnley Grammar School, Dover Secondary School, Dundee High School, Guildford Grammar School, Horsham Grammar School, Larne Grammar School, Maidstone Grammar School and Portsmouth Grammar School were all to be found among the cadets of the RMA and RMC, but this did little to change the social structure of the regular officer corps.[26]

This pattern had changed little by the last year of the war. *The Public Schools Yearbook* recorded that between December 1917 and December 1918 there were 1,010 cadets at the RMA and RMC

[24] Francis Law, *A Man at Arms: Memoirs of Two World Wars* (London: Collins, 1983), 39.
[25] *Ibid.*, 42.
[26] H. F. W. Deane and W. A. Bulkeley Evans (eds.), *The Public Schools Yearbook: The Official Book of Reference of the Headmasters' Conference* (London: Year Book Press, 1916), 419–25.

combined. Of these, sixteen had attended Bedford, fifty-two Cheltenham, twenty-two Clifton, eighty-three Eton, thirty-three Harrow, twenty-two Haileybury, twenty-six Marlborough, thirty-five Rugby and seventy-six Wellington, demonstrating the continuing importance of the major public schools with a pre-war officer-producing tradition. By contrast, 138 of these cadets came from a total of 88 schools which the Head Masters' Conference did not appear to consider to be public schools. While most of these eighty-eight schools were grammar schools, the curiosities of the Head Masters' Conference system meant that this list included Trinity College Glenalmond and the Leys School, Cambridge, which would now be regarded as leading public schools.[27] It is therefore obvious that the social structure of the regular army officer corps continued in an Edwardian pattern during the Great War. Indeed, the most plebeian cadet of the intake of May 1918 appears to have been W. G. Barker, whose father was Bandmaster of the 5th Dragoon Guards, an occupation which would still have been considered lower middle class by any standards of the day. It is telling that Barker secured a King's Indian Cadetship, meaning that his father was relieved of all expenses connected with his time at Sandhurst.[28]

The entrance examinations to the RMA and RMC remained very similar to those which had existed pre-war. Although in August 1914 it was decided to dispense with oral and laboratory tests, these had been reinstated by 1916. For entrance to the RMC, a candidate had to sit compulsory examinations in English, English history (from 1558 to 1901) and geography, mathematics A (elementary) and French or German. He would then have a choice of sitting no more than two papers from a range of subjects: French or German, Latin, Greek, science (physics and chemistry), mathematics B (intermediate) and mathematics C (higher). Candidates for the RMA had to sit the same compulsory papers as those for the RMC, along with mathematics B (intermediate) and science (physics and chemistry). RMA candidates could also sit one additional subject: German, French, Latin, Greek or mathematics C (higher). Such examinations were designed for those who had attended a public school, and their chances in the competitive examination were helped by the fact that the headmasters of schools which belonged to the Head Master's Conference retained powers of nomination to the RMA and RMC

[27] Problems of the definition of a public school are evident in Anthony Seldon and David Walsh, *Public Schools and the Great War: The Generation Lost* (Barnsley: Pen & Sword Military, 2013), 11–13.

[28] Deane and Bulkeley Evans (eds.), *The Public Schools Yearbook*, 425–9; RMAS Archives, RMC Intake Register for May 1918; and *The Times*, 19 April 1918.

throughout the war, for a small number of their pupils a privilege which was not extended to other schools.[29]

Given the nature of these entrance examinations, if a young man wanted to become a professional soldier, looking forward to the post-war period, then the use of a crammer was a sensible economic decision. Competition for regular commissions remained fierce throughout the war, with one cadet claiming that in the entrance examinations for the July 1915 intake to Woolwich, 600 candidates were competing for 150 places.[30] In the RMC intake for November 1915, one of the few for which detailed information on the cadets survives, at least seven successful cadets were prepared by 'crammers'. Crammers were tutors who specialised in preparing men for the RMA, RMC and, often, also the Civil Service Examinations or entry to Oxford and Cambridge Universities. Some crammers operated as full-time commercial businesses. For example, W. N. Cobbold and W. L. B. Hayter operated West Wratting Park in Cambridgeshire with three resident tutors. The firm's advertisement in the *Public Schools Yearbook* of 1916 claimed that between June 1914 and September 1915, fifty-six of their candidates had secured places at Woolwich, Sandhurst and in the new Royal Navy examination. Other crammers operated this business as an addition to their main occupation. Thus, C. R. Billyard-Leake noted in his application to the RMC that he had been educated at Wellington College and by a crammer, Rev. E. S. Garnier of Guidenham Parsonage, Atteborough, Norfolk, who evidently carried out private tuition in addition to his normal parochial duties.[31]

One of the cadets who entered the RMC in November 1915 was F. C. Hitchcock. His attendance at the RMC seems very strange as prior to his arrival at Sandhurst he was serving as a second lieutenant with a Special Reserve commission in the 2nd Leinster Regiment on active service in France. Presumably, Hitchcock attended the RMC solely to secure a regular commission. Indeed, the *London Gazette* belatedly noted that he 'relinquishes his commission on appt. to a cadet-ship at the R. Mil. Coll[ege].'[32] Strangely, he makes no reference to his time at the RMC in his memoir, the period 8 November 1915 to 14 July 1916 simply appearing with a blank and Hitchcock noting that in early July 1916 he was posted back to the 2nd Leinster Regiment from the 3rd Battalion,

29 Deane and Bulkeley Evans, *Public Schools Year Book*, 1916, 378–85; and *The Times*, 13 August 1914.

30 IWMSA 10699, Brigadier J. M. Rymer-Jones.

31 RMAS Archives, Application Form for RMC Intake for 26 November 1915; and Deane and Bulkeley Evans, *Public Schools Yearbook, 1916*, 768.

32 Supplement to the *London Gazette*, 23 June 1916, 6225.

based in Victoria Barracks, Cork.[33] Hitchcock served out the war in this battalion, reaching the rank of captain, and in 1924 was still serving as a captain, then in the East Surrey Regiment, to which he had transferred on the disbandment of the Leinster Regiment in 1922.[34] Hitchcock's experience appears to have been almost unique. Only one other officer seems to have relinquished a reserve or temporary commission to qualify, as a cadet, for a regular commission. This was Second Lieutenant G. M. L. Smith, who held a temporary commission in the King's Own Scottish Borderers and left them in July 1916 to take up a cadetship, presumably at the RMC.[35]

The pre-war TF had relied largely on local gentry, professionals and businessmen to provide its officer corps. As Helen McCartney demonstrates in her study of the Liverpool Territorials, this remained the case throughout the war.[36] The formation of the Officer Training Corps (OTC) had provided a formal process for amateur soldiers to receive commissions. However, a number of class corps refused to take commissioned officers from outside their own ranks, insisting that commissions should go to their own rank and file, a system that quickly broke down in wartime as many of them were commissioned into other units and senior regular or New Army officers were posted to them.

Despite the fact that many TF senior officers had considerable regular army experience and that a number of TF units essentially became officer training units early in the war, there remained a 'glass ceiling' on promotion for TF officers.[37] As late as February 1918, only ten Territorials were commanding brigades, none any higher formations, and throughout the entire war, only three reached the highest Staff Grade of GSO1.[38]

While the role of the OTC in officering the New Armies has been rather over-estimated, notably by Gary Sheffield and Peter Simkins, who were writing before the release of the officers files at the National Archives (TNA), OTC cadets did form a large section of the wartime officer corps, especially in the first two New Armies.[39] While Field Marshal Lord

[33] RMAS Archives, Application Form for RMC Intake for 26 November 1915; and F. C. Hitchcock, *'Stand To': A Diary of the Trenches 1915–1918*, 128–9.

[34] *London Gazette*, 22 February 1924, 1572.

[35] Supplement to *London Gazette*, 14 July 1916, 7080.

[36] For a detailed discussion of the officer corps in two battalions, see H. B. McCartney, *Citizen Soldiers: The Liverpool Territorials in the First World War* (Cambridge University Press, 2005), 42–56.

[37] It has been calculated that 16 per cent of TF Commanding Officers were ex-Regulars on the outbreak of war. P. E. Hodgkinson, 'British Infantry Battalion Commanders in the First World War', unpublished PhD thesis, University of Birmingham, 2013, vol. I, 35.

[38] I. F. W. Beckett, 'The Territorial Force', in Beckett and Simpson, *A Nation in Arms*, 141.

[39] G. D. Sheffield, *Leadership in the Trenches: Officer-Man Relations, Morale and Discipline in the British Army in the Era of the First World War* (London: Macmillan Press in association

Kitchener may have been suspicious of the TF as a whole, the possible contribution of the OTC was recognised very early in the war. As early as 10 August 1914, advertisements appeared in the press asking for 2,000 cadets or ex-cadets of OTC units for temporary commissions.[40] A study of the OTC, published early in the war, estimated that from the outbreak of war until March 1915, the OTC had provided 20,577 officers, with a further 12,290 OTC cadets serving in the ranks. Within these overall figures, not surprisingly, there were considerable variations. Within the Senior Division, Cambridge University OTC was deemed to have provided 3,000 officers over this period, Oxford University OTC 2,000 and the University of London OTC 500. At the other end of the scale, Aberdeen University OTC had provided just thirty-six officers. Within the Junior Division there were similar, though not as extreme, variations. Charterhouse School OTC provided 411 officers despite not being regarded as an 'Army School' before the war. Eton College OTC provided 350, when its pupils numbered 980, and Haileybury College OTC provided 272 at a time when its pupil numbers were around 500; but Hertford Grammar School OTC provided just ten and Hillhead High School, Glasgow, OTC just fifteen.[41]

Figures for the war as a whole are impossible to ascertain, and the statistics available in some unit histories are confused by the conflation of OTC cadets with all students who received commissions from a particular university. It should also be remembered that Senior Division OTC units could train men who were not university students. However, some figures are clear. The University of London reported that 4,218 former cadets and 89 former officers of their OTC contingent served as officers during the Great War. Trinity College Dublin stated that 1,040 students and 450 other men were commissioned due to service in their OTC before or during the war. The Queen's University of Belfast had 680 members of their OTC contingent commissioned during the war.[42] Durham University claimed that up to May 1917 its OTC had seen 1,277 cadets commissioned, 128 posted to Officer Cadet Battalions and 446 joining the ranks.[43]

with King's College London, 2000), 37; and Peter Simkins, *Kitchener's Army: The Raising of the New Armies, 1914–1916* (Manchester University Press, 1988), 217–22.

40 *The Times*, 10 August 1914.

41 A. R. Haig-Brown, *The O.T.C. and the Great War* (London: Country Life, 1915), 99–106; and Deane and Bulkeley Evans, *The Public Schools Year Book, 1916*, 114, 142.

42 *University of London Officer Training Corps, Roll of War Service 1914–1919* (London: Military Education Committee of the University of London, 1921), 353; University of Dublin, *Trinity College, War List* (Dublin: Hodges, Figgis, 1922), viii; Queen's University of Belfast Archives, QUB/B/1/2/6, Senate Minutes, 20 November 1918.

43 *The Times*, 28 August 1917.

The instruction provided by the pre-war OTC units had varied considerably. J. M. L. Grover, who ended the war as an instructor in the 12th Officer Cadet Battalion, felt that his field days at Winchester had been little more than 'a good day out' but that the annual camp had provided some proper military training.[44] By contrast, J. M. Rymer-Jones, who was to rise to the rank of brigadier, felt that the OTC at Felstead, in which he had gained his Certificate A, had been 'nonsense really'.[45]

In the Senior Division OTC contingents, experiences could vary widely. To use two random examples, Arthur Samuels, commissioned into the 11th Royal Irish Rifles on its formation, had served in the Dublin University contingent for almost five years when war broke out, gaining his 'A' and 'B' certificates and serving periods of attachment with the 2nd King's Own Yorkshire Light Infantry. Samuels had been appointed a second lieutenant in the corps in December 1912 and a lieutenant on the unattached list of the TF in June 1914.[46] At the other extreme, George Smyth, a barrister and graduate of Trinity College Dublin, enlisted in the University of Dublin OTC on the outbreak of war and was quickly commissioned into the 6th Royal Irish Rifles.[47] Many of those who were appointed to commissions largely or solely on the basis of their OTC experience did not possess their 'B' or, in some cases, even their 'A' certificates. Of course, other factors often decided the appointment of these men: many were from influential local families who would have had little difficulty in securing commissions in any case. Ironically, one of these was Arthur Samuels, whose father was a judge.[48]

Such varieties of experience were not always picked up when commanding officers or adjutants of university OTC contingents recommended men for commissions. It is clear that at some universities candidates were carefully scrutinised before being recommended to the War Office. This was most obvious at Cambridge University, where the Vice Chancellor, as chairman of the Board of Military Studies, established a special war committee on 6 August 1914. This body interviewed Cambridge students who were applying for commissions in *viva voce* examinations and worked long hours up until 6 September, when the initial rush subsided. A similar system seems to have been established at Oxford University.[49] Elsewhere, the situation was more chaotic. While

44 IWMSA, 46, J. M. L. Grover. 45 IWMSA, 10699, Brigadier J. M. Rymer-Jones.

46 Personal file of Captain A. P. I. Samuels (TNA, WO339/13357), University of Dublin, *Trinity College, War List, February 1922*, 181.

47 TNA, WO339/11541, Personal file of Captain G. B. J. Smyth.

48 A. P. I. S[amuels] and D. G. S., *With the Ulster Division in France*, 76.

49 Hew Strachan, *History of the Cambridge University Officers Training Corps* (Tunbridge Wells: Midas Books, 1976), 140–1; and J. M. Winter, 'Oxford and the First World War',

OTC units were to continue to function throughout the war and, indeed, were to take on an important role in training temporary officers, at the start of the war many lost key personnel to other units. At the University of Leeds, Captain J. H. Priestly, the commanding officer, left to take up other military duties almost immediately on the outbreak of war, and the senior NCO was posted to the 8th West Yorkshire Regiment in November 1914.[50] The Queen's University of Belfast OTC quickly lost Captain J. D. M. McCallum, who was acting adjutant of the unit, to the 8th Royal Irish Rifles, which seems to be the reason why so few former cadets of this OTC had their applications for a commission properly endorsed.[51] David Campbell, who was a member of the Dublin University OTC remembered receiving a letter from the university on 4 August 1914 inviting him to apply for a commission. He did so and was duly commissioned into the 6th Royal Irish Rifles. Only when he was being officially discharged from the OTC to take up his commission was it discovered that throughout the 1913–14 academic year he had not attended any drills with the OTC, and he was fined £5, the amount of the War Office bonus which the contingent had lost by his absenteeism.[52]

As the war went on, it appears that OTC cadets were not necessarily seen as an asset by the War Office. In December 1915, the President and Secretary of the University of Leeds Military Education Committee had an unpleasant interview at the War Office, where a staff captain apparently stated that he regarded those who had enlisted in the OTC after October 1915 as 'Derby Dodgers' who had done so to escape attestation under the Derby Scheme. The Military Education Committee at Leeds University had already taken measures to resolve this problem, but by June 1916 it had been agreed with the War Office that, with the exception of medical students, no student over the age of eighteen and a half years of age would be retained as a member of the OTC. When students reached this age, they would be transferred to an Officer Cadet Battalion.[53] The Queen's University of Belfast OTC found itself in a similar position despite the decision not to extend the Derby Scheme or conscription to Ireland. In Belfast, the infantry unit of the OTC had

in Brian Harrison (ed.), *The History of the University of Oxford*, Vol. VIII: *The Twentieth Century* (Oxford: Clarendon Press, 1994), 8.

[50] University of Leeds Archives, University Committees Minute Book, 11; Military Education Committee minutes, 4 August 1914, 31 August 1914, 20 November 1914.

[51] TNA, WO339/13911, Personal file of Captain J. D. M. McCallum.

[52] D. H. Campbell (ed.), *Forward the Rifles: The War Diary of an Irish Soldiers, 1914–18: Captain David Campbell, M.C.* (Dublin: Nonsuch Publishing, 2009), 9–11.

[53] University of Leeds, Special Collections, Military Education Committee minutes, 3 December 1915 to 20 June 1916; and typescript, 'Leeds University Officer Training Corps. Memorandum of Interview at the War Office, Wednesday, December 1 1915'.

reached a peak strength of 240 in early 1916, but, following new War Office instructions, a large number of those who were not students at the university had to be discharged, reducing the unit strength to just ninety-six in November 1916.[54] Cambridge University OTC, which had provided so many officers to the New Armies, had only sixty cadets remaining at the start of the Lent Term of 1916 and became moribund at this point.[55]

While the TF as a whole suffered from a shortage of officers on mobilisation, a number of 'class corps' within the TF were soon providing officers to regular, TF and New Army units. Indeed, one of the major criticisms which can be made of how the British Army was expanded in 1914 and 1915 is that many of these 'class corps' were sent into the line to serve as ordinary infantry units when, from the start, it was clear that they provided excellent officer cadres. The Inns of Court Regiment had been organised as a TF battalion in 1908 but, on the outbreak of war, was already regarded as a unit of the Senior Division of the OTC. During the war, it was estimated that this unit provided 12,000 officers, and in early 1915 it was 5,000 strong. Originally recruiting those concerned with the legal profession, the regiment soon cast its net much wider. A recruiting notice of June 1915 stating, 'All members of the Corps, excepting the officers must be (a) members of one of the Inns of Court, or (b) of the Faculty of Advocates Scotland, or of the King's Inn, Dublin or (c) Oxford or Cambridge University men, Public School men or (d) gentlemen considered by the Commanding Officer to be specially eligible for membership.' It is telling that the two former members of the Inns of Court Regiment, who were interviewed by the Imperial War Museum, both went to minor private schools, which were not, in 1915, regarded as public schools and did not have OTC contingents, namely, Bedales School and St. Peter's School, York.[56]

The 1/28th London Regiment (Artists Rifles), where all officers had started their careers in the ranks and whose commanding officer noted that officers and men 'were of the same social class', were sent to France in late October 1914 and were serving in the front line with the 7th Division by early November. On 12 November, General Sir John

[54] Queen's University Belfast Archives, QUB/B/1/2/6, Senate minutes, 'Annual Report of Military Education Committee to Senate,' 22 November 1916.

[55] Strachan, *History of the Cambridge University OTC*, 145.

[56] Guildhall Library, London (NB: now transferred to London Metropolitan Archives but not re-catalogued by them at the time of this writing), ms. 17,686; records of Inns of Court OTC, 1915–17, Recruiting notice dated 3 June 1915; TNA, WO32/18661, 'Future of the Inns of Court and Artists Rifles'; Letter Lord Reading to Winston Churchill, 20 May 1920; IWMSA 9959, Interview with W. H. Wood; and IWMSA 11962, Interview with Roger Powell.

French as Commander of the BEF discussed with the regiment's commanding officer, Lieutenant Colonel H. A. R. May, the officer shortages in the BEF and asked for fifty-two men to be picked from the ranks of the Artists Rifles for immediate battlefield commissions as 'probationary officers'. May assured French, '[I]f we were to have the great honour of supplying young officers to the grand old "regular" Regiments then in France, I would undertake to pick out the very best men we had in the Regiment, and, I assured him, every Officer and N.C.O. in the Regiment would assist me to select the best.' Having selected his new officers, May then gave them a one-hour lecture on leading and serving and the privilege of taking the place of a young regular officer; he also tried to obtain enough copies of the *Field Service Pocket Book* for each of them. This rather desperate expedient was obviously seen to be successful, as ultimately the Artists Rifles provided over 10,000 officers during the war. The 1/28th London Regiment (Artists Rifles) provided seventy-five to one hundred officers per month from November 1914, and in November 1915 all three battalions of the regiment were recognised as OTC units.[57] W. T. Colyer, who was commissioned in January 1915 from the ranks of the 1/28th London Regiment (Artists Rifles), through the so-called suicide club, remembered that he had, initially, been concerned about his credentials to be an officer. But his section sergeant reassured him, saying

> [Y]ou'll be perfectly all right. You're a Public School man and your father washes probably every day and wears a collar and a coat at mealtimes. That's about all they want... You'll have some special training first. As a matter of fact the course you'll go through will be a sort of barrilised [i.e. bastardised] version of the most practical part of the Sandhurst course, with all the red tape and tommy rot cut out. Moreover you'll have what the Sandhurst bloke has never had, and that is a short but invaluable experience of being an ordinary private soldier on active service, which makes you one *better* than him!

Once selected for officer training, Colyer then underwent a five-week course at Bailleul with forty-nine other men from the Artists Rifles. This course included two attachments with regular units in the trenches and a ten-day machine gun course, along with classes on map reading, lectures from regular officers based on the *Field Service Pocket Book* and practical experience in drilling men.[58]

[57] H. A. R. May, *Memories of the Artists Rifles* (London: Howlett, 1929), 142–6; and Anonymous, *The Regimental Roll of Honour and War Record of the Artists Rifles (1/28th, 2/28th and 3/28th Battalions, The London Regiment, T.F.)*, 3rd edn. (London: Howlett, 1922), x–xv.

[58] IWM 76/51/1, W. T. Colyer, 'War Impressions of a Temporary Soldier', 395–409.

The Inns of Court Regiment and 28th London Regiment (Artists Rifles) were unusual in being recognised as OTC units, but a large number of other class corps provided a disproportionately large number of officers who were commissioned from their ranks. The Honourable Artillery Company could claim that over 4,000 of their members had been commissioned. The 14th London Regiment (London Scottish) claimed that 'some 3,000 non-commissioned officers and privates were taken for commissions in other units, and these were mostly taken from the 1st Battalion.' Keith Mitchinson suggests that the 5th London Regiment (London Rifle Brigade) had 1,339 commissioned during the war, 174 serving with the regiment itself. Jill Knight has calculated that the 15th London Regiment (Civil Service Rifles) had 967 of their men commissioned during the war. The yeomanry as a whole regarded itself as a 'class corps', and this was particularly the case with the older regiments formed in the 1790s. George Hay has calculated that the 1/1st Queen's Own West Kent Yeomanry and 1/1st Royal East Kent Mounted Rifles produced 248 officers during the war, while the Sussex Yeomanry had 216 men commissioned, the Glamorgan Yeomanry over 200 and the Northamptonshire Yeomanry 136.[59]

'Class corps' TF units could, initially, be very particular about those whom they accepted. Viscount Buckmaster, a lawyer practicing in London when war broke out, initially tried to enlist in the 1/28th London Regiment (Artists Rifles) and Inns of Court Regiment but was rejected for both due to poor eyesight, his true medical category in fact being 'C3'. He then resorted to learning the standard eye chart used by the army before attempting to enlist in the Honourable Artillery Company. Initially, all seemed to go well until he was asked to read the card backwards, when his memory failed him. Family influence intervened at this stage as Buckmaster's uncle, an officer in the Duke of Cornwall's Light Infantry, told him that he could get him a commission in his regiment. Buckmaster attended for an interview at the War Office and was passed as 'A1' at his medical as, rather than being asked to read off an eye chart, he was simply asked to tell the time from a mantelpiece clock and guessed the correct time. Showing the British Army's long-established tradition of placing square pegs in round holes, Buckmaster

[59] G. Goold Walker, *The Honourable Artillery Company, 1537–1987* (London: Honourable Artillery Company, 1987), 292; J. H. Lindsay, *The London Scottish in the Great War* (London: Privately published, 1925), 89; K. W. Mitchinson, *Gentlemen and Officers: The Impact and Experience of War on a Territorial Regiment 1914–18* (London: Imperial War Museum, 1995), 267; Jill Knight, *The Civil Service Rifles in the Great War: 'All Bloody Gentlemen'* (Barnsley: Pen & Sword Books, 2005) 232; and G. M. Hay, 'The British Yeomanry Cavalry, 1794–1920', unpublished PhD thesis, University of Kent, 2011, 232.

was appointed the sniping officer for the 7th Duke of Cornwall's Light Infantry in late 1915.[60]

Officer training during the war continued to owe a great deal to the TF. Colonel H. A. R. May, who had started the war as CO of the 1/28th London Regiment (Artists Rifles) noted, immodestly, but apparently truthfully:

> No one has had more experience in the rapid training of young men (not professional soldiers) to be Officers than myself, having (after over 30 years pre-war service) been engaged continuously in this task since the first day of War till the Armistice, and having trained *many thousands* during that time. The original syllabus of practical rapid training of the young Officers was devised by me in France and in substance was subsequently adopted by all Cadet Schools in the Army, and may I claim that the young Officers trained by me in France in the early days of the War (the first so trained) and subsequently those trained at No. 3 School of Instruction at Tidworth . . . were among the best in the Army.[61]

In addition, OTC units, which continued to function throughout the war, took on an important role in training officers after they were appointed to temporary commissions. The University of Leeds OTC established a School of Instruction, initially training thirty to thirty-five officers, under the officers and NCOs of the OTC in March 1915.[62] A similar School of Instruction was established at Queen's University Belfast in the autumn of 1914, and when this was wound up in February 1916, it was noted that ten courses had been run, training a total of 477 officers. However, J. H. Stewart-Moore, commissioned into a service battalion of the 36th (Ulster) Division, commenting on the usefulness of this course stated: 'I do not think that we learnt much that was useful but the course provided an opportunity for one or two pleasant tea parties.'[63]

When Lord Kitchener decided to raise his New Armies in August 1914, he was aware of the great problems that there would be in finding suitable officers to lead them. Each infantry battalion of the original BEF was ordered to leave three officers and a number of NCOs behind as a cadre for the new units, and 500 officers of the Indian Army who were home on leave were detained and posted to the New Armies.[64] These officers,

[60] Viscount Buckmaster, *Roundabout* (London: H.F. & G. Witherby, 1969), 116–34.

[61] TNA, WO32/18661, 'Future of the Inns of Court and Artists Rifles'; H. A. R. May, 'Artists Rifles O.T.C. Points to Be Considered in Framing New Regulations', undated but March 1920; May, *Memories of the Artists Rifles*, 164–6.

[62] University of Leeds, Special Collections, Military Education Committee minutes, 5 March 1915 to 14 February 1916.

[63] Queen's University Belfast Archives, QUB/B/1/2/6, Senate minutes; 'Annual Report of Military Education Committee to Senate', 22 November 1916; and IWM, J. H. Stewart-Moore, 'Random Recollections', 6.

[64] Simkins, *Kitchener's Army*, 212–3.

along with those recently retired and relying on the Reserve of Officers, meant that the first batch of New Army divisions contained a large proportion of professional officers. Peter Hodgkinson has calculated that 82 per cent of the commanding officers of K1 infantry battalions were regular officers. But these regular reserves were quickly exhausted, to the extent that the K2 battalions had 14 per cent of regular commanding officers, K3 6 per cent and the local raised 'Pals' units also just 6 per cent.[65]

It appears that at the field officer and subaltern level, the first batch of New Armies also had a high proportion of regular officers. N. E. Drury, posted to the 6th Royal Dublin Fusiliers, 10th (Irish) Division, noted that ten of the officers had previous military experience: six in the Royal Dublin Fusiliers, three in the Indian Army and one in the Rifle Brigade. Similarly, the 6th Royal Irish Rifles had fourteen regular officers out of a total of twenty-one in late 1914.[66] The 10th (Irish) Division seems to have had a more generous allocation or regular officers than the 13th (Western) Division in K1. There the 6th South Lancashire Regiment was deemed to be fortunate in having as many as seven regular officers, and Stephen Sandford's careful calculations comparing the two divisions suggest that while the 10th (Irish) Division had 12 per cent of its original officer corps who were regulars who had been commissioned through the RMA or RMC, it was only 5 per cent in the 13th (Western) Division.[67] In K2 the number of regular officers was already almost exhausted. It was claimed that in the 15th (Scottish) Division, '[a]t no time were there more than five Regular officers in any one brigade.'[68] Subsequent New Army formations were unlikely to receive as many serving regulars on their formation and had to rely on retired officers, unflatteringly termed 'dug-outs' or hastily commissioned civilians.

The term 'dugout' conjures up a Colonel Blimp–like image of a very senior and very retired officer. But in the small pre-war regular army, which had only a limited number of general and senior staff positions to fill, many able officers had retired when they were still comparatively young and when, as events were to prove, they were perfectly capable officers. A very good example is Oliver Nugent, who was a fifty-five-year-old full colonel on the outbreak of war but then unemployed, having

[65] P. E. Hodgkinson, 'British Infantry Battalion Commanders in the First World War', unpublished PhD thesis, University of Birmingham, 2013, 63.

[66] NAM, 7607-69-1, 'Diaries of Captain N. E. Drury', 1; and Stephen Sandford, *Neither Unionist nor Nationalist: The 10th (Irish) Division in the Great War* (Sallins, Ireland: Irish Academic Press, 2015), 55.

[67] Sandford, *Neither Unionist nor Nationalist*, 62; and Simkins, *Kitchener's Army*, 217.

[68] J. Stewart and John Buchan, *The Fifteenth (Scottish) Division 1914–1919* (Edinburgh: William Blackwood, 1926), 3.

recently completed his term as commander of the Hampshire Infantry Brigade, TF. In the normal course of events, he could have expected to be compulsorily retired, with no further appointment, particularly given his decision to take command of the Cavan Regiment of the Ulster Volunteer Force. On the outbreak of war, he took over the command of the Hull defences; in May 1915, he was posted to the 14th (Light) Division, to take command of the 41st Infantry Brigade. In September 1915, he was given command of the 36th (Ulster) Division, and he ended the war as a lieutenant general.[69] At the other extreme were officers such as Lieutenant Colonel G. S. Ormerod, who was appointed to command the 9th Royal Irish Rifles. He had retired from the Royal Munster Fusiliers as a major as long ago as 1904. While he brought considerable organisational skill to the formation of the battalion, his health soon broke down in the trenches, and he was invalided home in late 1915.[70] The man originally appointed to be Ormerod's second in command, F. P. Crozier, was a different type of 'dugout' officer, and the fact that he was re-commissioned at all was a reflection on the chaos that existed in the War Office in the early part of the war. Crozier had served in the ranks of Thorneycroft's Mounted Infantry in the South African War and, as a result of this, was commissioned into the 2nd Manchester Regiment. He then served a period of attachment with the West African Frontier Force. However, in 1908 he was forced to resign his commission for issuing dishonoured cheques. The outbreak of war found him serving in the Ulster Volunteer Force, and this was crucial in securing his appointment to the 36th (Ulster) Division. Despite this unpromising start, Crozier proved to be a very effective officer in trench warfare and was promoted to lieutenant colonel to replace Ormerod when he was invalided home. Crozier went on to command the 119th Brigade, though post-war appointments as Inspector General of the Lithuanian Army and commander of the Auxiliary Division of the Royal Irish Constabulary were less successful.[71]

Once the supply of regular and retired officers had been exhausted, the New Armies had to turn to civilians to fill their officer corps. There has been a tendency to believe that almost all these civilians had gained military experience in OTC contingents, but the release of the WO339

[69] Nicholas Perry (ed.), *Major-General Oliver Nugent and the Command of the 36th (Ulster) Division 1915–18* (Stroud: Sutton Publishing for the Army Records Society, 2007), 1–8.

[70] F. P. Crozier, *Impressions and Recollections* (London: T. Werner Laurie, 1930), 160; and War Office, *Army List, October 1908*, 2012b.

[71] Personal file of Brigadier-General F. P. Crozier (TNA, WO374/16997); Crozier, *Impressions and Recollections*; F. P. Crozier, *Brass Hat in No Man's Land* (London: Jonathan Cape, 1930); Charles Messenger, *Broken Sword: The Tumultuous Life of General Frank Crozier 1879–1937* (Barnsley: Praetorian Press, 2013), 7–142.

records at TNA demonstrate that the picture is much more complicated.[72] Essentially, the decision on who to commission in a unit came down to the unit's own commanding officer, and in most cases he completed the forms nominating a candidate for a commission following a brief interview with the candidate. In the 36th (Ulster) Division, different battalion commanders took very different decisions over whom they wanted as officers in their battalions. Lieutenant Colonel S. W. Blacker does not seem to have accepted a single OTC product into the 9th Royal Irish Fusiliers, preferring to appoint local gentry and businessmen who had served under his command in the Ulster Volunteer Force. By contrast, at least six former OTC cadets were commissioned into the 8th Royal Irish Rifles, presumably due to the influence of that battalion's adjutant, Captain J. D. M. McCallum, who pre-war had been an officer in the Queen's University of Belfast OTC. Similar fluctuation is evident in the case of the 14th, 15th and 16th Royal Warwickshire Regiment (Birmingham Pals), where only four OTC products were commissioned into the 15th Battalion, while ten were commissioned into the 16th Battalion.[73]

Some men were commissioned into New Army units on the basis of colourful military experience, often in amateur units. For example, of three officers commissioned into the 36th (Ulster) Division, G. W. Matthew had served for three years in the Northern Bengal Mounted Rifle Volunteers, George Barton had served for three years as a trooper in the Cawnpore Light Horse and Adrian Hulse had served in the Cape Mounted Rifles and the Malay States Volunteer Rifles.[74] Henry Richardson appears to have been commissioned into the 16th Royal Warwickshire Regiment on the basis of his service in Gifford's Horse in Rhodesia in 1896.[75] One officer of the same battalion, J. E. Holme, was commissioned due to his service in the French Foreign Legion, which he joined while on holiday in Paris on the outbreak of war, serving for three and a half months in it before he was transferred to the British Army.[76]

Some men gained their commissions almost on the old basis of 'recruiting for rank' which had essentially ended in the mid-1790s. H. C. Maclean,

[72] Martin Petter, '"Temporary Gentlemen" in the Aftermath of the Great War: Rank, Status and the Ex-Officer Problem', *Historical Journal*, XXXVII, 1 (1994), 136; and Sheffield, *Leadership in the Trenches*, 37.

[73] Timothy Bowman, 'Officering Kitchener's Armies: A Case-Study of the 36th (Ulster) Division', *War in History*, 16, 2 (2009).

[74] Personal files of Captain G. W. Matthew (TNA, WO339/14242), Captain George Barton (TNA, WO339/13923), Lieutenant Arthur Dawson Allen (TNA, WO339/14252) and Major Adrian Hulse (TNA, WO339/14050).

[75] Personal file of Henry Richardson (TNA, WO339/16500).

[76] Personal file of J. E. Holme (TNA, WO339/24265).

who was a barrister, normally resident in Streatham, was recommended for a commission in the 9th Royal Inniskilling Fusiliers by that unit's commanding officer on the basis that he had brought thirty-two Ulster Volunteers with him to enlist and had enlisted, in the ranks, with them as an example. John Wray, a solicitor's son from Enniskillen, Co. Fermanagh, similarly secured his commission on the basis of bringing in around 200 Irish National Volunteers to enlist in the 16th (Irish) Division. The future Prime Minister, Anthony Eden, gained his commission in the Yeoman Rifles of the King's Royal Rifle Corps on the basis of enlisting a sufficient number of suitable recruits in County Durham.[77]

Promotion from the ranks was another early way to fill vacancies in the New Armies. Just as the TF had 'class corps', so the New Armies developed some such units. It is therefore not surprising that, like their TF counterparts, these units provided a disproportionately high number of officers. The 16th Middlesex Regiment (Public Schools Battalion) had already had 1,450 men commissioned from its ranks by 1 July 1916.[78] D Company of the 7th Royal Dublin Fusiliers, which was formed by the Irish Rugby Football Union, was permitted by Lieutenant Colonel Geoffrey Dowling to elect two of their members as officers. The fact that one of these men was Ernest Julian, a barrister and professor of law at Trinity College Dublin, says much about the social composition of this unit.[79]

In other New Army formations, promotion from the ranks was not uncommon but inconsistent. Surviving WO339 files at TNA, Kew, suggest that the 36th (Ulster) Division had twenty-two officers appointed before August 1915 who had started their military careers as private soldiers in the division and eight private soldiers posted from other units. Otherwise there were widespread variations within the New Armies over commissioning from the ranks. In the 13th Royal Welsh Fusiliers, no fewer than thirteen of the officers had started their military careers as private soldiers in the battalion by August 1915. By contrast, the Bristol-raised 12th Gloucestershire Regiment did not number one commissioned other rank among its officers by August 1915 from this or any other unit. Some COs did not think that men who had served in the ranks of their units would make effective officers in these units; thus,

[77] Personal file of Lieutenant H. C. Maclean (TNA, WO339/14274); Terence Denman, *Ireland's Unknown Soldiers: The 16th (Irish) Division in the Great War* (Dublin: Irish Academic Press, 1992), 43, 50; Anthony Eden, *Another World 1897–1917* (New York: Doubleday, 1977), 64–5.

[78] J. E. Edmonds, *Military Operations: France and Belgium, 1916*, Vol. I (London: Macmillan, 1932), 435.

[79] Henry Hanna, *The Pals at Suvla Bay: Being a Record of 'D' Company of the 7th Royal Dublin Fusiliers* (Dublin: E. Ponsonby, 1916), 18.

H. M. Hewitt and E. L. Marshal both enlisted in the 13th Royal Irish Rifles but received commissions in the 9th Royal Inniskilling Fusiliers.[80]

These promotions from the ranks were not always meritocratic and often relied on various forms of patronage. When sending in his application for a commission in the 9th Royal Irish Rifles, W. L. Gorman, then serving as a private in the 6th Bedfordshire Regiment, was clearly acting on family connections as he wrote, 'Colonel Ormerod of the 9th. Battn. [Battalion], Royal Irish Rifles has informed me that he has a vacancy for a 2nd. Lieut.[Lieutenant].'[81] E. N. F. Bell, who was a student at the University of Liverpool on the outbreak of war and had enlisted in the 6th Royal Inniskilling Fusiliers, 10th (Irish) Division, was recommended for a commission by Lieutenant Colonel Ambrose Ricardo in his unit, the 9th Royal Inniskilling Fusiliers. Ricardo demonstrated the importance of regimental patronage when he stated, 'Mr. Bell's father served for 24 years in the R. [Royal] Inniskilling Fusiliers rising to the rank of Quartermaster. This would make a valuable young officer.' Ricardo was to be proved absolutely correct in this estimation, as Bell went on to win the Victoria Cross for his actions on 1 July 1916.[82] Charles Carrington, having failed to obtain a temporary commission in the Rifle Brigade, enlisted in the ranks of the 14th Royal Warwickshire Regiment (1st Birmingham 'Pals'). On leave, he went to see Colonel Addison of the 9th York and Lancaster Regiment, who had been billeted on his uncle. Addison arranged for him to get a commission in his battalion, and he was appointed to it in February 1915. Carrington stated, 'I was a better bargain for the York and Lancasters than I would have been for the Rifle Brigade the previous August, but still an innocent child.'[83]

A number of men were directly commissioned who did not have the OTC, educational or employment backgrounds that were expected of officers. Desmond Young, later to be known as the biographer of Field Marshal Erwin Rommel, quickly gained a commission in the 9th Kings Royal Rifle Corps by cycling over to the regimental depot and insisting on seeing the senior officer on the first day of the war. Having dropped out of both his degree at Oxford University (where he had never been a member of the OTC) and King Edward's Horse, where he had served as trooper, Young had, on the face of it, few claims for a commission.[84] Two of the

[80] Personal files of Lieutenant Holt Montgomery Hewitt (TNA, WO339/51204) and Captain Edward Leslie Marshal (TNA, WO339/57830).

[81] Personal file of Captain W. L. Gorman (TNA, WO339/16720).

[82] Personal file of Captain E. N. F. Bell (TNA, WO339/14809).

[83] Charles Carrington, *Soldier from the Wars Returning* (London: Hutchinson, 1965), 48–56.

[84] Desmond Young, *Try Anything Twice* (London: Hamish Hamilton, 1963), 46–134; and TNA, W0339/13553, Personal file of Major Desmond Young.

officers commissioned in the 36th (Ulster) Division had similarly slim qualifications. Both lived in areas of Belfast which were predominantly inhabited by skilled working-class families, and neither man had any previous military or Ulster Volunteer Force (UVF) experience or appears to have attended a grammar school. Colonel G. H. H. Couchman, the original commander of the 107th Brigade, endorsed both of these men's applications, and this may be why Major-General Oliver Nugent commented that commissions had been given to 'men of the wrong class' when he took command.[85]

In Ireland, political concerns were involved with the officering of the 16th (Irish) and 36th (Ulster) Divisions, which drew on the pre-war Irish National Volunteers (INV) and UVF, respectively, for much of their manpower. The 36th (Ulster) Division was formed in September 1914 following lengthy negotiations between Sir Edward Carson, the Irish Unionist leader, and Lord Kitchener. Ultimately, a number of concessions were made to Carson, principally that regular and reserve officers who had served in the UVF would be posted to the 36th (Ulster) Division and that men who had served as officers in the UVF would be recommended for commissions. The number of UVF officers or other ranks commissioned into individual battalions of the 36th (Ulster) Division varied considerably, though. In the 9th Royal Irish Fusiliers, raised largely in Co. Armagh, for which fourteen officers' files survive, seven were UVF officers and two of other UVF ranks. In the 12th Royal Irish Rifles raised in North Antrim, fourteen of the men commissioned had been UVF officers; this out of eighteen surviving files. However, elsewhere the picture was very different. In the 10th Royal Irish Rifles, raised in South Belfast, only three men were commissioned on the basis of UVF membership, out of a total of eighteen surviving files.[86]

Lieutenant General Sir Lawrence Parsons, appointed as GOC of the 16th (Irish) Division, was conscious that given the absence of OTC contingents at Catholic schools or universities in Ireland, he had a very thin basis of military expertise on which to draw. Also, the INV were, when war broke out, poorly organised and did not, in Parsons' view, provide a reservoir of part-trained officers. Parsons therefore decided to establish a cadet company in the 7th Leinster Regiment which between November 1914 and December 1915 produced 161 officers

[85] Personal files of Lieutenant D. B. Walkington (TNA, WO339/14295) and Lieutenant R. McLaurin (TNA, WO339/14277); and Letter, Nugent to his wife, 26 October 1915 (PRONI, Farren Connell papers, D.3835/E/2/5/20A).

[86] Timothy Bowman, 'The Ulster Volunteer Force and the Formation of the 36th (Ulster) Division', *Irish Historical Studies*, XXXII, 128 (2001), 509

for the division.[87] As Nora Robertson, Parsons's daughter, noted of the cadet company: '[A]s a means of training officers it could not have been more satisfactory nor, for the majority, more popular. But as a political device for a distracted leader trying to entice M.P.s, J.P.s, touchy publicans, and financial supporters to send their sons to an extremely dangerous and not very popular war it was, to say the least of it, rebuffing.'[88] Parsons' handling of Irish Parliamentary Party (IPP) Members of Parliament (MPs) who desired commissions was far from tactful, especially in the case of William Archer Redmond, MP, son of the leader of the IPP, John Redmond.[89] Colonel Maurice Moore, the Inspector General of the INV, noted of the cadet company: 'I admit a very good plan from his [i.e. Parsons'] point of view, but may mean the officering of the [Irish] Brigade by Unionists, whereas we want it as a training place for our officers to be ready after the war.'[90]

There were some similar problems in securing officers for the 38th (Welsh) Division. A senior administrator at the University of Wales noted in October 1914 that thirty OTC cadets from Bangor and fifty from Aberystwyth had already been commissioned. However, he went on to explain that pre-war Cardiff had failed to obtain permission to establish an OTC and expressed concern that '[s]ome men who have obtained Degrees with First Class Honours have joined as privates and many who have distinguished themselves as athletes.' Concerns were also raised concerning the availability of Welsh-speaking officers for the division. Brigadier-General Owen Thomas took a similar view to Parsons in his belief that men should enlist in the ranks before being considered for commissions. Indeed, a cadet company, similar to that raised by Parsons, seems to have been established in the 16th Royal Welsh Fusiliers.[91]

From February 1916, largely as a response to the introduction of the Derby Scheme, officer training became more formalised, and twenty-three Officer Cadet Battalions were established throughout the country. Between February 1916 and December 1918, these units produced 107,929 officers. The fact that a number were established in stately

[87] NLI, Ms.21,278, Parsons papers, list of officers.

[88] N. Robertson, *Crowned Harp, Memories of the Last Years of the Crown in Ireland* (Dublin: Allen Figgis, 1960), 126.

[89] Denman, *Ireland's Unknown Soldiers*, 48.

[90] N.L.I., ms.10,561/1-18; Moore papers, letter, Moore to Joseph Devlin, M.P., 7 November 1914.

[91] National Library of Wales, B23, 'Welsh Army Corps: Commissions in Above Corps', Letter Selyn Roberts to Major-General Sir Ivor Herbert, MP, 29 October 1914; Letter Brigadier-General Owen Thomas to Secretary, Welsh Army Corps, 23 November 1914; and printed pamphlet, 'Sixteenth Battalion of the Royal Welsh Fusiliers: Second University Company: Special Facilities for Promotion to Commissions'.

homes or Oxbridge colleges tended to reinforce the concept of the officer, even the temporary one, as a gentleman.[92] Accounts of service in these units are sparse, though the fact that the 19th Battalion produced its own magazine suggests that some level of esprit de corps was built up.[93] Alfred Duff Cooper, then a First Division Clerk at the Foreign Office, later a First Lord of the Admiralty and Secretary of State for War, was, finally, released for military service in June 1917. He had already met with the Regimental Adjutant of the Grenadier Guards and was under the impression that he had already been accepted for them when posted to officer training. However, on arrival at his Officer Cadet Battalion, he was most perturbed to be lumped in with men being trained for all regiments and even more shocked to be issued with a private's uniform and boots. Most of the men whom Duff Cooper was training with had started their military careers in the ranks, and he clearly found sharing a room with them a real shock: 'The strangeness, roughness and degradation of it all appalled me.'[94]

While the courses at Officer Cadet Battalions lasted for four months, it seems that a shorter six-week commissioning course continued to operate in France. F. N. Stansfield, who had enlisted in the ranks of the 19th Kings Liverpool Regiment (3rd Liverpool Pals) in September 1914, found himself selected by his commanding officer for officer training, and in February 1916 he was interviewed by his brigadier general and asked to fill in a form to join an OTC unit. In May 1916, Stansfield was sent to his commissioning course at a country house near St. Omer in France. As he wrote of his experiences there:

> There are Colonials Regulars, Terriers and Kitcheners, and they are all splendid fellows – young (20–30), alert, clear, brave and cultured. To be in their company is a privilege which does not come every man's way. Our instructors are absolutely the pick of the army – V.C.s, D.S.O.s and M.C.s and every one of them the perfect type of the perfect officer . . . The work is hard and the discipline strict . . . We have been told quite plainly what is expected of us – we have to train ourselves to become officers of the original type, i.e. not only officers but gentlemen, and quite half of our training here has had to do with the latter.[95]

Two professional groups, medical doctors and the clergy, could be commissioned into the army with no further specialist training.

92 Simpson, 'The Officers', in Beckett and Simpson (eds.), *A Nation in Arms*, 80–1.

93 Liddle Collection, University of Leeds, GS1842, H. Hemmings papers.

94 J. J. Norwich (ed.), *The Duff Cooper Diaries, 1915–1951* (London: Weidenfeld & Nicolson, 2005), 54–5.

95 Liddle Collection, GS 1528; F. O. Stansfield, 'My First Two Years in the Army, 1914–16', unpublished manuscript, 78.

However, the expansion of the Royal Army Medical Corps (RAMC) during the First World War created particular problems. When the original BEF sailed for France in August 1914, the RAMC contingent consisted of nearly 900 medical officers and 10,000 other ranks, whereas by March 1918, 13,284 medical officers alone were on active service, which demonstrates the massive expansion which took place. However, in the early months of the war there was considerable confusion over both how civilian doctors would be recruited to the army and the best way in which medical students could play their part in Britain's war effort. Mobilisation of the TF in August 1914 withdrew 2,000 medical doctors from civilian practice at a stroke, leaving a number of locum arrangements to be made very hastily. Lord Kitchener, when recruiting his new armies, spoke of men serving their country the best way they could, and this meant that some recruiting officers turned away medical students at the start of the war, and indeed, there are some examples of men having been enlisted and being discharged from the army to continue their medical studies. Early in the war, the War Office refused to enter into any formal agreements with the British Medical Association, which meant that some officers volunteered for the Red Cross and served overseas with this organisation. As the war continued, confusion over the supply of medical officers remained. The university authorities at Glasgow and Leeds took the view that while senior medical students in their fourth and fifth years of study should complete their degrees and qualify as doctors before joining the army, more junior medical students should enlist for combat service. When the Derby Scheme was introduced in 1915, this view was officially endorsed. The introduction of conscription proper in 1916 meant that third-, fourth- and fifth-year students were required to attest into the army but were then allowed to complete their studies, while first- and second-year students, and third-year students who had failed their examinations, were liable for general service. Not surprisingly, by 1917 there was a shortage of army doctors, exacerbated by the refusal of the War Office to use female doctors effectively. The War Office responded by allowing all those who had studied for two years as medical students before joining the army to return to their studies, and in 1918, any soldier or officer who had attended a recognised medical school for six months before enlistment was allowed to return to his studies.[96]

The numbers of clergy serving in the British Army during the First World War also increased massively. At the outbreak of war, there were

[96] Mark Harrison, *The Medical War: British Military Medicine In the First World War* (Oxford University Press, 2010), 1–122; and I. R. Whitehead, *Doctors in the Great War* (Barnsley: Leo Cooper, 1999), 32–107.

117 chaplains in the army, 89 of whom were Anglican. By the armistice, there were 1,698 chaplains, including 878 Anglicans, 389 Roman Catholics, 161 Presbyterians and 127 Wesleyans. Initially, the War Office was reluctant to increase the number of non-combatants serving with the BEF, and offers of service by clergymen were turned down. This attitude only changed in the spring of 1915, as the War Office came under pressure from both the Army Chaplains Department itself and from the Anglican hierarchy to increase the establishment of padres and as Lieutenant-General Sir Nevil Macready, the Adjutant General, saw the importance of chaplains in maintaining morale. As Edward Madigan notes: 'Over the course of the war the administrative organisation of the Army Chaplains' Department was skilfully adapted to the perceived needs of the vast citizen army and the number, and denomination, of chaplains increased correspondingly.'[97]

The expansion of the British Army as a whole saw the development or formation of a number of new technical corps. The Royal Flying Corps, which, of course, pre-dated the war, having been formed in 1912, underwent massive expansion. On mobilisation in August 1914 the Royal Flying Corps mobilised all of its slender resources to send five squadrons to France, while by November 1918 the Royal Air Force (RAF) had 99 front-line squadrons in France and 144 squadrons in the Mediterranean, the Middle East, India or at home service. When the RAF was put on a regular footing in August 1919, with the strength below that of its wartime peak, 1,065 officers were gazetted with permanent commissions.[98] This expansion of the officer corps occurred because unlike in the French and German military, where many pilots were NCOs, the British decided that commissioned officers were required to pilot aircraft.

The First World War officer corps of the Royal Flying Corps (RFC) awaits its historian, but the careers of a few notable officers are worth discussing here. Hugh Trenchard, who had transferred to the RFC from the Royal Scots Fusiliers as a major in 1912, probably saw the most spectacular promotion of any officer during the war, ending it as head of the newly created RAF, despite being, in the words of one of his

[97] Edward Madigan, *Faith under Fire: Anglican Army Chaplains and the Great War* (Basingstoke: Palgrave Macmillan, 2011), 56. See also Michael Snape, *God and British Soldier: Religion and British Army in the First and Second World Wars* (Abingdon: Routledge, 2005), 83–138.

[98] Hugh Driver, *The Birth of Military Aviation: Britain, 1903 to 1914* (Woodbridge: Royal Historical Society and the Boydell Press, 1997), 272; Charles Sims, *The Royal Air Force: the First Fifty Years* (London: Adam and Charles Black, 1968), 25; and Malcolm Cooper, *The Birth of Independent Air Power: British Policy in World War I* (London: Allen & Unwin, 1986), 47.

biographers, an 'indifferent pilot and dangerous tutor'.[99] James McCudden, one of the most famous air aces of the First World War, was killed in action in 1918 as a captain. He had started his career in the army as a boy soldier, a bugler, in the Royal Engineers before transferring to the RFC in April 1913 as a mechanic. He then served as an observer, with the rank of flight sergeant. He learned to fly in early 1916 and was commissioned on 1 January 1917. In writing the Foreword to McCudden's memoirs, Major-General J. M. Salmond noted that in August 1914 McCudden was regarded as one of the best engine-fitters serving in the RFC, and it seems that McCudden always insisted on servicing his own aircraft.[100] McCudden was clearly an exceptional man, but his case does suggest that the RFC recognised the importance of mechanical knowledge among its officer corps.

Indeed, the training programme outlined for RFC officers in early 1917 was an eight-month course, double the length of the normal Officer Cadet Battalion course, which included ordinary infantry officer training in drill as well as map reading, military law, interior economy, musketry, field engineering and first aid in the first two months before RFC-specific training. Attempts to cut this initial part of the course met fierce resistance from senior officers, who continued to believe in the importance of drill and ceremonial work in instilling discipline.[101] Somewhat surprisingly, it was left to a junior officer, Robert Smith-Barry, who, on the outbreak of war, was a mere second lieutenant in the RFC (Special Reserve), to develop a proper training system for the RFC as a whole, which he started in late 1916 when posted to command the 1st (Reserve) Squadron at Gosport. Smith-Barry, who had commanded the 60th Squadron in France from July to December 1916 as a major, had been appalled at the poor training which officer pilots posted to his squadron had received. Smith-Barry's philosophy of teaching was that pilots had to be trained, in dual-control aircraft, how to deal with serious potential accidents such as spins rather than simply being taught how to fly solo in ideal conditions. He also insisted on longer training time so that in 1918, when his training programme had been disseminated throughout the RFC, pilots were arriving at the front with an average time in the air of fifty hours, compared to just seventeen and a half hours in 1917, and had the excellent

[99] Vincent Orange, 'Hugh Trenchard', available at: www.oxforddnb.com.chain.kent.ac.uk/view/article/36552?docPos=2; and Andrew Boyle, *Trenchard: Man of Vision* (London: Collins, 1962).

[100] James McCudden, *Five Years in the RFC* (London: Aeroplane and General Publishing Company, 1918).

[101] TNA, AIR1/130/15/40/208, 'Syllabus for First Two Months Training in the RFC Officer Cadet Wing'.

AVRO 504 adopted as the standard training machine for the RFC. Smith-Barry ended the war as a brevet colonel for these efforts but does not seem to have been offered a permanent commission in the RAF; in the Second World War, he served as a ferry pilot.[102]

Some serving officers found it difficult to organise a transfer to the RFC. E. J. Furlong, who applied as an officer in the Royal Inniskilling Fusiliers to transfer to the RFC, remembered a difficult interview with his CO: '[H]e was very horrified that any one of his officers should want to leave his wonderful regiment to go into a hare-brained outfit like the Flying Corps and he promptly turned it down.' When Furlong reapplied two months later, his CO relented and 'finally said well if I was that sort of an officer who didn't realise the honour of being in his lot, I could go.'[103]

By the mid-1916, the Machine Gun Corps, which had been officially formed in October 1915 by taking machine gun sections out of existing infantry battalions, already had a strength of 4,000 officers and over 80,000 other ranks.[104] As one of the founders of the corps noted of the problems in developing an efficient officer corps for this new unit:

> It must be noted that the officers for the Corps were not selected for any special abilities and aptitude which would enable them to attain to proficiency as machine gunners. Though it has long been realised that a special type of brain and training were necessary both for engineers and artillery, it did not occur to anyone that the machine gun officer, whatever his other qualifications, must also be a ready mathematician, possess an instinct for map-reading, and have a mechanical bent. Owing to an entirely haphazard method of posting officers to the Machine Gun Corps, it was often found that they were deplorably lacking in those vital departments of general education which form the essential background to the quick grasp of the principles of machine gunnery. Both in the selection and training of officers, those deficient in mathematical knowledge and mechanical instinct cannot be made into efficient machine gun officers. As the need for covering fire, and the more scientific use of machine guns, impressed itself both upon the fighting units and the staffs of the training centres, the need for a higher inspectorate in the field for the furtherance of the science itself and for the elimination of unsuitable direction became clearer. During the year 1917, therefore, a machine gun officer was appointed to the staff of each Corps and, later divisional machine gun officers were also appointed.[105]

[102] www.rafmuseum.org.uk/research/online-exhibitions/taking-flight/historical-periods/lieutenant-colonel-robert-smith-barry.aspx; F. D. Tredrey, *Pioneer Pilot: The Great Smith Barry Who Taught the World How to Fly* (London: Peter Davies, 1976); and www.oxforddnb.com.chain.kent.ac.uk/view/article/72242.

[103] IWM, 15/08, Transcript of interview with E. J. Furlong, 19–20.

[104] G. S. Hutchinson, *Machine Guns: Their History and Tactical Employment (Being Also a History of the Machine Gun Corps, 1916 to 1922)* (London: Macmillan, 1938), 143–6.

[105] *Ibid.*, 172.

The Tank Corps was established in March 1916 very much as part of the nation in arms. Indeed, an early history described it as a 'citizen force' and went on to state, '[O]f the 20,000 odd souls that went to compose it, perhaps not more than two or three per cent were professional soldiers; and, where the General Staff officers on H.Q.s were almost without exception regulars, the whole of the administrative and engineering staffs with one solitary exception were drawn from various civil vocations.'[106] Initially, its officer corps relied on officer cadets with engineering experience drawn from the 18th, 19th and 21st Royal Fusiliers.[107] C. D. Baker-Carr was one of the founders of the Machine Gun Corps, and in late 1916 he was appointed to take command of the newly formed C Battalion of the Tank Corps. Writing of this command, Baker-Carr noted:

> [T]he nucleus personnel, from which I was to form a Battalion, consisted of a heterogeneous collection of men, not only from every branch of the Army, but also from the Royal Navy. The officers, including one regular officer of the R.A. and two regular infantry officers, were a wonderful body of enthusiasts. They were, however, but a small lump of leaven wherewith to leaven the large mass of raw material which was needed to bring the battalion up to full strength.
>
> A memorandum had been sent out to all units in the infantry and cavalry inviting officers and men to volunteer for service in the Tank Corps and we were overwhelmed with applications. In consequence, we found ourselves in the happy position of being able to pick and choose, with the result that a high standard of efficiency was established at the very start and never thereafter departed from.
>
> My battalion staff, to whom I can never be sufficiently grateful for their loyal support during the most difficult period, was a strange collection of men.
>
> My Adjutant came from a box-factory in Wallasey near Liverpool; my Equipment Officer (the most efficient and outrageous collector of unconsidered trifles in France) was a Welshman and the best-known beekeeper in Wales; my Reconnaissance Officer was a London lawyer; my Engineer Officer came from the Hillman car company of Birmingham; my Medical Officer from the South Pole, where he had been for the past two years with Shackleton; and my spiritual adviser from a remote parish in the depths of the country.[108]

While the British Army officer corps expanded its class base slightly during the war, two groups were explicitly barred from being granted commissions: women and black soldiers. In the women's services, the First Aid Nursing Yeomanry and Women's Auxiliary Army Corps, the solution was to develop an alternative rank structure for command within the units, with the clear understanding that no women would be in

106 H. J. Elles, 'Introduction', in Clough Williams-Ellis and A. Williams-Ellis, *The Tank Corps* (London: Country Life, 1919), x.
107 *Ibid*, 16.
108 C. D. Baker-Carr, *From Chauffeur to Brigadier* (London: Ernest Benn, 1930), 206–7.

a position to give orders to male soldiers.[109] With regard to black officers, Walter Tull is generally recognised as the one black soldier who managed to secure a commission in the British Army during the First World War, and indeed, this seems to be the case regarding units raised in the United Kingdom itself. However, it is clear that some men who, a contemporary Colonial Office official noted, were 'slightly coloured' did receive commissions in the British West Indies Regiment. This was not widely known at the time, and the opinion of a senior Colonial Office official was that the War Office should be left to explain why a colour bar existed as 'it won't hurt them while it will be damaging to the CO [Colonial Office].' Tull was British born but came from an impoverished background; indeed, he was brought up in an orphanage. However, he established himself as a professional footballer before the war, playing for Tottenham Hotspur and Northampton Town. Shortly after the outbreak of war he enlisted in the 17th Middlesex Regiment (1st Footballers Battalion), later serving as a lance sergeant in the 23rd Middlesex Regiment (2nd Footballers Battalion), seeing active service in France with both battalions. In 1917, Tull was sent back to Britain for officer training, and he was commissioned in May 1917, curiously into the special reserve rather than to a temporary commission, and posted back to the 23rd Middlesex Regiment as an officer. He was killed in action in March 1918.[110]

Once appointed to a commission, an officer could find himself sent on a number of courses; the training of New Army officers at University OTC units and the truncated Staff courses introduced from 1916 have already been alluded to earlier. Initially, there was a very ad hoc approach to training, based on various local initiatives. Viscount Buckmaster, posted to a New Army battalion of the Duke of Cornwall's Light Infantry, remembered being put through the basics of drill by Guards NCOs at Chelsea barracks for a brief period, along with a squad of other temporary officers, but still regarded himself 'utterly ignorant of all military matters' when he joined his battalion.[111] By contrast, Anthony Eden felt that he received a good military education at a 'strenuous course at an officers' school in the Eastern Counties' in early 1915.[112] Ivone Kirkpatrick, who was appointed to a commission in the 5th Royal Inniskilling Fusiliers (his father was recalled from retirement and commanded the 6th battalion of the regiment), based on his limited

[109] Janet S. K. Watson, 'Khaki Girls, VADs, and Tommy's Sisters: Gender and Class in First World War Britain', *International History Review*, 19, 1 (1997), 32–5, 41.

[110] Phil Vasili, *Walter Tull (1888–1918): Officer, Footballer* (London: Raw Press, 2009); and CO318/357/27 f.626, Letter H. S. Cox to Under Secretary of State, Colonial Office, 13 March 1918; and Memo by E.R.W., 20 March[?] 1918.

[111] Buckmaster, *Roundabout*, 120. [112] Eden, *Another World*, 67.

experience in the Downside School OTC, and probably some parental patronage, remembered, 'I was then sent to the Staff College at Camberley where I spent a month on an exceedingly strenuous officers' training course.'[113] By October 1915, more formalised courses of instruction were being held at the Staff College to train New Army and TF senior subalterns and junior captains how to take command of companies.[114]

As Simon Robbins notes, from 1915 onwards, large numbers of schools of instruction were established in the BEF. The original initiative for these seems to have come from General Sir Charles Monro, who first established them in Third Army. Monro was concerned by the levels of training of officers in France and set up one-month courses for already commissioned officers and NCOs. Many schools followed at Army, Corps and Divisional level, most set up in the winter of 1915–16, but as late as September 1917 there were only seventeen schools among twenty Corps, and most of their work seems to have involved training junior officers in platoon work. GHQ Schools were established throughout 1916 and 1917 and concentrated on specialist training of junior officers and NCOs so that they could become instructors in areas such as machine guns, trench mortars, sniping and bayonet training.[115]

A number of publications also appeared to help officers expand their professional knowledge. Many of these were produced by commercial publishers, without explicit War Office approval. A good example of an early work is *Quick Training for War*, written by Lieutenant General Sir Robert Baden-Powell, founder of the Boy Scout movement and hero of Mafeking. Baden-Powell's work was aimed at junior officers in the New Armies and, not surprisingly, drew heavily on the author's experience of soldiering in the South African War. This was a popular book, selling 65,000 copies in September 1914 alone and receiving widespread press reviews. The market for such 'unofficial' works seems to have continued throughout the war. An anonymous work, *The Subaltern's Handbook of Useful Information*, was in its third edition by January 1918. While this volume does, indeed, contain useful advice, it is interesting to note that nine pages were devoted to conduct, behaviour and mess etiquette but only three to 'The Defence'.[116]

113 Ivone Kirkpatrick, *The Inner Circle* (London: Macmillan, 1959), 3–4.
114 RMAS Archives, 'Staff College, 25 October 1915'.
115 Robbins, *British Generalship on the Western Front*, 90–1.
116 Robert Baden-Powell, *Quick Training for War: A Few Practical Suggestions* (London: Jenkins, 1914; new edition with Forward by Martin Robson, London: Conway, 2011); and Anonymous, *The Subaltern's Handbook of Useful Information* (Aldershot: Gale & Polden, 1918), 6–12, 61–3, 104–6.

Official doctrine publications were produced by GHQ of the BEF from March 1916, the first being, 'Notes for Infantry Officers in Trench Warfare'. Later volumes considered topics such as machine gun tactics, artillery-aircraft co-operation, counter-battery work, trench mortar use and defence against gas. In February 1917 a new Training Branch was established at GHQ which took responsibility for these publications, along with various schools of instruction. 'Instructions for the Training of Platoons for Offensive Action' was written by Major-General Arthur Solly Flood and appeared in February 1917. This is a particularly important work as Solly Flood drew on French tactics. Jim Beach does, however, seriously question the value of this doctrine. He notes that no manual on defensive tactics was produced before March 1918, considering this 'a serious indictment of the BEF's doctrine and writing process'. Beach also notes that most of those responsible for writing this doctrine were 'citizen soldiers'. Cuthbert Headlam had been a Clerk of the House of Commons and officer in the Bedfordshire Yeomanry pre-war, Edward Grigg was commissioned into the Grenadier Guards in February 1915 and had been colonial editor of the *Times*, and Lord Gorrell, commissioned in May 1915 into the 7th Rifle Brigade, had been the editor of the *Times Educational Supplement*. Beach considers the last pamphlet issued, 'The Division in the Attack' of October 1918 to have 'anchored itself in an established and familiar doctrine' raising serious questions about the nature of any 'learning process' in the BEF over the course of the war.[117]

Some officers were not found to be capable of exercising their duties properly during the war. In total, 4,048 officers were tried by courts-martial between 4 August 1914 and 30 September 1918, with the main offences being absence without leave and drunkenness. Of those officers tried by general courts martial abroad between 4 August 1914 and 30 September 1918, 2 were sentenced to death (one for murder), 14 to various periods of imprisonment, 77 were cashiered, 449 dismissed, 379 forfeited seniority and 939 were reprimanded.[118] What is noticeable, when compared to the sentences passed on other ranks, is how the traditional concepts of honour were still thought to apply to an army largely composed of temporary officers. The disgrace of being cashiered out or dismissed was seen as more of a deterrent than a lengthy prison sentence, although, when conscription was introduced, officers who suffered these punishments could, in theory, be forced to serve in the ranks.

[117] Jim Beach, 'Issued by the General Staff: Doctrine Writing at British GHQ, 1917–18', *War in History*, 19, 4 (2012), 464–91, esp. 474, 490.

[118] *Statistics of the Military Effort of the British Empire*, 643–61.

As an alternative to such formal disciplinary procedures, officers could be posted home or to another theatre of operations. In British military terminology, this was known as 'stellenbosching' as those officers found to be incompetent in the South African War had been sent to the remount department at Stellenbosch, where it was felt they could do little harm. Most famously, this was what happened to Field Marshal Sir John French in December 1915. The government, concerned that French could raise a political storm, especially if his shaky personal finances were exposed by unemployment, transferred him to the newly created post of Commander in Chief Home Forces.[119] General Sir Horace Smith-Dorrien's decision to disobey orders and make a stand at Le Cateau on 26th August 1914 during the retreat from Mons earned him lasting enmity from Field Marshal Sir John French. Smith-Dorrien was removed from the command of Second Army in April 1915, supposedly for displaying 'pessimism' during the Second Battle of Ypres. The then Chief of Staff of the BEF, 'Wully' Robertson, supposedly broke this news to Smith-Dorrien with the words, 'Orace, you're for home.' Smith-Dorrien took command of First Home Army in June 1915 and in November 1915 was appointed GOC East Africa, an appointment he never actually took up due to ill-health.[120]

Stellenbosching, in the true sense of the word, was more evident at the lower officer grades, when officers were sent to training and garrison units on home service, when they were seen to be unsuited to command in an active theatre of operations. When Major-General W. B. Hickie took over command of the 16th (Irish) Division in early 1916, he decided to replace six of his battalion commanders. Of these, two were compulsorily retired, and Lieutenant Colonel D. L. Hartley of the 7th Royal Irish Rifles went to the Royal Defence Corps as a section commandant. But of the others, Colonel J. S. Brown of the 8th Royal Irish Fusiliers went home to command the 86th Training Reserve Battalion; Lieutenant Colonel W. E. G. Connolly of the 9th Royal Dublin Fusiliers became CO of the 2nd Garrison Battalion, Royal Irish Fusiliers; and Lieutenant Colonel H. J. Downing of the 8th Royal Inniskilling Fusiliers was posted to the 10th Reserve Battalion, East Lancashire Regiment.[121] The case of Lieutenant Colonel W. E. G. Connolly is an interesting one and demonstrates how reluctant the military authorities were to dispense with

[119] Holmes, *The Little Field Marshal*, 307–15.

[120] I. F. W. Beckett, *The Judgement of History: Sir Horace Smith Dorrien, Lord French and 1914* (London: Tom Donovan, 1993), vii–xxi; and S. J. Corvi, 'Horace Smith Dorrien', in Beckett and Corvi (eds.), *Haig's Generals*, 183–207.

[121] Timothy Bowman, *Irish Regiments in the Great War: Discipline and Morale* (Manchester University Press, 2003), 121–3.

an experienced officer's services, even when his professionalism had been seriously questioned. When sending Connolly home, Hickie had commented:

I have to report that I consider Temp. Lt. Col. [Temporary Lieutenant Colonel] W. E. G. Connolly (retired Major Royal Marines) unfitted for the command of a Battalion, and I beg that he may be relieved at once, from the command of the 9th. Royal Dublin Fusiliers ... I can recommend an officer, now serving with the Division, for the appointment.

As this Battalion is very shortly for a tour of duty in the trenches I beg that I may be empowered to send Lt. Col. [Lieutenant Colonel] Connolly Home [*sic*] pending the receipt of authority for his relief ... He is not educated up to the requirements of modern War ... The Battalion is not well trained or as efficient as it should be. I cannot recommend Lt. Col. [Lieutenant Colonel] Connolly for employment for training purposes. I do not recommend that his services be dispensed with, as there may be work in his late branch of the Service in which he might be useful.

When Connolly was sent to take command of the 2nd Garrison Battalion, Royal Irish Fusiliers, it was on home service. Incredibly, when it was sent to Salonika in 1917, Connolly was left in command. He was finally retired in May 1917, having carried out a poorly planned and costly trench raid.[122]

The massive expansion of the British Army in the opening months of the war, along with the heavy casualty lists in the original BEF, saw some fairly desperate expedients adopted to find officers, once the rather flimsy reserve of officer cadets generated by the OTC had been exhausted. Among this chaos, a curious 'business as usual' routine was established at the RMA and RMC after the first six months of war. When the commissioning of temporary officers was formalised through the Officer Cadet Battalions in 1916, created as much due to the problems of introducing conscription as to a desire to create a uniform training programme, temporary officers were being trained in four months, while those at RMA and RMC were still undergoing a full year's instruction, which was increased later in the war to eighteen months. Tensions between temporary, TF and regular officers were exacerbated by the 'glass ceiling' which non-regular soldiers hit in promotion, with few being advanced beyond lieutenant colonel. The commissioning of men for newly formed, and supposedly specialist, corps, especially the Machine Gun Corps and Tank Corps, was on a decidedly ad hoc basis.

[122] TNA, WO339/7608, Personal file of Lieutenant Colonel W. E. G. Connolly. Of the commanding officers relieved in 16th (Irish) Division this is the only file available.

Similarly, the post-commissioning training provided to all officers during the Great War was decidedly patchy, and it remains unclear why many officers were selected for specialist or staff training in the first place. The class basis of the army officer corps did change during the war, but not to the extent sometimes imagined, and women and black soldiers remained barred from commissions.

3 A Nation in Arms

Regulars, Territorials, Volunteers and Conscripts

Prior to 1914, discussion on army reform had often touched upon the material difference between the British voluntary system of enlistment and the continental mass-conscript armies. In Europe, the modern concept of a 'nation in arms' is invariably dated to the proclamation of the law of *réquisition*, popularly known as the *levée en masse*, by the French Committee of Public Safety in August 1793, although forms of conscription had existed earlier. The successes of the French citizen armies begat emulation elsewhere, although not always in the French sense of military service being rewarded with full citizenship. To the Prussian military reformers after 1806, for example, the adoption of 'universal' service was a catalyst for social and political change, although this was to be stillborn. After 1815, the concept came under widespread attack as monarchs and restored monarchs sought to re-establish the political reliability of professional long-service armies, albeit that the system of short-service conscription survived in Prussia. The rhetoric of the nation in arms was no longer to be taken too literally, and insofar as a genuine mass citizen army existed, it was to be found only in Switzerland and the idealism of socialists such as Jean Jaurès. In Britain the idea of universal military service also had its exponents, with pressure increasing for the introduction of some form of conscription as Britain's political isolation became more apparent. To the potential military advantages – although a short-service conscript army was unsuitable for the defence of a far-flung empire – the apparent physical deficiencies of many recruits during the South African War added seemingly compelling social reasons for military training. Some form of compulsory military training was endorsed by the Wantage Commission in 1892, by the Norfolk Commission in 1904 and even by the Army Council in April 1913. Formed in 1902, the National Service League also pressed for compulsion, but conscription remained anathema to the wider public, all five parliamentary bills introduced to implement it between 1908 and 1914 failing comprehensively.

There was a degree of mild militarism within society encouraged by the educational system and by a great deal of the popular culture at all levels that identified with imperialism and Social Darwinism. Significantly, R. B. Haldane and his military advisers took some note of the Swiss system, and Haldane certainly envisaged the creation of the Territorial Force (TF) not only as an alternative to conscription but also as a specifically British version of a nation in arms. It would be a 'real national army' welding a unity between army and society, while the new County Territorial Associations would promote military virtues in general within local societies. While not in any sense equivalent to continental military systems, in that the voluntary system was clearly preserved, the specifically British approach to the nation in arms still embodied the sense of the army drawing upon the nation as whole in exigencies. So it ultimately proved to be, albeit that there had to be a recourse to conscription when the limits of the voluntary system were reached.

Traditionally, once war was imminent, it is usually assumed that there is a readiness and even eagerness to accept its challenge among many of Europe's peoples. It was commonplace in Britain in the 1920s to stress the inevitability of war. Caroline Playne's *The Pre-War Mind in Britain*, published in 1928, spoke of the mood as being one of infectious mental contagion which 'swept down the mindless, expectant, half-frightened, wondering crowds, and .... swept down progressives, earnest people, intelligent people as well'.[1] Such a reaction has been attributed to the incipient militarism of pre-war society fuelled by nationalism, imperialism and Social Darwinism. How else, it is reasoned, could the pre-war expectations of international solidarity have been so easily overcome?

Yet, in the case of Britain, the public had little time in which to react to events, and the contribution of the popular mood to actual events in July and August 1914 was limited. There was no noticeable sense of impending foreign crisis in the British press until 29 July, attention having been fixed largely on the continuing Irish Home Rule crisis. The final descent into war unfolded over the Bank Holiday weekend, the news of the German ultimatum to Belgium reaching London on the morning of Bank Holiday Monday, 3 August.

In Manchester at least, the opposition to intervention on the part of *The Manchester Guardian* reflected the fears of the local and influential business community as to the economic consequences of involvement. Its editor, C. P. Scott, noted: 'We care as little for Belgrade as Belgrade does for Manchester.'[2] The Governor of the Bank of England, Lord Cunliffe, also warned against war. The Chancellor of the Exchequer, Lloyd

[1] Caroline Playne, *The Pre-War Mind in Britain: An Historical Review* (London: Allen & Unwin, 1928), 329–30.

[2] Ian F. W. Beckett, *Home Front, 1914–18: How Britain Survived the Great War* (London: National Archives, 2006), 11.

George, noted on 31 July that Cunliffe had 'pleaded with him with tears in his eyes, "Keep us out of it. We shall be ruined if we are dragged in!"'[3] An immediate crisis in foreign-exchange markets had a knock-on effect, in turn, for the London Accepting Houses and the Bank of England. With investors forming long queues to convert bills of exchange into gold, the bank lost £6 million – 16 per cent of its reserves – in just three days. The Bank Holiday was extended until Thursday 6 August to allow the bank to take the necessary measures to retain financial control.

There were anti-war demonstrations in a number of cities and towns, including Birmingham and Ipswich, and a small demonstration for peace in Trafalgar Square on 2 August, at which the volatile nature of the public mood saw one speaker pushed off the platform by youths. King George V certainly recorded on 1 August that the public mood was against intervention. Even those largely Bank Holiday crowds that greeted the declaration of war in London were perhaps no more than 10,000 strong in a city of 7 million inhabitants. Many people would not have learned that Britain was at war until receiving their newspapers on 5 August. Interestingly, the King estimated that the crowd outside Buckingham Palace was larger on 6 August than on any previous day since its first appearance on 2 August, and at its greatest on 9 August, when he judged it to be about 50,000 strong. As elsewhere in Europe, the London crowd at least was composed primarily of middle-class youths.

There was little sympathy for Serbia, Asquith himself telling the Archbishop of Canterbury as late as 31 July that the Serbs deserved a 'thorough thrashing'.[4] While a more emotive issue, even the fate of Belgium was more significant for the Cabinet than for many others in Britain. Having declined the government's request on 3 August to cut short the annual holidays, the South Wales Miners Federation did so again even on 5 August. The federation only accepted an additional hour's work per day requested by the government and coal owners on 1 September. It is suggested from an analysis of the national and provincial press that the middle class were more in favour of intervention than the working class, London more in favour than the provinces, the young more in favour than the old, Anglicans more in favour than Nonconformists and men more so than women.[5]

[3] John Keiger, 'Britain's "Union Sacrée"', in Jean-Jacques Becker and Stéphane Audoin-Rouzeau (eds.), *Les sociétés européennes et la guerre de 1914–1918* (Nanterre: Université Paris-X Nanterre, 1990), 39–52, at 43.

[4] Hew Strachan, *The First World War: A New Illustrated History* (London: Simon & Schuster, 2003), 16.

[5] Adrian Gregory, *The Last Great War: British Society and the First World War* (Cambridge University Press, 2008), 25.

In 1914, the regular army's rank and file were not that experienced. Only 4,192 men had over fifteen years' service, and 46,291 had registered under two years with the colours. In 1914, indeed, between 50 and 60 per cent of the mobilised war strength of the British Expeditionary Force (BEF) comprised recalled reservists. The losses in the course of 1914 struck the old army heavily: in the Ypres salient between 14 October and 30 November 1914 alone, the BEF suffered 58,155 casualties, including 2,621 killed. In most cases, there was barely one officer and thirty men left in infantry battalions from those who had embarked in August 1914.

When Lieutenant-General Sir Richard Haking inspected the 2nd Royal Welsh Fusiliers in March 1916 following an earlier visit to a New Army battalion that same day, he was delighted to find a number of old regulars: 'He chatted and chaffed, pinched their arms and ears, asked how many children they had, and if they could be doing with leave to get another. As he passed from one 1914 man to another he dug his elbow into the CO's ribs and exclaimed, "You're a lucky fellow." When it was over he said to the CO, "That's been a treat. That's the sort we've known for thirty years."'[6] In a way that suggests that the regular army had all but disappeared, but, of course, the ethos remained. When the 2nd Royal Welsh were transferred to the 38th (Welsh) Division in February 1918, with even fewer old regulars left, and having just received large drafts from two disbanded New Army battalions, the Commanding Officer (CO) pointedly reminded all of the battalion's 'regular' status. It was still possible to enlist on the pre-war regular terms of enlistment throughout the war, although most wartime recruits were also enlisted as regulars, albeit on a new short-service engagement for three years or the duration. In March 1919, a total of 51,243 men were serving on 'normal' regular engagements with one or more years to complete. Recruiting for the Special Reserve also remained open throughout the war. An addition to the regular reserve, the Special Reserve had enlisted men prior to the war for six years' service, and this could be extended by a further four years, although not beyond the age of forty; former regular reservists, however, could serve in the Special Reserve until the age of forty-two.

Even if the pre-war British estimates of wartime wastage rates had been realistic – an expected 40 per cent for the first six months and 65 to 75 per cent for the first twelve months contrasted with the reality of 63 per cent in the first three months of the war – pre-war assumptions regarding manpower requirements were imperfectly formulated. The regular army stood at 247,432 officers and men in August 1914, the addition of

[6] J. C. Dunn (ed.), *The War the Infantry Knew, 1914–19*, 2nd edn. (London: Jane's, 1987), 185.

reservists (340,303) and the TF (245,779) bringing its total strength to 733,514.[7] Indeed, as already suggested, the greater proportion of the BEF would have to be found upon mobilisation from the reservists. Thereafter, the TF would be the means of expansion, but they were only liable for overseas service if they chose to take the so-called Imperial Service Obligation (ISO). In 1914, just 18,683, or only some 7 per cent, had done so – including only five complete units – although at least the County Territorial Associations (CTAs) provided ready-made machinery for wartime expansion.

Whatever assumptions had been made prior to the war, all were set aside by the appointment of Kitchener as Secretary of State for War in August 1914. Kitchener had not served at home since 1883 and was wholly unfamiliar with any pre-war arrangements. The Unionist politician Leo Amery aptly described him as a 'great improviser but also a great disorganiser'. This was particularly seen in Kitchener's distaste for the TF, whom he told Sir Edward Grey was a 'town clerk's army'.[8] Contemporaries suggested that his view of 'amateurs' had been influenced by the experience of seeing ineffective French citizen armies during the Franco-Prussian War, while he probably also distrusted the measure of independence enjoyed by CTAs and the potential for local nepotism in appointments. He told Violet Asquith that he preferred men with no military knowledge to those with 'a smattering of the wrong thing', and told Sir Charles Harris that 'he could take no account of anything but regular soldiers'.[9] His attitude effectively spelled the end of any pre-war plans to expand through the CTAs, as Kitchener resolved to raise his 'Kitchener' or 'New' Armies through the War Office. Briefly, under pressure of recruits, the responsibility for housing and preliminary training of the New Armies was vested in a committee headed by the former Unionist Secretary of State for War, St. John Brodrick, now Lord Midleton. Midleton turned to the CTAs, but his committee was relieved of its duties on 7 September 1914 and invitations to the CTAs to help rescinded.

Nevertheless, there was more to Kitchener's reasoning than simple prejudice.[10] There were no actual practical plans for expansion through

[7] *Statistics of the Military Effort*, 30.

[8] Leo Amery, *My Political Life*, 3 vols. (London: Hutchinson, 1953–5), Vol. II, 23; Lord Grey, *Twenty Five Years, 1892–1916*, 2 vols. (London: Hodder & Stoughton, 1925), Vol. II, 68.

[9] Peter Simkins, *Kitchener's Army: The Raising of the New Armies, 1914–16* (Manchester University Press, 1988), 41.

[10] Much of what follows on the TF is drawn from Ian F. W. Beckett, 'The Territorial Force', in Ian F. W. Beckett and Keith Simpson (eds.), *A Nation in Arms: A Social Study of the British Army in the First World War* (Manchester University Press, 1985), 128–63.

the CTAs, and Kitchener believed they would be swamped by having to train and recruit simultaneously. Similarly, Kitchener was reluctant to put pressure on married men to volunteer for service abroad, the TF containing not only a high proportion of married men but also those underage for overseas service: Territorials could enlist at seventeen compared to eighteen in the regulars, with overseas service only being permitted at the age of nineteen.

The issue of the ISO was clearly a factor. On 10 August an invitation was extended to complete Territorial units to volunteer for overseas service, and on 21 August, units where 80 per cent had volunteered were authorised to recruit to war establishment: two or more units with less than the required percentage could combine to produce service units. The latter proved unattractive, and from 31 August, second-line units could be raised where 60 per cent of the first line had volunteered, enabling the first line to be completed from the second and to return their home service men to the second line as a nucleus. The 60 per cent requirement was more realistic. While there is evidence to show that between 80 and 90 per cent of many units responded immediately to the call to go overseas, commitments made by some COs proved highly optimistic. In what was to become the 51st (Highland) Division, for example, the 75 per cent acceptance rate officially recorded fell significantly when individuals had to signify their assent on paper. One brigade that had supposedly volunteered to a man all opted subsequently for home service. In the 4th Royal Scots, 90 per cent of an 'artisan company' volunteered but only 15 to 20 per cent of a 'banker's company'. Only about 50 per cent came forward in the Civil Service Rifles (15th London Regiment) and around 58 per cent in the 4th Oxfordshire and Buckinghamshire Light Infantry. The response in the London brigades only improved after the Bishop of London 'harangued' the men in their training camp.[11] In the 1st Buckinghamshire Battalion, Oxfordshire and Buckinghamshire Light Infantry, the numbers were unequally distributed between companies. While 600 men volunteered, a further 240 declined to do so, many older NCOs or men with families. Labelled 'Never Dies' by the commanding officer, they were deprived of equipment and sent back to form the nucleus of the 2/1st Bucks Battalion. Not surprisingly, they resented their treatment, and greater understanding borne of experience was displayed when the 2/1st Bucks was asked to take the obligation in April 1915: 140 men, mostly elderly or unfit, still declined to do so. On 21 September 1914, a general duplication of the first line was authorised

[11] K. W. Mitchinson, *England's Last Hope: The Territorial Force, 1908–14* (Basingstoke: Palgrave, 2008), 210–11.

and a third line established in November 1915 as first-line units went overseas, and this was extended to cover all units in March 1915. The original designations of Imperial Service, First Reserve and Second Reserve units was changed in February 1915 to 1st, 2nd and 3rd Line units. The nomenclature of battalions to indicate the lines, *viz.*, 1/1st, 2/1st and 3/1st had been prescribed a month earlier, while original 'territorial' designations of brigades and divisions were discontinued in May 1915 and numbers substituted. Thus, the South Midland Division became the 48th (South Midland) Division.

Physical fitness was another crucial factor: 15 per cent of the 1st Montgomeryshire Yeomanry and 20 per cent of the 6th West Yorkshire, for example, were declared unfit for overseas service. It was also the case that pre-war Territorials could and did enlist for home service only until March 1915, and the pre-war Territorials could and did seek their discharge at the end of their original term of service until May 1916. Incomplete recruiting figures for Caernarfonshire suggest a ratio of home to foreign enlistments of four to one between September and December 1914.[12] Lloyd George advised his son, Gwilym, to opt only for home service, and there were 82,588 home servicemen still borne on TF returns in August 1915. Over 159,000 pre-war Territorials would have been entitled to discharge between 1914 and 1917 under normal peacetime conditions. It is not possible to estimate how many did so rather than accept a month's furlough and a bounty upon re-engagement for another four years or the duration. But there are examples of men taking a chance on discharge. Ironically, many of those opting for home service achieved faster promotion because they were more experienced than new recruits. By contrast, many of those units that did volunteer immediately found themselves marooned in India for the duration on poorer ration scales, poorer allowances, with inferior equipment, and little prospect of active service, the 43rd (Wessex), 44th (Home Counties) and 45th (2nd Wessex) Divisions being despatched to the sub-continent between September and December 1914. Pre-war time-expired Territorials serving in India were not then allowed to complete service at home. After 11 December 1915, no more direct recruiting was permitted into the TF except for a few specified units.

Yet a further legislative difficulty was that the form that Territorials signed in assenting to overseas service specified that they would remain with their own unit and could not be subsequently transferred to another. Amalgamating or disbanding Territorial units was also theoretically

[12] Clive Hughes, 'Army Recruiting in Gwynedd, 1914–16', unpublished MA thesis, University of Wales, 1983, 166.

Figure 4. 1/1st Royal Buckinghamshire Hussars, King's Head, Aylesbury, August 1914.
Source: From Authors' Collections

illegal. Following the failure of legislation in April 1915, a new form to permit transfer was issued in May 1915 to all new recruits as well as to all who had already signified assent. It was said by Lord Derby – the 'King of Lancashire' – to be 'murdering' Territorial recruitment.[13] As it happened, Derby's influence was such that while the complaints of London units were aired in the House of Commons in March and April 1916, county and regional identity was maintained in Western Command until 1918, although this also reflected its larger and more homogeneous nature. In the event, clauses were included in the Military Service Act of May 1916 to remove the anomaly. Amid increasing evidence of the breaking down of the drafting system by 1916, a constant loss of trained personnel damaged the efficiency of second-line TF units, contributing to perceived failures by the 53rd (Welsh) and 54th (East Anglian) Divisions at Suvla Bay on the Gallipoli Peninsula in August 1915. Second-line units continued to have a poor reputation. Temporary amalgamations of many Territorial units took place in the wake of heavy casualties in 1915 and became more permanent in 1916, while second-line Territorial units took the brunt of reductions on the re-organisation of the BEF amid the

[13] Randolph S. Churchill, *Lord Derby: King of Lancashire* (London: Heinemann, 1959), 185–6.

general manpower shortages in early 1918, leading to an increasing sense of powerlessness on the part of CTAs. Most CTAs were reduced to administering separation allowances and welfare funds and, from 1916, the Volunteer Force.

Above all, however, Kitchener was preoccupied in 1914 with possible German invasion, against which the TF was the principal defence. Use of the TF to expand the BEF would disorganise the force for its home defence role, as its division into first-line overseas and second-line home service units was already judged to be doing in September 1914. Despite pre-war dismissal of invasion fears by the Admiralty, there were genuine fears following the German capture of Antwerp on 10 October. Kitchener expected the danger to continue until at least January 1915, and even Churchill and the First Sea Lord, Fisher, were alarmed. By 12 November, there was some expectation of a German attempt on the east coast within the next six weeks, with a likely date assumed to be 20 November, when moon and tides were right. Kitchener's scrapping of existing home defence plans had not materially contributed to home defence organisation either, pre-war expectations of engaging an invading enemy inland being replaced by a concept of meeting an invasion on the beaches that had been consistently rejected by defence planners since the 1880s. Some 30,000 men, mostly TF, were spread accordingly along the east coast. The Admiralty chose not to disclose a German appreciation it had obtained that greatly exaggerated the strength of British defences, and fears were sustained by the press and by the German bombardment of Scarborough and other northeast towns in December 1914. By January 1916, it was still believed that the Germans could land up to 160,000 men before the Royal Navy could intervene, the scale assumed by pre-war invasion enquiries being only 70,000 men. The scale was not reduced until December 1917, when it was set at 30,000, before a final adjustment down to 5,000 was made in September 1918.

Kitchener was eventually reluctantly persuaded to allow the TF to 'fill the gap' in France and Flanders in the winter of 1914–15 before his New Armies were ready to do so. By the end of December 1914, some thirty-three TF units were in France and Flanders, including twenty-two infantry battalions. The total of battalions rose to forty-eight by February 1915, and the first complete division – the 46th (North Midland) Division – arrived that same month. Meanwhile, the failure to use the CTAs clearly resulted in duplication of effort and competition, both in recruitment and in finding equipment, damaging to both the TF and the New Armies. When voluntary direct enlistment in the TF ceased in December 1915, some 725,842 men had enlisted in it, or approximately half the number enlisted in the New Armies in the same

Figure 5. Recruits of 2/1st Royal Buckinghamshire Hussars, Market Street, Buckingham, November 1914.
Source: From Authors' Collections

period. Indeed, compared to 267 regular or reserve battalions and 557 New Army battalions in existence during the war, there were 692 TF battalions.

Unfortunately, it was also the case that the raising of the New Armies was almost entirely haphazard in the absence of any coherent manpower policy. Kitchener himself had no clear idea of how many men might be needed and never articulated how he had discerned that the war would last at least three years. On 6 August 1914, Parliament was asked to sanction an immediate increase of 500,000 men, Kitchener making his appeal for the 'first 100,000' on 7 August. A figure of seventy divisions is usually cited as the ultimate intention, but this was not adopted by a Cabinet sub-committee until August 1915, Kitchener having spoken of thirty divisions on 31 August 1914, forty-six to fifty on 8 September 1914 and sixty in June 1915. It is usually suggested that the figure of seventy divisions was chosen for its approximation to the pre-war strength of the French and German armies at sixty-two and eighty-seven infantry divisions, respectively.[14] The official figure was adjusted downwards to sixty-two divisions abroad and five at home in February 1916 and then to fifty-seven abroad and ten at home in April 1916. In terms of overall

[14] F. W. Perry, *The Commonwealth Armies: Manpower and Organisation in Two Worlds Wars* (Manchester University Press, 1988), 9.

numbers, Parliament sanctioned a further 500,000 increase on 9 September 1914, another million on 12 November 1914 and an upper limit of 4 million men in December 1915. The figure was adjusted retrospectively and for the last time to 5 million in December 1916.

Between August 1914 and November 1918, 4,970,902 men were enlisted in the British Army, of whom 2,466,719 were volunteers and 2,504,183 were enlisted after the introduction of conscription in January 1916. The latter figure, however, includes those who enlisted in the regulars and the TF, as well as those attested under the Derby Scheme: actual conscripts brought in by the application of successive Military Service Acts numbered 1.3 million. With the existing forces in August 1914, that yielded a wartime total of 5,704,416 men in the army at one time or another, approximating to 22.1 per cent of the entire male population of the United Kingdom (thus including Ireland).[15] The effort between 1914 and 1918 compares to 19.4 per cent of the male population serving in the armed forces as a whole during the Second World War (in which 4.6 million men served). Thus, with the possible exception of the almost twenty-three years of continuous warfare between December 1792 and June 1815, the Great War represents the greatest degree of military participation Britain ever experienced. Nonetheless, it needs to be recognised that roughly half the men of military age did not enlist, and roughly half of those who did serve spent half the war as civilians.[16] To these figures can be added 2.8 million men from the Empire. France, however, initially mobilised approximately 4.4 million men and eventually mobilised about 8.4 million, while Germany initially mobilised 5.2 million men and eventually mobilised 13.2 million.

The 'rush to the colours', however, was quite arbitrary, and the impact accordingly varied. Fifteen per cent of all wartime enlistments did indeed take place in the first two months of the war, but the response was not immediate. It has been almost precisely dated to the period between 25 August and 9 September 1914. Initial confusion was not assisted by a lack of news from France until the publication in the *Times* on 30 August of the sensational 'Amiens Despatch' by Arthur Moore, accompanied by a telegram from Hamilton Fyfe of the *Daily Mail* reporting the retreat from Mons. Moore's earlier report on Mons, published on

15 *Statistics of the Military Effort*, 156–9, 363–4.

16 Central Statistical Office, *Fighting with Figures: A Statistical Digest of the Second World War* (London: CSO, 1995), 38–9; M. Greenwood, 'British Loss of Life in the Wars of 1794–1815 and 1914–18', *Journal of the Royal Statistical Society*, 105 (1942), 1–16; Laura Ugolini, *Civvies: Middle-Class Men on the English Home Front, 1914–18* (Manchester University Press, 2013), 7.

25 August, had already been doctored by the head of the Press Bureau, F. E. Smith, to emphasise the need for recruits. German atrocity stories had also surfaced, and on 24 August the highly influential Derby approached the War Office with a suggestion to raise Pals battalions of men from the same communities, factories, and so on. Derby first mentioned the actual term 'Pals' in a public meeting at Liverpool on 28 August. The idea had actually originated in the War Office as early as 14 August, and the 'Stockbrokers Battalion' (10th Royal Fusiliers) had begun to recruit on 21 August following a conversation two days earlier between the newly appointed Director of Recruiting at the War Office, Sir Henry Rawlinson, and Major the Hon. Robert White at the Travellers' Club in Pall Mall.[17]

Together these factors seem to have accounted for the great increase. Only 51,647 men had enlisted in Britain prior to 15 August 1914, but 174,901 were enlisted between 30 August and 5 September. A total of 179,680 men enlisted in the first week of September, with the 33,204 who enlisted on 3 September being the highest recorded for any single day, exceeding a year's pre-war enlistment rate. The most fruitful recruiting period was over by 9 September as the news from France improved, and there were increasing rumours that recruits were suffering discomfort in improvised accommodation. It also appeared that men were no longer required, deferred enlistment having been introduced in view of the accommodation problems with men enlisted in the Reserve and sent home on 6d per diem. Since many had given up employment to enlist, Asquith was compelled to announce an increase to 3s.0d per diem to deferred entrants on 10 September. The War Office also tried to regulate the flow on 11 September by arbitrary variations in physical requirements, raising the five-foot, three-inch height requirement set on 8 August to five feet, six inches, though the upper age limit was increased from thirty to thirty. At least 10,000 men already enlisted were rejected on arrival at their units under the new regulations. On 23 October, the War Office lowered the height requirement to five feet, four inches and extended the upper age limit to thirty-eight or forty-five for former servicemen. On 14 November it was dropped again to five feet, three inches, and the first 'Bantam' units were raised from men down to five feet, zero inches, the first being the 1st and 2nd Birkenhead Bantams (15th and 16th Cheshire Regiment). A Durham miner who had walked all the way to Birkenhead in the attempt to enlist had taken his story to the local Member of Parliament (MP), Alfred Bigland: potential recruits were offered a rail warrant to Birkenhead from any recruiting office in the

[17] Simkins, *Kitchener's Army*, 83–4.

Figure 6. New Army recruits at Peterborough, 12 October 1914.
Source: From Authors' Collections

country, and 1,098 had done so by 27 November.[18] The height requirement generally was lowered to five feet, two inches in July 1915 and the age limit extended to forty, but it was already apparent that the voluntary system was failing.

It is also clear that the process of enlistment was exceedingly complex with wide regional and local variations. Initially, Wales and Scotland, for example, found proportionally more recruits than England. Within England, there were considerable variations. By November 1914, it was reported that while southern Scotland had produced 237 recruits per 10,000 of population, the Midlands 196 per 10,000, Lancashire 178 per 10,000, London and the Home Counties 170 per 10,000 and Yorkshire and the North East 150 per 10,000, the South West had found only 88 per 10,000 and eastern counties only 80 per 10,000. Comparison of enlistment rates in Bristol, Glasgow, Hull, Liverpool, Norwich, and Nottingham show equally wide discrepancies.[19]

[18] Peter Simkins, '"Each One a Pocket Hercules": The Bantam Experiment and the Case of the 35th Division', in Sandars Marble (ed.), *Scraping the Barrel: The Military Use of Substandard Manpower, 1860–1969* (New York: Fordham University Press, 2012), 79–104.

[19] J. M. Osborne, *The Voluntary Recruiting Movement in Britain, 1914–16* (New York: Garland, 1982), 138–44.

Of course, patriotism played its part, and there was more than one kind of patriotism, deriving from a complex web of individual loyalties. Other factors were equally important. One was certainly family situation. Inefficiency by the War Office in paying out adequate separation allowances discouraged married men from enlisting. Agitation began in September for the rates paid to pre-war regulars – 11s.1d a week for a wife without children and 1s.9d for each boy under fourteen and each girl under sixteen – to be increased and to be paid weekly rather than monthly. Concessions were duly made with effect from 1 October 1914, but the War Office struggled to cope with the unprecedented increase in numbers so that the charitable organisation, the Soldiers' and Sailors' Families Association, had been compelled to deal with over 932,000 separate claims on their funds by December 1914. Others with dependants also took time to put their domestic affairs in order. Equally, there were those only too glad to escape family or, indeed, humdrum routine.

The propaganda effort of the Parliamentary Recruiting Committee (PRC), officially constituted on 31 August, had some effect. It produced 2 million posters and 20 million leaflets by March 1915.[20] The impact of well-known posters, however, should not be exaggerated. The PRC's eventual output of 5.7 million posters and 14.2 million leaflets at a cost of £240,000 represented less than Rowntree's of York had spent on advertising a cocoa brand in 1911–12.[21] Some caution must also be exercised with regard to the impact of women handing out white feathers. While they were often seeking vicarious participation through encouraging male enlistment, their 'unfeminine' efforts frequently resulted in a public backlash.[22]

Nonetheless, the significant voluntary effort that swung into operation alongside the War Office's own network of recruiting offices on the initiative of individuals and organisations such as the National Service League, the Primrose League, the Rural League, the Church Lads' Brigade, the British Empire Agency and the Mother's Union clearly had an impact. The Legion of Frontiersmen, for example, sponsored the 25th Royal Fusiliers, and even some CTAs raised battalions for the New Armies, including Cambridgeshire and the Isle of Ely, Denbighshire and Flint and East Riding. It was a measure of the inability of the War

[20] Roy Douglas, 'Voluntary Enlistment in the First World War and the Work of the Parliamentary Recruiting Committee', *Journal of Modern History*, 42 (1970), 564–85, at 568.

[21] Nicholas Hiley, '"Kitchener Wants You", and "Daddy, What Did You Do in the War?": The Myth of British Recruiting Posters', *Imperial War Museum Review*, 11 (1997), 40–58.

[22] Nicoletta Gullace, 'White Feathers and Wounded Men: Female Patriotism and the Memory of the Great War', *Journal of British Studies*, 36 (1997), 178–206.

Office to cope with expansion on its own, and, excluding the TF, 38 per cent of the 557 new service or reserve battalions raised between August 1914 and June 1916 were the result of initiatives by groups or individuals other than the War Office.

All manner of recruiting methods were employed. It has been suggested that very public recruiting meetings 'embodied spectatorship and participation in an explicit form, issuing an invitation to individuals to step across the line from one to the other'.[23] Yet, in Caernarfonshire, a canvass carried out by teachers, chapel elders and shopkeepers with local knowledge or influence was more effective than public meetings, though route marches were also tried through unresponsive areas. Generally, it has been suggested that the sheer theatricality of recruiting meetings as community 'occasions' held more symbolic significance than the actual military results.[24] Recruiting marches generally were much favoured. In the North West; Lord Derby made much use of a former miners' agent and anti-militarist, Joe Tinker, whom he had helped obtain a place in the Inns of Court OTC. At Preston in August 1915, a recruiting week included marching bands, a 'moving picture van', garden parties and fetes and appearances by a local Victoria Cross (VC) winner. The clergy were especially prominent, the great majority of the 20,000 local agents who acted for the Inns of Court in providing information on obtaining commissions being clergymen. The Archbishop of Canterbury refused to sanction the use of pulpits for recruiting, but many diocesan bishops were effective recruiters outside it, notably the Bishop of London, A. F. Winnington-Ingram. In Wales, even Nonconformist ministers spoke so strongly in favour of the war that many lost their congregations. In Scotland, recruiting posters and military murals were the first advertisements ever carried on trams in Glasgow, while a tramcar in Edinburgh became a mobile recruiting office. Recruiting vans were despatched elsewhere in rural Scotland, and the infant cinema also featured in recruiting efforts. In some cases, public-spirited employers such as the larger ironworks and shipbuilding firms in Middlesbrough, the Stroud Brewery Company and the sporting outfitters Aquascutum offered bonuses to their employees who enlisted.

Studies of Bristol, Birmingham and Leeds show a particular link with employment. Possibly as many as 480,000 men lost their jobs in Britain by the end of August 1914. Many others were placed on half time in the prevailing economic uncertainty at the outbreak of war: in any case,

[23] Gregory, *Last Great War*, 76.
[24] Kit Good, 'England Goes to War, 1914–15', unpublished PhD thesis, University of Liverpool, 2002, 142.

autumn was a traditional time of lay-offs in agriculture and the building trade. Labour exchanges certainly encouraged enlistment. In Bristol, 10 per cent of the workforce was laid off in July 1914 and a further 26 per cent placed on short time. In August, the Local Government Board instructed charities to refuse relief to those eligible for enlistment. Nine of every ten men laid off in the city enlisted, and Bristol's unemployment fell by a full 1.5 per cent. In Birmingham, 78 per cent of recruits in August 1914 came from the same working-class background that had been enlisted in peacetime, the majority from less secure employment subject to seasonal variations, though they were men slightly older than in peacetime.[25] In Leeds, textile and engineering workers were laid off, with 7,000 trade unionists reported as unemployed in August 1914. By September, enlistment had reduced the 10.25 per cent contraction in employment to 1.5 per cent.[26]

Significantly, enlistment dropped away rapidly once large government contracts were placed in the autumn for clothing, boots, munitions and other war essentials. Army pay was lower than that for most common occupations, and enhanced pay rates were only offered temporarily to recruits with particular skills such as artificers or motorcyclists. It was also the case that rising retail prices in the first eight months of the war were an additional incentive for men to stay in civil employment with better rewards. In Birmingham, male industrial employment had contracted by 10 per cent between July and December 1914, but there was actually now a labour shortage of 2.7 per cent, though some trades such as linen and pottery remained on short time until February 1915.[27] In Leeds, one of the larger engineering employers, Fowler's, which had laid off 1,700 men in August, was working overtime by the end of October: 1,145 men had indicated their willingness to join a Workers' Pals Battalion in early September, but only 100 then came forward to attest when asked to do so in December. In Leicester, increasing orders for the local boot trade may well have contributed to what was perceived to be a civic embarrassment in terms of the lack of response: only 2.6 per cent of those deemed eligible had enlisted by March 1915, leaving an estimated 60,000 men of military age in Leicestershire and Rutland not serving. The boot industry benefitted in Northamptonshire as well, with a similar impact upon recruitment.[28]

25 M. D. Blanch, 'Nation, Empire and the Birmingham Working Class, 1899–1914', unpublished PhD thesis, University of Birmingham, 1975, 341–67.

26 Patricia Morris, 'Leeds and the Amateur Military Tradition: The Leeds Rifles and Their Antecedents, 1859–1918', unpublished PhD thesis, University of Leeds, 1983, 316–17.

27 John Hartigan, 'Volunteering in the First World War: The Birmingham Experience, August 1914 to May 1915', *Midland History*, 24 (1999), 167–86.

28 Gregory, *Last Great War*, 88–9; Pierre Purseigle, 'Beyond and Below the Nation: Towards a Comparative History of Local Communities at War', in Jenny Macleod and

In the case of the South West, the abundance of the 1914 harvest and the land-holding pattern of many smaller farms with owner-occupiers prepared to offer incentives to agricultural labourers to remain on the land contributed to significantly low rates of enlistment compared to the national average. Outside of Plymouth and Exeter, the region was largely rural and geographically isolated, the poor communications impeding centralisation of the recruiting effort. Only seven service battalions were raised in the two counties, and in the case of those such as the 6th Duke of Cornwall's Light Infantry and 9th Devonshire Regiment, most recruits were from London, South Wales and the Midlands. In Plymouth, a quarter of the male workforce was already employed in the Devonport Dockyard, the workforce of which expanded significantly. Coastal communities generally in Devon and Cornwall also tended to be attracted to TF coastal defence units, the Royal Naval Reserve Trawler Section and the Royal Navy's South West Auxiliary Coastal Patrol.

There were additional reasons for a poor Devonian response, however, in the strong Liberal and Nonconformist tradition in the north and west of the county; the existing hostility of much of the local press to the Hon. Hugh Fortescue, the son of the Lord Lieutenant, who undertook to oversee the recruiting campaign; the delay in establishing a central recruiting committee until February 1915; and the resentment towards recruiting agents, who attempted to canvass individuals in their own homes. Recruiting posters were often vandalised. Ironically, the more co-ordinated effort in 1915, coupled with the impact of the German sinking of the *Lusitania* in May 1915, then resulted in a substantial increase in recruiting in Devon at the time it was trailing off elsewhere. Similarly, in Cornwall, while extraction industries such as china clay and, especially, tin were suffering economic depression from falling prices, the labour forces were well used to economic cycles of boom and slump. There had been substantial emigration to new mines in the Australia, South Africa and South America in the late nineteenth century, and men appeared prepared to await better times rather than enlisting. Among clay miners, too, there was some residual opposition to the authorities stemming from a bitter strike in 1913. When a specifically targeted campaign was mounted for the 10th DCLI in March 1915 as the skills-based 'Cornwall Pioneers', it was immediately much more successful.[29] The harvest is also suggested as a major factor in impeding recruitment in East

Pierre Purseigle (eds.), *Uncovered Fields: Perspectives in First World War Studies* (Leiden: Brill, 2004), 95–123.

29 Bonnie White, 'Volunteerism and Early Recruitment Efforts in Devonshire, August 1914 to December 1915', *Historical Journal*, 52 (2009), 641–66; Andy Gale, 'The West Country and the First World War: Recruits and Identities', unpublished PhD thesis,

Anglia and in the southern part of Kent. The 7th and 8th Buffs were both dependent upon recruits from London, although the 6th Buffs had one company formed by William Cory & Son, a Medway coal and coke transport company.[30]

Overall, the Board of Trade estimated that those on short time had declined from 26 per cent of the industrial labour force in September 1914 to only 6 per cent by February 1915. High wages may have discouraged enlistment among dockers, railway workers and miners, whereas low rates of employment may have stimulated recruitment among building workers. Yet, there was a high rate of enlistment from some industries such as engineering, chemicals and iron and steel not threatened by unemployment, and wage rates as such do not appear to have been a major factor overall in determining enlistment. By contrast, the response from industry did reflect the age structure of the labour force in differing sectors as well as purely local factors. As might be expected, young men tended generally to enlist before older men, but there was also a direct correlation between average age and enlistment. Thus, the highest percentage of the labour force aged between twenty and thirty-four in Britain was found among employees of omnibus companies (74 per cent), and they had also recorded the highest enlistment rate by July 1916 (47 per cent). Equally, agriculture and the railways had the oldest average labour force aged twenty to thirty-four (both 50 per cent) and produced the lowest rates of enlistment (22 and 18 per cent, respectively). It is suggested, therefore, that 'age was the largest single determinant of enlistment variations during the first year of the war.'[31]

In Gwynedd in Wales, some slate quarry owners refused to keep open the places of those who enlisted, whereas other owners threatened men with dismissal if they did not enlist. Faced with such uncertainties, increasing numbers of quarrymen simply took up employment vacancies in the railways, docks and mines. By contrast, both the North Eastern and Cardiff Railway Companies encouraged enlistment by inducements such as guarantees of post-war employment and welfare assistance to dependants, though the latter retracted its offers after four days when it became clear that under-manning might result from the enthusiastic uptake.[32]

University of Lancaster, 2010, 64–96; Stuart Dalley, 'The Response in Cornwall to the Outbreak of the First World War', *Cornish Studies*, 11 (2003), 85–109.

30 Nicholas Mansfield, 'Volunteering and Recruiting', in Gerald Gliddon (ed.), *Norfolk and Suffolk in the Great War* (Norwich: Gliddon Books, 1988), 18–31; Mark Connelly, *Steady the Buffs: A Region, A Regiment and the Great War* (Oxford University Press, 2006), 10–12.

31 P. E. Dewey, 'Military Recruiting and the British Labour Force during the First World War', *Historical Journal*, 27 (1984), 199–224, at 210–11.

32 Clive Hughes, 'The New Armies', in Beckett and Simpson (eds.), *Nation in Arms*, 100–25, at 102, 120.

From the beginning, there was also a degree of protectionism for key workers such as railwaymen and Admiralty employees. Railwaymen required written consent to enlist from their employers from 4 September 1914 onwards, and Admiralty workers were 'badged' with 'On War Service' badges from 26 September. Within six months, the Admiralty had issued over 400,000 badges. Those employed directly by the War Office in the Royal Ordnance Factories and other key munitions plants were also badged from March 1915 – about 80,000 had been badged by July – though there was no legal means by which those badged could be prevented from enlisting. The Ministry of Munitions then became the only authority for issuing badges in July 1915. Private firms had also issued badges, and these were declared illegal on 4 August 1915. Certificates of exemption replaced war service badges once conscription was introduced.

Others enlisted under the peer influence of what has been called social inheritance, joining because their friends had done so. The most obvious manifestation of this was the success of the Pals Battalions, of which 115 were raised including the Accrington Pals (11th East Lancashire), Barnsley Pals (13th York and Lancaster Regiment), Bradford Pals (16th West Yorkshire), Glasgow Corporation Tramways Battalion (15th Highland Light Infantry), Grimsby Chums (10th Lincolnshire), Newcastle Commercials (16th Northumberland Fusiliers), Oldham Comrades (24th Manchester) and Swansea Pals (14th Welsh Regiment). Lancashire and Cheshire raised twenty-four such local battalions, and both Yorkshire and the North East fifteen apiece. Not all were necessarily easy to recruit, the 'Tyneside Scottish' (20th Northumberland Fusiliers), only completing its establishment in November 1914 by accepting non-Scots. In the case of the First Salford Pals (15th Lancashire Fusiliers), there was strong competition from other Lancashire units, including the Manchester Pals (16th Manchester Regiment), which had started to recruit before the Salford Committee was formed. The second and third Salford Battalions (16th and 19th Lancashire Fusiliers) required companies to be raised in Eccles and Swinton, while a fourth battalion was not completed until July 1915. The Accrington Pals equally drew men from Blackburn, Burnley and Chorley.

There was effectively a class element to the Pals. Like the recognised Territorial 'class corps' such as the Inns of Court OTC (formerly 14th Middlesex Rifle Volunteers), the Artists Rifles (1/28th London Regiment) and the London Rifle Brigade (5th London Regiment), which had always attracted more upper-middle-class recruits, it was a matter 'less about who you served with, but much more obviously about who you didn't serve with'.[33] Five Pals battalions were drawn almost entirely from those educated at public schools, including, unsurprisingly, the Public Schools Battalion (16th Middlesex Regiment). The 16th Highland Light Infantry was comprised of former members of the Glasgow Boys' Brigade, and the 17th Highland Light Infantry was targeted at the commercial classes. The Birmingham City Battalions were specifically advertised as for non-manual volunteers only, recruiting in the city also being characterised in practice by the appeal of enlisting alongside friends from schools and a variety of class-based social and leisure clubs and organisations. It has also been postulated that regional and civic consciousness and identity played a distinct role. This was true of rural Sussex, where a relative newcomer to the county, Claude Lowther MP, of Herstmonceux Castle, raised three Southdown Battalions (11th, 12th and 13th Royal Sussex) from coastal resorts and down-land villages. Rather than the appeal to the quasi-feudalism evoked by the county's TF, which was dominated by the traditional rural elite, Lowther 'employed sentimental attachment to locality as landscape, rather than to family or estate'.[34]

It was also true of Hull, which had received city status in 1897 and which raised four city battalions, the first being the Hull Commercials (10th East Yorkshire), the four together later forming the 92nd Brigade in the 31st Division. The 11th, 12th and 13th East Yorkshire were respectively the Hull Tradesmen, Hull Sportsmen and Athletes and the splendidly evocative T'Others. In theory, the Hull Commercials were raised by the Lord Lieutenant of the East Riding and subsequent battalions by the CTA rather than by the city. There was, however, a sense of inward-looking identity and a conscious rivalry with the perceived recruitment efforts of Liverpool. The rhetoric in Hull was cast initially within a national framework. It became increasingly specific to the region after December 1914, with a new emphasis upon completing the city's TF units before becoming nationally orientated with the end of voluntary enlistment. Some caution must be exercised in generalising from these specific examples for 'the apparent endorsement of sub-national identities by the War Office in the designation of so many service battalions was not really an affirmation of region or locality, but an expression of faith in private sponsorship.'[35] It depended not on civic effort but on the

[33] Gregory, *Last Great War*, 78.

[34] Keith Grieves, 'Lowther's Lambs: Rural Paternalism and Voluntary Recruitment in the First World War', *Rural History*, 4 (1993), 55–75, at 69.

[35] Helen Townley, 'The First World War and Voluntary Recruitment: A Form for Regional Identity? An Analysis of the Nature, Expression and Significance of Regional Identity in Hull, 1900–16', unpublished PhD thesis, University of Sussex, 2007, 177.

willingness of individuals to bear the costs of raising them. Indeed, the War Office soon revoked local designations for battalions. Subsequently, as recruiting flagged, the War Office tried to revive the idea of locally raised units, but new formations averaged only five a month between January and July 1915.

Some reasons why men enlisted simply defy categorisation. Some may simply have enlisted on impulse. Sidney Rogerson, for example, who served in the 2nd West Yorkshire Regiment, described how his soldier servant had enlisted in an alcoholic haze after seeing a friend off to the front, never recalled enlisting, and '"when the sergeant comes and claimed" him next morning he was as surprised as his wife was annoyed.'[36]

As already suggested, Wales and Scotland certainly increased the proportion of their males under arms to a level largely matching that of England, with Scotland actually producing the largest proportion of recruits under voluntary enlistment within the United Kingdom. It might be noted that the voluntary tradition had been stronger in Scotland in terms of the Victorian rifle volunteer movement as well, although the Territorials remained the military arm of choice in 1914 and had the advantage of established drill halls from which to recruit. It did well, particularly in rural areas, whereas the concept of Pals was somewhat alien. Only seven Pals Battalions had been formed in Scotland by February 1915, one as already noted – the 15th Highland Light Infantry – being the result of the charismatic exertions of James Dalrymple, the General Manager of Glasgow Corporation Tramways. Moreover, there was a recognised military tradition in terms of the popular identification of kilted regiments as representing a 'martial race' with the expansion of empire. Vestiges of traditional clan loyalties to individuals such as Lord Lovat or Cameron of Lochiel had a role in the Highlands: a belief that some commitment had been made to a post-war redistribution of land to crofters and cottars led to considerable post-war unrest when this proved illusory.[37]

It was also the case that economic factors played a significant part, and in Scotland, it had little to do with the age or wage structures of industry. There had been considerable unemployment in Scotland in 1907–8 and a great deal of emigration between 1901 and 1911, amounting to 5.5 per cent of the population of military age. There had been an economic upswing in 1913, which persuaded many men to remain who might

[36] Sidney Rogerson, *Twelve Days* (London: Arthur Barker, 1933), 40.

[37] Ewen Cameron and Iain Robertson, 'Fighting and Bleeding for the Land: The Scottish Highlands and the Great War', in Catriona M. M. Macdonald and Elaine W. McFarland (eds.), *Scotland and the Great War* (East Linton: Tuckwell Press, 1999), 81–100.

otherwise have emigrated. But the war brought new uncertainty not just in terms of men immediately affected by unemployment or short-time working but also in terms of those who saw a potential future threat to employment. The expected seasonal contraction of the building trade would not be remedied by the usual autumn uptake, and shipbuilding orders were being cancelled. Some 8,000 miners had been placed on short time in Fife by 12 August. There were regional variations, however, for the east coast mines were more badly affected than west coast mines because the former immediately lost German and Baltic markets: while 36.5 per cent of East Lothian miners enlisted by August 1915, this fell to 20 per cent in Ayrshire. Some coal owners offered bounties to men to enlist. The other main industries of engineering and iron and steel also suffered considerable contraction in trade. Of thirty major industries surveyed by the Board of Trade in October 1914, twenty had produced a higher proportion of recruits in Scotland than elsewhere. In the first three months of the war, Scottish industry provided over 109,000 recruits, representing 13.5 per cent of the total in the United Kingdom. Rural Scotland also showed a higher rate of enlistment than comparable areas in England, but it was still noticeable that men in 'economically safe' sectors such as agriculture and commerce showed less inclination to enlist. In the longer term, as industry recovered and protection was extended increasingly to key industrial occupations, the overall balance of military service would shift more to those without such protection. In the shorter term, however, it has been suggested that Scottish enlistment in 1914 might be seen as a continuation of pre-war emigration.[38]

In the case of the Welsh and Irish, Kitchener's distrust of the possible politicisation of a proposed Welsh Army Corps and of the offers to raise units from the pre-war Ulster Volunteer Force (UVF) and the rival Irish National Volunteers (INV) put something of a blight upon enlistment. Under pressure from Lloyd George, who first mooted the idea on 19 September, the Welsh Army Corps was authorised on 10 October 1914. Kitchener had clear reservations about 'wild and insubordinate' Welsh troops.[39] There was an angry exchange between Kitchener and Lloyd George in Cabinet on 28 October over an order issued to the 2/1st Denbighshire Yeomanry prohibiting the speaking of Welsh in billets that spilled out into a wider confrontation over the units to be allocated to the Welsh Army Corps. Nevertheless, the Welsh Army Corps was permitted to incorporate several existing battalions, whereas a Welsh National

[38] Derek Rutherford Young, 'Voluntary Recruitment in Scotland, 1914–16', unpublished PhD thesis, University of Glasgow, 2001, 96–158, 195–9.
[39] Brock and Brock (eds.), *Asquith*, 298.

Executive Committee raised the additional new units required for what, in the event, emerged as only a single division – the 38th (Welsh) Division – rather than two. The formation projected a strongly nationalist image, with the prospect of Welsh officers and chaplains being used to stimulate recruitment. Nepotism was rife, with Lloyd George securing commanders of his own choice such as Brigadier-General Owen Thomas, a popular Welsh speaker. Thomas found commissions for his own three sons and furthered the military careers of Lloyd George's sons, Gwilym and Dick, Gwilym having opted for overseas service after all. Two other brigade commanders were Liberal MPs, as was another battalion commander. One of the brigade commanders, Ivor Philipps MP, whose previous service had been as a major in the Indian Army, was then promoted to command the 38th (Welsh) Division in January 1916. Attracting considerable prejudice on the part of regulars from its perceived political nature, the division was unjustly criticised for its performance at Mametz Wood on the Somme in July 1916, the stigma persisting throughout the war. In fact, it is difficult to identify any specific Scottish or Welsh service 'experience' substantially different from that of the remainder of the army.

In terms of recruitment to the British armed forces, the Irish case was unusual in a British context as recruitment was much more politicised and conscription was never introduced in Ireland. There is some disagreement about the number of Irishmen who enlisted in the British Army, and there will never be an exact figure on this as Irishmen who enlisted in Great Britain were generally not counted as Irishmen, whereas those from elsewhere in Great Britain who enlisted in Ireland or served in Irish units often were.[40] The most accurate estimates have been provided by David Fitzpatrick and Keith Jeffery; Fitzpatrick's figure is around 5,000 men higher, suggesting a total of 144,000 recruits during the war, in addition to 58,000 serving regulars or reservists on the outbreak of war.[41]

While David Fitzpatrick has sought to downplay the importance of politics and religion in Irish recruitment, stressing the importance of peer pressure, exerted through various 'fraternities', it is undeniable that politics played an important role. On the outbreak of war, the 10th (Irish)

[40] This is a problem when using government publications as a whole and in Irish National War Memorial, *Ireland's Memorial Records, 1914–1918* (Dublin, 1923). The destruction of around 50 per cent of British servicemen's records by enemy action in World War II means that it is impossible to calculate an exact figure.

[41] Jeffery, *Ireland and the Great War*, 7; and David Fitzpatrick, 'The Logic of Collective Sacrifice: Ireland and the British Army, 1914–1918', *Historical Journal*, XXXVIII, 4 (1995), 1017–30.

Division was established as the Irish component of the First New Army (K1), with recruiting being organised by the War Office through existing recruiting structures. However, as Stephen Sandford has shown, recruiting for this division was soon failing; by 29 August 1914, only 2,729 officers and men had joined the division, while the strength of the other five divisions in K1 ranged from 7,729 officers and men in the 12th (Eastern) Division to 13,272 in the 13th (Western) Division. Indeed, to bring the 10th (Irish) Division up to establishment, a large number of recruits were brought in from Great Britain, and it appears that somewhere between 30 and 40 per cent of the initial rank and file of the division were not from Ireland.[42] It became clear to Lord Kitchener that if Irish recruitment were to improve, then he would have to broker deals with John Redmond, the leader of the Irish Parliamentary Party (IPP) and Edward Carson, the leader of the Irish Unionists, in an attempt to tap the manpower of, respectively, the Irish National Volunteers (INV) and the Ulster Volunteer Force (UVF).

The Irish question, as a whole, was addressed in mid-September 1914 when Home Rule was placed on the statute book but with a suspending clause, meaning that it would not come into operation until the end of the war, when special provision would be made for parts of Ulster. Kitchener offered a range of specifically military concessions to the political leaders over symbols, badges and officer commissions. Contemporary Nationalist MPs had some justification in criticising how the War Office dealt with the 16th (Irish) Division in comparison to the 36th (Ulster) Division. Lieutenant-General Sir Lawrence Parsons, the GOC of the 16th (Irish) Division, did not see the INV as a particularly useful cadre and made few attempts to accommodate Nationalist sensitivities.[43] While both Redmond and Carson had pledged their support to the British war effort at the outset of war, both had some difficulty in carrying all their supporters with them. Redmond's parliamentary colleagues were not, as a whole, enthusiastic to take on the role of recruiting sergeants for the British Army, and the split in the volunteer movement, which saw around 12,000 men break away from the INV to form the Irish Volunteers, can, in retrospect, be seen as the first major challenge to Redmond's position by advanced Nationalists.[44] Similarly, Edward Carson was unable to

[42] Stephen Sandford, *Neither Unionist nor Nationalist: The 10th (Irish) Division in the Great War* (Sallins, Ireland: Irish Academic Press, 2015), 15, 20–1.

[43] Terence Denman, *Ireland's Unknown Soldiers: The 16th (Irish) Division in the Great War* (Dublin: Irish Academic Press, 1992), 38–58; Stephen Gwynn, *John Redmond's Last Years* (London, 1919), 173; and D. D. Sheehan, *Ireland since Parnell* (London: Daniel O'Connor, 1921), 286–8.

[44] Richard Grayson, *Belfast Boys: How Unionists and Nationalists Fought and Died Together in the First World War*, 2nd edn. (London: Continuum, 2009), 14–16; James McConnel,

carry all his followers with him, some of whom expected British duplicity over the Home Rule issue if large numbers of UVF members enlisted in the British Army and were posted overseas.[45]

Those who were members of the INV or UVF provided a high proportion of the Irish recruits to the British Army. British government figures suggest that up to 15 April 1916, 29,617 UVF members and 30,161 INV members had enlisted, whereas 57,863 men with no affiliation to either group had also joined up.[46] In absolute terms, this did not mean that INV or UVF members were exactly rushing to the colours. The UVF had a strength of something in the region of 100,000 men in July 1914 and the INV possibly as many as 180,000. This should not distractfrom the point that UVF members were considerably more likely to enlist than those from the INV.[47]

Economic factors were clearly important in men's decisions to enlist. T. P. Dooley, in considering Waterford as a case study, notes that unskilled labourers stood to increase their earnings by 154 per cent, with free food and clothing, by enlisting in the British Army.[48] Fitzpatrick has discounted economic motivations by noting the large numbers of skilled workers who enlisted in the British Army in the early months of the war. However, this fundamentally misconstrues the employment prospects of many skilled workers in this unusual period, and army attestation forms asked for a man's previous occupation on enlistment, which tended to drastically under-count the numbers of unemployed enlisting. In Belfast, uncertainty about future orders saw men laid off in both the shipbuilding and engineering industries during the first couple of months of the war. That other great staple of industrial Ulster, the linen industry, was badly affected by the stoppage of flax imports from Belgium and Russia on the outbreak of war.[49]

The Irish Parliamentary Party and the Third Home Rule Crisis (Dublin: Four Courts Press, 2013), 298–310; James McConnel, 'Recruiting Sergeants for John Bull? Irish Nationalist MPs and Enlistment during the Early Months of the Great War', *War in History*, 14, 4 (2007); and Michael Wheatley, *Nationalism and the Irish Party: Provincial Ireland 1910–1916* (Oxford University Press, 2005), 208–12.

45 Timothy Bowman, *Carson's Army: The Ulster Volunteer Force, 1910–22* (Manchester University Press, 2007), 163–89.

46 Statement on enlistments in Joseph Brennan papers, ms. 26,154, NLI. Fitzpatrick suggests higher figures of 32,105 INV and 30,738 UVF recruits but continues his figures until the end of 1917, presumably using the RIC County Inspectors' reports in TNA, CO904 series.

47 For a detailed discussion of the role of the UVF during the war, see Bowman, *Carson's Army*, 163–89.

48 T. P. Dooley, *Irishmen or English Soldiers? The Times and World of a Southern Catholic Irish Man (1876–1916) Enlisting in the British Army during the First World War* (Liverpool University Press 1995), 124.

49 Eric Mercer, '"For King, Country and a Shilling a Day": Recruitment in Belfast during the Great War, 1914–18', unpublished MA thesis, Queen's University of Belfast, 1998,

Figure 7. 36th (Ulster) Division parade, Donegall Square, Belfast, 8 May 1915.
Source: Courtesy of Public Record Office of Northern Ireland

Pals recruitment was not widespread in Ireland, and it can be argued that the failure to establish units specifically aimed at lower-middle-class or skilled working-class men served to undermine recruitment rates there. Indeed, as the war went on, the military authorities continually criticised farmers' sons and shop assistants for their unwillingness to enlist. D company of the 7th Royal Dublin Fusiliers formed by the Irish Rugby Football Union is the only proper example of a Pals unit raised in Ireland.[50] Attempts to form both University and Sportsmen's Battalions in the 36th (Ulster) Division on the pattern of the University and Public Schools and Sportsmen's Battalions raised in the Royal Fusiliers were stillborn.[51]

13–16; and Michael Moss and J. R. Hume, *Shipbuilders to the World: 125 Years of Harland and Wolff, Belfast, 1861–1986* (Belfast: Blackstaff Press, 1986), 175–96.

[50] Cyril Falls, *War Books: A Critical Guide* (London: Peter Davies, 1930), 112; and Hanna, *The Pals at Suvla Bay*.

[51] *The Northern Whig*, 7 September 1914, 16 September 1914, 21 September 1914 and 22 September 1914.

Until early 1916, when conscription was introduced into Great Britain but not Ireland, Irish recruitment patterns followed those of the United Kingdom as a whole, though at a much lower base, considerably below Ireland's share of the UK population. Irish recruitment reached a peak in September 1914 and then went into a sharp, if uneven, decline.[52] Recruiting in Ireland was an urban rather than a rural experience; from the outbreak of war until 15 October 1916, 130,241 men enlisted in Ireland; of these, 38,543 were from Belfast, 21,412 from Dublin and 8,360 from Cork. While the relatively high percentage of UVF members who enlisted in the British Army suggests that Unionists were more likely to enlist than Nationalists, this figure is skewed by the propensity of citizens of Belfast to enlist. Indeed, rural recruitment in Ulster was not noticeably higher than in the rest of Ireland.

Whatever the reasons for enlistment in the United Kingdom as a whole, the effect of what occurred in August and September 1914 was that certain groups were far more willing to enlist than others. Seen from the perspective of sectoral distribution of occupation, some groups in Britain bore a proportionally high share of the military effort. By February 1916, sampling surveys of the Board of Trade, though not entirely reliable, suggested that whereas over 40 per cent of those engaged in the professions, entertainment, finance and commerce had enlisted, less than 30 per cent of those in industry as a whole, agriculture or transport had done so. The entertainment sector showed the highest rate of response at 41.8 per cent and transport the lowest at 22.4 per cent. Thus, as has been remarked, overall, 'men engaged in commercial or distributive trades were in uniform and at risk for longer periods and in relatively larger numbers than were industrial workers, transport workers or agricultural workers.'[53] The lowest response was among textile and clothing workers, industries that were to enjoy wartime stimulus.

A number of groups also came under attack for alleged unwillingness to enlist. Professional sportsmen in particular were castigated for the perception that they had not come forward as much as their amateur colleagues. The amateur (and largely southern) rugby union was seen as more virtuous than the professional (and northern) rugby league: eleven Welsh, twenty-seven English and thirty Scottish rugby union internationals were to be killed during the war. In January 1915, *Punch* branded the football results as 'The Shirker's War News', professional matches having

[52] Keith Grieves, *The Politics of Manpower, 1914–18* (Manchester University Press, 1988), 8–17.

[53] Jay Winter, *The Great War and the British People* (Basingstoke: Macmillan, 1986), 37; Jay Winter, 'Britain's Lost Generation of the First World War', *Population Studies*, 31 (1977), 449–66.

continued. The Football Association had allowed use of all league grounds for both recruiting and military training. It now pointed out that of 5,000 professionals, some 2,000 had already enlisted, and 2,400 were married, so that only 600 could be considered as genuinely shirking.[54] Similarly, the Harmsworth Committee fixed its sights in April 1915 on the retail trade as ripe for combing out.

Of course, a short war had been anticipated, at least by the volunteers of 1914, although a few, such as Kitchener, had expected a rather longer conflict. The reality was not only massive casualties but also competing demands for manpower between the armed forces, industry and agriculture as the conflict became one in which it was just as vital to out-produce as to out-fight the enemy. Not surprisingly, the manpower pool available rapidly declined, with ever more desperate efforts to comb out every possible fighting man from the civilian population. The effective limit of volunteers was reached by December 1915, by which time it was clear that conscription must follow through a process of exhaustion, exhortation having already reached what has been characterised as enlistment by insult. But, as already indicated, conscription had long been an anathema in Britain. There was a long and agonised debate, the organisational milestones being the Householders' Returns in November and December 1914, the National Register in July 1915, and the Derby Scheme of October to December 1915.

An initiative of the PRC, the Householders' Returns were a failure, only 3.6 million being returned from the 8 million forms distributed. The formation of the coalition government in May 1915 substantially increased the likelihood of conscription because the Unionists generally favoured it. Walter Long, who became President of the Local Government Board, was a firm advocate of conscription, believing that the pressures on the agricultural labour force in his native Wiltshire made it absolutely essential to ensure that urban Britain was pulling its weight. Lord Milner, who remained outside the new coalition government, and who had become President of the National Service League in June 1915, also waged a high-profile campaign for conscription. Many Liberals instinctively opposed conscription as an affront to individual liberty, but Lloyd George and Churchill, who remained a minister as Chancellor of the Duchy of Lancaster until October 1915, supported it. As Minister of Munitions after May 1915, Lloyd George was equally convinced of the value of labour conscription. There was also a group of Liberal

[54] George Robb, *British Culture and the First World War* (Basingstoke: Palgrave, 2002), 169; Colin Veitch, '"Play Up! Play Up! And Win the War": Football, the Nation and the First World War, 1914–15', *Journal of Contemporary History*, 20 (1985), 363–78, at 375.

backbenchers who did not regard it as incompatible with Liberal principles, even interpreting it as a progressive measure when compared to the vagaries of the voluntary system. A surprisingly diverse group of between thirty and forty MPs was to form the nucleus of the later Liberal War Committee, which came into existence in January 1916, a week after the formation of the Unionist War Committee, and became the core of Lloyd George's Liberal supporters thereafter.

Neither Asquith nor Kitchener was convinced that the time for conscription had come, Kitchener fearing the potential decisiveness of the issue. A suggestion by Sir Ivor Herbert MP to register the manpower resources available was taken up by Lloyd George, the Unionists, and the Northcliffe press. The resulting National Registration Act of July 1915 was intended to ascertain the likely number of men and women available for war work, the 1911 census being out of date and without sufficient data for the purposes of estimating military service potential. As pressure increased, Asquith endeavoured to buy time with a new War Policy Committee to examine manpower issues, only for Kitchener to be forced to concede, when he appeared before the committee on 24 August, the likely need for conscription by the end of the year in order to meet his projected seventy divisions. Otherwise, the six-man committee's deliberations were of little utility, two minority reports being submitted by its members. Meanwhile, National Registration Day on Sunday 15 August 1915 required a massive voluntary effort on the part of some 40,000 canvassers to record information on all men and women between the ages of fifteen and sixty-five. It was not entirely successful. The calculation was that 5.1 million men of military age were not in the armed forces, of whom 2.1 million were single and 2.8 million married. Of the single, just over 690,000 were in essential 'starred' occupations, leaving 1.4 million single men available for service. Unfortunately, however, this ignored those previously rejected for military service on grounds of physical fitness and who were now back in the potential recruitment pool, thereby overestimating the manpower available.

There remained opposition to conscription within the membership of the Trades Union Congress (TUC) and the Independent Labour Party, as well as the pacifist No Conscription Fellowship, which had been formed in November 1914. None, however, had sufficient parliamentary support to prevail. Kitchener pronounced the voluntary system all but dead, but Asquith made one last attempt to retain it, appointing Derby, a conscriptionist, as Director General of Recruiting on 5 October 1915. Ten days later, the Derby Scheme was announced, whereby a canvass would be carried out based on the National Register. All those between eighteen and forty-one would be asked to attest their willingness to serve if called upon to do so. Single and married men would be classified separately, each divided into twenty-three age groups. The assumption was that the youngest married men would not be called before all single men had been enlisted. The first attempt to produce a schedule of 'starred' reserved occupations was undertaken by the inter-departmental Reserved Occupations Committee in the same month of October, employers being able to appeal for exempted status for employees to the tribunals established under the Derby Scheme. The scheme was another massive voluntary exercise, the Local Government Board also beginning to establish tribunals to adjudge appeals against attestation or call-up.

Asquith duly promised in the House of Commons on 2 November that no married man would be called up before all single men had been taken. The end date of the canvass was extended from 30 November until 15 December 1915. In view of Asquith's pledge, it was not surprising that those married came forward in larger numbers than single men. Only 1.1 million of 2.1 million single men considered available for service were prepared to attest willingly if called upon to do so, and only 318,533 of those willing were actually believed to be available: it had been expected that at the very least 500,000 men would be forthcoming. Of married men, 403,921 of 2.6 million were adjudged to be both willing and available. To give one example of local results, the Mid-Buckinghamshire Recruiting Sub-committee, organised by the local Liberal Party agent, reported on 16 December that 2,642 men had enlisted or attested a willingness to do so, but 1,485 were not considered to be available, and a further 1,521 had categorically refused to attest.[55] The results finally forced Asquith's hand, the decision being taken on 28 December 1915 to conscript single men: only the Home Secretary, Sir John Simon, resigned. Asquith had succeeded through ploys such as the Derby Scheme in keeping the coalition together, thereby avoiding an election and preserving his own premiership.

Technically, the Military Service Act, given the royal assent on 27 January 1916 and popularly known as the 'Bachelor's Bill', deemed all single men and childless widowers between the ages of eighteen and forty-one to have enlisted. The wide discrepancies in medical examination and the numerous exemptions granted by military service tribunals resulted in fewer men becoming available than anticipated. Between 1 March 1916 and 31 March 1917, for example, only 371,500 men were compulsorily enlisted, while some 779,936 were exempted. Of the 193,981 immediately called up in January 1916, 57,416 had failed to

[55] Ian F. W. Beckett, 'The Local Community and the Great War: Aspects of Military Participation', *Records of Buckinghamshire*, 20 (1978), 503–15, at 507.

appear by March 1916. According to the Official History, those refusing to appear climbed to 93,000 by July. This resulted in the unedifying spectacle of official round ups of likely-looking men at railway stations, parks and cinemas in the summer and autumn of 1916.[56] The attempt to call up married men who had attested under the Derby Scheme, in contradiction to Asquith's pledge, also led to increasing pressure, as did the Easter Rising in Dublin in April 1916, which required the diversion of yet more manpower to suppress.

The Military Service Act (No. 2), which passed all its parliamentary stages in nine days and received the royal assent on 25 May 1916, therefore extended conscription to all men between eighteen and forty-one. Inevitably, to the alarm of the Board of Trade, the War Office had taken the figure of 1.4 million men suggested by the National Register as the number it should be allowed to recruit. Prior to the National Register, the board had insisted that no more than 800,000 men could be spared for the army from trade. Though it revised this estimate upwards to 1.2 million in its submissions to the Cabinet Committee on the Co-ordination of Military and Financial Effort in January 1916, the board remained concerned at the damage that would be done by acceleration of call-ups to the 250,000 men per month the War Office was now demanding through its forecasts of 'wastage' at the front. The War Office was also proving uncooperative in returning skilled men to industry, as requested by the Ministry of Munitions. Though a Man-Power Distribution Board was established in August 1916 under the chairmanship of Austen Chamberlain, it had little success in reconciling competing demands for manpower and was wound up in November 1916.

Backed by Lloyd George, Derby was now pressing for full labour conscription, the Ministry of Munitions suggesting that it would need 250,000 to 300,000 more workers. In view of their calculation that there was a manpower deficit of 95,000 men and that the army would need 940,000 men in 1917, Robertson and the other military members of the Army Council also demanded that the age for military and civil service be raised to fifty-five. The manpower issue played no small part in generating the crisis that led to Asquith's downfall in December 1916. Asquith accepted a proposal for a Cabinet Committee to consider civil affairs in the same way that the War Committee deliberated on strategic matters. Lloyd George became chairman, but his instincts, and those of the Unionist members, Lord Robert Cecil and Austen Chamberlain,

[56] D. Hayes, *Conscription Conflict* (London: Shepherd Press, 1949), 213; Ian F. W. Beckett, 'The Real Unknown Army: British Conscripts, 1916–19', in Becker and Audoin-Rouzeau (eds.), *Les sociétés européennes*, 339–56; Trevor Wilson, *Myriad Faces of War: Britain and the Great War, 1914–18* (Cambridge: Polity Press, 1986), 400.

conflicted with those of the Liberal members, Walter Runciman and Herbert Samuel. Runciman absolutely refused to accept any labour conscription, and Asquith increasingly appeared to be procrastinating. Lloyd George proposed a three-man 'War Council' to take such means as necessary to conduct war policy and was backed by Andrew Bonar Law and Carson, the acknowledged leader of the Unionist War Committee. Asquith accepted it in principle on 3 December as he became aware of Unionist backing for Lloyd George. He indicated, however, that he intended to be chairman of such a committee. Warned that Lloyd George would resign on the issue, the Unionists insisted Asquith go, or they would also resign. Asquith now agreed to Lloyd George chairing a small committee but then retracted his support. Lloyd George resigned on 5 December 1916. Aware that the Unionist decision still stood if Lloyd George resigned, Asquith resigned himself on the assumption that Lloyd George would not receive sufficient backing to form a government. Bonar Law was invited to form a government by the King, which Asquith then refused to join. In any case, Bonar Law himself lacked sufficient resolve. Not all Unionists were overjoyed at the prospect, but there seemed little alternative, and Lloyd George duly became Prime Minister on 7 December 1916.

In the event, Lloyd George backed away from labour conscription as Prime Minister though Neville Chamberlain, the Lord Mayor of Birmingham and Austen's half-brother, was appointed as Director of National Service. Chamberlain favoured removing the exemptions of all born between 1895 and 1898 deemed fit for service, estimated at about 280,000 men. He received no Cabinet support. Accordingly, an entirely voluntary scheme of national service was implemented in February 1917 to encourage men to enlist in an 'industrial army' to replace those being enlisted through progressive cancellation of exemptions. Instead of the 500,000 volunteers anticipated by 31 March, only 114,000 had come forward. Just over 92,000 men were processed subsequently by employment exchanges, of whom half were already in protected occupations. It is suggested that only 388 men were actually directed into new employment.[57] An increasingly beleaguered Chamberlain resigned in August 1917 when it was proposed that his department take over responsibility for military recruiting.

The Army Council was now pressing again to conscript men up to the age of fifty-five or even sixty, but a committee chaired by Lord Rhondda, which had been set up to examine the issue in February 1917,

[57] Gerard DeGroot, *Blighty: British Society in the Era of the Great War* (Harlow: Longman, 1996), 101.

recommended only re-examining those previously exempted. It resulted in the Military Service (Review of Exceptions) Act of April 1917, which allowed for the combing out of more men from industry, agriculture and the mines, including many previously judged unfit and particularly those born between 1895 and 1898. Intended to remedy perceived deficiencies in army medical boards, the legislation produced 130,000 men in six weeks as a result of contentious re-examination of those previously exempted on medical grounds, those previously discharged from the army as unfit and Territorials exempted from overseas service on physical grounds. In some cases, exemption certificates had been obtained on the black market, which was the ostensible reason for the legislation, but widespread resentment led to a number of demonstrations, not least from the newly formed National Federation of Discharged and Demobilised Sailors and Soldiers (NFDDSS). The latter campaigned on the slogan, 'Every man once before any man twice.'[58] Two days before a by-election for the Abercromby seat in Liverpool in June 1917, at which there was a NFDDSS candidate, the government pledged that those men who had served overseas and had been discharged on medical grounds would not be re-examined. The Trade Card Agreement reached with the unions in November 1916, which had allowed the skilled unions themselves to determine which skilled men should be called up by issuing exemption certificates to their own members, was cancelled in the teeth of opposition from the Amalgamated Society of Engineers and other craft unions.

The Military Service (Conventions with Allied States) Act of July 1917 allowed for the conscription of British subjects living abroad and of allied citizens living in Britain, conventions being signed with Russia in July and with France in October. Sir Auckland Geddes, who had replaced Neville Chamberlain, calculated, for a new War Priorities Committee in October 1917, that 3.6 million men of military age remained outside the armed forces, but only 270,000 of those aged eighteen to twenty-five were sufficiently physically fit to be classed as category A, and probably only 150,000 to 160,000 of them were actually available once industrial requirements had been taken into account. In November, the War Office calculated its manpower deficit at over 437,000 men.

For the first time on 6 December 1917, a Cabinet Committee on Man-Power, consisting entirely of War Cabinet members, was established to consider manpower priorities. Rejecting the War Office calculations on 'wastage', it decided that the manpower deficit in the armed forces was

[58] Stephen R. Ward, 'Great Britain: Land Fit for Heroes Lost', in Stephen R. Ward (ed.), *The War Generation* (Port Washington, NY: Kennikat Press, 1975), 10–37, at 15.

between 500,000 and 600,000 and for industry a deficit of 400,000 men and 100,000 women. The army's demands, however, could be largely ignored on the assumption that there would be no offensive operations on the Western Front. The steady evolution of a war economy and of a manpower policy had steadily pushed the army to the bottom of the list of priorities. On 7 January 1918, the War Cabinet accepted the committee's priorities. Production of timber, iron ore, food, merchant shipping, aeroplanes and tanks all took priority over the army. Geddes was tasked with implementing the recommendations. The resulting Military Service (No. 1) Act of February 1918 removed any exemptions based on occupation. Geddes, however, did not use all the powers he had been given initially because the revised schedule for exemptions allowed for the minimum age of exemption in most protected occupations to be raised to twenty-three. The shortages prompted the reduction ordered in the number of infantry divisions in the BEF and in the size of those divisions in January 1918. In all, 161 infantry battalions – many second-line TF formations – were disbanded in the first two months of 1918.

There remains debate, and conflicting official figures, on how many men were retained in the United Kingdom and how many of them were realistically available for service when the German spring offensive began on 21 March 1918. This triggered the so far dormant provisions of the February legislation, cancelling the exemptions of all fit men under age twenty-three. It has been suggested that the Official History's figure of approximately a million men as potentially available is improbable, and at best, only 125,000 were trained, fit and old enough for immediate service.[59] The War Cabinet met on 23 March to consider emergency measures, and Geddes brought back proposals two days later. As a result, the Military Service (No. 2) Act of April 1918 extended the age range for call-up to those between eighteen and fifty and provided for the conscription of men up to the age of fifty-six if the need arose. It was assumed that raising the age limit to fifty would yield 250,000 men, of whom 60,000 would be immediately available. Geddes was also empowered by the legislation to extend his 'clean cut' to further groups of exempted men over the age of twenty-three. The Cabinet also took the decision on 23 March to reduce the age at which overseas service could be undertaken to eighteen and a half, making 30,000 trained men immediately available. Consideration had even been given to abolishing military service tribunals and to lowering the call-up age to seventeen. In the event, the legislation released about 9,000 men a week from munitions work, but casualties were then averaging over 31,000 a week.

[59] Perry, *Commonwealth Armies*, 28.

The April 1918 legislation also provided for the extension of conscription to Ireland. It was assumed that 150,000 men could be made available, though not, of course, immediately. Among those harbouring serious doubts as to the practicality was the Chief Secretary H. E. Duke. The government regarded an equality of sacrifice essential if exemptions were to be curtailed further in Britain, especially if tribunals were suspended. Passage of the legislation aroused considerable opposition from Irish MPs, but it was passed overwhelmingly. Irish conscription was never implemented as the danger in France waned, but the political impact of the enabling legislation was disastrous. It seriously undermined the constitutional approach of the IPP and led to the dominance of Sinn Fein within Irish nationalism.[60]

Had the war continued into 1919, the acceptance of the Man-Power Committee's priorities would have allocated only 170,000 new men to the army for the whole year. The final piece of legislation, the Naval, Military and Air Force Service Act of April 1919 retained compulsory service until 30 April 1920. Criteria for retention were set at a maximum age of thirty-seven with less than two wound stripes. In practice, however, it retained only some 80,000 young men already under training, since further call-ups had been suspended at the armistice and over 3 million men had been demobilised by the end of 1919. Shortly after the expiry of the legislation, Churchill, as Secretary of State for War and Air, announced that it was not necessary to repeal previous conscription legislation as the release of all remaining conscripts had been ordered. With the official termination of the war by Order in Council on 31 August 1921, all conscription legislation lapsed. The War Office had resumed recruiting on the pre-war regular terms of enlistment on 15 January 1919 in accordance with the Army Order promulgated on 10 December 1918, wartime servicemen being permitted to re-engage for terms of two, three or four years. By April 1919, in addition to those on 'normal' regular engagements, a total of 74,930 wartime servicemen had re-engaged, and 141,104 new recruits without wartime service had been enlisted.[61]

In theory, conscription should have equalised the burden after 1916, but, as elsewhere, although 'universal', conscription was always selective in practice. There were always going to be men exempted by virtue of

[60] R. J. Q. Adams and P. P. Poirier, *The Conscription Controversy in Great Britain, 1900–18* (Columbus: Ohio State University Press, 1987), 230–41; Adrian Gregory, '"You Might as Well Recruit Germans": British Public Opinion and the Decision to Conscript the Irish in 1918', in Gregory and Paseta (eds.), *Ireland and the Great War* (Manchester University Press, 2002), 113–32; Grieves, *The Politics of Manpower*, 188–92; and Richard Holmes, *The Little Field Marshal: A Life of Sir John French* (London: Jonathan Cape, 1981), 326–40.

[61] *Statistics of the Military Effort*, 385–93.

physical fitness, occupation or even nationality. Medical boards exempted over 1 million men in the last twelve months of the war when there was some pressure on doctors to lower rejection rates. It needs to be borne in mind that despite medical advances, 200 of every 1,000 infants still failed to survive the first year of life in urban areas such as Birmingham, Blackburn, Dudley, Great Yarmouth, Salford, Sheffield, Wakefield, Wolverhampton and York. Life expectancy of English males in 1910–12 was greater than before at 51.5 years, but there were still conditions of poverty and ill-health in working-class Britain in 1914 that would now be associated with third-world countries.[62] Notwithstanding the doubtful nature of the Ministry of National Service medical statistics, it was calculated that of the 2.4 million men medically examined in 1917 and 1918, only 36 per cent of the male population of military age was physically fit for service overseas (Grade I), although a further 22.5 per cent were fit for garrison duties, including labour and sedentary duties such as clerical duties or trades (Grade II), and 31.3 per cent for home duties, including labour and sedentary work (Grade III), leaving 10.3 per cent totally unfit for military service of any kind (Grade IV). There were considerable regional variations. Wales (46 per cent), Scotland (44.2 per cent), and Northern England, defined as Cumberland, Durham, Northumberland and Westmoreland (43.6 per cent), were adjudged to have the larger proportions of men characterised as Grade I, London and the South East the lowest. The South West (14 per cent) had the largest proportion totally unfit for service. The army itself classified men into five classes (A, B, C, D and E), the first three each sub-divided into three or four classes: A corresponded to Grade I; B1 and C1 to Grade II; B2, B3, C2 and C3 to Grade III; and the remainder to Grade IV. The army received only 407,973 Category A men in 1917 out of 820,646 recruits. In 1918, 372,330 men out of 493,462 were classed as Category A by the army, but it became increasingly the case that Category B men were fed into front-line units.

Rejection rates naturally reflected pre-war deprivation, but, in part, there was also an application of suspect criteria as to what constituted fitness: physical ability was too readily equated with stature. Partly, there was also social prejudice. Jews and, especially, Russian Jews were automatically rejected as inferior. Approximately 120,000 of the 300,000 or so Jews in Britain in 1914 were those who had arrived from Russia since the 1880s, many fleeing conscription as much as pogroms. Understandably, Britain's wartime alliance with Tsarist Russia posed a dilemma for Jews

[62] Jay Winter, 'Army and Society: The Demographic Context', in Beckett and Simpson (eds.), *Nation in Arms*, 193–209, at 195.

generally. Lingering anti-Semitism was evidenced by frequent attacks on Jews and their property in the general anti-alien atmosphere of wartime Britain, and the perceived failure of foreign-born Jews to enlist generated more. Jews were often turned away from recruiting centres in 1914 for all that the Jewish Recruitment Committee (later the Jewish War Service Committee) was encouraging enlistment, and the Rothschilds opened a recruiting office at their bank's headquarters in New Court in London's St. Swithin's Lane. The Chief Rabbi also indicated his belief that neither Orthodox Jews nor those belonging to the 'Cohens' sect could oppose military service on the grounds of conscience. The Anglo-Jewish establishment, however, did not have a particular understanding of Russian Jews, who were slow to respond. Problems were also encountered in terms of the provisos of sufficient Jewish chaplains and of kosher food. Following passage of the Military Service Act (No. 2), it was announced that 'friendly aliens' should either serve in the British Army or return to do so in their own country, the fear of compulsory deportations to Russia resulting in the creation of the Foreign Jews Protection Committee against Deportation to Russia and Compulsion. Fearing increased perceptions of the unwillingness of Russian Jews to serve, the Anglo-Jewish establishment and the Zionist Federation persuaded the government to allow the voluntary enlistment of Russian Jews, a scheme extended until October 1916. Of the 30,000 Russian-born Jews believed to be available for military service, only 632 attested by the deadline of 25 October, and only seventy-four enlisted for immediate service.[63] Compulsion, however, was not immediately applied as the result of the scheme's failure.

The British government had been negotiating a convention with the Russian government, which wanted its subjects returned for military service, even before the overthrow of the Tsar in March 1917. The latter event, however, simplified matters, and Russian Jews of military age became liable to serve in the British Army under the Military Service (Conventions with Allied States) Act of July 1917 unless they chose within twenty-one days to return for military service in Russia. Special tribunals were established in London, Manchester and Liverpool to adjudicate claims for exemption: in August 1918 it was alleged that many East End Jews held forged or stolen exemption certificates, the police discovering that of some 8,000 men stopped by the police on the streets of Stepney to explain their civilian attire, 640 had forged papers and 400 had stolen papers. A political and press campaign began, particularly in East London, for Russian Jews to be forced to enlist or face

[63] Harold Shukman, *War or Revolution: Russian Jews and Conscription in Britain, 1917* (Edgware: Valentine Mitchell, 2006), 12.

deportation. Some 7,600 applied to return to Russia, though only 3,500 appear to have done so. The ability to conscript Russian Jews then lapsed once the Bolsheviks concluded the Treaty of Brest Litovsk with the Germans, which took Russia out of the war altogether in March 1918.

Separately, a specifically Jewish Legion was raised in July 1917 for service in Palestine. First mooted in the autumn of 1914 by leading Zionists in Britain, including Chaim Weizmann and Asher Ginsberg (aka Ahad Ha'am), it was a development from Vladimir Jabotinsky's earlier Zion Mule Corps that had served at Gallipoli in 1915. The Legion eventually comprised the 38th, 39th and 40th Battalions, Royal Fusiliers. The 38th and 39th battalions included about 2,000 American and Canadian Jews, amounting to about 40 per cent of the total, the remainder being mostly conscripted Russian Jews, while the 40th Battalion was formed from Palestinian Jews, characterised at the time as 'Judeans'.

It is difficult to determine the precise numbers of Jews who served, the *British Jewry Book of Honour*, published in 1922, being unreliable. Conceivably, about 41,000 Jews served in the British armed forces, perhaps 10,000 or so before the introduction of conscription, and including at least 1,140 who served as officers. It is suggested that 1,941 Jewish servicemen were killed: five certainly won the VC. If accurate, and all the figures may be an underestimate, approximately 13.8 per cent of the Jewish population served compared with Anglo-Jewry's 11.5 per cent share of the wider British population.[64]

Coloured recruits were also generally rejected until the colour bar was theoretically lifted in June 1918. This was largely as a result of the implementation of the Military Service (Conventions with Allied States) Act in the United States since over 2,000 blacks registered, and it was thought that rejection would have an adverse impact on Britain's image there. The policy followed, however, remained haphazard in the extreme, as did the reluctance to accept coloured soldiers. It is difficult to know how many black Britons enlisted or were conscripted. There are some well-known cases such as Roy and Norman Manley, who joined the Royal Field Artillery, the latter a future Prime Minister of Jamaica. The former black professional footballer, Walter Tull, was commissioned into the

[64] Sasha Auerbach, 'Negotiating Nationalism: Jewish Conscription and Russian Repatriation in London's East End, 1916–18', *Journal of British Studies*, 46 (2007), 594–620, at 618; Harold Pollins, 'Jews in the British Army in the First World War', *Jewish Journal of Sociology*, 37 (1995), 100–11; Barry A. Kosmin, Stanley Waterman and Nigel Grizzard, 'The Jewish Dead in the Great War as an Indicator for the Location, Size and Social Structure of Anglo-Jewry in 1914', *Immigrants and Minorities*, 5 (1986), 181–92; Anne Lloyd, 'Between Integration and Separation: Jews and Military Service in World War I', *Jewish Culture and History*, 12 (2010), 41–60.

Middlesex Regiment and killed in March 1918. Police records for 285 coloured men apprehended in riots in Liverpool in 1919 reveal that forty-three had served in the armed forces during the war, although eighteen of the twenty-eight with army service had entered after the introduction of conscription. The experience of the British West Indies Regiment, raised at the suggestion of the Colonial Office in 1915, as a separate British Army formation was not a happy one, not least its relegation to labour duties. In passing, it should be acknowledged that the strength of the BEF included, from 1916 onwards, over 193,500 native labourers drawn from China, India, South Africa, Egypt, the West Indies, Malta, Mauritius, the Seychelles and Fiji. There were similar labour corps in Mesopotamia, East Africa, Egypt, Italy and at Salonika.

As for the military service tribunals that pronounced on claims for exemption from military service, they have often been perceived to be unduly influenced by military demands – a military representative was present at all hearings – and hostile to claims for exemption on the grounds of conscience. The 2,000 military service tribunals were organised in conformity with county, urban and rural district councils. Tribunals had been established for the Derby Scheme but merely to process postponement applications from those who had voluntarily attested their willingness to serve. Though based on the Derby model, these new tribunals were very different. After the local rural and urban tribunals, decisions could be taken to county appeals tribunals or, beyond that, to the central tribunal in Westminster, where the final decision rested. Advice was received from the Local Government Board, and amending legislation closed off avenues of interpretation over time. Not least, the tribunals had to take into account the frequent changes in the schedule of reserved occupations. But, in effect, they were 'sovereign entities, duty-bound to consider cases judiciously and impartially, but with no *de jure* obligation to answer for their decisions'.[65]

The tribunals were, again, the ironic product of an extraordinary voluntary effort on the part of local notable figures, including trade unionists and women, sitting once and perhaps twice a week or more. Businessmen were usually members, as in the case of the Northamptonshire County Appeals Tribunal, which had not only two union representatives of the National Union of Boot and Shoe Operatives but also the President of the Northamptonshire Boot and Shoe Manufacturers Association, boots and shoes being the dominant employment. Possibly between 20,000 and 40,000 men and women served on the tribunals. With a

[65] James McDermott, *British Military Service Tribunals, 1916–18: 'A Very Much Abused Body of Men'* (Manchester University Press, 2011), 4.

relatively small catchment area, the Calne Tribunal in Wiltshire met sixty times during the course of the war, but the Kingston-upon-Thames Tribunal met about 260 times, that at Croydon 258 times, that at Leeds 435 times, and that at Birmingham 1,765 times. At Calne, a total of 683 cases were heard, but at Bristol, over 41,000 cases were heard. The Northamptonshire County Appeals Tribunal met 162 times and heard 12,150 cases, while the Middlesex Appeals Tribunal considered 11,307 cases. With an absolute legal right to appeal, those conscripted could claim release from military service not just on the grounds of conscience but also ill-health, family commitments or by reason of employment in key occupations. In fact, no fewer than 750,000 from the 1.2 million single men deemed to have enlisted appealed: within the first month, almost 59,000 had been exempted and only just under 26,000 sent to the army. Appeal rates remained strikingly high throughout the war. In addition, those already 'badged' by government departments were automatically judged exempt. By April 1917, for example, while 780,000 men had been exempted by tribunals, a further 1.8 million had been exempted by other means.

An individual could represent himself or be represented by an employer, a relative or a solicitor: if unable to attend, he could submit his case in writing. The tribunals could either insist that the individual concerned join the armed forces or defer his entry, or they could exempt him. The precise meaning of the legislation was not always clear with regard to the conditions for 'absolute' exemption, and tribunals applied widely differing standards. At Huddersfield, 12,543 initial claims were heard in 1916, of which only 24.5 per cent were refused outright.[66] In Buckinghamshire, the percentage of cases dismissed between January and April 1917 varied from 3.5 per cent at High Wycombe to 45 per cent at Marlow, with an average across the county's twenty-two tribunals of 19.4 per cent.

Even those predisposed to view tribunals harshly through the prism of conscientious objection have acknowledged that proceedings were not as arbitrary as sometimes claimed, and members were 'civilian, middle class and public minded'.[67] Conscientious objection, indeed, has received disproportionate attention considering that only 16,500 claims for exemption were made on such grounds. Whatever the perception, there

[66] Cyril Pearce, *Comrades in Conscience: The Story of an English Community's Opposition to the Great War* (London: Francis Boutle, 2001), 314.

[67] T. C. Kennedy, *The Hound of Conscience: A History of the No Conscription Fellowship, 1914–19* (Fayetteville: University of Arkansas Press, 1981), 91; John Rae, *Conscience and Politics: The British Government and the Conscientious Objector to Military Service, 1916–19* (Oxford University Press, 1970), 57.

was often a contradiction between tribunal rhetoric and the actual decision-making process, leading to inconsistency between contemporary perception of harshness and the reality. There were many different kinds of conscientious objectors ranging from religious to secular and political conviction, which tribunal members often found it difficult to define or to comprehend. The attitude of the individual appellant counted for much, those prepared to undertake some form of work deemed of national importance being given considerable latitude. Demonstrably long-standing religious affiliation counted more than political or secular conviction. There was also something of a hierarchy in credibility, Anglicans and Catholics falling foul of their churches' general support for the war. Quakers were well understood and respected, but Christadelphian and Seventh Day Adventist beliefs were tested far more rigorously. In York, for example, where two Quakers sat on the tribunal, only 1.75 per cent of Quakers who came before it were refused exemption.[68] There was little sympathy generally for dogmatism on the part of secular objectors.

Of the claims on the grounds of conscience, 5,111 claimants were given absolute or conditional exemption by tribunals and a further 1,400 by the Army Council. A further 1,969 men exempted from combatant service declined to serve in the Non-Combatant Corps and were court-martialled. In addition, 6,312 men refused to appear for military service when conscripted, of whom 5,790 were court-martialled. Most accepted non-combatant service or Home Office work, while others were released on medical grounds. In all, 843 so-called absolutists spent two or more years in prison, with seventeen given death sentences, later commuted to life imprisonment, and 142 given life sentences: ten died in prison custody.

In reality, occupation was by far the most significant factor. By October 1918, by which time many grounds for exemption had been removed, there were still 2.5 million men in reserved occupations. Tribunals were ever mindful of local needs in terms of economic vitality, not least in rural areas, consciously mitigating national policy directives and indulging in their own interpretation of economic interventionism. Perceptions of community and family needs were often prominent, Auckland Geddes as Minister of National Service complaining in July 1917 that 'the present exemptions system is based almost entirely on individual or local considerations.'[69] The whole system was rooted in locality and thereby

[68] A. R. Mack, 'Conscription and Conscientious Objection in Leeds and York during the First World War', unpublished MPhil thesis, University of York, 1983, 193.

[69] Gregory, *Last Great War*, 108. See also Adrian Gregory, 'Military Service Tribunals: Civil Society in Action, 1916–18', in Jose Harris (ed.), *Civil Society in British History: Ideas, Identities, Institutions* (Oxford University Press, 2003), 177–90.

representative of a whole series of compromises between state and largely autonomous local communities and networks that characterised the war effort in such other areas as war charities or the arrangements made for Belgian refugees.

All tribunals recognised the need to maintain production, be it industrial or agricultural. Local economic conditions certainly took precedence at Leek in Staffordshire. At Kingston-upon-Thames, where the tribunal included a builder and two retired grocers, and the labour representative was an insurance agent, the tribunal showed some partiality towards the employees of both local printing firms and also, more surprisingly, a department store. In Wiltshire, the shortage of agricultural workers was acute, and the question of farmers' sons and the number of men required to run individual farms were particular issues. The official guidance issued in February 1917 was one skilled and able-bodied man for every team of plough horses, every twenty milk cows, every fifty head of stall or yard stock cattle, every 200 sheep on enclosed land, and every 800 sheep on mountain or hill pasturage. Mechanisation was accelerated after 1917, but skilled ploughmen and tractor drivers were still regarded as essential. At Audenshaw in Manchester, the seven tribunal members included the owner of a dye works, an employer from the leather dresser trade, a retired hat manufacturer and a union representative from the Clerks' Union. These were not dominant trades in a district where engineering and textile firms were well established, but the tribunal was generally well informed on local economic requirements and, increasingly, sensitive to 'the assumption of social stability through the maintenance of local services'.[70]

In Cornwall, the importance of wolfram determined which mines had their workforce protected. In Northamptonshire, the boot and shoe trade was seen as vital not only to the local economy but also to the war effort: English firms had supplied 26 million pairs of boots to the allied armies by July 1916 alone. Indeed, at the very moment the War Office was demanding that more men should be released from the trade in January 1917, its Army Contracts Department was placing large new orders, adding to the counter-pressure being exerted by the trade's own representative at the heart of the appeals machinery in the county. National interests were seen in Northamptonshire to be indistinguishable from local interests. Of those Kineton men considered by the Stratford-on-Avon Rural District Tribunal, 48.2 per cent were involved in agricultural and 25.8 per cent tradesmen.

[70] Keith Grieves, 'Mobilising Manpower: Audenshaw Tribunal in the First World War', *Manchester Region History Review*, 3 (1989–90), 21–29, at 26.

At the same time, however, conceptions of masculinity such as in the exemption of men employed in intrinsically pre-war gendered occupations such as butchery and baking also played their part. Bakers worked in the early hours and often half-stripped, while butchers invariably carried out their own slaughtering. Consequently, they were not seen as trades in which women could be employed as substitutes. Invariably, too, bakers and butchers were sole proprietors, such individuals as well as directing heads of small businesses active in the local economy presenting a particular dilemma to tribunals. In cases of serious financial hardship for dependants arising from conscription, appellants failing to gain exemption could apply to the Military Service (Civil Liabilities) Committee for assistance, although its funding for such commitments as rent, rates, insurance, interest payments and purchase instalments was limited to £104 per annum.

The cumulative effect of the way in which conscription was applied meant that there was no material change in the social composition of the British Army after 1916. The sampling surveys of the Board of Trade show that each of the occupational sectors remained in approximately the same relationship to one another with regard to the proportion of manpower enlisted in 1918 as in 1916. Thus, the average sector enlistment rate in commerce was 41 per cent in July 1916 and 63 per cent in July 1918, while in transport it was 23 per cent in July 1916 and 38 per cent in July 1918. Variations within particular sectors such as manufacturing also remained unchanged. Thus, the British Army was no more representative of society as a whole under conscription than it had been before its introduction.

The war obviously made a distinction between young and old or, more specifically, between men eligible for military service and those either too old or too young to fight. The issue of under-age enlistment – technically, anyone under age nineteen – has attracted some attention from popular historians. The only attempts to quantify the extent of such recruitment are unconvincing: one based on a sample of 1,000 pension records of under-aged soldiers who survived extrapolates a total of over 250,000, while another, based on just two school rolls, suggests over 360,000.[71] Young soldiers certainly became part of the equation with respect to home defence and training units. Home service men were passed to fifty-six Provisional Battalions after April 1915, these being designated for home defence duties in support of second-line Territorial formations

[71] Richard van Emden, *Boy Soldiers of the Great War*, 2nd edn. (London: Bloomsbury, 2012), 365; John Oakes, *Kitchener's Lost Boys: From the Playing Fields to the Killing Fields* (Stroud, UK: History Press, 2009), 27.

such as cyclist battalions already allocated for such a role. Third-line Territorial units were re-designated as reserve battalions in 1916 to assist in training replacements for Territorial units in the same way that Special Reserve Battalions were tasked with the same role for regulars units. The Fourth New Army was similarly broken up in April 1915 into such training units to prepare those destined for other New Army units. In September 1916, a new system of 112 Training Reserve (TR) Battalions came into being. In May 1917, fourteen TR battalions were designated as Young Soldier Battalions to deal with eighteen-year-old conscripts, who were then sent on to one of twenty-eight Graduated Battalions before being posted to a Special Reserve or Territorial Reserve Battalion prior to going overseas at age nineteen.

As for those over military age, the National Reserve was mobilised in August 1914 to supplement those available for static guard duties being undertaken by the Special Reserve. The National Reserve had evolved alongside the Territorial Reserve and the Technical Reserve (which included a Corps of Guides) in 1910. A Veteran Reserve had been urged on Haldane by John St. Loe Strachey, the editor and proprietor of *The Spectator*, as a means of involving ex-servicemen to supplement the TF in a home defence role. Haldane had also seen it as a means of embracing Territorials not prepared to re-enlist on the expiry of their service. Renamed the National Reserve in August 1911, it had reached a strength of about 200,000 by 1912, but only 14,000 were judged fit for active service (Class I) and a further 46,000 for garrison service (Class II).

While many fitter National Reservists enlisted in the TF or New Army in August 1914, a number of 'Protection Companies' were also deployed for static guard duties at 'vulnerable points' such as bridges, rail lines and reservoirs. The authorities were reluctant to use non-Class I or II men on such tasks, but many took their own initiative in mounting patrols. In 1915, the Protection Companies were re-designated as Supernumerary Companies of the TF, while CTAs were also authorised to release Class III men to the Volunteer Training Corps (VTC), many having already joined the latter force. The Supernumerary Companies and so-called Observer Companies were formed into the Royal Defence Corps (RDC) in March 1916, administered by the City of London CTA, to which the Graduated Battalions were also transferred in August 1917. Additionally, men in lower medical categories had been formed into Garrison Battalions in January 1916, and these, too, were transformed into RDC battalions in 1917. RDC duties included guarding the 100,000 prisoners of war in Britain.

Almost as soon as the war began, unofficial and illegal groups of Town Guards appeared in many areas through fears of possible German invasion of East Anglia. The first is usually acknowledged to be the group formed by the villages of Saughall and Mollington on the Wirral on 4 August.[72] On 6 August 1914, a letter to the *Times* from a Liberal member of London County Council, Percy Harris, suggested a London Defence Force be established. H. G. Wells and Sir Arthur Conan Doyle were also enthusiastic supporters of a new volunteer force. Three days after Harris's letter, Lord Desborough agreed to become president of an organising committee. Groups were already drilling in Buckinghamshire, Lancashire, Oxfordshire, Surrey and Sussex. Harris had made a somewhat unhappy allusion to the UVF in his letter, and the War Office promptly banned such groups. Following the intervention of General Sir O'Moore Creagh, Kitchener authorised the committee to instruct men not of military age in drill and musketry on 4 September. With invasion fears increasing and offers and requests for information flooding in, the committee transformed itself into the Central Association of Volunteer Training Corps, which received official status on 19 November 1914. It was stipulated that men of military age should not be enlisted unless they had genuine reasons for not joining the army; eligible volunteers would enlist in the army if required; no military ranks or uniforms would be used other than a 'GR' armlet; no expense should fall on the state; and a recognised military adviser would be appointed. Attendance at forty one-hour drills and attainment of second-class musketry standard would qualify for an efficiency badge. Those not attending at least twelve drills in six months would be required to resign. Not all groups accepted the War Office terms, that at Preston disbanding. The educated, professional middle classes were prominent, many corps being formed around golf clubs or larger city institutions. Small businessmen or shopkeepers in towns and villages formed additional corps, while one rather more unusual group of professionals was to be found in the Piano Trade Corps.

The VTC attracted controversy, being accused of shielding men who might otherwise have enlisted, and was also ridiculed for its public image. Deriving from the 'GR' armband they initially wore, they were variously characterised as 'George's Wrecks', 'Gorgeous Wrecks' and 'Genuine Relics'. The Marquis of Lincolnshire made an effort to improve the status with new regulating legislation, but it ran out of parliamentary time in

[72] K. W. Mitchinson, *Defending Albion: Britain's Home Army, 1908–19* (Basingstoke, 2005), 68. Much of what follows on the VTC is also derived from Ian F. W. Beckett, 'Aspects of a Nation in Arms: Britain's Volunteer Training Corps in the Great War', *Revue Internationale d'Histoire Militaire*, 63 (1985), 27–39; and John M. Osborne, 'Defining Their Own Patriotism: British Volunteer Training Corps in the First World War', *Journal of Contemporary History*, 23 (1988), 59–75.

October 1915, the provisions of the Volunteer Act of 1863 then being applied in March 1916. The Central Association became one of Volunteer Regiments and an advisory council to the Director General of the TF, whose staff Harris, now a Liberal MP, and Desborough joined, with local administration devolved to CTAs. There were advantages from the 1863 legislation in that discipline could be imposed by fines recoverable under civil law and in enabling officers to receive recognised commissions. Unfortunately, it also created an anomaly when military service tribunals began granting exemption from conscription if men joined the VTC for the old legislation allowed an individual to resign on fourteen days' notice. A new Volunteer Act in December 1916 closed the loophole, compelling men to serve for the duration and to undertake a statutory minimum number of fourteen (later ten) monthly drills. The force was divided into six categories, with those deemed efficient in sections A and B – men above and of military age – receiving an annual £2 capitation grant for equipment. It was rarely enough, and those of military age were often in protected occupations and unable to perform the drills required. Section C was for men under military age; Section D (abolished in 1918) for those unfit for service in other sections; Section R for railway workers who would not be available in an emergency; and Section P for special constables. There was something of a conflict of interest between the Volunteers and the Special Constabulary, which had attracted many men in 1914 and performed similar duties in guarding key points, and with special tasks in handling the evacuation of refugees and livestock in the event of a German invasion. In Leeds, for example, the Special Constabulary developed from a pre-war 'Citizen's League', eventually embracing some 3,250 men.

If the status of Volunteers who were also Special Constables resulted in friction with the police authorities, the arrival of 'tribunal men' also brought complaints from Volunteers that they were unwilling to complete drills, but tribunals often resisted attempts to pursue defaulters. Tribunals, however, were aware of the unrealistic nature of some War Office demands with respect to military training when long hours were being worked in essential occupations. Indeed, in November 1917, immunity from civil prosecution was extended to all those directed into the force by tribunals. By February 1918, from 285,000 Volunteers, 101,000 (35 per cent) were 'tribunal men', a proportion that increased to 44 per cent by the end of the war. From the point of view of the War Office, the Volunteers were simply shielding men from military service, the Adjutant General claiming in 1917 that 100,000 men had been lost to the army. In the course of 1917, it was agreed to reduce the Volunteer Force to 267,150 men in 274 battalions, with a thirty-eight battalions being reduced by amalgamation of weaker units and dismissal of the non-efficient.

The Volunteers were not capable of replacing troops in home defence, as a confused affair in March 1917, which may have been either a planned test mobilisation or simply a panic, proved. Yet they did useful service in guarding vulnerable points, manning anti-aircraft batteries and assisting the London Fire Brigade during air raids, digging the London defences, assisting with harvests, and providing transport for troops on leave or invalided home. Over 13,000 served in special service companies on the east coast in three-month tours to release more troops for the BEF between June and September 1918. In the case of the 1st Dublin Battalion, sixteen men became casualties, including four killed when coming under fire during the Easter Rising: one was the President of the Irish Rugby Football Union, Francis Browning. Probably over a million men passed through the Volunteers at one time or another, and the Central Association claimed that over 2,000 had enlisted by the end of 1915 and 600 had attested under the Derby Scheme. The force withered away in suspended animation from February 1919 onwards until formally disbanded in January 1920, although 18,500 men of the Motor Volunteer Corps, seen as useful for strikebreaking, were retained until March 1921.

War also made a distinction between men and women for, overwhelmingly, it was men who fought, but this did not mean that women did not contribute to the armed forces. Quasi-military organisations such as the Women's Emergency Corps and the Women's Volunteer Reserve were immediately created under the patronage of titled women, although they aroused suspicion through donning quasi-military uniforms, which appeared to take them beyond acceptable feminine roles. By 1916, however, there were some 10,000 women in such corps, and their ability to project themselves within the context of the volunteering tradition as represented, too, by the VTC brought increasing acceptance, thereby opening up the opportunity for women to join the army itself as auxiliaries.[73] Traditionally, the British Army had only employed women as nurses prior to 1914: the trend was continued by Queen Alexandra's Imperial Military Nursing Service (QAIMNS), the Territorial Force Nursing Service (TNS), the Voluntary Aid Detachments (VADs) and

[73] Susan Grayzel, 'The Outward and Visible Sign of Her Patriotism: Women, Uniform and National Service during the First World War', *Twentieth Century British History*, 8 (1997), 145–64; Krisztina Robert, 'Gender, Class and Patriotism: Women's Paramilitary Units in First World War Britain', *International History Review*, 19 (1997), 52–65; Krisztina Robert, 'Constructions of "Home", "Front" and Women's Military Employment in First World War in Britain: A Spatial Interpretation', *History and Theory*, 52 (2013), 319–43.

the aristocratic First Aid Nursing Yeomanry (FANY). Excluding the 74,000 VADs in 1914, there were over 2,000 other military nurses, a figure that reached over 18,000 by 1918.

There was considerable reluctance to use women in any other capacity, but their work in the munitions industry forced the army to reconsider. In April 1915, therefore, the Army Council authorised the employment of women as cooks and waitresses in Britain in Lady Londonderry's Women's Legion, which received official recognition in February 1916. It eventually numbered some 6,000 women. If women could replace men at home, then there was no logical reason why they should not do so overseas for all that Haig doubted women's ability to replace men under service conditions and their motivation for wishing to do so. There was also some debate as to whether women should wear uniforms. In March 1917, however, the first uniformed cooks of the new Women's Army Auxiliary Corps (WAAC) arrived in France. The 41,000 women who served in the WAAC – renamed Queen Mary's Army Auxiliary Corps in April 1918 – were mostly working or lower middle class. Consequently, there was a tendency to view them as lacking the more altruistic patriotic motivations perceived in their social superiors.[74]

Patriotism was not incompatible with wanting to earn better money, experience different work, escape domestic service or see a different country. The WAAC, however, quickly earned a totally unjustified reputation for immorality: a survey undertaken in March 1918 showed that of the only twenty-one pregnancies, two involved married women, and the great majority of the rest predated enlistment. Class had much to do with this, as well as fears of the consequences of women in uniform usurping masculine roles. Hostility to the WAAC also derived from resentment on the part of men behind the lines employed as clerks, cooks, drivers and storemen, who were now combed out for service at the front. The military as a whole never quite came to terms with the concept of women in uniform, and their status within the army remained ambiguous. The corps was disbanded in 1920, not being revived until the creation of the Auxiliary Territorial Service (ATS) in 1938. A Women's Royal Naval Service (WRNS) also came into existence in January 1918, followed by the Women's Royal Auxiliary Air Force (WRAAF) in April, but they did not attract quite the same hostility as the WAAC.

The Great War was not a unique experience for British society, but it certainly appeared to be so in terms of living memory of conflict. Its

[74] Elizabeth Crosthwait, 'The Girl Behind the Man Behind the Gun: The Women's Army Auxiliary Corps, 1914–18', in Leonore Davidoff and Belinda Westover (eds.), *Our Work, Our Lives, Our Words* (Totowa, NJ: Barnes & Noble, 1986), 161–81; Lucy Noakes, *Women in the British Army: War and the Gentle Sex* (London: Routledge, 2006), 61–81.

impact has similarly endured within British popular memory. The extent of military participation was greater than it had been for a century and on a scale that has not been exceeded since. There was an almost unprecedented voluntary response to the outbreak of war, but the demands of modern industrialised warfare also necessitated a unique recourse to conscription that had previously been applied both sporadically and also only in terms of home defence forces. In that sense, for the first time in its history, Britain was truly a 'nation in arms' between 1914 and 1918.

4 Citizen Soldiers

Discipline, Morale and the Experience of War

The impact of military service upon those who enlisted varied so much that there are distinct dangers in generalisation. There was no one typical experience: no one British battalion was quite like any other. It should certainly not be accepted that a handful of well-known sensitive intellectual, or otherwise literary-minded, wartime officers like Siegfried Sassoon, Wilfred Owen and Robert Graves were in any way representative of the army as a whole. The British Army was certainly not one which universally carried Palgrave's *The Golden Treasury* in its knapsacks, let alone the literary agent's contract. As has been commented, the army comprised 'essentially the British working man in uniform'.[1]

Cultural historians have tended to assume from the literary evidence that there was a universality of experience linking officers and men in a common community of spirit bred in the trenches. This is sometimes expressed as the concept of a 'war generation' or 'front generation'. It is argued from this largely post-war literary invention that the kind of high expectations supposedly shared by early wartime volunteers doomed them to disillusionment under the stress of 'machine-age' warfare. Unable to come to terms with the stark difference between the realities of the front line and the failures of those at home to comprehend their sacrifices, such men were prone to war neuroses. Thus, the introspection of the trenches supposedly created a kind of idealised community in which officers and men alike shared both during and after the war.

Clearly, there was a wartime process of bonding, often a continuation of the kind of social links familiar from workplace, schools, youth organisations and clubs and societies of all kinds. Old Comrades' Associations were invariably established after the war, but many struggled for members and, in any case, often only operated on the basis of an annual reunion. Regimental histories were also published. The issue of class, however, soon re-asserted itself, as did the role of women in men's lives. Reliance on literary sources or the subsequent careers of a few high-profile

[1] John Bourne, 'The British Working Man in Arms', in Cecil and Liddle (eds.), *Facing Armageddon*, 336–52, at 336.

individuals such as Harold Macmillan or the BBC's first 'disk-jockey', Christopher Stone, tends to perpetuate the idea there were no divisions within armies and assumes that the front line and the home front were quite separate spheres.[2]

Dealing first with the concept of a 'war generation', divisions between officers and men existed to an extent to suggest that if a war generation did exist, it was 'only for so long as it remained under fire'.[3] Even if officers were increasingly promoted from the ranks, shared front-line dangers, played football with their men or offered themselves up to ridicule at concert parties, rank conferred status and privilege, as trench literature made clear. Officers were differentiated in many different ways: from better rations, better dugouts, greater periods of leave, greater freedom of movement and even separate brothels and cinemas to doctors' assumptions that enlisted men were more liable to hysteria than officers.[4]

There were wide differences between service on different fronts and in different sectors. It is too often forgotten that the Great War was not fought solely on the Western Front. It can also be noted that it was not until 1917 that there were more British troops in France and Flanders than in the United Kingdom. Campaigning conditions on the Eastern Front, where the war was always more fluid, in Mesopotamia or East Africa, were quite different from those in France and Flanders. Nonetheless, whereas the casualty rate was one for every twenty-one men serving in Italy, one in twelve for Egypt and Salonika, and two in nine at the Dardanelles, it was five for every nine men serving on the Western Front.[5]

Even the Western Front, however, was not a theatre of unrelieved terror, deprivation, disillusionment and futility. For one thing, it can be argued that trench warfare conserved lives compared to more mobile warfare because trenches protected men physically if not psychologically from bombardment. British casualties in August 1917 during the Passchendaele offensive, for example, totalled 81,000, but 122,000 became casualties in the semi-mobile warfare of August 1918. For another, there were considerable differences between trench warfare in the flat waterlogged fields of Flanders, on the rolling chalk downs of the

[2] G. D. Sheffield, 'The Effect of The Great War on Class Relations in Britain: The Career of Major Christopher Stone', *War & Society* 7 (1989), 87–105.

[3] Richard Bessel and David Englander, 'Up from the Trenches: Some Recent Writing on the Soldiers of the Great War', *European Studies Review* 11 (1981), 387–95, at 393.

[4] P. J. Lynch, 'The Exploitation of Courage: Psychiatric Care in the British Army, 1914–18', unpublished MPhil thesis, University of London, 1977, 140–1.

[5] Keith Simpson, 'The British Soldier', in Peter Liddle (ed.), *Home Fires and Foreign Fields: British Social and Military Experience in the First World War* (London: Brasseys, 1985), 135–58, at 137–8.

Somme uplands, or on the forested slopes of the Vosges. Some sectors were considered quiet and others active. While it was on the Western Front, the 56th (1st London) Division spent 330 days at rest, 195 days in quiet sectors, 385 days in active sectors and only 100 days on actual active operations.[6] The Christmas Truce of 1914 is invariably remembered, but a 'live and let live' system existed in many sectors of the front. In any case, it was simply not the case that soldiers spent their entire service in the front line. Charles Carrington, for example, recorded of his service in the 1/5th Royal Warwicks in the course of 1916 that he spent 65 days in the front line, 36 days in close support to the front line, 120 days in reserve, 73 days at rest behind the liens and the remaining 72 days variously on leave, sick, travelling or attending courses.[7] In the line, too, it was perfectly feasible to make rational judgements as to the degree of risk involved in any particular activity, the live and let live system itself suggesting a degree of control.

The nature of modern warfare was such that the ratio between combatant and non-combatant troops altered considerably during the war as more and more men were required to supply the materials required to keep an army fighting. There is some limited evidence that skilled tradesmen and engineers were directed towards the Royal Engineers, Army Service Corps, and Royal Artillery and that those with animal skills also tended to go in the same direction. Overall, however, the British Army did not use its manpower very intelligently, frequently failing to re-assign those with particular technical skills where they might best be used. Of 180,000 former railwaymen in the army in 1917, for example, only 22 per cent were serving with transportation units.[8] It is possible that these units believed that they had sufficient numbers of skilled men, but there is some evidence of an increasing 'civilianisation' of the wider army labour force in such areas as transportation – both railways and inland water transport – and communications. Established in 1916, the Directorate of Labour attempted to work as a kind of labour exchange within the army, but labour units remained unpopular and a less than well-motivated billet for older and/or physically unfit men. Nonetheless, the ratio of combatant to non-combatant troops still changed from 83.3:16.6 in 1914 to 64.8:35.1 by 1918. The proportion of infantry and

[6] Evelyn Wood, *The Citizen Soldier* (London: privately printed, 1939), 49.

[7] Charles Edmonds [sc. Carrington], *A Subaltern's War* (London: Peter Davies, 1929), 120.

[8] David Englander, 'Manpower in the British Army', in Gerard Canini (ed.), *Les Fronts Invisibles: Actes du Colloque International sur La Logistique des Armées au Combat pendant la Première Guerre Mondiale* (Nancy: Presses universitaires de Nancy, 1984), 93–102; Richard Grayson, 'Military History from the Street: New Methods for Researching First World War Service in the British Military', *War in History* 21 (2104), 465–95.

cavalry also declined, while new branches such as the Tank Corps, the Machine Gun Corps and the Labour Corps emerged. Indeed, while the proportion of infantry declined from 53.8 per cent of the army to 31.9 per cent between 1914 and 1918, the Labour Corps embraced 14.3 per cent of the army by 1918. Moreover, within the combat arms, the percentage of infantry declined from 64.6 to 49.2 per cent. The percentage of men serving in the Royal Garrison Artillery had also increased from 1.0 per cent of the army to 6.4 per cent by 1918, reflecting the shift towards heavier firepower.

At the front itself, there were divisions between officers in fighting units and staff officers, between the different arms and branches of service, and between specialists such as machine gunners and the infantry. Trench mortar crews firing off their weapons, for example, might easily endanger ordinary riflemen, who would expect a tit-for-tat barrage across no man's land. Royal Engineers would make demands on the infantry for labour when the infantry were supposedly at rest. There were differences, too, between divisions, some being regarded as 'holding' formations and others as 'assault' divisions. Above all, there were differences between regulars, Territorials and New Army volunteers. The New Army volunteers were initially viewed with something akin to contempt on the part of many regulars. Major-General Henry Wilson, for example, spoke of Kitchener's 'ridiculous and preposterous army', while two regular privates, John Lucy of the 2nd Royal Irish Rifles and Frank Richards of the 2nd Royal Welsh Fusiliers, were equally critical.[9]

As the war continued, so the distinctions blurred as any pretence to draft men from a particular area to a particular unit was sacrificed to the military necessity of making losses good, a reduction in identity particularly resented among Territorial and Irish units. Based on the admittedly less than perfect snapshot provided by casualties recorded in *Soldiers Died in the Great War*, the proportion of those killed from the recruiting area of 1/8th Scottish Rifles declined from 79 per cent in 1915 to 40 per cent in 1918; in the 1/6th West Yorks from 68 to 15 per cent; in the 1/6th and 2/6th South Staffs from 85 to 64 per cent and in the 1/1st Bucks Battalion from 65 to 38 per cent. In terms of nationality, the decline in identity was also evident, from 91 to 88 per cent Scots in the Cameron Highlanders between 1915 and 1918 and from 58 to 51 per cent Welsh in the Royal Welsh Fusiliers. It was precisely the collapse of the drafting system under the pressure of casualties that led to the questions increasingly raised by

[9] C. E. Callwell, *Field Marshal Sir Henry Wilson: His Life and Diaries*, 2 vols. (London: Cassell, 1927), Vol. I, 178; John Lucy, *There's a Devil in the Drum* (London: Faber & Faber, 1938), 338–43; Frank Richards, *Old Soldiers Never Die* (London: Faber & Faber, 1964), 154, 212–13.

Members of Parliament (MPs) with regard to the violation of the pre-war commitment to retain the integrity of Territorial Force (TF) units.

Pre-war Territorials had a particular identification with locality and a sense of middle-class solidarity. During the war, close links were maintained with county and community through the uncensored provincial press. Indeed, Territorial units may have resisted a 'nationalisation' of the army longer than most, though, as battalion identity became more difficult to sustain, it was replaced by county identity, albeit it has been argued that regimental identity remained particularly strong in the 54th Division serving in the Middle East. It has also been suggested that at least among Liverpool Territorials, as social homogeneity declined, social status remained significant, with surviving middle-class men more easily promoted to positions of responsibility.[10] In part, regular criticism of the TF was due to the assumption that discipline was less pronounced in Territorial units as a result of the idea that officers and men were more likely to be social equals in civilian life and, therefore, discipline could not be based on rigid codes. It is a misapprehension to suppose that all TF units were 'class corps' with a preponderance of the middle class because there were many working-class formations, as in the 59th (2nd North Midland) and 62nd (2nd West Riding) Divisions. Clearly, though, many Territorials took pride in the appearance of a more relaxed ethos.

Even if these earlier divisions blurred as units were increasingly fed from the same pool of manpower, there still remained a distinction between those who had volunteered and those who had been conscripted after 1916. Distinctions were made additionally between 'Derbyites', eighteen-year-olds and older conscripts who had not attested a willingness to serve. But the universal impression of the conscript among contemporaries was a being of progressively declining intelligence, physique and ability. To those who had volunteered, it was self-evident that the unwilling could not have the same commitment as themselves. Soldiers perceived the resistance to the abolition of the Trade Card Agreement as an act of self-preservation on the part of trade unionists. The higher command also viewed the arrival of conscripts with some trepidation as drawing in 'many men who were temperamentally unfitted to be soldiers'.[11] As with all generalisations, too much should not be read into the stereotyped contemporary view of the conscript. Some of those who

[10] James Kitchen, *The British Imperial Army in the Middle East: Morale and Identity in the Sinai and Palestine Campaigns, 1916–18* (London: Bloomsbury, 2014), 123–50; Helen McCartney, *Citizen Soldiers: The Liverpool Territorials in the First World War* (Cambridge University Press, 2005), 55–6, 87–8.

[11] Major-General Sir Wyndham Childs, *Episodes and Reflections* (London: Cassell, 1930), 139.

believed that their domestic or professional responsibilities precluded voluntary enlistment had genuine difficulties in reconciling themselves to service. Clearly, some men had been unwilling to serve from baser motives, but there is no real evidence, as alleged at the time, of conscripts having a greater propensity towards indiscipline. Indeed, it has been suggested that one of the factors in the army's eventual success in 1918 was the supply of younger conscripts who 'ignorant and easily killed though they often were, blended with surviving natural leaders to keep the show going'.[12] In any case, conscripts were products of the same society as their fellow soldiers and had similar concerns.

What can be said of the experience of soldiers is that the actual welcome afforded new arrivals in a unit varied widely, and the conditioning of men depended almost entirely upon the unit in which they actually served. This might not always be the same unit, for there was a constant change of personalities. Men left units as casualties from battle or disease; they went on leave or on courses; they left to become commissioned and they were drafted to other units. Most units would steadily lose any real connection with the particular locality or social group from which they might have been raised. Of course, no man was in the front line continuously.

Many soldiers were exposed to colleagues from widely differing social backgrounds. Military service clearly broadened horizons. British society had been deeply divided before the war, and more refined recruits had to come to terms with a semblance of equality in the ranks. William Lintorn Andrews, a Dundee journalist serving in the 1/4th Black Watch, and others who had also purchased their own cutlery were astonished to be told that 'it was bad taste for us to differentiate ourselves in that way from the rougher men'. Similarly, a trooper from the 1/2nd County of London Yeomanry (Westminster Dragoons) recorded of sharing troopship accommodation with men of the 1/9th Manchester Regiment that 'their lack of manners and their filthy habits are more than we can stand.' A private in the 8th Norfolk Regiment found himself amid the 'riff-raff of England' who 'smell horribly some of them'.[13] For working-class recruits, however, the army might not be far different from the regimentation of the factory and, compared to civilian life, even offered compensations in the relief from drudgery. As indicated later, one explanation for the maintenance of British morale on the Western Front is that men were used to the subordination and tedium commonplace in industrial society. It is arguable, therefore, that most British soldiers would not have

[12] Shelford Bidwell and Dominick Graham, *Firepower: British Army Weapons and Theories of War, 1904–45* (London: Allen & Unwin, 1982), 117.

[13] Ian F. W. Beckett, 'The Nation in Arms', in Beckett and Simpson (eds.), *Nation in Arms*, 2–35, at 20–1; Simkins, *Kitchener's Army*, 207.

recognised the disillusionment said to have been experienced by those of literary sensitivities, who embarked upon war with high expectations in 1914.

The notion of separate spheres has also been dismissed as a 'modernist myth'.[14] Judging by the lack of disciplinary disturbances in the British Army until demobilisation, most wartime servicemen simply wished to return to civilian life as soon as possible because they had never really ceased to be civilians. There was certainly widespread criticism of civilians on the part of soldiers, for 'even the most radical of ex-servicemen believed in the existence of an unlimited supply of man-power composed of cunning shirkers and the like.'[15] British soldiers frequently showed their dislike for strikers. Yet, criticism of civilians did not imply a rejection of civilian society. The hostility towards shirkers common to most soldiers in most armies arguably reflected a disguised rural and lower-middle-class resentment of the privileges enjoyed by the urban working class in war.[16] The enormous volume of mail between front and home provided a vital bridge so that it was more a question of interaction than alienation. The constant movement also limited separation during the war between front and home, as men were released to or recalled from war-related industries. Moreover, the idea of separate military and civilian worlds was not one held by the authorities, who 'took pains to monitor the two-way traffic in ideas and influence'.[17]

It has also been argued on the basis of the reports sent back to grieving relatives in Britain by the British Red Cross Wounded and Missing Enquiry Bureau that civilians were not shielded as much as usually suggested from the more harrowing aspects of life at the front by a 'conspiracy of silence'. Indeed, they displayed a 'morbid curiosity about the exact circumstances surrounding their loved ones' deaths'.[18] Certainly, there was little attempt to hide the extent of casualties until at least the end of 1916 so far as the national press was concerned. The provincial press continued to publish full casualty lists throughout the war, as well as news of local servicemen. Accounts of the battlefield in

[14] David Englander, 'Soldiering and Identity: Reflections on the Great War', *War and History* 1 (1994), 300–18, at 317.

[15] David Englander and James Osborne, 'Jack, Tommy and Henry Dubb: The Armed Forces and the Working Class', *Historical Journal* 21 (1978), 593–62, at 619.

[16] John Horne, 'Introduction: Mobilising for Total War, 1914–18', in John Horne (ed.), *State, Society and Mobilisation in Europe during the First World War* (Cambridge University Press, 1997), 1–18, at 12.

[17] David Englander, 'People at War: France, Britain and Germany, 1914–18 and 1939–45', *European History Quarterly* 18 (1988), 229–38, at 236.

[18] Eric F. Schneider, 'The British Red Cross Wounded and Missing Enquiry Bureau: A Case of Truth-Telling in the Great War', *War in History* 4 (1997), 296–315, at 309.

the provincial press were invariably 'graphic and brutal' and the coverage of the care for and entertainment of wounded servicemen in local hospitals a constant feature, albeit there was a continuing emphasis on the heroism of local men. In short, the public 'both knew more and commemorated earlier' than supposed.[19]

Conscription was a major break with pre-war expectations in Britain, and the wartime experience of military participation as a whole had social and institutional implications. For the first time in a century, even if essentially civilians in uniform, very large numbers of troops were permanently visible to British society. With the delay in providing hutted accommodation in the autumn of 1914, they were also in close proximity to civilians. Reactions naturally varied on both sides, but in many cases the influx of men from different classes and from different regions was undoubtedly a cultural shock for householders in what was a markedly parochial society prior to 1914. One watch repairer on whom Territorials of the 2/5th Manchesters were billeted in Colchester 'expressed surprise that we could speak without using the dialect, and that we had good table manners'. Another in the 1/6th Gordon Highlanders in Bedford was asked 'if I didn't feel the cold night, on the hills with only my plaid to cover me while sleeping'. Another householder told the same Scot that the bath would be a 'great surprise for us, never having seen one before'.[20] The War Office was overwhelmed by complaints in 1914 and 1915 from civilians at the plight in which new recruits supposedly found themselves. At Bulford, one correspondent writing to Southern Command in August 1915 claimed that troops were begging for food. Certainly, camp life in the autumn and winter of 1914–15 could be distinctly uncomfortable. Ten per cent of those in the 51st (Highland) Division quartered around Bedford who contracted measles died in December 1914 and over 29,000 men encamped on Salisbury Plain were returned as sick each month from October to December 1914. It was rumoured that 2,000 Canadians had died from pneumonia or meningitis: up to January 1915, there were 1,508 cases of pneumonia among British troops, with 301 resulting in death. One of the serviceman's few rights was to refuse inoculation, and many defied the official campaign encouraging it until it was made effectively compulsory by refusing leave to those not inoculated.

With accommodation in short supply, soldiers were billeted routinely on civilians. It was far from the case that billeting parties were greeted enthusiastically, and increasingly, many householders became disillusioned

19 Michael Finn, 'Local Heroes: War News and the Construction of Community in Britain, 1914–18', *Historical Research* 83 (2010), 520–38, at 522 and 538.

20 Peter Simkins, 'Soldiers and Civilians: Billeting in Britain and France', in Beckett and Simpson (eds.), *Nation in Arms*, 165–92, at 173–4.

with the military presence despite the billeting allowances on offer. But it should also be noted that the presence of troops could be beneficial, Welsh seaside resorts actually competing to attract military camps during the slack autumn period of 1914. At Bournemouth, it was calculated that troops were spending £20,000 a week in the winter of 1914–15. The conflicting efforts of War Office, County Territorial Associations (CTAs), corporations and individuals to equip units also benefitted business, as did the erection of the many new army camps that sprang up. Official contractors made handsome profits, although local contractors also did well by undercutting them. Scandals were common. In Southern Command, for example, Army Service Corps personnel in Winchester were found to be selling off oats to farmers. At Sutton Veny in November 1915, a soldier was selling off freshly roasted meat to a canteen manager from the army contractors, Dickenson & Co., who sold it back to other soldiers as faggots.

It was not just a question of becoming aware of one's own country but of foreign countries as well. The exposure of British soldiers to French and Belgian civilians and vice versa had its own revelations. While there was a certain sympathy for the Belgians, British soldiers often commented adversely on the perceived lack of hygiene among French and Belgian civilians, the mercenary ways of these civilians and their own resentment at being made to feel unwelcome in countries they had come to defend. British soldiers tended to be regarded by French civilians, however, as cleaner than French troops and less overbearing. While benefitting from running *estaminets* and other trading ventures, employment as labour behind the lines and even help with harvesting as operations permitted, civilians naturally felt resentful of damage to crops, destruction of property such as barns and the frequent petty theft and looting. Claims against the British Expeditionary Force (BEF) rose steadily in line with the increase in troop strength. From January to May 1915, for example, claims totalled over 8.2 million francs, of which some 2.9 million francs' worth was accepted. From August to October 1916, however, claims totalled over 115.1 million francs, of which some 50 million francs' worth was accepted. For the period January to October 1917, a total of 281.14 million francs was claimed and 156.5 million francs paid out.[21]

Prostitution was a severe trial to the British military authorities. Significantly, the Women's Police Volunteers (WPV), created by Nina Boyle of the Women's Freedom League in September 1914; the

[21] Craig Gibson, 'The British Army, French Farmers and the War on the Western Front, 1914–18', *Past & Present* 180 (2002), 175–240; Craig Gibson, *Behind the Front: British Soldiers and French Civilians, 1914–18* (Cambridge University Press, 2104), 393–409.

Women's Police Service (WPS), a breakaway movement from the WPV established by two former militant suffragettes, Margaret Damer Dawson and Mary Allen, in February 1915; and the Women's Patrols Committee of the National Union of Women's Workers all began by patrolling in the vicinity of army camps. Subsequently, the WPS extended its activities to factories by agreement with the Ministry of Munitions in July 1915. The WPS 'copperettes' were particularly unpopular.

In 1916, some 19.2 per cent of all British Army hospital admissions were for sexually transmitted diseases (STDs). It was also claimed that the numbers thereby incapacitated were equivalent to a division a day by 1918.[22] In any given week, about 30 to 40 per cent had contracted STDs in England rather than in France.[23] Strenuous efforts were made through the pre-war National Council for Combating Venereal Disease to influence soldiers, but pre-marital sex was common in British working-class life. There was an assumption that French women were essentially immoral, and in many areas the BEF was filling the 'demographic breach' in the absence of French males. Realities had to be faced, and by 1917, there were 137 licensed brothels in thirty-five French towns, no British servicemen being actually barred from brothels until March 1918.

In Britain itself, the controversy that had surrounded the Contagious Diseases Acts in the Victorian period left the authorities wary of new legislation. Asquith had pledged to the Women's Freedom League in October 1914 that the Contagious Diseases Acts would not be revived. Pressure for action came primarily from Dominion governments, Australian cases of venereal disease in 1917 running at 144 per 1,000 men and Canadian cases at 158 per 1,000 in 1918 compared to the average of 34 per 1,000 men in the British Army as a whole. As a result, the Defence of the Realm Act (DORA) was extended in terms of its provisions on sexual behaviour. Regulation 40D in March 1918 enabled prosecution of women infecting soldiers, even if the woman was married to the serviceman so infected and he had infected her first. Public uneasiness soon undermined the measure, the extension of the suffrage to women leading to the establishment of a committee to examine the issue in October 1918: its deliberations were suspended by the armistice, and Regulation 40D was abrogated in late November.

Naturally enough, the army attempted to divest soldiers of civilian values and 'recreate them in the army's image' by inculcating appropriate

[22] *Official History of the Great War: Medical Services: Hygiene of the War*, 2 vols. (London: HMSO, 1923), Vol. I, 20; *Official History of the Great War: Medical Services: Casualties and Medical Statistics* (London: HMSO, 1931), 74.

[23] Craig Gibson, 'Sex and Soldiering in France and Flanders: The BEF along the Western Front, 1914–19', *International History Review* 23 (2001), 535–79.

military values. But citizen soldiers 'were not social blanks waiting for the army to write its will upon them'.[24] While it was quite feasible for long-service volunteers to be conditioned, amid rapid and continuous wartime expansion, it was far harder to separate the temporary soldier from civilian values. Initially, civilian perceptions and a lack of familiarity with military disciplinary codes saw unrest in the New Armies, though more trouble was ameliorated by the patriotic enthusiasm of the volunteers and the kindness of the public towards them. In the case of many Pals Battalions, the civic structures supporting them meant that they were spared the worst of the conditions suffered by others because they often remained close to their place of origin until hutted accommodation was ready. For many men, however, there was a degree of shock on arrival at camps in the autumn of 1914 and with the lack of equipment and organisation found there. The long hours spent in drill, physical training and route marching were also immensely taxing. These problems were then exacerbated by wet weather in October and November that badly affected the more exposed camps before hutted accommodation was ready. Equally, the existing barracks and depots pressed into service quickly became overcrowded with new recruits: Salamanca Barracks at Aldershot, intended for 800 men, housed over 2,000 recruits in September 1914, the beds having been removed to accommodate more men sleeping on the floors.

There was a 'siege' of Hoxton barracks by hundreds of women in August 1914 when the 1/7th London Regiment was unexpectedly confined to barracks overnight for the first time. Up to 250 men at a time slipped away from Welsh Territorial units to tend their allotments in January 1915. Others simply attempted to go home from camps such as Purfleet, Shoreham and Preston. South Wales miners accommodated at the latter marched through the town to advertise their grievances in September 1914 with banners proclaiming, 'No Food, No Shelter, No Money'. Men from the 25th Division held mass meetings and refused to parade over the poor accommodation at Codford. Grievances were readily communicated to families, the local press and to MPs, as in the case of a 'strike' by men in the Sportsman's Battalion (24th Royal Fusiliers) at Tidworth in September 1915 over poor food. Such difficulties owed much to the delay in issuing uniforms, men still appearing for some weeks in civilian clothes, or substitutes such as the grey uniform issued to the Welsh Army Corps or the 'Kitchener blue' serge that began to be supplied by the Quartermaster General's Department in late September and which led to some men being ridiculed as looking like

[24] Bourne, 'British Working Man in Arms', 337.

postmen, tram guards or convicts. Khaki was simply the expected clothing of the soldier, carrying with it positive associations of physicality, masculinity and military modernity. Like much else, rapid expansion severely taxed uniform supply: in March 1916 it was announced that rather than a 'normal' annual provision of 1.9 million sets of uniform (boots, shirts, socks, tunic and trousers), 117 million sets had been produced since 1914 at a cost of £65 million.[25] Leather equipment was in particularly short supply, with most New Army battalions having to wait four months after receiving their khaki uniforms, and it was often of poor quality. In many cases, men had to make do with old tin water bottles, the 7th Oxfordshire and Buckinghamshire Light Infantry using window blind cords as bandoliers for them, while the 2/12th London Regiment made use of beer bottles and had school satchels as haversacks. In November 1914, the 'First New Army' had only a third of its requirements of modern service rifles, the rest being either old weapons or wooden dummy 'drill purpose' rifles. Broomsticks and poles substituting for rifles were commonplace, and ammunition was also wanting.

While the war clearly exposed men to experiences very different from those at home, however, it could never sever the link of a citizen army with civilian life, nor could it eradicate the social or regional diversity that had existed in civilian society. At the same time, however, the nature of civilian life was not unhelpful. A sense of community and social cohesiveness was well engrained through the shared experience of adversity and a spirit of mutual support epitomised by such organisations as the friendly societies. There was also a predisposition in British working-class popular culture that made light of hardship. It might be characterised either as a phlegmatic acceptance of fate or sheer bloody-mindedness but was commonly observed with a sardonic, vulgar humour. This factor ideally complemented the significance of the small 'primary group' – a small group of individuals bonded together by their service – in maintaining morale. In the same way, the increasing division of the army into 'specialisms' reproduced the small-scale nature of much of British industry, where even larger enterprises routinely divided men into work gangs. Men were used to making life bearable and were well suited to the challenges of war, relying on civilian values and not those of the army to see them through.

Industrialised warfare certainly increased the degree to which men were exposed to concussion and sensory deprivation, derived from heavier and more prolonged artillery bombardment. The battlefield had also become

[25] Jane Tynan, *British Army Uniform and the First World War: Men in Khaki* (Basingstoke: Palgrave Macmillan, 2013), 74.

progressively more 'empty' as the range of weapons increased, thus distancing soldiers yet further from a ready identification of the enemy. In turn, these newer pressures undoubtedly heightened the impact of those experienced by soldiers in earlier wars, such as the effects of sleep deprivation and exhaustion, the fear of mutilation or death, the guilt fears of survivors, anxieties felt for friends or family and so on. Morale could equally be damaged by a whole range of other factors, such as insufficient motivation, poor training, boredom, the lack of creature comforts such as adequate food and quarters, the debilitating effects of climate or disease and the lack of confidence in officers.

Nonetheless, whatever the increased pressures of the modern battlefield, morale and fighting spirit could still be built upon traditional military remedies: the appeal to patriotism, religion or honour; good leadership; discipline; rewards such as medals; accurate information; good medical arrangements; adequate leave arrangements; efficient administration; realistic training; rest and palliatives such as the rum ration (1 ounce per man per day) or cigarettes in appropriate measure. In the case of training, on average, New Army battalions had at least 9.4 months of training before they were committed initially to the Western Front. They had also had at least an inkling of what lay ahead from the many practice trench systems dug. The so-called Loos trench system at Blackpool, for example, used over the winter of 1914–15, subsequently became a wartime tourist attraction. But there was also the appeal to the regiment and its identity, as characterised by the rallying call of Lieutenant-Colonel Elstob on 21 March 1918: 'The Manchester Regiment will hold Manchester Hill to the last.' Similarly, there was the notice in Mansel Copse cemetery on the Somme: 'The Devons held this trench, the Devons hold it still.'

The role of religion in particular has been re-examined, and the war did increase religious observance, if not belief, but most soldiers' contemporary and later accounts hardly mention it. Much depended upon the calibre of individual military chaplains attached to units. Based on a survey of the 9th Loyal North Lancashire Regiment, it is suggested that perhaps only between 6 and 9 per cent of soldiers were active Christians. Catholic chaplains, mostly working-class Irishmen, had better rapport with ordinary soldiers than Anglicans, who were seen as authority figures and whose chaplains were kept out of the front line until 1916.[26]

Religion might be regarded as one of a number of 'coping strategies' by which men adapted to the dangers of active service, including the

[26] Richard Schweitzer, *The Cross and the Trenches: Religious Faith and Doubt among British and American Great War Soldiers* (Westport, CT: Praeger, 2003), 117.

calculation of risk, humour, superstition and 'a highly positively biased interpretation of the trench environment' by which men tended routinely to overestimate their chances of surviving death or mutilation. A kind of fatalism kept men inured to violent death. Perseverance – 'sticking it' – was a military version of a shared ideal of courage in British culture that transcended class, gender and national divisions. Civilians tended to cling to the more traditional concept of chivalry and self-sacrifice epitomised by the pre-war examples of the *Titanic* and Robert Falcon Scott and the continued emphasis upon the heroic in contemporary popular media and art resulting in a near 'canonisation' of front-line soldiers. Even for soldiers, experience of war did not erode the resonance of the rhetoric of sacrifice.[27] In addition, the cultivation of the 'primary group' was of inestimable value in maintaining morale under any circumstances. Such groups shared hardship, a common culture of songs and a particular language of service slang. Moreover, some men enjoyed the experience of war.

Not unexpectedly, the maintenance of morale was of crucial significance to military leaderships, and all armies undertook extensive monitoring. General Headquarters (GHQ) tended to use the relatively crude indices of the incidence of trench feet, shell shock and crime.[28] Trench journalism was also monitored. A total of 107 such newspapers circulating among the British and Dominion units in France and Flanders have survived, including such titles as *The Dump* (23rd Division), *The Gasper* (Royal Fusiliers), *The 5th Glo'ster Gazette* (1/5th Gloucesters), *The Mudlark* (1st Bedfordshire), *The Outpost* (17th HLI) and *The Wipers' Times* (12th Sherwood Foresters). British trench journals appear mainly to have been the work of junior subalterns and middle-class NCOs: of the 107 newspapers, the authors of sisty-six have been identified, comprising twenty-seven edited by officers, twenty-five edited by other ranks, and fourteen with joint editorship.[29] They were largely self-censored, though there was also a degree of loose censorship at battalion and divisional levels. Even claimed circulation figures are relatively small, with a print-run average of under 5,000: the highest circulation appears to have been

[27] Alex Watson, *Enduring the Great War: Combat, Morale and Collapse in the German and British Armies, 1914–18* (Cambridge University Press, 2008), 100; Edward Madigan, '"Sticking to a Hateful Task": Resilience, Humour and British Understandings of Combatant Courage, 1914–18', *War in History* 20 (2013), 76–98, at 82; Alex Watson and Patrick Porter, 'Bereaved and Aggrieved: Combat Motivation and the Ideology of Sacrifice in the First World War', *Historical Research* 83 (2010), 146–64.

[28] J. Brent Wilson, 'The Morale and Discipline of the BEF, 1914–18', unpublished MA thesis, University of New Brunswick, 1978, 31–4, 42, 47.

[29] John Fuller, *Troop Morale and Popular Culture in the British and Dominion Armies, 1914–18* (Oxford: Clarendon Press, 1990), 7, 11.

that of the *7th Manchester Sentry* with a reputed run of 26,000 in the Egyptian theatre. Thus, although circulation may have been boosted in the sense that an issue may well have been read aloud to a group of men, it is entirely conceivable that many soldiers never saw one at all. Thus, the 'documented readership remains elusive.'[30]

Compared to German trench newspapers, those of the BEF had far less emphasis upon justification of the war since the Germans were occupying Belgian and French territory and the British felt 'little need to prove to themselves that they were fighting a defiance and just war'.[31] In fact, the British publications evinced little interest in Belgium or France beyond a carnal attraction towards any local females. An interest in women, and particularly nurses, was common to all trench journalism. Compared to the French and German trench newspapers, which were mostly serious in tone, however, those of the BEF displayed an unrelenting humour and, often, mock defeatism. The emphasis was primarily on the unit as a community steeped in a common culture across the social divides, as reflected in shared jokes, sporting interests and entertainments, itself persuasive of a way of life worth fighting for.

The military authorities were likely to derive more useful information on the state of morale from surveying the results of censorship of the extraordinary quantities of service mail common to all armies. In the case of the British Army, this amounted by 1916 to 12.5 million letters and 875,000 parcels a week, overseas postage being just 1s.0d for civilians and 1s.2d for soldiers. Prior to Christmas 1916, the BEF on the Western Front alone received 4.5 million parcels. In all, the army shipped 320,409 tons of mail to the BEF between 1914 and 1918. Some problems arise with the use of censorship reports because the balance in men's lettersg between self-censorship and self-expression is 'unknowable'.[32] There were certain matters such as sexuality and bodily functions that were rarely mentioned. Often, too, the content was platitudinous, aimed at consolation towards, or reassurance of, the civilian recipient. Unfortunately, few British reports based on censors' material have survived, though there are reports for the Indian Army. Those which do survive suggest that conclusions drawn by the military authorities were often based on limited sampling. One report in September 1917, for example, was based on an examination of 4,552 'green envelopes'. These were a restricted special

30 Englander, 'Soldiering and Identity', 304.

31 Robert Nelson, *German Soldier Newspapers of the First World War* (Cambridge University Press, 2011), 8.

32 Michael Roper, *The Secret Battle: Emotional Survival in the Great War* (Manchester University Press, 2009), 93; Joanna Bourke, *Dismembering the Male: Men's Bodies, Britain and the Great War* (London: Reaktion Books, 1996), 21–2.

issue first introduced in March 1915 of one per man per week that enabled soldiers to write about private matters and that were not censored in the usual way by regimental officers but only liable to be examined at base. That represented only 0.26 per cent of the troops then serving in France and Flanders, of which twenty-eight, or 0.61 per cent, of the sample expressed complaint or war weariness. A second report from December 1917 drew on a larger sample of 17,000 combatant troops, again only 1.32 per cent of men in the combatant arms.[33] Bread and butter issues were dominant in such reports. There were concerns, for example, over the prices of cigarettes in the First Army in October 1916, complaints of monotonous food in the Fifth Army in November 1916 and the infrequent and uneven distribution of leave generally that same month.

Food generally has been identified as a central concern and obsession in soldiers' contemporary letters and diaries and subsequent memoirs. The initially relatively generous ration scale could not be sustained, and there was a downward trend from September 1914 onwards with particular reductions in protein and fats and frequent substitution. In 1914, the daily fresh meat ration had been one pound, four ounces. By 1918, this had been reduced to one pound for a man in the front line, twelve ounces for those on lines of communication, and ten ounces in military camps at home. The daily fresh vegetable ration remained at eight ounces throughout, but this was not always forthcoming, and 'scrounging' and poaching were common. It also made the arrival of food parcels from home especially significant for morale. Indeed, the army was far less well nourished than has sometimes been assumed. Not unexpectedly, the army operated within the boundaries of 'early twentieth century nutritional science where calorie count was paramount, and there was only a partial awareness of the true complexity of a healthy diet'. Accordingly, boils, sore gums and bad teeth were frequent occurrences.[34]

All armies suffered morale problems. In the British Army, military crime invariably rose after heavy casualties, with particular problems during the first winter of the war, following the near destruction of the old regular army during First Ypres, and during the winter of 1917–18 following Passchendaele. Absence without leave and drunkenness

[33] Peter Scott, 'Law and Orders: Discipline and Morale in the British Armies in France, 1917', in Liddle (ed.), *Passchendaele*, 349–68, at pp. 359–60.

[34] Michael Senior, 'The Price of Fags', *Stand to* 78 (2007), 30–1; Royal Archives, GV/Q2521/V/148; Rachel Duffett, 'A War Unimagined: Food and the Rank and File Soldier of the First World War', in Jessica Meyer (ed.), *British Popular Culture and the First World War* (Leiden: Brill, 2008), 47–70; Rachel Duffett, *The Stomach for Fighting: Food and the Soldiers of the Great War* (Manchester University Press, 2012), 231.

remained relatively high throughout the war. Self-mutilation was not a significant problem, but for any who were intent on evading danger, the Army Suspension of Sentences Act in 1915 ensured that deliberate crime would not result in avoidance of front-line duties. There was some increase in crimes that had been relatively unknown in the pre-war army, such as sodomy and murder, that was attributed to the influx of wartime servicemen.

There was something of a collapse of morale within the British Fifth Army during the opening of the German spring offensive on the Western Front in March 1918, although the figures available for sickness, crime and discipline for the Fifth Army between April 1917 and the start of the German offensive show little signs of any serious morale problem.[35] Even the experience of Passchendaele, however, had not dented the continued belief by British soldiers that they would ultimately triumph. Consequently, they met the German onslaught in March 1918, many fighting until surrounded or overwhelmed. Fortunately, logistic support generally remained functioning, and sufficient reinforcements were fed into the battle to ensure that a wider collapse did not occur.

There were some instances of collective indiscipline, the best known being the events at the 'Bull Ring' base camp at Etaples between 9 and 15 September 1917, although it has been much exaggerated in popular accounts. The disturbances were due to poor food and accommodation and the failure of elderly officers to keep in check NCOs, who subjected new drafts and men returning from convalescence alike to an unnecessarily brutal training regime. A series of demonstrations was held after a military policeman shot into a crowd and killed a soldier: subsequently, one man was executed, ten received terms of hard labour and over thirty received field punishments.

Mutiny is not necessarily an appropriate description of all forms of collective disobedience towards military authority. Some might be better characterised as strikes, particularly when involving citizen soldiers. While military authorities readily ascribed mutinies to external influences, most resulted from long-term mundane 'bread and butter' grievances concerning pay, leave or conditions. Often these were exacerbated by poor administration and a failure of communications between officers and men. Not only did armies truly march on their stomachs, as Napoleon once observed, but soldiers were perennially interested in defending or acquiring privileges.

[35] David Englander, 'Discipline and Morale in the British Army, 1917–18', in Horne (ed.), *State, Society and Mobilisation*, 132–6.

There is usually little evidence of the kind of political motivations often alleged by the authorities. Two mutinies involving British colonial contingents are typical examples. It has been argued that a mutiny among West Indian troops at Taranto in Italy in December 1918 was an early manifestation of indigenous nationalism. It arose, however, primarily from unfavourable comparisons with the pay of British troops and from the use of the West Indians as dock labour. The mutiny among the men of the 5th (Native) Light Infantry of the Indian Army at Singapore in February 1915 resulted in the death of thirty-two Europeans and the public execution of thirty-seven mutineers. It was blamed on Sikh Ghadarite subversion and the influence of German prisoners of war from the cruiser, *Emden*, and other internees held on the island. In reality, while rumours of the regiment's impending despatch to fight in Mesopotamia provided the trigger, internal divisions between Indian officers and men lay at the root of the mutiny. The situation was compounded by poor rations and the strained relationship between the commanding officer and the other British officers.

A mutiny in the 36th (Ulster Division) in September 1915 was primarily due to a mistaken belief that men would be sent overseas without prior home leave, while that in the 49th Brigade of the 16th (Irish) Division in April 1918 was a result of being broken up to reinforce other brigades. Generally, it might be noted that morale and discipline in Irish formations were little different from those of the rest of the British Army, though it has been suggested that the supposed martial and aggressive qualities of the Irish placed more pressure on Irish formations in static trench warfare. The 'Indianisation' of the 10th (Irish) Division in the Middle East in 1918 – by which British units were sent back to Europe and replaced within formations by Indian Army units – was due both to the need for experienced soldiers in France and the high rate of malarial disease within the division. It was not due to any perceived fears of political unreliability. Irish reserve battalions were removed from Ireland in 1918 as a precaution in the event of conscription having to be enforced by military means, but there was no evidence of Republican infiltration. Nor had the 1916 Easter Rising had any discernible impact on Irish units.[36]

It has been suggested that such a major crisis of morale as the French mutinies in April 1917 or the collapse of the British Fifth Army in March 1918 tended to occur in all armies, except that of the Germans, between two and half and three years after real entry into the war. If Britain's baptism of fire is counted from the battle of Loos in September 1915,

[36] Timothy Bowman, *Irish Regiments in the Great War: Discipline and Morale* (Manchester University Press, 2003), 85–6, 127–31, 169–71, 174–8, 194–9.

when New Army divisions were first used, then March 1918 fits well. Equally, it is argued that, with the exception of Germany, there is a correlation between the occurrence of collapse and the total number of combat deaths equalling the number of fighting infantry, such an occurrence signifying that the odds of individual survival had passed from possibility to probability of death. Again, the French mutinies and March 1918 fit well.[37] Yet, unlike the armies of France, Italy, and Russia in 1917 and, ultimately, even Germany in late 1918, the British did not suffer total or near-total collapse. Some comparison with the French is instructive.

French soldiers had consistently more hatred for the Germans than did British soldiers.[38] There is no evidence that the British were better fed than the French, who were actually allowed more leave, particularly after Pétain's reforms in 1917, while Dominion contingents got better pay than British soldiers. Nor were the French harassed behind the lines while 'at rest' in quite the way British troops were, although the French still complained of such harassment. The French were spared 'bull', of which British trench newspapers routinely complained. Nor did the French pursue the 'active front' policy of British trench raiding, which did have some beneficial impact, provided that raids were well planned but a negative one if not. The first trench raid is sometimes suggested to have been mounted by the Indian Corps on 9–10 November 1914, although it is generally accepted that the 1st Worcesters mounted the first true raid on 2–3 February 1915. Established as part of a policy of 'wearing out fights' by Haig in December 1915, raids, feint and 'Chinese attacks', bombing raids, silent and stealth raids, patrols and fighting patrols – the terminology was varied but the activity often indistinguishable – could be undertaken for a variety of reasons, including the gathering of intelligence, disrupting the enemy and pinning enemy reserves. One of the so-called SS (Stationery Service) training manuals, SS107, *Notes on Minor Enterprises*, was issued in March 1916. It would appear, however, that raids were not necessarily as frequent as supposed. In 1916, for example, it has been suggested that in First Army there were, on average, of just over five raids per corps per month and only 1.5 per division per month. They were also seen as necessary in inculcating an aggressive spirit in troops. The problem was that they often resulted in significant losses in the raiding parties, often among the most enterprising officers and men. There has been an increasing debate among historians as to the

[37] John Keegan, *The Face of Battle* (Harmondsworth, UK: Penguin, 1978), 276–7; John Keegan, *The First World War* (London: Hutchinson, 1998), 372.
[38] Fuller, *Troop Morale*, 38–40.

value or otherwise of raids. In 1932, in outlining the war's lessons, the Kirke Committee deemed raiding a mistake, but it has been argued that, in terms of imparting new military kills, the balance sheet 'might just be read in favour of raids'.[39]

Yet, clearly, there were differences between the British and French, which contributed arguably to the greater stability of the British. Drill and coercion clearly assisted, and so too did regimental tradition and the local identity of units. Divisional loyalty also became marked in at least some parts of the British Army. In some divisions, such as the 17th, 29th, 30th, 38th, 40th, 50th and 55th, the divisional badge seems to have become a particular mark of self-esteem. Major-General Hugh Jeudwine of the 55th (West Lancashire) Division, for example, claimed of its Red Rose badge that 'no more dreaded a punishment could be awarded for slackness . . . than to order the individual to remove the rose from his shoulders or the unit to erase it from its transport.'[40] The 19th Division awarded a highly prized 'White Butterfly' badge to battalions that had distinguished themselves. Yet it is not the case that all divisions produced post-war histories. British medical care was superior to that of the French, and French officers showed none of the concern for their men's welfare so inculcated in the British system.

Working-class soldiers both accepted and expected the imposition of discipline because, in British society, the working class routinely extended deference, which was not regarded as subservience, to social superiors in return for paternalism. It has been suggested, indeed, that paternalism might be better characterised as 'maternalism' given the tendency of officers and men to nurture each other since, for example, the batman cared for his officer and comrades looked after each other. Dispersal certificates of demobilised officers suggest about 36 to 39 per cent of British officers were lower middle or even working class in origin by the end of the war but were just as imbued with the traditional paternalistic approach to other ranks. It was also the case that, whatever the social origin of an officer, the differentiation between officer and ordinary soldier reinforced the continuity of social conventions.[41] Paternalism tended to create something of a culture of dependency among British soldiers but also mitigated the harsher aspects of the disciplinary code.

39 Connelly, *Steady the Buffs*, 91. See also Senior, *Haking*, 79–82, 273–90.

40 McCartney, *Citizen Soldiers*, 81. For comparison with the French generally, see Fuller, *Troop Morale*, passim.

41 Roper, *Secret Battle*, 166; G. D. Sheffield, *Leadership in the Trenches: Officer-Man Relations, Morale and Discipline in the British Army in the Era of the First World War* (Basingstoke: Macmillan, 2000), 31–2; Christopher Moore-Blick, *Playing the Game: The British Junior Officer on the Western Front, 1914–18* (Solihull: Helion, 2011), 160.

In many ways, British popular culture was exported with the army. An extensive British welfare network of divisional and regimental canteens, YMCA, Salvation Army and Church Army rest huts provided a variety of recreational activities and comfort funds. The cinemas, music hall and other concerts and bathing parties so often mentioned in British memoirs do not figure in those of the French. In Britain, troop entertainment was organised by the YMCA and, from 1917, by the Navy and Army Canteen Board. Overseas, the YMCA and the army itself were responsible. Bizarrely, the YMCA even linked with the Folk Dance and Song Society to sponsor folk dance centres behind the lines, though its image of the rural idyll contrasted somewhat with most soldiers' own identification with, and desire for, the music of commercial mass urban culture familiar from the gramophone, public house and music hall. Annual sales of gramophone records generally in Britain rose from 3.3 million in 1914 to 5 million by 1919, and the keenness to acquire the latest songs from home was another enduring and powerful link to civilian society. Nor did the French have the divisional sports meetings, the boxing tournaments, horse shows, football and cricket matches which, incidentally, provided men with an opportunity to embarrass officers without incurring penalties. Football in particular became officially accepted as institutionalised rest. At Salonika, British officers were even able to indulge in archaeological investigations.[42]

There were large numbers of trade unionists in the British Army's rank and file, but they rarely figured in wartime disturbances. It is significant in this regard that the list of grievances in the twelve-point petition drawn up by the Soldiers and Workers Council established among units stationed at Tunbridge Wells in Kent in June 1917 – the only other such councils were at Birmingham and Swansea – was not only almost entirely concerned with the mundane issues of daily military life but also equated grievances with the rights of the citizen. It has been described, indeed, as displaying 'pre-eminently the voice of the respectable working man'.[43] Disturbances at Shoreham in September 1917 were prompted by the scale of rations, the higher pay of Canadians stationed nearby and the cancellation of leave trains to Brighton to save fuel.

Both the Army Council and War Cabinet recognised in September 1917 that those disturbances that had occurred had resulted from issues such as pay and leave, as publicised in the *Daily Mail* and by the

[42] Nick Hiley, 'Ploughboys and Soldiers: The Folk Song and the Gramophone in the British Expeditionary Force, 1914–18', *Media History* 4 (1998), 61–76; Alan Wakefield and Simon Moody, *Under the Devil's Eye: Britain's Forgotten Army at Salonika* (Stroud: Sutton Publishing, 2004), 155–8.

[43] Englander and Osborne, 'Jack, Tommy and Henry Dubb', 604–5.

self-proclaimed soldier's champion, Horatio Bottomley, in *John Bull.* Some attention had been given in earlier years to using chaplains and the YMCA to begin a kind of low-level patriotic instruction. A more formal educational scheme was authorised in February 1918, although not finally implemented until August, by which time the restoration of mobile warfare both limited its effect and its necessity. An education officer was appointed on a full-time basis to each army, divisional and base headquarters, with a part-time officer attached to each brigade staff.

Where trade unionists did emerge much more prominently was in the post-war demobilisation disturbances in January 1919. The disturbances began at Folkestone on 3 January, where an estimated 2,000 men marched on the town hall to protest delays in demobilisation. It spread to other bases in Kent and then to camps around London and beyond. A total of forty-seven different incidents have been identified in Britain and a further four in France at Calais, Dunkirk, Le Havre and Etaples. The beginning of demobilisation on 11 January brought the protests rapidly to an end. Many of those serving in the base camps particularly affected were specially enlisted volunteer tradesmen, who had been enjoying a regime that became a model for post-war civil labour relations. Compared to trade unionists, survivors of the regular army continued to appear prominently in wartime disturbances and suffered a disproportionate number of wartime executions.

Under the provisions of the British Army Act, a total of 346 men were executed during the war, of whom 291 were serving with British regiments, twenty-five were Canadians and five New Zealanders (two of whom were actually Australians), with the remainder foreign labourers. Taking into account all executions up to the suspension of the death penalty in 1924, and including civilians and prisoners of war executed for various offences, the total comes to 438. A total of 117 Australians were condemned to death but could not be executed under the provisions of the 1903 Australian Defence Act, to the frustration of many Australian commanders as much as to the British. The US Army executed thirty-five men between April 1917 and June 1919, only ten of whom committed offences in France, these all being for murder or rape. The Belgians executed eighteen soldiers and the Germans supposedly forty-eight soldiers. In some respects, therefore, the application of discipline was harsher in the British than other armies. The number of military police expanded from 405 in 1914 to 13,414 by 1918, the ratio increasing from one military policeman to every 3,306 soldiers to one to 292.[44] The

[44] G. D. Sheffield, 'British Military Police and their Battlefield Role, 1914–18', *Sandhurst Journal of Military Studies* 1 (1990), 33–46.

British had twenty-seven capital offences in their military code compared to just eleven in the German Army and two in the French Army, but the British criminal code was harsher than that of many continental states. The Germans also consciously softened many penalties in April 1917. At least 750 Italian soldiers were executed during the war, some by lot since the concept of decimation was reinstated. Indeed, 141 Italians were summarily executed in November 1917 alone in the effort to arrest collapse after Caporetto, and it is usually suggested that there were probably at least another 200 to 250 such summary executions during the war in addition to the official figure. Figures are uncertain for the French Army but may be around 700 and unknown for the Austro-Hungarian and Russian Armies.

Only 10.8 per cent of death sentences actually imposed by British courts martial on white soldiers were confirmed, albeit compared to 76.9 per cent in the case of the Chinese Labour Corps. Nearly forty of those executed had previously been sentenced to death, and two of them twice previously. Others had previously served, or had had suspended, sentences of imprisonment for capital offences.[45] Although it has been argued that the process was biased against Irishmen, colonial labourers and those deemed mentally degenerate or 'worthless',[46] it should also be noted that standards in the conduct of courts martial differed little from those in pre-war civil courts. The British command modified the much harsher line taken by New Zealand commanders. It is also the case that there was a decreasing use of the death penalty with the conscious revival in the field, especially among British units serving in Italy, of the concept of 'pious perjury' to mitigate the recourse to capital punishment as the army became more dependent upon conscripts. In Italy, desertion was 'often downgraded to absence'.[47]

Disproportionate attention has been devoted in Britain to the relatively minor matter of wartime executions (affecting 0.006 per cent of the wartime army as a whole) largely through the popular perception that those executed must all have been suffering from 'shell shock'. Indeed, the public campaign for pardons for all save murderers upheld by the British government in 2006 was profoundly unhistorical, a matter of faulty popular memory imposing contemporary values on the past. 'Shell shock' itself was a term first coined by Dr (later Lieutenant-

[45] Bowman, *Irish Regiments*, 13–15, 203.

[46] Gerard Oram, *Worthless Men: Race, Eugenics and the Death Penalty in the British Army during the First World War* (London: Francis Boutle, 1998), 17–18, 28–31, 60–73, 84–112.

[47] Gerald Oram, 'Pious Perjury: Discipline and Morale in the British Forces in Italy, 1917–18', *War in History* 9 (2002), 412–30, at 426.

Colonel) Charles Myers in *The Lancet* in February 1915. Similar psychological disorders had been observed in previous wars, but there was no agreed theory, diagnosis or therapy relating to the condition among medical practitioners, who were divided between physiological and psychological concepts of mental health. At one extreme, Dr L. R. Yealland used electric shock treatment at the National Hospital for Paralysed and Epileptic in London's Queen Square, while Dr R. G. Rows at the Maghull Hospital in Liverpool employed an analytical approach. There was a concern, however, that disturbed servicemen should not be consigned to institutions previously intended for pauper lunatics, and a series of special war mental hospitals was opened in Britain, such as Palace Green in Kensington and Lord Derby's War Hospital at Warrington. Nine existing asylums were also taken over in the Asylum War Hospital Scheme. Ironically, Myers himself had no qualifications in psychiatry, medical or experimental psychology, having been a member of the prewar Industrial Fatigue Research Board and of the National Institute of Industrial Psychiatry.

The predominant medical view was that of the practitioners of biological, deterministic medicine rather than those of the relatively new and controversial fields of psychiatry and psychology. The similarity of the condition with the kind of 'hysteria' normally associated with female mental disorders in itself contributed to the coining of the word 'shell shock'. Before the war, too, distinction had been drawn between traumatic neurosis, which qualified for pension rights, and traumatic hysteria, which did not. There was also a tendency to regard it as a matter of class and character, officers suffering from 'shell shock' and other ranks from varying manifestations of hysteria or hereditary mental illness. Even Dr W. H. R. Rivers, the best-known practitioner of the new psychoanalytical treatment, subscribed to the view that officers were less prone to hysteria, hence the 'country house' approach of Rivers at Craiglockhart.[48] In view of the widely divergent medical views, it was relatively easy for the military authorities to associate the condition with cowardice and malingering, a phenomenon identified before the war in industrial compensation claims. It has been suggested that there were some 325,000 psychiatric casualties during the war, 143,000 of them cases of shell shock, but this represents only 5.7 per cent of the army's military manpower.[49] War neuroses probably accounted for about 36 per cent of subsequent post-war disability pensions to servicemen.

[48] Denise Poynter, 'Regeneration Revisited: W. H. R. Rivers and Shell Shock during the Great War', in Matthew Hughes and Matthew Seligmann (eds.), *Leadership in Conflict, 1914–18* (Barnsley: Leo Cooper, 2000), 227–43.

[49] Watson, *Enduring the Great War*, 43, 239–40.

Ultimately, shell shock became a useable political issue, which meant different things to different people. It was recognised formally as a condition by the post-war War Office Committee of Enquiry into Shell-Shock, but, dominated by conservative practitioners such as Sir Frederick Mott, the committee produced a report that was highly ambiguous in its findings. It should be noted, however, that the committee was satisfied that only 186 men were sentenced to death for cowardice – the offence usually associated with shell shock – and only eighteen of these men actually were executed.

Other than mutiny or the disintegration of an army under the pressure of enemy action, the most obvious sign of military collapse was desertion or mass surrender. Surrender could be a distinctly risky practice given the propensity of soldiers to kill rather than take prisoners, although prisoners were an important source of intelligence on the Western Front, and great lengths were taken to obtain them in trench raids. Approximately 397,000 British soldiers were captured during the war, around 177,000 of them on the Western Front. While most of the latter were captured in March 1918, 21,000 of them on 21 March 1918 alone, the highest proportion of British troops surrendering rather than fighting to the death actually occurred in 1914: the ratio of soldiers captured to soldiers killed was 8:1 in August 1914 compared to 5:1 in March 1918. As with casualties generally, the fluidity of mobile warfare was more likely to lead to men being cut off and under less supervision than more static warfare. Pre-war regulars and especially recalled reservists were also probably less well prepared for the intensity of conflict than more intelligent, better educated and better prepared wartime volunteers.[50] The near collapse to apathetic surrender of the 1st Royal Warwicks and 2nd Royal Dublin Fusiliers at St. Quentin on 27 August 1914 is well known.

Of the British and Dominion POWs in German hands, a total of 11,978 died, while 575 escaped and fifty were released. The death rate was relatively high at sixty-seven per 1,000, a total of 1,280 dying from pneumonia.[51] Nonetheless, captivity was 'less violent than front line infantry life'.[52] Employing prisoners as labour immediately behind the front line flouted the conventions, which permitted the use of rank and file prisoners of war as labour in other circumstances. British POWs were placed in labour companies behind the front line for the first time in May

[50] *Ibid.*, 143–7.

[51] Mark Spoerer, 'The Mortality of Allied Prisoners of War and Belgian Civilian Deportees in German Custody during the First World War: A Reappraisal of the Effects of Forced Labour', *Population Studies* 60 (2006), 121–36.

[52] Heather Jones, *Violence against Prisoners of War in the First World War: Britain, France and Germany, 1914–20* (Cambridge University Press, 2011), 24.

1916 supposedly as a reprisal for British employment of German POWs at Rouen and Le Havre. Supposed French mistreatment of German captives and a British refusal to limit the employment of POWs to thirty kilometres behind the front then resulted in British captives being employed immediately behind the front line in March 1917. Following agreement between Britain, France and Germany, they were then removed a distance of at least thirty kilometres behind the lines in June 1917. In March 1918, however, the Germans reneged on the agreement. Violence towards prisoners was also officially sanctioned when deemed to be in operational interests, its use by the Germans becoming sufficiently routine and widespread to become entirely 'disproportionate to the intended result'.[53] Violence also increased towards British POWs held elsewhere.

In theory, these and other provisions of The Hague Convention such as prohibiting close confinement and allowing for parole should have applied to all prisoners. Subsequently, the Stockholm Protocol set minimum standards for food and accommodation in December 1915. Further agreements on repatriation of the disabled or their transfer to internment in neutral states were signed at conferences at Copenhagen, Stockholm and Kristiana in 1916 and 1917. There was provision for the exchange of the blind, amputees and the facially disfigured from March 1915 onwards, with the mentally disabled being exchanged after May 1917. Similarly, 'barbed wire disease' was recognised by an Anglo-German agreement at The Hague in July 1917. In December 1917, agreement was reached at Berne for the exchange of prisoners over the age of forty-eight who had been held for eighteen months or more.

In practice, it was often difficult for the International Red Cross's Prisoner of War Agency to inspect all camps in all belligerent states regularly. The United States and, then after 1917, Spain also had a role in supervision of arrangements, but the Spanish in particular had few representatives or resources available. Officers tended to be treated better than ordinary soldiers, though former privileges were inevitably eroded. In the case of the 6,482 British and Dominion officers who became POWs during the war, there were no clear War Office orders as to whether it was a duty to attempt escape or otherwise. Generally, escape was not seen as an officer's duty, but choices varied according to individual attitudes, and although escapers were in a minority, there were actually more successful British escapes in the Great War than in the Second World War. Moreover, the subsequent popularity of published escape narratives in the inter-war

[53] Heather Jones, 'The Final Logic of Sacrifice? Violence in German Prisoner of War Labour Companies in 1918', *The Historian* 68 (2006), 770–91, at 782.

years was to influence greatly the next generation of POWs in the Second World War so that escape became regarded more as duty. Generally, prison camp life was one of daily grind alleviated by what entertainment could be improvised. In camps holding British prisoners, freemasonry flourished. The Turks were notoriously brutal to captured British and Indian soldiers in Mesopotamia.

It has been suggested that the British women who served close to the front developed a different concept of gender from the women who remained at home. Proximity to combat, especially for nurses, evinced 'a solidarity or comradeship with [men] that overrode all distinctions'.[54] In one sense, this merely reinforced post-war gender barriers by emphasising the desire of feminists to distance themselves from masculine concepts of war. Moreover, it has been suggested that the essential division between men, who fought, and women, who did not, also widened the gender gap. As might be expected, there was a class distinction in perceptions of the war experience among women themselves.

Viewing the military experience in the Great War as a whole, it could be argued that for those not actually maimed physically or mentally by the war, wartime service had neither an overtly positive nor negative impact. Surveys undertaken by the Ministry of Labour in the 1920s show no discernible differences in rates of unemployment among ex-servicemen and those who had not served despite assumptions by many contemporaries that ex-servicemen were shouldering unemployment disproportionately. The post-war literature of disillusionment that appeared between 1928 and 1935 represented only a small fraction of the extensive creative writing that emerged from the war, only one-fifth of which was the work of combatants, with a quarter the work of women. Much of the work usually identified as anti-war was actually ambiguous in its response to the conflict, and that which was more clearly anti-war was the product of a particular mind-set.

Nonetheless, there was the legacy of the maimed, widows, orphans and other dependants. Figures vary, but there were approximately 722,700 British war dead, representing 11.8 per cent of those mobilised and 6.3 per cent of males aged between fifteen and forty-nine. The army's share of deaths was 573,497, with a further 1,642,469 men wounded. There were an additional 203,000 war dead from the Empire. It has been argued that the effect was dysgenic in that some sectors of society had volunteered in greater proportion than others, and so many working-class

[54] Susan Kingsley Kent, 'Love and Death: War and Gender in Britain, 1914–18', in Frans Coetzee and Marilyn Shevin-Coetzee (eds.), *Authority, Identity and the Social History of the Great War* (Providence, RI: Berghahn Books, 1995), 153–74, at 165.

men had been either physically unfit or exempted by reason of employment. Moreover, officers suffered proportionally more dead than other ranks, the ratio of officers killed to other ranks being 14.2:5.8 in 1914–15, 8.0:4.9 in 1915–16, 8.5:4.7 in 1916–17 and 6.9:4.0 in 1917–18. Officers also died in a greater proportion to the proportion of officers within the army. This apparent confirmation of a 'lost generation' of the future sociopolitical elite, however, was offset by the greater fertility among poorer classes and the greater availability of contraception to their social superiors.[55] Over 192,000 war widows' pensions had been granted by 1921, including provision for over 344,000 children. There had been 41,000 amputations in the army during the war, 69 per cent of a leg, 28 per cent of an arm, and 3 per cent both arms and legs.[56] In 1921, some 1.1 million men were in receipt of war disability pensions, a total of 36,400 being considered to have 100 per cent disability. The figure climbed to 2.4 million by 1929. In 1927 it was suggested that more than 4,000 ex-servicemen had developed epilepsy and more than 42,000 tuberculosis. Those suffering from war neuroses accounted for 36 per cent of those awarded disability pensions in the 1930s. There were still 3,000 limbless veterans of the Great War living in Britain in 1977 and still 27,000 in receipt of disability pensions three years later.[57]

The sense of loss could hit harder as those originally listed as missing were found subsequently to be dead, as with some 25 per cent of the 28,000 bodies of British soldiers found for the first time between 1921 and 1928, at which point the memorials to the missing in France and Flanders alone contained over 268,000 names. Bodies are still being found and sometimes identified. A total of 251 bodies, mostly Australians, killed at Fromelles in July 1916 were found in German burial pits in 2008 and re-interred in a new cemetery in 2010: 124 have so far been identified by DNA.

[55] Jay Winter, 'Some Aspects of the Demographic Consequences of the First World War in Britain', *Population Studies* 30 (1976), 539–62; Jay Winter, 'Britain's Lost Generation', 449–66.

[56] Bourke, Dismembering the Male, 33.

[57] Francis W. Hirst, *The Consequences of the War to Great Britain* (Oxford University Press, 1934), 298–99; Lyn Macdonald, *The Roses of No Man's Land* (London: Michael Joseph, 1980), 303–4. For war victims generally, including widows and dependants, see Peter Banham, *Forgotten Lunatics of the Great War* (New Haven, CT: Yale University Press, 2004); Deborah Cohen, *The War Come Home: Disabled Veterans in Britain and Germany, 1914–39* (Berkley: University of California Press, 2001); Peter Reese, *Homecoming Heroes* (London: Leo Cooper, 1992); Jeffrey Reznick, *Healing the Nation: Soldiers and the Culture of Caregiving in Britain during the Great War* (Manchester University Press, 2004); Fiona Reid, *Broken Men. Shellshock, Treatment and Recovery in Britain 1914–1930* (London: Continuum, 2011); Julie Anderson, *War, Disability and Rehabilitation in Britain: Soul of a Nation* (Manchester University Press, 2011); and Angela Smith, *Discourses Surrounding British Widows of the First World War* (London: Bloomsbury, 2012).

Potentially, there was a risk of political difficulties arising from any grievances on the part of ex-servicemen. Prior to the war, British labour had been particularly suspicious of state welfare provision, cherishing the self-help mechanisms of the friendly and co-operative societies and demanding of the state only the right to work for adequate wages. The tradition of voluntary organisations and self-help continued to be evident in the readiness to support war charities of all kinds, no less than 18,000 new such funds springing up during the war to join established charities such as the Red Cross, which collected over £22 million in Britain during the war.[58] Rather similarly, separation allowances for servicemen's wives were initially administered by the privately run Soldiers' and Sailors' Families Association, only being taken over by the Ministry of Pensions in 1916. State interference in terms of wartime dilution of labour and manpower control had been unwelcome to many. Wartime sacrifice, however, demanded appropriate reward rather than simply a restoration of the pre-war status quo, even if many also wanted diminution of state intervention once the war had ended. An enhanced level of state welfare provision was to be expected.

During the war, governments had been as careful to maintain surveillance of veterans as of civilians. In most cases, ex-servicemen were a force for conservatism in one way or another. The demobilisation disturbances in Britain in January 1919 had a limited political element linked to the possibility of service against the Bolsheviks in Russia. The great majority were related solely to demands to go home or to familiar grievances over food, compulsory church parades and working hours. Those involved in the demobilisation disturbances wanted not only to leave the army but also to sever all contact with it. Thus, most British ex-servicemen were indifferent to attempts by some veterans' organisations to forge a radical political movement.

Ex-servicemen certainly had grievances. Many tended to display some cynicism towards the 'honoured dead', casting themselves as the 'neglected living'. The pensions issue was not well handled in Britain, no statutory rights being granted until late 1919. It had been intended to pay pensions from reparation receipts, but the latter were not forthcoming. James Hogge MP had campaigned for disability pensions as early as 1917, but there was less public sympathy after the war, and with 58 per cent of the unemployed being former servicemen, it was harder still for the disabled. The seriously disabled failed to benefit from schemes such as the King's National Roll, intended to encourage employers to take on disabled ex-servicemen. There was a struggle over the kind of artificial

[58] Simon Fowler, 'War Charity Begins at Home', *History Today* 49 (1999), 17–23.

limbs that would be supplied, the authorities favouring wood over more expensive alloy: in the end, alloy was seen to be cheaper in the longer term. In the case of the psychologically damaged, a show of official concern went hand-in-hand with the reality of government trying to limit financial liabilities, a specialist on 'malingering' advising the Ministry of Pensions. Some 12,000 men were accommodated in asylums in 1922: more often than not, families were left to cope with little official help. Re-integration of the disabled was also largely left to voluntary efforts such as Oswald Stoll's War Seal Mansions, the Actresses' Franchise League's Star and Garter Homes, Mrs Gwynne Holford's Roehampton Hospital, the Lord Roberts Workshops and the Enham (now Enham Alamein) Colony founded by the Quaker, Fortescue Fox, in Hampshire. The British Limbless Ex-serviceman's Association (BLESMA), founded in 1932, was radicalised but had fewer than 2,000 members. Lord Reith of the BBC, himself a facially scarred veteran, employed similarly scarred men in the Addressing Department of *The Radio Times*, responsible for sending out copies of the magazine to subscribers. Thus, while the public often tended to lose interest in their plight, the dependence of the war disabled upon private philanthropy at least still suggested that their sacrifice was largely recognised.

The National Association of Discharged Sailors and Soldiers (NADSS), formed in Blackburn in September 1916; the National Federation of Discharged and Demobilised Sailors and Soldiers (NFDSS), formed in London in April 1917; and the Comrades of the Great War (CGW), formed in August 1917, were created as pressure groups in response to the government's ad hoc approach to such matters as pensions, rehabilitation and disabilities. Both NADSS and NFDSS were mildly radical, loosely sympathising, respectively, with the Independent Labour Party and the Liberals. By contrast, Lord Derby encouraged CGW as a Conservative riposte after the NFDSS put up a candidate against Derby's son in a by-election in Liverpool in June 1917. Twenty-nine candidates were put up by NADSS and NFDSS in the 1918 election, and one, Robert Barker from NADSS, was elected for Sowerby in West Yorkshire. Far more radical was the Soldiers', Sailors' and Airmens' Union (SSAU). Formed in January 1919 with the support of *The Daily Herald* as an association of socialist servicemen, it was supposedly about 10,000 strong. In actuality, it had few members and was successfully infiltrated by the A2 Section of the Adjutant General's Department. It was moribund by June 1919, only one issue of its journal, *The Forces*, ever appearing. There were also two even more radical splinter groups from NFDSS, the National Union of Ex-servicemen (NUX), formed in May 1919, and the International Union of Ex-servicemen (IUX), formed in Glasgow the same month.

Fragmentation of the movement resulted in bitter rivalries, such as that which led to a serious riot at Luton in Bedfordshire during supposed 'peace celebrations' in July 1919, when the town hall was gutted. As it happened, however, most involved in the disturbances at Luton and similar incidents at Doncaster and Swindon were not ex-servicemen. Moreover, even the more radical veterans baulked at close co-operation with industrial militants who had stayed at home while they fought.

Much of the basis of veterans' grievances was removed by government concessions on pensions in August 1919, followed by preferential treatment at labour exchanges and official encouragement of assistance to ex-servicemen by voluntary agencies. By July 1921, NADSS, NFDSS and CGW had combined in a new British Legion under Haig's leadership. Haig's initial involvement had been with the Officers' Association, started in January 1920 to provide for the many wartime officers of lesser means, some 25,000 former officers being among the unemployed. How far the British Legion was Haig's creation is a matter of debate. Certainly, a crucial role was also played by Thomas Lister of NFDSS, James Howell of NADSS, George Gosfield of CGW and Sir Frederick Maurice of the Officers' Association, which also joined the Legion. The Legion rejected political partisanship. Through the participation of some ex-officers, it also replicated the army's hierarchy, albeit often to the annoyance of former rank and file members, who were wary of the anti-socialist theme of the leadership. Indeed, *The Daily Herald* and other left-wing newspapers were apt to refer to the Legion as 'Haig's White Guard'.

If slow, the Legion's growth was steady with, by 1938, just over 409,000 members, many of whom were disabled. While there was some thought of being a political pressure group, the Legion soon became effectively a charitable organisation. The Legion's first Poppy Day in November 1921 began the annual process of raising funds for ex-servicemen after the success of a similar poppy appeal for American ex-servicemen by the American Legion. Indeed, poppies became the biggest annual charity appeal in inter-war Britain, gross receipts rising to over £578,000 by 1938: the Legion was spending about £1 million per annum on welfare. Increasing unemployment rendered many unable either to join or to participate in the Legion's social activities, and there was a distinct correlation between membership and unemployment patterns across the country. Generally, there were at least 300,000 unemployed unskilled ex-servicemen for much of the inter-war period. While, therefore, the Legion generated its own internal dynamic as a charity, it had little influence and appeared increasingly outdated.

With the appearance of the British Legion, the other radical veterans' groups simply disbanded. Indeed, the closest comparison of any British ex-servicemen's organisation with those abroad is arguably the 7,000 members of the Black and Tans and the 1,418 members of the Auxiliary Division of the Royal Irish Constabulary (RIC), both recruited to fight in the Anglo-Irish War of 1919–21. In June 1922, ex-servicemen in Tonypandy, a town famously though inaccurately known for the supposed order for troops to open fire on striking miners there in 1910, offered their services to the King to serve anywhere in the empire following the IRA's murder of Field Marshal Sir Henry Wilson. Ironically, Wilson's two assassins were ex-servicemen. The record of the Black and Tans together with the experience of the 1919 disturbances led to some fears that men had become generally brutalised through the war, as was also to be the case with the Freikorps in Germany. Some former activists in the veterans' movement became associates of Oswald Mosley's British Union of Fascists (BUF) in 1932. The BUF had some similarity of philosophy with the NUX and IUX, but Mosley did not seek to recruit veterans exclusively, and relatively few were drawn to his movement.[59]

One specific measure taken for the relief of British ex-servicemen was in land settlement schemes, initially seen as a response to the task of rehabilitating disabled veterans. Provision was made for three experimental domestic colonies by the Small Holdings and Allotments Act of 1916. The war ended before any wider scheme had been implemented, and the scheme in Britain was killed off by financial retrenchment in 1921. Over the country as a whole, only some 24,000 candidates had been accepted by 1921, of whom only just over 9,000 had been allotted smallholdings. By 1923, the total had risen to about 19,000, while, in Scotland, some 6,000 allotments were provided for ex-servicemen.

In Ireland, it was believed that local authorities in the south, which had become dominated by nationalists, could not be trusted to house ex-

[59] For British veterans, see Englander and Osborne, 'Jack, Tommy and Henry Dubb', 593–621; David Englander, 'Troops and Trade Unions, 1919', *History Today* 37 (1987), 8–13; David Englander, 'Military Intelligence and the Defence of the Realm', *Bulletin of the Society for the Study of Labour History* 52 (1987), 24–32; David Englander, 'The National Union of Ex-Servicemen and the Labour Movement, 1918–20', *History* 76 (1991), 24–42; Stephen R. Ward, 'Intelligence Surveillance of British Ex-servicemen, 1918–20', *Historical Journal* 16 (1973), 179–88; Stephen R. Ward, 'Great Britain: Land Fit for Heroes Lost', in Stephen R. Ward (ed.), *The War Generation: Veterans of the First World War* (Port Washington, NY: Kennikat Press, 1975), 10–37; Stephen R. Ward, 'The British Veterans Ticket of 1918', *Journal of British Studies* 8 (1968), 155–69; Niall Barr, 'The British Legion after the Great War: Its Identity and Character', in Bertrand Tithe and Tim Thornton (eds.), *War: Identities in Conflict* (Stroud: Sutton, 1999), 213–33; Niall Barr, *The Lion and the Poppy: British Veterans, Politics and Society, 1921–1939* (Westport, CT: Praeger, 2005).

servicemen, while state promotion of a scheme would give ex-servicemen a stake in the status quo. In the event, the scheme to provide smallholdings or cottages was affected both by post-war financial retrenchment and the creation of the Free State in 1921. After negotiation with the Free State and establishment of the Irish Soldiers' and Sailors' Land Trust in 1922–3, the scheme was limited to 3,672 dwellings, of which 2,626 were in southern Ireland and 1,046 in Ulster. The target was only met in 1933, although the trust survived until 1987. Unemployment was to prove higher among ex-servicemen in southern Ireland than in the rest of the United Kingdom due to Sinn Féin's pressure on employers not to hire them, while cottages and smallholdings were vandalised. There were also instances of intimidation and murder, at least 120 ex-servicemen being killed in the south between 1919 and 1924.

With failure of the domestic settlement scheme, imperialists such as Lord Milner and Leo Amery, appointed as Colonial Secretary and Under-Secretary, respectively, in January 1919, promoted soldier settlement as an imperial policy. In April 1919 it was announced that free passage to the Dominions would be granted for ex-servicemen and their dependants for a year from January 1920; the deadline was extended subsequently to March 1923. In all, some 37,199 ex-servicemen accompanied by 48,828 dependants took up the free-passage option, accounting for 12 per cent of British emigration to the Empire between 1919 and 1922.[60] Fears of dislocation after the war had prompted similar schemes within the Dominions themselves.

With additional hopes of reducing rural depopulation, Canada began an assisted colonisation scheme in February 1917, and a Soldier Settlement Act was passed in May 1917. Ex-servicemen from Britain were offered the chance for selective immigration to reinforce homogeneity after the problems experienced with aliens during the war. As a result, there was a revitalised effort under the Soldier Settlement Act of 1919. Under the British and Canadian schemes, almost 25,000 soldier settlers did try agriculture, of whom almost 11,000, or 43 per cent, were still on the land in 1931. Moreover, even where the veterans failed, many of the farms were resold to other immigrants. Consequently, soldier settlement in Canada was by no means a total failure.

A New Zealand scheme was initiated as early as October 1915 under the Discharged Soldier Settlement Act, the government settling just over 9,000 Anzac veterans by 1919–20. The cost aroused opposition since the

60 Kent Federowich, 'The Assisted Emigration of British Ex-Servicemen to the Dominions, 1914–22', in Stephen Constantine (ed.), *Emigrants and Empire* (Manchester University Press, 1990), 45–71.

state was buying cultivated land at inflated prices when large areas of Crown land remained undeveloped. Some New Zealanders opposed British veteran immigration unless carefully controlled, but, in fact, only just over 13,000 ex-servicemen and dependants, or 15.5 per cent of the total, went to New Zealand on free passage. As elsewhere, depressed prices hit in the 1920s, and government curtailed the acceptance of ex-servicemen unless they were already assured employment and accommodation. Settling soldiers, however, gave a stimulus to town planning in New Zealand.[61]

There was a similar attempt to increase British veteran migration to South Africa in order to restore British numbers after the failure of earlier attempts encouraged by the English-speaking Unionist Party. Afrikaners opposed preference given to ex-servicemen at the expense of poor whites, and the South African government was understandably wary of the scheme. Consequently, only 6,064 ex-servicemen and dependants, or 7 per cent of those taking up free passage from Britain, went to South Africa. A small number of British veterans also settled in Kenya and Southern Rhodesia. In Australia, British veterans were also welcomed, and the 37,000 ex-servicemen or dependants opting to take free passage to Australia were by far the largest proportion, at 43.7 per cent of the total.[62]

Commemoration lies outside the scope of this book, but it can be noted that while some early Armistice Days were the focus of protest by unemployed ex-servicemen, as in Liverpool and Dundee in 1921, ex-servicemen's groups more generally regarded Armistice Day as a day of festivity in the early 1920s. Indeed, the resulting public controversy led to the cancellation in 1925 of the former annual Victory Ball in the Albert Hall, its replacement in 1926 being a performance of a requiem for war charities and, then in 1927, by the first Festival of Remembrance. If commemoration was a positive or even frivolous activity for some, there was also that general means by which many men recognised their wartime service through attending annual reunions of divisional and regimental old comrades' associations and through the purchase of the plethora of divisional and regimental histories that appeared in the 1920s and 1930s.[63] The British Army's post-war recruitment was relatively buoyant,

[61] J. M. Powell, 'Soldier Settlement in New Zealand, 1915–23', *Australian Geographical Studies* 9 (1971), 144–60.

[62] Kent Federowich, '"Society Pets and Morning Coated Farmers": Australian Soldier Settlement and the Participation of British Ex-servicemen, 1915–29', *War & Society* 8 (1990), 38–56.

[63] Keith Grieves, 'Making Sense of the Great War: Regimental Histories, 1918–23', *Journal of the Society for Army Historical Research* 69 (1991), pp. 6–15; Keith Grieves,

providing little evidence of any immediate revulsion against matters military.[64]

If the impact of the war upon the individual was not as great as has been supposed, it is certainly clear that in the case of the British Army, expansion had little impact on the army as an institution. In that sense, the army differed little in the 1920s from what it had been in the Edwardian era, and some undoubtedly welcomed a return to 'real soldering' on the frontiers of Empire. But, although it was not until the Kirke Committee was established in 1932 that there was a formal enquiry to establish the military lessons of the Great War, the experience of wartime expansion, and of coming to terms with citizens in arms on a massive scale, would stand the army in good stead for the next global conflict.[65]

'Remembering an Ill-fated Venture: The 4th Battalion, Royal Sussex Regiment at Suvla Bay and its Legacy, 1915–39', in Macleod (ed.), *Gallipoli: Making History*, 110–24; Helen McCartney, 'Interpreting Unit Histories: Gallipoli and After', in Macleod (ed.), *Gallipoli: Making History*, 125–35; Dan Todman, *The First World War: Myth and Memory* (London: Hambledon, 2005), 187–90.

64 Keith Jeffery, 'The Post-War Army', in Beckett and Simpson (eds.), *Nation in Arms*, 211–34.

65 For the inter-war period, see Brian Bond, *British Military Policy between the Two World Wars* (Oxford, UK: Clarendon Press, 1980); David French, *Raising Churchill's Army: The British Army and the War against Germany, 1919–45* (Oxford University Press, 2000).

5 British Strategy and the British Army

Writing to a young woman with whom he was obsessed – Venetia Stanley – the Prime Minister, Herbert Asquith, set down on 2 August 1914, as much for his own benefit as for hers, the respective obligations and interests underlying the British position in respect to the deteriorating diplomatic situation in Europe. Austria-Hungary had declared war on Serbia on 28 July, and Germany had declared war on Russia on 1 August. On the same day that Asquith was setting down his thoughts, Germany had invaded Luxembourg and demanded passage for its troops through Belgium. Britain was a guarantor of Belgian neutrality under the Treaty of London of 1839, though the Foreign Office had concluded that this did not require Britain to go to Belgium's assistance in all circumstances. Some pre-war British military and naval planners had themselves contemplated violating Belgian neutrality, if necessary to do so, in order to take a war to Germany. There was also some debate on how substantial a violation of neutrality would need to be in order to trigger a British response. In addition, there was an expectation on the part of the Foreign Secretary, Sir Edward Grey, that he could mediate successfully. In view of the difficulties of carrying the Cabinet on intervention, it was only the threat of resignation by Grey and Asquith that had brought an honouring of pre-war naval commitments to France on 2 August to safeguard the Channel while the French fleet deployed to the Mediterranean. As late as 31 July, only two Cabinet ministers supported intervention, with five for neutrality and twelve as yet undecided. The Cabinet had rejected sending the British Expeditionary Force (BEF) to France on 29 July and did so again on 1 August. There was little sympathy for Serbia, extending to Asquith himself, and the public mood was still generally against intervention. Moreover, the French were so far from confident of British assistance materialising that they had not actually included the BEF in their line of battle despite the staff planning that had taken place since the initiation of talks between the British and French general staffs in 1905.

In Asquith's own mind at least, there was an obligation to defend Belgium but none actually owed to France and Russia beyond the 'long standing and intimate relationship' with the former, although even these tentative alliances really dated only from 1904 and 1907, respectively. Britain's interests, however, in preventing the elimination of France as a great power and in preventing Germany from establishing any hostile bases on the Channel coast were paramount.[1] It was simply not in Britain's long-term strategic interests to allow Germany either to dominate the Low Countries and the Channel ports or to upset the balance of power in Europe. Nor is it likely that, even if Germany's immediate war aims had been limited by a need to ensure British neutrality, a victorious Germany would not have soon threatened British interests. It has been argued that firmer British diplomatic action in the 'July crisis' following the assassination of the Archduke Franz Ferdinand at Sarajevo on 28 June 1914 would have had an additional deterrent effect on Germany. This appears highly unlikely. While an increasingly unfashionable view, and unpleasant though the consequences were for Britain, it was a necessary war in contemporary terms.

Effectively, it was the German ultimatum to Belgium rather than the actual German invasion of France and Belgium on 3 August that triggered the British ultimatum to Germany, which expired at 11 PM on 4 August 1914. Irrespective of whether there was actually a moral obligation to support France, the German demands on Belgium certainly let Asquith off the hook with regard to Liberal opposition to a continental involvement and in terms of establishing a degree of popular support for war. In the event, only two Cabinet ministers resigned.

The question remains, however, of how Britain had gone from a situation of 'splendid isolation' at the end of the nineteenth century to one of potential commitment to a continental involvement. To a large degree, it was a consequence of the South African War. Rather than the three- or four-month campaign requiring no more than 75,000 men originally expected, it had taken thirty-two months, the expenditure of £230 million and the eventual deployment of 448,000 men from Britain and the Empire to overcome what amounted to a handful of farmers. The Boers had never fielded more than about 42,000 men and, following the defeat of the main Boer field army in February 1900, never more than about 9,000 on commando. By March 1900, there was but a single regular battalion left in Britain. Though drawing on the manpower of its white colonies, Britain had been otherwise totally diplomatically isolated.

[1] Michael and Eleanor Brock (eds.), *H. H. Asquith: Letters to Venetia Stanley* (Oxford University Press, 1982), 145–7.

Significantly, over 2,500 foreign volunteers from Europe – including an Irish contingent – and the United States had fought for the Boers. Additionally, by 1900, Britain had already been outstripped by both Germany and the United States in industrial production in such areas as coal, pig iron and steel, continued British primacy resting more upon financial capital, shipping and primary products than manufactured goods or new technologies. Thus, from a situation in 1899 where Britain was responsible for 38.3 per cent of global manufactured exports and 20.8 per cent of global manufactured output, its share had declined, respectively, to 31.8 and 15.8 per cent by 1914. Britain's growth rate between 1870 and 1913 was 1.6 per cent per annum, while Germany's was 4.7 per cent and that of the United States some 5 per cent.[2]

It has been argued that financial primacy in world trade, and the extent of its Empire, could not compensate Britain for longer-term decline, and it masked the strategic and political implications. Britain, therefore, was less able to out-build naval opponents with her former ease or compete realistically with continental powers when numbers secured by conscription were the yardsticks of military power.[3] Yet, conversely, it has been maintained that British weakness has been exaggerated, for the impact of its predominance in global finance has been underestimated: sterling was the preferred international currency and its reserve currency. Britain controlled 70 per cent of global cable communications, and its merchant marine remained the largest in the world, giving Britain a stranglehold over the infrastructure of global trade.[4]

Yet, there were certainly contemporary fears of decline. In January 1904, for example, the geographer, Sir Halford Mackinder, contended that there was now a correlation between geographical and historical generalisations, suggesting the decline of maritime power and the emergence of a strategic Eurasian 'heartland' that would determine international development through size and numbers. There were particular concerns that the 'two-power' standard that had governed naval expenditure since the Naval Defence Act of 1889, by which the Royal Navy would maintain a number of capital ships equal to the combined strength of the next two largest navies – then France and Russia – was increasingly

[2] Marcello De Cecco, *Money and Empire: The International Gold Standard, 1890–1914* (Oxford: Blackwell, 1974), 26; Aaron Friedberg, *The Weary Titan: Britain and the Experience of Relative Decline, 1895–1905* (Princeton, NJ: Princeton University Press, 1988), 25.

[3] Paul Kennedy, 'Strategy versus Finance in Twentieth Century Britain', *International History Review* 3 (1981), 44–61.

[4] Keith Neilson, 'Great Exaggerated: The Myth of the Decline of Great Britain before 1914', *International History Review* 13 (1991), 695–725; Niall Ferguson, *The Pity of War: Explaining World War I* (London: Allen Lane, 1998), 33–5.

unsustainable given new American and German naval construction since the 1890s. There had already been a certain acceptance of reliance upon American goodwill in the western hemisphere. The Anglo-Japanese Treaty of January 1902 not only addressed global diplomatic isolation but also offset any Franco-Russian naval threat in Far Eastern waters, as well as avoiding any weakening of capabilities in European waters.

In opening the Colonial Conference in June 1902, the Colonial Secretary, Joseph Chamberlain, pointedly remarked: 'The Weary Titan staggers under the too vast orb of its fate.'[5] Chamberlain anticipated that the white colonies would help to pick up the military burden of imperial defence, but he was also to launch his campaign for tariff reform in May 1903 in the expectation that a system of imperial preference – free trade within the Empire – and of tariffs to counter European and American protectionism would establish an economic bloc to rival Germany and the United States. The latter campaign failed to draw sufficient public support and contributed to the defeat of the Unionist government at the polls in January and February 1906. The former aspiration also remained largely unfulfilled. The idea for an 'imperial pool' of troops was aired at the 1902 Colonial Conference, but only the New Zealand Prime Minister, Richard Seddon, whose 1900 Defence Act already permitted the transfer of volunteers into such an imperial reserve for service overseas, gave it much support. Seddon envisaged the cost being borne by the imperial government, but this found little favour with the Colonial Defence Committee or the Secretary of State for War, St. John Brodrick, and the proposal foundered. The 1907 Colonial Conference was more positive in advancing ideas for greater military integration, though New Zealand and South Africa were more co-operative than Canada or Australia. At the Colonial Conference in July 1909, summoned chiefly as a result of Australian and Canadian naval aspirations, the colonies were persuaded to adopt British unit establishment scales and equipment and regulations, as well as also establishing an imperial general staff. *Field Service Regulations* were imperial documents and imposed a common doctrine at least in theory. In practical terms, however, little had been achieved in terms of colonial and Dominion participation in War Office strategic planning by 1914. More had been achieved in naval terms.

There had also been increasing and unrealistic demands from the Indian military establishment for substantial reinforcements to be available for Indian defence. The Viceroy, Lord Curzon, suggested in 1901 that 30,000 men would represent only an immediate reinforcement in the

[5] Friedberg, *Weary Titan*, 116.

event of a Russian attack on India, and a further 70,000 men would be required to follow. Even the strong former advocate of Indian priorities, Field Marshal Lord Roberts, now Commander-in-Chief at the War Office, indicated in 1904 that no more than 48,000 men could be sent to India in an emergency. The ever-increasing forecasts of the reinforcements needed by Lord Kitchener as Commander-in-Chief in India between 1902 and 1911 – ultimately amounting to 160,000 men in the first year of a war with Russia and 300,000 more in the second year – was one of the factors that prompted the government to seek the diplomatic solution of the Anglo-Russian entente of 1907. Kitchener's earlier demands had already contributed to the renewal of the Anglo-Japanese alliance in 1905, the negotiations embracing the unlikely possibility of deploying Japanese troops on the North West Frontier.

Far from being motivated by some far-sighted assessment of an emerging German threat, the military reforms of the new Liberal Secretary of State for War, R. B. Haldane, were driven by economic considerations in the light of the costs of the South African War, the annual estimates having peaked at £92.3 million in 1902 and still reaching £69.4 million in 1903. Haldane announced an absolute ceiling of £28 million in January 1906. The estimates then came in at £27.7 million in both 1907–8 and 1908–9. Recurring financial retrenchment was hardly a novel experience for the army. The BEF of six infantry divisions and one cavalry division represented the maximum number that could be formed from forces maintained at home for draft-finding purposes, and the divisional scales conformed entirely to the pattern of the Indian Army. It reflected precisely the assumption of the Director of Military Operations (DMO), Sir James Grierson, in July 1904 that 'great' divisions gave flexibility since 'it was impossible to foretell whether our field army will be employed in India, Canada, South Africa, or elsewhere'.[6] Then Quartermaster-General, the future Chief of the Imperial General Staff (CIGS), Sir William Nicholson, similarly argued in March 1906 that war organisation should not be predicated on a single contingency and that divisions were more flexible than the corps some were suggesting were more suited to European campaigning and could easily be combined.

Grierson's stance is particularly significant given his role in the Anglo-French staff talks in 1905–6 that are generally viewed as a dramatic departure from previous strategic assumptions. What might be termed

[6] John Gooch, 'Haldane and the National Army', in Ian F. W. Beckett and John Gooch (eds.), *Politicians and Defence: Studies in the Formulation of British Defence Policy, 1845–1970* (Manchester University Press, 1981), 69–87, at 74.

the prevailing strategic orthodoxy in the War Office prior to the South African War was encapsulated in the Stanhope Memorandum of December 1888, which had answered previous military demands by providing firm guidance as to the contingencies for which the army might be required to plan and the purposes that it fulfilled. It famously ordered priorities as aid to the civil power in the United Kingdom, the provision of drafts for India, the provision of garrisons for colonies and coaling stations, the provision of two corps for home defence and the possible employment of one of the corps in a European war, though this was deemed so improbable that nothing need be done to prepare for such an eventuality. The juxtaposition of priorities was entirely logical in the light of prevailing circumstances, reflecting contemporary fears and the strategic views of the majority of Stanhope's advisers.[7] Traditional considerations continued to feature in strategic calculation. The newly established Committee of Imperial Defence (CID), part of the 'managerial revolution' in defence ushered in by the South African War and intended to provide strategic advice to the Cabinet, still considered the defence of India at fifty of its eighty meetings between 1903 and 1905. It also conducted three major invasion enquiries between 1903 and 1914. The Royal Navy's position that invasion was impossible was accepted by the CID in 1903 and 1908, yet it still recommended in October 1908 that two of Haldane's six regular divisions be retained in Britain after mobilisation and re-iterated this in a further enquiry in April 1914. Two divisions were indeed initially held back in Britain in August 1914.

Those diplomatic agreements reached with France in April 1904 and Russia in August 1907 not only reflected alarm at Britain's diplomatic isolation but also a growing concern that Germany threatened the European status quo. The entente with France implied no real commitment, but in April 1905 a war game played in the War Office suggested that if the Germans were to invade Belgium, any British intervention must be swift if there was any hope of it being effective. On 19 December 1905, while the general election campaign was being fought, an informal caucus from the CID – the so-called Whitehall Gardens Sub-committee – agreed that the British should intervene in such circumstances and authorised the General Staff to seek military staff talks with the French General Staff. Of the four members of the sub-committee, only two were regular members: Sir George Clarke, the secretary to the CID, and Captain Charles Ottley, the Director of Naval Intelligence. The third, Lord Esher, had only just become a permanent member, and the fourth present – Sir John

[7] Ian F. W. Beckett, 'The Stanhope Memorandum of 1888: A Reinterpretation', *Bulletin of the Institute of Historical Research* 57 (1984), 240–7.

French commanding the corps at Aldershot – was not a member of the CID at all. As it happened, Grierson, had come to the same conclusion independently and was also keen to approach the French. He joined the others in their deliberations in January 1906, contacts with the French being established through the agency of the military correspondent of the *Times*, Charles Repington, and the French military attaché in London, Colonel Victor Huguet. A meeting of the CID itself on 6 January 1906 endorsed the talks in the face of what appeared to be Admiralty indifference to Clarke's enquiries concerning a possible alternative amphibious strategy against Germany. It became a matter of whether any British expeditionary force should be placed in Belgium or with the French Army in the event of war. Talks, which had never been authorised, were concealed from most members of the incoming Liberal government. Their continuation was a War Office initiative – Grierson's successor as Director of Military Operations (DMO), Sir John Spencer Ewart, maintained the contacts – since the First Sea Lord, Sir John Fisher, withdrew Ottley from the deliberations in January 1906, and Clarke also dropped his support for an overt continental commitment.

A Military Needs of the Empire Sub-committee of the CID considered the resulting plans for intervention in October 1908 at the War Office's request as a consequence of tensions between France and Germany and Austria-Hungary's annexation of Bosnia and Herzegovina. Fisher believed the exercise to be something of a sham intended merely to improve the War Office's financial position, and it has been suggested generally that the Admiralty's own potential war plans were rejected by default because they were never fully articulated.[8] While the CID resolved on 24 July 1909 that the War Office should continue planning to send four infantry divisions and one cavalry division to France if it was attacked by Germany, this did not amount in any way to a government endorsement of such a course of action. Moreover, the Admiralty's plans for an alternative economic strategy were discussed.

The War Office scheme remained a plan only in principle until Henry Wilson became DMO in June 1910 and assiduously worked in drawing up detailed mobilisation schedules and plans. Under these plans, the BEF would be concentrated at Mauberge, a general assumption being that any German advance into Belgium would be confined to the area south of the Meuse. At a celebrated meeting of the CID on 23 August 1911, consequent upon the Agadir crisis in Europe, Wilson effectively demolished the Admiralty case presented by his namesake, the First Sea Lord, Admiral of

[8] John Gooch, *The Plans of War: The General Staff and British Military Strategy, c. 1900–16* (London: Routledge & Kegan Paul, 1974), 287–8.

the Fleet Sir Arthur Wilson, who had been brought back from retirement when Fisher resigned in January 1910. Arthur Wilson had shown no particular interest in ongoing Admiralty planning for economic warfare against Germany, was badly prepared for what he assumed was only another War Office ploy for additional funding rather than a serious discussion of strategic options and was fatally drawn into a muddled discussion of his personal ideas for an amphibious strategy against the German coast that had no Admiralty backing.

The meeting is invariably seen as a pivotal success for the War Office with momentous consequences, not least for the Royal Navy. The Home Secretary, Winston Churchill, and French, now CIGS, demonstrated, however, a concern that the British should not be too closely tied to the French Army and should be free to co-operate more with the Belgians. For all Wilson's skill in presenting the case for the so-called WF ('With France') Plan, neither the existence of his schedules nor his machinations did of themselves commit the British government to military intervention. Those like Churchill who favoured intervention on the continent were made wary of the opposition among many of their own Cabinet colleagues when the nature of the contacts between the British and French general staffs was finally revealed in November 1911.

Moreover, within the army, some like Sir John French remained attracted to what is sometimes called the 'Belgian option' as likely to serve British strategic interests better than simple subordination to French military planning. The meeting of the CID in 1911 had not actually finally determined future strategy since no decision had been reached. In any case, the CID was not an executive body, and only the Cabinet could take a decision on continental intervention as and when circumstances arose to suggest its necessity. The only immediate result was the replacement of Reginald McKenna as First Lord of the Admiralty by Churchill and Churchill's near clean sweep of the Admiralty's naval leadership that in itself was of considerable significance for naval planning. French, of course, had taken part in the deliberations of the CID sub-committee on strategic choices that had examined the Belgian option in 1905 and which had also actually initiated the first staff conversations with the French. Though he had kept in touch with Grierson, French did not take part in the subsequent discussions that led to the conclusion that the WF option was preferable due to the Belgians rebuffing British approaches for fear of it compromising their neutrality. The difficulty with the 'Belgian option', indeed, lay in the general uncertainty as to Belgian intentions. The Belgians again rebuffed British approaches in 1912 to the extent that, in 1914, the Belgian Army deployed against a possible British invasion as well as against French and German intervention. The preliminary planning that was undertaken also suggested that the BEF would still need to disembark at French ports whatever the final destination, and there were serious doubts as to the efficiency of the Belgian Army.

Before the war, Sir John had invariably appeared sufficiently friendly in contacts with French officers observing British manoeuvres for them to assume his general support for close co-operation. Sir John was motivated rather more by the wish to maintain independence from the French high command, since Britain would clearly be the junior partner in a wartime alliance. Indeed, he had expressed just such a belief during the deliberations of another CID sub-committee in January 1909, at which point he also favoured holding the BEF in reserve, perhaps at Amiens, so that it might be available for operations in Belgium. In short, though French was a continentalist, he was also a nationalist intent on using the BEF in British rather than French interests.

The strategic debate was unresolved, and there was an extraordinary meeting of a so-called War Council on 5 August 1914. A variety of prominent military and naval officers – eighteen persons were present – were summoned to meet with Asquith, Churchill and the acting Secretary of State for War Haldane and debate the options afresh, notwithstanding the fact that all mobilisation plans were geared to a concentration at Mauberge. Wilson characterised the assembly as 'an historic meeting of men, mostly entirely ignorant of their subject'.[9] To Wilson's dismay, French was able to resurrect the Belgian option by arguing for landing the BEF at, or marching it to, Antwerp, although he also suggested that it might be concentrated in a reserve deployment at Amiens in order to see how matters developed. The commander of I Corps, Sir Douglas Haig, similarly suggested delaying the dispatch of the BEF for at least three months, albeit on the grounds that it would be beneficial to await the arrival of British and imperial forces from overseas. Though Wilson admitted that some thought had been given to a concentration at Amiens, Antwerp was deemed impossible both on logistic grounds and also through naval fears of operating in confined waters. It was tentatively agreed to send the BEF to France but to leave any decision as to its line of operations until after the French had been consulted. A second meeting of the War Council on 6 August endorsed an earlier Cabinet decision that day to dispatch only four of the six infantry divisions of the BEF before the defence of Britain had been properly secured. French as well as Kitchener, who was appointed Secretary of State for War on 5 August,

[9] William Philpott, *Anglo-French Relations and Strategy on the Western Front, 1914–18* (Basingstoke: Macmillan, 1996), 8.

continued to press for concentration at Amiens. On 12 August, however, Wilson and a French delegation finally persuaded Sir John and Kitchener to concentrate at Mauberge as originally intended. The episode demonstrated Sir John French's continuing commitment to the idea of operating on the allied left flank, a concept revived subsequently with movement of the BEF to Belgium in September 1914 amid the German operations to seize Antwerp.

Soldiers like French do not conform readily to the older perception that a 'revolution' had occurred in British military planning between 1902 and 1905. There were British politicians, too, for whom a strategy of strictly limited liability, confining British effort to imposing an economic blockade and bankrolling the French and Russians to undertake the main effort on land, was an attractive option in 1914. It has been argued that the adoption of a strategy of attrition in the summer of 1916 spelled the end of a real alternative strategy in British policy circles that was associated principally with the Home Secretary, Reginald McKenna, who was to become Chancellor of the Exchequer in May 1915, and the President of the Board of Trade from August 1914 to December 1916, Walter Runciman. Previously, as President of the Board of Agriculture, Runciman had presided over one of the pre-war committees intended to mitigate the likely consequences of the disruption of North Sea trade in the event of war.

McKenna and Runciman saw no advantage in raising a large army or risking economic exhaustion, believing that the best way to sustain the entente would be by continuing to bankroll it and to maintain the economic blockade by capitalising on Britain's maritime strength. A strategy of 'limited liability' or 'business as usual', it promised maximum advantage at minimum cost with continued economic primacy after the war since domestic production and overseas exports would be maintained.[10] McKenna suggested in December 1915 that victory would be assured if 'we retain unimpaired our power to assist in financing, supplying and carrying for the Allies, but retention of that power is probably the most indispensable element of success'. Rather bitterly, the CIGS, Sir William Robertson, described it in January 1916 as 'to find out what is the smallest amount of money & smallest number of men with which we may hope, some day, to win the war, or rather not to lose it'.[11] In part, while their arguments were economic rather than specifically strategic, it could be

[10] David French, 'The Rise and Fall of Business as Usual', in Kathleen Burk (ed.), *War and the State: The Transformation of British Government, 1914–18* (London: Allen & Unwin, 1982), 7–31.

[11] David French, *British Strategy and War Aims, 1914–16* (London: Allen & Unwin, 1986), 247.

said that McKenna and Runciman echoed the concept of a 'British way in warfare' from the period of the eighteenth century when, supposedly, Britain had acquired its Empire and defeated France by using the Royal Navy to impose a blockade and utilising the army to seize colonies. The concept of such a maritime strategy had been given currency by the naval historian and theorist Sir Julian Corbett in *Some Principles of Maritime Strategy* in 1911, while the efficacy of sea power had been greatly publicised in the 1890s by the works of American naval theorist Alfred Thayer Mahan. A 'British way in warfare', however, had little historical substance, for Britain had only been able to prevail in its great power wars with the assistance of allies: the only war lost was that for America, when Britain was without a continental ally. It had also always been necessary to dispatch sizeable forces to fight on the continent.

Limited liability, however, should not be confused with limited effort in terms of the naval contribution to the war and the conflict outside Europe. McKenna, indeed, thought more in terms of Britain fighting to the limit of its financial capacity. Moreover, it has also been argued that the Admiralty – McKenna had been First Lord prior to Churchill – had developed a sophisticated concept of economic warfare by 1912 since it was well recognised that the blockade system used in the French Revolutionary and Napoleonic Wars was no longer relevant to an age of global trade. Therefore, it is suggested, rather than the previous assumption that the Admiralty planned the defeat of the High Seas Fleet at sea or the other means of applying maritime power such as through amphibious operations or a slow strangulation by blockade, the Admiralty intended to impose a swift dislocation of the German economy. Hinted at by Fisher at the Military Needs of the Empire Sub-committee in 1908, it is contended that this Admiralty plan had been under development since 1907. Notwithstanding the apparent result of the CID meeting in August 1911, therefore, the CID's Trading with the Enemy Sub-committee, chaired by Lord Desart, had begun work in January 1911. Its report, formally adopted on 6 December 1912, endorsed the idea that the German economy would be swiftly strangled by closing down trade through Belgium and the Netherlands and taking control of the British merchant marine to prevent strategic materials being traded through neutrals. In the event, concern for neutral opinion – not least that of the United States – led the Foreign Office to oppose the Admiralty's plans. Other government departments were also to resent Admiralty interference, as did business and a banking sector already alarmed by the general disruption in financial markets once economic measures were duly implemented on 5 August. Consequently, they were then significantly diluted in a series of Cabinet discussions between 13 and 21 August 1914 so that, instead of economic warfare, it was a less effective blockade that was implemented. It might be added, however, that this revisionist version of an Admiralty economic strategy rests on a problematic reading of some of the documents, the contention that no one believed in a lengthy war and that the Admiralty eschewed all idea of amphibious operations.[12]

Naval blockade, as Corbett had recognised long before, could not result in any swift German economic collapse. Intensification also required the neutralisation of the German High Seas Fleet. This was desirable in any case but was difficult to achieve when the Germans declined on most occasions to contest a naval battle in the North Sea. There was also a greater possibility of the British losing the war through naval action than by winning it. Britain itself was less self-sufficient and more vulnerable to counter-economic warfare than in the past. Blockade, indeed, only began to make an impact once a Ministry of Blockade was established in February 1916 and, more crucially, the United States ceased to be a neutral in April 1917. Just as the Admiralty's alternative economic warfare strategy, if it truly existed, failed to materialise, so the raising of the Kitchener 'New Armies' also effectively undermined any strategy of 'business as usual' predicated on minimum social and economic mobilisation. Bankrolling the entente and raising the new armies also made Britain increasingly dependent upon American money and materials.

Realities constrained choices for politicians and soldiers alike. Effective strategy required the appropriate employment of resources in order to achieve particular national political objectives. It followed that strategic objectives should match the desired political objectives and that there should be consistency between strategic means and political ends so that both strategic and political objectives were equally achievable. Objectives should be commensurate with the resources available to achieve them. In practice, lack of resources or, more frequently, disagreement between and within competing military and political leaderships, and between coalitions, over objectives greatly complicated the formulation of effective strategy.

The traditional view of wartime strategic decision-making in Britain has been that of the clash between 'Westerners' and the 'Easterners'. In Britain it was an image that was relentlessly cultivated in the so-called battle of the memoirs in the 1920s and 1930s. Briefly stated, the traditional argument was that once deadlock occurred on the Western Front in

[12] Nicholas Lambert, *Planning Armageddon: British Economic Warfare and the First World War* (Cambridge, MA: Harvard University Press, 2012), 155–81, 216–31. See the critique of Lambert in Matthew Seligmann, 'The Renaissance of Pre-First World War Naval History', *JSS* 36 (2013), 454–79.

the autumn of 1914, politicians were motivated to seek a new strategy to break that deadlock. Their earlier easy transference of control over strategy in August 1914 to the soldiers now rebounded because the latter were unwilling to divert manpower from the Western Front to other theatres. Soldiers regarded the latter as 'side-shows' irrelevant to the main effort. To use the oft-repeated phrase of defenders of Sir Douglas Haig's strategy as Commander-in-Chief of the BEF from December 1915 onwards, the war could not be won without 'engaging the main body of the main enemy in a continental war'.[13] Soldiers like Haig and Sir William Robertson, the CIGS between December 1915 and February 1918, therefore, were characterised as 'Westerners'. Politicians like Churchill and David Lloyd George, who was Chancellor of the Exchequer in 1914, were 'Easterners', convinced of the desirability of finding an 'indirect approach' through such campaigns as the Dardanelles between February 1915 and January 1916 and that at Salonika from October 1915 onwards.

The strategic direction of the war in Britain was certainly punctuated by major civil–military disputes not only over the side-shows but also over the conduct of the two main British offensives on the Western Front, the Somme between July and November 1916 and the third battle of Ypres – popularly known as 'Passchendaele' – between July and November 1917. To a large extent, the fault lay in the lack of effective governmental machinery for strategic decision-making. The CID had been a relatively useful mechanism, but the War Council, which emerged from it in November 1914, proved unsatisfactory. No memoranda were circulated, there was no regular agenda, meetings were infrequent and there was no proper record kept of decisions. In theory, the War Council's decisions were not binding on the Cabinet, but the latter was effectively bypassed by Asquith's reliance upon Churchill, Lloyd George and Kitchener. As one junior minister remarked in March 1915, the only real difference between the War Council and the Cabinet was Kitchener, Churchill and Lloyd George dominating proceedings in front of 'a different set of spectators'.[14] While McKenna and Runcimann clung on to a policy of holding back Kitchener's New Armies, they were to be increasingly marginalised in any case by the way in which the Cabinet was bypassed by the War Council.

When war broke out, Kitchener was on home leave from Egypt, where he was British Agent and Consul General. Kitchener had genuine strategic insights and famously anticipated that the war would last at least three years. Indeed, generally, there were few policy makers in Britain who

[13] John Terraine, *The First World War*, 2nd edn (London: Leo Cooper, 1983), x.

[14] David French, *British Economic and Strategic Planning, 1905–15* (London: Allen & Unwin, 1982), 176.

believed that the war would be over quickly. Haig also suggested a war of months, if not years, in August 1914, and Churchill, too, suggested in a memorandum to Admiralty colleagues on 8 August that they must envisage at least a year of war. Unfortunately, however, grown increasingly autocratic and secretive in his overseas appointments, Kitchener had little time for the niceties of Cabinet debate and did not feel obliged to discuss his decisions with either politicians or subordinates. Such a situation left the initiative within the War Council in the hands of those characterised as 'strategic entrepreneurs', namely, Churchill, Lloyd George and the increasingly influential secretary to the CID and now the War Council, Maurice Hankey.[15] The result was the Dardanelles campaign.

The nascent General Staff had also been effectively dismembered by the despatch of so many of its members to become the staff of the BEF. Those who remained deferred to Kitchener's massive authority. The CIGS, Sir Charles Douglas, who had succeeded French upon the latter's resignation over the Curragh affair in March 1914, died of overwork in October 1914. Douglas's successor, Sir James Wolfe Murray, fully lived up to Churchill's characterisation of him as 'Sheep' Murray. When asked by the enquiry into the Dardanelles campaign in 1917 why he had never expressed an opinion on it in the War Council, Wolfe Murray replied that Kitchener 'was a man who had a very overwhelming personality, we will say, and was a man of very great experience, and it did not appear to me that he, having, so to speak, taken the whole thing in hand and working on it almost entirely himself, to be necessary or desirable that I should interfere'. Indeed, the minutes of the War Council show that when directly asked by Grey on one occasion to offer his view on the Dardanelles, Wolfe Murray 'replied that he had no suggestions to make'.[16] Effectively, then, the man deemed to be the professional head of the army as CIGS constantly deferred to Kitchener as if he was merely chief of staff to the minister to the extent that the post hardly existed. Given the particular staff reductions that had hit the Directorates of Military Training and Staff Duties and the way in which Kitchener also interfered constantly in the work of the Quartermaster General, the post of DMO should have been the most influential in formulating strategic ideas. Unfortunately, again, the DMO, Charles Callwell, recalled from retirement, made no attempt to question Kitchener's judgement and was largely ignored by him. The Admiralty staff was equally silent when confronted by Churchill. The Junior Lords of the Admiralty met only twelve times in the first ten months of the war, while Prince Louis of Battenberg's successor as First Sea Lord, Sir John Fisher, brought back

[15] Gooch, *Plans of War*, 299. [16] *Ibid.*, 305–6.

from retirement, remained silent despite his serious misgivings about the whole concept of the Dardanelles.

The Dardanelles expedition arose from separate memoranda circulated by Churchill, Lloyd George and Hankey in December 1914 to find an alternative to the deadlock evident on the Western Front. Hankey's Boxing Day Memorandum on 26 December 1914 posited an attack on Ottoman Turkey, which had entered the war on the German side in October, in the belief that the uncommitted Balkan states would be encouraged to join the entente because they would gain from the dismemberment of Austria-Hungary and expulsion of Turkey. Coincidentally, Churchill produced his paper on the future of British strategy on 29 December, graphically posing the question, 'Are there not other alternatives than sending our armies to chew barbed wire in Flanders?'[17] At this stage, however, what Churchill had in mind was an amphibious assault on the German coast through Schleswig-Holstein with a preliminary operation to seize the island of Borkum as a base for these operations. After having seen Hankey's memorandum, he remarked on the similarity of the analysis, referring to his earlier wish to have the Dardanelles attacked as soon as the Turks had come into the war: he had ordered bombardment of the Turkish defences of the Dardanelles on 3 November. Nonetheless, a further memorandum from Churchill on 31 December still favoured an attack on Borkum. That same day, Lloyd George suggested two possible courses of action: first, an attack on Austria-Hungary with the assistance of the Balkan states by landing at Salonika or on the Dalmatian coast and, second, an attack on Turkey through Syria.

Despite pre-war assessments of the difficulties of forcing the Dardanelles, Churchill contacted the British Commander-in-Chief in the Mediterranean, Rear Admiral Carden, on 3 January 1915, asking for a view on the possibility of naval operations against the Dardanelles. Meanwhile, the various ideas for an alternative strategy were discussed more fully by the War Council on 8 January, at which Lloyd George took the lead in urging action against Austria-Hungary through Salonika or Ragusa (Dubrovnik). While feeling it was not the time to diffuse strength elsewhere, Kitchener indicated that if it was so decided, then Salonika was probably the least objectionable target, though he also suggested that the Dardanelles was the best choice, particularly as it would help the Russians. The Russians had appealed for help against the Turks, who were pressing them heavily in the Caucasus, on 2 January. Yet Kitchener

[17] Martin Gilbert, *Winston S. Churchill*, Vol. III: *1914–1916* (London: Heinemann, 1971), 226.

also proposed his own idea for an attack on Alexandretta in Syria. The next meeting of the War Council on 13 January discussed Sir John French's desire to take Zeebrugge, but Churchill also reported that Carden had replied on the previous day to the question posed him earlier by suggesting the use of older capital ships to force the Dardanelles methodically. It was resolved to plan for an advance towards Zeebrugge but also to consider naval action in the Adriatic and definite plans to take the Dardanelles and Gallipoli peninsula leading to the fall of Constantinople. The Zeebrugge scheme itself was a revival of the 'Belgian option' but fell on Kitchener's reluctance to commit either Territorial Force (TF) or New Army formations to active operations prematurely.

Agreement on naval action against the Dardanelles had been adopted with very little examination of the strategic issues involved, since all agreed that it was important to do something somewhere. There were to be further papers in favour in February, including a highly professional paper from Hankey on 2 February 1915, which listed five major strategic arguments and four economic arguments for the expedition, all primarily linked to the need to open communications with Russia. There were too many assumptions, however. Could a fleet actually capture a city? Would Italy, Greece, Romania and even Bulgaria commit to a Balkan League as a result of entente action at the Dardanelles? Could Russia be materially assisted through such an operation? Did Germany depend upon her Austro-Hungarian and Turkish allies to the extent that 'knocking the props under her', as Lloyd George expressed it, would trigger its collapse? In the event, the operation was finally authorised on 19 February. When the naval operations were deemed to have failed on 18 March, Kitchener was persuaded that the army must assist by landing on the Gallipoli Peninsula and committed the 29th Division, the last regular division available. That in itself was symptomatic of the lack of trained manpower available in 1914. Two more divisions – the 7th and 8th – had been formed in September and October 1914 from regular battalions serving overseas, with the 29th then being formed from more distant imperial stations only after Territorial units had arrived to replace them. The initial landings on 25 April and the subsequent landing at Suvla Bay in August 1915 succeeded only in reproducing the deadlock on the Western Front. Gallipoli was abandoned on 8–9 January 1916.

The failure of the naval and military campaigns at the Dardanelles, coupled with Admiral Lord Fisher's resignation as First Sea Lord and the impact of the publicity given the BEF's shortage of shells on the Western Front, coincided with other domestic political events. Lloyd George wanted more state intervention – not least in control of the supply of liquor – while both Asquith and Unionist leader Andrew Bonar Law wanted to avoid the possibility of an election as dissatisfaction grew among both Liberals and Unionists. A diffident and lethargic figure at the best of times, Asquith had relied on the desire of his Liberal colleagues to cling to office. He also feared that an election would lead to a split in his party. Bonar Law equally feared losing control of his backbenchers and felt a place in government would assuage them and cement his own leadership. In any case, an election was an uncertain business given that the electoral register was out of date and that local constituency organisations had been gravely weakened by enlistments of key agents. Members of Parliament (MPs) generally found it difficult to retain contact with their constituents, and, in January 1915, 184 MPs were themselves serving in the forces.

The crisis resulted in Asquith forming a coalition government on 25 May 1915. He had insisted in the House of Commons only on 12 May that such a coalition was 'not in contemplation'.[18] The War Council now gave way to the Dardanelles Committee, originally comprising six former members of the War Council and five Unionists but without serving officers other than Kitchener. In theory, its responsibilities were confined to strategy and diplomacy in the eastern Mediterranean. It got little information from the War Office, met less frequently than the Cabinet and 'its command over policy was correspondingly slight'.[19] On 25 November 1915, following Unionist pressure on Asquith to refine the machinery further, the Dardanelles Committee begat the five-man War Committee, comprising Asquith, Lloyd George, McKenna, and the Unionists Arthur Balfour and Bonar Law. The CIGS and First Sea Lord customarily attended, and minutes produced by Hankey in the form of 'conclusions' were circulated.

Failure at the Dardanelles also prompted a reconstitution of the General Staff on 22 September 1915 when Kitchener was absent from the Dardanelles Committee, a pronounced 'Westerner', Sir Archibald Murray, becoming CIGS. As part of the wider reconstruction of the high command, consequent upon declining confidence in both Kitchener and Sir John French, French was succeeded by Haig on 19 December 1915. Robertson replaced Murray as CIGS four days later, Bonar Law having particularly urged taking more heed of professional military advice. This marked the resurrection of the post's autonomy from the Secretary of

[18] Cameron Hazlehurst, *Politicians at War, July 1914 to May 1915: A Prologue to the Triumph of Lloyd George* (London: Jonathan Cape, 1971), 231.

[19] John Turner, 'Cabinets, Committees and Secretariats: The Higher Direction of War', in Burk (ed.), *War and State*, 57–83, at 60.

State. Robertson's terms were that the CIGS should be regarded as sole military adviser to the War Committee, which would be presented with reasoned advice on the military implications of policy proposals. Lord Curzon, who had been a member of the Dardanelles Committee and remained a member of the Cabinet, but was not on the War Committee, warned that the CIGS might now become the de facto commander-in-chief and also feared that the Cabinet would be bypassed. Kitchener also resisted remaining at the War Office himself if removed from any executive role in the direction of the war. It was agreed that orders from the War Council would be issued by the CIGS but under the authority of the Secretary of State for War, a formula that was sufficient to persuade Kitchener to remain at the War Office. Robertson immediately moved to strengthen the professionalism of the General Staff by bringing in more capable directors but also soon discontinued detailed briefings to ministers, substituting a weekly 'summary', which Hankey for one considered 'an insult to the intelligence of the War Committee and the Cabinet'.[20]

Robertson also made it clear that the Western Front should be regarded as the main theatre of operations and fully supported the recommendations already made by Murray to withdraw from the Gallipoli Peninsula. Though seen as archetypical 'Westerner', however, Robertson was conscious that Britain was part of an alliance and that it 'could make its most effective contribution to the alliance by concentrating its resources in France', a process that could only be cumulative through the necessity to resort to attrition given the impossibility of a breakthrough on the Western Front.[21] Indeed, Robertson was always a supporter of what might be termed the 'step by step' or 'bite and hold' approach in terms of operational strategy on the Western Front, in which short infantry advances would be supported by a weight of artillery firepower in achieving limited objectives. Like Robertson, both Sir Henry Rawlinson and the artillery adviser at General Headquarters (GHQ), John DuCane, had been early advocates as a result of their evaluations of the lessons of Neuve Chapelle in March 1915. If applied consistently between 1915 and 1917, such an approach would have been far more effective and far less costly than Haig's obsession with a strategic breakthrough. Haig never engaged truly with any alternative operational strategy to his own unrealistic ambitions, but, unfortunately, though equally senior in rank, Robertson felt unable to press his views on Haig, primarily it would seem for fear that he must present as united a front as possible towards the politicians. Haig,

20 David Woodward, *Lloyd George and the Generals* (London: Associated University Presses, 1983), 80–2.
21 French, *British Strategy and War Aims*, 161–2.

it would appear, believed that Robertson's function was simply to supply him with men and keep the politicians off his back.

Kitchener, already shorn of responsibility for munitions by the creation of a new Ministry of Munitions under Lloyd George in May 1915, was confined to administrative matters until his death by drowning in June 1916, when HMS *Hampshire*, carrying him on a mission to Russia, struck a German mine off the Orkneys. The extent of Robertson's power was clear to Lloyd George when he succeeded to the War Office on Kitchener's death. Robertson himself was not averse to veiled references in his private correspondence to the benefits of military dictatorship.[22] But, unlike the situation in Germany, the British military leadership did not aspire to the control of anything other than strategic policy. When Lloyd George became Prime Minister in December 1916, though he was able to neutralise any potential interference on the part of the King, his ability to impose his own strategic views was circumscribed through the weakness of his political position and lack of any majority support within Parliament. Leading Unionists such as Walter Long and Austen Chamberlain had only agreed to join the new government on condition that the high command was left alone. The same condition applied to Curzon, one of the five-man War Cabinet now also established.

Accordingly, Lloyd George resorted to subterfuge in attempting to outmanoeuvre Haig and Robertson and to force one or both to resign, notably at the Calais Conference on 27 February 1917, where he proposed subordinating Haig to French General Robert Nivelle. At what was ostensibly a conference to discuss railway transport problems on the Western Front, Nivelle was introduced to outline the plans for his new offensive. Lloyd George had previously secured the War Cabinet's agreement to a single command for the operation at a meeting three days earlier that neither Robertson nor Secretary of State for War Derby had attended. Lloyd George had also concealed his intentions from King George V. A British representative, whom Lloyd George indicated would be Henry Wilson, would be attached to Nivelle's headquarters, leaving Haig as a glorified adjutant. According to Edward Spears, when the command arrangements were revealed, Robertson's face 'went the colour of mahogany, his eyes became perfectly round, his eyebrows slanted outwards like a forest of bayonets held at the charge'.[23] Hankey proposed the compromise by which Haig would pass under the general direction of Nivelle, but for the one offensive only. He would also retain

[22] David Woodward (ed.), *The Military Correspondence of Field Marshal Sir William Robertson, Chief of the Imperial General Staff, 1915–18* (London: Bodley Head for Army Records Society, 1989), 40–1.

[23] Edward Spears, *Prelude to Victory* (London: Jonathan Cape, 1939), 143.

operational command over the BEF and have the right of appeal to London against any instructions that he considered would compromise his army's position.

Lloyd George's failure was despite the establishment of the War Cabinet, which theoretically offered him far more influence over decision-making. The War Cabinet had a permanent secretariat under Hankey and eventually increased to seven members. In addition, Lloyd George established his own secretariat – the 'Garden Suburb' – as a further independent source of advice. In practice, however, Lloyd George often scrapped the War Cabinet's agenda on short notice, and despite Hankey's efforts, its meetings were far from businesslike. In October 1917, for example, one observer commented to Robertson that the meeting he had attended had not proved very edifying, to which Robertson retorted, 'They were very good today. You should see them after an air raid.'[24] In reality, the War Cabinet strongly resembled the War Committee, albeit with clearer overall authority. Moreover, the War Cabinet, through its War Policy Committee, proved unwilling to halt operations that had manifestly failed to meet its stated criteria for continuation in the case of the Passchendaele offensive in 1917. In October 1917, Lloyd George turned instead to seeking advice from Sir John, now Lord, French and Sir Henry Wilson as a means, as French's private secretary put it, of 'clipping Robertson's wings'.[25] They duly backed the Prime Minister's preference for operations elsewhere than the Western Front such as Palestine, and both urged a new high-level inter-allied committee to co-ordinate strategy and the allocation of resources. Robertson threatened to resign and was backed by leading Unionists, but Lloyd George then threatened his own resignation.

Robertson was certainly doing his utmost to prevent Palestine from soaking up more resources, and it has been suggested that Sir Edmund Allenby's report on 9 October 1917 that an additional thirteen divisions were needed to take Jerusalem was cooked up with him. It has been countered that Allenby was suitably cautious as a newcomer to the theatre of operations in responding to intelligence reports that the Turks were planning their own offensive in Palestine.[26] In the event, there was a

24 David French, 'A One-Man Show? Civil-Military Relations in Britain during the First World War', in Paul Smith (ed.), *Government and Armed Forces in Britain, 1856–1990* (London: Hambledon, 1996), 75–109, at 82.

25 Keith Jeffery, *Field Marshal Sir Henry Wilson: A Political Soldier* (Oxford University Press, 2006), 200.

26 Matthew Hughes, *Allenby and British Strategy in the Middle East* (London: Frank Cass, 1999), 35–40; Matthew Hughes (ed.), *Allenby in Palestine: The Middle East Correspondence of Field Marshal Viscount Allenby* (Stroud: Sutton Publishing for Army Records Society, 2004), 10.

Turkish offensive but towards Baku in the Caucasus, and Jerusalem fell to Allenby on 9 December 1917. The German spring offensive on the Western Front in March 1918 stymied any further opportunity for Lloyd George to pursue wider aims in Palestine, with Allenby's best troops diverted back to France and replaced with raw formations from India.

The collapse of the Italian army at Caporetto in October 1917 finally enabled Lloyd George to divert troops from France. On 7 November, the entente conference at Rapallo agreed on the establishment of a Supreme War Council (SWC) at Versailles. It proved a formal counter-weight to the CIGS, Robertson recognising immediately that while the SWC had no executive powers, he would be held responsible for any military plans proposed by it. In February 1918, a dispute between Robertson and Lloyd George arose over control of an allied reserve by the SWC and, specifically, under Ferdinand Foch as chairman of its Executive War Board. Robertson insisted on being placed on the Executive War Board of what he termed the 'Versailles Soviet' or on Henry Wilson, whom Lloyd George had appointed British representative to Versailles, being designated his deputy. Complicated negotiations ensued with the King, Haig, and the Unionists. It became clear that Haig would not resign if Robertson was sacrificed, and on 11 February 1918, Lloyd George trapped Robertson into either remaining CIGS with reduced powers or going to Versailles as British representative. Refusing both posts, Robertson resigned on 16 February 1918 and was replaced by Wilson, although Haig and Nivelle's successor, Philippe Pétain, were able to block the creation of a general reserve.

The dispute provided the background for a new confrontation over manpower policy. The DMO at the War Office, now Sir Frederick Maurice, a strong ally of Robertson, was informed by Wilson that he would be replaced on 20 February. Maurice's relief was arranged for 20 April 1918, his last assignment as DMO being a visit to GHQ in France from 14 to 16 April. Maurice already believed that Lloyd George was deliberately retaining men in Britain rather than committing them to France and Flanders, a view widespread at GHQ and which had already brought press attacks on Lloyd George. On 9 April, a speech by Lloyd George suggested that the strength of the BEF was greater on 1 January 1918 than it had been on 1 January 1917. It was re-iterated in the House of Commons by the Under Secretary of State for War on 18 April. Bonar Law then also declared on 23 April that the recent extension of the British front had been the result of government pressure. Having received no reply from Wilson, whom he had told that the statements were inaccurate, Maurice wrote to the press, his letter appearing in five national newspapers on 7 May 1918. Maurice contended that the extension of the front had been a decision of the SWC, that there were fewer troops in France in 1918 than 1917 and that there were fewer British troops in Palestine than also stated. Responding to a vote of censure moved by Asquith on the issue, Lloyd George suggested that the figures had come from Maurice's own department. Lloyd George won the vote easily, and Maurice was forced into retirement. The correct figures had been sent to Lloyd George in time for the debate, but he chose not to use them and always afterwards claimed that he had never seen them. In 1956 it was finally revealed that Lloyd George had deliberately misled Parliament. While he had wished to prevent Haig wasting lives, it was also true that there was now a proper manpower policy, that as many men as available were sent to France once the German spring offensives began in March 1918 and that the soldiers themselves also manipulated figures to justify continuing offensives. Some 88,000 men had been sent home on leave by GHQ on the very eve of a German offensive that had been anticipated. The War Office itself had taken the decision to bolster other arms and services in preference to infantry and, bizarrely, classed machine gunners and tank drivers as non-combat arms. While not excusing Lloyd George's conduct, he clearly believed 'a military conspiracy was under foot'.[27]

The prospect of the British and French armies being split apart by the German spring offensive in March 1918 finally forced Haig to accept the appointment of Ferdinand Foch as allied supreme commander at the Doullens conference on 26 March 1918, though Haig and Pétain retained tactical control over their own troops. The offensive also enabled Lloyd George to establish a new 'X' Committee consisting of himself, Wilson and Lord Milner, who had become Secretary of State for War in April 1918, to discuss strategy prior to meetings of the War Cabinet. Like the War Policy Committee before it, the 'X' Committee could take decisions without reference to the War Cabinet though it was little used after July 1918. Interestingly, Wilson as CIGS also 'believed there were some things the War Cabinet had better not know'.[28] Haig's position remained insecure, but there was no acceptable alternative, and by the summer the entente was on the offensive, although no one expected the war to be won in 1918.

While continuing tensions between civilians and soldiers were thus clearly evident, there were frequently other factors that were equally significant in shaping strategic decisions. One was the need to accommodate coalition partners. Every belligerent fought in order to win or, at

[27] Woodward, *Lloyd George and the Generals*, 297.

[28] David French, *The Strategy of the Lloyd George Coalition, 1916–18* (Oxford: Clarendon Press, 1995), 220.

least, not to lose, and therefore, there was an essential unity of purpose between coalition partners. Having an ally was an insurance against defeat. Each state, however, had its own reasons for entering the war and would have, or develop, its own particular objectives, serving its own national interests. Consequently, war aims within a coalition could conflict with those of allies. Some partners within the coalition were likely to be more powerful than others in terms of military or economic resources and in a better position to impose their own aims on the alliance. The balance of power was by no means static. Even if a common strategic aim could be agreed on, it was still likely that national considerations would render actual operational co-ordination difficult because such issues as unity of command, amalgamation of forces and pooling of material resources all implied at least a partial surrender of national sovereignty.

The entente developed a relatively elaborate system of inter-allied committees by the end of the war, numbering twenty-five in total. Initially; however, there was no formal machinery for strategic or political co-ordination beyond a few meetings between Sir John French, the French Commander-in-Chief, Joseph Joffre, and the Commander of the French Fifth Army, Charles Lanrezac, and others during the first campaign of the war. Co-ordination was accordingly weak, as epitomised by the muddle over the defence of Antwerp in October 1914 when British, French and Belgian forces were theoretically co-ordinated by Foch. Asquith and his French counterpart, René Viviani, did not meet until 6 July 1915, while Kitchener met Joffre and the French Minister of War, Alexandre Millerand, only five times in the first twelve months of war. Coinciding with the first meeting of the British and French Prime Ministers, the first inter-allied military conference was held at Chantilly on 7 July 1915. Other conferences followed, but there was little co-ordination between the decisions reached at the military conferences and those at the political conferences.

The actual exercise of allied command over different nationalities remained difficult, compounded in some cases by ignorance of languages. French became the accepted language at allied conferences, but practical problems extended to the British calculating artillery barrages in yards per minute and the French in metres per minute.[29] More French generals spoke German than English: Lord Derby, sent as British Ambassador to Paris in 1916, could not speak French. In any case, French soldiers who could speak English generally declined to do so. Sir John French, who had experienced particular problems dealing with Lanrezac, confided to his

[29] Elizabeth Greenhalgh, *Victory through Coalition: Britain and France during the First World War* (Cambridge University Press, 2005), 4–5.

confidante, Winifred Bennett, in April 1915 that 'Truly, I don't want to be allied with the French more than once in a lifetime.' Robertson in October 1916 also found allies 'a tiresome lot'.[30] The French pressed the idea of a unified command on a number of occasions, and at Calais in July 1915, the British accepted in principle that Joffre should determine the force, objective and date of any joint offensives in France. Haig always resisted any joint command arrangements, though he worked well enough with Pétain.

While a significant development, the SWC was by no means entirely satisfactory. Commanders-in-chief could attend but were not members and had no vote, although the French, who would have preferred unity of command, solved the problem by making Foch's chief of staff, General Maxime Weygand, their military representative to the council. In the crisis of the German spring offensive in 1918, supposed unity of command was forged at Doullens. Doullens, however, did not define Foch's responsibilities satisfactorily, and at Beauvais on 3 April 1918 Foch got powers of strategic direction. Yet tactical control remained with the component field commanders. Foch's authority was extended to the Italian front on 14 April, but the Italian Chief of Staff, Armando Diaz, strenuously resisted his authority.

Arguably, British strategic interests were sacrificed to wider alliance considerations in August 1914, but Sir John French was invested by Kitchener with instructions that made clear that his command was an independent one and that he had direct recourse of appeal to the British government in the event of difficulties. French exercised his discretion in September 1914 in requesting withdrawal from the Aisne to Flanders, which would greatly ease the supply problems by positioning the BEF closer to the Channel ports as well as enabling the British to support Antwerp. The lines of communication had certainly been disrupted to a major extent during the 'great retreat' to the Marne in August, and the French had not always proved amenable to giving the BEF any kind of priority in the use of their railway system while on the Aisne. Sir John himself later suggested that he had become anxious about the security of the Channel coast on 16 September when it was reported that the Germans were already on the allied left flank. According to Asquith, French would also be able to carry out 'a great outflanking march' and sweep to a line across Belgium from Brussels to Cologne, relieving Antwerp en route.[31] Relations with Joffre had become strained, not

[30] John Gooch, 'Soldiers, Strategy and War Aims in Britain, 1914–18', in Barry Hunt and Adrian Preston (eds.), *War Aims and Strategic Policy in the Great War* (London: Croom Helm, 1977), 27.

[31] Brock and Brock (eds.), *Asquith*, p. 256.

least when Sir John had interpreted his obligation to ensure the safety of the BEF and of the Channel ports in terms of continuing to retreat towards Amiens and Le Havre in late August rather than participating in Joffre's planned counter-offensive. In the event, political necessity had led the Cabinet to dispatch Kitchener on 1 September to order French to remain in the line. The meeting did little to ameliorate French's antagonism towards Kitchener, who chose to wear his Field Marshal's uniform for the occasion, or to reverse the mutual distrust between French and Joffre.

In terms of the impact of coalition politics on British military strategy, the supposed division between 'Westerners' and 'Easterners' is somewhat artificial since there was much common ground between them, particularly with respect to the position of Britain within the entente. Both soldiers and politicians recognised the importance of holding the entente together in order to defeat Germany. They also intended to ensure that Britain would become the strongest partner in the coalition in order to be able to impose its own terms on enemy and allies alike. As Kitchener expressed it, '[O]ur Army should reach its full strength at the beginning of the third year of the War, just when France is getting into rather low water and Germany is beginning to feel the pinch.'[32] Britain was the strongest economic partner in the anti-German coalition until the entry of the United States and the strongest naval partner throughout. Therefore, her principal effort would be confined initially to blockading the Central Powers and bankrolling and supplying the French and Russians.

In this light, it could be argued that the primary motivation behind the Dardanelles campaign was to assist the Russians, who, as indicated earlier, appealed to Britain for assistance on 2 January 1915 in drawing Turkish forces away from the Caucasus. It was vital to keep Russia in the war lest its collapse release German and Austro-Hungarian troops for the West or, indeed, Turkey. Like other assumptions connected with the campaign, this begged the question of whether Russia could have been satisfactorily supplied with more war materiel in the event of the Black Sea route being opened. In turn, the British decision to contest the Dardanelles affected French strategy because the initial plan for a British naval assault appeared to challenge further the command arrangements in the Mediterranean when operations in defence of Egypt had already been excluded from French control. The apparent British interest in striking at Alexandretta, the major entrepôt for Asia Minor, as well as the Dardanelles, also rang alarm bells in Paris because the French had

32 David French, 'The Meaning of Attrition, 1914–16', *English Historical Review* 103 (1988), 385–405, at 388.

long coveted controlling the trade routes centring on the port and believed their intended post-war influence over Syria threatened. Under an agreement hammered out between Churchill and the French navy minister, Victor Augagneur, the British gained control of the Dardanelles operations in return for dropping the idea of an expedition to Alexandretta. Kitchener's decision in March 1915 to send the 29th Division to Gallipoli in itself caused considerable friction, for it was being committed where it might contribute most to British interests rather than those of the French, who had been insistent that British reinforcements should go to the Western Front. Kitchener was fundamentally out of sympathy with French plans and enjoyed an increasingly frosty relationship with Millerand. The immediate result was that Joffre withdrew from an intended French attack in Artois, leaving the BEF to attack without allied support at Neuve Chapelle in March 1915.

Similarly, it could be argued that the British joined in the Salonika campaign in 1916 because the French and Russians requested their participation rather than because there was any confidence that such a venture could assist Serbia, under attack from German, Austro-Hungarian and also Bulgarian forces once Bulgaria had come into the war on 11 October 1915. The Salonika campaign itself has been characterised as 'a vital requirement of French domestic political stability' in finding a worthwhile command for the radical republican general, Maurice Sarrail.[33] The British continued to support it largely as a means of preserving Aristide Briand's ministry. At the same time, however, just as the French did not trust the British to act alone at the Dardanelles, the British could not afford to allow the French to act alone at Salonika. Ultimately, Salonika did not receive further British reinforcements as the campaign was seen in London to be in French rather than British interests.

Ironically, the adoption of a strategy of attrition on the Western Front – a touchstone of the post-war 'Westerners' versus 'Easterners' debate – was not originally intended to cost British lives but to conserve them, since the brunt of the continental war would fall on the French and Russians. The politicians, indeed, convinced themselves that attrition did not imply full-scale British frontal assaults on German positions. In a sense, it was a limited strategy for unlimited objectives. What then went wrong was that the very heavy losses suffered by the French and Russians in 1914–15, and the realisation that the Germans would not oblige by attacking in the West, made it increasingly clear that the future of the entente depended upon Britain's readiness to play a major role in the

[33] David Dutton, 'The "Robertson Dictatorship" and the Balkan Campaign in 1916', *Journal of Strategic Studies* 9 (1986), 64–78, at 64.

continental land war. The French and the Russians were increasingly less inclined to wait patiently and perhaps indefinitely for the British Army to arrive when much of their national territory remained in German hands, and their own manpower resources were depleted.

Thus, the British offensive at Loos in September 1915 was mounted primarily for the political purpose of sustaining French and Russian morale, especially in light of the Russian defeat at Gorlice-Tarnow, operations at which had begun in May 1915. Kitchener remarked that 'unfortunately we have to make war as we must, and not as we should like to'.[34] Ultimately, Britain's increasing commitment to the land war was to be reflected in the length of the Western Front held by the BEF, which increased from the twenty-four miles held in November 1914 to 123 miles by February 1918.

By April 1916, most British policy makers were reluctantly convinced that the war might end either in an indecisive peace or possibly even a German victory if the British did not participate fully in the combined offensive planned by the allied military representatives at Chantilly between 6 and 8 December 1915. Britain's finances were under increasing strain, and the Cabinet was warned in January 1916 that if the war was not won by the end of the year, bankruptcy threatened. It was also at least theoretically possible that either France or Russia might be ready to negotiate a separate peace with the Germans, who had made peace overtures to both as early as the winter of 1914–15. The French were also suffering heavy losses at Verdun, where the German offensive had opened unexpectedly on 21 February 1916. Significantly, Asquith revealed to the War Committee on 7 April that French Finance Minister Alexandre Ribot had said that 'if France did not get the required assistance, she could not go on. She must put up the shutters.'[35] It has been suggested, however, that both McKenna and Robertson found agreement in seeing the coming offensive in terms of a continuance of a 'limited and gradualist approach'. Robertson saw the offensive as limited in scope and part of a longer-term strategy of attrition, while McKenna, who came close to resigning as Chancellor, could also view a limited offensive as not jeopardising continued reliance on naval and economic strength to wear down the Germans. Haig saw the offensive in very different terms and 'made a mockery of any suggestion that the Somme was compatible with a strategy of limited liability, resulting in a use of resources so prodigal as to create havoc with any notions of gradualism inherent in the thinking of either Robertson or McKenna'.[36]

[34] George Cassar, *Kitchener: Architect of Victory* (London: William Kimber, 1977), 389.

[35] French, *British Strategy and War Aims*, 184–5.

[36] Hew Strachan, 'The Battle of the Somme and British Strategy', *Journal of Strategic Studies* 21 (1998), 79–95, at 93.

Thus, the ground was laid for the opening of the Somme campaign on 1 July 1916, representing a compromise between Joffre's desire that the British carry out an attritional blow before his own planned offensive and Haig's desire to attack in Flanders in a combined operation with the Royal Navy. It has been argued that the Somme offensive was 'the culmination of a long series of measures, ploys and discussions, by which the French had attempted to draw the British more fully into the war effort in France'.[37] While the French believed that the BEF had limited offensive capability and, therefore, could only act in concert with their own armies, Haig was convinced that the French could not last another winter and that his army must make the decisive effort. On 20 January 1916, Haig and Joffre agreed that the main British offensive would be north of the Somme, preceded by a preliminary limited British attack on the Somme in April and the main French effort there in June. Within three days Joffre asked for a second limited attack in May. Haig countered by reducing the scale of the preliminary operations. Given a lack of Belgian co-operation, Haig increasingly came round to a Somme offensive, he and Joffre agreeing on 14 February 1916 to forego any significant preliminary operations prior to two weeks before the main offensive. The Somme was chosen as a battlefield because this was where the British and French sectors of the front lines met and because Anglo-French co-operation appeared to offer the best chance of success in what had hitherto been a quiet sector. In the event, French participation was far less than originally planned because of the opening of the German Verdun offensive on 21 February. It also led to the re-appearance of the Flanders plan, though the prolongation of Verdun soon brought the realisation that there would be little French participation in any British summer offensive. Haig contemplated reviving the Flanders offensive, but Joffre declined to allow the British 'to go it alone in the north'.[38] Ironically, Haig finally decided on a Somme offensive when it appeared that elements within the French government were ready to accept his own earlier decision to delay operations.[39]

It is certainly true that the Verdun offensive persuaded a reluctant British government to authorise the Somme offensive on 7 April 1916. It was not specifically intended to take pressure off Verdun, however, because the strategy had been agreed on before the opening of the German offensive, though it was later claimed by Haig that it was

[37] Roy A. Prete, 'Joffre and the Origins of the Somme: A Study in Allied Military Planning', *Journal of Military History* 73 (2009), 417–48, at 419.

[38] William Philpott, *Bloody Victory: The Sacrifice on the Somme and the Making of the Twentieth Century* (London: Little, Brown, 2009), 83.

[39] J. P. Harris, *Douglas Haig and the First World War* (Cambridge University Press, 2008), 207–8.

continued in order to help the French. While Joffre did initially request help and Haig agreed to take over more of the front, Joffre was assuring the British by May 1916 that they need not advance the date of the offensive as matters had stabilised. In June, Philippe Pétain, now commanding at Verdun, requested the date of the offensive be brought forward, but the success of the Russian Brusilov offensive on the Eastern Front then eased pressure as German formations were withdrawn from the Western Front. Joffre now suggested postponement of Haig's offensive. Haig refused to delay beyond 29 June.

Subsequently, Haig declined to concur with Joffre's desire to make more of the initial successes on 1 July on the southern sector of the front where the British and French had been side by side. His conduct of the offensive thereafter also indicated no intention to accept French views. In practical terms, too, Anglo-French co-operation was marred by arguments over details and lines of demarcation with the result that there was 'no interdependence' between the two armies' plans.[40] Moreover, the British effort was continued for four months after the Germans had ceased to attack at Verdun. Robertson, himself highly cautious over the likely results of the offensive and worried about casualty levels, had assured the War Committee on 30 May that there was no intention of trying to break through the German lines. Indeed, as was to happen with the Third Ypres offensive in 1917, there was remarkably little attempt by the politicians to impose any effective control over the offensive. As it happened, the Chief of the German General Staff, Erich von Falkenhayn, had anticipated that Britain would be forced into an offensive by his own offensive against the French, but the British effort was stronger than he had expected. For a brief period in August and September 1916, attrition seemed to be working, with Haig claiming results on the Somme, the Italians claiming to have inflicted heavy losses on an Austro-Hungarian offensive, the Brusilov offensive in the east and Romania's entry into the war. By November, hopes had been dashed by the failure of the Somme offensive and the swift crushing of Romania.

In some respects, the reluctant agreement to allow the Passchendaele offensive to proceed in the summer of 1917 was partly founded in Haig's promise that this would bring a morale-boosting victory but also in the belief that if the British stood idle, the spectre of defeatism would spread through the entente. The Tsar had abdicated in March 1917, and the new Provisional Government in Russia had called in May for a peace without annexations or indemnities. The Russian collapse, the French mutinies

[40] Elizabeth Greenhalgh, 'Why the British Were on the Somme in 1916', *War in History* 6 (1999), 147–73, at 159.

following Nivelle's disastrous offensive and the challenge of the German revival of unrestricted submarine warfare in February 1917 all placed Britain in a precarious position, even if the United States had come into the war in April. The War Cabinet, having previously rejected any idea of peace without victory, was resolved in August 1917 to negotiate if the Germans evacuated Belgium. Coupled with the outbreak of revolution in Russia, indeed, and the fact that American troops could not yet arrive in force, the French mutinies meant that Britain was now the dominant partner in the alliance.

The concept of a Flanders offensive was of long standing, as suggested by the pre-war 'Belgian option' and the resurrection of the Zeebrugge scheme, which was considered anew both in the autumn of 1915 and early 1916. Interest in the Belgian coast resurfaced in the autumn of 1916 when the Admiralty became concerned by the potential for raids on Channel shipping by German cruisers and destroyers operating from Ostend and Zeebrugge. Cross-Channel troop transports were temporarily suspended. After a meeting of the War Committee on 20 November 1916, Asquith had presented Haig with an unsigned memorandum conveying its conclusion that great importance was attached to depriving the Germans of Ostend and Zeebrugge. The surface threat remained more significant than that posed by German submarines, hence the lack of reaction to the alarm about submarines voiced by the First Sea Lord, now Jellicoe, in a meeting of the War Policy Committee on 20 June 1917, since the adoption of convoys had already greatly reduced the submarine menace. Haig, however, conceived of an offensive to force the Germans to fight for the Channel ports rather than simply withdrawing from the existing front line as they had withdrawn to the new defences of the Hindenburg Line prior to the Nivelle offensive.

Lloyd George was apprehensive of the likely results of Third Ypres, but his hands were tied by the reaffirmation of the primacy of the Western Front at the entente conference at Chantilly in November 1916 and by Nivelle's failure. Discredited by the latter after his machinations at the Calais conference, Lloyd George was in no position to argue his strategic preference for shifting resources to the Italian front. He was forced, therefore, to accept the conclusions of a military conference at Paris on 4–5 May 1917 that the soldiers should determine the timing and nature of the allied offensives for the year. It was assumed that the objectives would be limited and that the French would participate fully. It took sixteen meetings between 11 June and 20 July 1917 for the specially convened War Policy Committee, which had been established on 8 June, before half-hearted support was given to an offensive in which few had any faith. Its deliberations have been characterised as 'a depressing catalogue of prevarication and indecision'.[41] Robertson was also sceptical but felt a residual loyalty to Haig and preferred the Flanders offensive to Lloyd George's Italian scheme because it would still advance his expectation that attrition would work in the end. Haig had sufficient doubts about Robertson's support to suggest to Lloyd George in June that Robertson be moved to become chairman of the Admiralty Board. The offensive was agreed to on condition that a step-by-step approach would be adopted and that it should be discontinued if it proved too costly. Indeed, the offensive was presented to the committee on such a basis, though Haig always aimed at a significant strategic breakthrough. Third Ypres was also justified – though primarily in retrospect – on the grounds of relieving pressure on the French, the true state of the French army being concealed from ministers. Far from trying to take pressure off the French, Haig repeatedly urged them to participate more fully and believed that German strength was sufficiently weakened to achieve a decisive victory. In the event, while the offensive began on 31 July 1917, the War Policy Committee did not reconvene until 24 September. Hankey recorded in his diary on 15 August that Lloyd George was 'obviously puzzled, as his predecessor was, as to how far the Government is justified in interfering with a military operation'.[42] While Haig remained stubbornly wedded to a failing offensive, the politicians also manifestly failed to halt the operations when their worst fears were being realised.

With the failure of the offensive, which he had never expected to prove a knockout blow, Lloyd George determined to husband remaining manpower resources and economic staying power until the arrival of the Americans in force could enable a decisive effort to be mounted in 1919. In that way, the British Army would not totally exhaust itself, preventing the military and political balance within the entente from swinging entirely in the favour of the United States. In other words, the British would still have sufficient soldiers left alive to retain some diplomatic leverage in the peace talks.

In the event, following the failure of the German spring offensives in 1918, the entente counter-attacked in the summer. In October, when the Germans appealed to Woodrow Wilson for an armistice on the basis of his Fourteen Points, it posed a serious challenge for the British in terms of whether it would be better to continue the war in the expectation of a more complete victory. Alternatively, however, if the war continued, then American influence would increase yet further. South African statesman

41 Matthew Hughes, 'Command, Strategy and the Battle for Palestine, 1917', in Ian F. W. Beckett (ed.), *1917: Beyond the Western Front* (Leiden: Brill, 2009), 113–29, at 120.

42 French, *Strategy of Lloyd George Coalition*, 130.

and member of the War Cabinet Jan Smuts argued cogently on 24 October 1918 that in an 'American peace', the United States 'will have taken our place as the first military, diplomatic and financial power of the world'.[43] Accordingly, the British accepted the terms proposed only on the understanding that President Wilson's demands for freedom of the seas, the future of German colonies and the question of indemnities would not be settled until the subsequent peace conference.

While the needs of coalition partners might or might not influence strategic decisions, each belligerent's own concept of its national interests most certainly did. Britain, France and Russia adopted a joint Declaration of London on 5 September 1914, which rejected concluding a separate peace and accepted the need for consensus in formulating peace terms. As the war continued, however, national war aims, whether regarded as essential, desirable or merely useful, became an important means by which domestic morale could be sustained for further sacrifices. In the process, war aims became a maximum negotiating position, but their use as bargaining counters in itself tended to lead to escalation of demands because no belligerent could be seen to accept lesser gains. Aims were best kept fairly vague in order to avoid the possibility of failure to achieve them appearing as defeat. Unfortunately, vagueness might suggest to domestic opinion that the gain was not worth the sacrifice: as has been nicely expressed, '[t]he flower of British and French manhood had not flocked to the colours in 1914 to die for the balance of power'.[44]

In the case of a number of members of the entente such as Belgium, France and Russia, the national interest dictated that national territory occupied by the enemy after the war's first campaigns must be retaken. For Britain, too, the most obvious early war aim was the restitution of Belgium, although adherence to the entente also implied acquiescence in general to French and Russian aims, which served British interests less well than safeguarding the Channel ports. The question of precisely what else Britain was fighting to achieve was raised systematically for the first time only amid the fleeting optimism of August and September 1916. It was soon clear, however, that the rather vague expression of a war being fought to destroy 'Prussian militarism', a theme used by Asquith in his speech on war aims at the Guildhall on 9 November 1914 and on other subsequent occasions, masked differences of perception.

On the part of the soldiers, there was a determination to inflict a sufficiently clear military victory on Germany to deter future aggression. At the same time, there was a certain ambivalence towards what might be

43 *Ibid.*, 276–7.

44 Michael Howard, *Studies in War and Peace* (London: Temple Smith, 1970), 104–5.

termed total victory because, as Haig put it on 2 January 1918, 'few of us feel that the democratising of Germany is worth the loss of a single Englishman'.[45] Indeed, the British military leadership as a whole believed that nothing would be gained by stripping Germany of her colonies or imposing crippling economic indemnities in view of the need to re-establish an effective post-war balance of power in Europe. However, both the Colonial Office and the Admiralty were keen to take German colonies to ensure the future security of the Empire. Generally, too, politicians sought a more total victory than the soldiers in order to be able to restructure Germany, the crusade against Prussian militarism becoming a major theme of British wartime propaganda. Nonetheless, most British policy makers recognised that after the war Germany would be required to balance France and, especially, Russia. The Russian collapse in 1917 saw a modification of attitudes towards the balance of power, with a renewed sense of the need to strengthen France, since Russian defeat suggested greater opportunities for Germany to increase its own post-war power. Austria-Hungary was hardly regarded as an opponent at all, and while no one was especially committed to its preservation, it was seen as a useful barrier to Germany's eastern ambitions. Thus, it was only belatedly, with the failure to detach Vienna from Berlin, that Britain came round to the view of allowing self-determination to prevail.

Of greater importance was the future security of the Empire, for fighting alongside the French and Russians did not automatically extinguish older imperial rivalries. Winning the war for Britain meant increasing security against both current enemies and current allies. In this context, the breakup of Ottoman Turkey was increasingly seen as desirable. Middle Eastern oil resources were vital for a Royal Navy now fuelled by oil rather than coal. It was the need to secure Persia and to deflect Russian interest from acquiring German or Austro-Hungarian territory – yet keeping Russian military effort concentrated on the Eastern Front rather than the Caucasus – that persuaded the British government to allow the Russians the post-war control of Constantinople in the Straits Agreement on 12 November 1914, to which France also agreed in April 1915. Similarly, Britain could not afford France acquiring Syria without adequate compensatory protection for British interests in Egypt and Mesopotamia. Thus, a limited demonstration by the Indian Army was mounted in November 1914 to occupy Basra in the Persian Gulf to reassure the Gulf rulers of British protection against the Turks, the Indian government having despatched the force to Bahrain even before

[45] Robert Blake (ed.), *The Private Papers of Douglas Haig, 1914–19* (London: Eyre & Spottiswoode, 1952), 277.

Turkey entered the war. It also had the advantage of reassuring the Gulf rulers of British protection.

It was not until April 1915 that an interdepartmental committee was tasked with determining what actual British war aims – quaintly characterised as 'desiderata' – should be in the event of victory over the Turks. Primarily forced on London by knowledge of Russian territorial demands, the deliberations of the de Bunsen committee recommended post-war zones of influence with Britain securing Mesopotamia and Haifa as a terminus for the Baghdad railway the Germans had been constructing and which it was now intended Britain should control. An additional consideration was that the Sultan in Constantinople claimed the Caliphate, aspiring to supreme global authority over Sunni Islam, whose adherents represented the greatest proportion of Muslims. Over 100 million Muslims lived under British control, hence the willingness to encourage the religious and territorial aspirations of the Hashemite Sherif of Mecca, Hussein (Husayn), who also claimed the Caliphate. It was not appreciated in London or Cairo that Hussein would see the British offer of the Caliphate as an offer of an extensive Arab kingdom, while the British interpretation of correspondence that passed between Hussein and Kitchener's successor as Agent and Consul General in Egypt, Sir Henry MacMahon, in October 1915 differed from that by Hussein. In any case, the subsequent Sykes-Picot agreement in January 1916 effectively partitioned the Ottoman Empire in the Middle East between Britain and France. Any promises made to Hussein were also dependent on an Arab revolt against the Turks, which began in June 1916 with British support.

The desire to ensure British prestige in Muslim eyes encouraged extension of the campaign in Mesopotamia to an advance upon Kut in June 1915 with an inadequate force. The advance to Kut became one on Baghdad in November 1915, but within two days, the over-extended expedition was forced to retreat back to Kut, where, surrounded, it was compelled to surrender in April 1916. Saving face after such a disaster was an additional stimulus for the renewed British offensive towards Baghdad in the spring of 1917, but this was also accelerated by fears that the Russians intended to move on Baghdad themselves through Persia. The expansion of the campaign was thus perceived by British politicians as essential to preserve Britain's status as an Asiatic and global power. Russia was still seen as presenting a threat to India, while any German and Turkish victory would equally threaten not only India but also Egypt. As Curzon and Austen Chamberlain argued in September 1916, loss of prestige in Mesopotamia 'would greatly increase the risk of *jehad* on the [North West] Frontier. The force saved in Mesopotamia would be much less than the force required in that event in India.'[46] After the war, Robertson, who had always favoured only defensive operations in Mesopotamia, was to suggest that the issue of British prestige had been exaggerated, but given the civil–military tussle in London, it is not surprising that the politicians fell upon the concurrence of their views with those of 'the men on the spot' in terms of the Commander-in-Chief in India, Sir Charles Monro, and the Commander-in-Chief in Mesopotamia, Sir Stanley Maude, both of whom urged the capture of Baghdad. Once Baghdad was taken, the campaign was extended to the Euphrates Valley to secure its agricultural resources and thereby to sustain the logistic and other costs of occupation.

The British offensive into Palestine in the spring of 1917 aroused both French and Italian suspicions of British aims. In turn, it also encouraged publication of the Balfour Declaration in November 1917, recognising the Zionist desire to establish a national home in Palestine. It was partly triggered by fears that Germany might preempt any British public declaration of support for the Zionists. The War Cabinet viewed it in terms of short-term political advantages. It did not occur to Balfour that there would be any Arab reaction, and he observed that 'planting a minority of outsiders upon a majority population, without consulting it, was not calculated to horrify men who worked with Cecil Rhodes or promoted European settlement in Kenya.'[47] The resulting problem, as Henry Wilson remarked in June 1919, was that the British had made 'so many promises to everybody in a contradictory sense that I cannot for the life of me see how we can get out of our present mess without breaking our word to somebody'.[48]

Actual public declaration of British war aims was speeded by the German announcement on 12 December 1916 that they were willing to discuss peace terms. The British rightly judged the German approach as an attempt to split the entente but could not afford outright rejection, which might strengthen German support in the United States. In response, therefore, the British and French called for the restoration of Belgium and Serbia, the evacuation of German occupied territory, indemnities for war damages and self-determination for subject nationalities within the Austro-Hungarian and Ottoman Empires. They also accepted President Wilson's proposal for a post-war League of Nations.

[46] Andrew Syk (ed.), *The Military Papers of Lieutenant-General Frederick Stanley Maude, 1914–17* (Stroud: Sutton Publishing for Army Records Society, 2012), 155.

[47] William Mathew, 'War-Time Contingency and the Balfour Declaration of 1917: An Improbable Regression', *Journal of Palestine Studies* 40 (2011), 26–42, at 27, 38.

[48] Keith Jeffery, *The British Army and the Crisis of Empire, 1918–22* (Manchester University Press, 1984), 122.

Additional pressure was exerted by the collapse of the Tsarist government in Russia in March 1917 and the call by the new Provisional Government in May for a peace without annexations or indemnities. By the summer of 1917, the Russian defection, the French mutinies and the challenge of German unrestricted submarine warfare placed Britain and the entente in a precarious position. Thus, though Austro-Hungarian overtures for a separate peace were eventually rejected, the War Cabinet, which had previously rejected the idea of peace without victory, resolved in August 1917 that they would negotiate if the Germans evacuated Belgium. Passchendaele was waged against the background of the Reichstag Peace Resolution calling for a settlement based upon no annexations or indemnities, to which the British responded by a demand for democratisation of Germany in advance of any negotiations. Papal mediation was also rejected later in August, as was a further German approach in September.

Nonetheless, in response to the publication of a letter on 29 November 1917 by the former Unionist Foreign Secretary, Lord Lansdowne, calling for peace, Lloyd George suggested in a major speech at Caxton Hall on 5 January 1918 a certain willingness to compromise. Italy's claims on Austria-Hungary would not be supported unless justified, and while Belgium, Serbia and Romania should all be restored, there should not be an automatic expansion of states in the Balkans despite the need to recognise self-determination within the Austro-Hungarian and Ottoman Empires.

Self-determination, of course, was a two-edged sword for the British in view of the situation in Ireland, but with great imperial proconsuls like Milner and Curzon in the War Cabinet and many of Milner's disciples within government, it was always evident that Turkey would be dismembered. There was a 'new imperialism' at the heart of government.[49] At the same time, the establishment of preferential tariffs over the expanded Empire would strengthen Britain's future economic position. Moreover, viewing the prospect of the war continuing into 1919, some, like Henry Wilson and Leo Amery, argued that Britain could act on the defensive in the west and seize the initiative in the east, expanding British influence to the Caucasus, Armenia and the Caspian as an appropriate buffer zone between a German-dominated eastern Europe and a British-dominated Asia and Middle East now that Russia had collapsed. Thus, in 1918–19, British forces were pushing into Persia and towards Baku and Batum in the Caucasus, 'Dunsterforce' briefly occupying Baku.

[49] Paul Guinn, *British Strategy and Politics, 1914–18* (Oxford: Clarendon Press, 1965), 193.

With the negotiation of the Treaty of Brest Litovsk between Germany and the Bolsheviks in March 1918, matters looked black for the entente, and tentative negotiations were opened by Britain with both Austria-Hungary and Turkey. With the opening of the German spring offensive on the Western Front, however, these negotiations speedily collapsed. The British had extended some assistance to those within Russia likely to continue the war against the Germans at the end of 1917 in order to keep the Ukraine out of German hands and thus blunt the threat to British interests elsewhere. Neither Britain nor France had many troops to spare, however, and they therefore pressed President Wilson and the Japanese to intervene in Russia. The revolt against the Bolsheviks in May 1918 by the Czech Legion, recruited from former Austro-Hungarian prisoners of war, provided a useful opportunity because the Czechs were distributed along the Trans-Siberian Railway and had seized the port of Vladivostock. Woodrow Wilson was apprehensive of such an enterprise but was persuaded by July 1918 that the Germans must be forced to retain large numbers of troops inside Russia for fear of tilting the balance in the West before the Americans could arrive in force. As a result, 7,000 US troops were landed at Vladivostock in August 1918, together with 70,000 Japanese. British troops had earlier landed at Murmansk in March 1918 and had penetrated trans-Caspia from Mesopotamia and Persia. British, French and American troops also landed at Archangel in August 1918.

The matching of strategy and policy, therefore, was a complex affair of balancing resources, interests and priorities in a war being fought on an unprecedented scale so far as both soldiers and politicians were concerned. In October 1916, Robertson summed up what he saw as the essential problem from the military perspective:

> Where the politician goes wrong is in wanting to know the why and the wherefore of the soldier's proposals, and of making the latter the subject of debate and argument across a table. You then have the man who knows but who cannot talk discussing important questions with the man who can talk but does not know, with the result that the man who knows usually gets defeated in argument and things are done which his instinct tells him are bad.[50]

[50] French, *Strategy of Lloyd George Coalition*, 287.

6 The Western Front, 1914

The British official historian, Brigadier Sir James Edmonds, judged the British Expeditionary Force (BEF) despatched to France in 1914 as 'in every respect . . . incomparably the best trained, best organised, and best equipped British Army which ever went forth to war.'[1] Edmonds was not given to hyperbole, and such a judgement has been understood as a ringing endorsement of the professional rigour and dedication of the British Army. However, Edmonds's conclusion is slightly misleading. Although undoubtedly the product of many well-developed professional minds that had studied, debated and refined systems for the British Army in the years since 1902, the BEF that crossed to France was on many levels a flawed instrument. Exploring the BEF's juddering introduction to battle and its initial reactions to trench stalemate reveals the strengths and weaknesses of the British Army in sharp relief.

Determining the proficiency with which the BEF attempted to come to terms with the challenges thrown down by war involves many factors internal and external to the British Army itself. A major external problem was that of time. Plunged headlong into battle in August 1914, it was given little chance to consider and profit from its experiences in an easy and effective manner for the simple reason that it was continually engaged with the enemy due to the unexpected development of flank-less trench warfare on the Western Front. It was only very slowly that the officers and men of the BEF could begin to pick their way through this novel situation and provide a response. As Sir John French was to write in his memoir, *1914*, 'No previous experience, no conclusion I had been able to draw from campaigns in which I had taken part, or from a close study of the new conditions in which the war of today is waged had led me to anticipate a war of positions. All my thoughts, all my prospective plans, all my possible alternatives of action, were concentrated upon war of movement and manpower.' At the time, too, French had written to a friend in evident

[1] Sir James Edmonds, *Military Operations, France and Belgium, 1914*, Vol. II (London: HMSO, 1925), 10–11.

astonishment in December 1914 that 'modern weapons have completely revolutionised war. It is quite different from anything which you and I have known. A battle is siege on one side and a fortress defence on the other, but on a gigantic scale.'[2]

Understanding what had happened and what could be done about it shaped much of 1915 as trench warfare at least brought about some lulls in activity. Appreciating experiences and implementing improvements, however, were two entirely separate activities determined by Britain's lack of preparation for large-scale continental war and lack of an overall strategic vision. In these circumstances, the internal culture of the army and, in particular, its intellectual ability to come to terms with the new situation had the ability, at the very least, to ameliorate some of the difficulties caused by factors beyond its control. The higher commanders of the BEF were given a particularly difficult challenge by the nature of the warfare that unfolded from August 1914 onwards. Examining the initial ways in which they sought to overcome these difficulties provides a vital audit of its pre-war culture and nature.

The commencement of full mobilisation on 3 August 1914 created much hard work, but it was largely coherent thanks to Major-General Henry Wilson's carefully laid plans. Meticulously drawn up since 1910, Wilson's mobilisation scheme was a masterful blueprint. It was so flexible that it coped easily with a number of changes. The Territorial Force (TF) had gone into summer camp in late July, necessitating a two-day delay from 7 to 9 August as they had to be brought back to their depots before being despatched to wartime stations. Fog in the Channel required a 24-hour delay at one point, and subsequently, following the retreat from Mons and the closure of Boulogne on 26 August, the entire base of operations was switched from Le Havre and Rouen to St. Nazaire and Nantes until mid-October. Yet, within the first 24 hours, a train ran into Southampton every ten minutes, only one being late and by just five minutes. For nineteen consecutive days, Southampton handled ninety trains a day with an average of thirteen ships sailing. By 26 August, a total of 65,814 officers and men had been transported successfully to France.[3]

Given the army's lack of numbers, mobilisation had also entailed the sending of thousands of telegrams calling reservists back to the Colours: between 50 and 60 per cent of the entire BEF consisted of reservists, the

[2] Field Marshal Viscount French, *1914* (London: Constable, 1919), 11; French to Hutton, quoted in Philip Towle, 'The Russo-Japanese War and British Military Thought', *Journal of the Royal United Services Institute for Defence Studies* 116 (1971), 64–8.

[3] Ian F. W. Beckett, 'Going to War: Southampton and Military Embarkation', in Miles Taylor (ed.), *Southampton: Gateway to the British Empire* (London: I. B. Tauris, 2007), 133–48, at 143.

Army Reserve standing at some 146,000 men compared to the regular army at home with a strength of 138,000 men. The war establishment of an infantry battalion was twenty-eight officers and 1,031 other ranks. The 1st Gloucestershire Regiment, for example, needed 600 other ranks and nine officers from the reserve in order to be brought up to strength in 1914, and the 1st Northumberland Fusiliers received 641 reservists on 6 August, of whom over 200 had to be returned to the depot for additional training. The 1st Black Watch also required 500 reservists, with 200 men left behind at the depots as under age for overseas service.[4] Although lacking the sharpness of existing regulars, these reservists did understand the standards required and the BEF's system and thus had the ability to become highly effective soldiers once they re-found the rhythm. However, it also needs to be pointed out that the regular army was rather less experienced than commonly believed. In 1914, only 4,192 regulars had over fifteen years of service, while over 46,000 had under two years of service.[5] The recall and drawing up of the full war establishment created a force of just over 150,000 men organised as one cavalry and six infantry divisions. As has been said of this striking force, however, 'there is no military problem to which the answer is six divisions.' The BEF, of course, had not been shaped by strategic and operational factors but by financial expediency; it represented what the Secretary of State for War between 1905 and 1912, R. B. Haldane, could create within the parameters of his government's policy.[6] Even this small force, however, was not destined to embark in its entirety as a result of the unexpected War Council decision on 6 August to retain the 4th and 6th Divisions at home, 4th Division only proceeding to France on 23 August and 6th Division on 8 September. As already indicated in Chapter 5, it was even less clear when mobilisation was ordered what was intended to be the actual role of the BEF given the disagreements evident in the deliberations of the War Council.

[4] John Mason Sneddon, 'The Company Commanders', in Spencer Jones (ed.), *Stemming the Tide: Officers and Leadership in the British Expeditionary Force, 1914* (Solihull: Helion & Co, 2013), 314–31, at 326–7; Edward Spiers, 'The Regular Army', in Ian F. W. Beckett and Keith Simpson (eds.), *A Nation in Arms: A Social Study of the British Army in the First World War* (Manchester University Press, 1985), 38–60, at 56.

[5] *Statistics of the Military Effort of the British Empire during the Great War* (London: HMSO, 1922).

[6] For a discussion of the role of Haldane in the creation of the BEF, see Edward Spiers, *Haldane: An Army Reformer* (Edinburgh University Press, 1980), 48–91; John Gooch, 'Haldane and the "National Army"', in Ian F. W. Beckett and John Gooch (eds.), *Politicians and Defence: Studies in the Formulation of British Defence Policy, 1845–1970* (Manchester University Press, 1981), 69–86; Ernest M. Teagarden, *Haldane at the War Office* (New York: Gordon Press, 1976).

Of course, compared to the great continental conscript armies, the BEF was tiny. Moreover, its commanders had little experience of handling large formations in the field. While the French and German armies possessed twenty and thirty-five corps headquarters, respectively, in peacetime, the British had but one, namely, that at Aldershot. Only three serving regulars had commanded it – French, Sir Douglas Haig, who took it to war in August 1914, and Lieutenant-General Sir Horace Smith-Dorrien, now commanding Southern Command in Britain. Of the 12,738 regular officers in the army, only 908 had received any staff training, and 22 per cent of them were casualties by May 1915. The belated development of the staff had also resulted in staffs serving commanders in contrast to the German system, where the staff and not the commanders were the real centre of authority. British staff officers could not issue orders on their own authority. Rigid demarcation in staffing terms also saw a division between those responsible for operations and intelligence and those tasked with personnel and supply functions. It might also be argued that command itself was not sufficiently well understood in terms of finding the balance between guidance and control of subordinates, something all the more necessary when a lack of modern communications made empowerment of subordinates vital. Pre-war *Field Service Regulations* had implied decentralisation in command but had not defined it clearly and, in any case, assumed a well-trained staff.[7]

The BEF began crossing to France on 12 August 1914, where its two corps were gradually assembled as cohesive entities. An early shock was the death from a heart attack of Lieutenant-General Sir James Grierson, Commander of II Corps, on 17 August. Grierson was widely regarded as a fine general and had proved a shrewd commander during pre-war manoeuvres, although it is doubtful events would have unfolded very differently had he lived.[8] Sir John French requested the services of Lieutenant-General Sir Herbert Plumer, General Officer Commanding (GOC) of Northern Command, as Grierson's successor, but Kitchener exercised his authority and insisted on Smith-Dorrien instead. French

[7] Peter Scott, 'The Staff of the BEF', *Stand To*! 15 (1985), 44–61; John Bourne, 'British Generals in the First World War', in Gary Sheffield (ed.), *Leadership and Command: The Anglo-American Experience since 1861* (London: Brasseys, 1997), 93–116; Niall Barr, 'Command in Transition from Mobile to Static Warfare, August 1914 to March 1915', in Gary Sheffield and Dan Todman (eds.), *Command and Control on the Western Front: The British Army's Experience, 1914–18* (Staplehurst: Spellmount, 2004), 13–38; John Hussey, 'The Deaths of Qualified Staff Officers in the Great War: A Generation Missing?' *Journal of the Society for Army Historical Research* 75 (1997), 246–59; N. Evans, 'The Deaths of Qualified Staff Officers, 1914–18', *Journal of the Society for Army Historical Research* 78 (2000), 29–37.

[8] Mark Connelly, 'Lieutenant-General Sir James Grierson', in Jones (ed.), *Stemming the Tide*, 133–50.

resented this intrusion by his old rival, Kitchener, but the decision caused a deeper problem. For reasons that are not entirely clear, Smith-Dorrien was not highly regarded by French, conceivably going back to when Smith-Dorrien had succeeded French in the Aldershot Command in 1907 and changed various aspects of the training regime. Kitchener was aware of the animosity but may have wanted a more independently minded officer free of French's own clique.[9] It was an antipathy to Smith-Dorrien, however, seemingly shared by Haig, while it so happened that Haig's Chief of Staff, Brigadier-General John Gough VC, had been on bad personal terms with the Chief of Staff of II Corps, Brigadier-General George Forestier-Walker, since 1903.[10] Smith-Dorrien had a notoriously bad temper, and his own relationship with his chief of staff was fraught, to the extent that Forestier-Walker tried to resign on the evening of the battle of Mons. The BEF, therefore, was opening operations against the enemy with a high command team not fully fused together by mutual confidence and respect.

This lack of cohesion was mirrored within General Headquarters (GHQ) itself. In theory, his chief of staff should have led French's staff. Although the chief of staff had no absolute power invested in him, the position was widely regarded as one of *primus inter pares*. The incumbent in this particular instance, Lieutenant-General Sir Archibald Murray, was to have no such authority or status. Apparently, French had wanted Wilson, but his role in the Curragh Incident in March 1914 had caused the government to look on him with suspicion. There is no real evidence as to how Murray was appointed or by whom, but he was an experienced staff officer and he clearly lacked political baggage. Not to be outflanked, French ensured Wilson's presence by appointing him sub-chief. In turn, Wilson promptly brought with him almost his entire staff from his former post in the War Office's Military Operations Department, including Colonel G. M. Harper as head of operations, who proved especially obstructive in his dealings with Murray. Thus, Murray, who was by no means a particularly forceful character, was utterly undermined from the very start. After the war, indeed, Murray complained that Wilson's clique 'entirely ignored me as far as possible, continually thwarted me, even altered my instructions'.[11] Murray was also one of several staff officers

[9] Steven Corvi, 'Horace Smith-Dorrien', in Ian F. W. Beckett and Steven J. Corvi (eds.), *Haig's Generals* (Barnsley: Pen & Sword, 2006), 183–207; Spencer Jones and Steven J. Corvi, '"A Commander of Rare and Unusual Coolness": Lieutenant-General Sir Horace Lockwood Smith-Dorrien', in Jones (ed.), *Stemming the Tide*, 151–70.

[10] Ian F. W. Beckett, *Johnnie Gough VC: A Biography of Brigadier-General Sir John Edmond Gough VC* (London: Tom Donovan, 1989), 181.

[11] Murray to Deedes, 18 December 1930, quoted in Nikolas Gardner, 'Command in Crisis: The BEF and the Forest of Mormal, August 1914', *War & Society* 16 (1998), 13–32,

who suffered breakdowns under the strain of events, Murray's temporary collapse coming on 25–26 August: the GSO1 of 3rd Division shot himself on 26 August, and the future official historian, Edmonds, then GSO1 to 4th Division, broke down on 28–29 August.[12] Given Murray's marginalisation, Wilson proceeded to exert an extremely baleful influence on Sir John through his constant advice to follow French forces and to take the war to the Germans in an aggressive, offensive manner.

In line with Wilson's pre-war planning, the BEF duly concentrated on Maubeuge in order to protect the French left. Ironically, as already suggested, French had shared Kitchener's earlier reservations that Maubeuge was too far forward and therefore might serve to lessen the BEF's strategic and operational flexibility. Despite these reservations, both men agreed to the deployment in order to maintain entente uniformity. In French's case, the acceptance increased in enthusiasm the more he invested in Wilson's interpretation of the situation. Nikolas Gardner has borrowed the sociological term 'cognitive closure' to describe this mind-set.[13] Gardner suggests that GHQ revealed a weakness that was to beset it continually in its alarming propensity to ignore information contrary to its expectations and desires. Individuals who challenged the dominant view were marginalised and deemed to lack moral fortitude. Wilson's ability to convince French that offensive operations would end in success created a powerful atmosphere of cognitive closure in which he urged Sir John forward despite the fact that liaison between the Belgian, French and British forces was anything but smooth and coherent.

More worrying still was increasing evidence of a potent German threat. French's director of intelligence, Colonel George MacDonogh, doubted the interpretation being placed on German movements. Backed up by evidence from aerial reconnaissance, he argued that the Germans were in fact attempting to outflank the entente powers in a deep westward movement through Belgium. MacDonogh found himself largely disabled by Wilson's dominance. It was not to be the only time on which MacDonogh had difficulty in persuading GHQ to accept his reasoning. Wilson and Harper in particular tended to urge MacDonogh to give French only

at 19. See also John Bourne, 'Major-General Sir Archibald Murray', in Jones (ed.), *Stemming the Tide*, 51–69.

[12] Edmonds himself suggested that he did not do so until after 9 September, but this is erroneous. Compare Dan Snow and Mark Pottle (eds.), *The Confusion of Command: The War Memoirs of Lieutenant-General Sir Thomas D'Oyly Snow, 1914–15* (London: Frontline Books, 2011), 39; with Ian F. W. Beckett (ed.), *The Memoirs of Sir James Edmonds* (Brighton: Tom Donovan. 2013), xiv, 323.

[13] Nikolas Gardner, *Trial by Fire: Command and the British Expeditionary Force in 1914* (Westport, CT: Praeger/Greenwood, 2003), 40–1.

information that coincided with their interpretation. The taciturn MacDonogh was regarded with some suspicion as he was a convert to Catholicism, and he had refused to back the Goughs and their allies at the time of the Curragh Incident. There was to be a stand-up row between French and MacDonogh in September, MacDonogh threatening to resign, and further disagreements in both October and November 1914. Generally, field intelligence relied on 'reliable agents', Belgian civilians, captured Germans and their documents, patrols and aerial reconnaissance. Increasingly, as the 1914 campaign wore on, however, radio intercepts were to become more important. The British and French, for example, picked up over fifty German messages transmitted in plain language between September and November 1914, and interception was to provide some warning of six full-scale German attacks during the First Battle of Ypres. The use of ciphers was in its infancy due to the cumbersome process, but some German ciphers, too, were being broken in October and November 1914.[14] On 22 August 1914, however, using cavalry and Royal Flying Corps reports, MacDonogh managed to persuade French that the situation in front of the BEF was far from simple or clear.

By this date, the BEF was, in fact, in front of Charles Lanrezac's French Fifth Army sitting to its right and in danger of marching even further away from French forces. Further, the BEF was also scattered around the vicinity of Mons. French therefore decided to concentrate his exposed forces. He ordered Lieutenant-General Sir Edmund Allenby's Cavalry Division on his extreme left to form up on II Corps' left and I Corps to close up to II Corps' right. Even at this point French was not set on a defensive mode and was seriously contemplating a resumption of the advance on the following day. What changed his mind was the shocking news that Lanrezac's army had been hit hard and was certainly not going to close up to the BEF. Lieutenant Edward Spears, the British liaison officer at Fifth Army HQ, made this very clear to MacDonogh, who, in turn, forcefully pointed this out to French. French now moved to halt the BEF's advance along the canal at Mons, but it was still uncertain whether this represented a temporary pause or a total re-think of the BEF's position. On meeting Allenby and his two corps commanders early on the morning of Sunday 23 August, French informed them that three German corps were in proximity.

[14] Michael Occleshaw, *Armour against Fate: British Military Intelligence in the First World War* (London: Columbus Books, 1989), 287; David French, 'Sir John French's Secret Service on the Western Front, 1914–15', *Journal, of Strategic Studies* 7 (1984), 423–40; John Ferris, 'The British Army and Signals Intelligence in the Field during the First World War', *Intelligence and National Security* 3–4 (1988), 23–48.

Surprisingly, given the seriousness of this news, he then left for Valenciennes to inspect the 19th Brigade well away from the centre of events.

This nonchalance was not shared lower down the chain, for the men of the BEF were already engaged in strenuous attempts to fortify their positions. The first British units had arrived in Mons on 21 August, having advanced in hot, sunny weather. The infantry was hard pressed to maintain its momentum, burdened down with kit and tested by the uneven, cobbled roads. As cavalry patrols entered Mons, they questioned Belgian civilians on the local situation. On the following day, the rest of the BEF began to arrive and took up positions along the Mons-Condé canal, which ran across the northern tip of the town in a broad, inverted U-shape northwards towards Nimy, placing Mons in a small salient. West of the canal the line was held by Smith-Dorrien's II Corps, while Haig's I Corps covered the eastern end where the canal made a lazy turn towards the north-east. Rather than follow the line of the canal, however, Haig's line pulled away from it, forming a diagonal in a south-easterly direction in order to protect the BEF's flank.

It was not an easy position to defend due to the numerous small slag heaps and mix of industrial and residential buildings which interfered with fields of fire. Major-General Sir Charles Fergusson's 5th Division was most handicapped, being placed in an area where the slag heaps were numerous, yet none compensated by providing commanding observation, and a series of meandering ditches and lanes. Aided by residents of Mons, the British soldiers sought to improve the situation by erecting barricades and digging trenches. By this point aerial reconnaissance had shown clearly that major German forces were marching straight towards the British positions. In fact, eight German divisions of Alexander von Kluck's First Army were advancing with six of them aimed, albeit completely unwittingly, straight at the 3rd and 5th Divisions of II Corps.

Action commenced the next day, Sunday 23 August, in a haphazard and incoherent manner as surprised German units stumbled onto the British positions. The experiences of the 4th Royal Fusiliers holding the bend in the canal at Nimy typified the battle. At first they were utterly stunned by the abundance of targets as German soldiers came on in tight bunches. Using the musketry skills so regularly practised, the fusiliers poured in devastating fire. It was soon noticed, however, that the Germans could bring their howitzers into action, whereas British gunnery was hindered by the close country and lack of observation. German troops also altered formation, learning that dispersal was much safer

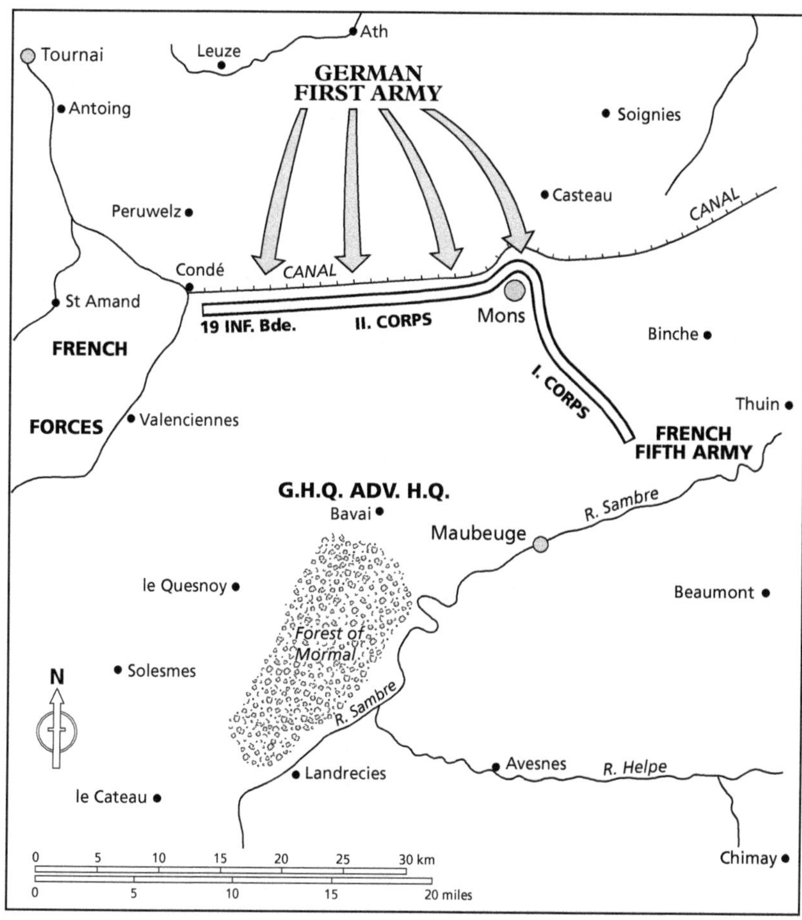

Map 1 Battle of Mons, 21–23 August 1914

than masses. Using their sheer weight of numbers and heavier hitting power, the Germans began to cross the canal, but it was by no means an easy passage. By evening, Smith-Dorrien's II Corps was exhausted and had suffered nearly 1,600 casualties but had inflicted a heavy check on Kluck's forces.[15]

[15] Gardner, *Trial by Fire*, 46–65; J. Paul Harris, *Douglas Haig and the First World War* (Cambridge University Press, 2008), 66–72; John Terraine, *Mons: Retreat to Victory* (London: Batsford, 1960), 78–98.

Salvation occurred for the heavily outnumbered BEF only partially through its combat skills. More important still was Sir John French's sudden understanding of Lanrezac's intentions for Fifth Army. As evidence of Lanrezac's retreat mounted, French's desire to stand, fight and advance drained away. In the early hours of 24 August, French ordered an immediate retreat of the BEF, and a highly skilful disengagement was carried out. Even so, orders for a full retreat confused the corps and divisional commanders as most expected French to return to an offensive mode. Sir John's mercurial temperament and only partial grip on the reality of the situation had created a situation of misunderstanding and doubt. Unable to think clearly and quickly, French finally decided that he would conform to Joffre's request to form a line with the Fifth Army from Valenciennes to Maubeuge; fortunately, he rejected his earlier plans, which involved either a withdrawal to Amiens or refuge in the hopelessly outdated fortress of Maubeuge. French then acted decisively, sending a telegram at 1.40 AM to his corps commanders, making it clear that I Corps should cover II Corps' retreat. Unfortunately, Smith-Dorrien did not receive this telegram, but Haig did at around 2.00 AM.[16]

With Smith-Dorrien lacking precise knowledge of French's intentions and unable to clarify matters until he was able to meet with Haig, 24 August proved to be a hard day for II Corps. It was unable to shake off Kluck's attentions entirely, forming as it did the extreme left hand of the entire entente line. As the two corps continued their retreat during 25 August, they came to the barrier of the Mormal forest, which forced II Corps to the western side and I Corps to the east, thus dividing them from direct, physical contact: Haig was misled into believing the routes through the forest were in too poor a state to support the passage of troops and equipment. In the evening, elements of the German advance guard clashed with Haig's 4th (Guards) Brigade in Landrecies. Haig was deeply concerned by these reports, believing them to be extremely serious. It was a state of mind very probably induced by sickness, but it caused French to conclude that his right hand was in more danger than his left. Haig, in effect, ignored the order to cover II Corps' retreat, even when Smith-

[16] Some debate surrounds the precise nature of the instructions given by French to his corps commanders. Richard Holmes, *The Little Field Marshal: A Life of Sir John French*, 2nd edn. (London: Weidenfeld & Nicolson, 2004), 220, implies that French did not make his intentions clear, which is repeated in Hew Strachan, *The First World War: To Arms* (Oxford University Press, 2001), 222. However, although Gardner, *Trial by Fire*, 48, condemns French for leaving too much to the hard-pressed staffs of I and II Corps, he, like Harris, *Haig*, 72, refers to the 1.40 AM telegram, as does Edmonds, *Military Operations, France and Belgium, 1914*, Vol. I (London: Macmillan, 1922), 97–8.

Dorrien made his way to Haig's headquarters to request assistance, by which time Haig's formations were already in retreat from Landrecies. Subsequently, he attempted to conceal the extent to which his actions had diverted from GHQ's intentions. The seven days in which I and II Corps were to be out of contact were the most critical period of the retreat.[17] French's misconception of the situation increased the misery on II Corps, which had spent almost three days in continual combat. As his units stumbled into Le Cateau during the early hours of 26 August, and realising that daylight would make it impossible to slip away easily, Smith-Dorrien decided to turn and fight the Germans. His intention was to bloody the German muzzle and then recommence the retreat in somewhat better order. French was not at all happy with this decision, believing that it recklessly imperilled the corps, and thus it further deepened his distrust of II Corps' commander. Smith-Dorrien, by contrast, felt sure that he was carrying out the only possible course of action in such extreme circumstances. In addition, he probably felt some confidence that Haig would act to protect his right flank. Wishing to provide as much fire support as possible, 5th Division moved its guns forward among the infantry. In turn, this made both the guns and the infantry in their immediate vicinity much more liable to German counter-battery fire. Once again, British soldiers fought with a mixture of great skill and intense ferocity, suffering 7,812 casualties in the process.[18]

Throughout the battle, II Corps fought alone unaided by Haig. Although much of this failure can be attributed to a collapse in communications between the two corps, Haig has been condemned for his failure to march to the sound of the guns, which were clearly audible at his headquarters.[19] The result of the battle was that Smith-Dorrien was able to resume the retreat. The fact that he then managed to put considerable distance between himself and his pursuers is attributable not just to the intensity of his men's resistance but also to the profound failure of German reconnaissance and intelligence to discover and interpret British intentions properly: Georg von der Marwitz's German Cavalry Corps failed to pursue II Corps, and the Germans continued to believe that the British were moving south-west rather than south. After the war, French's notorious memoir, *1914*, grossly misrepresented Smith-Dorrien's stand at Le Cateau,

[17] Gardner, 'Command in Crisis', 13–32; Harris, *Haig*, 72–82.
[18] Gardner, *Trial by Fire*, 46–65; Harris, *Haig*, 66–72.
[19] Harris, *Douglas Haig*, 76.

but the general consensus was that Smith-Dorrien had thereby saved the BEF.[20]

Despite this escape, there was no let-up for the BEF as the retreat continued to place an immense strain on all ranks. Especially hard hit were the many reservists who had softened up during their years of civilian life. The sudden reversion to march discipline in active service conditions was a profound shock. But it was not just the reservists who found it tough, as even serving regulars found it difficult. Some reached breaking point, such as the commanding officers of the 1st Royal Warwickshires and 2nd Royal Dublin Fusiliers, Lieutenant-Colonels J. F. Elkington and A. E. Mainwaring, who planned to surrender at St. Quentin on 27 August but were stopped by the intervention of a staff officer, Major Tom Bridges. Both were cashiered, but Elkington subsequently regained his rank after distinguishing himself as a private soldier in the French Foreign Legion.[21]

As the BEF trudged south in a trance-like state, the force's supply services strained to ensure supplies of food, water and ammunition. It was an intensely difficult task in the congested roads made worse still by the fact that the BEF had drifted a long way from its formal lines of communication. A potentially greater problem was the fault-line lying at the core of the BEF's logistics in the structural division between the Quartermaster-General's (QMG's) staff and that of the Inspector-General of Communications (IGC). The QMG, Major-General Sir William Robertson, resided at GHQ, whereas the IGC had his own entirely separate office. Although this issue had been raised at a pre-war staff meeting, it had not been resolved, revealing the lack of attention the British Army paid to the issue of supply. Fortunately for the BEF, Robertson as QMG and Major-General F. S. Robb, the IGC, worked well with each other, and Robertson in particular managed to maintain a tight grip on the situation. Robertson wished to change the command structure both so that Robb would be responsible for supplies only as far as the BEF's railheads, with the QMG taking responsibility for all supply matters thereafter, and also so that the IGC would be subordinate to the QMG. Such a situation, however, was not realised until September 1916.[22] Thus, the BEF survived despite its system, not because of it.

Fixated on keeping his force together, Sir John French's earlier optimism had evaporated completely and had been replaced by an equally

[20] Ian F. W. Beckett (ed.), *The Judgement of History: Sir Horace Smith-Dorrien, Lord French and "1914"* (London: Tom Donovan, 1993), vi–xxvi.

[21] The best analysis of this episode is in Peter Scott, *Dishonoured: The Colonels' Surrender at St. Quentin* (London: Tom Donovan, 1994).

[22] John Spencer, '"The Big Brain in the Army": Sir William Robertson as Quartermaster General', in Jones (ed.), *Stemming the Tide*, 89–108.

strongly held feeling, that of grievance against his French ally. This see-sawing of emotions impervious to intellectual grip and objective thinking seriously undermined French's capabilities as a commander. Deeply scarred by Lanrezac's failure to inform him of his retreat, French fell back on his instructions from Kitchener. These made clear that in the event of defeat, he should retreat along his line of communications to the coast. British strategic independence now came to the fore again with even Wilson believing that a retreat homeward might be useful. On 30 August, French therefore announced that he planned to pull the BEF out of the line for ten days to rest and refit at a location west of Paris. The gap thus created in the entente line would have forced Michel-Joseph Maunoury's French Sixth Army to close up with Lanrezac's flank, subsequently compelling Joffre to forfeit the chance of enveloping the oncoming German forces.

French's intransigence and refusal to comply with Joffre's demands led to Anglo-French discussions at the highest levels with the result that Kitchener went to France and personally ordered Sir John to co-operate. Revealing further his lack of grip, French descended into rage at Kitchener's use of his field marshal's uniform when visiting as a civilian in his role of Secretary of State for War. An important issue about Britain's strategic and operational independence was therefore reduced to a point of military protocol and etiquette.

By now the wider military situation was beginning to alter. From 31 August, Joffre had become aware that Kluck was going to pass east of Paris, and French General Headquarters (GQG) slowly began to realise the potential for a counter-offensive into the German flank. Aerial reconnaissance then proved decisively to both Joseph Galliéni, the Military Governor of Paris, and Joffre that the German forces were exposing their right flank along the line of the River Marne. By contrast, German intelligence was still extremely sketchy, and it remained largely oblivious to the developing threat, convinced, as it was, that the BEF was a thoroughly defeated force unsupported by any powerful and cohesive French units.[23]

The BEF's retreat finally came to an end on 5 September some fifteen miles southeast of Paris. Its enormous trek was over, having covered nearly 200 miles in thirteen days. The opportunity for rest and reorganisation was utilised, which improved morale immensely. Joffre's plan was

[23] Gardner, *Trial by Fire*, 92–102; Strachan, *To Arms*, 250–61. The adverse German assessments of the BEF generally have been repeated in Terence Zuber, *The Mons Myth: A Reassessment of the Battle* (Stroud: History Press, 2010).

for the BEF to advance between Maunoury's Sixth Army to its left and Louis-Félix Franchet d'Espérey's (who had replaced Lanrezac) Fifth Army to the right, thus providing French with the assurance that his flanks were well protected. Maunoury went into battle on 5 September, surprising the German forces. The assault was followed up the next day by the BEF and French Fifth Army. After so many days retreating, most British soldiers interpreted the reversion to the offensive as a positive step. It proved to be a relatively comfortable day for the BEF as the advance was barely interrupted by the Germans. Moving in a north-easterly direction, the BEF augmented by a modest French contingent advanced through the Forest of Crécy and up to the line of the Grand Morin River and its confluence with the Aubetin. The next day the Grand Morin was crossed, and much evidence was found of a very hasty German retreat, which further boosted morale. The momentum was carried into the 8 September when the BEF crossed the Petit Morin and even reached the Marne at some points. Happily for the BEF, it was advancing into a gap between the German First and Second Armies and thus met minimal resistance. Crossing the Marne in force on 9 September, the BEF found that the Germans were retreating still further.

In the face of these entente moves, the Chief of the German General Staff, Helmuth von Moltke, decided to withdraw to the River Aisne and prepare field fortifications. By 13 September, both the German First and Second Armies had crossed to the right bank of the Aisne and were holding the heights that dominated the river. The realisation that the Germans were melting away caused French and Franchet d'Espérey to order a vigorous pursuit of the enemy. However, both found that their subordinate commanders advanced only cautiously. The BEF has been particularly criticised for its tardiness in the advance from 5 to 13 September.[24] These criticisms fail to take into account the utter exhaustion of men and horses, the impact of cold, wet weather on tired men and the new-found respect for an enemy possessing impressive firepower assets.

By 12 September, elements of the BEF had closed up on the Aisne, and some had even crossed it. On the following day, more British units followed with surprising ease, finding that the Germans had not thoroughly destroyed all bridges and only partially troubled by inefficient enemy artillery fire. But, having crossed, few British troops did anything with great intent. This further failure to move with decision haunted Haig in particular, who remained sensitive to the accusation that he did not exploit his initial advances with sufficient boldness. Command failures made themselves apparent throughout the battles of the Marne and the

[24] Harris, *Haig*, 86.

Aisne. It is clear that GHQ staff took a long time to recover composure after the spell of optimism was broken. Although there was a recovery of morale and fighting spirit among the front-line troops once the retreat ended and they had had a chance to snatch some rest, GHQ staff seemed to remain in a state of almost total paralysis. There was little effective attempt to co-ordinate the actions of the corps and divisions, meaning that the BEF often moved piecemeal during the battle of the Marne and subsequent advance to the Aisne. Of particular concern was the increasing problem of co-ordinating infantry and artillery, leading to friendly-fire incidents. The 1st Division War Diary for 10 September 1914, for example, recorded British artillery firing on their infantry and ascribed the error to the absence of 'any mutual system of intercommunication arranged between the infantry and the [artillery] Brigade originally detailed to support the attack'.[25]

When confidence was recovered and the pursuit to the Aisne urged, it was often achieved through unnecessarily costly attacks as artillery ammunition was bled dry, although it was being understood that there must be more dispersion in infantry attack. However, at Ypres, Major-General Sir Thompson Capper's 7th Division tended to dig in on forward slopes where they were more vulnerable to artillery fire.[26] Lacking cohesion and resolve, the BEF handed the advantage back to the Germans. Although all German infantry attacks were disposed of using the musketry skills shown at Mons, the British found the enemy artillery much harder to deal with as it began to pound their positions and crossing points with great accuracy. Insufficiently equipped with howitzers, the British had no real response to the German artillery dominance. With neither side possessing a definitive advantage, both were now digging trenches on a much grander scale in order to hold onto their positions and free up men for alternative operations. As Hew Strachan has commented, 'Bitterest of ironies, trench warfare was adopted to enable mobile operations to take place [elsewhere].'[27]

After nearly a month of inconclusive trench warfare during which the BEF suffered 18,922 casualties (12 September–3 October), attention was switched back to Belgium and the possibility of winning the war on this still-open flank. For Britain, two prospects opened up. First the chance to

25 Quoted in Gardner, *Trial by Fire*, 82.

26 Spencer Jones, 'The Thin Khaki Line: The Evolution of Infantry Attack Formations in the British Army, 1899–1914', in Michael Locicero, Ross Mahoney and Stuart Mitchell (eds.), *A Military Transformed? Adaptation and Innovation in the British Military, 1792–1945* (Solihull: Helion & Co, 2014), 83–96; Ian F. W. Beckett, *Ypres: The First Battle, 1914* (Harlow: Pearson Education, 2004), 72, 91–2.

27 Strachan, *To Arms*, 261.

shorten the BEF's lines of communication and concentrate the force in an area of extreme interest to the safety of Britain; second was the opportunity to exert its strategic flexibility and independence by deploying a newly formed Royal Naval Division and the newly constituted IV Corps consisting of the 7th Division and the 3rd Cavalry Division, Sir John French favouring the opportunity of resuming the offensive on the open flank. Such intentions coincided roughly with Joffre's desire to use this last remaining open space on the Western Front. The problem was that the Germans had much the same idea, so the vastly unequal relationship in the force-to-space ratio, which had been present throughout the campaign, was to be repeated on an even more concentrated scale.[28]

The Royal Naval Division was despatched with the intention of assisting Belgian forces in the defence of Antwerp, which appeared ever more problematic. Arriving on 2 October, its position was supposed to be bolstered by the despatch of IV Corps under Lieutenant-General Sir Henry Rawlinson, which began disembarking at Zeebrugge on 6 October. Realising that marching on the rapidly collapsing city of Antwerp would place his division in extreme danger, Capper of 7th Division advanced to Ghent instead. From there Capper assisted in the Belgian Army's withdrawal from its line north of the city and the extraction of the last remnants from Antwerp: part of the 1st Naval Brigade interned itself in the Netherlands rather than surrender to the Germans, and part of the Royal Marine Brigade was captured. Rawlinson's corps now fell back onto the bulk of the BEF, which was gathering around the Belgian town of Ypres, making contact on 14 October. The BEF had been brought up from the Aisne largely by railway, the transport of I Corps alone involving fifty-one trains for combatants and thirteen for supplies.[29] IV Corps now reverted from its independent role to one under GHQ's command. Once again, friction was to mar the internal management of the BEF as French was piqued by Kitchener's decision to create an independent force in the first place and annoyed still further by the choice of Rawlinson, another officer he doubted, for command. Smooth command was further complicated by IV Corps' lack of staff officers and cobbled-together status. No one had any kind of relationship or experience of working as a team. Inadequate command structures such as this could only be compensated by superlative performances from the officers and men at the sharp end. This the BEF achieved time and again during the battles of 1914.

Unfortunately for the BEF, GHQ once again fell victim to cognitive closure. Ignoring reports that German forces were gathering in strength, French was again convinced that vigorous offensive action would bring

[28] For the 'Race to the Sea', see Beckett, *Ypres*, 12–25. [29] *Ibid.*, 17.

about great results. However, it must be stressed that French was being subjected to an almost continual stream of offensive-minded plans from General Ferdinand Foch, who had been appointed the Northern Army Group Commander by Joffre, and his immediate subordinate, General Victor d'Urbal. Both men were convinced that a path could be forced through Roulers and on to Thorout. It was in this atmosphere that French arranged the BEF around Ypres. A little after IV Corps took up its position, I Corps was ordered forward to a line north-west of Ypres near the Ypres-Yser canal. To I Corps' left and slightly to its front was a French Territorial Division, which, in turn, was supported by a French cavalry corps providing the link to the Belgian Army on the entente's extreme left. On I Corps' right and slight front was Rawlinson's IV Corps, which then gave way to Allenby's newly created Cavalry Corps, with the British line completed by the III and II Corps stretching down to Givenchy-La Bassée. Sir William Pulteney's III Corps had been constituted from the 4th and 6th Divisions on 31 August.

French had ordered Rawlinson into action on 18 October, much to the latter's dismay. Reports of strong German forces to his front had convinced Rawlinson that an attempt to advance on Menin in great strength would be folly. As a result, he advanced only cautiously. Disgruntled by this seeming lack of dash, French angrily ordered another attack for the following day. Rawlinson duly carried out his orders but was repulsed by the Germans. Under intense pressure, the 3rd Cavalry Division was even forced to give some ground. Fortunately for Rawlinson, French decided against continuing assaults with the IV Corps and turned his attention to Haig's I Corps.

Before I Corps could carry out any kind of offensive action, it first had to deal with a furious German assault on 21 October. Once again, the Germans played into British hands by failing to co-ordinate their infantry and artillery and sending in dense clumps of infantry. Superior British musketry ripped the German assaults to pieces, particularly at Langemarck, where the hard-pressed 7th Division managed to hold its own. Assessing the situation, French did not believe that he could order an advance and requested General Antoine de Mitry, commander of the French cavalry corps, to pay particular attention to Haig's flank. D'Urbal now insisted on a renewed assault, but Sir John declined to assist. On 22 October, French troops attacked alone to very little effect. At the same time, another German assault fell on Haig's 1st Division. Thinly strung out along an extended line, the men of Major-General Samuel Lomax's 1st Division provided another example of excellent musketry. When the line buckled in the middle, a well-executed counter-attack by Brigadier-

General Edward Bulfin's 2nd Brigade retrieved the situation. Haig and his corps had performed extremely well.

Although German strength showed no obvious signs of lessening, Foch insisted that a counter-attack be mounted. French was prepared to accept Foch's demands because he shared d'Urbal's belief that the opposing forces were now finely balanced in Belgium and that even a slight tip of the balance in the entente favour could force the Germans back to Ostend, unhinging their entire position. Similar thoughts were pervading the German high command with Moltke's successor, Erich von Falkenhayn, concentrating on maintaining assaults along the Yser and south of Ypres. The hard-hit 7th Division holding Gheluvelt found itself in the path of a major German assault on 24 October. Already tottering under its weight of casualties, the division was put under immense pressure. Between 22 and 24 October it suffered the loss of 120 officers and 2,700 men; by 24 October, total officer casualties amounted to 45 per cent, while the other ranks' losses stood at 37 per cent.[30] Rawlinson vented his frustrations in a bleak assessment for French, in which he claimed that excessive demands were being made on his corps. Predictably, French's temper over-boiled, and it was only assuaged by Rawlinson's profuse apology. French gained his revenge by moving the 7th Division to Haig's command and returning Rawlinson to Britain in order to instruct the new 8th Division on current active conditions. This move seemed to diffuse the situation, for Rawlinson returned to active command on 12 November without too much difficulty.

Having managed to fend off such desperate attacks, Foch, d'Urbal and French were all convinced that the balance had now tipped in the entente's favour. Revealing their adherence to pre-war concepts of combat, all three believed that they had weathered the fury of the enemy's assault, which, in turn, made them vulnerable to counter-attack. Driven by such thinking, Haig's and Rawlinson's corps' were ordered into action on 25 October with the intention of supporting the assault of the French IX Corps. Pressure was undoubtedly put on the Germans, but at no point was there anything like a clean break through the enemy positions or major readjustment of its line. Indeed, German counter-attacks continued to exert equal pressure on British positions. Despite this ebb and flow, French remained convinced that the underlying situation remained the same: German strength was lessening. His attempts to maintain the offensive over the next few days did little to alter the situation noticeably other than to continue the attrition on the BEF.

[30] *Ibid.*, 93.

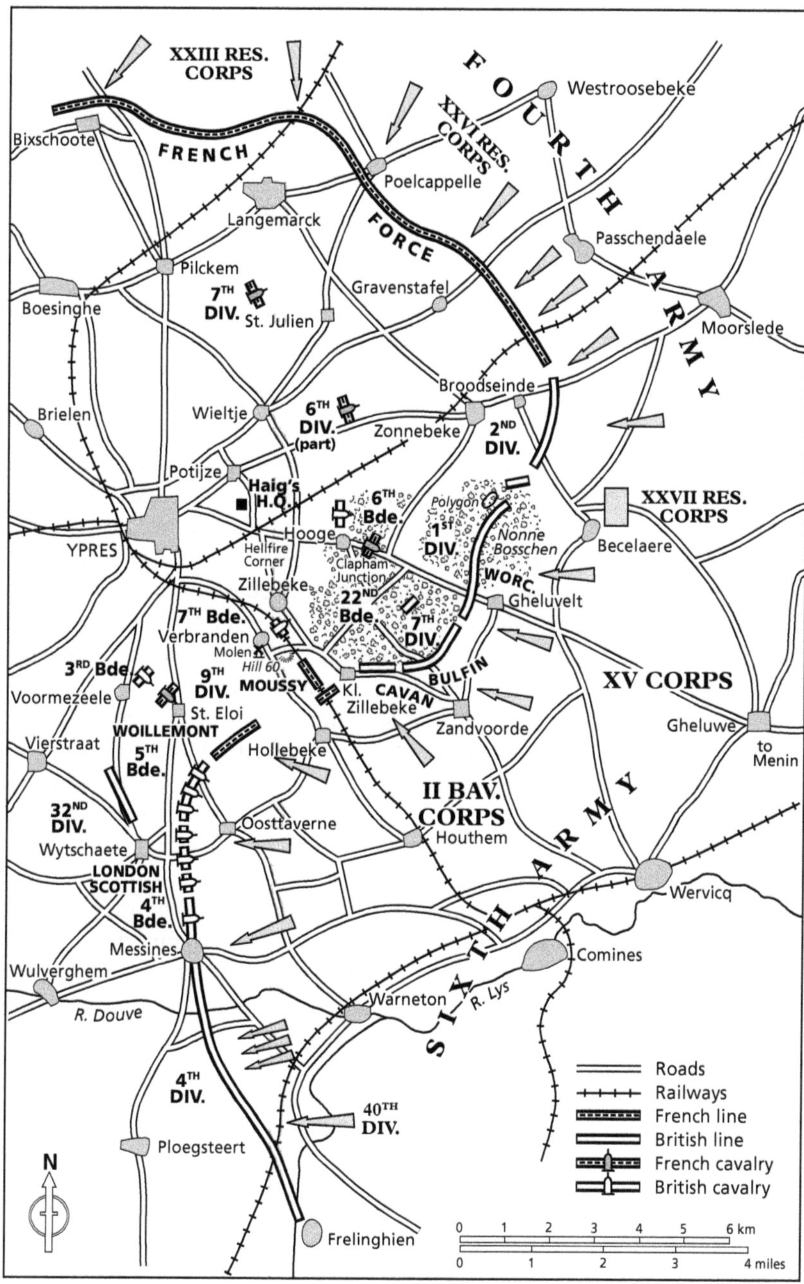

Map 2 First Battle of Ypres, 31 October 1914

Both the German and entente forces were now involved in a desperate spiral of escalating violence, with each convinced that the next big punch would cause great results. This spiral became even more intense with the inundation of the coastal region from Nieuport to the Yser embankment. Achieved by the opening of the lock gates and sluices by Belgian engineers between 21 and 28 October, the floods destroyed any chance of using the area for major offensive action.[31] In turn, this meant that even more military power was forced into the Ypres front. Falkenhayn created a new force consisting of the XIII, XV and II Bavarian Corps, 26th Division, 6th Bavarian Reserve Division and I Cavalry Corps, all under General Max von Fabeck. Eager to open a new line of assault, Falkenhayn directed it to the south of Ypres to attack in a north-westerly direction between Messines and Gheluvelt along the Menin road. Haig's I Corps lay astride the road with Allenby's cavalry corps to his immediate right.

The German assault commenced on 29 October and in another day of furious fighting pushed I Corps back along the Menin road. Although hard pressed, British units struck back in equally desperate counter-attacks which had some success. Revealing the utter lack of reality that was engulfing many senior commanders in this phase of the war, French still felt that significant gains could be made through offensive action. It was a spirit Haig decided to ignore, ordering his corps onto the defensive. With Fabeck's force now in place, another powerful assault fell on Haig's men on the following day which caused him to appeal to General Pierre Dubois, commander of the neighbouring French IX Corps, to shore up the defence at Zandevoorde. At the same time, Allenby's corps was being forced back. Throughout these assaults it was the power of the German artillery that caused most problems for the British. Lacking heavy guns, they were often powerless to respond until the German troops showed themselves. Firing in close support of defending British infantry ensured that the British optimised the power of their guns, but it left them vulnerable to the heavier German pieces. With the artillery's help, the British infantry was then given the opportunity to deploy its immense fire discipline and ability to make every round count.

Crisis arrived on 31 October with I Corps put under intense pressure. Command almost broke down when a German shell hit Hooge Chateau, killing and wounding a significant portion of the staffs of the 1st and 2nd Divisions, including Lomax of the 1st Division, who was to die of his wounds in April 1915. French was in the area and visited Haig's

[31] For the inundations, see Ian F. W. Beckett, *The Making of the First World War* (New Haven, CT: Yale University Press, 2012), 12–30; and Paul van Pul, *In Flanders Flooded Fields* (Barnsley: Pen & Sword, 2006).

headquarters at the White Chateau, where he found all in an extremely grave mood. Both French and Haig were to exhibit great anxiety during the course of the day. Fortunately, the situation was being shored up by the famous assault of the 2nd Worcesters. Moving south-east from a line due north of the Menin road, they forced the Germans off the Gheluvelt crossroads. This minor epic was a triumph of the strengths of the BEF. The close relationship Brigadier-General Charles Fitzclarence VC, Commander of the 4th (Guards) Brigade, had with his fellow officers in the 2nd Division gave him the ability to plan, order and co-ordinate the counter-attack, which was then seen through with great gallantry. In the intensity of battle, tactical command had become the preserve of brigadiers such as Fitzclarence and Bulfin and even lieutenant-colonels, with higher commanders often forced to react to their decisions rather than shape them.[32] The personal leadership qualities displayed at Ypres, while admirable in themselves and necessary to the BEF's survival, came at a heavy price. Major-General Hubert Hamilton of 3rd Division had been unnecessarily killed earlier on 14 October while well forward. Fitzclarence would be killed on 12 November, and the reckless courage of Capper of 7th Division throughout the operations at Ypres was to foreshadow his death at Loos in September 1915. Haig's much vaunted ride up the Menin road on the afternoon of 31 October just after the recovery of Gheluvelt was also symbolic of the exercise of personal leadership, although few troops would have seen Haig, and it actually deprived I Corps of its commander when the command structure had been severely weakened by the loss of the staffs of 1st and 2nd Divisions.[33]

From this point the first battle of Ypres began to unwind, but it did not splutter out quietly with the British, particularly Haig's I Corps, facing major tests on 11 and 12 November. Once more, on 11 November, the situation was retrieved by the action of a single battalion, the 2nd Oxfordshire and Buckinghamshire Light Infantry driving elements of the Prussian Guard from Nonneboschen.[34] The stress the battle caused on the BEF was immense. On 12 November, 1st Division was reduced to sixty-eight officers and 2,776 other ranks (OR). In the 1st Brigade the numbers had been whittled down to four officers and 271 OR, but despite

[32] Michael Locicero, '"A Tower of Strength": Brigadier-General Edward Bulfin', and Spencer Jones, '"The Demon": Brigadier-General Charles Fitzclarence, VC', both in Jones (ed.), *Stemming the Tide*, 211–39, 240–62.

[33] Gardner, *Trial by Fire*, 207–31; Harris, *Haig*, 103–4; Beckett, *Ypres*, 177–8. See also John Hussey, 'A Hard Day at First Ypres: The Allied Generals and their Problems, 31 October 1914', *British Army Review* 107 (1994), 70–89; John Hussey, 'Haig's Ride up the Menin Road at First Ypres on 31 October 1914: Did He Invent the Whole Story?' *Bulletin of the Military Historical Society* 46 (1995), 21–9.

[34] Beckett, *Ypres*, 166–71.

this, the over-stretch on British manpower meant that the 1st Brigade still had to find a battalion for front-line duty. Between 14 October and 30 November, 58,155 men, the majority infantry, were made casualties. Of the eighty-four infantry battalions at Ypres on 1 November 1914, seventy-five had fewer than 300 men, while eighteen had fewer than 100, and only nine exceeded 300.[35] By 30 November, too, 842 officers had been killed since August, with a further 688 missing and 2,097 wounded.[36] The situation also took further toll of French's psychological strength. He descended into another gloom which caused Kitchener to raise the idea of replacing him at an Anglo-French conference.

The desperation of the fighting at Ypres makes it easy to lose sight of the fact that the BEF was heavily engaged further south during the same period. Battles of equal fury were fought out on II Corps' front between Neuve Chapelle and La Bassée. The landscape of the region made all operations extremely difficult. Flat, boggy, interspersed with numerous drainage ditches and intersected with thick hedgerows, movement was difficult and easily spotted from any vantage point. Joffre had hoped that the BEF's II and III Corps would help to save the important industrial city of Lille, but it fell on 12 October before British forces could intervene, although Armentiéres was held. Already much weakened by its fighting and particularly deficient in officers, II Corps found itself locked in a series of exchanges which drained away its resources still further. Continually urged into aggressive action, II Corps took part in intense fighting to regain Givenchy and move on Aubers Ridge. Doubtless feeling the gaze of French upon him, Smith-Dorrien demanded action, and when the costly fighting proved inconclusive, he removed Sir Charles Fergusson, commander of 5th Division, for his failure. In turn, this placed pressure on its brigadiers and battalion commanders to produce results. Faced with a series of thankless tasks, the only useful response many felt able to make was that of setting an example of extreme personal courage. Precious human resources were therefore frittered away in a series of ill-conceived attacks. In this depressing atmosphere can be seen the first glimpses of the intellectual sterility that descended on many higher-level commanders for the next few years, namely, that the only real measure of intent was the number of casualties. It was a factor which made itself particularly felt when there was either a poor or client relationship between commander and subordinate. The nadir for 1914 was reached

[35] Edmonds, *Military Operations*, Vol. II, 449, 466–7.

[36] Peter Hodgkinson, 'The Infantry Battalion Commanding Officers of the BEF', in Jones (ed.), *Stemming the Tide*, 293–313, at 305.

when Neuve Chapelle was lost on 27 October, and French ordered a series of attacks to recover it. Smith-Dorrien's approach perhaps revealed his scepticism, for he split his men into two groups. One was allocated the recapture of Neuve Chapelle, while the other was put to work on the preparation of a second line of defence. The attack was to be carried out by British, French and men from the newly arrived Indian Corps.[37] Given this mix of languages and experience, it is hardly surprising that confusion surrounded the planning. This was made all too clear when the artillery bombardment lifted and only four companies (47th Sikhs and 20th and 21st Companies, Sappers and Miners) left their trenches to make the attack. Unsurprisingly, Neuve Chapelle was not recovered. On the night of 29–30 October, French withdrew much of the exhausted II Corps into reserve under his personal control and thus effectively relieved Smith-Dorrien of his command duties. Between 12 and 31 October, II Corps lost men at an alarming rate. The 3rd Division suffered 219 officer and 5,616 OR casualties, with its 8th and 9th Divisions reduced to less than half their original establishments.[38] The pre-war assumption had been a wastage rate of 40 per cent in the first six months of a war and perhaps 65 to 75 per cent in the first twelve months: the reality was 63 per cent in the first three months alone.[39]

Contrary to many popular understandings of Great War commanders, all European armies had considered the high probability of mass casualties in any future war due to the power of modern weapons. The totally unexpected thing was the lack of decision and mobility after such an intense blood-letting. Lieutenant-General Sir Nevil Macready, the Adjutant-General, put total BEF casualties between the commencement of the campaign in France to 30 November at 89,864. This figure exceeds the original establishment of the first seven infantry divisions, which numbered 84,000 men. The BEF's ability to stay in the line was due to the rapid despatch of reinforcements totalling 109,272 men. In addition, both Territorial units and the Indian Corps boosted the numbers of the BEF.[40]

Such reinforcement and the need to create a more efficient supply and command system saw the creation of two armies on 25 December. First Army was commanded by Haig and comprised I, IV and the Indian

[37] Coverage of the Indian Army's contribution to the war lies outside the scope of this book, but for the Indian Corps and its tribulations on the Western Front, see George Morton-Jack, *The Indian Army on the Western Front: India's Expeditionary Force to France and Belgium in the First World War* (Cambridge University Press, 2014).

[38] Edmonds, *Military Operations, 1914, Vol. II*, 222; Beckett, *Ypres*, 101–13.

[39] David French, *British Economic and Strategic Planning, 1905–15* (London: Allen & Unwin, 1982), 26.

[40] Strachan, *To Arms*, 278.

Corps; Second Army was placed under Smith-Dorrien and consisted of II and III Corps and the 27th Division. The two cavalry corps, Lieutenant-General Sir Michael Rimington's Indian and Allenby's British, came under direct GHQ control. This seemingly impressive move had two distinct weaknesses. First, no British commander or staff officer was in anyway prepared for an army system, as opposed to a divisional one. Indeed, the functions of corps were not clear, let alone armies. French had delayed the introduction of army-level commands precisely because he believed that they would impose an unacceptable additional level of command between corps commanders and himself, and he preferred adding more divisions to corps. Even when the two armies were created, he saw them primarily as administrative structures. By contrast, Haig did not regard an army headquarters as a mere post office, emphasising in December 1914 that his corps commanders should not deal directly with GHQ on operational matters.[41] Secondly, many of the reinforcements despatched from Britain lacked full training and had very little experience being Special Reservists and Territorials. Fortunately, winter weather ensured a lull in operations which at least gave the later arrivals a chance to adapt to conditions on the Western Front gradually.

Of perhaps far greater concern to the BEF was the issue of ordnance and logistics, which showed no signs of immediate improvement. The BEF's munitions supply was a particular worry, for it was the result of a systemic weakness and so was unlikely to be fixed quickly or cheaply. It was a system that had emerged during the South African War when British forces had suffered similar supply problems. Sir Francis Mowatt had chaired a committee appointed to investigate the issue of ammunition manufacture and supply, and most of its proposals were accepted in 1904. However, they were based on the assumption that a six-division army and one cavalry division would have to be kept in the field for a campaign similar in duration to that experienced in South Africa. No particular allowance was made for a continental war. This may have been excusable given Britain's foreign and military policies of the time, but more worrying was the failure to revise the figures in the wake of rearming with a quick-firing gun. Some significant revisions were made in 1912 when the need to increase small arms ammunition was accepted. This decision is revealing for it implies both the continuing demand for economy and the belief that the infantry fire fight was the decisive element in battle.

41 Barr, 'Command in Transition', 13–38; Andy Simpson, 'British Corps Command ion the Western Front, 1914–18', in Sheffield and Todman (eds.), *Command and Control*, 97–118.

Ammunition production was mainly vested in three small state-owned factories at Woolwich, Waltham Abbey and Enfield Lock. The placing of tenders with other firms was technically possible but had to be arranged by the Finance Department of the War Office at the request of the Master-General of the Ordnance. It was a system that was in no way prepared for the situation met on the Western Front in the autumn of 1914. In 1914, the production capacity of the Royal Ordnance Factories was limited to 10,000 rounds per month for thirteen- and eighteen-pounder guns and 4.5-inch howitzers and only 100 rounds per month for the heavier sixty-pounder guns. Total reserves for each gun were most abundant for the eighteen-pounders (486,000 rounds), but this translated into only 324 rounds for each gun at that calibre. There were 129,600 rounds available for the 4.5-inch howitzers. Once again, the situation was most constricted for the sixty-pounder guns at 24,000 rounds, or twenty-four for each gun. The Mowatt Committee drew up projections of expenditure and replacement requiring 400 to 500 additional rounds for each calibre after the first six months. However, all these preparations and calculations were made meaningless within the first few months of the war. In theory, each eighteen-pounder was supposed to have 1,000 rounds available, of which thirty-three would be retained in the United Kingdom and 500 manufactured within six months. At battery level, however, there were only 176 rounds available. Moreover, if the gun was fired at the preferred Rate 4 (four rounds per minute), the entire stock envisaged for each gun for the first six months of war would have been exhausted in fewer than seven hours of continuous action.[42]

The inability to envisage the actual scenario had significant effects on the BEF's ability to fight effectively. III Corps ran out of ammunition entirely for its heavier sixty-pounders and 4.5-inch howitzers on 15–16 September. On 10 October, French reported that he had only six rounds per day for his eighteen-pounders, nine for the sixty-pounders and eleven for the 4.5-inch howitzers. Compared to an average expenditure on the Aisne of fourteen rounds day, that at Ypres from 21–24 October had reached seventy-six rounds a day. With only 150 rounds per gun left in the theatre of operations and only seven per gun per day being received from Britain, an order was issued on 24 October restricting expenditure to thirty rounds a day for the eighteen-pounders and fifteen rounds a day for 4.5-inch howitzers. In II Corps, Smith-Dorrien

[42] Jonathan Bailey, 'British Artillery in the Great War', in Paddy Griffith (ed.), *British Fighting Methods in the Great War* (London: Frank Cass, 1996), 2–29, at 25; Jonathan Bailey, *The First World War and the Birth of the Modern Style of Warfare* (London: HMSO and Strategic and Combat Studies Institute, 1996), 9; Edmonds, *Military Operations, 1914*, Vol. II, 12–14.

specified that artillery should only be used against infantry attack or easily identifiable vulnerable targets. Limits for the eighteen-pounders were lifted to fifty rounds per day on 26 October but remained for 4.5-inch howitzers. Batteries were allowed to exceed daily limits as the intensity of operations at Ypres increased. Indeed, on average, guns were firing off eighty rounds per day, with some batteries reporting firing as many as 1,200 in twenty-four hours. Between 21 October and 22 November, I Corps expended 54 per cent of all the eighteen-pounder shells it would fire during the entire war.[43]

Kitchener, who had always seen war with Germany as a prolonged and expensive affair, immediately ordered the Royal Ordnance Factories to move to full capacity, and the private sector was flooded with contracts. However, this had unfortunate consequences on quality control and the procurement and supply of the vital raw materials necessary for shell production. At the same time, the vital need for new guns was realised, and on 12 October the issue was discussed at the first meeting of the new Cabinet Committee on Munitions. It was reported that contracts had already been placed for thirty-two heavy, forty-eight medium and sixty light howitzers. In order to meet the immediate shortfall, guns, including obsolete marks, were scraped together from every store and sent to France.[44]

Thus, by December 1914, all types of guns used by the BEF were chronically short of ammunition, with daily demand outstripping supply. Once again the sixty-pounder guns were in the most worrying position, with no ammunition delivered in December despite a twenty-five rounds per gun per day requirement by this stage. The position was complicated further by the decision to opt for a mixture of shrapnel and high-explosive (HE) shells, as prior to this point all field guns fired nothing but shrapnel. This chronic lack of howitzer, heavy and long-range artillery ensured that much of the artillery was engaged in hitting enemy infantry at the First Battle of Ypres. Counter-battery work was therefore left to the obsolete 4.7- and 6-inch howitzers, showing how little importance was attached to this task in 1914. It betrayed the fact that artillery had been seen primarily as a close support weapon, the Royal Field Artillery being somewhat unscientific in its approach to gunnery before the war. There was no artillery organisation above divisional level, and artillery advisers at corps level had no staff.[45] Certainly there had been a serious underestimation of the need for heavier-calibre guns. In August 1914, indeed, there had been only fifty-four such guns available, comprising twenty of

[43] Beckett, *Ypres*, 87–9. [44] Edmonds, *Military Operations, 1914*, Vol. II, 12–14.
[45] Bailey, 'British Artillery', 23–5.

the heavy sixty-pounders, sixteen of the notoriously unreliable quick-firing 4.7-inch guns adopted at the time of the South African War, sixteen of the old 6-inch howitzers, a single 6-inch gun and a single experimental 9.2-inch howitzer. Any counter-battery work was initially to be entrusted to a Royal Navy armoured train with just one 6- and two 4.7-inch guns since naval ammunition was more plentiful. No HE shells were provided for the eighteen-pounders until 19 October, the difficulty of the gun's flat trajectory amid the deep and narrow valleys of the Aisne becoming all too apparent.[46]

As indicated earlier, the 5th Division deployed its guns alongside the infantry at Mons and suffered heavily as a result, losing a third of its divisional total, while the 3rd Division fared better by keeping its guns behind the infantry and out of sight of the Germans.[47] The propensity for artillery to fight in the open was also displayed at Néry on 1 September, albeit that L Battery, Royal Horse Artillery, was caught in the open unexpectedly at dawn. In the defensive battles of 1914, such use of artillery probably maximised its effectiveness and assistance to the infantry, albeit at great cost. The artillery was simply too busy plugging gaps to engage in counter-battery work, but in any case the mobility implicit in the Royal Field Artillery's (RFA's) pre-war tactical expectations were of increasingly less relevance as static warfare developed. Slowly, the artillery began to pull back during the course of October with the beginnings of a system for fire support. The front was divided into sectors with the guns under command of the relevant infantry, which could then call down 'SOS' fire by a pre-arranged signal – usually flares because telephone cable was in short supply. At a higher level, Haig had improvised a more centralised fire reserve for I Corps on the Aisne, and as heavier guns arrived, they were allocated to corps level. The problem remained that other than the sixty-pounder, German 5.9-inch howitzers seriously outranged the BEF's guns.[48] Smith-Dorrien for one had grasped that 'our only certainty of advancing successfully is by siege methods, that is to say by assault preceded by sap and overwhelming artillery preparation, or by the latter alone.'[49]

It was not just ammunition that was in short supply. Virtually everything the BEF needed for simple survival, let alone operations, was difficult to procure. Existing manufacturers in Britain could produce only 47,000 rifles a year in 1914. In December, Master General of the

[46] Beckett, *Ypres*, 32–3.
[47] Sanders Marble, *British Artillery on the Western Front in the First World War* (Farnham, UK: Ashgate, 2013), 45–6.
[48] *Ibid.*, 49–56.
[49] The National Archives (TNA), WO 159/15, Smith-Dorrien to von Donop, 20 December 1914.

Ordnance, Major-General Stanley von Donop, was forced to remind Robertson that it was imperative to retrieve the rifles of casualties after one divisional commander, Major-General Henry Beauvoir de Lisle of the 1st Cavalry Division, had expressed to Kitchener his surprise that it was necessary to do so.[50] Entrenching tools, barbed wire and sand bags were also in short supply, the pattern of trenches at Ypres being short and usually disconnected and without dugouts or cover: the first consignment of sand bags arrived only on 28 October. Lacking tools and time, the infantry rarely had the chance to prepare a second position, while forward positions were often separated by between 200 and 400 yards. In most cases, therefore, small groups of British soldiers had fought separate actions. Gaps could be covered by artillery and by crossfire from other positions in the day but were vulnerable once the light began to fade, the available artillery being dug in where possible on reverse slopes and reserves for counter attack held under cover in woods.[51]

Living in scattered, hastily-prepared positions, the onset of winter weather made the need for boots all the more pressing. By 18 December 1914, the War Office had placed orders for 7.8 million pairs and still had 1.9 million to place but was already 692,000 pairs in arrears. These estimates were based on the size of the force up to September 1915 and compared with the 250,000 pairs required annually before the war.[52] These shortages were mainly problems in production, but they were compounded by distribution difficulties once sent to France. The BEF needed more berthing space to unload the supply ships, more railway line and motorised and horse transport to ensure distribution from the railheads and more effective use of the inland waterways. All of this needed to be managed by a system in which the QMG and IGC were still not fully co-operative and inter-dependent pieces of machinery. Matters were then compounded by the arrival of the Indian Corps and the elaborate rationing requirements necessary to meet the demands of its races and religions.

Tactically, the BEF was in a state of confusion by December 1914. Undoubtedly, the BEF's professionalism was shown to be a priceless asset acting as a highly significant force multiplier. The long hours spent improving musketry, the tight interior cohesion of battalions and their ability to work with neighbours in brigades were shown to be invaluable as the BEF often tottered but never crumbled. The British Army's desire to retain operational and tactical flexibility was

[50] French, *British Economic and Strategic Planning*, 139, 171; TNA, WO 159/15, von Donop to Robertson, 1 December 1914, and Robertson to von Donop, 3 December 1914.

[51] Beckett, *Ypres*, 75–6.

[52] Ian Malcolm Brown, *British Logistics on the Western Front, 1914–1919* (Westport, CT: Praeger, 1998), 65.

also shown to be useful. As noted earlier, at First Ypres, the situation at Gheluvelt was altered by the grip and vision of the men on the spot who took the right decisions in extremely trying circumstances. However, much of the BEF's most impressive work in 1914 was spent in defensive reaction to the actions and tempo of the enemy. As a force, it rarely imposed its understanding of offensive action on the enemy, and offensive action was at the heart of its pre-war thinking and training. When it did so, it was usually in the form of counter-attack, and the results were often bloody and inconclusive.

At the higher command levels the situation was mixed. French had shown himself to be too inconclusive, inconsistent and mercurial to be a truly effective commander-in-chief. At the corps level, Haig increased in confidence after a hesitant start. He undoubtedly benefitted from being given more operational freedom than other commanders, most notably Smith-Dorrien and Rawlinson, thanks to French's idiosyncratic approach to generalship. In addition, the enormous advantage of having a settled staff used to working alongside each other in the only permanent corps of the British Army allowed him to shine all the more during the stressful first battle of Ypres. Finally, close collaboration with the French during that battle also provided I Corps with assistance at vital moments. All these factors combined to boost Haig's reputation, but he tended to reap the benefits alone with too few examining the individual elements behind the success. None of Haig's fellow corps commanders shared quite the same level of qualities, personal and corporate, or accidents of circumstance. Smith-Dorrien performed very well during the retreat but was far less effective when put under pressure to maintain offensive operations in October. Rawlinson and Pulteney were also to show inconsistencies, although both men were significantly more handicapped by the even greater degree of 'ad hocism' present in their commands. With the overwhelming majority of British commanders and staff officers unused to co-ordinating anything higher than a division or two, the BEF's command performance was never going to be smooth or easy. It is a tribute to the professional qualities of all in the BEF, regardless of how intellectually vibrant or far-sighted they were, that the force held together and played a not insignificant role in a campaign involving armies far larger and more powerful than itself.

By Christmas 1914, an enormous challenge had been thrown down before the BEF and its higher command in particular. First, and on the grand strategic scale, it was necessary to continue with the war but as a junior military partner. Second, it would have to do so in operational circumstances largely unforeseen before 1914 – flank-less warfare. Third, it had to continue fighting despite staggering shortages of vital munitions and equipment. Finally, and intellectually most difficult given this combination of circumstances, it had to determine how much of its pre-war approach to war and combat had failed the test of war utterly, how much needed simple revision and how much was directly applicable. Responding to such a grand conundrum effectively and quickly was the unenviable task of the BEF in 1915.

7 The Western Front, 1915

The British Expeditionary Force (BEF) entered 1915 as a force in flux. Although the manpower strength of the British Army was expanding massively, training and equipping over a million volunteers was a very slow process, meaning little relief from the overstretch in France and Belgium could be expected from the 'New Armies' in the immediate term. In addition, it was a year of competing strategic priorities with the British government's decision to open operations against the Ottoman Empire at Gallipoli and in the Balkans in Salonika, which distracted focus from what the majority of Britain's generals believed to be the decisive front in France and Belgium (see Chapter 5 for further details). Replacing losses was therefore a case of calling upon the few regular units left scattered around the Empire, deploying all available reservists and despatching Territorial Force (TF) units to the Western Front as swiftly as possible. The precarious manpower situation was matched by that of equipment and supplies. Every unit in France and Belgium had to husband very carefully all items of kit while British industry slowly geared itself up to full production. Yet none of these obvious deficiencies won any major concessions from Britain's entente partners. Led by Joffre, French generals and politicians were keen to prosecute the war with great vigour in 1915 in order to eject the Germans from France. This determination was made stronger still by the belief that Russia needed energetic support to assist its recovery from the checks of 1914 and convert its potential into war-winning power. As very much the junior player in the entente, British strategic freedom in terms of land operations was limited. While the British War Council explored other options, most notably the viability of attacking Ottoman Turkey, the BEF in France and Belgium was tied to French military thinking and caught in an operational bind. Deficient in military strength, it lacked political influence among its French collaborators.

Whether Sir John French liked it or not, the BEF was destined to remain in the shadow of its much larger partner for the foreseeable future. Although he still had the ability to appeal to his political masters in

London, this was a blunt weapon, for the War Council was well aware of Britain's military weakness, leaving it highly unlikely to challenge French supremacy. During 1915, the BEF desperately sought to make war as it could. Although this meant fighting at a disadvantage, the high command of the BEF often accentuated the problem by failing to balance the strategic conundrum through clear-sighted concentration on the possible. Instead, French demands for support were too often translated into operationally unachievable objectives.

With Russia under pressure from strong offensives by the Central Powers and much of France's industrial heartland under German occupation, the onus was on the French and British to attack as soon as the winter weather lessened. Joffre requested French's support in his plan for offensive action on the Western Front. With the British now firmly occupying a series of field fortifications consisting of trenches and breastworks from Ypres to the La Bassée Canal just south of Givenchy, Joffre stressed the value of operations in the area north of the canal. As originally conceived, the battle was to be conducted jointly by the BEF and the French Tenth Army, which was located immediately south of the canal. In order to facilitate this action, the French requested the relief of their troops to the immediate north of Ypres. However, French declined to do so, citing his own lack of adequately prepared resources, but remained enthusiastic about offensive action. In response, Joffre and the Tenth Army Commander, Louis de Maud'huy, postponed operations in the area. Joffre's decision appears to have been a further expression of doubt about the BEF's willingness to do its share of the fighting. Much discontent had been caused in mid-December 1914 when the British mounted extremely half-hearted assaults in the southern Ypres sector in support of a French offensive. Far from being deterred by this snub, French pressed on with preparations for an assault at La Bassée. With Kitchener convinced that little could be achieved in France for the time being and directing the government to instead look at other fronts, French probably saw offensive operations as a way of refocusing the government's attention on the Western Front.

The lessening of large-scale action during the mid-winter months had done nothing to alleviate the BEF's supply problems. As already suggested, facing up to the nature of trench warfare demanded weapons that were not part of the British Army's standard armoury in 1914. Somewhat ironically for a war made awful by the might of modern industry and technological developments, the desperate needs of the winter of 1914 were of a 'back to the future' nature. The men of the BEF required timber on a vast scale to revet and duckboard trenches and lines of communication, make bivouacs and gun platforms and a host of other tasks. Waking

Figure 8. A group from 1/1st Buckinghamshire Battalion, Ploegsteert, June 1915.
Source: Courtesy of Soldiers of Oxfordshire Museum

up to the urgent demand, the government eventually established a Home-Grown Timber Committee in November 1915 to maximise domestic production and free up precious shipping space used for importing supplies. Weapons systems long thought defunct or of limited value were suddenly needed. In October 1914, French requested 4,000 hand and 2,000 rifle grenades per month, respectively, but only 280 grenades a month were being produced. By December 1914, Robertson, Rawlinson and Smith-Dorrien were all urging the Master General of the Ordnance, von Donop, to supply not only grenades but also trench mortars, the latter being especially needed to counter German *minenwerfer*.[1] Again, only twelve mortars – improvised from boring out six-inch shell bodies – with 545 rounds were despatched to the BEF in December 1914. No department within the War Office was tasked with invention, although von Donop clearly had responsibility for all munitions. Fortunately, the BEF showed enough ingenuity to improvise weapons, and many men were soon at work in cottage-industry munitions production.

Various suggestions for new munitions tended to be handled through a section – FW3 – of the Directorate of Fortifications and Works or the

[1] The National Archive (TNA), WO 159/15, von Donop correspondence with BEF officers.

Inspectorate of the Royal Ordnance Factory at Woolwich. Generally, the Royal Laboratory at Woolwich proved unequal to the task of providing novel munitions, and von Donop allowed Lieutenant Colonel Louis Jackson of FW3 to begin to do so. A Special Reserve officer of the Royal Engineers, Lieutenant E. S. R. Adams, was appointed Experimental Officer to the Chief Engineer of the BEF in October 1914 and began working on hand grenades, with Royal Engineers Field Companies improvising in the field. The first field workshop – the Béthune Bomb Factory – began work in November 1914, producing an improvised mortar and a grenade devised by an officer of the 21st Company, Sappers and Miners, based on a 1913 Indian Army design. The First and Second Armies established workshops in 1915, as later did Third Army, while GHQ established an Experiments Committee in June 1915. It was Captain Henry Newton of 1/5th Sherwood Foresters, an electrical and mechanical engineer in civil life and a prolific wartime novel munitions inventor, who devised a rifle grenade while with Second Army Workshop. Re-designated FW3a in early 1915, Jackson's section then became the Trench Warfare Department of the newly created Ministry of Munitions in June 1915, splitting at the end of the year into the Trench Warfare Research and Trench Warfare Supply Departments. Although not without difficulties, the supply of novel munitions greatly increased. A total of 11.6 million grenades, for example, were supplied in the second half of 1915 alone.[2]

More often than not, however, out and out civilians rather than even those temporarily in uniform, like Newton, made significant contributions. William Mills, for example, was one such civilian engineer whose grenade, devised in February 1915, was based on a pre-war Belgian design. Another was Wilfrid Stokes, Chairman and Managing Director of Ransomes and Rapier of Ipswich, whose three-inch mortar was adopted in September 1915 after various trials and changes. Eventually, 11,421 of these mortars would be manufactured together with 1,123 of the four-inch model used for smoke projectors.[3]

It was also recognised that infantry small arms firepower had to be improved through increased numbers of heavy machine guns and the Lewis gun. Prior to the war, the British had seen the heavy machine gun as a cross between a defensive weapon and a firepower reserve. There were good reasons for this thinking. The weight of the heavy machine gun

[2] Anthony Saunders, 'A Muse of Fire: British Trench Warfare Munitions, Their Invention, Manufacture and Tactical Employment on the Western Front, 1914–18', unpublished PhD thesis, University of Exeter, 2008, 64–82, 104–11.

[3] Saunders, 'Muse of Fire', 138–40; Peter Scott, 'Mr Stokes and His Educated Drainpipe', *The Great War* 2 (1990), 80–95.

made it difficult to manoeuvre easily, and its ammunition demands posed a significant supply problem. As a result, British thinking about the machine gun atrophied, and there was little understanding of its tactical flexibility and potential in 1914. But the BEF should not be condemned as the only combatant unsure as to the best way of using the weapon. None of the other major combatants were much further forward, and all were forced to reconsider its deployment in the light of direct experience. This tactical malaise was still apparent in early 1915, for although there was a real desire to increase radically supplies of the Vickers-Maxim heavy machine gun, the demand was still not based on a particularly sophisticated understanding of its use. Rather the sheer desperation to maximise firepower was the over-riding and rather prosaic reason behind the request.

Much the same can be said of the motivations behind demands for the Lewis gun. In fact, it was not much lighter than the Vickers, although it could be moved swiftly from front-line trench to no man's land to captured enemy positions. Its pan-fed ammunition also encouraged its operators to consider targets and ammunition supply more closely, and this chimed in with British thinking about achieving a balance between accuracy and rate of fire. The infantry firepower experts of the British Army, led by Major N. R. McMahon, had explored the potential of automatic rifles and came to sophisticated conclusions as to its use in pre-war debates. However, few of these debates had penetrated the army as a whole. Thus, the ability of the Lewis gun to provide immediate tactical fire support facilitating movement was only gradually grasped by the bulk of the army under active service conditions.

Regardless of the lack of definition concerning their precise operational and tactical uses, the demand for the Vickers-Maxim and Lewis guns far outstripped supply. At the outbreak of war, the BEF possessed a total of 1,963 machine guns in service and reserve. Realising the need to increase supply significantly, Vickers Armstrong was asked to expand production. In September 1914, however, only forty per month were being supplied, although this doubled to eighty per month in November 1914. As a British-based arms manufacturer experienced in meeting government contracts and working to a fixed, proven design, for Vickers Armstrong this issue seemed far less problematic than the supply of Lewis guns. The British Army adopted the weapon on the eve of war based upon an experimental design and rapidly placed an initial order for 250 guns, which was soon increased to 1,250, with its US production company. Unable to shift rapidly from prototype marks to mass production, the company did not commence work on the contract until November 1914. Both manufacturers then experienced shortages of skilled labour, which caused further significant delays, although, because the Lewis gun was also produced in Belgium before the war, the flight of many of its workers to Britain in 1914 at least provided a nucleus of operatives familiar with its production for BSA in Birmingham. However, by July 1915, instead of the 1,792 Vickers and 1,500 Lewis guns ordered, only 1,022 and 621, respectively, had been delivered. Nonetheless, the first Lewis Gun School was established in June 1915, with two to four weapons generally being available per infantry company by mid-1916. The Machine Gun Corps was established on 14 October 1915, with a Machine Gun School for the Vickers at Grantham in November 1915 and another at St. Omer in December 1915. The Machine Gun Corps enabled each brigade to have a machine gun company.[4]

All these new weapons required vast quantities of small arms ammunition (SAA), which was another product in short supply. In August 1914 there were 400 million SAA rounds in stock, but active service quickly eroded the available stock. A further squeeze was experienced when the New Army divisions commenced training. The only way to keep up shipments to France was to curtail New Army musketry practise considerably. By June 1915, 101 million rounds per month were being produced, and as with all other forms of ammunition, contracts were placed in the United States. This meant projections of 300 million rounds per month from 1916 but little immediate relief from a dire situation. In April 1915, there were only 137 SAA rounds per rifle on the lines of communication; by September, there were 133. On 27 September, GHQ sent an order for 43 million rounds of SAA immediately, in addition to the 20 million already promised for weekly despatch. By this point the battle of Loos had opened, and GHQ was desperate to bring the figure up to 200 rounds per rifle, the establishment levels, as soon as possible. The BEF was therefore forced to make war in extremely straightened circumstances.[5]

The first major British assault on German positions since the advent of trench warfare was ordered against the village of Neuve Chapelle. For French and Haig, the operation had the potential to push the Germans off the Aubers Ridge and possibly even imperil the German grip on Lille. French's confidence was such that he ordered his two cavalry corps to prepare to exploit a major victory and even went as far as briefing the two

[4] Tim Travers, 'The Offensive and the Problem of Innovation in British Military Thought, 1870–1915', *Journal of Contemporary History* 13 (1978), 531–53; Paddy Griffith, 'The Lewis Gun Made Easy: The Development of Automatic Rifles in the Great War', *The Great War* 3 (1991), 108–15; Edmonds, *Military Operations, 1915, Vol. I* (London: Macmillan, 1927), 58.

[5] Edmonds, *Military Operations, 1915*, Vol. I, 58.

cavalry corps commanders, Allenby and Rimington, in person. Understanding the optimism of French and Haig is difficult, especially when both men knew they would be attacking without immediate French assistance and that ammunition was likely to be a problem. Even more intriguing was Haig's decision to delegate planning for the operation to the relevant corps commander, Rawlinson. Given Haig's confidence and the fact that it was the first major assault of his own First Army, his insistence on delegation seems odd. This passing on of authority was promptly mirrored by Rawlinson, who asked his divisional commanders to come up with a scheme. Somewhat ironically, Haig then rebuked Rawlinson for taking this stance and urged him to direct matters more forcefully.[6]

Haig's criticisms of the initial plan produced by Rawlinson and Major-General F. J. 'Joey' Davies of 8th Division were perceptive: the scheme was too complicated as it involved pincer assaults on the village and thus made the attacking troops vulnerable to both enfilade fire and friendly fire casualties as they converged. This shook Rawlinson into action, and he set to work preparing a plan based on frontal assault. The result was interesting for its absorption of lessons about fighting on the Western Front. Rawlinson believed that surprise, very careful artillery preparation and good communications were the essential elements. In terms of artillery preparation, he exploited aerial photography and thorough mapping to assist in the efficiency of fire. Aerial photography proved very useful, but no one appeared to notice the construction of concrete pillboxes well to the rear that would prove a serious obstacle to any exploitation or defence of newly captured positions. He also wanted a very short bombardment designed to neutralise the enemy while the infantry advanced on their trenches. Realising the difficulty of hitting certain key points in the German line, Rawlinson also requested as many mortars as could be found in order to achieve the right kind of weight and trajectory of shot. As part of his artillery plan he committed some guns, thirty-seven of the 340 gathered, to counter-battery work. To ensure surprise, Rawlinson insisted on secrecy throughout and the concealment of all preparations. In certain areas, therefore, Rawlinson worked effectively, thoughtfully and imaginatively. Where he diverged most completely from Haig's

[6] For the planning of Neuve Chapelle and detailed analysis of the operations, see Edmonds, *Military Operations, 1915*, Vol. I, 74–88; Harris, *Haig*, 113–21; Robin Prior and Trevor Wilson, *Command on the Western Front: The Military Career of Sir Henry Rawlinson, 1914–1918* (Oxford: Blackwell, 1992), 19–43; Shelford Bidwell and Dominick Graham, *Firepower: British Army Weapons and Theories of War, 1904–45* (London: Allen & Unwin, 1982), 74–9; Marble, *British Artillery*, 71–7. On Haig's command style, see Nick Lloyd, 'With Faith and Without Fear: Sir Douglas Haig's Command of First Army during 1914', *Journal of Military History* 71 (2007), 1051–76.

wishes was in his half-hearted response to his chief's desire to exploit northwards and take Aubers Ridge. For Rawlinson, the best result of the operation was nothing as grandiose as an advance on Lille. The rectification of a nasty little salient in the British line would suit him given the BEF's material limitations. Rawlinson's lack of confidence in the wider potential of the operation meant that he and Haig were pursuing different intentions, which had the potential to cause confusion once the operation commenced.

Although Rawlinson might have been far less sanguine than either French or Haig over the chances of breakthrough, all three men knew that the battle was in the hands of the artillery. Unfortunately for the BEF, not only were the right types of guns and ammunition in short supply, but the accuracy of fire was also open to question, especially when firing indirect and guided by the map. At this point in the war British artillerymen worked on the basis that accurate firing actually meant that for every 100 shells fired 50 per cent would fall in the near proximity of the target rather than precisely on it. The immense difficulty of accurate shooting is a crucial element in understanding the early problems of the BEF and involved a number of interlocking issues. Achieving even a semblance of accuracy was a lengthy process dependent on the firing of registration shots, which were then adjusted by a forward observation officer (FOO). But consistently achieving perfect sight lines for FOOs and continual communication with the guns were difficult. Firing by the map had been introduced, but this process required plentiful, up-to-date and accurate maps which was equally difficult to achieve in 1915. Some maps were out by nearly 150 yards. A systematic Royal Engineers' survey of the British sector had commenced but could not be hurried. Of more immediate help was the deployment of aircraft, which had the capability to improve observation immensely and correct errors of the map through aerial photography. In turn, weather was crucial for effective aerial survey and was also an important factor in the working of the guns themselves. Thus, guns registered on their target might find that atmospheric conditions had altered their fire by the time the bombardment was due to commence. Much of this knowledge was understood by the Royal Artillery, but the degree to which it was understood evenly and consistently is less clear, and this meant that some odd decisions were made. Particularly strange was the statement of Major-General John Du Cane, artillery adviser at GHQ in 1915, who stated that he had no need of Royal Flying Corps (RFC) reports on wind direction and speed. Unfortunately for the Royal Artillery, the Garrison Artillery, which was the most scientific branch of the corps, was also the most unfashionable and least influential, and so its methods were not incorporated easily into the

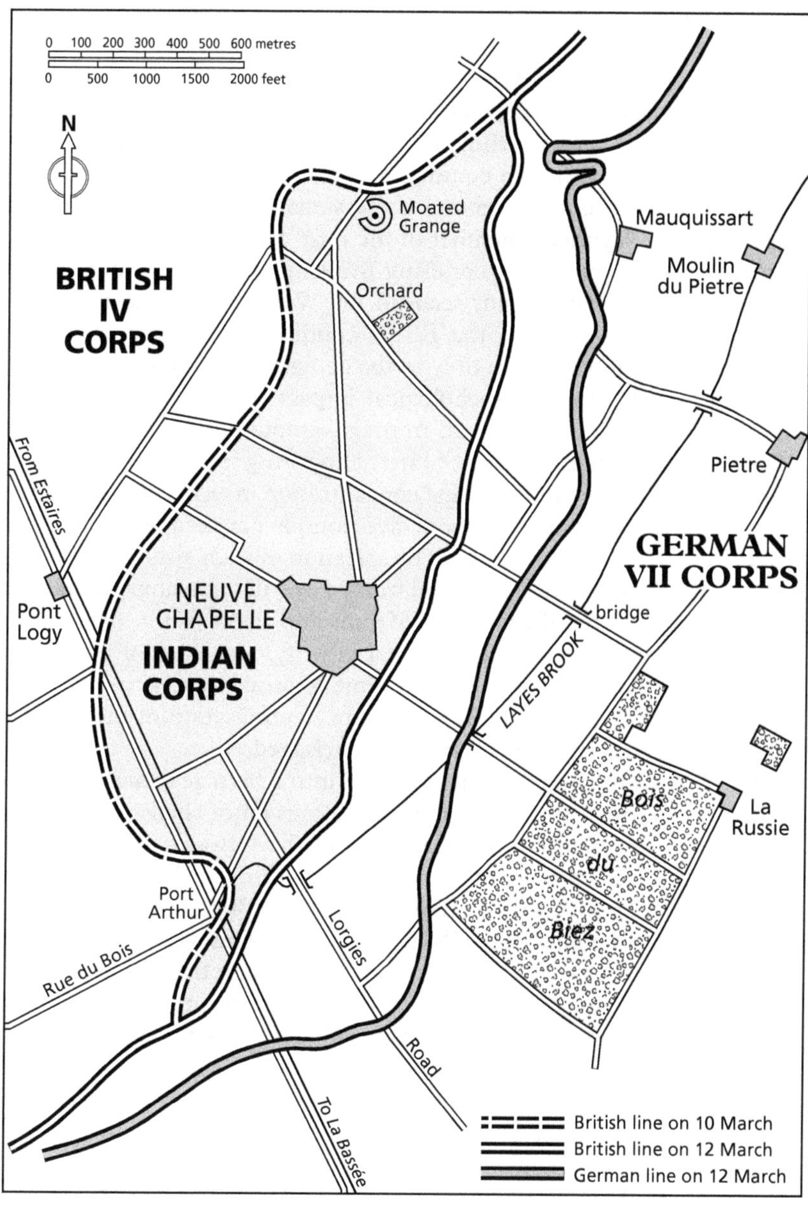

Map 3 Battle of Neuve Chapelle, 10–12 March 1915

ethos of the regiment. All this combined to make the artillery an erratic instrument in 1915.

The attack commenced at 7.30 AM on 10 March as the thirty-five-minute bombardment of the German front-line trench opened. It seemed miraculous to the men watching it. Despite the many criticisms that can be made of the British high command at this period, the bombardment was a tribute to the planning and professionalism of the force. Indeed Captain G. C. Wynne, a member of the post-war British official history team and not a man given to praising British efforts lightly, identified it as the greatest bombardment seen on the Western Front to that date: no easy achievement given the BEF's condition.[7] The success of the initial attack owed much not only to the actual weakness of the German defences but also to the psychological impact of the concentration of firepower over only a 2,000-yard frontage, amounting to the delivery of 288 pounds of high explosive per yard of opposing trench in such a short period of time, although the actual concentration in terms of the German front-line trenches had been about five pounds per yard when all other artillery tasks were factored out. The selection of such a short bombardment by Rawlinson, when Haig had wanted one of three hours' duration, was not just a matter of a shortage of guns and shells. Wire cutting with shrapnel had been seen as the greatest priority, and thirty-five minutes had been calculated as the minimum time required to achieve it. Neuve Chapelle, therefore, proved an exercise in neutralisation of the defence rather than its destruction, as had been envisaged.

At 8.05 AM, the bombardment turned into a barrage some 300 yards behind the German front line, meaning a curtain of shells was fired in order to prevent German reinforcement of the forward trenches. This tactic worked well, and the infantry of the 25th Brigade had stormed the front line by 8.15 AM, with men of the 2nd Rifle Brigade then managing to advance up the main street of Neuve Chapelle. This was good progress, but reporting it back to Rawlinson took a very long time. These delays revealed another major weakness in all Western Front operations: the fragility of communications once the attacking troops left the trenches, for telephone cables run out by the attackers were all too vulnerable to being cut. The success of the 25th Brigade was not replicated elsewhere, for on the far left the situation was nowhere near as positive, with the 23rd Brigade held up by uncut wire. On the far right, the Indian Corps made solid progress in the Port Arthur salient and up to Neuve Chapelle village itself and were thus in touch with IV Corps. Fighting continued through

[7] Captain G. C. Wynne, *If Germany Attacks: The Battle in Depth in the West* (London: Faber & Faber, 1940), 25.

the afternoon, but the vast majority of the successes had already been achieved. By nightfall, an undoubted victory had been won. The German defences had been penetrated to a depth of 1,200 yards and widened from the initial 1,500 to 4,000 yards, putting the IV and Indian Corps on the German VII Corps' reserve line by the end of the day. But it was precisely the sort of limited victory Rawlinson expected, and nowhere along the entire front was there the prospect of useful exploitation by infantry, still less cavalry.[8]

The day had revealed much of great importance. First and foremost, it had been made clear that the right type of artillery bombardment could greatly assist the infantry in penetrating the German front line. By the same token, it had also shown that the artillery was tautly stretched providing this support and was far less effective hitting second- and third-line targets. Intimately connected with this point was the issue of communications. Once the infantry went forward, maintaining meaningful communications between front-line troops and those in the rear was almost impossible. The lack of accuracy and precision in the information flow is fully revealed by Capper's 10.40 AM request for permission to push 7th Division through the 23rd Brigade position, believing that opposition on this section of the front had been overcome. Fortunately, Rawlinson was aware that no advance had been made here and was able to rule against such a move. Higher commanders were therefore paralysed, and by the time they put together a response to a request, the situation had either already moved on significantly or the communications with the component parts of their response had failed. This situation emphasised the onus placed on forward commanders to direct the tactical flow of battle but deprived them of the means of gaining assistance for their decisions. A good example of this disconnection between the macro and micro direction of the battle can be found in the actions of Lieutenant-Colonel E. R. R. Swiney of the 1/39th Garhwal Rifles. Observing the situation in the Port Arthur salient, he became aware of an assault on its north face by the 1st Seaforth Highlanders. Reacting with great speed, he assembled the remaining four platoons of his own battalion and ordered two companies of the 13th London (Princess Louise's Kensington Regiment) to support the attack on the trench from their position. By his actions, he divided the German fire and ensured that the trench was assaulted from front and flank. However, utterly unable to call upon artillery or trench mortar support quickly and direct it accurately, the men had to make the assault over open ground unassisted. The Germans then inflicted heavy casualties before their position was overwhelmed.

[8] Prior and Wilson, *Rawlinson*, 44–56.

Here was an officer of great tactical sense making a shrewd decision, but bedevilled by the hiatus in communications technology.

Throughout the day, Haig remained upbeat, requesting the rest of 2nd Cavalry Division to join the 5th Cavalry Brigade at Estaires during the afternoon. At nightfall, Haig was no less confident of major success, and at 11.30 PM ordered the resumption of operations at 7 AM, maintaining the objective of securing Aubers Ridge. However, the situation was not quite as promising as it seemed, for although the German front-line troops had been largely destroyed, reserve units were already taking possession of the strong points at Pietre West, forming blocks in the Bois du Biez and occupying an old trench from Pietre West to the German front line. During the course of the night, more German reserves were rushed in, reducing the likelihood of any further meaningful British advance. With these movements the Germans established another theme of battle on the Western Front: the defending side always had the ability to recover and stabilise more quickly than the attacker. Unlike the attacking British, the Germans were not trying to advance through unfamiliar trenches and traverse a smashed no man's land. Unlike the British, the Germans were not trying to reverse fire-steps in trenches nor clear them of dead and wounded to create space for fresh troops to come through. Advancing from their own local lines of communication, the Germans could funnel in men, ammunition and stores more effectively than their enemies. The German defenders also had a much clearer idea of where the British were likely to be – in their old trenches – whereas the British, and especially the British artillery, were left guessing at the precise nature of hastily improvised new field works. Aerial reconnaissance was useless at night, and dawn on 11 March broke misty. The offensive was therefore going to be renewed in a state of command and control disarray.

The British assault commenced at 7 AM with a fifteen-minute bombardment. The infantry then attacked and failed disastrously. Unable to register on new targets due to misty weather, with FOOs desperately trying to make sense of the new German defences, the British bombardment was ineffective. In response, significantly reinforced German artillery fire destroyed British positions and men and also played havoc with communications. Rawlinson was informed of the situation, but his only response was yet another bombardment, and he asserted with increasing inflexibility that assaults must go ahead. However, his determination was tempered by the men on the spot. His divisional commanders were unwilling to contemplate further attacks unless the artillery preparation was more effective. Rawlinson shrugged aside Davies' apprehensions and ordered an assault on Pietre West, which duly came to nothing. On the right, after a desperate round of orders, counter-orders and disorder, the

1st Worcesters attacked alone and were routed, advancing no further than fifty yards from their own trenches. So devastating was the German response that the CO of the 2nd Northants simply refused to let his men attack. Indian Corps assaults were similarly ill-fated and resulted in useless loss of life.

At the end of the day, both Haig and Rawlinson seemed unable to grasp that the opportunity for further advances had passed, and both men took out their ire on their subordinates. Davies was blamed for not moving vigorously enough, and Haig believed that the troops had done nothing all day. Rawlinson seems to have forgotten entirely his original formula for success – well-planned artillery bombardments as the vital prerequisite for infantry assaults. Showing a staggeringly poor grip on reality, Haig ordered further action for the next day. This time the Germans pre-empted the British by making a heavy bombardment on British lines at 4.30 AM. Revealing that the fog of war drifts both ways, the bombardment largely missed the British front-line positions and fell on those to the rear. At 5 AM the Germans assaulted, assisted by the thick mist, but were repulsed with heavy casualties by British rifle and machine gun fire. A few hours later the British once again attempted to advance. The commanders of British and Indian units on the spot appear to have been most half-hearted in their attempts, lacking as they did any conviction in their orders. A further round of assaults in the afternoon was equally desultory, and after discussion with his corps commanders, Haig called off the offensive at 10.40 PM.

In continuing the offensive beyond the first day, French and Haig caused the loss of more valuable British and Indian regulars. First Army casualties amounted to around 13,000, with the majority suffered in Rawlinson's IV Corps. In return, they had inflicted roughly the same number on the Germans, but the majority of these probably came during the Germans' ill-conceived assault on 12 March.[9] Assessing the command performance of the BEF in the light of Neuve Chapelle is a tricky task. Nearly all had shown inconsistencies. Haig had rightly criticised Rawlinson's initial plans but then clung to over-optimistic assessments despite the evidence. In the Indian Corps, Lieutenant-General Sir James Willcocks had done his best to nurse along his men shocked by the extremity of the violence and the physical conditions of the Western Front. Rawlinson moved from initial caution to somewhat bizarre insistence on the maintenance of the offensive. He may have felt that the severely jolted defenders were susceptible to follow-up assaults, which would compensate for weaknesses in the artillery preparation. If this was the case, he should have been disabused by afternoon on day

[9] Harris, *Haig*, 124–31; Prior and Wilson, *Rawlinson*, 68.

two. Reacting sharply to the accusation that a great opportunity had been fumbled, Rawlinson directed the blame at Davies, stating that he had failed to follow orders and exploit the situation correctly. Rather than meekly accept the rebuke from a senior officer, Davies defended himself spiritedly and cited Rawlinson's actual orders. The unpleasant little scene was ended by Haig privately scolding Rawlinson for trying to scapegoat subordinate officers but publicly defending him. In the highly personalised world of the British Army, this move effectively made Rawlinson beholden to Haig. Thus, the man who had not imposed on Haig his revised understanding of battle on the Western Front in the planning stages was highly unlikely to find the moral courage to do so in the future.[10]

Having fought their first major battle under conditions of trench warfare, the senior commanders of the BEF were given the chance to digest its progress and distil the lessons. Contrary to many popular understandings of the British Army in this period, clear thinking was possible. Even before the battle commenced, some were moving towards a better perception of the operational problem posed by the Western Front. On 9 February 1915, Robertson, now Murray's successor as Chief of Staff at GHQ, commenced the gestation of the Neuve Chapelle plan by requesting schemes for offensive action from the two army commanders. It was accompanied by his memorandum of a day earlier in which he stated that breaking through the German line was highly unlikely. Rather, he argued that operations should be aimed at more modest achievements through the infliction of a steady attrition on the Germans achieved 'by a slow and gradual advance on our part, each step being prepared by a predominant artillery fire and great expenditure of ammunition'.[11]

Rawlinson was obviously sympathetic with this thinking, writing of Neuve Chapelle to Kitchener, 'Had we been content with the capture of the village & stopped at the end of the 1st day our losses would have been only 2,300 & we should have killed twice that number of Germans.'[12] Writing to the King's assistant secretary, Clive Wigram on 25 March, Rawlinson used the phrase, 'bite and hold':

> Bite off a piece of the enemy's line … and hold it against counter attack. The bite can be made without much loss, and, if we choose the right place and make every preparation to put it quickly into a state of defence, there ought to be no difficulty in holding it against the enemy's counter-attacks, and inflicting on him at least twice the loss that we have suffered in making the bite.[13]

[10] Ian F. W. Beckett, 'Henry Rawlinson', in Beckett and Corvi (eds.), *Haig's Generals*, 164–82.
[11] Quoted in Harris, *Haig*, 112.
[12] Quoted in Beckett, 'Rawlinson', 174.
[13] Quoted in Harris, *Haig*, 129.

Aware of the weaknesses in his approach, Rawlinson pointed out that it required artillery and ammunition resources Britain did not yet have and that it would not work quickly, ensuring a long war. He missed one further flaw, the strategy depended on the Germans reacting to British bites rather than ignoring them.[14]

Du Cane had come to similar conclusions, but on a much more elaborate scale, and he was prepared to share them more widely. In a GHQ memorandum he produced a highly insightful analysis of Neuve Chapelle. He identified the inability of the attacking infantry and covering artillery to communicate with each other after the initial advance without leaving a sufficient pause for reorganisation. During this lull in operations, the enemy had the chance to react and stabilise the position. According to Du Cane, the answer to this conundrum was the 'step-by-step' approach. This involved selecting a piece of line both strategically important to the enemy and suitable for the deployment of all the BEF's arms. The formula was then that of the initial stages of Neuve Chapelle: carefully prepared and executed artillery bombardment on limited targets followed by infantry assault to suppress the remaining defenders. Unlike Neuve Chapelle, there would be a pause while the position was consolidated, counter-attacks repelled and then prepared for the next stage. This process was to be repeated continually until the enemy was exhausted, at which point the decisive moment would come ready for the final breakthrough and exploitation phase. As Paul Harris has said, Du Cane's idea was 'not so much "bite and hold" as "bite and bite"'.[15]

Like Rawlinson's suggestions, Du Cane's relied upon the expenditure of enormous amounts of ammunition and deployment of vast quantities of material none of which were in adequate supply at this point. Unlike Rawlinson's approach, it did not depend on reaction by the enemy but was about maintaining the pressure on the enemy at one point. Du Cane had made a significant point in one other way. His understanding of battle was a modification and extension of British pre-war thinking. This was *Field Service Regulations* (*FSR*), Part II, on a longer and more elaborate time frame. But like *FSR*, Part II, and so much of British military thought, there was still a gap between operational sense and tactical instruction. What Du Cane's operational analysis did not provide was useful advice on the best way for infantry to cross no man's land and come to terms with the enemy. This was still caught in the rather confusing terminology of

14 For 'bite and hold', see Harris, *Haig*, 125–31; J. Paul Harris and Sanders Marble, 'The Step by Step Approach: British Military Thought and Operational Method on the Western Front, 1915–17', *War in History* 15 (2008), 14–42.

15 Harris, *Haig*, 131.

Infantry Training, 1914, which will be discussed further in Chapter 8. However, these responses show that the British Army was capable of lucid analysis. It was up to its highest commanders to match the analysis to performance and practice. It was in the course of 1915 that GHQ began to produce training pamphlets, about ninety appearing by the end of the year, albeit many were primarily for home consumption by units under training rather than disseminating lessons at the front.[16]

There was no immediate opportunity to put any lessons into effect due to the shortage of ammunition. The initial bombardment at Neuve Chapelle saw the firing of 61,219 rounds of artillery ammunition from a First Army stockpile of 216,340 rounds: thus, nearly a quarter of the supply was expended in one bombardment. It also consumed the equivalent of seventeen days' supply of shells. During the spring of 1915, the production and supply lines were hard pressed maintaining three-fifths of the regulation quantity determined after the South African War. Forced to place contracts with a range of firms few of which had any specialist knowledge of ammunition manufacture, the War Office invariable faced problems in terms of both quantity and quality. The process of fuse manufacturing proved particularly difficult. At the end of May 1915, less than half the contracted consignments of eighteen-pounder ammunition fitted with the correct fuse had been produced; it was a problem that persisted well into 1916. On the surface, matters seemed to improve markedly. By April 1915, eighteen-pound ammunition supply was 225,000 rounds per month compared with 3,000 in July 1914. However, this disguised the fact that the most pressing need was for high-explosive (HE) shells. By May 1915, of the 481,000 HE rounds ordered, only 52,000 were actually delivered. Much of the limited production capacity was also wasted in supplying eighteen-pound HE shells, which were not particularly effective on deep dugouts. This imbalance was only gradually rectified, meaning that the real shell shortage in April and May 1915 was that of heavy artillery ammunition.[17]

It was in this scenario that the British and French faced a serious crisis on the Ypres front.[18] Falkenhayn wanted to achieve a local success on the Western Front and gain a better position for threatening the Channel coast. A sinister adjunct to the attack was his decision to use the banned weapon of asphyxiating gas. Senior commanders on the British and French side had ignored warning of a gas attack. Working on scraps of information and with absolutely no grasp on the real

[16] Marble, *British Artillery*, 108. [17] Edmonds, *Military Operations, 1915*, Vol. I, 56.
[18] *Ibid.*, 158–70; Cyril Falls, *The First World War* (London: Longman, 1960), 90–3; Basil Liddell Hart, *The Real War* (London: Hutchinson, 1934), 183–92.

horrors of chemical warfare, it is perhaps unfair to condemn the commanders on the spot too fiercely for their lack of serious anti-gas preparations. By 22 April, 6,000 cylinders containing 160 tons of gas had been emplaced facing the positions held by French Territorial, Zouave and Algerian units at Langemarck. Flanking them was the recently arrived 1st Canadian Division, with the rest of the Ypres salient arc held by the British 5th, 27th and 28th Divisions. The gas was released at 5 PM that afternoon and soon caused panic among the French troops, who abandoned their positions, creating a gap of 8,000 yards in the defences. Some Canadian troops were also gassed, but they were rapidly reinforced and their line extended. Fortunately, many German units dug in on their new line and did not press forward their advantage. This was a major mistake as the Germans lacked substantial reserves in the area: it was a case of now or never. This failure to advance and exploit the initial tactical success serves to confirm the problem of the attacker on the Western Front and also shows that the inability to deepen a penetration was by no means a British preserve.[19]

In the wake of the assault, the British rushed in three battalions ('Geddes Force') to fill the gap. Foch, as the French Army Group Commander, sent forward three reserve divisions for counter-attack. These assaults were easily repulsed by the Germans when launched on 25 April. The British also took part in a series of equally hastily arranged attacks, which came to nothing against strong German resistance. Fearful that his hard-pressed British and Indian troops were now far too exposed to German artillery on their newly won high ground, Smith-Dorrien wished to withdraw to a better defensive line, making this position clear to GHQ on 27 April. Although the decision made good military sense and may well have been accepted from any other commander, French exploded with anger at his old enemy Smith-Dorrien. Believing that Smith-Dorrien had once again failed, French relieved him of command and appointed V Corps commander, Lieutenant-General Sir Herbert Plumer, in his place (formalised on 6 May). Revealing French's inability to divide his personal distaste for Smith-Dorrien from his professional status, Sir John then accepted Plumer's proposal to carry out Smith-Dorrien's planned withdrawal.[20]

Before this could take place, however, Foch requested that the British hold their position and await the outcome of further French attacks on 1 May. When these failed, French gave the order to withdraw to a new

[19] John Keegan, *The First World War* (London: Hutchinson, 1998), 214.
[20] Corvi, 'Smith-Dorrien', 183–207.

position, which was completed on 3 May. Following up on the British withdrawal, the Germans launched a ferocious assault on the Frezenberg Ridge on 8 May. Over the next six days the two sides locked in a desperate struggle in which the British were gradually pushed back. Overlooked by German artillery spotters and desperately outnumbered in terms of heavy artillery, the British infantry put up yet another magnificent defence and kept German gains to a minimum. On 24 May, the Germans switched their attention to the Bellewaarde Ridge. The attack was not entirely unexpected and was driven off. The second great battle of Ypres came to an end. It was not a moment too soon, for the Second Army was straining under the immense weight of casualties and expenditure of ammunition. Between 22 April and 31 May, the British suffered 2,150 officer and 57,125 other ranks (OR) casualties in the Ypres salient. It had, however, once again shown the effectiveness of the defensive even when heavily out-gunned. This lesson was easy to miss in a battle overshadowed by the use of gas and the dismissal of Smith-Dorrien.[21]

The Germans had used gas again after the initial attack on 22 April. The Ferozepore Brigade of the Indian Corps' Lahore Division suffered a gas attack on 26 April, as did the 12th Brigade on 1 and 2 May around Hill 60. There was another gas attack on the four-mile frontage on 24 May. German artillery had actually had the greatest impact during the operations, but the British calculated that they had suffered about 8,000 gas casualties. This was almost certainly exaggerated, and even the most primitive and improvised gas mask – namely, wads of cloth soaked in urine – had been relatively effective. Following the visit to France of two scientists, John Scott Haldane and W. Watson, the first 'black veil respirator' based on cotton pads soaked with thiosulphate was issued in May, followed shortly by the first gas hood, wool helmets of viyella dipped in thiosulphate, and then by the P (phenate) gas helmet. The British, however, failed to appreciate the difficulties the Germans had experienced in handling chlorine released from cylinders and drew too favourable a view of the likely impact of gas in the future from an experiment hastily organised at Runcorn on 4 June 1915. The first Special Companies RE were formed in July 1915 to deal with the use of gas rapidly expanded under the direction of Major Charles Foulkes, who became gas adviser to GHQ, his own headquarters and laboratories situated at Helfaut near St. Omer.[22] Ultimately, despite some sixty-three different types of gas being utilised by belligerents during the course of the war, soldiers

[21] Edmonds, *Military Operations, 1915*, Vol. I, 355.

[22] Simon Jones, '"Under a Green Cloud": The British Response to Gas Warfare', *The Great War* 1 (1989), 126–32, and 2 (1990), 14–21; Simon Jones, 'Gas Warfare: The British Defensive Measures – The Second Battle of Ypres', *Stand To!* 14 (1985), 15–23.

became better protected against gas than any other weapon and capable of operating in a gas environment.[23]

Somewhat surprisingly given the stress the battle imposed on the British, First Army managed to launch an offensive while the struggle around Ypres was still raging. French felt the pressure to resume the offensive after a conversation with Kitchener convinced him that unless major results were achieved soon, the Cabinet would move more resources to the Dardanelles. With Joffre also desirous of further assaults, French agreed to support General d'Urbal's Tenth Army with an attack on Aubers Ridge. In preparing for the offensive, Haig let First Army know that he expected it to be part of a decisive series of operations in conjunction with its French partner. There was certainly nothing half-hearted about the preparations. Haig intended to use all three of his corps. On the southern (right) front, the Indian and I Corps were to attack a front of 2,400 yards, while Rawlinson's IV Corps was directed on Fromelles. Ignoring his lack of faith in a pincer attack at Neuve Chapelle, Haig accepted a gap 7,000 yards long between the two fronts. Each spearhead was to advance and converge on Aubers Ridge.[24]

This was only the initial stage leading to a rolling operation that would unleash cavalry. Despite these great expectations, Haig did have some concerns, for immediately before the battle he warned French that he did not have enough infantry to ensure effective exploitation. This appreciation revealed Haig's misconception of the problem. The real issue was the lack of sufficient guns and ammunition to hit the far more complex German defensive systems and yardage of trench. Originally, Rawlinson had wanted to limit the attack frontage to that which could be covered by the available six-inch howitzers, amounting to about 600 yards. The frontage was then progressively increased to 1,000 yards and to 1,500 yards with the vain hope that the deficiency of heavier guns could be compensated for by the lighter 4.5-inch howitzers and by eighteen-pounders firing HE shells. Good observation work had identified many of the new German machine gun emplacements and strong points. These were duly added to the artillery plan, but this merely watered down still further

[23] For the development of gas warfare generally, see Edward Spiers, *Chemical Warfare* (London: Macmillan, 1986); L. F. Haber, *The Poisonous Cloud: Chemical Warfare in the First World War* (Oxford: Oxford University Press, 1986); Donald Richter, *Chemical Soldiers* (London: Leo Cooper, 1972); Albert Palazzo, *Seeking Victory on the Western Front: The British Army and Chemical Warfare in World War I* (Lincoln: University of Nebraska Press, 2000); and Tim Cook, *No Place to Run: The Canadian Corps and Gas Warfare in the First World War* (Vancouver: University of British Columbia Press, 1999).

[24] The analysis of Aubers Ridge is drawn from Harris, *Haig*, 132–44; Richard Holmes, *The Little Field Marshal: A Life of Sir John French* (London: Jonathan Cape, 1981), 275–90; Prior and Wilson, *Rawlinson*, 77–93; Marble, *British Artillery*, 81–3.

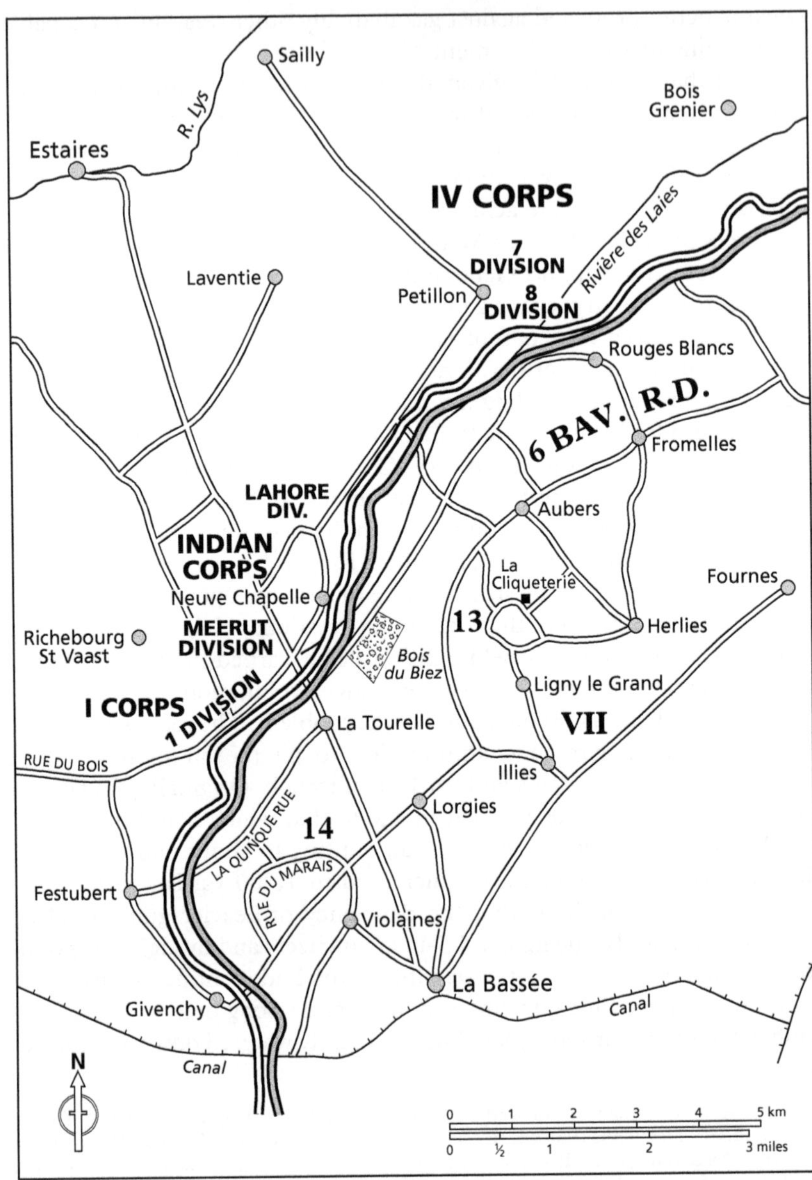

Map 4 Battle of Aubers Ridge, 9 May 1915 (positions at start of operations)

the shells needed to neutralise the German front line. Compared to the five pounds at Neuve Chapelle, only two pounds of HE was being put down onto each yard of German front line The Germans had also greatly strengthened their front-line defences as a result of Neuve Chapelle, while many of the 121 heavy guns and 516 field and medium guns were showing signs of wear and tear. As at Neuve Chapelle, the British bombardment was planned to be short and sharp, but it now had far more jobs to do. The assault was eventually ordered for 5 AM on 9 May, when a forty-minute bombardment was scheduled to open up on the German positions. In the trenches opposite the Indian Corps, the bombardment did not even force the Germans to keep their heads down.

The battle of Aubers Ridge was an unmitigated disaster for the British Army in France. For the most part, the original assault was stopped dead on the British parapet along the length of the front. Only in a very few places did small numbers of men heroically work their way into the German line. Largely untroubled by effective counter-battery work, the Germans responded ferociously by hammering the British front line and communication trenches. Haig was quickly made aware of these failures but ordered another assault for the afternoon. This too came to grief almost immediately. Yet another assault was pre-empted by a sudden, intense bout of German artillery activity, which utterly destroyed any chance of imposing order on the men in the front line. Very much displeased, Haig assembled his corps commanders at Indian Corps HQ and proposed either a night attack or one the next day. No one showed much enthusiasm for a night assault, so, by default, operations were scheduled to recommence the following day.

Capper having been wounded in a training accident, his temporary replacement, Major-General Hubert Gough, was commanding 7th Division. Gough was ordered to relieve the punch-drunk 8th Division but found it utterly impossible to get his men through the shambles in the trenches and form them up in time for an assault. This was duly reported to Rawlinson, who passed the information to Haig. Although Haig accepted this as a reason for postponement, he did not give up on the idea of renewing the assault on 10 May, scheduling a 4 PM zero hour led by I Corps and then reinforced by the Indians. Haig was forced to reverse this decision when clear information regarding the appalling chaos at the front, casualties and the power of the German artillery emerged. In relation to the numbers involved, the losses were two-thirds as heavy as those suffered on 1 July 1916 and included a considerable number of veterans. Around 11,500 casualties were inflicted on First Army; the assault did nothing to assist the French, and indeed, the Germans withdrew two divisions from behind this sector to prop up their defence against French assaults. Shocked and subdued by this check, French desperately needed a face-saving formula and found it in the shell shortage. He colluded with Charles Repington, the influential military correspondent of the *Times*, to ensure publication of the story. Run on 14 May under dramatic headlines, the report deflected attention from the BEF's performance and put the government under pressure. As already indicated in Chapter 5, the scandal combined with a series of other criticisms to play a role in ending Asquith's Liberal government and ushering in the coalition.[25] As noted earlier, there were undoubtedly severe shell shortages in France, but the important deficit was in heavy artillery ammunition and the guns to fire them. Had the deficiencies been as great as French implied First Army would not have been able to enter another battle almost immediately after the cessation of Neuve Chapelle.

Anxious to secure a much-needed victory, French now responded to Haig's desire to attack at Festubert. Equally anxious to deliver a victory, Haig revised his approach to battle. He acknowledged the wisdom of careful artillery preparation using heavy guns to destroy German strong points guided by effective observation of the shooting. Indeed, Haig wished every shot to be observed but then also said that bombardments should continue by night so as to demoralise the enemy. Although his revision of ideas revealed this contradiction, it was nonetheless a sign that his method was changing.

Once again, however, he planned a pincer assault. On the left, the Meerut Division (Indian Corps) and two brigades of 2nd Division (I Corps) were assigned a front of about 1,600 yards. On the right was Gough's 7th Division (now in I Corps) to attack a front of around 900 yards. The left-wing assault was to go in by night using their knowledge of the ground to make up for the difficulty of attacking in darkness. On the right, 7th Division was to advance at dawn as it was less familiar with the local landscape. A sixty-hour bombardment was planned to commence on 13 May using more than 100,000 rounds but concluding with a more rapid rate of fire that served to warn the Germans of the impending assault. This lengthy bombardment was then wisely confined to achieving a shallow advance of no more than 1,000 yards. All of this showed a step towards attacking more methodically and without excessive ambition.[26]

Rain interrupted the bombardment on 13 May, but it continued more effectively on 14 and 15 May, and at 11.30 PM on 15 May, the Meerut

25 David French, 'The Military Background to the Shell Crisis of May 1915', *Journal of Strategic Studies* 2 (1979), 192–205; Peter Fraser, 'The British "Shell Scandal" of 1915', *Canadian Journal of History* 18 (1983), 69–86; Turner, *British Politics*, 56–61.

26 For Festubert, see Harris, *Haig*, 145–8; Marble, *British Artillery*, 83–5.

and 2nd Divisions began their advance. Unfortunately, only the 6th Brigade of 2nd Division managed to achieve any of its objectives, while the Meerut Division could not penetrate the German position. To his credit, Haig stopped all further assaults on this front once he became aware of the position. By this point, 7th Division had commenced its assault (3.15 AM). Both the 20th and 22nd Brigades managed to advance, the 22nd Brigade even getting into the support line. This was a fairly respectable outcome compared with Aubers Ridge, but it left Haig with two small incisions in the German line. He therefore ordered 2nd Division to straighten the line by achieving a junction with 7th Division, leaving the commander of 2nd Division, Major-General Henry Horne, to decide on zero hour. However, the Germans rather pre-empted this with a voluntary withdrawal to a new line. The two British divisions were therefore able to link up but were in no position to penetrate further into the German line. Haig relieved both divisions, and the battle guttered out with much expenditure of shells and minor movements forward. The battle of Festubert cost the British between 16,000 and 17,000 casualties; about 800 Germans were captured and possibly 5,000 other casualties inflicted. The Germans also avoided the temptation to counter-attack too hastily and had relied on their artillery to break up the BEF's assaults. The battle was therefore neither a great success in terms of ground taken nor effective attrition. However, it had at least shown the French a dogged British supporting action, and no one had run away with grandiose exploitation ideas.

At this point British manpower expansion was occurring much more quickly than ammunition and materiel. The arrival of complete TF, New Army and Canadian divisions provided a considerable boost. The great difficulty was equipping them properly and completing their sketchy training. Such was the increase in numbers that a Third Army was created. Continuing his strategy of personality-driven appointments, French avoided giving Rawlinson command of the new force, preferring instead Sir Charles Monro.[27] Rawlinson undoubtedly took this as a sign of French's distaste for him, which, in turn, drew him even closer to Haig. It was therefore natural that Haig turned to Rawlinson when French requested a diversionary assault to support another of Joffre's offensives. Turning his attention away from the ground directly in front of Aubers Ridge, Haig identified the Rue d'Ouvert at Givenchy as a point of local tactical importance. This straight road lined with two-storey houses carefully converted into mini-strongholds by the Germans had resisted capture during the Festubert operations. Rawlinson was utterly pessimistic

[27] John Bourne, 'Charles Monro', in Beckett and Corvi (eds.), *Haig's Generals*, 122–40.

about the chances for success, but such was the depth of the master–client relationship with Haig that these concerns were never discussed with him frankly. Revealing a worrying inconsistency, Haig again urged full consideration of exploitation plans when it was clear that the assault was nothing more than a very minor affair with limited resources. As Sanders Marble has commented, it seemed more important to attack than to prepare properly.[28]

On 15 June, a forty-eight-hour bombardment commenced, three days later than originally scheduled due to alterations in French plans. As had been the case at Festubert, the bombardment was deliberate and progressed only slowly in order to maximise observation and interpretation of its effect. The majority of the twenty six-inch howitzers were put on to the German front line, and 4.5-inch howitzers were given wire-cutting duties for the first time. But instead of groping their way back to the reasons for success at Neuve Chapelle, where frontage of trench had been carefully tallied against available resources, this was a watered-down version of Aubers Ridge. The length of the front to be attacked was only slightly more modest than on 8 May, but the number of guns was not greatly increased: there were 190 guns for roughly 1,500 yards of front at Aubers Ridge compared with 211 guns for 1,300 yards on this occasion. Rawlinson's lack of faith in the plan may have been reflected in the choice of 6 PM as zero hour; attacking so late in the day had the advantage of maintaining observation of fire until the last moment, as well as forestalling any demands for too hasty exploitation.

When the attacking troops went in, a disaster unfolded. They found much wire uncut, which allowed only small and scattered numbers of British troops to penetrate the enemy line. Unsubdued German artillery and machine guns then swept no man's land, ensuring that the British were unable to resupply the small groups in the enemy line. It was a total failure, as the British were pushed back to their start line. Haig ordered another assault on 17 June using the 1st Canadian Division as reinforcement. The result was the same: IV Corps took 3,500 casualties for no ground. The Germans also defeated the assault using nothing but local troops. The battle of Givenchy therefore provided absolutely no aid to the French.[29]

In the aftermath of the battle, Haig insisted that he needed far more and heavier munitions, more trench mortars, better grenades and more balloons and aircraft to assist with observation. On the human front, he wanted to weed out unfit and burnt-out men, replacing them with

[28] Marble, *British Artillery*, 87.
[29] Harris, *Haig*, 148–52; Prior and Wilson, *Rawlinson*, 94–9.

vigorous, younger commanders. Although this was part of the answer, the problem required a deeper analysis from Haig. The initial response of Rawlinson was not much more encouraging. As in the wake of Aubers Ridge, he once again indulged in the unpleasant habit of questioning the will of his troops. A better-reasoned response was produced on 21 June when he suggested that German positions were now of such strength with such deep dugouts as to be almost impenetrable. In turn, this meant a readjustment of the artillery's task away from destruction and in favour of neutralisation. Rawlinson had come close to unlocking the secret of assaults on the Western Front: the artillery could cut wire, and then it could force the German defenders below the parapet until the infantry was on them; it could not hope to cause such devastation of the enemy lines that the infantry merely occupied smashed trenches and cleared away the remains of shattered men and corpses.

Putting such an approach into action depended on getting the right production and logistics framework in place, which required time. Unfortunately, the entente powers did not have that luxury in the summer of 1915. The British and French felt the onus to maintain pressure in the west in order to help their Italian and Russian partners. It was the precise nature of the assistance that caused problems. Joffre seemed to accept that the breakthrough was a difficult proposition and started to talk of 'nibbling' at the German position but at the same time maintained that great results were possible through large-scale offensive action, whereas Kitchener favoured attrition.[30] Although the two options seemed very different, a core issue connected them: whatever path Anglo-French strategy took led back to supply and logistics, and neither side took this seriously enough. The British had made some improvements in their system by the summer of 1915, especially that of divisional packing, meaning the preparation and forwarding of supplies from the bases determined by pre-calculated quantities. At the same time, however, the BEF still had a desperate lack of suitably qualified administrative staff officers. At brigade level, for example, only twenty-seven of 105 brigade majors in France in November 1915 were actually staff trained. A short four-week course on staff duties had been introduced in Major-General Richard Haking's 1st Division in mid-1915, but there were to be no staff

[30] For discussion of Joffre's position on the nature of offensive action and the seeming contradiction between limited offensives and breakthrough, see Robert Doughty, *Pyrrhic Victory: French Strategy and Operations in the Great War* (Cambridge, MA: Belknapp Press, 2005), 168; Jonathan Kraus, *Early Trench Tactics in the French Army: The Second Battle of Artois, May–June 1915* (Farnham: Ashgate, 2013), 26.

schools in Britain or France until 1916.[31] These deep weaknesses in the supply chains of both Britain and France were never discussed in depth by Joffre and French, which had the effect of fundamentally undermining strategic and operational planning in the summer of 1915.[32]

French's failure to press the issue of logistics, particularly ammunition supply, with Joffre did not mean he was unaware of it. Indeed, French was very gloomy about the possibilities of meaningful results in these circumstances and was even more dismayed by Joffre's identification of the Loos region as the focus of British efforts. The landscape around Loos was not conducive to effective offensive operations. As a coal-mining district, it was pockmarked with quarries, large slag heaps and winding towers, which gave the defenders excellent observation. These commanding positions were made all the more dominating by the flatness of the surrounding plain. Scattered between the slag heaps and mine works were small clusters of miners' cottages, which had been converted into strong points. Finally, the flat landscape lacked truly distinctive features, making the maintenance of direction by attacking infantry a trying task. These deep reservations became even greater when French started to question Joffre's real commitment to a great breakthrough battle around Arras. Revealing both the increasing insecurity of French himself and Britain's lack of confidence as the junior military partner on the Western Front, French still decided to support Joffre's plan.[33]

Like French, Haig was not at all impressed by the ground around Loos and felt that it offered little chance of success. Lacking the power to escape a commitment entirely, French instructed Haig to prepare a modest plan designed more as a demonstration than a full-scale assault. This approach chimed with Haig's own thinking. Reviewing the results of his previous offensives, Haig came to a variant on the conclusions reached by Du Cane, Rawlinson and Robertson. In agreement with them, he accepted the need for vast quantities of guns, munitions and men combined in a very carefully prepared plan. His departure from their thinking came over the intention and time-frame. Whereas Du Cane, Rawlinson and Robertson all worked on the concept of successive operations for limited objectives, Haig believed that he could telescope time by attacking

[31] Aimée Fox-Golden, 'Hopeless Inefficiency? The Transformation and Operational Performance of Brigade Staff, 1916–18', in Locicero, Mahoney and Mitchell (eds.), *Military Transformed*, 139–56.

[32] Brown, *British Logistics*, 90.

[33] For Loos, see Harris, *Haig*, 153–77; Holmes, *Little Field Marshal*, 295–306; *Marble, British Artillery*, 100–6; Nicholas Lloyd, *Loos, 1915* (Stroud: Tempus, 2006), esp. 213–30; Prior and Wilson, *Rawlinson*, 100–16.

across an extremely broad front, suggesting as much as 100 miles. This would suck in enemy reserves much more quickly and consequently buckle the line to breaking point within a shorter time, allowing the cavalry-led breakout and exploitation. Haig's thinking seems closer to Du Cane's than to Rawlinson's or Robertson's as both were clearly building upon the pre-war British concepts of battle and revising them to fit the current circumstances. The main difference was that Haig's mental concept of a broad front seemed to carry with it a consequent sense of stretching, and therefore thinning, of the depth of the German defences. Du Cane's was quite the opposite, containing a healthy respect for the depth of German defensive systems.

Knowing that Loos could not be such a battle and with French's instructions in mind, Haig duly informed his corps commanders of the need for modest plans at a meeting on 13 August. Haig was rightly concerned by the strength of the Hohenzollern Redoubt and requested that this problem be given particular attention. Hubert Gough, now commanding I Corps, worked on the idea of a vigorous rush to the enemy line after a preliminary bombardment. He believed that this would take Fosse 8 and the Hohenzollern Redoubt in the first bound, which would form the base for an advance between the redoubt and the Vermelles-Hulluch Road. This move would then allow for exploitation towards the quarries. True to form, Rawlinson's initial plan was more cautious and included slow sapping towards the enemy line to narrow the distances the attacking troops had to cover. Equally true to form, Haig was disappointed with Rawlinson's cautious approach but found much to commend in Gough's aggressive stance.

Unfortunately for the BEF, Joffre gained knowledge of French's determination to limit the scale of the offensive and demanded a greater vision. Kitchener now stepped in and ordered Sir John to act according to French wishes. This demand was duly passed on to Haig, who was then visited by Kitchener and told much the same. Haig now felt obliged to fall into line and told Kitchener that First Army would play its role but needed much more in the way of ammunition. This avoided the other crucial factor. First Army, and indeed the entire BEF, desperately needed more guns, especially heavy artillery.

From this point on an increasingly detrimental confusion of visions entered British planning. French and Haig now became convinced that a breakthrough battle was possible, opening the way for a deep advance with the line Douai-Valenciennes-Maubeuge as the ultimate objective. It has been suggested that the mental *volte face* carried out by both men was because they convinced themselves that circumstances had materially changed for the better since June and July.[34] A crucial element in this conversion was the potential of gas. Haig was deeply impressed by the gas demonstration he attended on 22 August. Over the next week, his faith in the new tool increased despite its immense flaws as a weapon. Released from cylinders, it was utterly reliant on wind speed and direction for effect, making it an extremely erratic implement at this stage in the war. Placing so much emphasis on this fragile technology also revealed a weakness in Haig's original thinking. Knowing that First Army was desperately short of artillery, the initial use of gas was a stopgap complement. In one bound it went from being a weapon of pragmatic expediency to one of decisive significance. Indeed, preparations for the use of gas and smoke were so extensive that they swallowed staff time which should have been devoted to the more important artillery plan.

French did little to keep this enthusiasm for gas in check by maintaining an ambiguous stance between grand and limited visions. This hovering uncertainty was summed up in the orders sent to Haig on 23 August telling him to

> support the French attack to the full extent of your available resources, and not to limit your action in the manner indicted in the above quoted letter [meaning the 'demonstration plan'] … [but then added] This instruction is not, however, to be taken as preventing you from developing your attack deliberately and progressively, should you be of the opinion that the nature of the enemy's defences makes such a course desirable.[35]

Given these orders, it is unsurprising that Haig confused the difference between the strategic need for an all-out assault designed to satisfy French demands with a tactically limited operation. This misunderstanding was compounded when Haig quoted the term 'to the full extent of your power' to subordinate commanders.[36]

Opportunities to clarify French's intentions never arose as he suffered from frequent bouts of ill-health in August and September. It took until 18 September for French to intervene more clearly, spelling out that he expected Haig to attack with commitment and energy, but in a carefully controlled manner and always with a close eye on the outcome of Joffre's operations.

A further lack of clarity arose over the role of the reserve units. For French, the reserves were there to be used once success was achieved, whereas in Haig's opinion they were a component in ensuring initial

[34] Holmes, *Little Field Marshal*, 300. [35] Quoted in Lloyd, *Loos*, 53.

[36] Holmes and Lloyd form different judgements on French's intention. According to Holmes, French was converted to the idea of decisive attack (*Little Field Marshal*, 300–1), whereas Lloyd believed that French was far more circumspect (*Loos*, 53).

success. Haig was keen that the thruster, Haking of 1st Division, should be put in charge of the new Reserve (XI) Corps, to which Haking was duly appointed on 4 September. He also wanted the precise position of the corps established. He met French on 18 September, where the two men disagreed over Haig's desire to have them well forward with the leading divisions at Noeux-les-Mines. French's reasons for holding back the reserves are not clear. Given his inconsistencies, it may well have been due to another sudden bout of pessimism leading him to put a brake on Haig's ambitions. Once again, the BEF's high command was undermined by a lack of clarity in the decision-making processes of its commander-in-chief and his ambiguous relationship with his senior subordinate. In effect, French was using the reserves as a way of keeping control over the battle rather than ordering Haig directly and clearly to manage it in a manner of which he approved. Haig certainly did not take this as a subtle hint to rein in his ambition and maintained his grand visions while taking the odd snipe at GHQ for its timidity. The eventual decision to place XI Corps at Lillers provoked fury in Haig. He sent an angry note to French, which caused him to give way, agreeing that they would be held 7,000 to 5,000 yards from the front. French's revision is not easy to explain, but it was clear that he still held ultimate authority over its use.

In order to make the assault, the BEF was put under great pressure. As the plans were increased in scale, it rapidly became the biggest venture the British had yet undertaken on the Western Front. The attack frontage represented a huge increase, standing at 11,200 yards compared with 1,450 at Neuve Chapelle and 5,800 at Festubert. Simple frontage hides the real problem for the guns, which had to hit more than one line of trenches. The full yardage of trench was therefore somewhere in the region of 36,000 yards. To tackle this very difficult task, the First Army was allocated 533 guns divided evenly between the two attacking corps (I and IV). For IV Corps, this represented a significant diminution of the 342 guns it had used for the attack at Neuve Chapelle. Although the bombardment at Loos was to be much longer and utilised more heavy pieces, the overall impact was significantly less because it meant one gun for every 141 yards compared with one gun for every six at Neuve Chapelle. As already indicated, at Neuve Chapelle during a thirty-five-minute bombardment, a total of 288 pounds fell on each yard of trench under attack. At Loos, a bombardment of 72 hours spread over four days saw only forty-three pounds falling on every yard of trench. Loos was therefore only one-fifth as heavy as Neuve Chapelle in terms of weight and in terms of shells per yard of trench, it was only one-seventh as heavy.[37]

[37] Prior and Wilson, *Command on the Western Front*, 111–12.

On the issue of ammunition supply, First Army received 650,000 shells for the field artillery (roughly 1,000 per gun) and 100,000 shells for the howitzers and heavy guns (400 rounds per gun).[38] Because the supply of guns was so limited, they had been put under great pressure all year and by September were showing defects, meaning that many were out of action. Hurriedly made ammunition was also problematic with a high number of duds. Gas was in equally short supply and thus was unable to fill the gap. Almost by accident this deficiency led the British to smoke shells and candles, which were rightly regarded as the ideal way to neutralise German machine gunners. The utter poverty of supply is revealed in the fact that the British lacked adequate supplies of even these substitutes for a substitute. As Sanders Marble has commented, the artillery plan 'was reduced to hitting key points, firing as much as possible on other targets, and hoping for the best'.[39]

An important step forward was the centralising of artillery control under corps Brigadiers-General Royal Artillery (BGRA). This at least ensured that all artillery within a corps worked to a set plan, and only the counter-battery work was allotted differently. However, no system of inter-corps co-operation or uniformity was imposed. Thus Brigadier-General Noel Birch (I Corps) worked a different system from that of Brigadier-General Charles Budworth (IV Corps). Birch wrote out a comprehensive, step-by-step fire plan, whereas Budworth identified the tasks and then devolved much of the detailed planning to group commanders. Budworth was probably hamstrung by his ambiguous position. Lacking faith in his own BGRA, A. H. Hussey, Rawlinson had taken Budworth from his post at 1st Division. He did so, however, without formally relieving Hussey and instead left Budworth to work around Hussey. Further confusion was created by the fact that the heavy artillery batteries were under First Army control, as was counter-battery work. This revealed the low priority given to counter-battery fire, with only sixty-one guns allocated to the task and only thirty-four given to the two attacking corps. As a consequence, counter-battery work was desultory, and too many batteries took German artillery silence as a sign of success. Interestingly, however, there was one new feature of the artillery plan in the attempt to incorporate a lifting barrage. It would appear that the first unheralded attempt had been made in a small operation at Hooge on 16 June in which the bombardment lifted from the German front line trench to the support trench and then to the communications trenches. It is unclear whether the Commander Royal Artillery (CRA) of the 6th Division, G. Humphreys, or the artillery adviser of VI Corps, W. L. H.

[38] Lloyd, *Loos*, 100. [39] Marble, *British Artillery*, 102.

Paget, devised this, or whether or not there had been any observation of French methods. A lifting barrage was to be used all along the front at Loos, though in very different ways, with, for example, one brigade keeping the barrage on the German front line for three minutes beyond zero. It was not a major factor at Loos (and it would be further refined as the 'creeping barrage' in 1916) the overwhelming difficulty being the lack of communications and the inevitability of reliance on pre-arranged timetables that might not reflect the tactical reality on the ground.[40]

These uneven artillery arrangements reveal Haig's lack of grip on artillery matters. He had simply gathered as many guns as possible and then worked on the assumption that they could provide significant assistance to his plans. It was a strange method given the perfectly sensible conclusions he had already reached on the vital need for accurate and overwhelming artillery fire. Lacking overall cohesion, the bombardment then proved patchy in its results, a problem compounded by the lack of system linking infantry observations of its effect and the gunners themselves. Aerial observation also needed refinement as certain areas of the line were under-studied, whereas others attracted more than one aircraft. The dry conditions further inhibited effective bombardment by throwing great clouds of chalk dust obscuring observation. This meant precious shells continued to be fired on sectors where there was uncertainty as to the effect. On 23 September, the weather became wet and cloudy, sustaining the problem of observation. On 24 September, conditions were much better, and the fire became both more intense and more effective.

Infantry preparations were equally inconsistent. The uncertainty over the actual intentions of the battle was reflected in ambiguous orders. Many of the attacking brigades were confused as to their final objectives, with the only clarity being the onus to attack to the utmost. Loosely set objectives were confused still further by the lack of co-ordinated planning and tactical thinking. The attack at Loos was to be spearheaded by two hurriedly raised and trained New Army divisions (the 9th and 15th), backed by a Territorial Division (the 47th), which was also regarded as an unknown quantity, and the remnants of the regular army (1st, 2nd, and 7th Divisions). Given this immense mix of troops with their differing levels of training and experience, it is amazing that no one felt it necessary to sketch out at least some over-arching tactical guidelines. Even if it was assumed that everyone had at least passing knowledge of *Infantry Training, 1914*, some revisions to take account of trench warfare should have been produced and distributed. This lack of uniformity was summed up in the fact that the 2nd, 9th and 47th Divisions wisely constructed

[40] Marble, *British Artillery*, 88–91, 103–4.

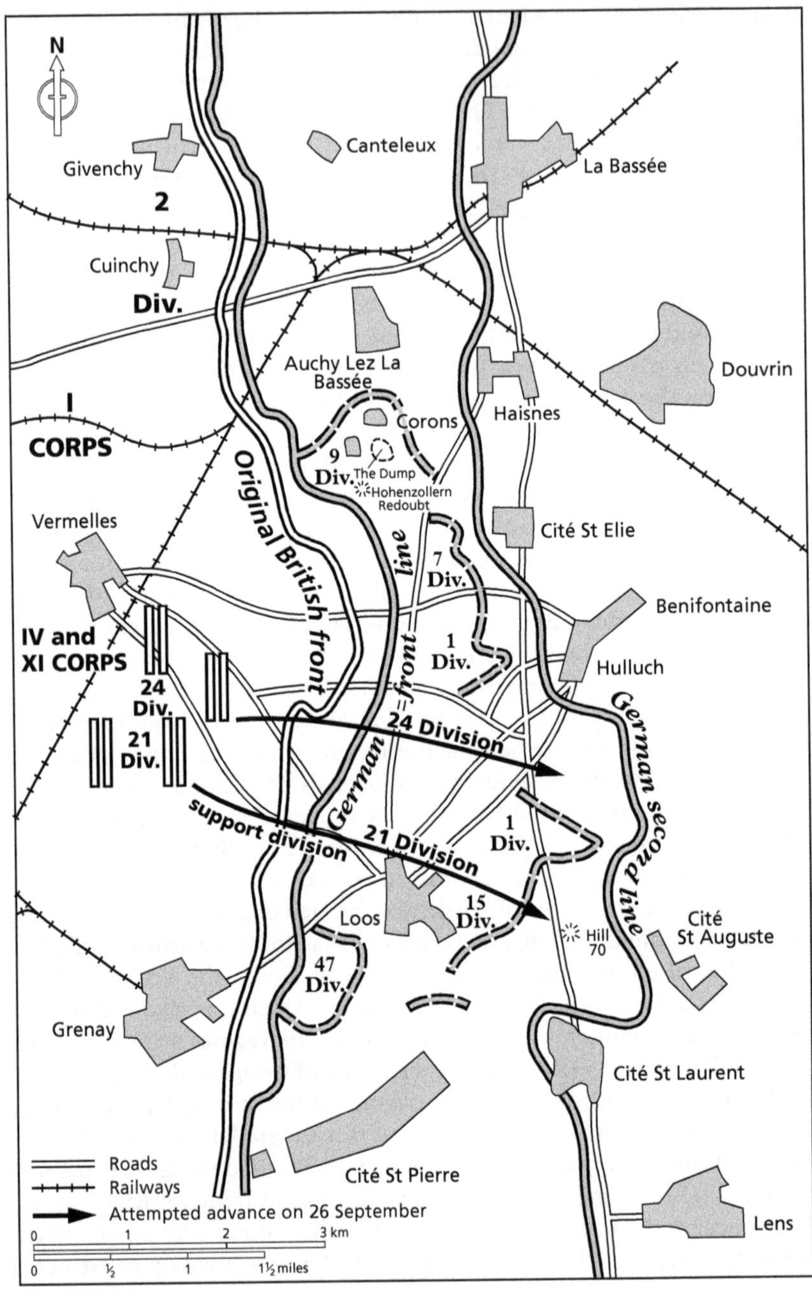

Map 5 Battle of Loos, 25–26 September 1915

models of the ground to be attacked, using them to familiarise the men with their tasks, but no one made this good idea binding on the other three divisions. Rather shockingly given the wrangles over the reserve divisions, they were also given very little preparation. The support and equipment required to launch them into battle smoothly were not thought through by anyone in responsibility. Few of those responsible for the good governance of the corps from the rear area to battle emerge from the affair creditably, and the welter of recriminations in the wake of XI Corps' disastrous showing in the battle appear to be attempts at denying culpability.

The final element of uncertainty was the weather. With so much now dependent on the gas, a huge amount had been staked on a completely uncontrollable variable. The pressure was all the greater given the fact that the requirement to support the French assault gave little leeway over the start date of the offensive. After much wrangling with the French, it was agreed that the British could delay until 25 September, but no later. In the event, the conditions on 25 September were not optimal for a gas release, being mildly favourable at the most, but the weight of expectation was such that Haig gave the order to commence the assault.

At 5.50 AM an intensive bombardment opened up on the German front, and the gas was released. On the extreme right of the British line, the assault of the Territorial 47th Division went well, with the defensive flank quickly put into place. This success can be put down to the fact that on this sector the artillery had done well cutting German wire thoroughly, and the combined gas and smoke cloud blinded the defenders. Determined to capitalise on these advantages, the well-prepared Territorials advanced at great speed and overran the German positions before the defenders had a chance to react. To the 47th Division's immediate left was the New Army's 15th Division. Rawlinson had allocated this raw unit the tricky task of clearing Loos village, cross Hill 70 and advance a further three miles. The wind was in the right direction on its front, and the combination of gas and smoke along with well-cut wire helped the division forward. By 7.30 AM, Loos had been penetrated and was being cleared, and an hour later the troops were advancing on Hill 70, and it was quickly overrun. Rawlinson was much exhilarated, but he had not considered the true situation. There had been considerable casualties in the division, its brigades had become much intermixed and the men were drifting towards Lens rather than maintaining the line of advance. This was realised by officers on the spot, who wanted to consolidate Hill 70 first and bring the situation under control. However, too many men had set off in the direction of Lens. Once over the crest of the hill, German fire from Cité St Auguste and Lens, both protected by thick belts of wire, brought the advance to a halt. Unsupported by friendly artillery fire, there was little that now could be done except dig in and attempt to consolidate. In the event, German troops responded first putting in a counter-attack at 11.30 AM. The Germans rapidly increased their strength to four battalions and forced the British back over the crest of Hill 70. Rather than entering the battle as exploitation troops, 15th Division's reserves now did so with the sole intention of stabilising the position and consolidating the ground held. Rawlinson's left-hand assault led by 1st Division had a much tougher day. After hard fighting, it forced its way up to the Lens-Hulluch Road, where it consolidated, having suffered many casualties.

On Gough's I Corps front, the progress of the attacking units was generally more mixed. Assigned the task of left-hand flank guard, the men of Horne's 2nd Division were forced to cross a landscaped littered with craters and shell holes. This forced them to bunch as they advanced between the obstacles, which made them easy targets for German fire. In addition, the lingering gas and smoke cloud and large sections of uncut German wire clustered the men still further as they sought clear observation and passage through to the German lines. The new P (phenate) helmet, designed in case the Germans were to use phosgene or hydrogen cyanide, contained stronger chemicals that affected the men wearing them, as well as providing more limited visibility than the earlier hood. Despite these immense difficulties, the men fought their way into the line but then found it increasingly difficult to maintain all their toeholds. The spearhead of Gough's assault was 9th Division in the corps' centre against the Hohenzollern Redoubt. On the division's 26th Brigade front, the wire protecting the redoubt had been well cut, allowing the troops to fight their way into the position. However, the 28th Brigade to its left came up against uncut wire and intact German machine gun positions, which destroyed its advance. I Corps ordered the brigade to make a fresh assault, but the bombardment commenced and concluded long before the ruffled brigade had had a chance to compose and prepare itself. The renewed attack then went off in a ragged manner as units received their orders at different times, and unsurprisingly, it came to nought. 7th Division, once more under Capper's command, led the right hand of the corps' assault. It found the wire to its front almost completely uncut, but with great skill and courage, the men fought their way into the German line and cleared it. Capper, however, was mortally wounded while characteristically well forward.

Given the weaknesses of the British bombardment and the patchy effectiveness of the gas and smoke candles, the BEF had produced an extremely creditable performance. After such exertions, however, they rapidly lost operational momentum during the afternoon. The Germans were moving in reserves at a much quicker rate than the British, and the failure to pinch out all the strong points also allowed them to pour in enfilading fire, disrupting all attempts to consolidate or exploit. In addition, the utter failure of British counter-battery work meant that the German artillery was free to interdict British movements across no man's land and blast likely forming-up points. Matters looked very different at First Army HQ; Haig was absolutely convinced that the door had swung open and offered a tantalising view of wide-open spaces. He was particularly interested in 15th Division's success and thought this was the area where the enemy line was about to snap. The vision obscured reality, however, for immediately behind Hill 70 lay untouched, well-wired German defences into which fresh soldiers were being poured. Eagerly pursuing what he perceived to be great opportunities, Haig had clearly forgotten the leeway French's orders implied.

Haig now wished to hurry the two reserve divisions – 21st and 24th – of XI Corps into action. He was largely unconcerned that they were absolutely raw Kitchener divisions as he believed the Germans were incapable of a disciplined defence. As a result of this optimism, already overloaded staffs worked immensely hard to make and disseminate meaningful plans. The expectations of the BEF's senior commanders surpassed utterly the realities of the actual machinery at their disposal and the reactions of the enemy. Thus, 26 September 1915 was another disaster for the British Army in France. Utter confusion reigned in the 21st and 24th Divisions, which were thrown into battle without proper support and suffered 8,200 casualties in the process.[41]

The rest of IV Corps' front achieved nothing. The catastrophic failure of the two reserve divisions has tended to overshadow the fact that command and control broke down across the British front that day. On Hill 70, the 45th Brigade managed to reach the crest, but the 62nd Brigade broke and ran taking 15th Division with them. For a while, it even looked like Loos village itself might be surrendered, but the troops rallied and re-occupied their positions. Along I Corps front a series of poorly co-ordinated assaults achieved equally little. (By the same token, the Germans were clearly not masters of battlefield arts, as they persisted in equally poorly planned counter-attacks, which were largely rebuffed by even the most exhausted British troops.) The artillery plan had not

[41] Edmonds, *Military Operations, 1915*, Vol. II, 342; Mike Senior, *Haking: A Dutiful Soldier – Lieutenant-General Sir Richard Haking, XI Corps Commander, 1915–18* (Barnsley: Pen & Sword, 2012), 42–73.

provided sufficiently for renewed bombardments, and the batteries that were moved forward on 25 September became vulnerable to German counter-fire on 26 and 27 September, the Germans retaining good observation over the battlefield as a whole.

Having experienced such a disappointing day, Haig was prepared to scale back the scope of British operations. However, renewed pressure from the French ensured that the battle would grind on for a further three weeks. Little short of chaos seemed to reign in I Corps as Gough persisted in ill-considered attempts to clear the Hohenzollern Redoubt. Major-General Edward Bulfin, 28th Division Commander, whose hard-pressed troops were at the butt of these directives, believed that Gough completely misunderstood the scale of the tactical problem. Rather than reflect on his own methodology, Gough took the same line as Rawlinson at Neuve Chapelle and blamed his subordinate. Haig shared this view, and it played a major role in ensuring the diversion of the supposedly dud 28th Division to Salonika. A final series of costly assaults occurred on 13 October, which achieved very little of material value. British losses at Loos were high. Over the course of the battle, the British suffered some 50,000 casualties, including over 6,000 confirmed dead and 16,000 missing. Disaggregating the figures and attributing them to the various stages of the fighting is difficult, but one reasonable estimate is that the majority were suffered on 25 September, with figures that could be as high 19,000. Indeed, it can be suggested that 25 September 1915 was as lethal as 1 July 1916 in that average divisional losses were 1,058 at Loos compared to 1,107 on the first day of the Somme.[42] In return, around 5,000 German fatalities were inflicted. Loos cannot be read as anything other than a failure.

Attempts were made to learn lessons, one from the fiasco of the reserves being the need for far better traffic control behind the front by the staffs of the QMG and the Provost Marshal.[43] An assessment by Rawlinson's Chief of Staff, Brigadier-General A. A. Montgomery, suggested, *inter alia*, the need for reserves to be held closer to the front line, the importance of a defensive flank to an attack, the problem of brigade and divisional headquarters being too close to the front where they might be shelled and, above all, the need for more careful preparation. In any case, Montgomery believed that there was little chance of 'breaking through in one rush'.[44] Both Rawlinson and Haig concluded that speed by advancing troops was essential in the 'race to the parapet', and Haig noted that a

[42] Lloyd, *Loos*, 156, 218. [43] *Ibid.*, 220.

[44] *Ibid.*, 226–7; Harris and Marble, 'Step by Step Approach', 14–42; Tim Travers, 'Learning and Decision-Making on the Western Front, 1915–16: The British Example', *Canadian Journal of History* 18 (1983), 87–97.

final intensive bombardment had only alerted the enemy to the imminence of the assault. But Haig also concluded that a longer bombardment was necessary to cut the wire and destroy enemy defences. Some lessons were to be taken on board, others were to be ignored, when Haig, Rawlinson and Montgomery combined to plan the Somme offensive in 1916. The failure to learn was partly due to the absence of any real mechanism for disseminating lessons but also to a prevailing mind-set, which Tim Travers has summed up as a 'more and more syndrome' of simply increasing the size of an offensive rather than seeking alternative solutions.[45]

In the aftermath of the battle, Haig and French indulged in a heated debate over the reserve divisions. In essence, the two men repeated the misunderstandings that had clouded the issue before the battle. Haig insisted to Kitchener, and others, that an enormous opportunity had been missed because of French's incompetence. By failing both to position the reserve divisions close enough to the battlefield and then holding onto them until far too late, French had turned a great victory into defeat. The controversy helped to topple Sir John from his position. French found it difficult to fend off these accusations, lacking as he did the necessary political skills. Even if he had possessed them, it is doubtful that they would have worked by the autumn of 1915. Since the beginning of the war, French had alarmed too many people in authority with his capricious temperament. Starting in September 1914 with the threat to pull the BEF out of the line, continuing with the see-sawing judgements during the first battle of Ypres and then compounding it all by his collusion in the shell scandal story, French seemed too unstable for high command.

The case against him appears to have been strengthened considerably by Robertson, who arrived in London in October 1915 to give GHQ's view on strategic matters. As a well-respected administrator with a clear-thinking mind, Robertson's doubts about French's performance must have been extremely persuasive. With the King also deeply concerned following a visit to France and briefings from Haig, Gough and Haking, Asquith was presented with a clear signal. While Asquith accepted that French must go, at this point it was unclear as to who should replace him. Robertson was a possible candidate, but he was aware of his own lack of field command experience and strengths as an administrator. This paved the way for Haig to take the post of Commander-in-Chief, with Robertson's talents given their natural outlet as Chief of the Imperial General Staff. It was a command team the military, the politicians and

[45] Travers, 'Learning', 93.

the King could all support warmly. Asquith duly persuaded French to resign, and Haig formally succeeded him on 19 December 1915.[46] Haig brought with him a new staff team and a determination to succeed on the Western Front. He was also aware of the fact that 1916 was likely to be significant in the military relationship between Britain and France, as Britain's mobilisation at last began to realise the potential of the nation. However, it was a strength that required thoughtful and correct application.

The BEF's introduction to continental warfare in 1914 and 1915 proved confusing and contradictory to its officers and men. At one and the same time the experience conformed to pre-war expectations and utterly shattered them. On the positive side, the British army's reliance on solidly trained, long-service professionals proved vital. The cohesion between officers, NCOs and men at the battalion level and in the established pre-war brigades and divisions was invaluable. They fought desperate battles as effective teams with men on the spot well able to take important tactical decisions, which then had significant outcomes on the fighting. More ambiguous was the performance of higher command. Unused to warfare on this scale, and certainly unused to the proliferation of corps and armies, many British senior officers were unable to determine the precise degree of grip and perspective required to manage their forces effectively. A number of causes lay at the heart of this problem. Pre-war British governments never gave the army clear and absolute instructions on its role in a continental war. In turn, no British government showed any particular desire to increase the size of Britain's standing army significantly, which then ensured a lack of experience at commanding large-scale units. Further problems were created by the government in its search for alternative ways of prosecuting the war, which led to manpower and materials being allocated to expeditions against the Ottoman Empire in the eastern Mediterranean. Finally, the British staff training system was undermined by this strategic malaise. It theorised about command styles which it could never reinforce with practical lessons in manoeuvres or exercises and at the same time failed to prepare men in the minutiae of routines and systems required to make a modern, continental army operate effectively.

Combat then proved every bit as bloody, desperate and intense as both pre-war professionals and military correspondents and writers had ever imagined. What none imagined was that such concentrated violence

[46] Harris, *Haig*, 178–85; Senior, *Haking*, 51–6; Peter Bryant, 'The Recall of Sir John French', *Stand To!* 22, 23, and 24 (1988), 25–9, 32–8, 22–6; Ian F. W. Beckett, 'King George V and His Generals', in Matthew Hughes and Matthew Seligmann (eds.), *Leadership in Conflict, 1914–18* (Barnsley, UK: Pen & Sword, 2000), 247–64.

might lead to stasis. Moreover, it led to stasis before the British had managed any great offensive action, thus leaving their own pre-war thinking largely untested. With the advent of trench warfare, the BEF had to find ways of applying offensive principles in an operational scenario utterly different to that expected. Lacking everything necessary to make such operations smooth, particularly heavy artillery and ammunition, the BEF's attempts at offensive action were largely failures. However, every battle offered the opportunity to learn lessons, and here is where certain British commanders failed, which created knock-on effects into 1916 and 1917. Some British soldiers spotted the problem of attacking the entrenched Germans on the Western Front quickly and offered solutions based on intensive and accurate artillery preparation, intelligent estimation of the enemy's ability to recover and stabilise his position and the depth of the enemy's defensive positions. Most admitted the distinct weakness that the process would be long and gradual and that it relied upon guns and munitions the BEF simply did not have at that point in the war. Doing nothing until the men and kit arrived was not an option, and this goes some way towards explaining the bloody and inconclusive battles of 1915. It does not, however, provide the whole explanation. In particular, it does not explain Haig's failures. As the man most often called upon to spearhead British operations, his performance was crucial to the BEF's effectiveness, but it was curiously inconsistent and erratic. It is very easy to over-personalise the argument about Haig and, in the process, fail to put his performance in its correct contexts. Often forced to fight battles at times and places not of his choosing due to Britain's junior military status, and lacking the necessary men and equipment, the operations were never going to be easy. But when these are taken into account, the curious inconsistency still remains. Haig often showed signs of understanding the nature of the problem in front of him but then losing his grip on it as expressed in over-optimistic targets.

Haig's experiences in South Africa have often been cited as crucial to the development of his overall military outlook, and they do appear to have overshadowed his understanding of operations on the Western Front. South Africa taught Haig what well-entrenched, proficient riflemen covered by good artillery could do in the defensive, and he brought this healthy knowledge of modern defensive capabilities with him in 1914. However, what he could not imagine from his South African experiences was the sheer depth of the defences on the Western Front and the ability this gave defenders to prolong a battle. In this respect, Haig's vision was very similar to that of French. Both men were highly professional officers who dedicated much thought to the problems of modern soldiering, but both were trapped by the South African war when assessing the situation on the Western Front. It was this weight of experience which allowed French to state, after stressing the vital need for more heavy guns and ammunition, that he could

> break thro' this tremendous *crust* of defence which has been forming and consolidating throughout the winter: once we have done it I think we may get the Devils on the run. How I should love to have a good 'go' at them in the open with lots of cavalry and horse artillery and run them to earth.[47]

French's original emphasis gave him away: *crust*. Both he and Haig seemed unable to escape the vision of a 'defensive crust'. The Boers had caused havoc to the British using defensive crusts which had crumbled before determined, well-organised and well-led assaults. What both men failed to grasp with sufficient clarity was that the Germans may have started with crusts, but these rapidly gave way to thick *layers* of defence. It was a misunderstanding that plagued British performance in 1916, as will be seen.

Finally, in order to understand the BEF's performance in its full context, it is necessary to look at it in comparison with the French and Germans. As has been noted, the Germans often played to the BEF's strengths, showing very little tactical or operational subtlety or skill despite the advantages of a larger force, more trained staff officers, greater quantities of artillery and intensive preparation for continental war. Aside from any discussions on the wisdom and thoroughness of German strategy, it is clear from the German operational and tactical performance in 1914 and 1915 that confusion was deep and widespread. Although Falkenhayn sought to clarify German operational approaches in 1915, his ability to ensure understanding and compliance on all his subordinates was limited.[48]

The French were no more consistent, effective or insightful. The realities of war were hideous for the French Army and forced upon it immediate revisions of its tactical and operational doctrine.[49] Many French commanders took note and altered their approach, but the intense onus on the offensive due to the wider strategic situation pressured the French armies into dreadfully costly battles in 1915. As in all armies, the unforeseen circumstances put down a fierce challenge, which stirred up debate and discussion. Much of 1915 was spent in playing out experimental approaches to the flank-less warfare on the Western Front. All the combatant armies hoped that, in 1916, they would apply formulas refined through these experiences to decisive effect.

[47] Quoted in Holmes, *Little Field Marshal*, 294. [48] Strachan, *To Arms*, 232–41.
[49] *Ibid.*, 227–30.

8 The Western Front, 1916

For the British Expeditionary Force (BEF) in France and Belgium, 1916 was a crucial year in which it was severely tested in a battle of great intensity and duration. The year highlighted fully the strengths and weaknesses of the British Army and proved immensely important in distilling lessons about the nature of combat on the Western Front. At the same time, the British also found it a year of instability and ironies which hindered the process of drawing clear conclusions from the recent fighting, which then had knock-on effects into 1917. These centred on the disparity between the gross growth of British strength on the Western Front in terms of manpower, weapons and munitions, on the one hand, and its extreme lack of experience, thorough training, familiarity with weapons systems and quality of munitions, on the other. This expansion of British military might then put an even-greater strain on higher command and staff systems which had never before grappled with operations of such scale and complexity. Compounding this difficulty was the ultimate strategic irony on the Western Front in 1916, namely, that far from dictating the pace to the Germans through a French-led combined offensive, the German assault at Verdun reversed the situation. All of a sudden the 'adolescent' British Army was expected to carry the weight of the offensive while lacking the necessary skills (at all levels) to perform it. These factors made 1916 bloody and traumatic while also imparting much hard-won knowledge to a maturing BEF.[1]

The battle of the Somme emerged from the entente's agreements to mount assaults on the Russian, French and Italian fronts by March 1916. Joffre favoured an Anglo-French assault on the Somme. As the point of

[1] John Turner, *British Politics and the Great War: Coalition and Conflict, 1915–1918* (New Haven, CT: Yale University Press, 1992), 94–100, 121–4; French, *British Strategy*; Robert T. Foley, *German Strategy and the Path to Verdun. Erich von Falkenhayn and the Development of Attrition, 1870–1916* (Cambridge University Press, 2005), 181–208; Hew Strachan, 'The Battle of the Somme and British Strategy', *Journal of Strategic Studies* 21 (1) (1998); and William Philpott, *Bloody Victory: The Sacrifice on the Somme and the Making of the Twentieth Century* (London: Little, Brown, 2009).

juncture between the two armies, it allowed for easy collaboration between the two; it was also relatively untouched and so added the possibility of surprise and a front not already thoroughly ploughed by gunfire and therefore made impassable. Of particular concern to Joffre was the need for preliminary offensives designed to wear down the Germans before the main assault. Anxious about French manpower, Joffre felt that this initial stage should be carried out by the British. Haig was rightly concerned by this aspect, given the BEF's continuing shortages of shells and guns. Wishing to maintain strategic flexibility, Haig did not commit fully to the Somme battle for a considerable time, maintaining the options of either a campaign in Flanders alone, a Somme campaign alone or a combination of the two.

In this rather opaque atmosphere, the German offensive opened at Verdun in February. It placed immense pressure on the French, but Haig believed that it was being used as a convenient excuse for placing more responsibilities on the British. At first Haig tried to use the battle as a way of forcing Joffre to accept the strategic wisdom of a British offensive in Flanders, a region of continuing importance to British security. But Joffre was not to be moved and remained convinced that the Somme front offered the best prospects. Realising that the BEF would be expected to play the major role in the Somme offensive, Haig sought to have it delayed until late summer. This wish even gained the backing of Georges Clemenceau, Chairman of the Military Committee of the French Senate. Fearing disastrous repercussions from a hastily planned and executed summer offensive, he preferred to strike only when all preparations were thoroughly made. Somewhat ironically, at much the same time, Haig became more willing to accept an early-summer offensive, probably driven by concerns that the longer the delay, the greater would be the diminution of the French contribution. Joffre's concept was finally accepted in May, and planning for an Anglo-French offensive on the Somme commenced. Despite this ultimate binding of visions, no adequate mechanism was created for ensuring co-ordination of the Anglo-French forces, which meant that both armies carried out their own planning and preparatory work in almost total isolation. This defect was never remedied throughout the campaign and resulted in what Elizabeth Greenhalgh has called a joined, rather than joint, battle.[2]

[2] Elizabeth Greenhalgh, *Victory through Coalition: Britain and France during the First World War* (Cambridge University Press, 2005), 71. See also Elizabeth Greenhalgh, 'Why the British Were on the Somme in 1916', *War in History* 6(2) (April 1999), 147–73; Greenhalgh, 'Flames over the Somme: A Retort to William Philpott', *War in History* 10(3) (2002), 335–42; William Philpott, 'Why the British Were Really on the Somme: A Reply to Elizabeth Greenhalgh', *War in History* 9(4) (2002), 446–71.

Determining the extent to which the British saw the forthcoming offensive as the decisive campaign of the war is a difficult one and is made more intricate by the differing views of politicians and soldiers. It has been argued that the advice of both Kitchener and Robertson to Haig to view the forthcoming campaign as one of highly methodical, step-by-step phases is evidence of a cautious approach in which Haig was being steered towards a limited vision. At the same time, there is evidence to suggest that many influential members of the government believed that 1916 had to be the decisive year in order to ensure the stability of the British economy.[3] These opposing interpretations make outright condemnation of Haig's increasingly ambitious vision for the battle difficult to sustain comprehensively. Whatever the actual desires of the British government, however, the real issue seems to have been Haig's failure to clarify the intentions of the battle in his own mind. He veered between seeing it as a wearing-out battle and a decisive offensive throughout May 1916. This confusion was encapsulated in a letter to Robertson on 28 May in which he stated his desire to gain a good line for the 1917 campaigning season and not get bogged down in the valley beyond Poziéres and Le Sars, but then he reiterated his need for cavalry to exploit a general retreat by the Germans. To be fair to Haig, he should not be beaten too harshly for being ready to exploit any great success should it occur. However, there was a difference between having the exploitation tools at hand as a contingency and commencing operations with the full expectation that they would be used. If such inconsistencies were perceived in London, no one seems to have worried sufficiently to exert greater influence on Haig.

By the summer of 1916, the BEF had swollen to a force of nearly 1.5 million men divided into five armies. The force allocated to the assault, Fourth Army, had come into being in February 1916 under Rawlinson and was supported by a Reserve Army under Sir Hubert Gough in close proximity. Haig therefore ensured that two loyal subordinates had major roles in the battle. One, Rawlinson, had emerged from the battles of 1915 with a patchy record but had been made largely dependent upon Haig as a patron. The other, Gough, with his cavalryman's sense of flair and high-tempo operations seemed perfect for the exploitation of success. The two armies were broken down into twelve corps, thirty-eight infantry divisions and five cavalry divisions. The bulk of the infantry divisions were New Army, whose training and standard of

[3] The views are summed up neatly in J. P. Harris, *Douglas Haig and the First World War* (Cambridge University Press, 2008), 204–13; John Turner, *British Politics and the Great War. Coalition and Conflict, 1915–1918* (New Haven, CT: Yale University Press, 1992), 94–100.

preparation were distinctly variable. Given the endemic lack of experience and trained staff officers across the army, a major weakness was the corps system. Unlike in the emerging Dominion corps (Canadian and Australian) and the Indian Corps, British divisions were not permanently attached to corps. Instead, they were rotated and moved into corps as needed for particular purposes. With most raw infantry divisions desperately in need of some stability in order to learn lessons and get used to simple administrative routines, the rotation was deeply unsettling. No sooner had a division got used to the personalities and their approaches in one corps than they were shifted elsewhere and had to commence the process afresh.[4]

Perhaps even more worrying was the inconsistency in training across all arms, but most especially the infantry. The British Army had traditionally acted in a highly laissez-faire manner over the demands of training. Advice, often quite detailed and thorough, and information were supplied through pamphlets and memoranda, but the precise application was left in the hands of battalion commanders. In the pre-war years, both the strengths and shortcomings of this system were only properly highlighted during the annual summer and autumn exercise and manoeuvres season. Successive Inspectors-General provided carefully considered reports often highlighting neatly areas for greater attention. However, much of this useful feedback was made utterly redundant by the lack of a comprehensive mechanism for ensuring regular inspection of training with the intention of bringing about uniformity of standards. This situation was maintained in France and Belgium, but the potential for problems was now all the greater given the huge number of totally inexperienced officers and men who were often under the command of retired officers, so-called dugouts, who had been hastily recalled in 1914. Although these older officers at least provided a core of military experience, in many cases it was either too distant or irrelevant to current conditions. There was little Haig could do about the lack of military experience other than to ensure a rapid phasing out of dugouts deemed unfit for further active service and their replacement by younger, sharper men. But he could have done something about ensuring unity of training standards more quickly. The fact that he did not should not necessarily be deemed an oversight on the part of an unthinking commander but can be judged as a significant fault in the wider culture of the British Army.

[4] See Andy Simpson, 'British Corps Command on the Western Front, 1914–1918', in Gary Sheffield and Dan Todman (eds.), *Command and Control on the Western Front: The British Army's Experience 1914–18* (Staplehurst: Spellmount, 2004), 97–118.

This lack of co-ordination and effective oversight undermined the value of the tactical advice given to infantry through the two key pre-Somme BEF training manuals, *Training of Divisions for Offensive Action* (SS109) and Fourth Army's *Tactical Notes* (the 'Red Book'), both issued in May 1916. Although both pointed out that the preferred assault formation was waves, options were available within this structure. Each battalion could choose whether to attack with a frontage of either two or four platoons giving a depth of four or eight waves spaced no more than 100 yards apart. The philosophy underpinning this position was designed to give the attacking wave weight of firepower combined with flexibility, for the gap between waves would allow commanders to assess the situation to their immediate front and prevent a jam occurring on a stalled front. Much emphasis was also placed on the need to move fresh successive waves through and onto the next objective, reflecting the knowledge that attacking troops quickly exhaust their physical and mental strength and cannot be expected to assault more than a strictly limited number of objectives. In order to assist in the successful execution of the assault, the 'Red Book' hinted that a specialist platoon structure divided between 'fighting', 'mopping' and 'carrying' tasks was the best system.[5]

Critics of the BEF's preparations for the Somme battle have suggested that the wave/linear formation was too crude and inflexible, particularly for dealing with an enemy defensive system made up of trenches covered by strong points. Those who take a more positive view have argued that a false distinction has been drawn, for flexibility was inherent in the wave system, which allowed the infantry to realign into different formations once the first wave had achieved the initial break-in by use of its concentrated but not overly dense firepower. But this flexibility was both a strength and a major weakness. On the positive side, high-quality infantry units appreciated the opportunity to develop their own approach effectively. The downside of such flexibility was that it left the large numbers of units inexperienced in the assault, as opposed to trench-holding, with no firm sense of direction. In some divisions and brigades, this was provided clearly and effectively by senior commanders, but in others, it was much more hesitant and patchy. Infantry preparation was then further weakened by the expectation that the bombardment would do much of the work for them, undermining intensive and uniform thought on tactical preparation.

[5] For the debate on tactics in 1916, see Paddy Griffith, *Battle Tactics on the Western Front: The British Army and the Art of Attack, 1916–1918* (New Haven, CT: Yale University Press, 1994), 52–64.

With the question of firepower ever more significant in the light of the battles of 1915, important developments in the organisation of weapons systems were implemented, designed to give the infantry direct support. This restructuring led to the formation of the Machine Gun Corps (MGC) in October 1915. Although the move deprived the infantry of direct heavy machine gun support, it did allow machine gun enthusiasts to indulge in a quite spectacular leap of the tactical imagination. The massing of machine guns opened the way for a hybrid form of fire power. Placed under brigade control, MGC battalions had many of the attributes of artillery. Like artillery, collected Vickers-Maxims could be used for a range of fire tasks: interdicting, deep barrages, flanking fire, direct and indirect fire. Unlike most artillery pieces, they could be moved, re-sighted and got back into action quickly. The main drawback was the lack of mobility beyond the original front-line trench. The weight of the gun, its tripod, accessories and ammunition plus its high profile meant it could not accompany the initial assault. However, the infantry still required the weight and accuracy of machine gun fire and required a substitute. This was found in the Lewis gun.

Developed in 1911, the Lewis gun was trialled by the British in 1912 but was not adopted. This was not for lack of interest but from confusion over the precise role of automatic fire and was therefore part of a wider debate in the British Army about the nature of fire power in modern war. The opening battles of the war proved to the British that weight of fire was vital but did not refine the tactical debate as to its use. It led to a situation in which there was immense demand for automatic-fire weapons without a true understanding as to the best way of using them. As the battles of 1915 revealed fully the mobility problems of heavy machine guns, the Lewis gun was gradually introduced as the infantry owned and operated alternative. There was much initial resistance to this move on behalf of the infantry which resented the loss of the continuous fire provided by the belt-fed Vickers-Maxim for the more staccato effect of the pan-fed Lewis. This was compounded by the extreme shortage of Lewis guns throughout 1915, and it was only in December 1915 that production stepped up markedly and reached 200 per week. This allowed most battalions to be issued with two to four guns by the battle of the Somme. However, trained Lewis gunners were always in short supply, placing great stress on the specialist training programmes. A second reason for resistance to the Lewis gun was caused by misunderstanding of terms. Having given up true machine guns in the Vickers-Maxim, infantry battalions were understandably often less than pleased with its replacement because they were judging it in like-for-like terms. However, the Lewis gun was in reality much more akin to an automatic rifle than a machine gun, so the comparison was not truly valid. This confusion of thinking affected many across the BEF regardless of rank, as reflected in the fact that it was only in the immediate run-up to the Somme battle that Fourth Army began to emphasise the importance of the Lewis gun as an automatic rifle. By this point, though, it was probably too late to ensure an even understanding of this important distinction.

Given the uneven nature of the infantry's tactical grip, devising a plan which balanced its capabilities with that of the artillery was essential. This was all the more important given the strength and depth of the German positions on the Somme which consisted of two main positions. The first was on the forward slope of a long chalk ridge and incorporated many villages converted into fortresses. Deep dugouts allowed easy and safe access to the trenches, and the whole was covered by two thick belts of wire. Behind this lay a second line of redoubts and fortified villages situated on the reverse slope, which could not be seen by British observers on the ground. This position, too, was strongly wired. Unknown to the British during the early planning and preparation stage, the Germans were also engaged in the construction of a third position about 3,000 yards further back.[6]

Rawlinson's initial plans were cautious and sensible. In line with the ideas he had been developing since the battle of Neuve Chapelle, he believed that only a step-by-step assault would prove effective against defences of such strength and depth. Working closely with his Chief of Staff, Major-General Archibald Montgomery, the two men discussed the situation with their corps commanders, who seemed to share their sense of caution, and then produced an initial plan. This first draft called for an assault by ten divisions on a front of 20,000 yards between Serre in the north and Montauban in the south. Nothing more than the German first line was to be attempted in the opening stage. Successful capture of this position would then afford significantly improved observation on the second position, opening the way for the next phase of operations. In the meantime, the newly won positions were to be consolidated immediately and German counter-attacks beaten off. Sitting on the highest points of the chalk ridge, Rawlinson might then be able to turn the second German line from the north. For Rawlinson, the operation was not about breakthrough, at least in the initial phases; rather it was a mission to gain ground with the intention of killing Germans in large numbers. It was sensible as far as it went, but at this point it lacked detail in terms of barrage arrangements and the nature of infantry–artillery co-operation.

[6] For the planning of the Somme battle, see Harris, *Haig*, 216–23; Robin Prior and Trevor Wilson, *The Somme* (New Haven, CT: Yale University Press, 2005), 35–57.

Repeating the short, intensive bombardment that had been so successful at Neuve Chapelle was no longer an option given the density of the German wire, but Rawlinson did not appear to rule out such an approach entirely. At the same time, he seemed to believe that destruction of the German positions was possible when closer examination of the available information on the strength of the enemy field works should have shown otherwise.

The plan was sent to Haig, who made various criticisms. Firstly, he was concerned that it did not provide enough assistance to the French through its lack of depth, which might expose them to heavy flanking fire. His second criticism made far less military sense. Worried that it was too cautious and lacking in surprise, Haig stated that a shorter bombardment followed by a rapid assault would shake the German defence and open the way for penetration of the second line in quick succession. Given all the evidence about the difficulty of achieving effective artillery fire and the problems of ammunition supply, this showed a lack of grip on the technical aspects of gunnery. There was also the problem of maintaining effective command and control and, through it, momentum after an initial break-in. Successfully overrunning two strongly held positions, even if the second one was less likely to contain a sufficient garrison, in one day was extremely optimistic thinking. Unfortunately, the nature of the relationship between Haig and Rawlinson precluded a frank debate about the pitfalls in Haig's suggestions. The result was an odd compromise. Rawlinson accepted a doubling of the depth of advance from 1,250 yards to 2,500 yards, but his mind appeared to remain focused on a much more limited operation. By contrast, Haig's vision expanded, and somewhat ironically given his earlier injunctions to tie the plan to French thinking, it developed into something very different. From the initial point of rolling up the line from north to south in order to assist the French, he moved in favour of shifting the focus of the advance northwards to clear Arras through cavalry action. He believed that Gough could force a passage to Bapaume, some ten miles beyond the German front line, and swing northwards, causing havoc in the enemy rear. Here was a clear example of Haig's inability to see Western Front defences as anything more than a crust.

Having moved towards a much more ambitious vision, it was now absolutely vital that the artillery was capable of assisting the infantry forward. In terms of artillery plans, Fourth Army revealed that it was moving forward while veering sideways at the same time. In order to support the artillery's work, an impressive degree of airpower was deployed. By 1 July, Fourth Army had sixty-eight observation aircraft allocated to it. Of these, thirty were allotted to counter-battery spotting, sixteen to trench bombardments, nine to aerial photography and thirteen as contact patrols to assess the advance of the infantry, while five kite balloons were also brought forward to assist in observation for the heavy artillery. To protect the observers, ten squadrons were deployed, ensuring local air supremacy, which gave much freedom of action to the reconnaissance flights.

Assembled to exploit this advantage was by far and away the most impressive concentration of guns for a British offensive. Over a thousand guns and howitzers were deployed, including 182 heavy guns and 245 heavy howitzers backed by 288 medium and twenty-eight heavy trench mortars. However, many of the guns had already seen intensive use in 1915 and were thus by no means in tip-top condition for the new offensive. There were, at least, enough shells for the guns, thanks to the massive expansion in ammunition production. A French contribution of forty heavy guns and howitzers and sixty seventh-five-millimetre field guns completed the seemingly impressive collection. Unfortunately, those lacking a technical engagement with artillery were so awed by the numbers that it overshadowed careful assessments of tasks and yardage to be bombarded. Haig had been warned that his howitzers, in particular, would be too tautly stretched, but he seems to have concluded that this did not constitute a major handicap. Major-General Budworth, Rawlinson's artillery commander (MGRA), drafted the first ever Army Artillery Operations Order, which was designed to address this problem by highlighting the range of tasks to be taken into consideration. He also worked out detailed plans for ammunition supply utilising a hugely improved local network of roads and railways. To exert command and control over the system, 50,000 miles of telephone cable was laid, with about 7,000 miles buried six feet below the surface to protect it from German bombardment. As the BEF lacked the physical labour required to complete these essential preparatory tasks, the infantry was often deflected from its training schedules to provide the vital muscle power.[7]

Much less effective than this elaborate command infrastructure was Budworth's attempt to ensure tactical conformity. Here a further inherent weakness in the British system of flexibility can be detected. As with the infantry, senior commanders were loathed to define precisely methods and approaches for the artillery. Budworth therefore fell back on fairly generalised statements about types of targets and their relative importance. In the process, he failed to allocate particular types of guns to particular tasks or number of shells required for particular targets. It can be rightly argued that to do so would draw a senior co-ordinating

[7] Harris, *Haig*, 233–6.

commander into a labyrinth of calculations, information and detail much better left to corps and divisional officers. By the same token, Budworth could have demanded detailed responses from subordinate artillery officers and assessed their overall plans. There appears to have been little of this type of exchange during the preparatory phases. This allowed Budworth's recommendation that the infantry should follow a moving artillery barrage to be interpreted in a number of different ways. Some corps and divisions opted for the sophisticated and still emerging technique of the creeping barrage in which the infantry advanced in close proximity to a falling curtain of shells. Although this tactic required a great deal of fortitude on the part of advancing infantry, forced as they were to assault while friendly shells exploded very close to them, it had the great advantage of working to a simple, pre-arranged timetable and kept the enemy in place until the infantry arrived. In addition, partially trained infantrymen would have been much better served by the creeping barrage as it would have clarified greatly their passage of no man's land. The alternative tactic was a bombardment built on fixed lifts and advances. This approach was particularly well suited to inexperienced gunners, of which the BEF had many in 1916, as it moved from one clearly delineated line to another. Its great disadvantage was that it had much greater potential to leave the infantry well behind if any problems were met by the attacking troops. Revealing the stilted way in which information passed up and down the command chain of the BEF in 1916, the preference of both Major-General Sir Noel Birch, Haig's artillery adviser at GHQ, and Budworth in favour of the creeping barrage never became apparent further down the chain.

Originally planned to last five days, but extended to a full week due to poor weather conditions, the initial bombardment commenced on 24 June. The effect certainly looked and seemed impressive enough. Between 24 June and 1 July, 1,022,296 eighteen-pounder shells were fired and 95,677 by the six-inch howitzers.[8] Unfortunately for the BEF, judging the actual effect of the bombardment was much more difficult, as the weather was not particularly kind, with cloud and damp days affecting the work of the spotter aircraft. Desperate for information, patrols were sent out regularly to report on the accuracy of the artillery and state of German positions. The information gathered revealed a patchy scenario. In some areas, particularly the southern sections of the line, fire was accurate, with wire cut and significant damage to dugouts. On other sectors the situation was far less reassuring, revealing a story of inaccurate

[8] Captain Wilfred Miles, *Military Operations: France and Belgium, 1916*, Vol. II (London: Macmillan, 1938), 9.

or inadequate weight of fire and a disconcerting quantity of dud ammunition. Having expanded so rapidly, British ammunition supply had surrendered quality for quantity, and the depth of the problem became truly apparent during the battle. Most worrying was the lack of impression on German artillery, which always came back to life. Successful counter-battery fire was absolutely vital to the offensive. Experience had shown that infantrymen could often find a way into enemy trenches and then suppress their opponents. However, unless no man's land was safe from enemy gunfire, relief and re-supply were impossible. Yet it was the counter-battery aspect of the bombardment that was weakest planned and executed. Despite these clear problems, intelligence assessments continued to put an optimistic gloss on matters, which were accepted by Haig even though the raw material was copied on to GHQ and thus susceptible to independent analysis.

This inefficient analysis and flow of intelligence allowed an atmosphere of confidence to reign in the vast majority of British infantry divisions. Nearly every man was ready to advance and sure of success, even if it meant hard fighting and severe casualties. Eleven British divisions from five corps were to make the initial assault in collaboration with XX Corps of General Fayolle's Sixth Army to the south, while in the north, VII Corps of Third Army was to make an assault designed to draw fire and protect the flank. Rawlinson had wanted a dawn attack, but in order to maintain cohesion with the French and as a way of controlling raw infantry, zero hour was fixed for 7.30 AM. At 7.20 AM the bombardment was due to reach its height of intensity before lifting to further targets at the moment the infantry assault commenced. The last dramas before zero hour were the blowing of five mines under the enemy position. All bar one were due for detonation at 7.28 AM, but Major-General Sir Aylmer Hunter-Weston of VIII Corps gained permission to explode a very large mine near Beaumont Hamel at 7.20 AM.

The advance of the British infantry at 7.30 AM on 1 July 1916 was met by strong German resistance. But, contrary to popular perception, the infantry assault by no means consisted solely of long lines of men slowly plodding towards their doom. Some men advanced into no man's land before zero hour, some were covered by a nascent form of creeping barrage and some advanced at the rush. Regardless of the precise degree of sophistication in infantry tactics, the result was largely the same along the length of the line: utter failure. In the north, Third Army's diversionary assault certainly drew German fire, but without lessening its impact anywhere else along the line. In yet another disastrously conceived pincer attack, two Territorial divisions, the 46th and 56th, were shredded for no gain. To its immediate south, VIII Corps suffered an equal catastrophe.

The blowing of the mine at 7.20 AM provoked the shaken but coherent German defenders into life. They manned their trenches and were ready when the advancing British came marching up the slope. Uncut wire and machine guns crumbled the assault in short order. Lieutenant-General T. N. L. Morland's X Corps was immediately to the south and achieved some initial successes. Revealing the lack of tactical uniformity across the British front, the 36th Division put some troops into no man's land before the barrage lifted and then advanced at great speed. They overran the German trenches before the defenders could man the parapet and then swamped the Schwaben Redoubt. Agonisingly, all of these successes were reversed through the failure of flanking units to advance against the wall of German resistance. The left-centre section of the assault was covered by Lieutenant-General Sir William Pulteney's III Corps. The 8th and 34th Divisions here met disaster assaulting from their trenches across a very broad no man's land against the two fortified villages of Ovillers and La Boisselle. All these attacks made north of the Albert-Bapaume Road thus came to bloody, awful grief.

South of the road there was much more success. By nightfall, Horne's XV Corps was on the verge of taking Fricourt through the advance of divisions on either flank. To his corps' immediate south was Lieutenant-General Sir Walter Congreve's XIII Corps. Here the 18th and 30th Divisions advanced from specially constructed assault trenches which were well out into no man's land and behind a well-planned barrage. It carried the two divisions through the German front line and maintained contact with the French, who were equally successful.

As with all earlier actions, the flow of information from the front was staccato and inconsistent. Haig and Rawlinson became spectators at a game glimpsed through fog. By nightfall, neither man was sure where the British line now stood, nor the extent of the casualties, which were in the region of 20,000 dead and 40,000 wounded.[9] With both unable to intervene in any meaningful way, the opportunity to exploit the success on the southern sector was lost. Given the fall-out from the battle of Loos, it was ironic that there remained an equal lack of clarity over the use of the Reserve Army and the local reserves of each corps. After a struggle with GHQ, Rawlinson had gained control over Reserve Army but then ignored it and made little attempt to integrate it into his plans. Here it is possible to gain glimpses of a more confident Rawlinson. He argued his case for control of Reserve Army doubtless knowing that Haig could hardly refuse given his interpretation of Loos. By making so little preparation,

[9] Prior and Wilson, *The Somme*, 112.

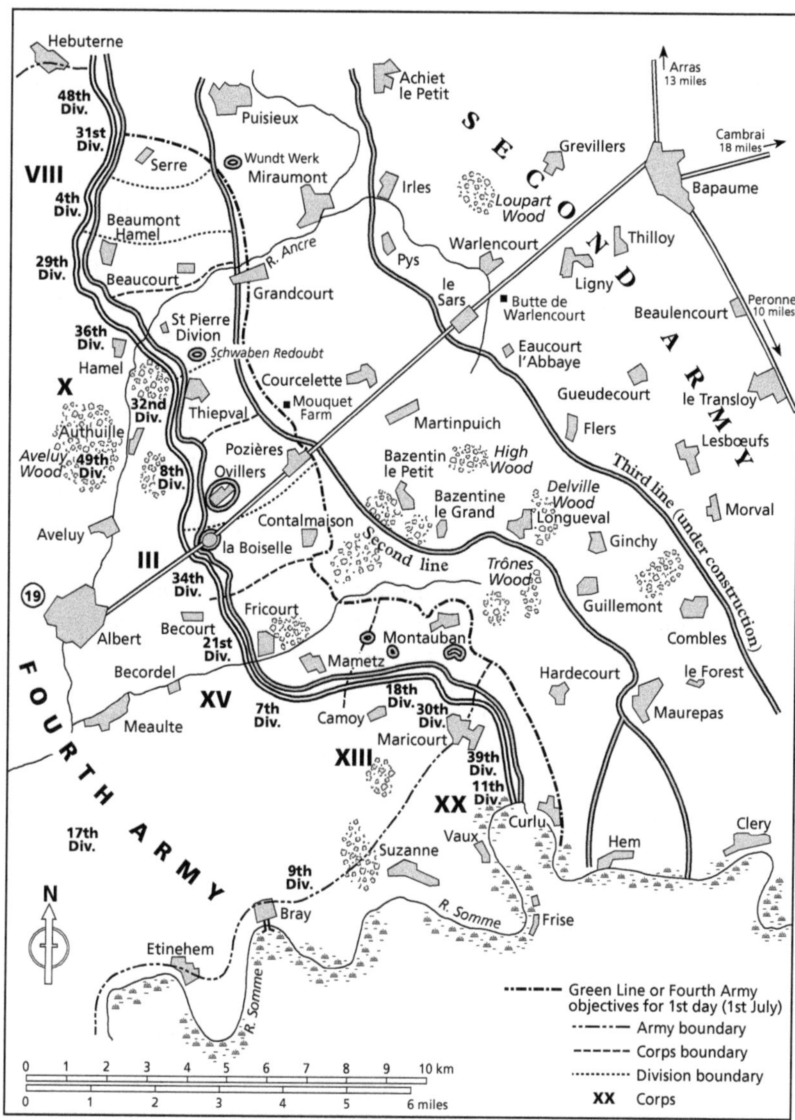

Map 6 Battle of the Somme, 1 July 1916 (objectives and positions)

Rawlinson also imposed a break on Haig's ambitions through alternative means. But having given little thought to its successful integration into his command structures and plans, he deprived himself of the chance to exploit the southern sector successes either through XIII Corps' reserve

9th Division, which was too widely dispersed for rapid response, or Reserve Army itself. There was certainly little chance of getting the cavalry forward given Rawlinson's dispositions, but even if it had been held further forward, whether it could have arranged to move cohesively and opportunely is debatable. Rawlinson was almost certainly caught off-balance by the success, as the main focus was on the Albert-Bapaume Road, and it was this area that contained the bulk of the British reserves.

The tragic disaster suffered by the British on 1 July is difficult to explain simply and easily. The length and depth of front were certainly major problems. The front stretched the available guns and ammunition too thinly and thus undermined the artillery preparation. Haig had forcefully driven forward the idea of deep advances, but it was Rawlinson who first identified such a long front. These competing ideas of deep versus long and shallow advances created a fault line at the heart of the planning process which was never resolved. The two men moved along different axes with dreadful consequences for the attacking troops. It can be argued that these differences of emphasis need not have been disastrous in themselves. If this is accepted, what seems all the more worrying is the failure by both men and their staffs to interpret the intelligence reports from the front during the preliminary bombardment. In this material was enough information to undermine *both* visions of the battle. Instead, cognitive closure descended again which effectively eradicated any attempt to reassess. Explaining the disaster of 1 July in terms of personal flaws may also fail to address the wider context, which has to be understood fully. Haig and Rawlinson were acting under certain constraints. Reacting to the demands of his political masters, Haig felt the need to deliver a major success. Moreover, he felt the need to do so on a battlefront not of his choosing with an imperfect military instrument which later on became the main, rather than supporting, player. Undoubtedly, these were daunting circumstances and cannot be disregarded lightly. However, it was precisely because of these circumstances that Haig and, through him, Rawlinson should have taken a very firm grip on the planning in which the capabilities of the BEF within the realities of 1916 were the driving factor.

Unsure of the precise position on the night of 1 July, the only thing Haig and Rawlinson knew for certain was that the second German line had nowhere been so clearly penetrated that Gough's Reserve Army could be rushed into action. But with scraps of information to hand revealing the successes on the southern sector, Haig moved quickly to make this the major focus of British efforts. This was in marked contrast to Rawlinson's muddled thinking, in which he identified the centre and north as the priority areas, thus running the risk of hammering pointlessly in a sector already in chaos due to the choke of dead, wounded and shocked men in the trenches. Haig's decisions wisely negated this approach, and instead, he shifted responsibility for the centre and northern sectors to Gough and instructed Rawlinson to concentrate on exploiting the situation south of the Albert-Bapaume Road. This clarity of thinking and intention of exploiting success rather than reinforcing failure made a good deal of sense. But it contained two drawbacks. First, all previous operations revealed the difficulty of exploiting initial successes, so dealing with the German second line was unlikely to be a quick or easy affair. Second was the reaction of Joffre and the French. Having been assured that the British were making a major effort to assist their partner, any scaling back of operations was likely to be seen as a betrayal. To his credit, Haig remained calm when Joffre duly exploded with rage at a meeting on 3 July. Standing his ground, Haig insisted that the southern sector must become the major focus of British activity. Unfortunately, although this decision placed the emphasis of the battle on the point where British and French troops were in close contact, it did nothing to ensure better collaboration and co-ordination between Rawlinson and Fayolle's armies.[10]

Whatever the failings of 1 July and Anglo-French co-operation, the opening of the battle was taken very seriously by the Germans. Seven German divisions were diverted to the Somme front by 2 July, and a further seven were despatched on 9 July. The initiative was being wrested from Falkenhayn, unpicking his Verdun strategy and Germany's hopes of breaking up the entente in 1916. Clinging to a policy of counter-attack, Falkenhayn's commanders threw German soldiers forward regardless of circumstances, where they met fierce resistance from British troops. Aided by aerial supremacy and the rapid reconstruction of good German positions, British soldiers were able to put up solid defences of their gains and impose great losses on the enemy. The German Second Army suffered 40,187 casualties in the first ten days of the battle as they sought to regain lost ground and stabilise their position.

Rawlinson's focus now shifted to the Bazentin Ridge, but before operations could commence on this feature, Fourth Army had to secure a series of intermediate objectives. Many of these actions were hastily prepared, narrow-front assaults which often allowed the Germans to pour in flanking fire, resulting in limited British gains for high casualties. This erratic

[10] For the next phase of the battle, see Harris, *Haig*, 238–59; Prior and Wilson, *The Somme*, 119–90.

path towards the Bazentin Ridge cost Fourth Army 25,000 casualties between 2 and 13 July.[11] Two opposing arguments have been put forward over this phase of operations. The first emphasises the dire consequences of abandoning systematic preparation, minimising British advantages and maximising German powers of resistance. By contrast, the second stresses the lack of tempo in thoroughly organised assaults and their subsequent failure to keep the enemy continually wrong-footed. In particular, it is emphasised that aggressive probing would have revealed weaknesses capable of immediate exploitation by troops at hand without the need for elaborate preparation.[12]

With the British government and particularly the new Secretary of State for War, Lloyd George, keen to see evidence of significant results, Haig had to be careful in his appreciation of the fighting and predictions for the future. Robertson asked Haig for an overview and was told that the advance in the southern sector promised to unhinge the German centre but would take several weeks to achieve. Doubting whether such responses would placate the Cabinet, Robertson re-emphasised his belief in a steady offensive with well-defined, limited objectives in a letter to Haig's Chief of Staff, Launcelot Kiggell. Whether Robertson thought he might influence Haig through a member of his staff is unclear, but the sheer fact that a veiled criticism should take this form reveals a lack of clarity in the professional relationship between Robertson and Haig. In reply, Kiggell implied that Robertson should refrain from intervening in operational matters and confine his role to managing the War Office and the politicians on behalf of GHQ in France.

As the British line slowly moved towards the Bazentin Ridge, Fourth Army staff began the process of planning an assault on the position. A major consideration was the width of no man's land on XIII Corps' front measuring some 1,500 yards. Rawlinson's solution was to order the attacking troops deep into no man's land under the cover of darkness to be ready for a dawn assault. To assist the infantry, a preliminary bombardment commenced on 11 July and lasted three days. Although the number of guns employed was considerably fewer than on 1 July, they were supporting only four divisions as opposed to eleven, ensuring a bombardment some five times more intensive than that of the ill-fated

11 Prior and Wilson, *Rawlinson*, 187.

12 The best examples of these two positions are Robin Prior and Trevor Wilson, who contend strongly that the period between 2 and 13 July lacked any semblance of command and control, and J. P. Harris, who has highlighted the advantages of seizing the initiative and the fact that the British did not do this consistently enough. See J. P. Harris, *Douglas Haig*, 241–2; Robin Prior and Trevor Wilson, *Command on the Western Front: The Military Career of Sir Henry Rawlinson, 1914–1918* (Oxford: Blackwell, 1992), 187–90, 203–7.

first day on the Somme. Haig was initially unsure about the boldness of a complicated night assembly and argued for a narrow-front attack. Backed by his corps commanders, Rawlinson held firm, and Haig accepted the plan with two provisos. Firstly, Haig sensibly insisted on attention to counter-battery fire. Secondly, he requested that the cavalry be committed only once it was clear they could be used effectively. Haig's uncharacteristic caution over the use of cavalry probably reflected his concern that the infantryman Rawlinson was not sufficiently qualified to employ them to best advantage. Despite this note of warning, once the bombardment commenced, Haig became convinced that a breakthrough was a distinct possibility within a relatively short time-scale and broadcast this understanding to Fourth and Reserve Armies.

The bombardment reached a crescendo at 3.20 AM on 14 July, and five minutes later the infantry stormed forward into the German first line. Moving with speed and with little ground to cover, the infantry won the 'race to the parapet' and took the German positions in quick time. Facing Longueval, there was uncut wire which caused hard fighting, and the delay here caused Rawlinson to hesitate over the next move on this front with the result that the opportunity to capture High Wood quickly and easily was lost. Later in the day, 7th Division and elements of 2nd Indian Cavalry Division did manage to penetrate the wood and the area around it but could not force the Germans from it entirely. By the end of the day, a very solid success had been achieved, with the villages of Bazentin-le-Petit and Bazentin-le-Grand and most of Longueval in British hands for modest losses compared with 1 July, and in the process, far greater casualties had been inflicted on the Germans. In some sectors, particularly the southern portions of the line attacked, it did appear as if the German defences had been levered open with only scratch positions behind them. However, the ability of the defenders to improve and improvise positions of great strength in short order meant that the opportunity for breakthrough, if it existed, was too fleeting for the British to exploit.

The success on 14 July helped to cement Haig's reputation in the British press. With casualties running so high, it was important to balance the losses against victories and some sense of the overall flow of the battle. Despite growing personal doubts about Haig, it was Lloyd George who helped to ensured positive press comment. His fierce commitment to victory and his desire to connect war workers on the home front with the results of their contributions led him to encourage enthusiastic reporting on Haig and his armies. Although this helped to secure Haig's position among the members of the War Committee and wider cabinet, Robertson continued to harbour doubts and asked him whether the casualties were likely to amount to great results. Haig rather pre-empted receipt of the letter by sending a justification of the campaign to the government. He explained that pressure had been relieved on Verdun, that heavy losses had been inflicted on the enemy, that the campaign would continue into the autumn and that a further campaign might be required to break the enemy. Deliberately avoiding any talk of a breakthrough, Haig's caution appears to have been one designed to silence unfavourable comment and leave him with maximum independence to pursue his own course. With Royal confidence assured and no overt criticism expressed by Asquith, Lloyd George or Robertson, Haig was given that freedom.

Believing the Germans were significantly unbalanced by the advance on 14 July, Haig demanded another major blow within a week. Rawlinson was ordered to take High Wood, Ginchy and Guillemont and follow up with an assault on Falfemont Farm and Maurepas, creating elbow room at the point of connection with the French. On Reserve Army's front, Gough was instructed to take Pozières, ensuring the left flank of the operation. The order to continue operations within a week of the major assault on 14 July shows how hard it is to plot a smooth and even learning curve or indeed any kind of curve at least in the GHQ perspective. Five corps were expected to prepare and plan for another night-time assembly, an assault and a comprehensive fire plan across a greatly expanded front line with many of the German positions on reverse slopes and thus much harder to observe. Overrun with demands, the staff work and organisation broke down. Once again, artillery was too thinly stretched and poor weather undermined aerial observation. The result was all too predictable: the assaults of 22–23 July were costly failures, with the 1st Australian Division's capture of Pozières the only redeeming feature.

Co-ordinating command now seemed to break down entirely in Fourth Army as the rest of July and much of August saw a large number of attacks mounted but in a piecemeal, haphazard way. Divisional attacks were often carried out only by a few scattered battalions inefficiently and insufficiently assisted by the artillery. These battalions then often found themselves caught by enfilade fire and, where successful, unable to exploit any small gains due to the utter inability to support them with fresh troops, trapped as they were by heavy German fire sweeping no man's land. Gough's Reserve Army proved no better and on most occasions notably worse. Haig was sufficiently perceptive to realise the problems caused by these un-co-ordinated assaults. After a failed Franco-British effort on 18 August, Haig wrote to Rawlinson requesting greater cohesion and method in the assault but then insisted that operations be maintained with all possible speed. Joffre's insistence that the British attack wholeheartedly in order to achieve a great success probably put pressure on

Haig to insist on tempo, but Haig's command style was still too inconsistent. Instead of ensuring clear direction based on military realities, Haig fluctuated between intervention in his subordinates' plans and leaving them to their own devices. Once again, the pre-war British military system can be identified as part of the problem. No one was used to high command at this level, and there had been no serious preparation for it. The lack of trained staff officers also denied Haig the mechanism to interact smoothly and easily with his subordinates. However, these deficiencies cannot explain his failure to set a consistent standard and approach to command.

The fragmentation of command was mirrored by an equally disturbing situation in supply. Of great concern was availability of ammunition. Although British industry was now producing the quantity, even if the quality varied enormously, there were significant distribution problems in France due to faulty logistics systems. Accentuated by the steep rise in British production and its priority despatch to France, enormous quantities of shells were unloaded in French ports, but here they became stuck in a bottleneck. On 5 July, Fourth Army was told that it could expect 56,000 eighteen-pounder rounds per day and 4,920 six-inch howitzer shells. (In order to achieve this, the allocation to other armies had to be cut to a dribble, and it even affected Reserve Army, which, despite its operational role, lagged far behind with 14,000 and 880 rounds, respectively.) However, by 11 July, there was such concern over the supply of heavy howitzer shells that daily allowances were strictly limited to twenty-five per fifteen-inch, fifty per 9.2-inch, 110 per eight-inch and 250 per six-inch gun. Only four days later, Fourth Army was once again warned about constrictions in ammunition supply, particularly as it wanted more attention paid to counter-battery work and well-supported infantry attacks. In mid-August, the ammunition situation was again cause for concern. For example, between 24 June and 18 August, XIII Corps' artillery fired off 1,942,132 rounds of all calibres weighing about 36,000 tons, seriously depleting Fourth Army's stocks. The demands placed upon the guns naturally led to equal problems with maintenance. By 23 July, the Germans had brought in more of their own artillery pieces, which then put an even-greater emphasis on counter-battery and consequently even greater stress on the guns. The repair and refitting of guns therefore became an urgent issue and led to shortages at the front. By 11 July, the situation was so bleak on XIII Corps' front that only 292 from the 357 guns available were actually fit for use.[13]

[13] Miles, *Military Operations, 1916*, Vol. II, 23, 64.

As the Anglo-French offensive wore on into August and with it the slow capture of the German second position, it demanded discussion of the next stage of operations. On 27 August, Haig and Joffre duly met to share ideas. Haig was somewhat perturbed by Joffre's insistence that a great offensive should be launched by 8 September at the latest. Haig was reluctant to move that fast, as he was still awaiting the build-up of the new tank units in France. Fears over the onset of autumn weather appear to have concerned Joffre greatly, leading the two men to agree on 15 September. The battle of Flers-Courcelette, which commenced on that date, was the largest assault since 1 July. In the main it was carried out by Fourth Army, but Gough's Reserve Army co-operated on the left and the French Sixth Army on the right. Rather disconcertingly, the aim was to overrun three lines, including a strong redoubt at Combles. Most of these positions were hidden from direct observation, placing the onus on good aerial spotting. Haig expected that many of these difficulties could be overcome by the use of tanks. As many other historians have noted, Haig was no technophobe, and he was an enthusiastic supporter of the tank project from the start. Deeply frustrated that none were available on 1 July, he was determined to get them into action as soon as possible. Such enthusiasm revealed that although Haig was willing to accept all forms of technological assistance, as was seen with gas, he lacked the ability to assess rationally their value and likely impact. Around fifty Mark I tanks were available for operations by mid-September. Weighing over twenty-eight tons, they were more than capable of crushing barbed wire and could suppress German machine gun positions either by simply rolling over them or using their machine guns or six-pounder gun (depending on variant). Unsurprisingly for a pioneering piece of technology which was moreover untested in actual combat, the tank suffered from some significant weaknesses. It was hard to manoeuvre and ergonomically disastrous for its crew, its speed was slower than infantry walking pace, it was vulnerable to direct hits from artillery and it was mechanically unreliable.[14]

Rawlinson was reasonably impressed by a demonstration but did not wish to rely on this untested weapon, placing his faith in artillery and a step-by-step approach in which tanks were launched after the first line had been captured. Revealing his lack of grip on the realities of the tank, he believed that they could be deployed in darkness, which was impossible given their severely limited vision. This was not, however, the grounds on which Haig rejected Rawlinson's first plan. Rather it was

[14] For next phase of the battle, see Harris, *Haig*, 259–65; Prior and Wilson, *Rawlinson*, 227–49.

the usual complaint that Rawlinson was being too cautious. Haig urged boldness and once again insisted that the opportunity for breakthrough had presented itself with the promise of decisive results. In this instance, Haig's insistence on attacking all three lines in one day probably did not dissipate the British bombardment greatly. Unable to reach the German third line, the British guns concentrated on the first and second lines. Much more worrying was the decision to open gaps in the bombardment for 'tank lanes'. Fearful of hitting the lumbering machines in the sectors where they were allocated to attack, no bombardment was allowed. The attacking soldiers in these sectors were therefore made utterly dependent on the arrival and advance of the tanks. If mechanical failure stopped them, the assault troops would advance alone against unsuppressed German defenders.

The preliminary bombardment commenced on 12 September, hampered by poor weather on the following day. At 6.20 AM on 15 September, the assault commenced. After the desultory and costly results of August, a great success was achieved. A 9,000-yard stretch of the German first line was overrun, as well as 4,000 yards of the second line, capturing six square miles of enemy ground. Casualties were lighter than 1 July but still significant, which greatly lessened the chance of rapid exploitation. The tanks provided mixed results. In some sectors they terrified the Germans into flight, but in other areas they failed to arrive, which proved particularly disastrous on the Quadrilateral Redoubt sector, where the attacking troops had little chance of penetrating such a strong point without tank or artillery support. In addition, the French failed noticeably and were in no position to maintain the offensive. Follow-up attacks on 16 September were ragged and achieved little value, and it was clear that a pause was required, although the Quadrilateral Redoubt finally fell on 18 September.

Poor weather and delays in French preparation forced a postponement of the next major operation from 21 to 25 September. This time the assault was aimed at one line of trenches only running through the fortified villages of Gueudecourt, Lesboeufs and Morval. Able to smother the German line with fire in a bombardment around 40 per cent heavier than that on 15 September, the British infantry followed their barrage into the German lines and overran the vast majority of the positions in quick time and with few casualties. The following day, Gough launched an attack on Thiepval and the Schwaben Redoubt in which the village finally fell, and after several days of bitter fighting, the entirety of the redoubt was subdued. In this attack, Major-General Sir Ivor Maxse's 18th Division played a major role and enhanced further its growing reputation as an elite unit. Maxse had not only been thorough in his preparations, but he had also been able to utilise an increasingly sophisticated BEF which was emerging from a brutal apprenticeship. British artillery was by now maturing, giving the infantry the vital assistance it needed to maximise its own growing tactical skill. Of particular importance was the increasing ability to deploy the creeping barrage. Use of the creeping barrage had developed during the summer and by the early autumn was widely advocated as the best way to protect infantry and destroy German machine gunners who had quit their trenches to establish positions in shell holes. But, as the August fighting around Guillemont had shown, unless a creeping barrage searched the ground thoroughly, the shell holes and craters could give adequate protection to determined soldiers, which went some way towards compensating for the generally weaker state of the new German defences. The creeping barrage evolved during the battle from its initial rate of 150 yards per minute and one or two rounds of shrapnel from each eighteen-pounder, which had proved too fast, to a rate of fifty yards per minute and three rounds of shrapnel per minute. (This would slow down still further later in the war, with rates of thirty-three and twenty-five yards per minute adopted intermixing four rounds of shrapnel.) Armed with this much more effective approach, an understanding of the artillery as an instrument of neutralisation and suppression rather than destruction and devastation was slowly emerging.

By late September, the persistency of the British combined with the growing tactical and technical expertise of the infantry and artillery was exerting extreme pressure on the Germans. It was noted that German soldiers were surrendering more freely and fighting less fiercely. So concerned was the German high command that it relieved all six divisions between Thiepval and Combles in the wake of the 15 September assault. Desperate to hold onto their positions, the Germans worked frantically to complete new defences. Aerial reconnaissance revealed evidence of two further German lines under construction behind the Transloy Line, but it was clear that they were incomplete. Here seemed the moment to maintain the pressure and perhaps achieve the great breakthrough. Haig was certainly keen to make the attempt and believed that the opportunity could be maximised by a much broader assault than those delivered since 1 July which would swamp German powers of resistance and recovery. Planning commenced for assaults by Third Army at Gommecourt, Reserve Army at Beaumont Hamel and Fourth Army to breach the Transloy Line and turn towards Cambrai.[15]

A number of factors combined to undermine the potential of this plan. First was the weather: it rained heavily between 2 and 5 October and thus

[15] For final phase, see Harris, *Haig*, 266–70; Prior and Wilson, *Rawlinson*, 250–60.

turned the battlefield and supply areas into a morass. This had an impact on aerial reconnaissance and also accentuated the logistics problems of the BEF, which were becoming acute by this time. Using every available moment given to them, the Germans once again revealed the advantages of the defender by rotating men quickly and working intensely on their new positions. The Germans also refined their new tactic of keeping machine gun positions well back in order to avoid the worse effects of the creeping barrage. In these unpropitious circumstances, costly and fruitless British assaults were launched on 7, 12 and 18 October. On Fourth Army's front, the British were now obliged to continue attacking regardless of the reality of breakthrough due to their dreadful positions in a valley bottom. The men could not sit out the winter in such a poorly drained spot overlooked by German artillery observers. A further round of assaults was ordered, with efforts made on 23, 28 and 29 October which inched the line forward in a few places. Conditions degenerated rapidly, leaving the trenches in an appalling state and making relief and resupply acts of intense labour. Haig was informed about the dreadful conditions at the front but was insistent that the offensive had to be maintained. In one sense he was correct: the impossibility of remaining in the valley meant advance or retreat. He was also still under pressure from Joffre to achieve a resounding success, and he may well have felt the first signs of Lloyd George's increasing concern at the cost of the Somme campaign.

Haig's determination to order fresh assaults led to dissent from his subordinate commanders. When Rawlinson ordered Lieutenant-General Lord Cavan, Commander of XIV Corps, to prepare for operations, Cavan responded by stating forcefully his objections, pointing out that those who ordered it clearly had no idea of the actual state of the ground. Unimpressed by Rawlinson's inference that failure on 3 November was due to problems at XIV Corps' headquarters, Cavan insisted that Rawlinson come forward to see the position for himself. Rawlinson was duly persuaded by his visit and informed Haig of the situation. After initial concurrence, Haig changed his mind following a meeting with Foch and ordered further attacks. Fourth Army's assaults on 5 November achieved nothing for 2,000 casualties. To its left, Gough's Fifth Army (as Reserve Army was now designated) was also making preparations for a November offensive. Working on shorter lines of communication due to the lack of significant advances on this sector, Fifth Army was able to deploy its resources more easily, and for once, Gough's planning staff were given the time and space to prepare properly. On 13 November, a well-executed assault on limited objectives supported by 282 heavy guns and a handful of tanks wrested Beaumont Hamel from the Germans by the late afternoon of

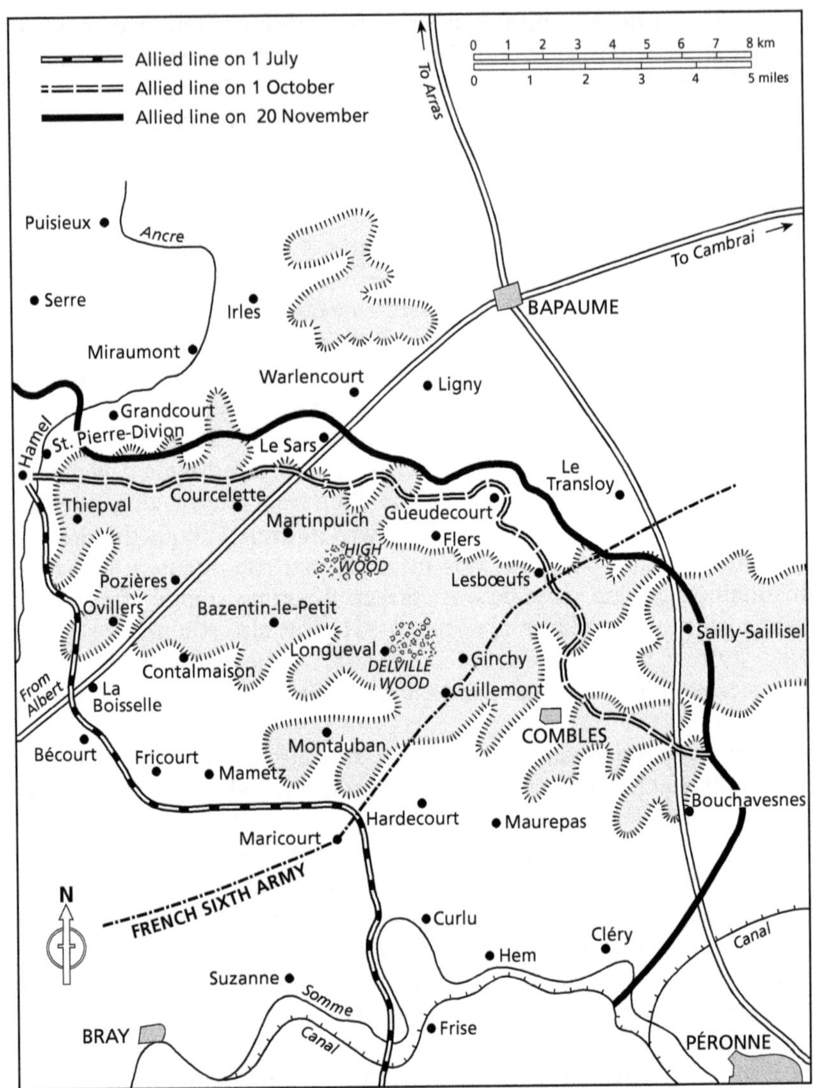

Map 7 Advances on the Somme, July–November 1916

the following day.[16] Renewed efforts were made on 18–19 November in steadily deteriorating weather, including heavy snow storms, but to little effect. With this coda, the battle of the Somme came to an end.

[16] Harris, *Haig*, 270.

The colossal struggle on the Somme played an important part in shattering Germany's strategy for 1916. Pressure on Verdun was relieved, the Germans were unable to switch major resources to the Eastern Front and the German army was hammered remorselessly. The scale of the failure was apparent by August, when Falkenhayn was sacked and replaced by Paul von Hindenburg and Erich Ludendorff. Confident of bringing order to affairs in the west after their success in the east, neither man had a simple answer to the increasing power of the BEF. Forced onto the defensive and committed to increasingly futile counter-attacks and often exposed to British and French artillery fire for prolonged periods, the morale of German troops suffered. Picking a way through the labyrinth of casualty assessments is tricky, but it is likely that some 500,000 casualties were inflicted on the Germans while the British suffered 420,000 and the French 200,000. Given the strength and depth of the German defences and the fact that the Germans were facing a largely novice army on 1 July, these ghastly figures may be taken as something approaching an entente victory.[17]

Haig had been forced to accept an offensive on the Somme and to maintain it once it commenced in order to maintain solidarity with the French. While resisting some of Joffre's most strident demands, Haig had nonetheless provided support for the French Army at a time when it was under great stress. Unfortunately, the mechanisms for entente interaction were neither extensive, logical nor subtle, and so the British and French did not maximise their combined power on the Somme. None of this can be blamed on Haig. He was attempting the very tricky task of serving his government loyally while addressing the needs of his partner force.

Much more problematic for the entire British high command was the achievement of operational cohesion and efficiency. Here again, factors outside the control of Haig and his army and corps commanders cannot be ignored or underestimated. The employment of largely raw troops backed by far more plentiful but not yet overwhelming and certainly not uniform quality ammunition and guns constituted significant handicaps. Communication problems could also prove crippling. Regardless of the incredibly intricate systems devised to keep higher commanders informed of the progress of battle, communications almost inevitably failed, leaving them groping towards an understanding of the actual situation. Given this obvious information gap, the insistence that so many assaults be carried out in a hurry by troops unfamiliar with the ground supported by artillery unsure as to its role and targets reveals a major weakness in the command structures of the BEF. The awful regularity with which ill-planned penny-

[17] *Ibid.*, 271.

packet frontal assaults were made on German positions makes it very difficult to avoid the conclusion that British operations could have been made more effective, and it is to Haig that much of the difficulty can be traced. Haig and his GHQ never attempted to work within the parameters of the possible given the limitations of the BEF with sufficient logic and clarity. Placing the blame for this on external factors, most notably French pressure to launch a great offensive, only goes some way towards explaining the problem. Serving the French and working within the limitations of the BEF were possible through tightly controlled operations for limited objectives. As Fourth Army revealed on numerous occasions during the battle, significant, if shallow, gains could be achieved, causing the Germans great loss and disorientation. By insisting so often that the moment of breakthrough and decision was at hand, Haig imposed demands on his subordinates which they could not achieve. More worryingly still, it revealed an inability to learn from previous experiences stretching back to 1915 and the earliest British offensive operations against strongly entrenched opponents.

At the army level, Rawlinson and Gough were equally erratic. Rawlinson's overall grasp of the Western Front's logic remained sound, but his grip was often weak, while Gough revealed similar attributes to Haig but in a more volatile manner, alternating between micro-management of details and lackadaisical direction of the over-arching scheme. Unsurprisingly, this uneven approach affected corps command, the vital link between the grander visions of army and GHQ and the operational performance on the ground. Despite increasing evidence of dialogue between corps HQs and divisions, too often corps remained reluctant to devolve decision-making. This was partly driven by sound reasoning, as the unit commanding the contact flights and deploying the heavy artillery, it had both far more immediate knowledge as to the overall situation and the ability to intervene. But, by the same token, it took until late into the battle for corps commanders to begin to realise that an important part of their role was the routing of information forward to inform local decision-making on a continual basis rather than simply demanding it for use further up the chain of command.[18]

For the British infantry, so often forced to attack in highly unpropitious circumstances, the experience of the Somme brought the tactical dilemmas emerging since the pre-war years towards a conclusion which pointed the way towards greater flexibility and effectiveness in the following year.

[18] For varying assessments of the battle, see Foley, *German Strategy*, 251–8; Harris, *Haig*, 270–3; Prior and Wilson, *The Somme*, 300–15; Gary Sheffield, *The Somme* (London: Cassell, 2003), 151–64.

The problem of infantry tactics in 1915 and 1916 was that no one was quite sure what they were meant to do in no man's land other than advance on the enemy trenches. On the surface this made a great deal of sense: the enemy was largely invisible in his own trenches and was usually engaged in rapid defensive fire. The only way to silence the enemy was to get at him as quickly as possible. In effect, the British threw away the vital preliminary to the main, decisive assault – the infantry fight for fire supremacy, which was such a large part of pre-war training and thinking. This slip in tactical thinking was understandable. Pre-war training was largely based on the idea that the infantry would be able to come to terms with its infantry opponents on essentially similar terms. A few hours into the battle of Mons, the British infantry found out that this was not the case. Artillery and infantry fire combined with such intensity as to undermine significantly any concept of infantry-led fire supremacy. The battles of 1915 then saw a seemingly natural, and therefore unconscious, shift to the idea that in the conditions of flank-less trench warfare, artillery acted as the instrument of fire supremacy. Thus, when the whistles blew in the trenches, it was taken as the decisive moment for the all-out infantry assault. What every infantry assault in 1915 then seemed to show quite clearly was that the artillery never won the battle for fire supremacy neatly and completely. The infantry needed to return to the idea of the struggle for fire supremacy and fire and movement within the scenario of no man's land. Feeling the way back to this path took the vast majority of 1915 and 1916. Even the highly sensible Fourth Army 'Red Book' of May 1916, with its urgings to rehearse different types of assault formations and emphasis on platoons detailed for specialist tasks implied that the real work commenced once the troops were in the enemy trenches. The passage of no man's land was a matter of importance in terms of formation in order to keep cohesion, but was not fully considered as a battlefield in itself.

In pre-war training, great emphasis was placed on the maintenance of high morale and fighting spirit as the vital psychological springs to force men forward in the final assault. Although this concept has often been derided as a failure to understand the nature of a fire-power-dominated battlefield, the essence of infantry is to close with the enemy, and this does require an intense effort of the personal will even in highly technologically advanced armies. (If this human-driven element to battle could be replaced completely, armies would relinquish the need for medals and personal honours.) The main weakness in the pre-war British system was that the training manuals were extremely hazy on when the moment of fire supremacy had been reached, thus indicating the moment for the decisive assault. Most front-line officers, NCOs and men were given only the vaguest sense of how to judge this crucial indicator, which, in turn, reflected confusions running to the top of the army.

Once the unconscious understanding that the lifting of the barrage meant the achievement of something like fire supremacy and was therefore the moment of the decisive assault had sunk into the minds of the high command, it opened the way for judgements on the moral qualities of the attacking troops. Those who failed to make it across no man's land lacked drive and morale. This perhaps goes someway to explaining the somewhat shocking comments made by Haig and Rawlinson on units deemed to have skulked in their trenches rather than attack. In turn, this fed the process by which number of casualties was taken as a sign of intent and commitment. However, this is the point where a failure to intellectualise externally an interior, subconscious logic became deeply detrimental to the BEF, for if casualties became a yardstick of intent, it should have revealed the immense dangers of crossing no man's land. These dangers were then an important critique on the concepts of fire supremacy and how it was achieved and judged. Analysing the nature of infantry assaults should then have led to a much quicker revision of both infantry and artillery tactics. The British undoubtedly learnt a lot, particularly during 1916, when many aspects of the fighting crystallised sufficiently, but a properly functioning brain and centralised nervous system would have achieved it quicker and implemented change more efficiently. Change in this instance did not actually mean something brand new (and therefore something very easy to identify in hindsight), but a revisiting of pre-war concepts in order to reshape and clarify. It was also intimately linked to artillery tactics, for 1915 had seen the BEF wander down the cul-de-sac of destructive fire. Once the artillery was conceived of as a hammer beating enemy resistance to a pulp, it necessarily undermined perceptions of the infantry. With the introduction of creeping barrages during the Somme campaign, the BEF had, in effect, accepted neutralisation, rather than destruction, as the overall aim. (It would, however, take time for this perception to penetrate the BEF fully.) In its turn, neutralisation meant the infantry once again had a tactical role before it reached the enemy front line.

Creating revised infantry tactics was not difficult for the BEF. Revealing the intelligence and flexibility of the BEF, once new training manuals were demanded, highly useful and intelligent responses were put together. The weakness was once again the lack of a co-ordinating authority to ensure uniform dissemination. By the same token, the infantry could only use new weapons and fresh tactical ideas effectively both in no man's land and in the enemy trenches if it was given a chance to do so. That chance was supplied by the artillery in particular through counter-battery work and through the ever-growing sophistication and power of its bombardments. At the start of the Somme battle, too much emphasis was placed on utter destruction of too many targets. The thinning out of the gun line, especially the heavy artillery, then led to disastrous results for the attacking infantry. As has been stressed, during the course of the battle, the creeping barrage came to be used far more extensively and proved far better at protecting the infantry. Running alongside this development came the ever-greater understanding of the need for effective counter-battery work. To carry out these two tactical tasks effectively, the artillery had a number of pre-requisites. Firstly, the gunners required to carry out the orders needed to be proficient and confident of their roles. This confidence emerged only gradually because, in effect, many of Fourth Army's gunners completed their training as a result of direct experience in battle. Secondly, the supply of guns and ammunition had to be of high quality and sufficient quantity. Both elements were highly problematic during the battle. The difficulty of distribution from the French ports had been noted in 1915 and was put under immense stress by the late summer and autumn of 1916. By the winter, the situation was reaching the point of desperation. Too many skilled watermen and railway operatives had been combed out of the support services to make good losses among front-line troops for the efficient running of the BEF's highly complex supply needs. In addition, too little clear thinking had been applied to the best way of ensuring efficient distribution of all types of supplies to the front line. This crisis in BEF logistics was to be met in a novel manner before the winter was out and led to a wholesale restructuring of the BEF's logistics system (as will be discussed in Chapter 9).

The third pre-requisite was the need for precise information on enemy positions. Much of this was supplied by aerial reconnaissance. The Royal Flying Corps (RFC) certainly fought extremely aggressively and well to ensure aerial supremacy for the British during the battle. Taking the offensive in strength, the RFC kept German aircraft well away from the front lines. Having won supremacy, the observation aircraft were then worked very hard indeed. During the course of the battle, they registered 8,612 targets and took over 19,000 photographs, from which 420,000 copies were made. Communication between air and ground was also made more effective, with wireless playing an increasingly important role. By mid-November, over 300 aircraft were equipped with wireless transmitting to 542 ground stations. Pointing the way towards future operations, the RFC then assisted the infantry and the artillery by direct use of its own firepower in bombing raids. Nearly 300 bombing raids were made during the course of the battle in which 176,000 bombs were dropped. However, all air activity was weather dependent, and when it closed in, the efficiency of British assaults often dropped markedly.[19]

The battle of the Somme was therefore an extremely complex process. During its course, the sharp end of the BEF gained much in the way of experience and expertise. Artillery and infantry began to unlock the tactical secrets of the Western Front and were capable of limited but highly successful actions. Much of this progress was made in a volatile strategic and operational atmosphere in which the higher levels of British command were often found wanting. Although forced to maintain the battle for the sake of Anglo-French unity, Haig could have achieved this end through a much subtler approach to operations. Greater clarity from GHQ might then have allowed Rawlinson's better qualities as a methodical step-by-step commander to flourish more clearly. Instead, the continuing confusion as to the aims of the battle led Rawlinson to act in a highly hesitant and indecisive manner. He often anticipated problems but did very little to work his way round them or advise his subordinates effectively. Assessing the extent to which this command malaise affected the morale of the men at the front is extremely difficult. Led to believe that the battle would end the war in short order, the protracted slugging match tried the resolve of the BEF deeply. The fact that it emerged from the battle scarred but solid is an immense tribute to the cohesion of British society and the paternal spirit that infused the British Army. Perhaps ironically, it seems that those most shocked were those furthest from the front line. The British government realigned significantly in the winter of 1916 as Asquith, who had led the coalition from its inception over a year earlier, was removed by an internal coup in which the Unionist party backed Lloyd George for the premiership. Lloyd George was dismayed by the lack of progress on the Somme and was determined to see the war prosecuted in what he believed to be a more efficient way in 1917. This resolution then had a profound effect on the shape of British operations on the Western Front in the following year.

[19] Miles, *Military Operations, 1916*, Vol. II, 566–7.

9 The Western Front, 1917

With hindsight, the battle of the Somme can be judged a victory for the Anglo-French coalition, but at the time it was difficult to make that case comprehensively. The soldiers on the ground had the doubtful satisfaction of showing the Germans, and indeed the French, that the British Army could fight solidly and continuously. It was also possible to point out the physical gains in terms of ground won. However, looking for clear and obvious advantages beyond these rather limited points was a challenge. This was certainly the way the new Prime Minister, David Lloyd George, looked at the situation. As a self-confessed layman in military terms, Lloyd George failed to see any obvious clear victory when set against with the enormous expenditure of life and materiel. In an attempt to ensure that Lloyd George achieved the correct perspective, both General Headquarters (GHQ) in France and Robertson in London stressed the benefits which appeared intangible in the immediate context of a map of the Somme region but had nonetheless been achieved. Chief among these was the emphasis on German morale and the erosion of German fighting power elsewhere, particularly at Verdun, which added up to a significant step in the attrition of German strength. Suspicious about the validity of this argument, Lloyd George remained unconvinced, particularly as it appeared that Haig wished to re-open the Somme offensive in the spring. Believing that the war on the Western Front had not been fought with maximum efficiency, he was determined to change its course in 1917 and believed that this was best done through much closer collaboration between the British Expeditionary Force (BEF) and the French armies. This vision ran contrary to Haig's conception, and the two men engaged in a struggle for mastery over strategy for the rest of the year (and, indeed, the remainder of the war). The military outcome of this tussle was a year of intensive activity on the Western Front for the BEF in order to meet the differing strategic aims of its political and military masters.[1]

[1] French, *The Strategy of the Lloyd George Coalition*, 40–66; Turner, *British Politics*, 152–65; D. R. Woodward, *Lloyd George and the Generals* (East Brunswick, NJ: Associated University Presses, 1983), 116–59.

Lloyd George's move to the premiership did not transform his relationship with Haig; rather, it deepened suspicions and doubts that had grown during the course of 1916. These reservations were then expressed in a highly unproductive manner as Lloyd George turned to both General Foch and Sir John French for 'independent' military advice. His faith in French military advice remained even after the sacking of Joffre and Foch in December 1916, and he turned his attention to Joffre's successor, Robert Nivelle. Nivelle quickly enchanted Lloyd George through a combination of his grand scheme to win the war in short order and fluent English. Won over by Nivelle's vision of a violent assault on the Chemin des Dames in which the BEF would play a supporting role – a concept highly attractive to the British Prime Minister, horrified as he was by the human cost of the Somme – Lloyd George was happy to accept Nivelle's demand that the BEF by formally subordinated to him for the duration of the offensive. The details of the scheme were then worked out at the notorious Calais Conference of February 1917. Haig was horrified that he had been made a component part of a foreign army and was no longer immediately responsible to His Majesty's Government in London. To assuage Haig's doubts, it was agreed that he retained the right to appeal to London if he felt it necessary and that the arrangement was valid for the length of the forthcoming operation, after which it would lapse immediately.

Without perhaps realising it, Haig had actually emerged somewhat stronger from the conference rather than humiliated and constricted. If Nivelle's scheme failed, he could distance himself from it very easily while also claiming a major slice of any victory. Lloyd George, by contrast, had failed to exert civilian control by making compromises with Haig and had discovered that he could not expect much support from senior British military figures in any plan to rein in Haig. Military developments on the Western Front then diminished Lloyd George's visions still further as much of Nivelle's thinking was undermined by the significant German retreat to the Siegfried Stellung which commenced in late February and was completed in early April. On the Somme, the Germans fell back across an 18,000-yard front facing Fifth Army, providing a clear indication that the battle was an entente victory of sorts. It was part of a series of well-planned withdrawals to a new and highly sophisticated defensive system stretching from Arras to the Aisne at Soissons. This move shortened the German line significantly, freeing up fourteen divisions. Hampering the entente advance to the new positions was the fiendish brilliance of the German disruption campaign: every road and track was destroyed or blocked, villages were razed and sources of fresh water poisoned. Virtually every aspect of Nivelle's detailed planning was made irrelevant by this move, and yet little was done to re-think the scheme from first principles.

Haig's overall understanding of the war in spring 1917 was very much shaped and dominated by the information provided by his intelligence chief, Brigadier-General John Charteris. Charteris is a controversial figure who has been blamed for feeding Haig overly optimistic interpretations of the information processed by his team, which then led to inaccurate understandings of German strength and morale on the Western Front. In the wake of the Somme, Charteris was certainly emphasising the depressed state of German morale, both military and domestic. But it was hard to put a positive gloss on the tottering condition of the Tsarist armies and indications of a less than robust outlook among French forces. Worse still, some intelligence reports suggested that the German armies on the Western Front were recovering their cohesion after a few months respite from major action. It was in this contradictory and unsettled atmosphere that Haig commenced planning for the BEF's supporting role in the Nivelle offensive.

In terms of implements, Haig had at his disposal infantry and artillery that had emerged from the Somme sobered but tempered by battle and with much greater knowledge of its roles. The lessons of the Somme were being incorporated into the infantry through an influential series of publications which marked an important development towards greater tactical uniformity. SS135, *Instructions for the Training of Divisions for Offensive Action*, was issued in December 1916. It digested many of the themes of an earlier publication, *Preliminary Notes on the Tactical Lessons of the Recent Operations* (SS119 issued in July 1916), and General Jacob's (II Corps) reflections of September. Revealing that the lessons of 1915 and the Somme had found their clearest expression yet, the pamphlet laid much stress on the need to follow a creeping barrage as quickly and closely as possible. Once in an enemy defensive system, infantry units were advised to deploy all their fire power and work in close co-operation with the Stokes mortars to suppress strong points and machine gun emplacements. Meticulous and methodical, almost plodding, preparation was the *zeitgeist* of the publication. In February 1917, two months after the appearance of SS135, perhaps the most important British training pamphlet of the war was published and issued, SS143, *Instructions for the Training of Platoons for Offensive Action*. Buttressing *Instructions for the Training of Divisions for Offensive Action* and infused by the lessons learnt during the Somme fighting, it too emphasised the need to close with the enemy as quickly as possible once an assault commenced. The pamphlet also called for a radical restructuring of the infantry's basic building block, the platoon. Four specialised fighting sections were created, thus expanding the army's now well-established but still largely unregulated training system. One section was dedicated to bombing, the second provided the Lewis gun team, the third was the rifles, and the fourth, the rifle-grenadiers; overall direction of the platoon was provided by a small HQ section. Tactically, the platoon ethos was now very flexible, as it was designed to use its weapons mix to subdue any enemy position left intact after a barrage. Platoons were instructed to lead with their riflemen and bombers screened by a line of scouts. If a resilient enemy was encountered, these sections were to swing towards the flank while the rifle-bombers and Lewis guns provided covering fire from the front. Once on the flank, the riflemen and bombers were then to close in while still under the cover of the rifle-bombs and Lewis guns. Although these tactical recommendations still conformed to an idea of linear/wave tactics, the essential lessons of probing for the soft flank was imparted.

The artillery had also advanced considerably since 1 July 1916. During the Somme battle, nearly 25 per cent of guns revealed faults, and vast numbers of dud ammunition were fired. By the spring of 1917, British industry was supplying shells and guns in far greater numbers and, perhaps more importantly, in far greater quality. In addition, a vital new component was added, the 106 Fuse. The 106 Fuse was a reliable instantaneous, or grazing, fuse which exploded on immediate contact rather than burying itself before detonation. This meant that wire entanglements could be shelled more effectively, and there was less likelihood of turning the battlefield into a cratered morass. When combined with the creeping barrages pioneered on the Somme, these new developments gave the artillery the ability to suppress the enemy more effectively than ever before.[2]

Servicing the demands of the BEF had placed an enormous strain on its logistics systems in 1916. The task of bringing order to GHQ's somewhat chaotic arrangements was given to a civilian expert, Sir Eric Geddes, who had been Deputy General Manager of the North Eastern Railway before the war. Given a free hand by Lloyd George and Haig, Geddes examined every aspect of the BEF's logistics, applying his immense professional expertise. Centralising the entire operation in the office of Director-General of Transportation, he comprehensively reordered the BEF's creaking system. Railways were reorganised, with control taken away from the French in a move that relieved the hard-pressed French greatly.

[2] Griffith, *Battle Tactics*, 95–100; Jonathan Bailey, 'British Artillery in the Great War', in Paddy Griffith (ed.), *British Fighting Methods in the Great War* (London: Frank Cass, 1996), 23–49; John Lee, 'Some Lessons of the Somme: The British Infantry in 1917', in British Commission for Military History, *Look to Your Front: Studies in the First World War* (Staplehurst: Spellmount, 1999), 79–88.

Recognising the need for more capacity, Geddes ordered 1,200 miles of track, 2.7 million sleepers, 7,000 wagons, sixty-one locomotives and 100 broad-gauge tractors. Wishing to diversify delivery from the railhead, Geddes lessened dependence on the lorry by improving the light railway network. At the same time he reformed the position in the ports, restructuring the way they worked to ensure rapid unloading and distribution of materiel. Refurbishment, repair and maintenance systems also came under his observation and were made more efficient. Within a short space of time, Geddes revolutionised a desperate situation and played a major role in ensuring the BEF's operational capacity in 1917 and 1918. Somewhat ironically, Geddes' very success brought other problems with it. The ability to supply the guns with vast amounts of ammunition led them to wear out much more quickly, while the more efficient use of trains, lorries and wagons also led to greater demands for coal, oil, petrol, lubricants and forage.[3]

It was with this infrastructure and set of implements that the BEF began its preparations to support the French. Haig identified the Arras front and Vimy Ridge as an important target, covering as they did the railway junction of Cambrai. Facing the BEF was the German Sixth Army under Colonel-General von Falkenhausen. Close surveillance on the German defences in this area had revealed the existence of a very strong entrenchment, the Drocourt-Quéant Line, which lay some six or seven miles from the British front and was thus beyond artillery range. The depth of these defensive positions meant that it was impossible to attempt breakthrough in one go: only systematic operations well supported with munitions could break down the German positions.[4]

With this awareness of German strength and doubtless mindful of the disasters of 1 July caused by over-ambitious targets, Haig's subordinates planned meticulously and realistically. A particularly difficult proposition was the capture of the German strong point of Vimy Ridge, which fell to Lieutenant-General Sir Henry Horne's First Army. Horne was a gunner and protégé of Haig but one more reminiscent of Rawlinson than Gough in his cautious approach. It was an understanding of battle Horne shared with his immediate subordinate, Lieutenant-General Sir Julian Byng, Commander of the Canadian Corps. Although a cavalry man who had already commanded both the Cavalry and IX Corps before moving on to what was, in effect, the Canadian National Army in France, Byng had no doubt that the dash had to be replaced by steadiness. Byng's hallmarks were thoroughness and sensible caution. Given the task of capturing

[3] Brown, *Logistics*, 138–51.
[4] For planning of Arras, see Harris, *Haig*, 300–7; Gary Sheffield, *Forgotten Victory*, 159–62.

Vimy Ridge, his corps staff began a comprehensive round of planning and preparation. Achieving this high degree of efficiency in the administration and structuring of the Canadian forces was part of a long and on-going process which had commenced almost as soon as the first Canadian troops arrived on the Western Front. Although the Canadians had shown immense bravery and endurance at Second Ypres, the Canadian Expeditionary Force was dogged by political interference from Sam Hughes, the Minister of Militia in Ottawa, poor equipment in the Ross rifle, a lack of qualified staff officers and erratic training and reinforcement procedures. Sorting through these issues took much time and patience and, as many Canadian academics have demonstrated, required the professional input of a good number of British soldiers to achieve.[5] The resulting plan demanded an advance by all four divisions covered by a comprehensive bombardment which placed particular attention on counter-battery work and a deep creeping barrage for the day of the assault.

To the south, Byng's fellow cavalryman, Allenby, planned to use Third Army to make a four-and-a-half mile leap in a single day, capturing Monchy-le-Preux on the high ground with its excellent visibility over the battlefield. Third Army's attack front was nearly ten miles long, stretching from Farbus Wood just south of Vimy, in the north covered by Sir Charles Fergusson's XVII Corps; Aylmer Haldane's VI Corps stood in the centre, while the southern-most point was Croiselle, where Sir Thomas Snow's VII Corps was to assault. In all, an eleven-day artillery bombardment was planned, consisting of seven days of wire cutting which culminated in a four-day final bombardment. The assault was due to commence at 5.30 AM with the first of a four-phase infantry attack which would climax in a final advance at 3.30 PM. This artillery plan was not Allenby's original intention. Wishing to utilise the element of surprise, Allenby was keen to cover his advance with a hurricane bombardment. Haig was much less convinced by this element of the plan. Unlike disagreements with the phlegmatic Rawlinson, this one had the potential to deteriorate given Allenby's volatile nature. Another problem was the fact that Allenby shared Haig's lack of verbal dexterity, which led to further misunderstandings. Haig's artillery adviser, Major-General J. F. N. Birch, was particularly worried that a short bombardment would fail to cut wire and provide too

[5] See e.g. Tim Cook's two-volume study of the Canadian Expeditionary Force, *At the Sharp End. Canadians Fighting the Great War 1914–1916* (Toronto, Ontario: Viking, 2007); and *Shock Troops. Canadians Fighting the Great War 1917–1918* (Toronto, Ontario: Viking, 2008). Also see his study of the problems created by Sam Hughes, *The Madman and the Butcher: The Sensational Wars of Sam Hughes and General Arthur Currie* (Toronto, Ontario: Penguin, 2011).

little opportunity for observation of effect. In reply, Allenby insisted that he had carried out thorough experimental tests and was convinced the approach could work. With neither side wishing to back down, Haig outmanoeuvred Allenby by replacing his artillery adviser with Major-General R. St. Clair Lecky, a man compliant with GHQ wishes. Given fresh advice, Allenby could do little but heed it.

In order to ensure operational tempo with fresh men delivering each assault in strength, divisions were instructed to leapfrog through each other. This required excellent planning and preparation and was an ambitious approach revealing a good degree of self-confidence in Third Army staff and its corps. GHQ prepared for success by giving Allenby two cavalry divisions for exploitation purposes. An additional cavalry division was also allotted to Gough's Fifth Army immediately to the south, while GHQ held on to a further cavalry division for its own use. It was at this point that the planning process began to show signs of inconsistency. To contemplate use of the cavalry in open country meant that the German fourth line had to fall, and yet this was well beyond the British artillery, meaning that its subjugation was in the hands of the infantry. Even if this was achieved, there was still the Drocourt-Quéant Line to consider, meaning that the chances of breakthrough into open country were negligible. Given this scenario, it was remarkable that very little attention was given to the handling of operations after the first day. This curious anomaly may have been a hangover from the initial Somme planning. In the spring of 1916, pretty much everything was staked on the idea of operations becoming fluid within twenty-four hours, which created the assumption that somehow momentum and success could be maintained with very little detailed preparation. Such a mentality can be defended on the grounds that it was impossible to predict exactly where the opportunity might open up, which then demanded a highly flexible command structure. However, there is a big difference between flexibility underpinned by sensible contingency planning and a scenario vacuum. This is precisely what occurred in the wake of 1 July. In effect, the British had no real plan to cope with either great success or great disaster and were forced into improvising an over-arching operational scheme. Much the same occurred here, but with one very important divergence in thought: in the run-up to 1 July, the emphasis was undoubtedly on breakthrough from top to bottom, but before Arras, a bite and hold, break-in mentality held sway. Given this clarity of vision, it might be argued all the more strongly that the logical corollary of such thinking should have been more detailed plans for continuing operations.

Nonetheless, such inconsistencies should not detract from the undoubted advances in planning and preparation which revealed a marked improvement on 1916. Aware that increased artillery activity might alert the Germans, the concealment of troops became a high priority. This came in the form of the expansion of the ancient tunnel and cellar network under Arras by labour units which provided the British with excellent cover. Not only did this keep the troops from prying eyes, thus confusing the Germans as to the actual intentions of the British, it also protected them from the still bitter weather and allowed them to be well fed before their final emergence. Nearly 25,000 soldiers were concealed from the Germans in this manner, going some way towards compensating for the loss of aerial supremacy in the spring of 1917. The swing of the air war back in the favour of the Germans was a considerable concern, jeopardising as it did observation and intelligence gathering. The Royal Flying Corps (RFC) fought back hard to give the gunners the information they needed, but at high cost, losing about 275 aircraft and suffering 421 casualties.

The artillery benefitted enormously from both the work of the RFC and the greater attention given to target prioritising. On 1 July 1916, the BEF attacked 27,000 yards of frontage with fourteen divisions. On 9 April 1917, the BEF also attacked 25,000 yards of frontage with fourteen divisions. But, for Arras, the BEF had the ability to commence with a creeping barrage and a density of guns almost three times greater: 963 guns, or one per twenty-one yards, as opposed to 455, or one per fifty-seven yards for the opening of the Somme battle. Used in a rigorous and imaginative way, the artillery never paused for long and fired off irregular harassing bombardments designed to disorient the Germans and interrupt relief and resupply missions. Gas and tear gas were also intermingled, particularly in intensive counter-battery work. As a further supplement to fire power and in direct support of the infantry, sixty tanks were gathered, including a small number of the new Mark II design.[6]

In comparison with 1 July 1916, 9 April 1917 was a great day for the BEF in France, and such was the thoroughness and efficiency of the BEF's preparation that its assault began long before Nivelle was ready to move. Covered by a thorough creeping barrage and well-placed standing bombardments and in a few places assisted by tanks, the British infantry fought its way forward impressively. Byng's Canadians took the vast majority of Vimy Ridge, while on the Third Army front a greater portion of the first three phases was fulfilled, and 5,600 prisoners were brought in. At no point, though, had the fourth line been reached.[7] Heavy snow disrupted the tempo, meaning that the opportunity to push on and

[6] Harris, *Haig*, 306. [7] Sheffield, *Forgotten Victory*, 164.

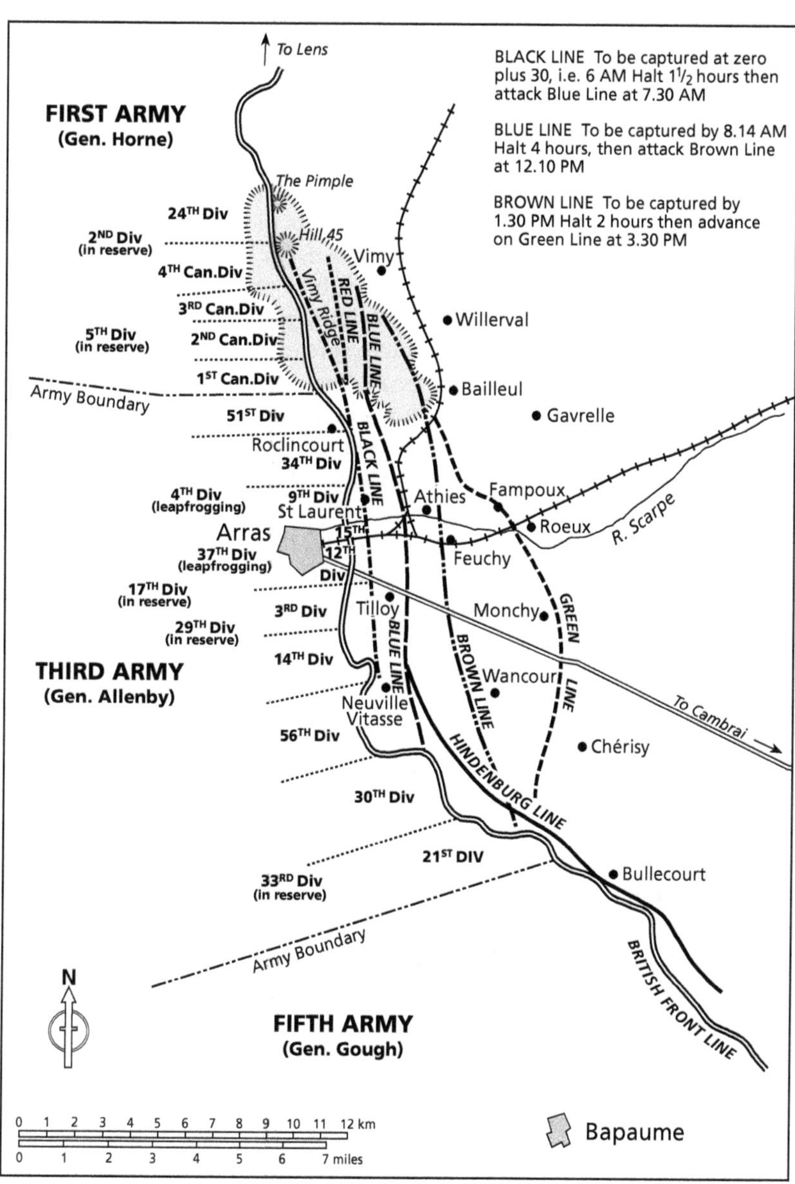

Map 8 Battle of Arras, 9 April 1917

take Monchy-le-Preux was lost. In addition, many British soldiers revealed their naivety in what was called 'semi-open' warfare as first experienced in the later stages of the Somme fighting. Once the foremost German defences were dented, advancing British soldiers often found either incomplete or improvised positions in front of them. This required a slightly different set of skills to the ones learnt so dearly during much of the fighting on the Somme. In 1916, the crafts most in demand were the clearing of German dugouts and trenches using teams of bombers covered by close-range rifle fire. Prioritising these tactics left British troops slightly unsure as to the best way of advancing once trench lines became ragged and the defenders more widely spread and often advancing, or retiring, to new positions across open ground. Dealing with this form of defence required accurate medium- and long-range rifle fire, greater sophistication in appreciation of targets and deployment of fire and movement tactics. Once again, the BEF was left with the need to retrace its steps to its pre-war training, revise it for current conditions and restructure training accordingly. Fortunately, the flexible, mutually supporting platoon system sketched out in the new manuals was equally applicable to this kind of warfare. However, once again, the lack of a central training authority meant that this connection was not made in a uniform, cohesive manner but piecemeal as units reflected on their own experience.

The situation at the end of the day was therefore highly impressive in terms of ground gained, prisoners taken and casualties suffered. But the day was much more ambiguous if judged as a springboard for further action, for the failure to prepare thoroughly for future operations now became apparent. Delighted with the day's successes, Haig wanted Allenby to press on and urged him to unhinge Monchy-le-Preux from the south. Having spent so much time preparing for the initial stages and thinking of little else, however, Third Army and its subordinate units showed little ability to move over to a rapid tempo battle, and 10 April was largely a day of tidying up rather than moving on determinedly. Anxious to regain the initiative, Allenby ordered the cavalry into action, but its advance was broken up and achieved little. Allenby was extremely frustrated by the ebbing away of the initiative and tried to will his men forward through the urgency of his communications. He was undoubtedly correct that the front-line units were sluggish in maintaining the momentum, but they were undermined by the lack of advance preparation, and even if they had responded quickly, it is debatable whether the next set of German defences could be overrun easily without rigorous artillery preparation.

From GHQ's perspective, the battle still promised much which seemed to be proven on 11 April when Monchy-le-Preux fell, providing dominance over the surrounding countryside and a further impressive haul of prisoners. Far less satisfactory was Gough's failure to take Bullecourt in a botched operation which caused much resentment among the Australian troops involved. A day later this seemed to be balanced by more good news when the Canadians cleared all of the Vimy position, but the momentum was now well and truly lost. If the battle of Arras had stopped at this point, it would have been designated a significant victory reflecting well on the BEF's entire structure. Artillery preparation was thorough and flexible using a thousand more guns to hit targets along a line 2,000 yards shorter than 1 July, firing an additional 36,000 tons of shells in the initial bombardments (88,000 for Arras as opposed to 52,000 for 1 July).[8] Well-trained men using sound tactics and an array of weapons were launched onto a surprised enemy which held its counter-attack units too far behind the lines. All of this thorough preparation had been aimed at breaking into the German defences and achieving highly advantageous fresh positions. The performance of the BEF revealed that it was fully capable of doing this by April 1917. What it could not do was maintain the tempo and use its strengths effectively after a set-piece action. Once again, the high command had confused itself by not creating an adequate central link between the immediate operational scenario and the desired end game.[9]

The lack of that element should have urged caution and ushered back the proven qualities of methodical preparation if operations were to be maintained. Unfortunately, Haig did not seem to realise that the moment to halt had come and insisted on further, immediate operations. This insistence was enacted in a contradictory manner, for he urged Allenby to be both methodical in preparation and pursue the enemy energetically. Into this confused command scenario came a shame-faced Nivelle. He was forced to admit to Haig that his forces were still not ready but that he would launch his offensive if Haig approved it. With this rather pathetic whimper, Nivelle showed that his position had greatly altered since February. The self-confident director of entente efforts on the Western Front had made the action of his forces dependent on those of the original supporting act. Haig stood by Nivelle loyally, stating that the British would continue to attack in order to assist French operations.

On the eve of the much-postponed French assault, 15 April, Haig sensibly ordered an operational pause while the next phase of attack was prepared. This move saved Allenby from further embarrassment at the

[8] *Ibid.*, 162.

[9] See in particular I. M. Brown, '"Not Glamorous, But Effective": The Canadian Corps and the Set-Piece Attack, 1917–1918', *Journal of Military History* 58(3) (July 1994); A. P. Palazzo, 'The British Army's Counter Battery Staff Office and Control of the Enemy in World War I', *Journal of Military History* 63(1) (1999), 55–74.

hands of his corps commanders, for on the previous day his subordinates in VI and VII Corps had refused to order assaults designed to reach the River Sensée. Unable to prepare thoroughly for this demanding task in poor weather, the divisional commanders given the tasks had made their views clear to their immediate superiors. A resolution was agreed calling for more time to plan and co-ordinate, particularly given the fact that Monchy-le-Preux had been lost to a counter-attack on the previous day. The resolution was then despatched directly to Haig over the head of Allenby. Such an extraordinary lapse in discipline, chain of command and etiquette revealed the depth of feeling and appears to have triggered Haig's decision to pause.

Doubtless in reaction to this somewhat shocking state of affairs, Gough, Horne and Allenby were invited to a conference with Haig on 16 April. He confirmed the decision to pause but stated that it be brief, for the offensive was to be re-launched on 18 April. This attack, carried out by Third Army with the objective of Guemappe, was envisaged as a preliminary designed to open the way for all three armies to combine in a fresh assault on 20 April. In the event, nothing happened, as both Horne and Gough protested their inability to mount significant operations in the face of continuing heavy snowfall and freezing conditions. In the meantime, the French offensive had been launched, and although Nivelle's plans led to some gains, compared with the great expectations, results were small and casualties heavy. Haig was then made aware that the failure to deliver the great breakthrough promised had had a deeply unsettling effect on the French Army, but precise details were extremely hazy.

Over the next few days Haig gained more information on instability in the French Army with some hints at a collapse in discipline. This news made him increasingly fearful that entente offensive operations would come to a grinding halt on all fronts, leaving the Germans with the initiative. Somewhat ironically, he found that Lloyd George for once wholeheartedly agreed with his opinion, whereas Robertson walked a middle path. Aware that the suspension of all aggressive activity was unwise, Robertson was nonetheless keen to urge prudence and method. This belief was rehearsed in a letter to Haig on 20 April in which he stressed once again a step-by-step approach to operations on the Western Front. While counselling caution, Robertson also went on to express his doubt that 1917 would prove decisive for the entente. Probably sent in knowledge of the declining returns from the Arras battle, it was a clear signal to Haig to rein in his ambitions. But such advice did little to alter Haig's opinion. He stuck by his decision to maintain the offensive at Arras based on his fear that the French could stall completely and do nothing for the rest of the year and his conviction that he had severely rattled the Germans and could continue to do so.

The renewed assault commenced at 4.45 AM on 23 April with the Third Army attacking astride the River Scarpe, while the First Army attacked in the direction of Gavrelle, which duly fell after hard fighting. On Third Army's front, fighting was severe, and the line moved forward only after an intense struggle. The artillery support was greatly undermined by having only patchy knowledge of German positions and an even more slender grip on enemy artillery locations. Haig was aware of the slow progress but remained determined to push on, telling Allenby to take the Drocourt-Quéant Line by the end of the month. Having made this significant demand, Haig somewhat undermined the chances of achieving it by stating that he could provide no fresh troops. With the battle degenerating into an increasingly bitter struggle, Haig now demanded support from Nivelle and the French government. He wanted assurances that the French would maintain offensive action. While making these points clear, he ordered Horne to capture Arleux and Oppy with Allenby taking Roeux and Greenland Hill. These operations were to open the way for an advance to the Drocourt-Quéant Line. Thrown into hastily arranged assaults, the attacks of 28 April were costly and largely fruitless, with the only major success being the fall of Arleux.

Receiving news that Nivelle was about to be sacked did not dampen Haig's enthusiasm. He ordered a fresh round of assaults for 3 May, but this time the Drocourt-Quéant Line was not included in the vision. Instead, Haig's intention seemed fixed on improving his local position by achieving a line from Lens to Riencourt via Greenland Hill. To achieve this, First, Third and Fifth Armies were to participate in a major offensive. Engineering harmonious co-operation proved difficult when I Anzac Corps in Fifth Army insisted on an earlier start time than Third Army. To solve this dispute, Haig arbitrarily split the demands and ordered a 3.45 AM zero hour. First and Third Armies were then left trying to rearrange their assaults at the last moment with all too predictable consequences. The fighting on 3 May provided a dismal epilogue on the battle. Lacking adequate preparation time, the artillery was once again unsure of its targets, fatally undermining its potential in ragged bombardments of little assistance to the infantry. Tangible results were minimal as only Fresnoy was captured, which was then lost five days later, and the Australians were outraged by Gough's handling of the assault at Bullecourt. Still unwilling to shut the battle down, Haig ordered further attacks at Bullecourt, deepening the rift between I Anzac Corps and Gough in the process as all came to nought. Bloody fighting did wrest Roeux and its chemical works from the Germans on 11 May, but it was hardly a resounding end to the contest.

A battle with the potential to wear down the Germans and significantly improve the British position had been allowed to spiral out of control. The British suffered some 150,000 casualties and inflicted between 79,000 and 85,000 in return in what was the bloodiest battle of the war for the British in terms of average daily casualties.[10] By April 1917, the BEF was a much-refined instrument of war capable of complex and imaginative operations. However, it could only achieve results if it was given time and space for its elaborate preparations. This army, the product of experience on the Somme, revealed these immense strengths on 9 April. In less than a year since the start of the Somme, it had become a brilliant exponent of set-piece battles. These strengths were then undermined utterly by the insistence with which Haig maintained operations long after they had ceased to be effective and sapped the morale of a force which had shown such mental and physical resilience and skill.

A significant result of the battle was the final collapse of relations between Haig and Allenby. Haig had shown concern at Allenby's failure to launch the cavalry in the wake of the initial successes and his seeming inability to co-ordinate attacks properly after 9 April. This led Haig to intervene more directly in an attempt to exert influence. However, the poor relations between the two men created even greater confusion in the planning and execution of assaults. As noted earlier, with the resolve of his divisional commanders hardening against further operations, Allenby was forced to concede the need for a pause, but this undermined his relations with Haig still further. Unfavourable comparison with Gough then added to Allenby's problems, and after pointing out the futility of maintaining the offensive, Haig became convinced that Allenby had to be removed. In June, Byng took over Third Army, and Allenby was given command of the Egyptian Expeditionary Force. This command implosion can be attributed to two causes: the clash of personalities compounded by the command culture of the British Army. As on the Somme, when difficulties over Rawlinson's approach to command were highlighted, Haig acted inconsistently, interfering on occasions and leaving well alone at other points. Such a style must have confused and irritated a volatile character like Allenby. However, both men were also victims of the British Army's command culture and in its utter lack of relevance to large-scale operations which were so far beyond its usual focus. In creating an umpiring mode, which was very well suited to smaller-scale operations where prolonged exposure to enemy responses was minimal, British commanders had little real

[10] Harris, *Haig*, 325.

sense of how to interact effectively with each other in a scenario which demanded continual action and reaction over an extended period.

It can be argued that Haig's decision to maintain the offensive at Arras revealed his subordinate position to the French and a loyal exercising of his remaining powers. Even within the confines of this argument, however, Haig could have done better. As on the Somme, showing solidarity with the French and supporting French forces to the utmost did not have to mean a continuous chain of ill-considered, ill-prepared assaults. Rather, carefully planned and controlled expressions of the BEF's power and strengths might have given a far clearer signal to the enemy of its own weaknesses and thus proved more useful to the French. Operational tempo was obviously a casualty of this approach, and this is the argument most often used against this alternative. But there is no way of judging just how quickly the BEF could have put on powerful, limited operations at Arras because it was never given the chance to see through such a method. The real pity of Arras was that in maintaining it the BEF was deprived of the services of many of its battle-hardened and attuned Somme veterans who could have been of great service in Haig's major strategic desire of the year, a Flanders offensive.

An attack in Flanders had much to recommend it. Defending the only substantial Belgian town left in the hands of the entente (albeit in ruins) was important for purposes of entente solidarity. However, the line around it was unfavourably sited, with the Germans generally holding the imposing high ground. In these conditions, even relatively small advances had the potential to make a significant difference to the defence of Ypres. The town was also the shield for much of the BEF's communications network spreading out from the Channel ports, so an advance from the salient would have provided greater security to the BEF's logistics infrastructure. Finally, the growth of German submarine activity from Ostend and Zeebrugge added to the attractions of a Flanders campaign as it would open the way for the clearance of the Belgian coast and provide some relief for the Royal Navy.[11]

Planning for an offensive at Ypres developed over a long period and remained the preferred option for Haig, but it was one he was forced to defer for reasons of Anglo-French solidarity until the summer of 1917.

[11] The decision-making processes behind Messines and Third Ypres have been much discussed by historians. For a range of views, see Harris, *Haig*, 328–39, 349–54; Turner, *British Politics*, 199–204; John Turner, 'Lloyd George, the War Cabinet, and High Politics', in Peter H. Liddle (ed.), *Passchendaele in Perspective: The Third Battle of Ypres* (London: Leo Cooper, 1997), 14–29; Robin Prior and Trevor Wilson, *Passchendaele: The Untold Story* (New Haven, CT: Yale University Press, 1996), 25–54.

A mix of ideas had been studied, including supporting amphibious operations along the coast. One of the most promising was the use of mines. Lieutenant-General Sir Herbert Plumer, Commander of Second Army which covered the Ypres sector, had encouraged mining activity to support a two-pronged offensive. Plumer working in close co-operation with Major-General C. H. 'Tim' Harington, his meticulous Chief of Staff, devised a cautious, limited plan divided into a number of phases hinging on the detonation of a series of mines. In the first phase, the high ground south of Ypres was to be captured along a line from Hill 60 to the Messines Ridge, while another army to the north took the Pilckem Ridge. Once this was achieved, a two-pronged attack would be made on the Gheluvelt Plateau before a shift to the north-east in order to strike towards the coast. This phase of operations could then be assisted by amphibious landings.

Although the eventual result of this plan was impressive, both Plumer and Harington stressed continually the difficulty of fighting through the German defensive positions and requested more artillery than the BEF actually possessed to achieve it. Haig was not entirely convinced and requested additional opinions on the plan, putting it to Rawlinson and Major-General Archibald Montgomery, his Chief of Staff at GHQ. Both men doubted the possibility of attacking Messines and Pilckem simultaneously, stressing lack of men and guns. Instead, Rawlinson suggested dividing the initial phase into two stages, with the first assault on Messines before switching to the Pilckem Ridge three days later. Insisting on a pause made a good deal of sense, but three days was still far too short to move and re-site artillery and register the guns on new targets. He also believed that the coast was far too ambitious a goal and suggested that the town of Roulers, some twelve miles from the British front line, might be reached but only after very heavy fighting.

Haig was not happy with this advice either. He regarded Plumer and Rawlinson as far too cautious, which also revealed his inability to comprehend fully the logistical demands grandiose schemes placed on the BEF's infrastructure. He was more impressed with an idea put forward by Colonel Norman Macmullen of GHQ's operations staff, who suggested a simultaneous attack on all three positions with the task of clearing the plateau assigned to a large tank force. Brigadier-General Hugh Elles and his staff on the Tank Corps studied the proposal but quickly pronounced it unfeasible due to the very boggy and heavily wooded ground. But this sort of ambitious, lightning-strike approach was much more to Haig's taste. Keen to ensure that dynamism remained the key, Haig divided the operations between Plumer and Gough. To Plumer's Second Army he entrusted the limited offensive of clearing the high ground south of Ypres.

But it was to Gough and Fifth Army that he turned for the more ambitious part of breakthrough in the central and northern sector.

Before actual operational planning could commence, Haig needed the approval of the British government. Although Lloyd George's doubts about Haig were plain, the stock of the BEF's Commander-in-Chief was remarkably high in the rest of the War Cabinet and government. Many were impressed by the early stages of Arras, and many could also see the wisdom behind Haig's insistence that the Western Front should not be allowed to slip into passivity due to the failure of the French Army. The final selling point was the ever-increasing threat of German submarines. With the Admiralty deeply concerned about shipping losses, Haig's plan and its promise of greatly disrupting German submarine activity looked very attractive. In these circumstances, Lloyd George found himself with little alternative but to accept the proposal for an offensive in Flanders.

The decision to allow the offensive was made at an Anglo-French conference in May 1917, but there were differing understandings of the nature of the agreement. Lloyd George and Robertson worked on the assumption that a major British offensive could only go ahead if given full and tangible support by the French Army. By contrast, Haig felt that he had been given authority to launch an offensive regardless of French intentions. His actual plans may also have confused Lloyd George, for they were a mixture of the limited and the grand. His written outlines implied a careful attrition of the enemy before any attempt at breakthrough, but the precise methodology for achieving the first and judging the moment for the latter was vague. In Haig's own mind the greater vision was very important, and he once again believed that he was on the verge of making the decisive move of the war on the Western Front. Haig now told his army commanders to prepare for a two-phase offensive. The first was the attack on the Messines-Wytschaete Ridge, after which the focus would switch to the north with the intention of unhinging the German position in Belgium. This firm intention remained undisturbed by the news that the French Army would not support the offensive with much more than artillery demonstrations. Haig appears to have kept this information to himself while also informing commanders down to corps level that the forthcoming offensive made 'the possibility of the collapse of Germany before next winter . . . appreciably greater'.[12]

Building on his earlier plans, Plumer was ready for operations against the Messines-Wytschaete Ridge by June. He was faced by three

[12] Quoted in J. P. Harris, *Douglas Haig and the First World War* (Cambridge University Press, 2008), 341.

impressive German defensive lines. Strongly wired and supported by concrete pillboxes, two of these lines sat on the ridge, with the third on the reverse slope. Set against these strengths were two main weaknesses. The first was the susceptibility to mining, and the second was the fact that the ridge was overlooked by Kemmel Hill in the British rear, and the RFC had once again achieved aerial supremacy. Working with great precision, Second Army planners gathered 1,510 field pieces and 756 heavy guns with 144,000 tons of ammunition stockpiled in its dumps supplemented by 428 heavy mortars.[13] It was a triumph for the newly revised British logistical system in which an immensely complex preparatory phase was carried through efficiently. This gave Second Army a two-to-one advantage over the Germans in field artillery and five-to-one in heavy artillery. Initially, Haig made only two significant interventions, both of value. Firstly, he insisted that greater time be allocated to wire cutting, and secondly, he requested that the whole of the ridge be taken in one operation. Given the logistical support he had given Second Army with its overwhelming local supremacy, this was not unreasonable. However, his final request was more problematic. He wanted not only the ridge taken in one leap but the third (Oosttaverne) line taken as well. Plumer had set this as an exploitation target if all went according to plan but had not made it a formal part of his expectations for the day. By insisting on this target, Second Army was forced to revise a great deal of its planning, which caused much additional pressure.

The preliminary bombardment commenced on 21 May and gradually grew more intense. Assisted by good observation, the British artillery was able to cut vast swathes of wire and smash German trenches. Although the Germans poured in more artillery resources, the quality of the counter-battery work was very good and ensured only desultory responses. Three corps, X in the north, IX in the centre and II Anzac in the south were brought up to attack along a 17,000-yard frontage. All three rehearsed the men intensively, with formations and leapfrogging techniques given great attention. The supporting tanks were then brought up in great secrecy and placed close to the line. The final awesome shock for the Germans was the detonation of the nineteen mines under their lines. When they were blown at 3.10 AM on 7 June, they threw enormous columns of earth, rock and smoke into the air, and the sound was audible in London. No sooner were the mines blown than the British artillery recommenced with even greater fury. It proved too much for the surviving German defenders. Most meekly surrendered to the first attacking troops they met, and the first line fell easily. Fresh troops then came through

[13] Harris, *Haig*, 342.

for the second objective, which was also taken; the resistance here was noticeable but was overcome with relative ease. In most cases the next objective was also attacked with fresh troops supplemented with tanks. Some hard fighting took place during this phase, with 16th Division experiencing a rigorous struggle for Wytschaete village. This brought Second Army into visual contact with the Oosttaverne line, which was scheduled for assault at 1.10 PM.

Luck now turned against the British forces. With so many men swarming forward, the trenches were full, making them excellent targets for the remnants of the German artillery. Virtually every shot caused casualties and disrupted attempts to organise the final advance of the day. Concerned at the rapidly collapsing command and control situation, Plumer postponed the assault for two hours. This did little to clarify the matter, and little was actually achieved. Fighting continued for a further week, after which the Oossttaverne line was finally overrun. Second Army suffered 25,000 casualties during the battle in return for 23,000 German casualties (a conservative figure almost certainly much higher) and 7,354 men taken prisoner.[14] It was an immense victory for the BEF and reflected the same lesson as 9 April: when given adequate time to prepare and unrestricted ammunition supplies, it was a magnificent exponent of the set-piece battle.

Buoyed by the great success of 7 June, Haig felt vindicated in maintaining the pressure for an offensive. He also felt that having been severely shaken, the Germans should be pursued without delay. Switching his attention to the Gheluvelt Plateau, he asked Plumer to commence operations against it at once. Plumer was willing to take on the task, but requested a three-day pause to move artillery and ammunition. Given the immense logistical effort made for Messines, three days was nowhere near sufficient to ensure the smooth unfolding of operations. Revealing Haig's continuing lack of grip on the nuts and bolts of logistics, he appears to have been unconvinced by this reasoning. In response, he took Plumer's two northern corps and placed them under Gough. Having only just established his headquarters in the salient, Gough promptly asked for time to consider the situation. By the time he responded on 14 June, the moment for any rapid exploitation of the victory by operations elsewhere had disappeared, if they ever existed in the first place. Haig's acceptance of this conclusion can be read in two ways: it constituted either a willingness to consider the advice of two experienced generals or is a sign of intellectual inconsistency in his understanding of the actual situation.

[14] *Ibid.*, 347.

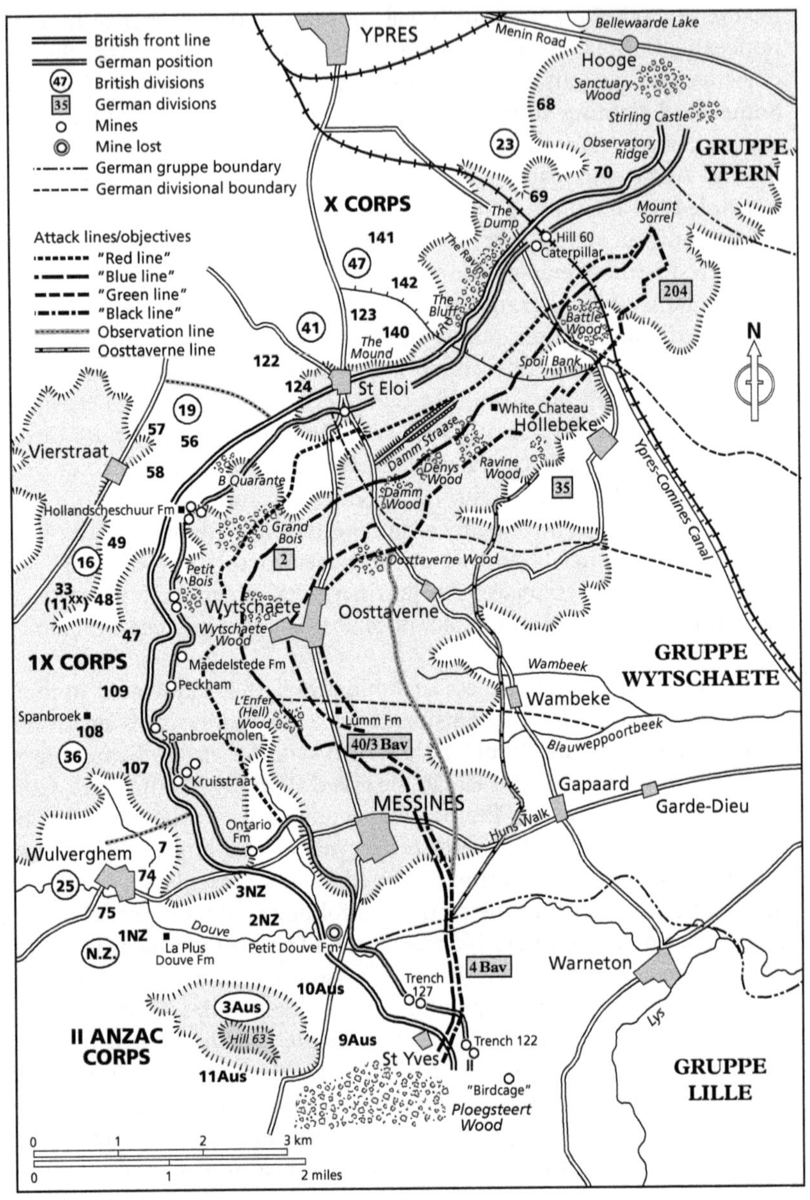

Map 9 Battle of Messines, 7–14 June 1917

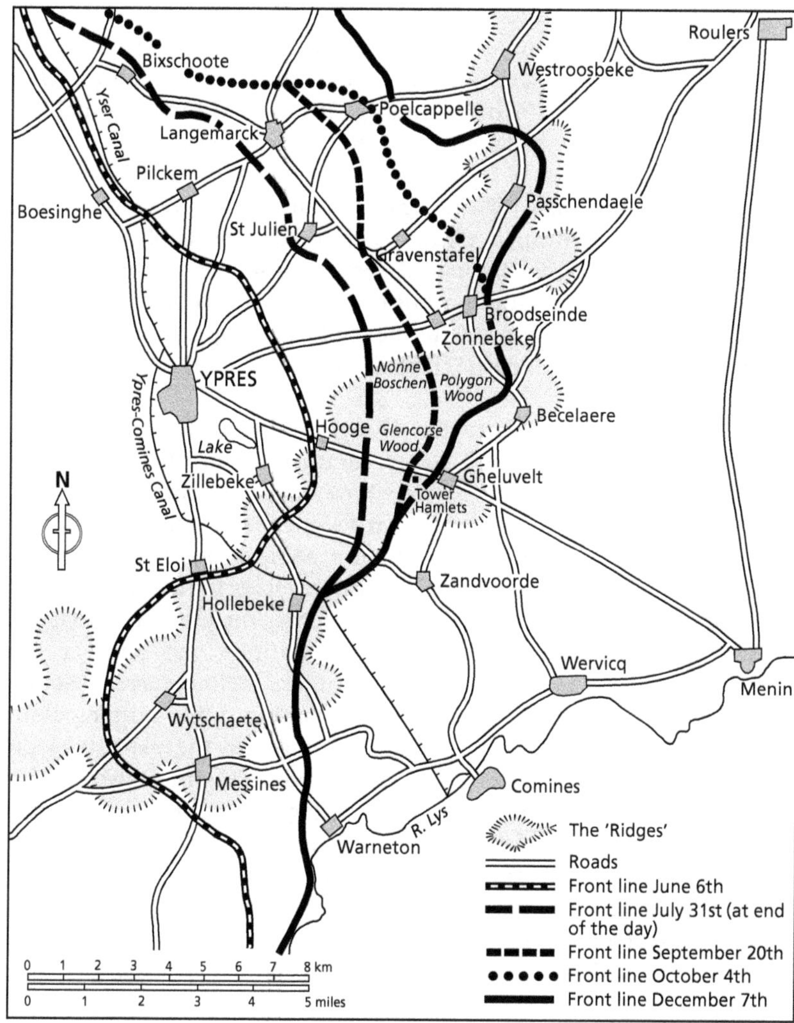

Map 10 Third Battle of Ypres ('Passchendaele'), 31 July–10 November 1917

Regardless of the success achieved at Messines, a mood of caution was still apparent in sections of the British Cabinet. Knowledge of the breakdown in French military discipline was emerging, expectations of great efforts from the Russians were low and the military build-up of the United States was still a long way from maturity, it having entered the war only two months earlier. Added to this was Lloyd George's concern at the war weariness on the home front. He wanted something to cheer the British people, but at very cheap cost in terms of casualties. Haig sought to reassure the War Cabinet by stressing Germany's inability to withstand another onslaught delivered with power and persistence. Few were convinced that Germany could be beaten in 1917, and yet no one made a decisive stand against Haig's interpretation. Lloyd George led the confirmed doubters, but Haig probably persuaded others by declaring that he would keep a close eye on the offensive and would not let casualties mount up if the gains were minimal. Still unsure of a final decision on the next phase of operations, the War Cabinet deferred the decision until the views of the French were gained.

In the meantime, Haig ordered Gough to commence planning. He had certainly given the Fifth Army commander an unenviable task. German defensive positions around Ypres were extremely strong and deep. The first line, mostly on forward slopes, was rather lightly held and regarded more as a trip-wire than a point of decisive resistance. Behind this was a line running along the reverse slope of the Pilckem Ridge from Bixschoote southwards and across the Gheluvelt Plateau. About 2,000 yards to the rear of this position was another line stretched from Langemarck to Gravenstaefel before turning southwards across the plateau. Next was the Flandern I line running along the front of the Passchendaele Ridge down onto the plateau to the bottom corner of Polygon Wood. Scattered across this system were hundreds of pillboxes mostly well camouflaged against aerial observation. Having launched the offensive at Messines, the British also paid the price in terms of German reinforcements. General Sixt von Arnim was assigned Colonel von Lossberg, a fortifications expert, to give him additional advice. His immediate decision was to begin construction of two further defensive positions behind Flandern I on the reverse slopes of the Passchendaele Ridge.

Aerial supremacy negated many aspects of these new defensive systems, as the British gained a good deal of information about their precise locations and nature, with German artillery of particular interest, from aerial photography. However, increasingly sophisticated camouflage and the use of dummy battery sites, as well as regular rotation of batteries, made the supply of accurate information about enemy artillery difficult later on in the battle. The British also commenced the battle with a good margin of artillery supremacy, gathering 1,422 field and 752 heavy guns under Fifth Army's control. French First Army was also prepared to lend its resources, adding a further 240 field and 300 heavy guns to the collection, while to the south British Second Army provided support from 240 field and 112 heavy pieces.[15]

After careful study of the area, Gough eventually decided to assault from Houthulst Forest on his left to the Kleine Zillebeke Road on the right. Gough planned to subdue German defences with a lengthy artillery bombardment before an infantry assault originally scheduled for 25 July. The infantry attack was to be led by nine divisions from Fifth Army and two from the French First Army. Contrary to the simple stereotype of Gough, he did not consider breaking through the German line a simple task requiring only the application of dash and desire. He was well aware that attacking each line of defence would be extremely difficult and require much hard fighting. Further, he was also aware that offensives rapidly ran out of steam after the first day. At this point, the clarity of Gough's thinking became blurred as he believed the solution was to set deep targets for the first day in the hope of severely jolting the German defences before the next punch was delivered. He therefore demanded an advance of between 4,000 and 5,000 yards on Z-day, taking his forces to the line Langemarck, Broodseinde, Polygon Wood, completely overrunning Pilckem Ridge and a portion of the Gheluvelt Plateau in the process. After a mere half-hour pause, the next phase was to commence with an assault on the second line. A four-hour pause was then planned as the prelude to an advance to the Steenbeek and the clearance of Polygon Wood.

This plan was much more ambitious than anything Rawlinson or Plumer had earlier considered possible and also seems to have been much more to Haig's taste. However, not all at GHQ approved. Brigadier-General John Davidson, Head of the Operations Staff, was concerned by the depth of the advance and wrote a paper outlining the risks and advocating shallower assaults which could be covered more effectively by the artillery. An element of confusion now entered the debate, for Gough responded rather favourably to the paper. He did not condemn it out of hand and stated his agreement with the principle of step-by-step limited operations, but he reiterated his desire to bite deeply on the first day. Davidson was then rather surprised to find that Plumer seemed sanguine about Gough's initial objectives. After the war, the precise positions taken by all players in the run-up to Third Ypres became a matter of much heated debate which appears to have encouraged embellishment and the passing off of hindsight judgements as contemporary insights which has made it difficult to understanding exactly what was discussed and agreed. Regardless of the fine details, what does seem

[15] *Ibid.*, 356.

apparent is that a fog of confusion was descending over the intention of the battle and the methods by which it should be fought. No one seemed completely clear as to whether the battle was one of carefully managed attrition of the Germans through deliberately limited assaults or one designed to bring about breakthrough in short order. Haig certainly seemed to soothe his doubters by implying the former but then encouraging thinking about the latter. It is on these grounds that Haig has been accused of duplicity over Third Ypres, but given his inability to maintain a consistent vision of battle, such accusations may well overstate the clarity of his thinking in 1917.

With the BEF planning to launch its third offensive of the year and its second in the Ypres sector, a massive amount of preparatory work had to be completed in June and July. A major blow was the withdrawal of fighter squadrons to assist in the defence of London which undermined the struggle to maintain aerial supremacy. Poor weather then hampered observation and had an impact on the effectiveness of the artillery. To further undermine the British, the Germans switched batteries regularly, weakening the effect of the counter-battery fire. As a whole, the impact of the bombardment was mixed. In some sectors it proved excellent at cutting wire and smashing trenches thoroughly, and even pillboxes built to the latest designs proved unable to withstand the immense power of the British artillery. But, along the Passchendaele Ridge, much of the German artillery remained intact, and the reliance on aerial observation for targets on the Gheluvelt Plateau inevitably watered down the impact of the bombardment in this sector given the wet, cloudy weather. Not entirely convinced that the artillery had done its job, General Anthoine of French First Army requested a postponement which Gough backed. Haig reluctantly agreed to do so, which resulted in Z-day being shifted to 31 July.

Even at this late stage, full consent for the offensive had still to come from London. It took until 18 July for Haig to get a good indication from Robertson that his plans were likely to be approved, but he added that Lloyd George was still very keen on an Italian offensive as an alternative. Two days later Haig was given the final go-ahead, but many probably hoped to take a 'wait and see' approach in which the battle would only be allowed to continue if it met expectations either through dramatic advances or clear attrition of the Germans. Robertson certainly appears to have been advocating these kinds of limitations and warned Haig on more than one occasion to keep the battle well in hand.

The first assaults on 31 July commenced at 3.50 AM on a murky morning. On the extreme left, things went very well. French First Army shot forward and took its limited objectives very quickly and cheaply. To its right stood Lord Cavan's XIV Corps, which had already infiltrated across the Yser Canal, having found that the artillery had done well in suppressing the remaining German batteries with gas. Cavan's leading divisions reached the western bank of the Steenbeek efficiently, but they could not advance to their final objective because most of the pillboxes on the eastern bank were still intact. The success was continued along this arc of the British front, for Maxse's XVIII Corps advanced across the Steenbeek and almost made contact with Gravenstafel. Next in line was Lieutenant-General H. E. Watts' XIX Corps, which made a significant advance to the St. Julien spur. None of these successes had come particularly cheaply, however. Although no unit suffered disastrous losses, the German defence had comprehensively shaken the cohesion of the attackers, leaving little prospect of immediate further successes.

The situation was a lot more mixed on the right. Attacking the Gheluvelt Plateau, Lieutenant-General Sir Claud Jacob's II Corps managed to take the German front line without too much difficulty but then found itself bogged down in the mires and smashed woods beyond. Contact was lost with the creeping barrage, allowing the German artillery to retaliate in concert with the surviving machine gunners in the pillboxes. In turn, Second Army was unable to provide much in the way of effective flank support. With such a shallow bite having been taken out of the Gheluvelt Plateau, the remaining Germans were left free to enfilade XIX Corps to the north. When these blows were followed up with counter-attacks, the British line sagged back, losing significant positions such as St. Julien in the process. Although the attack had by no means met all of Gough's initial demands, it was a great success, especially when compared with the first day on the Somme a year earlier. British and German losses were at least equal (27,000) and possibly much higher on the German side, and significant ground had been taken.[16] The major disappointment was the failure to make a real impression on the Gheluvelt Plateau. The pattern was now clear: a set-piece attack devised within an appreciable lead time could deliver results. Ignoring the fact that the battle had not achieved its ambitious initial targets, Haig ordered the maintenance of the offensive. Intelligence reports drawn from interrogation of German prisoners convinced him that the German Army was disintegrating. Whether this was an accurate assessment or not was made largely irrelevant by the weather. The BEF had the immense ill-fortune of suffering from freakishly wet weather, which made a mockery of every effort to maintain the offensive. The rain ruined artillery observation and

[16] *Ibid.*, 366.

made the movement of men and supplies intensely difficult, especially once the old front lines were crossed.

Gough's command now revealed the inconsistencies that hampered so much of British high command thinking. Sensibly, he did not allow himself to believe that further deep advances were likely and ordered modest operations designed to improve the situation along the front. This decision was all the wiser given the new German tactic of counter-attacking only once they were sure British assaults had reached their conclusion. This allowed the Germans to react when British soldiers were at their most exhausted physically and mentally. However, the timetable was completely out of kilter with the conditions. Setting 2 August as the day for renewing the assault, II Corps was ordered to capture its second objective of 31 July. A second phase of operations was scheduled for 4 August in which II, XIX and XVIII Corps would capture their third objectives of 31 July while XIV Corps took Langemarck. Davidson was perturbed once again and provided a critique of Gough's plan, urging the moving forward of fresh divisions and to wait for the weather to improve. Haig saw the wisdom in this suggestion and ordered Gough to delay.

The next assault commenced on 10 August in better weather, but there had not been enough time to ensure effective artillery fire, resulting in a very shallow advance in exchange for 2,200 casualties in the two attacking divisions. Rather than remain concentrated on the task of clearing the Gheluvelt Plateau, which was the key to the salient, Gough switched his attention back to the northern arc on 16 August. Despite further heavy rain, the French First Army and XIV Corps advanced well, taking Langemarck, while XVIII Corps took St. Julien, but the right and centre saw no advance of note at a cost of a further 15,000 casualties.[17] There was another brief pause before major operations recommenced on 22 August, when XVIII, XIX and II Corps assaulted to very little effect. Refusing to halt, Gough ordered more attacks as the rain fell in torrents before finally suspending operations on 27 August.

As in the later stages of the Somme and Arras battles, assaults in such unpromising circumstances tried the patience and morale of both the planning staff at corps and divisional levels and the men who did the actual fighting. Gough's abrasive methods caused much disquiet among the units under his command, which filtered back to Haig. At first, Haig felt able to ignore the growing frustrations due to the stream of good news from his intelligence chief. Charteris maintained his habit of feeding his superior the kind of news he wanted to hear. Backed with this see

[17] Prior and Wilson, *Passchendaele*, 104.

mingly credible information, Haig fiercely fought off Robertson's doubting letters. But Haig was also becoming aware of Gough's failure to bring order to the situation, particularly his inability to concentrate on the Gheluvelt Plateau. In this atmosphere, Haig shifted his army boundaries on 24 August, extending Plumer's front to the Gheluvelt sector. Gough did not appear to take the implied criticism to heart, for he kept the Fifth Army hammering away at the St. Julien spur in a series of narrow front attacks reminiscent of worse practice on the Somme until 10 September. Haig was made aware of the lack of progress in these assaults by Kiggell, which may have played a significant role in his decision to halt further Fifth Army operations.

The alteration in the army boundaries was formalised on 28 August, and Plumer at once sketched out his ideas for the capture of the Gheluvelt Plateau. As before Messines, he promised no deep advances and a slow operational tempo. This vision was accepted, revealing just how far expectations had dropped and just how far the desperation for evidence of solid achievement had risen. Plumer held other advantages. All now realised that the weather was vital and that nothing should be attempted until it improved markedly. Finally, Plumer had a vast array of artillery to support him. Fate was also much kinder to Plumer than it had been to Gough, for almost immediately the weather improved and remained dry for the next three weeks. Second Army went about preparations for a series of very short steps covered by immensely powerful barrages. This firepower advantage evened out the German strength in manpower and was used to great effect when the assault commenced on 20 September. A wall of fire 1,000 yards thick was poured onto the German positions, effectively cutting off the forward defences entirely. Behind this bombardment, I Anzac and X Corps of Second Army advanced alongside XVIII and V Corps of Fifth Army. The attacking troops penetrated to a depth of about 1,250 yards, but even this well-planned operation revealed the intense difficulty of achieving easy victories on the Western Front, for the British suffered some 21,000 casualties but inflicted at least as many in return. The number of British casualties has led some to re-evaluate the laurels heaped on Plumer for this victory, as the losses were higher than those experienced on 31 July for the capture of less ground despite the considerable advantage of more guns and good weather for observation. The disparity in judgements is probably because of the pre-battle expectations of both operations. Gough promised so much that anything short of breakthrough was always going to look bad: he took more ground than Plumer but not his final targets.[18] Plumer, however, had taken the Gheluvelt Plateau, which Gough singularly and miserably failed to do in August and never claimed once that he was going to do anything other than bite and hold a manageable piece of the German line.

Having gained this key victory, Haig once again let his imagination flare into life. He ordered the clearance of the Gheluvelt Plateau with assaults on Zonnebeke and Polygon Wood and completed by the capture of Poelcapelle with the operations commencing on 26 September. Although Plumer was prepared for a series of step-by-step advances, Haig's timetable still presented a great challenge to his planners and men. Artillery had to be moved forward and registered quickly and its prodigious stocks of ammunition brought up alongside. In a massive tribute to all involved, the assault on Polygon Wood duly commenced on 26 September. Launched after a single day's bombardment of pulverising power, four corps from Second and Fifth Armies advanced in a series of short steps. Stopping to consolidate well within the range of British guns and while the infantry was still fresh, the Germans were invited to counter-attack. They obliged with appalling results, suffering huge casualties in assaults easily repulsed by British defensive fire. Tactically, the Germans had been fooled by Plumer into making moves the exponents of scientific attrition longed for. On the minus side, the advances were so shallow as to have no effect on German artillery and so did nothing to further British counter-battery work.

These minor victories only served to befog the situation for the War Cabinet in London and contributed to a deadlock in civil–military relations, but in the strangest of ways. Robertson was caught in a web of contradictory thoughts and emotions. On the one hand, he was deeply suspicious of Lloyd George and believed in the solidarity of professional soldiers against ill-advised demands from civilian politicians. On the other, he was sympathetic to Lloyd George's doubts about the Flanders campaign and the wisdom of Britain remaining on the offensive alone rather than husbanding resources until the Americans arrived in force. Gripped by these opposing forces, Robertson slipped into paralysis, inviting the criticism of both Haig and Lloyd George. With the War Cabinet in London unable to assess clearly whether the situation in Flanders promised any great result, decision-making ground to halt. It was this malaise which allowed the offensive to continue.

In Flanders, the effect of Plumer's successes was to whet Haig's appetite for bolder moves. He took the victories as a sign that German resistance was crumbling and breakthrough operations were now in order.

[18] *Ibid.*, 113–31.

Setting the Passchendaele Ridge as the immediate objective with the intention of pushing tanks and cavalry on to Roulers, Haig asked Plumer and Gough to submit their requirements. Tactfully, but firmly, both Plumer and Gough insisted that step-by-step operations should remain the order of the day until the Passchendaele Ridge was taken. Haig firmly overruled this interpretation of the situation. He wanted Passchendaele taken quickly. Plumer reacted by planning the capture of the Broodseinde Ridge as a preliminary to the clearing of Passchendaele. Commencing at 6 AM on 4 October, the British caught the Germans forming up for an attack. Packed tightly in their forward positions, the British artillery minced them. Over 4,700 prisoners were taken as German morale seemed very badly dented.[19] Another shallow jump was made, securing a useful position for further advances, but the luck ran out as the weather broke again.

The rain poured incessantly between 4 and 9 October, liquefying the entire battlefield and making all movement an act of intense labour and stress. At the same time, it utterly destroyed observation of enemy positions, and the unstable ground made it hard to use the guns effectively. Fuelled by Charteris' insistence that the Germans had been bled down to the last of their reserves, Haig believed the situation demanded firm action regardless of the conditions. He set 8 October as the date for the next advance clearing the Passchendaele Ridge. The assault was to be across a broad front with French First Army attacking east of Houthulst Forest, Fifth Army contributing two corps and Second Army three. The crucial task of taking Passchendaele was given to II Anzac Corps in Second Army in an advance of nearly 1,000 yards.

In the appalling conditions, it proved utterly impossible to move forward all the artillery pieces and bring them into action. Supported by only a thin and ragged bombardment, the attacking infantry made little headway except on the flanks. Somewhat strangely given his usual cautious approach, Plumer agreed with Haig's desire to press forward. A fresh assault was made on 12 October. Once again, the troops advanced into a morass covered by a thin bombardment. The result was disastrous: 13,000 casualties were suffered for no appreciable gain.[20] Plumer reverted to type at this point and recommended the cessation of operations on Second Army front. Driven by Charteris' reading of the intelligence, Haig refused to admit that the door of opportunity had closed and at the very least wanted Passchendaele village as a preliminary to clearing the entire ridge.

[19] Harris, *Haig*, 375. [20] Prior and Wilson, *Passchendaele*, 169.

He did, however, concede the need for a pause before the next assault. Lieutenant-General Sir Arthur Currie brought his refreshed Canadian Corps up for the attack. The reluctance of Plumer and Gough to become involved in further operations allowed Currie to dominate planning and shape the operation to his own liking. His plan was for a series of short 500-yard steps covered by an immense array of artillery. On 26 October, the Canadians set out on their first step and were successful. However, on their flanks, the Australians hardly moved at all, while XVIII Corps' experiences to the left were so dreadful that even Gough was shaken. Gough and Plumer were now of the opinion that operations could continue only once winter frosts solidified the ground once again. Haig disagreed, stressing his satisfaction with the first phase of Currie's plans. Currie's corps returned to action on 30 October and successfully dragged itself forward another 500 yards, while XVIII Corps suffered once again. Haig finally put Fifth Army out of its misery by shutting down operations on its front. The Canadians now ground on alone, reaching Passchendaele village on 6 November, and extended their gains slightly on 10 November. Success did not come cheaply for the Canadian Corps: between 26 October and 10 November it suffered about 12,000 casualties.[21] An elite unit had been bled badly for very little return. Worse still, the victory was utterly meaningless, for the ridge was not cleared in its entirety and the position was untenable in the face of a determined German counter-stroke.

Justifying Third Ypres, especially its final stages, is a difficult task. Arguing that the taking of the Poelcappelle-Passchendaele/Broodseinde lower slope line meant that the Passchendaele Ridge had to be assaulted in order to avoid the problem of being caught on the low ground does provide an immediate and viable reason for the very last stages of the battle. However, this ignores the fact that a much more realistic assessment of likely progress should have been made long before this stage. As on the Somme in October 1916, the British higher command allowed the BEF to stick its neck on the chopping block, which, in turn, demanded the final agonising assault on the higher ground. Therefore, accepting the order to capture Passchendaele as evidence of the British high command's detached and lucid thinking is not convincing. Exonerating the British high command by placing the blame firmly on Lloyd George for allowing the offensive to continue

[21] Tim Cook, 'Storm Troops: Combat Effectiveness in the Canadian Corps in 1917', in Peter Dennis and Jeffrey Grey (eds.), *1917: Tactics, Training and Technology* (Canberra, Australia: Army History Unit, 2007), 43–61.

seems equally unconvincing. The case against Lloyd George rests on the fact that he lacked the moral courage to turn his convictions into a firm stand against Haig and the battle and was therefore at least equally culpable in its awful conclusion. However, this interpretation invests Lloyd George with a great deal more individual power and influence than he actually held. Working as *primus inter pares* with some extremely influential and experienced statesmen, many of them Unionist rather than Liberal, did not give him enormous leverage, which turned decision-making into a slow and tortuous process.

On the plus side, given the fact that the British were attacking frontally against extremely deep defences, the tactical performance on the ground was excellent. But this hints at one of the tragedies of Passchendaele: as with Arras, battle-hardened veterans were wasted, and the morale of the survivors was damaged. Judged by any of the terms under which the battle was launched, it is possible only to reach bleak conclusions. The German Army was clearly not bled to the point of no return, large amounts of strategically useful, as opposed to locally valuable, ground was not won and indeed ended with the British clinging to a useless asset. The value of Passchendaele as a launch pad for further offensives was also a rather hollow argument for two reasons. Firstly, it could only be realised if the morass to its rear was made thoroughly traversable. This was a major operation requiring vast amounts of scarce pioneer labour. Secondly, the width of front of the Passchendaele Ridge would require considerable extension in order to make it a suitable springboard. In stressing the undoubted tactical brilliance revealed in the battle, some historians have pushed this interpretation to argue that the BEF imposed tactical bankruptcy on the Germans, forcing them to chop and change between approaches continually without ever finding a successful response to the British. However, accepting the argument that the battle placed a strain on the Germans which put them into a highly reactive mode is not the same as agreeing that they were completely defeated or that German military intellect was utterly checkmated by the experience. Indeed, the first experiments in German infiltration tactics can be identified in some of the later counter-attack operations. Citing relief of pressure on the hard-pressed French is also a little unconvincing, for this was largely a post facto justification which did not play an important role at the time. In terms of positives, the operational and tactical brilliance of the BEF was exhibited. The officers and men of the BEF revealed clearly that when given reasonable chances of success, they had the ability to defeat the Germans comprehensively. It can also be seen as a strange sort of victory and improvement on the Somme insofar as British casualties were lower at 275,000, while German losses were in the region of 200,000.[22]

Third Ypres put a great strain on Haig's reputation in London, even among those who had confidence in him. Considerable doubts were expressed about the quality of Charteris and the differences between his optimistic interpretations and the generally sober ones provided by his opposite number at the War Office, Macdonogh, were noted. With Britain experiencing a wave of war weariness and gloom, Haig found his ability to shape strategy much weakened, which was shown in the transfer of British units to the Italian front. As part of the strategy to curb the power of Haig and Robertson, Lloyd George also gave enthusiastic support to the newly established Supreme War Council (November 1917) in Paris. Haig needed a success to redeem his reputation. Fortunately for him, at precisely the moment when Passchendaele was staggering towards its painful end and doubts about Haig's competence were being raised more insistently, planning was taking place for a fresh operation on Third Army front. The origins of the battle of Cambrai have been disputed and become enmeshed in the glamour and mystique of the tank. The Tank Corps staff certainly suggested a plan for a large-scale tank raid on ground more suitable for their machines than that of the Ypres salient, but it is unclear whether this thinking had any direct impact on the final design used at Cambrai.[23]

In fact, plans for an attack in the Cambrai sector originated with schemes devised by Fourth Army in April 1917. These were inherited by General Sir Julian Byng, who replaced Allenby as Third Army commander in June 1917. At first Byng envisaged extremely limited operations as a way of ensuring that the corps and divisions under his command did not atrophy and maintained a cutting edge. The pace and seriousness of planning increased significantly in the autumn of 1917 when Brigadier-General H. H. Tudor, Commander of Artillery in 9th Division, put forward ideas for a new type of bombardment programme. Drawing on

22 Prior and Wilson, *Passchendaele*, 195. Virtually every aspect of the Third Battle of Ypres has been subjected to vigorous debate. For a good overview on the quality of British command, see Ian Beckett, 'The Plans and the Conduct of the Battle', in Liddle (ed.), *Passchendaele in Perspective*, 102–16. For generally positive assessments of British performance, see John Lee, 'The British Divisions at Third Ypres', in Liddle (ed.), *Passchendaele in Perspective*, 215–26; Gary Sheffield, 'Haig and the British Expeditionary Force in 1917', in Dennis and Grey (eds.), *1917*, 4–22. For less optimistic views, see Prior and Wilson's condemnation of politico-military muddle in *Passchendaele*, 194–200; Robert T. Foley, 'The Other Side of the Wire: The German Army in 1917', in Dennis and Grey (eds.), *1917*, 155–78; Harris, *Haig*, 381–2.

23 For the strategic background to the battle of Cambrai and its planning phases, see Harris, *Haig*, 383–98; Bryn Hammond, *Cambrai, 1917: The Myth of the First Great Tank Battle* (London: Weidenfeld & Nicolson, 2008), 51–80.

experience and refining it, Tudor argued for no preliminary bombardment and an infantry attack covered by an intensive barrage and extensive counter-battery fire. In a further refinement, he advocated the registration of guns away from the front line before covert movement forward to firing positions. Such a complex fire plan was only possible because of the enormous advances made in mapping and the detection of German artillery through flash spotting and sound ranging. The technical brilliance of the BEF and its ability to instigate and integrate new technologies and techniques are illustrated most clearly in Tudor's appreciation. For the scheme to work, wire cutting had to be effective, especially on the dense belts which protected the Hindenburg Line. A hurricane bombardment was unlikely to achieve this no matter how well delivered, which made tanks a crucial component. Assisted by tanks and an intensive, completely unexpected bombardment, the infantry would fight forward and swamp the German defences. Originally, Tudor saw this as IV Corps' operation alone designed to seize and hold a small section of the St. Quentin Canal near Cambrai.

Byng took up the idea and discussed it with Brigadier-General Hugh Elles of the Tank Corps. Elles was enthusiastic. The ground was firm and as yet largely undisturbed by heavy shell fire, which made it perfect terrain for the tanks. Backed up by intelligence reports assuring a mere two German divisions opposite, Byng saw the potential of overwhelming the enemy and sending in cavalry after capturing bridges on the canal. Confident in his plan, Byng sent it to GHQ and was encouraged to work it up further. On 13 October, Haig gave definite approval to the scheme and promised the infantry reinforcements requested by Byng. Assured of the assets required, Byng expanded his plan to break through the enemy's front in a surprise attack, taking Cambrai, Bourlon Wood and the crossings of the River Sensée, the release of the cavalry and an advance north-east. The boldness of this concept, which was probably a selling point to Haig, was a remarkable statement from a man who had built his reputation on meticulously planned limited operations.

Haig then intervened to alter certain elements of the plan. He did not believe that the cavalry should become involved in the capture of Cambrai and advocated its use as a screening force around the town cutting it off from immediate support. He also insisted that Bourlon Wood, sitting on high ground overlooking Cambrai, should be taken on the first day. In taking this decision, Haig switched the main focus of attention away from Cambrai itself to the ridge to its north-west. Haig seems to have hoped that the capture of the Bourlon Ridge would open the way to the north and the rolling up of the German line in the direction of the Arras front. Although this aspect of his thinking can be criticised given the strength of the force available to Byng, the capture of Bourlon Wood and the ridge was not in itself a wasted exercise as its dominant position allowed its masters great influence over the surrounding area. Realising that gaining permission for another assault on the Western Front from Lloyd George might prove difficult, Haig justified it by stating its ability to drain German resources possibly allocated for offensive action against the French. This reasoning contradicted his earlier assertions that German manpower was reaching a crisis point through his actions at Third Ypres. However, it seems to have worked and revealed the equal lack of cohesive oversight exerted by Lloyd George and the War Cabinet.

The degree of preparation for Cambrai was extremely impressive. Men rehearsed with the tanks in carefully planned training schemes; tanks were fitted with fascines to provide trench crossing points; and most impressive of all, men, munitions and weapons were kept secret from the enemy through highly complex camouflaging schemes and brought up to the front line using carefully prepared routes according to an extraordinarily comprehensive timetable. Thick fog also helped the British conceal their intentions from the Germans, but in this instance it was not quite as disruptive to the RFC as it might have been due to the fact that there was no preliminary artillery activity to witness. All bombardment planning was carried out on the basis of maps already produced and shaped by previous aerial observation.

The offensive commenced at 6.20 AM on 20 November. Five divisions from the IV and III Corps were detailed to make the assault across a six-and-a-half-mile front, and just over a thousand artillery pieces were assembled to provide the bombardment. Avoiding the mistakes of 15 September 1916, the artillery plan abandoned tank lanes firing a relatively straight-forward lifting bombardment well in advance of the infantry. Abandoning the creeping barrage in this way was a well-reasoned decision. Firstly, the sheer surprise of the bombardment falling with great intensity was regarded as enough to disorient the Germans. Secondly, the tanks were capable of providing the immediate infantry protection given the favourable nature of the ground. The opening bombardment silenced the German batteries almost completely, and the great admixture of smoke shells helped to keep many German defenders disoriented. Across the front, advances were impressive. The most significant achievement of the day was 62nd Division's leap of four miles from its starting position. To its right, the 51st Division started very well but could not clear the Hindenburg support system easily, with strong resistance met at Flesquières, where German gunners specially trained in anti-tank fire checked the advance. The inherent communication problems of the war now intervened again. All could see that outflanking the village was the best option, but arranging it efficiently while in action proved impossible.

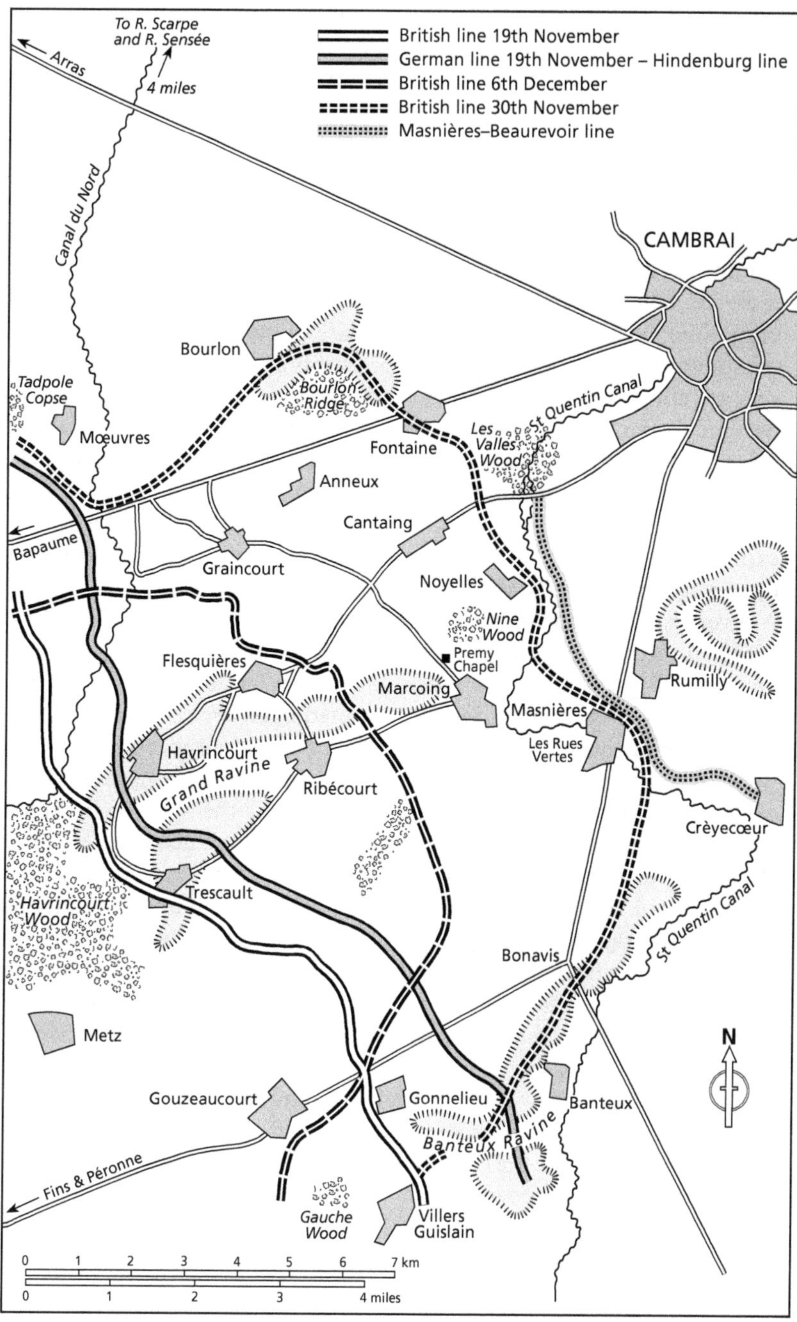

Map 11 Battle of Cambrai, 20 November–7 December 1917

On III Corps' front, 6th Division took Marcoing and combined well with the 20th Division, which then advanced on Masnières. To their south, 12th Division also moved forward well, securing the right flank at Lateau Wood. Having broken deep into the German defences, it was then found that penetrating the Beaurevoir line was generally beyond their capabilities. Despite this check, it was clear that the German defensive system had been given a severe jolt, and there were some opportunities for cavalry exploitation. By 1917, the cavalry was in a mixed condition. Much thought had been given to the issue of making it a more effective player in static warfare by some very sharp minds. At the same time, lack of obvious and immediate utility had led to drains on its manpower and horses. But perhaps the biggest problem was that of speedy communications. No matter how sophisticated the cavalry became in reaching the front line and traversing the old no man's land prior to deployment, it meant nothing if the cavalry was not given clear instructions delivered rapidly. Where cavalry did get into action on 20 November, results were mixed. Although it was the only real weapon of exploitation available in 1917, cavalry was not fully in syncopation with the actual conditions of the Western Front.

A very good day's work was carried out by Third Army on 20 November, especially given the fact that it was in many ways a large-scale experiment. Over 4,000 prisoners were taken and around a hundred guns, and a formidable German defensive position had been breached, even though not broached entirely and split open.[24] This was the rub. At no point was there a real opportunity for either deepening or widening the advance aside from local improvements. With little in the way of immediate reinforcement, Byng could not expect to make much headway, especially given the usually rapid reaction from German reserve units. Having been devised as a grand smash and grab raid, it is an immense pity that Haig and Byng did not decide to rest on what they had grabbed. The result of the decision to maintain the offensive was a series of increasingly desultory British attacks delivered over the next few days. Some local gains were made, but against strengthening and well-co-ordinated German resistance. Given that the original planning for the battle had stressed a major review after forty-eight hours to consider the wisdom of further operations, it is unclear why this useful proviso was ignored. Haig continued to press for the capture of Bourlon Wood and the ridge despite declining British manpower.

Much of the continued hammering at the German defences was once again built on the logic that German resources were reaching crisis point.

[24] Harris, *Haig*, 400.

This vision had proved incorrect throughout 1917, and with the situation in the east looking increasingly favourable, the Germans were reversing the manpower situation through transfers to the west. On 30 November, the Germans announced that they were as yet a far from beaten force by launching a major counter-attack at Cambrai. Using specialist storm-troops, low-flying aircraft and their own variant on surprise artillery bombardments, the Germans stormed forward. After achieving great initial successes, the Germans were reminded of the lesson they had inflicted on attacking infantry: the advantages of the defences. British resistance stiffened, and the German advance was checked. It was not achieved lightly, however. Third Army suffered 7,000 casualties; the vast majority of them were prisoners, showing the speed with which the Germans had overrun British positions, and 150 guns.[25] That such a blow could fall on Third Army reflected very poorly on the state of intelligence gathering and analysis. The battle wore on for a few more days and finally guttered out in mid-December.

Cambrai can perhaps be best described as a score draw. In terms of ground and guns gained and lost and casualties inflicted, the balance sheets are almost identical. The battle also revealed valuable lessons regarding the use of artillery, tanks and infantry working in close harmony and served as a reminder on the difficulties of getting cavalry into action, although it did nothing to prove conclusively its days were over. More worryingly, it revealed once again a high command structure unable to judge finely the position on the ground. Communication difficulties can be used as a partial explanation, but they cannot be made the sole reason. Having experienced so many similar scenarios, Haig should have been aware of the pitfalls of maintaining an offensive, especially one that was always designed as a limited operation carried out by a general new to command at the army level.

Thus, 1917 was a highly active and often traumatic year for the BEF. Three great battles were fought which made intensive demands on all the BEF's component parts. Among the positive elements was the continuing growth in know-how and experience at all levels. Due to the massive expansion of the BEF in 1915 and 1916, many of the commanders at both higher and middle-ranking levels as well as their staffs had had very little experience of conducting operations on such a large scale. Detecting their strengths and weaknesses did not become clear until 1917, when they had had sufficient opportunity to prove themselves. Haig himself believed that it was not until 1917 that the shuffling of the

[25] Hammond, *Cambrai*, 340–1, 429.

command personnel really settled down into an effective team. However, the weeding out of the unfit and incompetent also seemed to involve deeming men failures on highly controversial grounds. Many commanders were removed for their supposed lack of drive and fighting spirit which was judged on dubious criteria and minimal contextual information such as failure to take particular enemy positions. These men were often dismissed very curtly and, in turn, created a strained atmosphere in which brigadier-generals and divisional commanders forced their units into action in highly unfavourable circumstances.

As has been seen, when given ample preparation time, the BEF's arms, especially its infantry, air force and artillery, could combine to spectacular effect. The flip side of the successes achieved was that they often caused the higher command to lose sight of the original pre-requisites for such victories. All too often hastily prepared assaults supposedly in pursuit of a rapidly deteriorating enemy met disaster, leading to heavy casualties among the hugely valuable assets of highly trained and experienced troops. Those troops trained according to the latest advice contained in the imaginative and intelligent manuals continued to do so almost entirely according to the standards and interests of their battalion commanding officers. Fortunately, it seems from battlefield performance that training quality was generally improving due to the increasing experience of the BEF, but there was still no agency dedicated to ensuring common minimum standards. This omission had the potential to become far more problematic given the need to fill holes in units with sketchily trained conscripts drawn from the United Kingdom. On a wider level, it was the issue of fresh manpower that was becoming all the more important by the end of the year given the differing strategic visions of Lloyd George, Haig and Robertson. The impasse reached over the most effective allocation and distribution of manpower came at a critical moment, for it coincided with a significant shift in German fortunes. By Christmas 1917, the Germans were on the verge of victory on the Eastern Front, which provided the opportunity to switch manpower to France and Belgium. With the United States still far from transforming its potential into actual military power at the front and Anglo-French forces recovering from severe losses, the strategic situation in the west was critical. Given this threat, it was absolutely vital that the BEF maintained internal cohesion and had a clear understanding of its role in the new year. Unfortunately for the BEF, there was little sign of such clarity emerging after the upheavals and dramas of 1917.

10 The Western Front, 1918

Battered by the Third Battle of Ypres and shocked by the reversal at Cambrai, the British Expeditionary Force (BEF) and its commander were under considerable strain by the dawn of 1918. The BEF had played an increasingly large role in the war since the Somme battle of 1916 and had suffered great losses in terms of men and materiel, but nowhere in France or Flanders was there a clear and consistent sign that its sacrifices had weakened the Germans beyond recovery. This lack of evidence created the conditions for the wholesale re-examination of British strategy so desired by Lloyd George and others sceptical that the Western Front offered the potential for decisive victory. Desperate to impose civilian and, more particularly, his own authority over the shape of British strategy, Lloyd George used the lack of success in the battles of Ypres and Cambrai against Haig and Robertson. For Lloyd George, the moment had come to curb the influence of the British Army's two most important generals in order to ensure a comprehensive reappraisal of Britain's position and the state of the war. Unfortunately for the BEF, Lloyd George's review came at a moment when the significance of the Western Front was greater than ever. With Ludendorff determined to wage a final, decisive campaign in the west, the men of the BEF required clarity of thought from their political and military masters. Unused to the concept of the strategic defensive, the BEF needed careful preparation, mental and physical, for the role. It could not afford the luxury of a protracted debate over its mission in France and Flanders.[1]

Although Haig was aware of Lloyd George's increasing disquiet over the lack of progress in the Third Ypres campaign, it was the failure of Cambrai that precipitated the crisis in the relationship between Lloyd George and the Haig-Robertson partnership. Lloyd George was particularly angry at the success of the German counter-attack at Cambrai, for it

[1] For British perceptions of the strategic background, see French, *Strategy of the Lloyd George Coalition*, 171–92; David Stevenson, *With Our Backs to the Wall: Victory and Defeat in 1918* (London: Allen Lane, 2011), 492–500; Woodward, *Lloyd George and the Generals*, 190–281.

had been claimed that the Germans had no surplus manpower after being severely stretched at Passchendaele. It was compounded by the fact that intelligence reports suggested that the Germans had not yet transferred much in the way of manpower from the Eastern Front. With British civil–military relations now very much strained, Lloyd George hoped to use the Cambrai debacle to oust both Robertson and Haig while at the same time outflanking them by using the new Supreme War Council established at Versailles as an alternative focus for strategic discussion, advice and planning. The Secretary of State for War, Lord Derby, was not willing to play a role in such a move, but he was prepared to remove some of Haig's General Headquarters (GHQ) staff. As Lloyd George realised that he was unable easily to topple Haig, the option of purging his closest associates at GHQ seemed the best way of curbing his power. Indeed, while Lloyd George canvassed names of potential successors to Haig in January 1918, the South African statesman sitting in the War Cabinet, Jan Smuts, and its secretary, Maurice Hankey, could only suggest Lieutenant-General Claud Jacob of II Corps, although Plumer and Rawlinson were also mentioned.[2]

It was against this background that Byng completed his preliminary report on the Cambrai reverse. He stated that Third Army HQ had been expecting a German counter-attack and put the blame for failure onto his front-line soldiers: 'I attribute the reason for the local success on the part of the enemy to one cause and one alone, namely – lack of training on the part of junior officers and NCOs and men.'[3] Despite Byng's reluctance to accept that any of the higher commanders were to blame, over the next three months all three corps commanders involved were removed from their posts (Snow, Woollcombe and Pulteney). For all his many strengths as a commander, Byng's actions rather tarnish his reputation, as it seems unfair and inaccurate to blame the men under his authority for failures he and his own staff could have avoided through more effective action.[4]

But it can be argued that the real problem was at GHQ. Once again, Haig's intelligence chief, Charteris, had totally misunderstood the strength and intentions of the Germans on this section of the front and therefore provided no kind of advance warning. He deliberately suppressed evidence of the arrival of a German division before the battle,

[2] Tim Travers, *How the War Was Won: Command and Technology in the British Army on the Western Front, 1917–18* (London: Routledge, 1992), 34–5; Tim Travers, 'The Evolution of British Strategy and Tactics on the Western Front in 1918: GHQ, Manpower and Technology', *Journal of Military History* 54 (1990), 173–200.

[3] Harris, *Haig*, 414.

[4] Nikolas Gardner, 'Julian Byng', in Beckett and Corvi (eds.), *Haig's Generals*, 54–74, esp. 67–72.

apparently so as not to deter Haig from his intention to attack. This failure of interpretation and effective communication was a hallmark of Charteris' relationship with Haig. Rumours of this unbalanced and inefficient collaboration had spread widely, and it made Charteris vulnerable to a Prime Minister increasingly irate at the perceived weaknesses of GHQ.[5] Charteris was duly removed and replaced by Sir Herbert Lawrence, formerly the commander of 66th (East Lancashire) Division. A second high-profile casualty was the Quartermaster-General, Sir Ronald Maxwell, who had long since lost the confidence of those familiar with the BEF's earlier logistics problems, if not that of Haig. Maxwell's poor health was used as an excuse to remove him, and Lieutenant-Colonel Sir Travers Clarke replaced him.[6] Other important new appointments were the able Brigadier-General John Dill as Director of Military Operations and Major-General Guy Dawnay as Head of the Staff Duties Section.

The final adjustment was the replacement of Lancelot Kiggell, Haig's Chief of Staff. Somewhat ironically, Kiggell fell just at the moment when he had become a convert to the methodical, step-by-step battle under the guidance of his colleague, 'Tavish' Davidson, Dill's predecessor as Director of Military Operations at GHQ. This had caused him to doubt Gough's approach at Third Ypres and make efforts to contain the visions of the Fifth Army commander. However, he had never been particularly robust in his dealings with Haig and by December 1917 was clearly in a state of poor health. Derby warned Haig about Kiggell's condition, but he seemed reluctant to take this hint. When Haig finally relented, he indicated that he would like to promote Butler, Kiggell's deputy, but Derby refused to accept this idea doubtless because Butler was regarded as an equally malleable replacement. The need to replace Kiggell then caused further disruption at GHQ, for the newly appointed Lawrence was regarded as the best man for the job. He therefore left his position as Intelligence Chief to be replaced by Brigadier-General Edgar Cox, who was Deputy Head of Intelligence at the War Office. The extremely capable Cox was to suffer enormous strain during the German spring offensives and drowned while swimming alone off Berck Plage on 26 August 1918. He was replaced in mid-September by Sidney Clive.[7]

Whether this new staff team was the powerhouse that stabilised the BEF in the crisis moments of the German spring offensive and brought it to victory during the Hundred Days can be debated, but it certainly

[5] Despite the uneven relationship between Haig and Charteris, this should not be taken as the sole determinant of British intelligence work, as Jim Beach's research has shown.

[6] Brown, *British Logistics*, 180–1. [7] Beach, *Haig's Intelligence*, 44–61.

fulfilled Lloyd George's desire to bring greater rigour to Haig's GHQ relationships. This was particularly true in the case of Sir Herbert Lawrence. Son of a Viceroy of India and a former cavalryman, Lawrence had resigned from the army in 1903 over his lack of promotion and subsequently became a highly successful businessman. He re-joined the army in 1914 and gained a good reputation as a commander before proceeding to GHQ. These attributes gave him the self-confidence to engage with Haig more robustly than his predecessor.[8]

Lloyd George did not stop at this rearrangement of GHQ. Continuing the tactic of focusing on close collaborators, he turned his attention to Robertson. Believing that Robertson deliberately undermined comprehensive discussion of British strategy, Lloyd George worked hard to invest more executive power in the Supreme War Council. He was particularly keen to create an entente General Reserve under the direction of General Foch. Seeing this as a move designed deliberately to undermine the post of Chief of the Imperial General Staff (GIGS), Robertson resigned and was replaced by Sir Henry Wilson. This turned out to be a pyrrhic victory for Lloyd George for two reasons. Firstly, the Haig-Robertson relationship was nowhere near as strong and mutually supportive as Lloyd George suspected. This was shown when Haig proved remarkably compliant over the General Reserve concept, thus demonstrating that Lloyd George had by no means prized apart a significant alliance. Worse still for Lloyd George, Wilson was no more biddable a Chief of the Imperial General Staff than Robertson and quickly revealed that his supposed differences with Robertson were ones of detail and emphasis rather than core principles.

It was against this backdrop of mutual suspicion and misunderstanding that the War Cabinet attempted to liaise with the army over the vital issue of manpower. Unfortunately for Haig and the BEF, given the magnitude of the threat hanging over them, the suspicion Haig had created in London over his handling of the Passchendaele and Cambrai campaigns meant that Lloyd George had little sympathy for GHQ's manpower demands. Desperate to limit Haig's ambitions, to exploit the alleged advantages offered by other fronts and to maintain the British war effort on the home front, the distribution of manpower was a major problem for Lloyd George. Wanting a more 'scientific' management of Britain's human resources, Lloyd George established a Manpower Committee to determine priorities in the winter of 1917. The conclusions reached were not particularly generous to the army, and the situation was exacerbated by the decision to withhold 120,000 men in Britain as a 'general reserve'.

[8] Travers, *Killing Ground*, 85–97, 191–18; Todman, 'Grand Lamasery', 39–70; Robbins, *British Generalship*, 119–20, 129, 135–6.

Criticism can certainly be levelled at Lloyd George for his failure to appreciate German offensive capabilities, but the situation facing him was far from clear. Haig had been somewhat ambiguous in his assessments of actual German potential and intentions, which was partly the result of underestimations of troop transfers from the east. This seeming lack of concern was reflected in the decision to allow leave arrangements to continue unhindered, which meant that 88,000 men were in Britain when the German offensive commenced in March.[9] The confusion over manpower was therefore based on miscalculations, misunderstanding and suspicion on the part of both the government and GHQ. But there can be little doubt that the BEF was desperate for reinforcements, having suffered such high losses in 1917. On 1 January 1918, the BEF was 70,000 men short of establishment, but on that date there were 38,225 officers and 607,403 men trained and ready for service in Britain.[10]

Lloyd George was unwilling to release these men, convinced as he was that they would be assigned to futile offensive operations. Lloyd George's reluctance to hand over men was not merely a question of public confidence in his ministry if further bloody, and ultimately fruitless, offensives followed but also that of the British war economy. Maintaining the war effort required a very delicate balancing act of manpower resources, which was becoming increasingly problematic given the army's insatiable appetite for men. In the event, over the course of the crucial period between 21 March and 31 August 1918, 544,000 men were despatched to the front from Britain.[11]

Stabilising the BEF's manpower situation was all the more pressing given the indicators of declining morale such as increased drunkenness, desertion and other forms of ill discipline. In order to convince Lloyd George of the scale of the manpower problem, the War Office produced a plethora of statistics. Unfortunately for the BEF, Lloyd George was highly dubious of all War Office calculations and forecasts by this stage, believing that they had been manipulated deliberately to suit Robertson. A further complication was the debate on German strength and intentions. Knowledge of the transfer of German divisions was widespread, and Haig discussed it with the War Cabinet on 7 January. It was noted that thirty-two divisions could be transferred at the probable rate of ten per month, making March a potentially dangerous time. The discussion then moved on to consider the likelihood of a German assault and whether the British or French Armies would be the main targets. Revealing a degree of insouciance about German

[9] Stevenson, *With Our Backs*, 52, 260.
[10] Martin Middlebrook, *The Kaiser's Battle. 21 March 1918: The First Day of the German Spring Offensive* (London: Allen Lane, 1978), 25.
[11] Stevenson, *With Our Backs*, 66.

intentions, Haig was guarded about supporting the French should they be attacked and expressed a desire to attack in Flanders. Robertson was most alarmed by Haig's seeming lack of concern at the possibility of a major German offensive and persuaded him to add his signature to an appraisal written up after the meeting highlighting just such a scenario. This did little to create a positive impression on Lloyd George, who viewed this sudden about-face as typical of Haig's woolly minded lack of focus. Haig then committed a further faux pas at a lunch with Lloyd George and Derby on 9 January, at which he expressed his confidence that Germany was down to its very last manpower reserves and that risking these scarce resources in a full assault would be a desperate gamble. He added that if the Germans did pursue an all-out offensive, the blow would most likely fall on the French. This again implied that he was fairly sanguine in his appreciation of German intentions, and this certainly did not seem like a desperate call for men.

Somewhat ironically, in this instance, Lloyd George was happy to accept GHQ's scepticism on the possibility of a major German assault, for it allowed him to justify a lower priority for the Western Front. Understanding Lloyd George's precise thinking is difficult given the stream of information coming his way, but he probably wanted to play a waiting game during 1918, in which American power was firmly established in France as the vital pre-requisite for offensive action in 1919 or even 1920. But, by focusing so intently on the longer game, Lloyd George and the War Cabinet omitted to concentrate sufficiently on the immediate term. This misreading nearly caused complete disaster when the German spring offensives commenced.

With the manpower issue at an impasse, the War Office was forced into desperate expedience. GHQ was ordered into a radical restructuring of the BEF. Brigades were reduced by one battalion each, and the number of divisions contracted from sixty-two British and Dominion in the autumn of 1917 to fifty-eight by mid-January 1918; the cavalry divisions were also reduced from five to three. The actual figures vary from source to source, but it would appear that 134 British infantry battalions were lost through disbandment, amalgamation or conversion, reducing the strength of the army by about 70,000 by January 1918 compared with its position a year earlier.[12] Rearrangement was, of course, a time-consuming and disruptive process compounded by the fact that the government forced Haig to extend the British line in response to French requests. Although Haig was

[12] Harris, *Haig*, 433; Simon Justice, 'Vanishing Battalions: The Nature, Impact and Implications of British Infantry Reorganisation Prior to the German Spring Offensives of 1918', in Locicero, Mahoney and Mitchell (eds.), *A Military Transformed*, 157–73.

aware of these long-standing and repeated demands, he had used the Third Ypres campaign, Cambrai and the assignment of troops to Italy as diversions to avoid taking on the responsibility. Haig was extremely concerned at this extension southwards to the region of Ailette-Soissons-Laon Road, believing that it stretched his resources by increasing the British front by 30 per cent from ninety-five to 123 miles. Holding an extended front with greatly reduced numbers was a severe strain made more intense by the need for extensive work on new defences. Training almost ground to a halt as men spent long, hard hours digging fresh trenches, laying wire and filling sandbags in bitterly cold weather. Unsurprisingly, this contributed to the dip in morale that was so carefully monitored by the War Cabinet.

Although the reorganised divisions concentrated fire power within the contracted brigade structures, this probably meant little to the men working hard on the new defences. Noting the defensive tactics of the Germans, the BEF adopted a similar system based on three interlocking zones: forward, battle and rear. The forward zone was a trip-wire of dispersed but mutually supporting posts designed to harass the enemy, alert other units and gradually crumple backwards into the 'battle zone'. The battle zone was then to be the anvil on which attackers were hammered, for it was to be at least 2,000 to 3,000 yards deep on specially selected heavily wired ground. The defenders in the battle zone were to be supported by corps- and army-level counter-attacks to ensure local supremacy and the decisive halting of an assault. The rear zone, four to eight miles further back, was a final backstop line similar in structure to the forward zone.[13] According to the orders issued in XVIII Corps, divisions were to be responsible for preparing the forward zone, corps the battle zone and armies the rear zone.[14]

This highly sensible and intelligent response was, unfortunately, fraught with flaws.[15] The over-arching concept behind the system was never fully understood by the BEF as a whole, once again revealing a disturbing inability to disseminate information clearly and thoroughly. Thus, although the system demanded that the forward zone be lightly held given its relative lack of importance, some divisions packed it with the majority of their men, leaving little for the main battle. In a continuation of the confusion of command, even as prescriptive a commander as Hubert Gough, when confronted by differences in the distribution of their formations between Maxse of XVIII Corps and Butler of III Corps,

[13] For British preparations, see Middlebrook, *Kaiser's Battle*, 65–105.
[14] Simpson, *Directing Operations*, 137. [15] Travers, *How the War Was Won*, 50–70.

simply chose to instruct them to settle it among themselves.[16] A further block to widespread and uniform understanding of the concept was the difficulty of getting the BEF to reverse its tactical thinking in such a short space of time. Having spent almost the entire war considering ways of attacking positions, fewer front-line officers and men could immerse themselves in the mentality of the defence. This was in stark contrast to the Germans, who had been perfecting defensive systems for the best part of three years. There is no doubt that the dissemination of lessons learned was far superior in 1917–18 than in previous years, and the compilation of doctrinal training manuals was moving from a committee-based approach to a dedicated editorial team within GHQ's Training Branch. SS210, *The Division in Defence*, however, was still not completed in March 1918 and only appeared in May, by which time it was too late, although there is some evidence that its conclusions were at least considered valuable.[17] In any case, there remained the long-term problem of commanders choosing if and when they took notice of such official publications.

The British were therefore not psychologically prepared for the form of defence they had chosen. Used to the idea of fighting in line, the concept of separated posts and redoubts was alien. Many men expressed dislike of the 'bird cages' implied by a non-linear defence based on strong points.[18] In addition, many raw recruits felt extremely isolated by this strategy once the fighting began, and they sometimes proved hard to hold together. Platoon commanders, usually separated from their company and battalion commanders, carried a tremendous burden of responsibility. Often misunderstanding the nature of the defensive scheme, they decided to stay put and fight it out to the death or surrender when the situation was hopeless rather than execute a methodical, fighting withdrawal. As Edmonds noted in the official history: 'No warning seems to have been given to any brigade or battalion commanders, and therefore none to the lower ranks, that in certain circumstances there might be an ordered retreat.'[19] There was also a misunderstanding as to the likely nature of German offensive tactics. Assuming that they would mirror those used by the Germans in the Cambrai counter-attack and at Caporetto, it was believed that simply reproducing German defensive

[16] Ian F. W. Beckett, 'Hubert Gough, Neill Malcolm and Command on the Western Front', in Bond (ed.), *Look to Your Front*, 1–12.

[17] Jim Beach, 'Issued by the General Staff: Doctrine Writing at British GHQ, 1917–18', *War in History* 19 (2012), 464–91.

[18] Stevenson, *With Our Backs*, 52.

[19] Sir James Edmonds, *Military Operations France and Belgium, 1918*, Vol. I (London: Macmillan, 1935), 258.

tactics as experienced at Third Ypres would be sufficient to stop German progress. Haig, indeed, was concerned primarily that the Germans would *not* attack.[20]

The final problem was that faced by Fifth Army, which had extended its front in accordance with the Supreme War Council's instructions. Dangerously overstretched, it had to complete new positions at immense speed due to a lack of preparations by the French. All these difficulties meant that by March 1918, the defensive preparations were patchy, particularly the rear zone, which often existed only on army maps with barely a trace on the ground. Third Army was somewhat better placed in terms of the completion of defences. Moreover, while Byng was holding twenty-eight miles with fourteen infantry divisions, Gough was holding forty-two miles with just twelve divisions.[21]

GHQ was well aware that Fifth Army faced a particular problem, and concerns intensified when intelligence reports identified the presence of General Oskar von Hutier's Eighteenth Army in the area. The British knew that Hutier was the mastermind behind the storming of Riga, and his sudden appearance in the west combined with other evidence of preparations put Fifth Army HQ and GHQ on the alert. Gough liaised with Davidson at GHQ, and both men identified the major problem of the devastated Somme battlefield, which lay to Fifth Army's immediate rear. It acted as a massive block on the easy distribution of men and materials and would hinder all movement in a battle. As a result of these discussions, both men agreed that Fifth Army might have to make a substantial retreat if put under severe pressure. However, the sense of this decision-making was somewhat undermined by GHQ's insistence on holding Peronne, which required yet more extensive work on defences. Gough was now swamped with orders to construct elaborate defensive positions over an extensive area with a small labour pool. The fact that no one at GHQ seemed capable of realising this does not reflect well on its decision-making processes.

Despite Gough's serious doubts about the task in front of him, he clearly did not raise them directly with Haig when they met for dinner on 15 March. Understanding Gough's motivations for remaining silent is difficult but may have been connected to an increasing sense of insecurity. His aptitude for command had been questioned widely in London during Third Ypres, and there had been calls for his removal. An additional reason for silence may also have come from Gough's understanding of

[20] Simpson, *Directing Operations*, 132–4; Tim Travers, 'A Particular Style of Command: Haig and GHQ, 1916–18', *Journal of Strategic Studies* 10 (1987), 363–76, at 372.

[21] Harris, *Haig*, 436–7.

Haig's overall appreciation of the situation, for he seems to have gained the impression that the real focus of the BEF was the Channel ports, so a defeat at the extreme south of the British line would not necessarily be catastrophic. Haig's dispositions certainly support this interpretation. Of his four armies on the Western Front, Fifth Army had by far the longest front to cover and was the hardest to support with reserve divisions (GHQ had allocated two to each army). Given that the intelligence assessments available to Haig suggesting an assault on Third and Fifth Armies, the concentration on the BEF's northern sector seems muddle-headed, albeit that ground could be more readily yielded there than in the north. A further complication was the commander of the extreme right hand of the BEF, Lieutenant-General Sir Richard Butler of III Corps. Butler took over this post on 25 February, having been a member of the GHQ staff. Placing a novice general in such an important position does not seem a particularly sensible decision. Once again, the role of GHQ appears an enigma. Rational, intelligent and useful decisions and assessments were undermined by contradictory actions.

Generally, GHQ had made a reasonable assessment of German strength, suggesting that the number of German divisions on the Western Front had risen from 147 in October 1917 to 187 by 21 March, when the actual figure was 191 divisions: in fact, most of the new divisions brought west were used to release those with Western Front experience from quiet sectors to spearhead the offensive. Cox, however, believed as late as 2 March that the main German effort would be against the French in Champagne. In that sense, GHQ Intelligence did not entirely fail, but it was less prescient than later claimed.[22]

By 19 March, GHQ intelligence was convinced that an assault would be launched on 20 or 21 March, which triggered a warning order to all units. It was a good assessment, for the German assault, code named 'Operation Michael', commenced at 4:45 AM on 21 March with an initial bombardment of five hours' duration followed by an infantry assault along a fifty-mile front straddling Third and Fifth Armies' positions, much as predicted by British intelligence. Supported by an overwhelming firepower superiority of some 10,000 guns and heavy mortars firing 3.2 million rounds, German infantry from seventy-six divisions rapidly overcame the twenty-six divisions and 2,686 guns of Third and Fifth Armies. The importance of artillery to German plans reveals that the

[22] Beach, *Haig's Intelligence*, 276–80, 301–2; David French, 'Failures of Intelligence: The Retreat to the Hindenburg Line and the March 1918 Offensive', in Michael Dockrill and David French (eds.), *Strategy and Intelligence: British Policy during the First World War* (London: Hambledon, 1996), 67–95.

celebrated brilliance of German infantry was as reliant on artillery as their British foes. In most cases, British resistance wilted instantly, such was the shock and violence of the German assault against overstretched resources. The forward zone failed as a trip-wire, overrun as it was in quick time, which then put immediate pressure on the battle zone. It has been calculated that 84 per cent of the British infantry were within 3,000 yards of the front line, with at least a third of the Fifth Army being overwhelmed in ninety minutes: of eight battalions in XVIII Corps, for example, barely fifty men got back to the battle zone.[23]

Moreover, to support infantry adequately against attacking infantry, artillery had to be no more than 2,000 yards from the front, which rendered it vulnerable. Many guns were lost, particularly heavy artillery that simply could not be pulled back quickly enough, while counter-battery work was entirely disrupted by the collapse of communications due to the weather conditions. Flash spotting and sound ranging also were impossible.[24] The amazing tempo of the assault is revealed in the fact that 21,000 prisoners were taken during the day: British troops had simply been given no opportunity to put up a meaningful defence. However, the magnitude of the German success should not be over-exaggerated. At no point had the Germans reached their final objectives. The battle zone had not been breached, albeit the extent of success made its retention problematic. In the northern sector, the progress was deemed disappointingly slow. Equally worrying was the scale of the casualties. Although the British experienced a disaster, losing some 500 guns and 38,512 men, the Germans suffered the usual experience of the attackers on the Western Front insofar as their 39,929 casualties exceeded those of the defenders.[25]

This scenario thus had similarities with British experiences in 1916 and 1917 in which the opening day of battles provided great successes intermingled with elements of great concern. Unlike the British experiences of 1916 and 1917, the Germans did not find the subsequent days much harder as more troops and guns poured in to hold back the offensive. The difference lay in precisely the factors identified as disturbing before the battle. The lack of easy communications across the old Somme battlefield combined with an absence of strong defensive positions meant that the British did not have the ability to shore up the over-extended Fifth Army. During the course of 21 March, Gough

23 Samuels, *Command and Control*, 217; Stevenson, *With Our Backs*, 52; Simpson, *Directing Operations*, 142.
24 Marble, *British Artillery*, 217–19; Bailey, 'British Artillery', 40.
25 Middlebrook, *Kaiser's Battle*, 52, 307–23; Michael Kitchen, *The German Offensives of 1918* (Stroud: Tempus, 2005), 80.

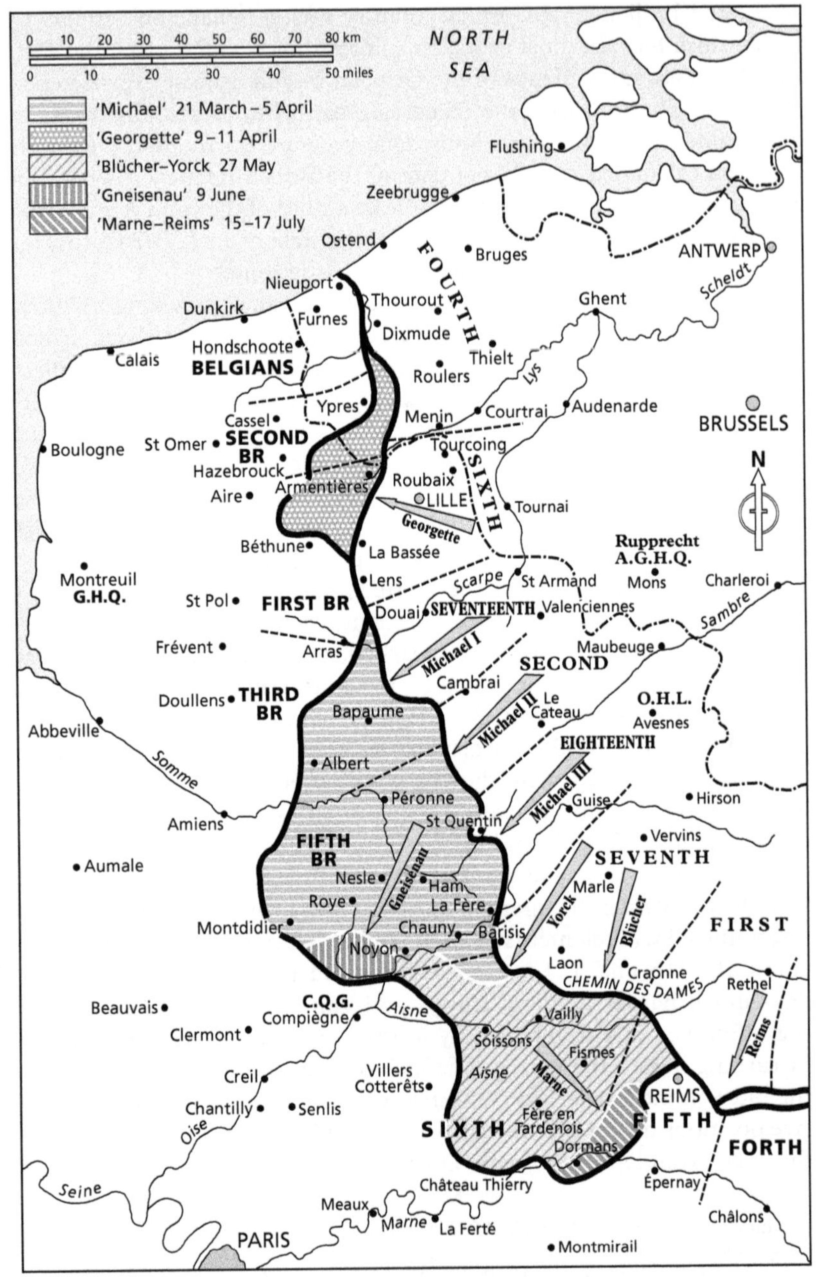

Map 12 German offensives, March–July 1918

frantically tried to exert control amid the wreckage of his command system, and although the Germans were less active on the following day, this still did not give Gough the time he needed to reorganise and bring order to his forces. He made no effort, however, to speak to Haig.[26] Left with little option, Gough had to devolve decision-making to his corps commanders, which led them, unsurprisingly in the circumstances, to advocate major retreats. Cohesion now collapsed completely as lateral communications broke down. Corps were therefore making unilateral decisions that often severely compromised the positions of their unwitting neighbours. Wishing to break contact and re-establish effective command, Gough ordered a retreat to the Peronne bridgehead position at 10:45 AM on 22 March, a decision confirmed by Haig at 2000 hours. Gough left decisions on withdrawal to the discretion of his subordinates. In any case, as the bridgehead position had never been given the attention it required, it was little more than a mark on the map.[27]

At just this moment a crisis on Third Army front began to emerge. Third Army had generally fought well and had restricted the Germans to modest advances. But Byng had emphasised a vigorous forward defence and thus had little in reserve to meet further emergencies. The problem came when German advances threatened to cut off completely his three divisions in the Flesquières salient close to the hinge with Fifth Army. When the Germans began to make progress against the salient's right flank, Third Army was forced to retreat northwest away from Fifth Army, thus threatening to open an irreparable breach between the two forces. The retreat of the two armies then left open the dangerous possibility that Amiens might fall and with it a major railway junction threatening the BEF's communications network. Amiens was vital in that it handled half the supplies coming from the main British supply ports of Rouen, Le Havre and Dieppe, as well as 80 per cent of all north-south traffic. Fortunately, the Germans did not initially make Amiens an objective.[28]

By this point, Pétain, Commander of French forces since Nivelle's ignominious collapse, was growing concerned. He was trying to assist the British in stabilising their right but was also convinced that a German assault was imminent against his own troops in the Champagne region. This ran contrary to Haig's assumption that the German aim was to sever the link between the British and French Armies. Haig was desperate to keep Pétain's attention on the actual crisis rather than a potential one and was worried that the French would not realise the full gravity of the

[26] Harris, *Haig*, 483. [27] *Ibid.*, 450–1.

[28] Peter Simkins, *From the Somme to Victory: The British Army's Experience on the Western Front, 1916–18* (Barnsley: Praetorian Press, 2014), 123–4.

situation before it was too late. News of the situation in France had reached London, where there was mounting concern. Lloyd George despatched Lord Milner to act as his personal emissary to assess the situation. The precise course of subsequent events is disputed in competing versions, and it appears that Haig subsequently wanted to give the impression that he had at no point lost control of the situation. What cannot be disputed is Haig's fixation on the need for maximum French assistance, a point he made to Sir Henry Wilson on the morning of 25 March when both men agreed to request a Franco-British conference to discuss the matter. Believing that Pétain might need to be overruled, Haig was very keen on high-level French political involvement. This desire was achieved, for on the following day a French team of Poincaré, Clemenceau, Foch and Pétain met Haig, Wilson and Milner at Doullens' town hall. Agreement was achieved on two crucial points. Firstly, Amiens had to be held, and secondly, Foch should be appointed as co-ordinating general to oversee operations. Although Foch's actual powers were left sketchy by the conference, he acted immediately by deploying the only card he had available at the time – the force of his own personality. He therefore visited Fifth Army HQ demanding more vigorous action, which no doubt seemed a fine gesture in his own mind but was merely annoying to an already hard-pressed Fifth Army staff. His next move was more positive as he issued orders directing more French troops to the assistance of the British.[29]

Haig seems to have been perfectly happy with this outcome. A major crisis on the BEF front was now regarded as an entente problem requiring a significant level of co-operation. The decision also came at the very moment that Operation Michael began to run out of steam. German troops had worn themselves out traversing the Somme battlefield and found that their logistical systems were collapsing under the strain of supplying men on the far side of a devastated region. British and French reinforcements were also pouring in, bringing stability to the entente line even if the situation remained grave. Ludendorff maintained Operation Michael until 5 April, but each assault revealed that it was rapidly dwindling in offensive power. Fifth Army held on very badly battered but never completely routed and driven from the field entirely. Although Fifth Army had suffered high casualties, the Germans lost somewhere in the region of 230,000 men, who could not be replaced and had not achieved a decisive breakthrough.[30]

[29] For differing interpretations of the Doullens conference, see Greenhalgh, *Victory Through Coalition*, 192–7; Greenhalgh, 'Myth and Memory: Sir Douglas Haig and the Imposition of Allied Unified Command in March 1918', *Journal of Military History* 68 (2004), 771–820; John Terraine, *Douglas Haig: The Educated Soldier* (London: Hutchinson, 1963), 422–5.

[30] Stevenson, *With Our Backs*, 68.

Somewhat ironically, just at the moment when the entente situation was improving, Gough found himself a casualty. On 28 March he was dismissed from command of Fifth Army and replaced with Rawlinson. Having aroused severe doubts by his conduct of earlier battles, Gough was fatally weakened by the disaster that befell Fifth Army, even if on this occasion he was by no means solely culpable and had done his best in extremely difficult circumstances. Haig certainly did little to protect Gough but did sweeten the pill by offering command of a newly constituted Reserve Army. Lloyd George was not prepared to countenance this and demanded that Gough be removed altogether. There was a need for a scapegoat, and Gough's already damaged reputation undermined his position. In the midst of this wrangling, Ludendorff launched a fresh offensive against First and Third Armies. 'Operation Mars' commenced on 28 March at 7:30 AM with a bombardment followed by nine assault divisions and was supported with fresh attacks against Fifth Army further south. Accurately predicted this time by British intelligence, the attack was largely unsuccessful as most German units did not employ the new storm-trooper tactics. This decision allowed the British to capitalise on their strengths, and the advance was brought to a halt by resolute troops in good defensive positions.[31] Haig offered his own resignation to Derby on 6 April but knew it was unlikely to be accepted, although it was actually taken more seriously than he imagined: as in January, there was no obvious successor.[32]

Despite the check of this new German assault, Haig remained anxious and was as keen as ever to maintain a solid Anglo-French barrier. A major boost to entente unity came on 3 April when a high-level conference was held at Beauvais attended by Lloyd George and Clemenceau as well as Pershing, Haig, Foch and Pétain. It was agreed that Foch would take charge of strategic direction while still leaving the national army commanders free to appeal to their governments. Haig expressed his feeling that a French offensive was the best response to the situation as it would disrupt German plans considerably. After initial agreement, the French did little to prosecute this idea, and the British floated alternative suggestions. The first was a request that the French consider taking over line from the British, and the second was the massing of French reserves in the Vimy area. The re-positioning of a French reserve was a response to intelligence reports which suggested a further assault on the British somewhere in the Arras-Cambrai area.

In fact, the British had got their interpretations slightly wrong. The target for the next German offensive was the Lys Valley, which opened the

[31] For discussions over the fall of Gough, see Travers, *Killing Ground*, 220–49; Harris, *Haig*, 461–4. For the next phase of the German offensives, see Kitchen, *German Offensives*, 99–136.

[32] Harris, *Haig*, 463.

possibility of a drive to the Channel ports and a subsequent unhinging of the British line. Believing the boggy ground of the Lys would make it unattractive, British planners had not given it a high priority. It was therefore not held in any particular strength and contained two low-quality Portuguese divisions among the defending troops. 'Operation Georgette' was launched on 9 April and quickly overran the Portuguese positions. There was still an assumption initially that it was only a diversion.[33] Soon, however, realising the gravity of the situation, Haig was concerned that his troops would be cut off in Armentières and stressed the need for French assistance once again. Unable to hold Armentières, Haig ordered it evacuated, but this opened the way to the important railway junction of Hazebrouck and threatened to expose the entire British left flank to defeat in detail. So agitated was Haig that he issued his melodramatic 'backs to the wall' message on 11 April. At Ypres, Plumer prepared to evacuate the Passchendaele salient and make a stand on the Pilckem Ridge. The sense of panic that seemed to be in the air was perceived by many French generals as a sign of weakness in their British counterparts that did little to bolster French confidence in their ally. Fortunately for the British, the Germans were once again losing momentum and, unable to take the high ground around Kemmel, could not evict the British from the Ypres salient entirely.

But there was little time to draw breath, for on the 24 April there were fresh attacks on the Amiens sector. Byng suggested that Cox had 'lost the German Army'.[34] The situation looked grim when Villers-Bretonneux fell, but a counter-attack by Australian and British troops in the early hours of the following morning stabilised the situation. The high-water mark of the German offensives against the British had been reached. Although British troops had been hard pressed and were intensely weary, nowhere had they been routed entirely and nowhere had a major gap opened up for any length of time. The British found good use for their cavalry as mobile fire power forces, which ensured that such gaps in the line were kept to a minimum. The defence had been led by a mix of veterans and inexperienced conscripts who had held together in the face of intense pressure. In all the engagements, the British were given a glimmer of hope, for by no means was every German assault made in the textbook storm-troop manner so admired by the advocates of the German Army. Instead, many had been delivered en masse with little tactical sophistication and consequently fell victim to British fire. Where successes were achieved, the Germans found their lack of mobility

[33] Beach, *Haig's Intelligence*, 292–3.
[34] Ferris, 'British Army and Signals Intelligence', 40.

crippling. Unable to ensure a regular flow of men and materiel across the devastated regions and stripped of effective cavalry, the Germans could not maintain momentum, allowing the British the time to recover.

By contrast, and despite the immense strain put on them, the British maintained mobility and logistical flexibility. The depth of the BEF's logistical infrastructure is revealed in the fact that it had the resources to fire off 5.5 million eighteen-pounder shells and nearly 1.5 million howitzer shells during Operation Michael. In terms of eighteen-pounder ammunition, this represented almost the entire stock available in the spring of 1916 for the Somme battle. In all, 859 guns were lost in three weeks, but the losses could be made good. In addition, throughout the German offensives, the BEF kept up supplies from the Channel ports to the artillery, and only 9.2-inch howitzer shells ever fell short of requirements. Over 555,000 tons of supplies were still in hand in November 1918.[35] Aware that he had reached deadlock in the north, Ludendorff suddenly switched his focus much further south. 'Operation Blűcher' was pitched against the French in Champagne on 27 May. Tragically for the British, the assault partially fell on units of IX Corps, which had been sent south to recuperate after their mauling further north. Filled with fresh conscripts and tired veterans, the divisions crumbled after an intensive German bombardment. Foch was rather confused by the attack, as it seemed to offer little hope of great success unless Soissons could be captured, which the Germans signally failed to do. A further heavy assault was delivered on 15 July but once again failed to achieve the decisive victory despite giving the French and Americans in the sector a severe shock. With the situation so fluid, Foch was anxious to gain more power, believing that his overview gave him a significant advantage which could be exploited only if he had the right to deploy and command troops more extensively. Haig was not particularly happy with this idea, but Lord Milner overruled him and provided the agreement of the British government on 7 June. This move towards still further cohesion of entente effort was a positive one and, combined with a number of other factors, added up to a decisive shift in advantage to the entente side. By the early summer of 1918, American divisions were finally in place, having been equipped and trained in trench routines. Secondly, the dreadful impact of Spanish influenza started to make itself felt. Worn down by years of short rations due to the effects of blockade, German troops were more susceptible to it than those of the entente. Already short of men following their offensive efforts, the Germans now saw disease adding to the attrition. Indeed, the British deliberately aimed their later

[35] Brown, *British Logistics*, 189–96; Stevenson, *With Our Backs*, 379.

operations on the Hamel and Amiens fronts knowing the Germans in this area had been badly affected by the influenza outbreak.[36]

The moment for counter-offensive was approaching. Both Foch and Haig were planning assaults by late June, and on 4 July, the Australian Corps under Lieutenant-General Sir John Monash attacked in a manner that revealed the enormous potential of experienced commanders and soldiers supported by abundant munitions of all types. The battle of Hamel was a small masterpiece of meticulous planning, the integration of a number of arms and confident battlefield performance by the troops on the ground. The village of Hamel and 1,000 prisoners were taken with minimal loss.[37] A fortnight later the French and Americans took up the offensive, launching assaults in Champagne.

Much trumpeted as heralding a new dawn for the BEF on the Western Front, Hamel can instead by read as a further evolution of the set-piece battle skills revealed so regularly in 1917. Perhaps the biggest novelty was the perception of those involved in authorising and planning the operation, for no one saw it as anything other than a minor affair that was not to get out of hand even if successful. It is this breakthrough in operational thinking, rather than the technicalities of the execution, which made Hamel a novelty. Content with the successes of the day, no one in the BEF insisted that the operation be maintained in the expectation and hope that a few days of improvised assaults would unhinge the whole German position. Hamel was therefore very different to Arras, Third Ypres or Cambrai. The action also revealed the strategic difficulties of the Germans. They had greatly increased the amount of territory under their control, but it overstretched their available manpower considerably. In addition, the hungry and tired German soldiers were now stuck in makeshift defences a long way from their well-prepared original positions from which they could operate with such confidence and skill. The strain was such that Ludendorff was forced to abandon plans for an offensive in Flanders, codenamed 'Operation Hagen', in order to deploy the troops and materiel elsewhere.

Looking for an opportunity to strike back, Haig was sympathetic to Rawlinson's suggestion that Fourth Army prepare for a major offensive, (As noted, Rawlinson had replaced Gough at Fifth Army on 28 March, and the force was then redesignated Fourth Army on 2 April.)[38] Rawlinson planned to assault just east of Amiens between the Somme and Luce Rivers and make a seven-mile advance to ensure the safety of

[36] Beach, *Haig's Intelligence*, 304–5. [37] Prior and Wilson, *Rawlinson*, 289–300.
[38] For the planning of the battle of Amiens, see J. Paul Harris and Niall Barr, *Amiens to the Armistice: The BEF in the Hundred Days' Campaign, 8 August–11 November 1918* (London: Brassey's, 1998), 59–86.

the city. Anxious to hit as hard as possible, Rawlinson requested the Canadian Corps to supplement the Australian and III Corps and French co-operation south of the Luce. Haig agreed to both requests and approached the French for help. The eventual result was a plan to strike hard without a preliminary bombardment in order to maximise surprise, with the infantry advancing under the cover of a creeping barrage assisted by tanks and aircraft. Foch was keen to provide maximum assistance and ordered Debeney's First Army to stage an equally grand supporting assault. Speed was now of the essence for Rawlinson as he was anxious to strike quickly lest the Germans withdraw before the punch was delivered. Accepting this possibility, Haig ordered Rawlinson to be ready for action by 8 August and at the same time requested that the attack aim for the Chaulnes-Roye line some twelve miles from the starting position and plan for exploitation towards Ham three miles further. Such interventions and scaling-up of objectives had been disastrous in 1916, but they were less dangerous than two years previously. The main reason was the overwhelming fire power the British were able to gather, which was then concentrated onto much weaker defences and delivered with the additional advantage of complete surprise. Fourth Army's guns were doubled to 1,000, and nearly 2,000 British and French aircraft were allocated to assist the assault, as well as 534 tanks.[39] The insistence on surprise meant that everything was assembled using great care, and the need for utter secrecy was stressed to all. Unusually, there was a deception plan, the Canadians leaving some formations in place while the bulk of the Corps was transferred from Arras to Amiens in just ten days in complete secrecy. Random silences on radio and field telephone networks and manipulation of signals traffic at army and corps levels added to the misleading effect.[40] The Germans threatened to spoil these meticulous preparations on 6 August when the newly arrived Württemberg Division commenced an assault on III Corps. Although disruptive, the attack by no means altered the wider situation, and Rawlinson remained on schedule.

The offensive opened at 4:20 AM on 8 August with the infantry attacking at 4:24 AM ably assisted by a well-planned creeping barrage, tanks and a highly effective counter-battery programme: some 95 per cent of all German batteries had been previously identified.[41] South of the Somme, the Australians and Canadians smashed their way forward, allowing cavalry and armoured cars to move through them and harass the rapidly retreating Germans. Both Dominion forces were by now

[39] Harris and Barr, *Amiens to the Armistice*, 74–5.
[40] Ferris, 'British Army and Signals Intelligence', 41.
[41] Harris and Barr, *Amiens to Armistice*, 106.

highly efficient organisations often deploying British staff officers in a well-integrated team which maintained consistency of approach, unlike British units, which were rotated regularly between corps. The Canadians in particular, backed up by fresh drafts after passing a conscription act, were kept up to strength and had become the cutting edge of the British imperial armies. North of the Somme, III Corps met stronger resistance; as a result, its attack was less impressive, which was unsurprising given the punishment it had received a few days earlier. The Royal Air Force (RAF. Formed as an independent force on 1 April 1918.) also had a jarring day, suffering heavy losses while trying the difficult task of low-level bombing of bridges, for which it was simply not equipped.[42] As had happened so often in 1916 and 1917, the following days were ones of rapidly diminishing returns. German resistance became better organised and more difficult to dislodge. Unlike previous battles, Haig revealed a clear grip and accepted Rawlinson's decision to close the battle down on 11 August. This sensible decision ensured that the victory remained a victory: Fourth Army and French First Army had taken just short of 30,000 prisoners and 400 guns. In return, Fourth Army had suffered about 20,000 casualties, but the overwhelming majority were wounded rather than killed.[43]

At this point the BEF revealed another significant advantage. Thanks to the productivity of its home front industries combined with the sophistication of its logistical infrastructure in France and Belgium, it now had the ability to switch to another sector. A year earlier the British had been unable to follow up their success at Messines with an immediate assault on the Pilckem Ridge. Now the situation was transformed. Revealing an embarrassment of materiel riches, Haig was able to consider a fresh assault delivered by his Third and Fourth Armies in conjunction with French First Army supported by 200 tanks. Although the British now had the ability to maintain an offensive in a flexible manner, it was not quite able to meet Haig's tempo, and it was not until 21 August that Byng was ready to commence. Once again, Haig revealed that he had learned much, for Byng was not put under undue pressure to hurry. When the assault commenced at 4:55 AM on 21 August, Byng's men moved forward and

[42] David Jordan, 'The Genesis of Modern Air Power: The RAF in 1918', and Alistair McCluskey, 'The Battle of Amiens and the Development of the British Air-Land Battle, 1918–45', in Gary Sheffield and Peter Gray (eds.), *Changing War: The British Army, the Hundred Days and the Birth of the RAF* (London: Bloomsbury, 2013), 191–206, 231–48.

[43] Prior and Wilson, *Rawlinson*, 305; Harris, *Haig*, 494–5.

took 2,000 prisoners for minor losses, but the day was by no means easy, with severe resistance encountered at Achiet le Grand. Anxious to keep up the pressure, Haig urged Byng forward much to the Third Army Commander's distaste. Any intention to maintain the offensive was then undermined by a German counter-attack in the area. Repulsed with relative ease, its failure unbalanced the Germans and opened the way for a further advance on 23 August, with the result that by the following day over 10,000 prisoners had been taken. It was at this point that the BEF's ability to dance around the ring like a good boxer and deliver blows at will was fully revealed, for on 26 August, Horne's First Army went over to the offensive, attacking successfully either side of the Scarpe. Haig had told army commanders on 23 August that they could take risks even if flanks were exposed and could allow discretion to subordinates in reaching distant objectives.[44]

By early September, First, Third and Fourth Armies were closing up on the Hindenburg Line. In the north, First Army prepared to break the Drocourt-Quéant Line, the formidable defensive position that had proved so stubborn in the Arras fighting of 1917. In a well-planned operation, the line was taken on 2 September, while in the south Monash pushed his forces through the Peronne–Mont St. Quentin sector. With these victories the BEF was brought another step closer to the edge of the main Hindenburg positions, having taken over 72,000 prisoners since August as well as nearly 800 guns. The next step was taken on 12 September, when Byng took the Havrincourt Spur. It was now up to Rawlinson to complete the task with Fourth Army. On the same day that Byng's IV and V Corps successfully brought Third Army to within sight of Cambrai, Rawlinson held a conference of his corps commanders. He put forward his plan to advance across a 20,000-yard front which would capture the old British front lines and bring his forces to the outposts of the Hindenburg Line from Epéhy in the north to Selency in the south. Fourth Army had a comfortable firepower and manpower supremacy over the German defenders, but the weather was poor, which affected observation.[45]

As with many of the assaults since 8 August, it was decided to dispense with a preliminary bombardment in favour of a creeping barrage heavily intermixed with smoke. When the assault commenced in mist and drizzle at 5:20 AM on 18 September, the central (Australian) corps advanced well, but the flanking corps were less successful. In the north, III Corps had to

[44] Harris, *Haig*, 496, 499. The full order is reproduced in John Lee, 'William Birdwood', in Beckett and Corvi (eds.), *Haig's Generals*, 33–53, at 48–9.

[45] For the planning of the next phase and comment on prisoners, see Harris, *Haig*, 500–7.

deal with a series of heavily defended fortress-villages, and in the south, IX Corps faced the equally formidable Quadrilateral Redoubt. The failure to take all these positions in one day revealed that despite fading German morale, it remained extremely difficult for infantry, no matter how skilled, to take strong defensive positions without a heavy, accurate bombardment. Despite these setbacks, the battle was still a success, with 9,000 Germans taken prisoner and the Hindenburg Line within reach.[46]

Haig, with Foch's agreement, now planned to bring all the BEF's armies into action while French and American forces launched separate, but interlocking, offensives. In effect, the British, French and Americans were now doing on the Western Front what entente strategy had demanded since the Chantilly conference of December 1915: close collaboration so as to deliver a continual rain of blows on the enemy. The new atmosphere of entente unity was such that Haig was prepared to allow Second Army to move from his command to that of the King of the Belgians in a Flanders Army Group. Facing the fifty-two infantry divisions (including two American) of Haig's five armies were sixty-three German divisions. This numerical disadvantage was more than balanced out by the extremely parlous manpower condition of most German divisions. However, the Germans had now returned to the Hindenburg Line, which had been constructed so carefully and formed part of a defensive scheme German soldiers understood so well.

On 25 September, the French and Americans attacked in Champagne. They made solid advances but could not press on largely due to inefficient staff work in the American Expeditionary Force (AEF), which led to severe logistical difficulties. On the BEF's front, action recommenced two days later when the Canadian Corps smashed its way across the Canal du Nord in a brilliant set-piece assault providing the central spearhead of the joint First-Third Army operation, which involved the co-ordination of infantry, artillery, engineers, machine guns, tanks and use of smoke and gas and ground-attack aircraft.[47] A day later, Second Army played its part in an impressive Flanders group assault, taking over 2,000 prisoners.[48]

While these assaults were going on, Rawlinson's Fourth Army was improving on the positions gained on 18 September. A well-planned attack by IX Corps on 24 September saw the Hindenburg Line outposts

[46] Harris and Barr, *Amiens to the Armistice*, 174–80.

[47] Simon Robbins, 'Henry Horne', in Beckett and Corvi (eds.), *Haig's Generals*, 97–117, at 108–10.

[48] Harris and Barr, *Amiens to the Armistice*, 201.

collapse and opened the way for a major assault on the main Hindenburg positions in the area, which appeared formidable in this area. Constructed at great expense during the winter of 1916, it utilised the St. Quentin Canal, which was 35 feet wide and contained six feet of mud and water. Much of it flowed in a deep, sheer-walled cutting fifty feet deep. This impressive obstacle was fronted on its western bank with thick belts of barbed wire, deep trenches and concrete machine gun emplacements. These defences were supplemented on the eastern side, where a series of heavily wired trenches had been constructed. On the northern half of Fourth Army front, the canal entered a 6,000-yard tunnel which was defended by a very strong forward line of multiple trenches and wire entanglements as well as three fortified villages, Bellenglise, Bellicourt and Bony. The one major weakness was the canal's valley bottom position. If an attacker gained the high ground to its front, then its defences could be exposed to accurate artillery fire. Fortunately for the British, a complete set of plans was found in a captured headquarters, and this gave Fourth Army staff the opportunity to exploit the few weaknesses in the position.

Revealing the degree of respect invested in the Australian Corps, Rawlinson asked Monash to draw up a plan despite the fact that only a portion of it was going to be committed to the battle. Monash believed that the tunnel sector was most vulnerable and wanted the American divisions to make the initial advance before two Australian divisions leapfrogged through. Given the inexperience of the American troops and the depth of the defences in this sector, presenting them with such a hard task is a little difficult to understand. Nonetheless, Rawlinson accepted the plan, but made the Australian advance to the final position contingent on success along the length of the line. The other alteration Rawlinson made was to insert a plan from Lieutenant-General Sir Walter Braithwaite, who argued that a division from his IX Corps should assault across the southern (open) portion of the canal, which would give Fourth Army more elbow room and a firmer flank on the eastern bank. Monash was highly sceptical about this idea, but Rawlinson insisted, revealing a much firmer grip on the planning than he had done during the Somme battle of 1916. This greater resolve was revealed again a few days later when he took the decision to relieve Butler (III Corps) due to increasing doubts over his competence. Haig accepted the advice and took the further step of relieving the entire corps and replacing it with Morland's XIII Corps.

Given the nature of the German defences, the attacking infantry had to be given every advantage. For this reason, 181 tanks were gathered, many of them with trench-crossing cribs. Cavalry and armoured cars were also brought up and detailed to work in collaboration with the ultimate objective of Valenciennes. The final element was a strong RAF deployment of over 300 aircraft.

Before the operation could commence, the US divisions needed to gain a better start line, but their assaults on 26–27 September did not go well. Some American troops managed to penetrate the German positions, but nowhere were objectives taken and held. This had an unfortunate repercussion on Fourth Army's fire plan as American commanders were convinced that large numbers of their troops remained trapped in the German trenches. In turn, this made them reluctant to put down a creeping barrage for fear of hitting their own men. Rawlinson was fully aware that such a decision might imperil the success of the American units due to attack on 29 September, but he was equally well aware of understandable American sensitivity on the issue and so allowed the initial bombardment line to be shifted eastwards by 1,000 yards.

Revealing the need to treat well-prepared positions thoroughly, a preliminary artillery bombardment commenced on 26 September. The bombardment used 1,044 field guns and howitzers and 593 heavy guns and fired shells totalling 27.5 million pounds in weight. By contrast, the assault on 8 August had only used 12.7 million pounds, thus revealing once again the excellent work of BEF's logistics arm.[49] The bombardment would deliver 126 shells per 500 yards of German trench every minute for eight hours. In all, 945,052 rounds would be fired.[50] However, the system was straining, and there were some delays in ammunition delivery. Moreover, there were still not enough guns to destroy all defences, and priority was given to counter-battery work, interdiction of rear areas, targeting of key points and cutting only gaps in the wire, the 106 Fuse being especially effective in detonating shells directly on the target.[51] The well-established tactic of intermingling gas and conventional shells to maximise confusion was used and heightened by the first British use of mustard gas shells, which were used exclusively against German artillery positions. Despite the great advances in British gunnery, the bombardment did not go entirely to plan due to poor weather hampering observation and the speed of ammunition supply. Labouring against these difficulties, the gunners could not quite deliver a perfect bombardment. In some sectors only a few lanes were cut in the wire, while the trenches opposite the 27th (US) Division were very patchily treated due to reasons mentioned earlier. On 46th Division's front, which was covered by fifty-four eighteen-pounders firing two rounds a minute and

[49] Brown, *British Logistics*, 198. [50] Prior and Wilson, *Rawlinson*, 363–74.
[51] Marble, *British Artillery*, 237.

eighteen 4.5-inch howitzers firing one round per minute, the guns managed to batter down the sides of the canal in some places, thus forming convenient slopping ramps for the infantry.[52]

The full assault commenced at 5:50 AM on 29 September. Given the nature of the obstacle in front of it, the performance of Fourth Army must be hailed as one of the greatest feats of British military history. Clad in 3,000 lifebelts taken from Channel steamers and carrying portable boats and assault ladders, as well as heaving lines, the 46th Division bounced across the canal, scrambled up the other side, leapfrogged two brigades through and then consolidated its positions. To its immediate north, the 30th (US) Division took Bellicourt behind a highly effective creeping barrage and pressed on. However, it did not consolidate all its gains, which meant that the following 5th Australian Division had to fight hard in mopping-up operations, destroying its tempo. These successes in the central-south section were not matched in the central-north sector, for the 27th (US) Division made little progress on its front, which meant that its supporting 3rd Australian Division had to fight for the initial objectives rather than perform its assigned role of exploitation. By the end of the day, some progress had been made, but at heavy casualties for not particularly advantageous positions. On the northern flank, III Corps had an equally frustrating day as it battered towards Vendhuille, making a modest advance. The inability to wrench open the entire position then meant that the exploitation arms of cavalry and armoured cars could not be unleashed. These elements of relative failure disappointed Rawlinson, who does not appear to have realised the amazing victory achieved by his troops. Given Rawlinson's often limited expectations, the fact that he believed more could have been achieved reveals his increasingly bullish nature. Less creditable was his irritation at the 27th Division, which he criticised for its lack of internal organisation.[53] Although there was some truth in this accusation, the magnitude of the task set before an inexperienced unit was the actual underlying problem.

The crossing of the St. Quentin Canal was, nonetheless, a great victory, which brought Fourth Army through the main Hindenburg positions on a 10,000-yard front to a depth of 6,000 yards, taking 5,300 prisoners.[54] Having lost this excellent defensive position, the Germans had few well-prepared defence lines on which to fall back, and the victory added to the speed with which German forces were crumbling. Thus, the entente

[52] *Ibid.*, 239.

[53] On the 27th and 30th US Divisions, see Mitchell Yockelson, *Borrowed Soldiers: Americans under British Command, 1918* (Norman: University of Oklahoma Press, 2008).

[54] John Terraine, *To Win a War: 1918, The Year of Victory* (London: Sidgwick & Jackson, 1978), 173–4.

assaults on 28 September led by the BEF had inflicted another major defeat on the Germans. The impact of the disaster, combined with Bulgaria's decision to seek an armistice, caused Ludendorff to have some sort of mental breakdown that afternoon. Forced to survey an increasingly bleak scene, he came to the conclusion that Germany had to seek an armistice as quickly as possible, and he requested that a new government be formed to pursue this objective. Although Germany now had one aim, the ability to shape it was complicated by protracted discussions between the army high command and politicians over the precise nature of the peace feelers and who was empowered to make them. It was made yet more intricate by the fact that there was no attempt to engage with the allies as a bloc; rather, all communications were directed to Wilson, who did nothing to encourage wider discussion, taking it upon himself to act as sole negotiator while hostilities continued in Europe.

Anxious to retain some semblance of controlling destiny, the Kaiser appointed the moderate Prince Max of Baden to the post of Chancellor with instructions to begin armistice negotiations with Woodrow Wilson. Such measures reveal the increasing sense of desperation in Germany, but they came at a moment when the entente effort was beginning to slow down. The Americans were utterly unable to overcome their logistical mess in the Argonne. Heavy rain had stalled the advance on the Flanders front, and the Canadians met rapidly stiffening resistance after bouncing the Canal du Nord so brilliantly, while Third Army was battering its way across the Schelde Canal in a steady rather than spectacular manner.

This left Fourth Army as the only instrument capable of sustaining Foch's desire to maintain pressure on the enemy. Over the next few days, Fourth Army managed to continue the offensive over its rambling front, sometimes only just, but its staff work and cohesion held together sufficiently for its subordinate units to fight their way through the Beaurevoir Line. At no point was the fighting easy, for the Germans were well aware that this was their last formal position in the region. Interrogation of prisoners revealed that they had been told to hold the position at all costs. By 5 October, Fourth Army was on the far side of the Beaurevoir Line and had the vision all had dreamt of since the descent of trench warfare four years earlier, open country. With the Germans retreating from the Armentières salient in the north, Haig could afford to feel satisfied. But his gratification was tempered by the increasing sensation that the bulk of the fighting was falling to the BEF, with the French and Americans failing to carry their fair share. This complaint appears to have been accepted by Foch, who promised to bolster French First Army to make it a more effective player on the BEF's extreme right flank.

Despite this sour note, Haig was determined to maintain the initiative and urged planning for a further round of broad front assaults. Efforts were concentrated on the region south of Cambrai involving a combined attack by Third and Fourth Armies supported by the French First Army. It proved a very tricky task, for Third Army had not advanced through the Beaurevoir Line, so the assaults required careful integration to ensure that they achieved full mutual support. In yet another tribute to British staff work and artillery professionalism, an excellent barrage covered the advancing infantry, and a thorough counter-battery programme silenced German guns. The result was a heavy defeat for the Germans on 8 October in which 8,000 prisoners were taken and three armies thrown into full retreat.[55]

Forced to evacuate Cambrai, the retreating Germans were harried all the way back to the River Selle by cavalry, tanks and RAF patrols. Anxious to provide an anchoring point for their disintegrating armies, the German high command then ordered all units in the region to go firm on the so-called Hermann Position I, a line of scratch trenches east of the Selle.

On 14 October, the Flanders Army Group went back on the offensive. Second Army played its part in ensuring a German retreat to the Lys. Units of Second Army then began to cross the Lys in strength on 18 October. By this point German command decisions were lacking relevance as they were often made redundant by the power and tempo of entente assaults. This was revealed when Ludendorff ordered the Northern Army Group to retire to the Hermann Position on 16 October, but a day later Fourth Army crossed the Selle and unhinged the position. For Rawlinson, the crossing of the Selle and suppression of its defensive lines were not an easy proposition despite the fact that it was nowhere near as strong nor deep as the earlier Hindenburg positions. He expected the Germans to put up a tough fight, knowing that blunting the spearhead of the entente armies represented the best way to gain favourable armistice terms. He was therefore determined to get his troops over the Selle efficiently, and this demanded a large artillery programme, which then slowed the operational tempo as his logistical train got to work. On 15 October, the preliminary bombardment opened. Despite throwing vast numbers of shells at the Germans, the bombardment was of patchy quality. Bad weather hampered reconnaissance, and so much of the firing was done on intelligent guesswork. It resulted in a battle that demanded all the infantryman's skills. Battalions fought their way forward on the murky morning of 17 October with their own weapons and under officers

[55] Harris and Barr, *Amiens to the Armistice*, 239.

making a plethora of important battlefield decisions in an immensely fluid day's fighting which ended with Fourth Army making solid gains and breaking into the main German positions. Over the next few days, Rawlinson maintained the offensive until, in conjunction with French First Army, he had driven the Germans back to the Sambre and Oise Canals.

The fighting resulted in the capture of a further 5,139 prisoners but had nowhere been a walkover.[56] The intensity of these engagements seems to have burst the bubble of Haig's optimism. From late September, Haig had been increasing in confidence but had been subjected to much less enthusiastic advice from Herbert Lawrence. Like Haig, Lawrence was convinced that the BEF was carrying a disproportionate share of the fighting, but unlike Haig, he saw it as a highly dangerous situation rather than a hindrance to efficient operations. Lawrence was concerned by the prospect of an overstretched BEF becoming vulnerable to counter-attack and left unassisted by allegedly timid allies. Haig seems to have perceived the hard fighting of 17 October in this perspective, which caused him to recommend lenient armistice terms to the government. Although he was confident that the BEF could maintain its immediate advance, he doubted whether the German Army could be defeated completely before it reached its own frontier. In raising this point, he stressed that the Germans might well be capable of dragging the war out well into 1919 and possibly 1920. Such a change of mood can be attributed to self-knowledge on Haig's part: aware that he had often caused tension by his over-optimistic claims, it is possible to argue that this dampening of expectations revealed a more reflective attitude made by a mind which had matured as a result of previous experiences. However, the speed of the about-turn implies an inability to read the situation with sufficient insight and thus reveals a weakness in Haig's approach to generalship. Once again, Haig seems to have been blinkered and lacked true vision; his judgement was made by too close a reference to the situation on the front of one of his armies and without enough consideration of the broader scenario. It seems to confirm the neat conclusion of Shelford Bidwell and Dominick Graham on Haig's command style:

> Haig's vision of a battlefield was rather like that of a fan in the stands of Murrayfield, where his native Scotland played England at Rugby football; or perhaps that of a man looking at the ground between the ears of a horse. His conception of the scale of it was too small, perhaps, and he expected to see too much.[57]

[56] *Ibid.*, 252; Jackson Hughes, 'The Battle for the Hindenburg Line', *War and Society* 17 (1999), 41–57.
[57] Bidwell and Graham, *Fire-Power*, 57.

At precisely the same time, Haig's opposite was revealing an even more dangerous lack of understanding. The pressure of the continuing entente advance was pushing Ludendorff to the limits of his mental endurance. In a fit of fatalism, he advocated a *levée en masse* and a fight to the last man. Such instability shocked even the Kaiser and led to his replacement on 26 October.

Regardless of Haig's concerns, the BEF was still pressing forward. Second Army made gains in Flanders, while Fifth and First Armies were pushing towards Valenciennes. The next step was to get Third Army across the Selle in force in order to close up to Fourth Army's forward positions. Byng planned his assault thoroughly, and when his forces advanced at 2:00 AM on 20 October, they achieved another stunning victory for the BEF. Over the next few days, the twenty-three British divisions and the one New Zealand division supported by two US divisions smashed their way forward taking 20,000 prisoners and 475 guns.[58] The next objective was Valenciennes, the last significant city before the Belgian border. First Army began its preparations, deploying Currie's formidable Canadian Corps to the centre. Taking Valenciennes was no simple matter. The southern approaches to the city were covered by two parallel streams, the Ecaillon and the Rhonelle. The Ecaillon was a stiff proposition, for it was fast flowing, had steep banks and was well wired. Despite these difficulties, when the 51st and 4th Divisions attacked in the early hours of 24 October, they were able to scrabble across and were close to the Rhonelle by the end of the day. Horne, commanding First Army, was now in an excellent position to attack Valenciennes from the south, but this meant dealing with the dominant feature of Mount Houy first. In discussion with Currie and Godley, Horne opted for a closely controlled assault unfolding in three phases. The first was the capture of Mount Houy, which would then set up an attack by the Canadian Corps to the outskirts of Valenciennes before ending in a combined assault by the Canadian and XXII Corps.

Preparations were made in the face of considerable German activity. Forceful counter-attacks had to be beaten off on 27 October, which revealed that the Germans in the vicinity were not yet utterly defeated. It was a foretaste of the intense fighting that took place on the following day when First Army's initial assault commenced. Mount Houy was contested with great vigour, and by the end of the day, 51st Division held only the lower slopes. This failure upset the timing of the next phase and also meant that the Canadians would have to include the mount in their plans. Deploying the deliberate method it had refined with such

[58] Terraine, *To Win a War*, 22.

skill, the Canadian Corps planned to advance under a sophisticated and heavy bombardment. Supported by a flexible logistics system capable of delivering munitions in abundance, the Canadian Corps fired 2,419 tons of shells between 31 October and 2 November as they saturated German positions and pushed the infantry through in another brilliant feat of arms. In effect, the Canadians had the support of one gun for every six men on a front of 2,500 yards.[59] The advance made the German grip on Valenciennes untenable, and they began evacuating the city on 2 November. First Army gradually realised that it was now involved in pursuit operations, but it was difficult to move forward with great speed due to the rolling, wooded country.

Third and Fourth Armies were also due to resume the advance and, like First Army, found that a new set of tactical problems was opening up. Instead of trench lines, the planning staff in both armies had to take careful note of the number of small villages, towns and geographical features in front of them. Of particular importance was the town of Le Quesnoy, the Sambre and Oise Canal and the Forest of Mormal. Although it has been pointed out that the thirty German divisions defending these positions were greatly under-strength, it should be noted that few of the twenty-one attacking British divisions were anywhere near their full strength either. Fortunately for the attackers, the British held the advantage in terms of artillery and could deploy tank and armoured car support. The mechanical units had suffered a good deal of attrition, but there were enough to play a useful ancillary role. Once again, the key to maximising the potential of these elements was identified in surprise, so in the days before the assault, the British artillery kept up its usual routine, and all preparatory activity was very well disguised. The autumn weather then brought its mixed fortunes. The low mist prevented useful aerial observation, but at the same time it helped to cloak the British troops. On the day of the assault, 4 November, the British were lucky that thick mist covered their initial advance, which then gave way to bright sunshine, allowing the air force to play a full part in operations.

It turned out to be another highly satisfactory day for Third and Fourth Armies. Le Quesnoy was taken in an impressive operation making elaborate use of Livens Projectors to throw cylinders of flaming oil at the ramparts and a carefully planned infantry envelopment covered by artillery. Patrols then pushed into the Forest of Mormal and found it deserted. A major achievement was the crossing of the Sambre and Oise Canal at a number of points. The 25th Division managed to straddle it

[59] Shane B. Schreiber, *Shock Army of the British Empire: The Canadian Corps in the Last 100 Days of the Great War* (Westport, CT: Praeger, 2005), 125; Bailey, 'British Artillery', 42.

using rafts, which then squeezed the Germans out of Landrecies, while 32nd Division led by its sappers had a fierce fight around Ors before securing a bridgehead. Across the front, German positions were prized open and the defenders thoroughly beaten, with around 10,000 taken prisoner.[60] Although the soldiers of the BEF did not know it, they had fought their last major battle of the war.

By 6 November 1918, Third and Fourth Armies realised that the German forces in front of them were in full retreat. The pursuit was maintained with the RAF's V Brigade having a particularly intense time engaging enemy transport. However, the advance was by no means uniformly easy. German rearguards often made hard work for the British, and on 8 November, the German 9th Division managed to prepare and attempt a counter-attack. When this was beaten off, enemy resistance crumbled, and the Germans took to flight so intensely that all contact was lost. To the north, Plumer was having an equally hectic time trying to follow up on German withdrawals from the Schelde, while Birdwood's Fifth Army pushed its cavalry patrols across the River Dendre. Famously, Canadian troops reached Mons late on the night of 10 November, thus bringing the BEF back to the spot where it started the war. At 11 AM the next day, the Armistice came into effect.

By the end of October, Germany and its armed forces were disintegrating. Forced to withdraw aid from its dependent allies, it was powerless to stop them breaking away to sign separate armistice agreements with the entente forces. Mutiny broke out in the Kiel naval base, and after inspecting the troops along the Western Front, Ludendorff's replacement, General Wilhelm Groener, recommended immediate negotiations with the entente before utter collapse. At the same time, President Woodrow Wilson informed the German government that Foch had been authorised to discuss armistice terms on behalf of the coalition powers. When the two sides met in a railway carriage at Compiègne on 8 November, Foch made no attempt to negotiate and instead dictated terms. The German Army was given the dignity of returning with its small arms and officers their swords, but all artillery was to be abandoned, the allies were to take bridgeheads over the Rhine and the naval blockade was to be maintained to ensure compliance. Deeply perturbed, the German delegates reported back to the new German Chancellor, Prince Max of Baden. Desperate to stabilise the situation and smooth internal and external relations, Max unilaterally declared the abdication of the

[60] Harris and Barr, *Amiens to the Armistice*, 283; Niall Barr, 'The Last Battle of the BEF: The Crossing of the Sambre-Oise Canal, 4 November 1918', in Sheffield and Gray (eds.), *Changing War*, 73–92.

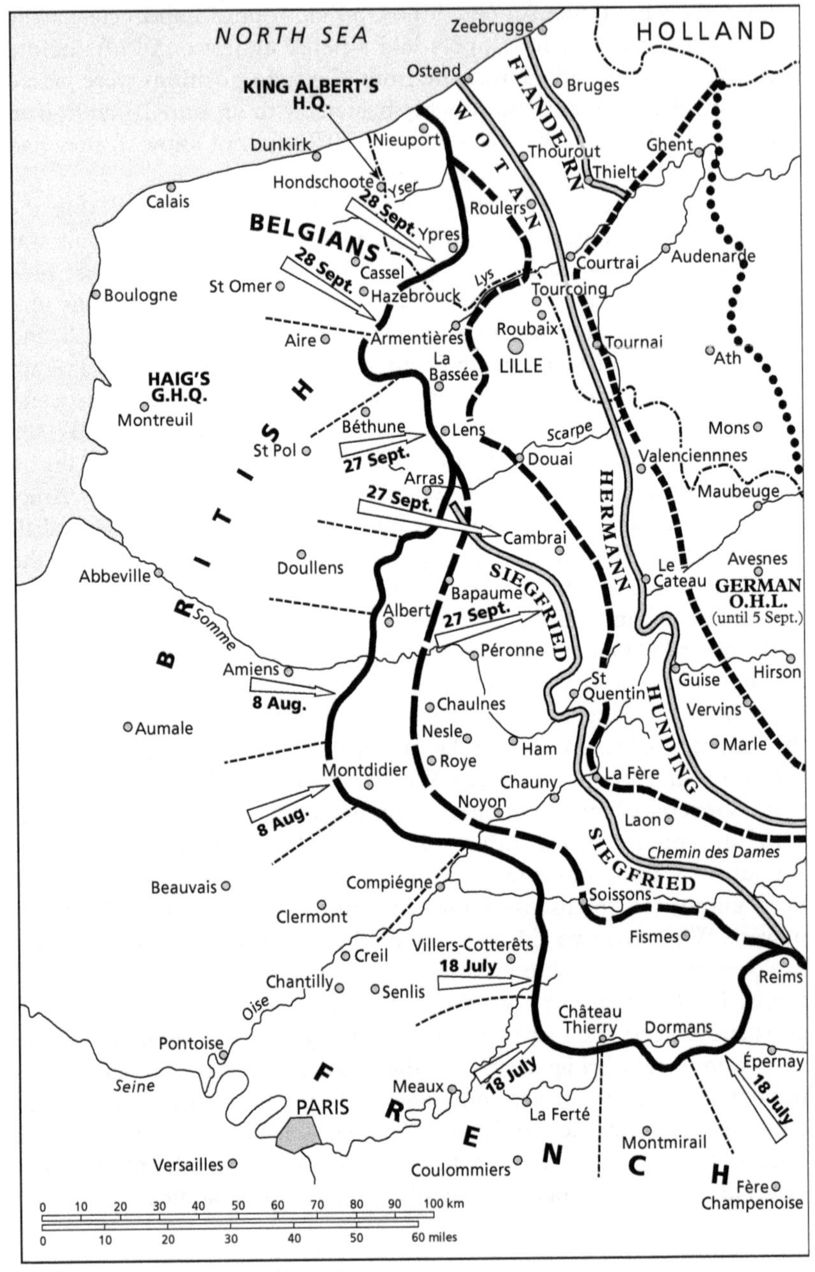

Map 13 Allied advances ('The 100 Days'), July–November 1918

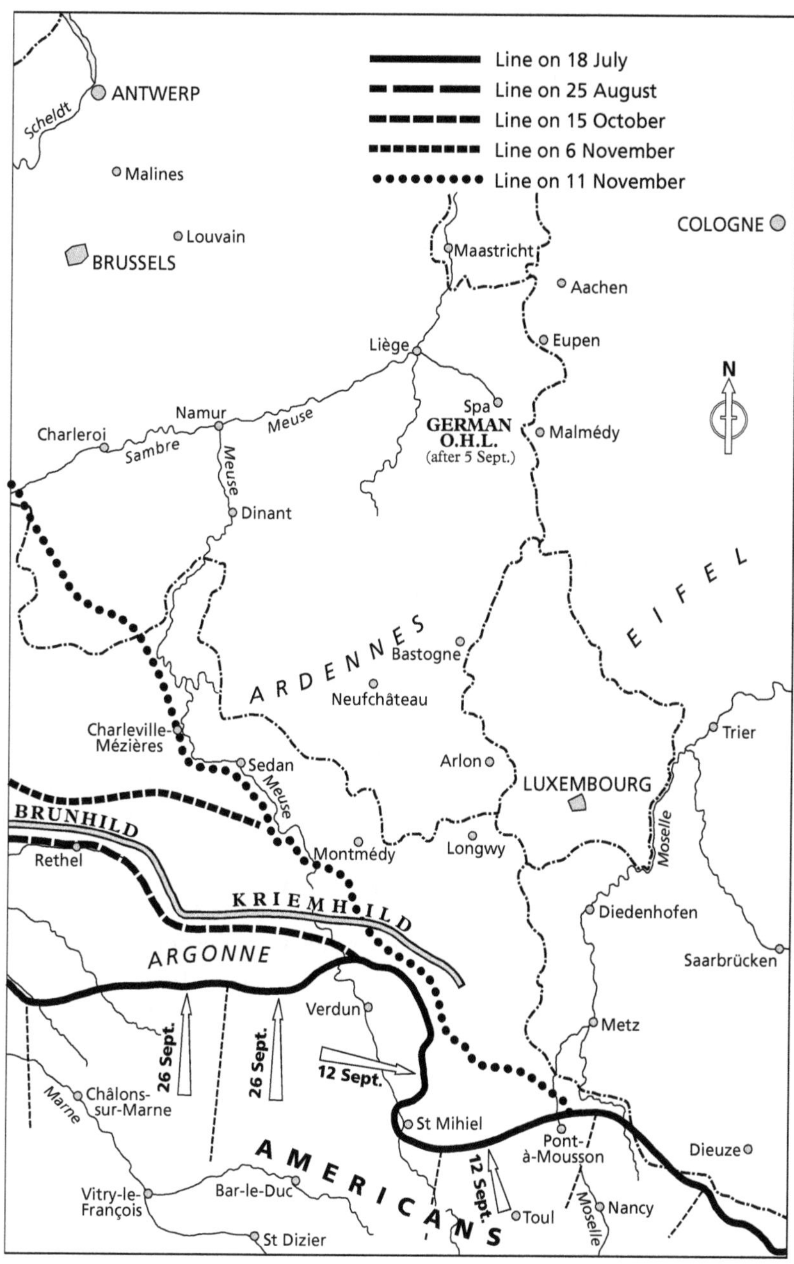
Line on 18 July
Line on 25 August
Line on 15 October
Line on 6 November
Line on 11 November
ANTWERP
Scheldt
Malines
Louvain
BRUSSELS
Maastricht
COLOGNE
Aachen
Liège
Eupen
N
Spa
GERMAN
O.H.L.
(after 5 Sept.)
Malmédy
Namur
Meuse
Charleroi
Sambre
Meuse
Dinant
EIFEL
ARDENNES
Bastogne
Neufchâteau
Charleville-
Mézières
Sedan
Arlon
Trier
LUXEMBOURG
Meuse
Moselle
BRUNHILD
Rethel
Montmédy
Longwy
KRIEMHILD
Diedenhofen
Saarbrücken
ARGONNE
Verdun
Metz
26 Sept.
26 Sept.
12 Sept.
Châlons-
sur-Marne
Marne
St Mihiel
Pont-
à-Mousson
Dieuze
AMERICANS
12 Sept.
Vitry-le-
François
Bar-le-Duc
Toul
Nancy
Moselle
St Dizier

Map 13 (cont.)

Emperor but did so in the immediate aftermath of his ministry's collapse. The Armistice would now come into effect with a new German government in place. But, at this point, the position of the Emperor was still uncertain, despite the new government reinforcing Max's statement by declaring Germany a republic. Wilhelm had already turned his back on civilian leaders, having taken the decision to consult with military headquarters. And it was Hindenburg and Groener who now advised him that the overwhelming opinion of the army was that he should indeed abdicate or else run the risk of open civil war in Germany. Revealing uncharacteristic humility and self-effacement, Wilhelm accepted the advice and agreed to leave for exile in the Netherlands. A response to the Armistice terms was now the first task of Frederich Ebert, first president of the new German republic, and he rapidly realised that he had no option other than to accept them. The German delegates at the front then duly signed the Armistice documents at 5:05 AM, which came into effect at 11:00 AM. Hostilities on the Western Front fizzled out with British troops going about their usual routines in a spirit of intense anti-climax.

By playing a major role in bringing about the Armistice, the high command of the German Army saved itself the extreme humiliation of utter disintegration in the field. Some entente generals, most notably Pershing and Mangin, argued that even this scintilla of dignity was too much and wanted a vigorous pursuit to the end. Two reasons militated against such a conclusion. First was the ability of entente logistics to maintain the offensive, for although the American, British and French armies had immense resources in terms of weapons, ammunition and (thanks to the Americans) manpower, all the coalition forces had strained their logistics systems to their utmost by November. Second was that by the autumn of 1918 the politicians and home fronts of both Britain and France were desperate to end the hardships forced by war, and sacrificing more of their soldiers in order to emphasise the scale of their victory seemed pointless.

The role of the BEF in the final advance to victory was considerable. Of the 385,500 Germans taken prisoner by the Americans, Belgians, British and French, the BEF took 188,700. The number of guns captured by the BEF was equally impressive, consisting of 2,840 from the 6,615 taken in total.[61] However, this disguises the American effort somewhat as a number of US Divisions fought as part of the British Armies. These figures also need to factor in the immense efforts of the Dominion

[61] Harris and Barr, *Amiens to Armistice*, 287–301; Terraine, *To Win a War*, 258.

divisions. The Australian and Canadian corps brought in a combined total of 54,391 prisoners, or just over a quarter of the BEF's total. The Canadian Corps had a particularly impressive end to the war. Having avoided major action in the German spring offensives, it was in a perfect position to reveal the strengths forged through years of internal cohesion and consistency of approach. In contrast, the Australian Corps was heavily involved in fierce defensive action and was, quite understandably, running out of steam by the autumn. At the same time, the New Zealanders and South Africans continued to perform to high standards despite operating in the interchangeable British corps system. Praise for Dominion units should not be taken as a sign that British divisions were failing to pull their weight. Most British divisions had fought to the point of exhaustion during the spring offensives and were being hurriedly reconstituted with raw conscripts at the point the advance commenced. The rapid integration of these troops and their ability to play a part, no matter how imperfect or partial, in the eventual victory is a tribute to the flexibility of the BEF's teeth units.

Using casualties as an indicator of military effectiveness is extremely difficult due to the impossibility of creating useful comparative statistics. On the surface, the figures look good for the Germans. On 21 March 1918, they suffered the usual experience of the attackers on the Western Front – their casualties exceeded those of the British defenders standing at 39,929 and 38,152, respectively. But thereafter the Germans bucked the trend. During the whole of Operation Michael the Germans suffered 239,800 casualties compared with 254,739 inflicted on the British and French.[62] This trend continued across the remaining German offensive efforts. But from mid-July and the resumption of the offensive by the entente forces, it becomes less easy to determine whether the usual pattern returned, for there is a welter of statistics with overlapping census dates. Taking the period August–October 1918, it can be determined that the Germans achieved a net advantage of 35,500 combat fatalities over the British. Therefore, it seems highly likely that the German Army re-imposed the Western Front orthodoxy until the Armistice. The re-emergence of this trend can be taken as evidence of the remarkable resilience and enduring professional standards of the German Army. But the inability to draw simple conclusions from casualty statistics is revealed when prisoners are factored in. German soldiers surrendered in vast numbers by the summer of 1918. In the last four months of the war, the BEF took almost as many prisoners as it had in the previous

[62] Stevenson, *With Our Backs*, 55, 68.

four years. Attributing this willingness to surrender to British military efficiency alone is, of course, highly problematic. By the same token, the impact of the BEF's steady, remorseless advance should not be discounted lightly. The experience of being pursued doggedly by a determined, well-supplied, competent foe must have been extremely demoralising for the exhausted German soldiers, especially as their leaders had so often belittled the quality of the BEF. Thus, the extent to which the German Army was a far from defeated force at the Armistice can be questioned. Although it can be argued that the German Army was defeated from within by the mental collapse of its high command, the fact remains that fewer and fewer German soldiers were prepared to make a determined stand by late October 1918, and the British-led entente advance was capable of dealing effectively with the last pockets of resistance.

The British forces on the Western Front had shown quite remarkable skill and imagination, which raises the issue of the considerable historiographical debate surrounding the British achievements in the 'Hundred Days' from 8 August to 11 November 1918. Broadly speaking, while some historians have focused variously on either operational or tactical improvements in British performance, others have stressed German failure as the greater factor in allied success. While operational explanations of British success have emphasised such factors as decentralisation of command, logistics and superiority of materiel, tactical explanations have embraced both the emergence of combined arms techniques and, alternatively and paradoxically, the significance of individual arms of service. Explanations resting on German failure, while equally varied, tend to condemn the BEF for continuing conservatism.[63] To all this must be added the greater co-ordination of allied armies following Foch's appointment and the abandonment of the idea of wider strategic objectives in favour of Foch's *bataille général* of a series of limited and localised attacks over a wide front that unlocked the deadlock and forced the Germans back.

There has been some emphasis upon the emergence of combined arms as a significant factor in British success and, indeed, of the emergence of 'modern battle'.[64] In reality, it is clear that this was by no means uniform across the BEF. Edmonds, indeed, was correct in suggesting that the Hundred Days consisted of a combination of more traditional set-piece

[63] There is an admirable summary of the different approaches in Jonathan Boff, *Winning and Losing on the Western Front: The British Third Army and the Defeat of Germany in 1918* (Cambridge University Press, 2012), 7–15.

[64] Jonathan Bailey, 'The First World War and the Birth of the Modern Style of Warfare', *Strategic and Combat Studies Institute Occasional Papers* 22 (1996), 13–21.

attacks on well-prepared defensive positions, attacks on field positions in semi-mobile conditions and outright pursuit. In the case of Third Army, for example, of 202 opposed attacks; not one saw the employment together of infantry, artillery, machine guns in close support or barrage, gas, tanks, cavalry and ground-attack aircraft. Cavalry appeared in just two attacks, gas in five, RAF ground attack in six, machine guns in forty and tanks in fifty. Infantry, however, were supported by artillery on 186 occasions.[65] Despite remaining an artillery-led force, the BEF's infantry proved that it was by no means simply an adjunct to heavy fire power. The 1918 offensives revealed that the infantry was capable of advancing with relatively few significant artillery assets. This was partly to do with the changing nature of the battlefield. In essence, the semi-open warfare experienced in the later stages of the 1916 and 1917 battles was the norm in the late summer of 1918. With the army on the march, the infantry had to survive with fewer large-scale, heavy bombardments and work their way forward supported by only immediate covering fire. This often required the infantry to deploy its full range of organic fire power assets from Lewis guns (which numbered thirty per battalion by July 1918) to rifles grenades (at least sixteen per battalion) while calling upon the close support of mortars and field artillery. With the Germans occupying scattered positions, the infantry had to consider even more closely the issues of outflanking and fire and movement. In defence and attack, the BEF required its infantry to show imagination, flexibility and dogged determination. Fortunately, the latter quality was often shown by both veterans and fresh conscripts. In terms of sophistication, the BEF certainly had an excellent blueprint in its training manuals, and it possessed equally good weapons in abundance by 1918, but it was continually undermined by the inability to ensure an overall quality in training and impart a cohesive, over-arching understanding of the infantry battle.

While it has been fashionable to stress the greater flexibility and skills of Dominion divisions, and notwithstanding contemporary criticism of the British by some Australian commanders, British infantry divisions generally stood up well to the challenges. After all, of sixty active divisions involved between August and November 1918, only ten were from the Dominions. Certainly, the standard of junior leadership was far better than the Official History later claimed, Edmonds's regular army prejudices perhaps coming to the fore when the decentralisation of

[65] Jonathan Boff, 'Combined Arms during the Hundred Days Campaign, August–November 1918', *War in History* 17 (2010), 459–78; Jonathan Boff, *Winning and Losing*, 36–8, 123–59.

command had unsettled older regulars.[66] It is also clear that the mix of surviving veterans and inexperienced conscripts did not impair the ability of the BEF to adapt. Indeed, it has been suggested that conscripts 'ignorant and easily killed though they often were, blended with natural leaders to keep the show going'.[67]

Adjusting to this form of warfare on a grand scale, however, was difficult given earlier experiences. British infantry units often remained obsessed with secure flanks and were not always comfortable with the concept of pushing on when neighbouring units appeared to be hung up or slowing down. It is difficult to be too condemnatory of such hesitation given the nature of the fighting in the great trench battles, but it also reveals once again the inability of the army to impose a cohesive, uniform training doctrine. This issue does appear to have been recognised, for in the spring of 1918 Maxse was appointed the Inspector of Training, replacing the former GHQ Directorate of Training. Considering that this had been in existence since 1916, its failure to set a consistent standard must be interpreted as either a black mark against its head, Brigadier-General Arthur Solly-Flood, or an indictment of British military culture. In fact, Solly-Flood had played an important role in overseeing the reorganisation of infantry platoons in 1917 and in restructuring the training system.[68] SS135, *Instructions for the Training of Divisions for Offensive Action*, was reissued in January 1918 as *The Training and Employment of Divisions, 1918*. It had several new features, including less emphasis upon hard and fast rules. It has been argued that a blend of it with the pre-war *Field Service Regulations I* made a significant base for the kind of operational and tactical flexibility that occurred in the Hundred Days.[69]

The difficulty, as always, lay in the varied nature of training within different formations and the diversity of command approaches. Pressure of events constrained training opportunities after March 1918, with the increasing tempo of operations militating against Maxse's efforts.[70] The combination of the beefed-up post in the form of an Inspectorate and the strength of Maxse's character opened up the way for a new attitude towards training, but the war ended before its work had matured, and it is therefore impossible to judge its impact. Such weaknesses should

[66] Simkins, *From the Somme to Victory*, 121–205; Simkins, 'Somme Reprise: Reflections on the Fighting for Albert and Bapaume, August 1918', in Bond (ed.), *Look to Your Front*, 147–62; Simkins, 'Co-stars or Supporting Cast? British Divisions in the Hundred Days, 1918', in Griffith (ed.), *British Fighting Methods*, 50–69.

[67] Bidwell and Graham, *Firepower*, 117.

[68] Robbins, *British Generalship*, 94–5, 107–10; Simkins, *From Somme to Victory*, 46–8.

[69] Simpson, *Directing Operations*, 155–75.

[70] Boff, *Winning and Losing*, 59–68.

temper any unconditional praise of the BEF in the final stages of the war. Irrespective of the attempts to bring about uniformity, however, decentralisation of, and flexibility in, command styles was undoubtedly helpful in allowing commanders to adapt to different circumstances and the increasing tempo, a result nicely characterised by Tim Travers as 'useful anarchy'.[71] Much depended, of course, upon the quality of leadership at battalion, brigade and divisional levels, and the emergence of younger commanders was significant: Roland Boys Bradford VC became a brigade commander (186th Brigade) at just twenty-five in November 1917, and Hugh Keppel Bethell became a divisional commander (66th Division) at thirty-five in March 1918. While these were exceptions, the average age of divisional commanders fell from fifty-five in August 1914 to forty-nine in November 1918.[72] In any case, centralisation had had limited appeal to those used to the pragmatism of the old regular army and 'the flexibility and professionalism that prided improvisation and empirical lessons drawn from experience, both past and immediate, over-elaborate doctrine and exhortation'.[73] Generally, it has been argued that divisional commanders were more and more important with both corps and army commanders less so, army commanders like Rawlinson even being largely spectators.[74] Clearly, there was increasing delegation to subordinate commanders, although, as with much else, there was little actual consistency in whether delegation resulted from top-down or bottom-up initiatives. This suggests continuing unevenness in any 'learning curve'.[75]

At the forefront of the BEF's advance to victory, too, was its artillery. By 1918, artillery fire could be adjusted according to temperature, the charge used, the velocity and direction of the wind, the age and wear of the gun and the type of shell and fuse.[76] Moreover, the techniques of sound ranging and flash spotting were fully developed. Despite the fact that advancing infantry often outstripped the ability of the heavy guns to keep pace, the BEF still found that it needed as many guns as it could muster. The fluid pace of operations in both defence and attack in 1918

[71] Travers, *How the War Was Won*, 149.

[72] Robbins, *British Generalship*, 64–5, 115–42; John Bourne, 'The BEF's Generals on 29 September 1918: An Empirical Portrait with Some British and Australian Comparisons', in Peter Dennis and Jeff Grey (eds.), *1918: Defining Victory* (Canberra, Australia: Army History Unit, 1999), 96–113.

[73] Connelly, *Steady the Buffs*, 225–6.

[74] Andy Simpson, 'British Corps Command on the Western Front' in Sheffield and Todman (eds.), *Command and Control*, 97–118; Peter Simkins, 'Building Blocks: Aspects of Command and Control at Brigade Level in the BEF's Offensive Operations, 1916–18', Sheffield and Todman (eds.), *Command and Control*, 141–71.

[75] Boff, *Winning and Losing*, 192–215, 249.

[76] Nick Lloyd, *Hundred Days* (New York: Basic Books, 2014), 34.

often placed much more emphasis on the rapid deployment of horse artillery in conditions much closer to those conceived in pre-war thinking. Lengthy barrages were simply not needed where the German defences were weak, the able artilleryman, Herbert Uniacke, in his capacity as Deputy Inspector General of Training, rushing out a series of new leaflets to encourage direct support for the infantry.[77] But, whenever the BEF came up against strongly held, well-prepared enemy positions, it found that it could not do without its heavy artillery. The attempt to take the Quadrilateral on 18 September was a notable example of an assault made on an elaborate enemy strong point which came to grief due to inadequate heavy artillery preparation. In this instance, the organic fire power and tactical skills of the attacking infantry were of little value without the vital support of a well-planned and well-executed heavy bombardment. The difficulties of keeping heavy artillery in action in rapidly changing circumstances were partially offset by the increasing use of gas shells. Although the British and French produced gas that was inferior to that of the Germans, their own variants proved to be sufficient against poor German gas masks. The increasing availability of gas shells and gas projectors then allowed the British to cover both their retreats and advances more effectively.

As has been noted, much of the success of the BEF in 1918 was due to its logistical strength. Committed to an artillery war, the BEF's logistics staff used artillery ammunition as the vital yardstick for its operational requirements. The emphasis on using artillery expenditure as the measurement of logistical endurance then made the BEF's operations less impressive in terms of ground gained than the German advances of the spring but far more secure and far less susceptible to counter-attack. The downside of this approach meant a loss of operational tempo, which often allowed the Germans to retreat in relatively good order, giving them time to block and destroy communications. Between August and November, for example, the Royal Engineers erected over 330 stock-span or rolled-steel-joint bridges over watercourses, or double the number erected in the previous four years of static warfare.[78] The logistical flexibility achieved by such efforts allowed Haig to switch positions almost at will, as noted, and thus ensured constant pressure on the German front. Maintaining

[77] Marble, *British Artillery*, 235.

[78] Lloyd, *Hundred Days*, 108. On the neglected issue of engineering logistics, see also Rob Thompson, '"Delivering the Goods": Operation Landovery Castle: A Logistical and Administrative Analysis of Canadian Corps Preparations for the Battle of Amiens 8–11 August, 1918', in Sheffield and Gray (eds.), *Changing War*, 37–54; Rob Thompson, 'Mud, Blood and Wood: BEF Operational and Combat Logistico-Engineering during the Third Battle of Ypres, 1917', in Peter Doyle and Matthew Bennett (eds.), *Fields of Battle: Terrain in Military History* (Dordrecht, the Netherlands: Kluwer Academic, 2002), 237–55.

the advance then placed great stress on the system, particularly once the railheads were left well in the rear. This put the emphasis onto motor lorries, which strained hard to deal with autumn conditions of greasy roads, fog, rain and drizzle. Nevertheless, lorries proved an invaluable link in the chain and their numbers increased enormously during the course of the conflict rising from 334 in 1914 to 33,560 by 1918.[79]

Understanding the nature of British thinking on logistics and the way it supported front-line operations has therefore got to be taken into account in any assessment of the supposedly greater quality of German tactical thinking and the extent to which the Germans were undefeated by the Armistice.

Improved communications also played its part, although there were still significant difficulties. To supplement earlier reliance upon telegraph and telephone, wireless had become more widespread by 1917 with the introduction of the British Field (BF) Trench Set, the Loop Set, and the Wilson Set, although all relied on spark technology and were vulnerable to damage and interference. Continuous-wave sets had then been introduced in 1917 but were largely confined to artillery counter-battery work. SS148, *Forward Intercommunications in Battle*, encapsulated lessons thus far learned in March 1917. More mobile operations in 1918 posed different problems: forty pigeon lofts were lost in March 1918, for example, with some corps exchanges trying to maintain links with multiple divisional headquarters along single cables. Advancing was potentially less of a problem in that cables did not have to be buried as consistently given the absence of German artillery, and wires could be salvaged more easily. Breakdown was still a reality, however, as at Epéhy on 18 September 1918. Nonetheless, communications were far more robust and flexible than before.[80]

These systems connected the key teeth-arms of the BEF, infantry and artillery, with their ancillaries in the form of tanks, armoured cars, aircraft and cavalry by 1918. Aircraft were vital in reconnaissance and performed an increasingly significant ground-assault role that was often extremely useful for the infantry. Their efficiency, however, was increasingly adversely affected by bad weather. Tanks and armoured cars could also support the infantry effectively, although they never became the cutting edge of the BEF's assaults. Despite being in demand, their lack of mechanical reliability meant that they were by

[79] Ian M. Brown, 'Feeding Victory: The Logistic Imperative behind the Hundred Days', in Dennis and Grey (eds.), *1918*, 130–47.

[80] Brian Hall, 'Technological Adaptation in a Global Conflict: The British Army and Communications beyond the Western Front, 1914–18', *Journal of Military History* 78 (2014), 37–71; Griffith, *Battle Tactics*, 169–75.

no means a panacea providing a powerful shield for the precious infantry, which often infantry attacked without much in the way of tank support.

At Amiens, 414 tanks – mostly the improved Mark V – started on 8 August, but only thirty-eight were available on 11 August and only six on 12 August. Even the newest and most improved types of tank had significant weaknesses as weapons of breakthrough and exploitation. The Mark V had a speed of only three miles per hour and a range of twenty-five miles. The Whippet (Medium A) could reach 8.3 miles per hour but could cross only narrow trenches. Tanks therefore remained best suited to supporting infantry in set-piece attacks, especially as the distance they were required to cover before reaching the point of attack had expanded from perhaps a mile in August to over twenty miles in November.[81] Apart from chronic mechanical unreliability, tanks remained vulnerable to artillery, armour-piercing machine gun rounds, and anti-tank rifles, while crews were still exposed to heat exhaustion, noise, and carbon monoxide poisoning. In addition, reserve crews were in short supply, with human losses in the Tank Corps amounting to 40 per cent between August and November 1918. But spares were also lacking because the emphasis had been given to production of tanks per se rather than keeping existing machines serviceable. Salvage was certainly possible, and some individual tanks were in action up to fifteen times, but tanks and armoured cars could not be kept running in large numbers indefinitely. Of the tanks available on 8 August 1918, some 55 per cent had been lost by 20 October.[82]

However, there is some discrepancy in the figures given for the number of tanks available at any given time since, while some tanks were being salvaged or repaired, others were in reserve or being used for training purposes. Indeed, it has been argued that tanks were more durable than usually assumed, with 800 salvaged between August and November, and could have been used much more effectively. Thus, there was an essential conservatism informing GHQ's conclusion in August 1918 that tanks were only 'a mechanical contrivance'.[83]

[81] Boff, 'Combined Arms', 466.

[82] Harris and Barr, *Amiens to the Armistice*, 297; Harris, *Men, Ideas and Tanks*, 186–7; Stevenson, *With Our Backs*, 217; Boff, *Winning and* Losing, 142.

[83] Tim Travers, 'Could the Tanks of 1918 Have Been War-Winners for the British Expeditionary Force?' *Journal of Contemporary History* 27 (1992), 389–406; Travers, 'Evolution of British Strategy and Tactics', 173–200' idem, *How the War Was Won*, 32–49. See also Robin Prior and Trevor Wilson, 'What Manner of Victory? Reflections on the Termination of the First World War', *Revue Internationale d'Histoire Militaire* 72 (1990), 80–96.

It is hard to quarrel, however, with the judgement of SS214, *Tanks and Their Employment in Co-operation with Other Arms*, which conceded in August 1918 that the tank was far from perfect in a technical sense.[84] What is apparent is that tanks became more scarce, the number of attacks made with their assistance steadily declining even though attacks with tank support enjoyed a high success rate. In the Third Army, for example, the number of attacks supported by tanks decreased from an average of over twenty-five with over ten tanks participating between 21 August and 3 September to fewer than five attacks and fewer than five tanks participating by 4 November.[85]

Like tanks and armoured cars, the value of cavalry is difficult to discern easily. At times it played an important role supporting the infantry, particularly in defence, and then acted as a weapon of exploitation from 8 August onwards and was certainly much in demand by the last few weeks of the war. It was hardly the fault of the cavalry that its manpower and horses had been whittled down so much by this point that it was unable to perform all of its allotted tasks evenly: it has been suggested that the entire Cavalry Corps had fewer men in late 1918 than the 1st Cavalry Division in 1914. More disconcerting for British command procedures was the fact that liaison between the cavalry and tank forces was minimal, which meant that the potential of these two arms to collaborate on the battlefield was not realised.[86]

The combination of structural weaknesses and rapidly changing circumstances meant that the BEF was never able to deploy all of its arms evenly in 1918. It therefore failed to develop anything like a unified approach to battle in which elements were neatly matched and balanced to produce maximum impact for most efficient input. Army and corps commanders were often forced to improvise with whatever they had to hand, reassured by the certainty that these components would not be undermined by insurmountable logistical difficulties. Nonetheless, this still translated into a high degree of combat effectiveness. In the Hundred Days, ground won stayed won, and moreover, the ground was of increasing strategic importance. As the BEF overran defensive systems, it successively opened up the Germans to defeat on a broad front and allowed them no respite even if the operational tempo was moderate rather than rapid. In 1918, the BEF experienced many scares and close-run things

[84] Griffith, *Battle Tactics*, 165; Beach, 'Issued by the General Staff', 485–7; Harris, Men, *Ideas and Tanks*, 166–71, 180–2.

[85] Boff, 'Combined Arms', 466; Boff, *Winning and Losing*, 142–5; Griffith, *Battle Tactics*, 166–7.

[86] Stephen Badsey, *Doctrine and Reform in the British Cavalry, 1880–1918* (Aldershot: Ashgate, 2008), 295–300.

before playing the major role in the entente's victory. Haig, his GHQ, armies, corps and divisions put on a team effort to achieve victory, and as in any good team, this did not necessarily mean brilliance at every level but the ability to show enough quality, consistency and cohesion to iron out weaknesses and maximise strengths.

11 Beyond the Western Front

The British military effort between 1914 and 1918 was dispersed throughout the globe. As if to underline this point, it is worth reflecting that the first shots fired by British troops in the conflict were fired on 12 August 1914 by troops capturing the German wireless station at Kamina in Togoland, and Paul von Lettow-Vorbeck did not surrender German forces in East Africa until 23 November 1918, when news reached him of the armistice in Europe. Excluding the experience of Dominion forces and Indian troops, which are beyond the scope of this book, a snapshot of the deployment of British infantry divisions on 1 November 1918 shows that while fifty-one were deployed in France, four were in Salonika, three in Italy, one in Palestine, one in Mesopotamia, three on garrison duty in India and four in the United Kingdom. At the same date, around 10,000 British troops, mostly soldiers of the King's African Rifles, were serving in German East Africa. British forces proper were to be involved in what were essentially colonial campaigns in Togoland, Cameroon and German East Africa, while Dominion troops from South Africa were responsible for the capture of German South-West Africa and Dominion troops from Australia and New Zealand first saw action in small-scale operations to capture German naval and wireless installations in the Pacific. Larger numbers of British troops were involved in the Gallipoli campaign, Mesopotamia, Palestine, Italy and Salonika. A token British force saw service, alongside Japanese troops, at the siege of the German naval base of Tsingtao in China.[1] British troops also had to deal with a domestic rebellion in Dublin in Easter week 1916.

Very small numbers of European British troops saw service in the campaigns in Togoland, the Cameroons and German East Africa. Most of the forces used in these campaigns were native troops drawn from the King's African Rifles (KAR) and the West African Frontier Force

[1] Robert Holland, 'The British Empire and the Great War', in J. M. Brown and W. R. Louis (eds.), *The Oxford History of the British Empire: The Twentieth Century* (Oxford University Press, 1999), 114–37. The best operational study of the war as a whole remains, Cyril Falls, *The First World War* (London: Longmans, 1960).

(WAFF). As discussed in Chapter 1, colonial parsimony meant that the KAR had actually been reduced in strength in the years leading up to the outbreak of the First World War. Nevertheless, this regiment was to expand to a strength of twenty-two battalions during the war. The WAFF saw a more modest expansion to eight battalions during the war, a reflection on the relative ease with which German forces were contained there. Significant contingents of the Indian Army also served in the African campaigns, and British forces were to be found acting in conjunction with French, Belgian and Portuguese troops. African manpower was tapped not just for the native regiments but also for logistics, with hundreds of thousands of African porters conscripted into service; a conservative estimate is that 50,000 of these men died through disease, overwork and malnutrition. The campaigns in Africa took on the character of the Victorian imperial campaigns in which so many British professional soldiers had learned their trade. The officer corps of the KAR and WAFF remained regular in composition long into 1915, while the New Armies in Britain were starved of a professional cadre.

The capture of Togoland proved to be a very straightforward operation, and it was conducted by Captain F. C. Bryant, temporary commander of the Gold Coast Regiment, with local forces. The major strategic asset which was captured was the powerful wireless transmitter at Kamina. The German forces in Togoland consisted merely of paramilitary police units numbering around 700 men and around 300 German reservists; thus, the acting German governor initially proposed neutrality to his French and British neighbours. On 9 August, two companies of the Gold Coast Regiment captured Lomé, just over the border in Togoland. British forces suffered no serious resistance until 22 August, but then columns became separated in the bush, and heavy casualties were taken from machine gun fire. On the night of 24–25 August, the Germans smashed the Kamina wireless station, and on the following day, German forces surrendered.

The Cameroons were rather better defended than Togoland, with twelve companies of locally raised Schütztruppen, 1,650 strong, with 205 white officers and NCOs. On the outbreak of war, these were augmented by paramilitary police and German reservists, which meant that ultimately German forces in the Cameroons could field around 8,000 men, 1,460 of them Europeans. The German defence plans drawn up in November 1913 focused the defence of the colony on the northern highlands, where the climate was better, disease less common and food supplies more plentiful. British intelligence on German intentions or indeed decent maps of the German colony were lacking on the outbreak of war.

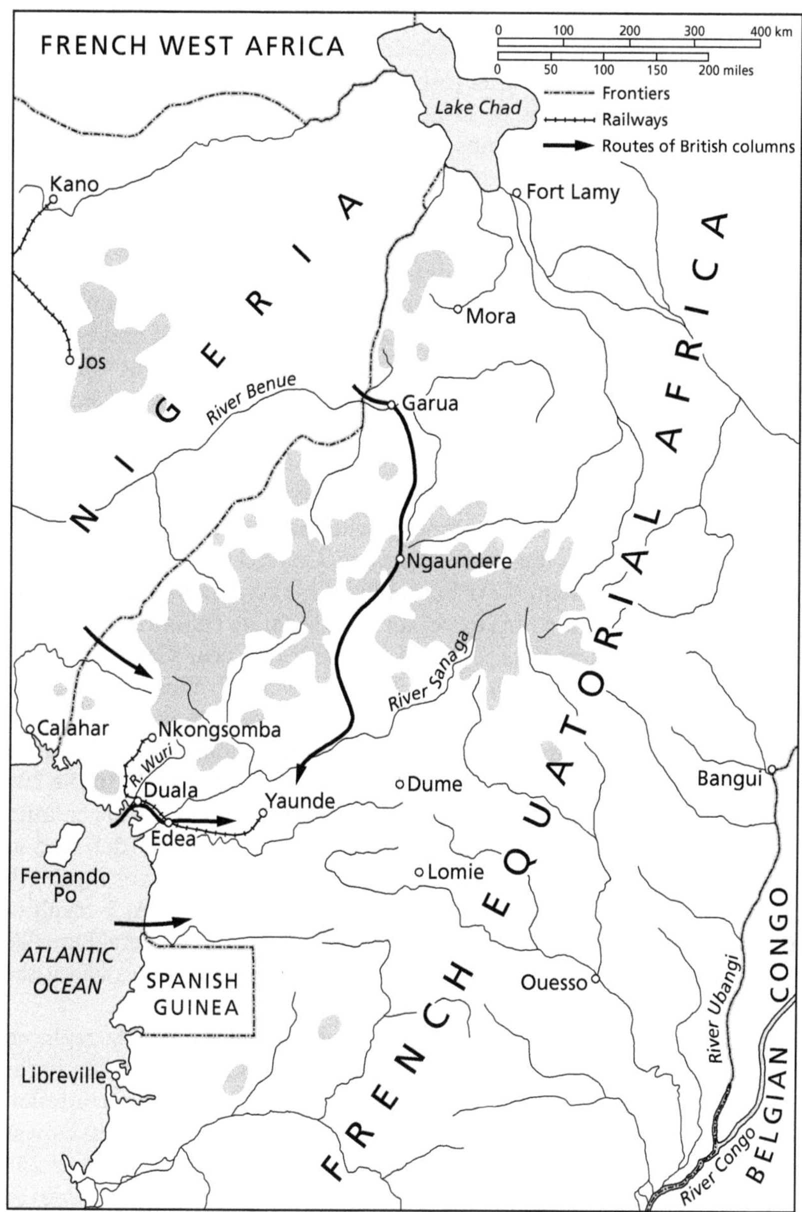

Map 14 The Cameroons

Britain's main concern in the Cameroons was to deny the use of Duala's wireless station and port facilities to German cruisers. Brigadier General C. M. Dobell, the Inspector General of the West African Frontier Force, who was in London on the outbreak of war, was put in command of the Cameroons Expeditionary Force (CEF), which contained a significant French contingent. Dobell's instructions were to seize Buea, Victoria and Duala on the coast, and initially the War Office did not envisage any further action, although it appreciated that the Germans would probably continue their defence from the interior of the colony. Dobell left Liverpool on the 31 August and collected his command, drawn from Gambia, Dakar, Sierra Leone, the Gold Coast and Nigeria, between 10 and 17 September. On the 25 September, the CEF had arrived at Duala, supported by Royal Navy cruisers HMS *Challenger* and *Cumberland*, and an ultimatum was presented to the German governor, informing him that the town would be bombarded if the colony was not unconditionally surrendered. The Germans abandoned Duala on the 26 September, and Dobell captured it without firing a shot.

In Nigeria itself, on the outbreak of war, Colonel C. H. P. Carter, CO of the Nigeria Regiment, WAFF, mobilised his command and, following pre-war plans, organised his forces into five separate columns, two based on Maidugari, one at Yola, one at Lkom and one near Calabar; by the end of August, these had all advanced into the North West Cameroons. Carter's force encountered strong German defences at Garua and Mora, and equipped with nothing heavier than 2.95-inch mountain guns, Carter was not able to reduce them. An attack on Garua on the night of the 30–31 August was driven back with heavy losses, and the whole Yola column was forced to retreat. Another British column was heavily defeated at Nsanakang on 6 September, losing over half of its men killed or captured, with only two officers and ninety native soldiers escaping. As a result of these reverses, troops had to be detached from Brigadier General Dobell's force and a purely defensive stance adopted by British forces along the whole Nigeria–Cameroon frontier.

In September 1914, Lieutenant Colonel Frederick Cunliffe replaced Colonel Carter as commander of the Nigerian Regiment and took charge of operations against the Northern Cameroons. The German commander, fearing that too many of his troops could be cut off if Garua was besieged, reduced the garrison to one and a half companies, around 250 men. So, when Cunliffe moved against Garua in June 1915, he enjoyed overwhelming superiority in manpower, having fourteen companies at his disposal. Also, since the first unsuccessful attack, the British force had been reinforced with two heavy guns, a naval twelve-pounder and a French ninety-five-millimeter. Once the heavy artillery opened up on

Garua, part of the garrison fled, and the rest quickly surrendered on 10 June 1915. After the rainy season, Cunliffe consolidated his position by capturing Banyo on 6 November 1915, no mean feat given its complex of sangars and mutual supporting defences.

In the south, British and French troops under Dobell were initially much less successful. An attempt to capture Jaunde failed as Dobell's troops faced stiff German resistance and the native porters disappeared as soon as shots were heard. Dobell's troops were also taking heavy casualties through disease and malnutrition, losing 25 per cent of their strength. Dobell retreated to Ngwe to regroup in June 1915 when the arrival of the rainy season made further operations impossible in any case. Dobell consolidated his position over the rainy season, and his forces captured Wum Biagas on 9 October 1915; supplied by motorised transport, this then became the forward operating base, which allowed for the British capture of Jaunde on 1 January 1916.

Between December 1915 and February 1916, around 7,000 German troops, mostly askaris, retreated into neutral Spanish Guinea, and Ebolowa fell to French troops on 19 January; this, in Dobell's mind, marked the end of German resistance. The final German garrison to surrender in the Cameroons was that in Mora in the far North of the colony. The 155-strong garrison there surrendered on 18 February 1916, when the men heard of the retreat of most of their comrades into Spanish territory.

The campaign against German East Africa was the most drawn-out campaign of the entire war, although the sustained defence of the colony is properly regarded as March 1916 to November 1917. The conquest of German East Africa was seen by the entente powers as less important than the conquest of the Cameroons, and only when South African troops were made available in large numbers did a sustained campaign really begin. Indeed, reflecting the importance of the South African contingent, Lieutenant General Jan Christiaan Smuts took command of the theatre in January 1916, and when he left to take up his seat in the War Cabinet, he was replaced by Major-General Jacob van Deventer. German forces in German East Africa were led by Lieutenant Colonel Paul von Lettow-Vorbeck, who emerged as one of the most capable commanders of the war and a leading practitioner of irregular warfare.

On the outbreak of war, the colony's governor, Heinrich Schnee, declared Dar es Salaam an open town, fearful that the Royal Navy would bombard it. By doing this, he essentially implemented the plan for the defence of the colony, which had been drawn up by the German General Staff and required the coastal areas to be abandoned and an active defence waged from the interior. Lettow, though initially having just fourteen companies of Schütztruppen and three of German

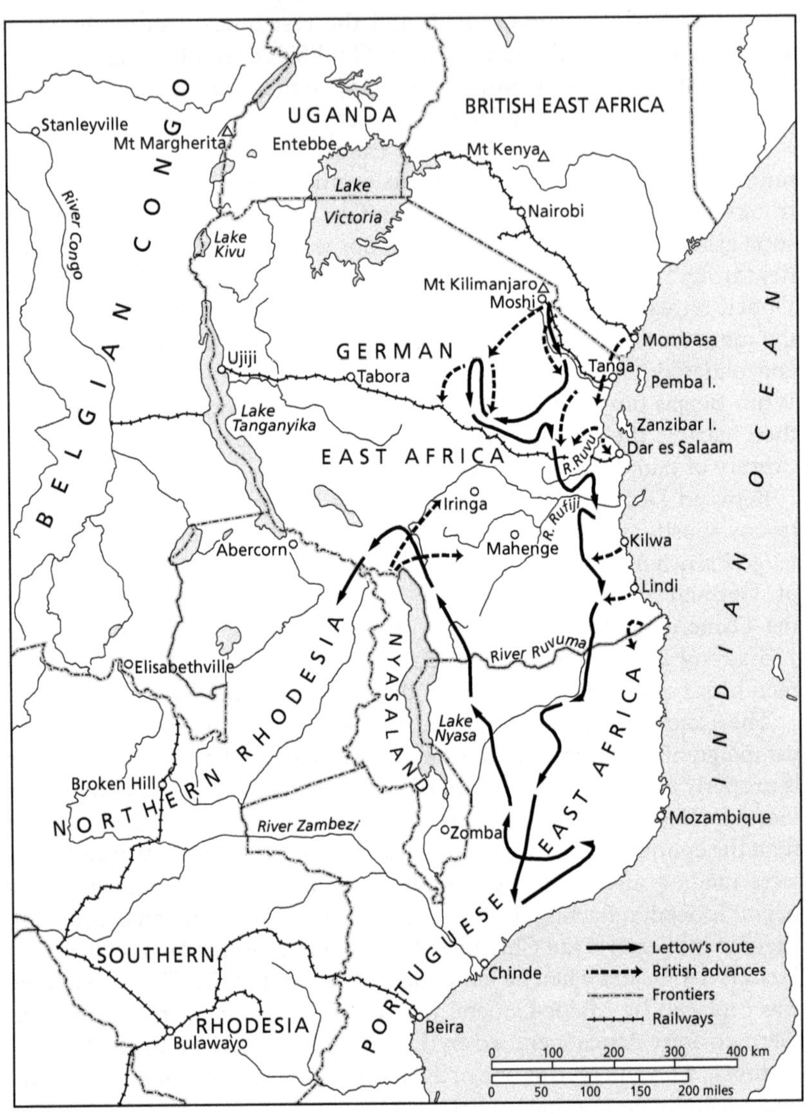

Map 15 East Africa

volunteers, believed that an offensive against British East Africa would relieve pressure against German forces, and on 15 August 1914, German troops captured Taveta, just over the frontier, and threatened the Uganda railway. Lettow was not convinced of the military utility of the local paramilitary police units, and it was to be 1917 until he incorporated them fully in his forces.

The first British attack against German East Africa came in November 1914 from Indian Expeditionary Force B (IEF B) under Major General A. E. Aitken. This force had mobilised at the outbreak of war, but shipping shortages had meant that it could not leave India until mid-October. On 2 November, this force arrived off Tanga, and given the earlier decision by the Germans to declare Dar es Salaam an open port, the British Commander believed that an ultimatum had to be delivered before he could begin offensive operations. On 2 November, the garrison of Tanga was a mere seventy-five men, while IEF B was 5,000 strong, but Lettow ordered Tanga to be held at all costs as he dispatched reinforcements. Over the night of 2–3 November, IEF B troops began landing but in a very poor position, in a mangrove swamp, leading to a narrow beach. The troops continued to land over the course of 3–4 November, establishing a beach head. On the German side, reinforcements started to arrive quickly, with Lettow himself arriving to conduct a stubborn defence in the early hours of 4 November. At midday on 4 November, Aitken ordered his two brigades to advance, but both soon came up against strongly defended German positions. Aitken ordered a frontal assault, and not surprisingly, against heavy machine gun fire, two of his battalions broke. After this ignominious defeat, Aitken decided to re-embark his force, and the force left on 8 November, having suffered over 800 casualties to the defenders 145.

Through 1915 the campaign in German East Africa was more of a naval than a military campaign, much British effort was expended to secure Lake Tanganyika, bringing two motorboats, HMS *Mimi* and *Tou-Tou*, overland in sections through the Belgian Congo, while the destruction of the light cruiser *Konigsberg*, which had sought shelter in the Rufigi River, was accomplished by Royal Naval units with the aid of aerial observation in July 1915. In 1916, the nature of the war changed in German East Africa as the Union of South Africa, having crushed German forces in South West Africa, was able to send significant military forces to East Africa. Smuts took command of a force of 20,000 men and had support from allied forces in the Belgian Congo and Nyasaland. Over the course of 1916, in what was essentially a war of manoeuvre, Smuts managed to expel German forces from most of the colony and captured the important Central Railway. However, faced with supply problems and disease, which reduced some of his units by 80 per cent, Smuts was unable to bring Letow to a decisive battle. In July 1917, when the rains ended, Deventer began his offensive against Lettow and had considerable success, forcing 5,000 German troops, under the command of Theodor

Tafel, to surrender on the 27–28 November. This halved Lettow's forces in one action, and Lettow himself led the remainder of his command into Portuguese East Africa. Living off the land and relying on captured ammunition and supplies, Lettow held out until the 23 November 1918, when news of the Armistice reached him.[2]

The German naval base of Tsingtao, in China, need not, in theory, have been defended at all as it could, under the terms of its foundation treaty, have been returned to the Chinese government, which would have protected German civilians and business interests and allowed German reservists in the Far East to return to Europe. This option vanished quickly when the colony's governor, Meyer-Waldeck, received a message from the Kaiser informing him, '[I]t would shame me more to surrender Kiaochow [*sic*] to the Japanese than Berlin to the Russians.' The British government originally wanted only Japanese naval support in the war to counter the threat from the German Far Eastern Squadron and was acutely aware of the concerns of the United States and the British Dominions about growing Japanese imperialism. When the Japanese assembled an army of 60,000 men and 100 siege guns to capture Tsingtao, which was defended by a mixed force of 184 officers and 4,390 men, many of them German reservists, the British government decided to send a token force, of one battalion of British troops, the 2nd South Wales Borderers, and two companies of the 36th Sikhs, drawn from the British garrisons at Hong Kong and Tientsin, under the command of Brigadier General Barnardiston. The inclusion of this force was rather resented by the Japanese, who saw it, rightly, as an attempt to frustrate Japanese imperial ambitions in China and provide substance to the British declaration on Chinese integrity of 18 August 1914. The first Japanese troops landed at Lungkow on 2 September, with the British contingent arriving at Laoshan Bay on 23 September. The siege of Tsingtao commenced on 22 October and ended in capitulation on 7 November. British losses in the 2nd South Wales Borderers were fourteen men killed or dead of wounds or disease and two officers and thirty-four men wounded.[3]

[2] Ross Anderson, *The Forgotten Front 1914–18: The East African Campaign* (Stroud, UK: Tempus, 2007); H. Moyse-Bartlett, *The King's African Rifles: A Study in the Military History of East and Central Africa, 1890–1945* (Aldershot, UK: Gale & Polden, 1956), 259–418; E. H. Gorges, *The Great War in West Africa* (London: Hutchinson, 1930); and Hew Strachan, *The First World War*, Vol. I: *To Arms* (Oxford University Press, 2001), 495–643.

[3] C. T. Atkinson, *A History of the South Wales Borderers, 1914–18* (London: The Medici Society, 1931); Peter Lowe, *Great Britain and Japan, 1911–15* (London: Macmillan, 1969), 178–98; Hew Strachan, *The First World War*, Vol. I: *To Arms*, 455–65; The

British action against the Ottoman Empire was seen in a number of theatres, most famously at Gallipoli, Palestine and Mesopotamia but also in defence of the Suez Canal itself in February 1915, where a Turkish attack was driven off, the Turkish soldiers in the three boats which actually crossed the canal being killed or captured, and against the Senussi in the Western Desert, who were finally defeated by a charge of the Dorset Yeomanry at Agagiya on 26 February 1916. While many of the actions against the Ottoman Empire relied heavily on Indian Army formations, it must be remembered that an Indian Army brigade consisted of three battalions of Indian troops with one battalion of British troops, so the British Army was intimately involved in these operations, even when there were no British formations per se involved in them.

Britain was formerly at war with the Ottoman Empire from 5 November 1914, though there was a period of hostile neutrality, most notably marked by the closure of the Dardanelles Straits against British shipping on 1 October. On 2 October, the Cabinet sanctioned the dispatch of IEF D to the Persian Gulf, the first element to land being the 16th Infantry Brigade of the 6th (Quetta) Division. It was felt that the presence of this force would protect key oil installations and reassure wavering British allies in the region. The 16th Infantry Brigade arrived at the British-protected island of Bahrain on 23 October and remained there until 31 October. When war with the Ottoman Empire was imminent, it was ordered to sail to Shatt al-Arah and prepare for an attack on the Faw Peninsula south east of Basra. On 6 November, the first elements of the brigade were landed on the peninsula, after HMS *Odin* had reduced an Ottoman fort opposing the landings, and the remainder of the brigade was disembarked at Abadan on 9 November. On 13 November, the 18th Infantry Brigade of the Indian Army also arrived. At this early stage of the campaign, there were already logistical issues as the 16th Brigade had left behind all its transport in India and the 18th Brigade had only brought along some camel transport. The initial landings and supply of these brigades were heavily reliant on locally procured craft. Action against Ottoman troops was also heavily reliant on fire support from the naval flotilla. On 21 November, following further instructions from the Cabinet, Basra was captured, which completed the initial objective of IEF D.

What were perceived as easy victories against the Ottoman troops up to this point, and with Basra essentially abandoned by the Turks, British policy makers in both London and Delhi were inclined to push for a

National Archive (TNA) WO95/5444, 'North China Command: Tsing Tao Expedition: Report of Operations, etc.'.

further advance which would consolidate the position around Basra and, hopefully, open the way to the capture of Baghdad. With some difficulty, due to the problems of river navigation at that time of year, the town of Qurna, fifty miles to the north of Basra and at the confluence of the Tigris and Euphrates Rivers, was captured on 9 December 1914. It was at this point that the Mesopotamian campaign started to evolve into a large-scale military campaign rather than the simple gunboat diplomacy with which it had started. Between March and September 1915, the towns of Amara and Kut on the Tigris and Nassariya on the Euphrates were captured with relatively small losses; Major General Charles Townshend's 6th Indian Division had just ninety-four men killed in their capture of Kut. However, this advance meant that forced IEF D, by this stage reinforced to corps strength, was already widely dispersed with over-extended logistics. An attempt by Townshend's force to capture Baghdad was defeated at the battle of Ctesiphon (22–26 November 1915) by superior Turkish forces. Of the 8,500 British and Indian troops who fought in the battle, more than half were killed or wounded, and the wounded had an agonising journey, in unsprung carts, through the desert, when evacuated to Kut. Townshend managed to extricate his defeated army in a fighting retreat back to Kut, where Townshend decided to await reinforcements and turned the city into an entrenched camp. Bolstered with reinforcements, Turkish forces besieged Kut, which held out for 147 days before finally surrendering on 29 April 1916. The situation for the besieged was desperate as food and medical supplies were exhausted, and trench systems were flooded in heavy rain, exacerbated by the fact that much of Kut was below river level. Attempts to relieve the city were frustrated, and its fall was a serious blow to British prestige, largely as the POWs were so poorly treated. Essentially ordered on a death march by Turkish commanders, who did not have the logistical support to transport them in any other way, and given insufficient rations and no medical help, 4,250 of the 11,800 men taken prisoner died in captivity.

Despite the increasingly desperate situation in Kut, the British situation in Mesopotamia as a whole was starting to improve in early 1916. The 3rd Lahore and 7th Meerut Divisions of the Indian Army along with the 13th (Western) Division all arrived as reinforcements. Major General Frederick Stanley Maude arrived in the theatre in command of the 13th (Western) Division, and in August 1916, as a Lieutenant-General, he took command of the entire Mesopotamian Expeditionary Force (MEF). Maude had served on the Western Front and at Gallipoli and had gained an insight into how a modern army should be organised. Maude did much to resolve the command and logistical problems that had dogged British efforts in Mesopotamia, even though this often meant that senior staff

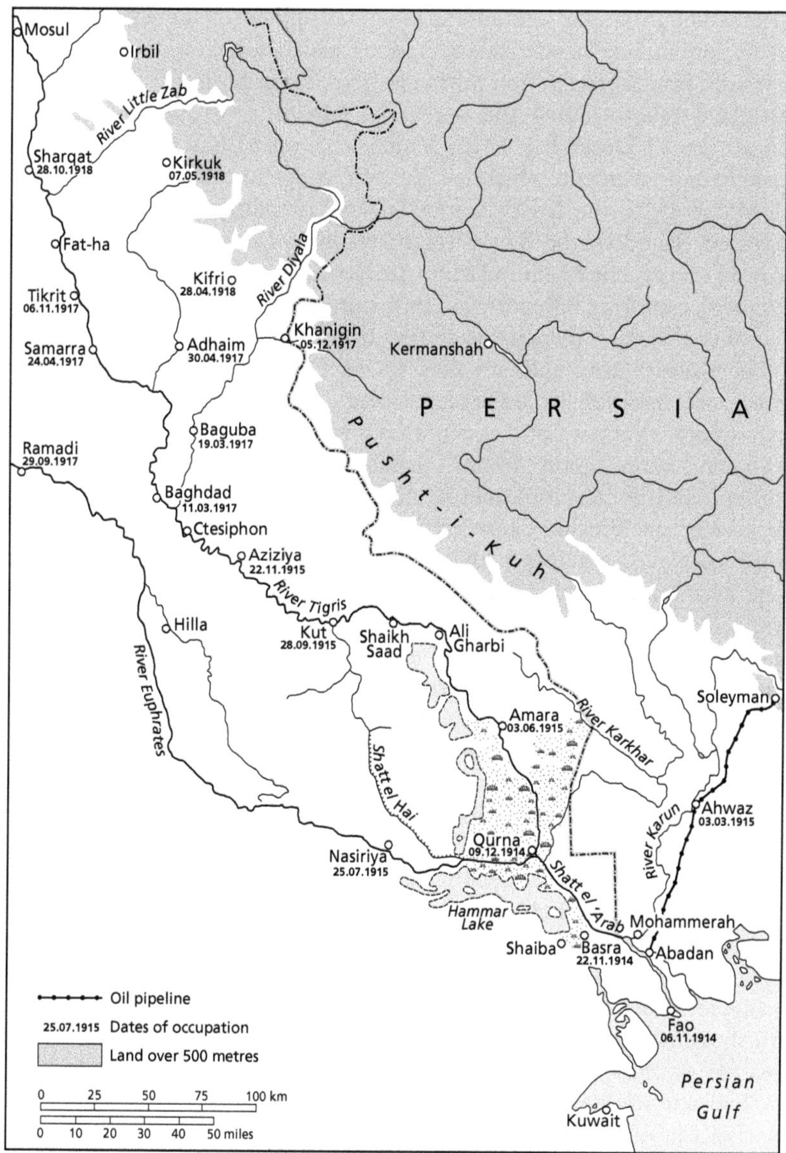

Map 16 Mesopotamia

officers thought he was demanding too much of them. Maude also resolved on the continuance of offensive operations, which he believed were essential to restore British prestige and were in any case a sensible policy given that his intelligent reports noted the numerical inferiority of opposing Turkish forces. On 23 December 1916, Maude recaptured Kut with a masterly enveloping movement, which led Turkish troops to evacuate the city. On 11 March 1917, the MEF, reinforced with two further Indian divisions, captured Baghdad, the Turkish garrison there having been denuded to provide reinforcements in Palestine. In November, the MEF made further advances, capturing Ramadi and Tikrit, but Maude himself was not to enjoy the fruits of victory, dying from cholera on 18 November 1917.[4]

The British Army units involved in the Gallipoli campaign performed with considerable ability at the tactical level, but this was frustrated by poor operational command and a confused strategic vision. Originally, it had been felt that the capture of the Turkish forts overlooking the Dardanelles Straits could be accomplished by the Royal Navy alone. As early as 3 November, on Winston Churchill's orders, as First Lord of the Admiralty, an Royal Navy Squadron bombarded the forts at Sedd el Bahr and Kum Kale with some success. This served as a warning to the Turks and saw preparations in the Gallipoli Peninsula accelerated, though it is worth noting that the defences of the Gallipoli Peninsula had been improved during the Balkan Wars, when a Greek invasion had seemed likely.

Admiral Sackville Carden, commanding the Eastern Mediterranean Squadron, took the view that the navy alone could force the straits if given sufficient ammunition and aerial reconnaissance. Carden envisaged a slow reduction of the Turkish forts, unaware that since November Turkish defences now relied primarily on minefields protected by field artillery. A more determined naval campaign commenced against the Dardanelles on 19 February 1915. Despite heavy shelling and early hopes, it was clear that British armour-piercing shells had made little impact, insufficient quantities of high explosive or shrapnel shells being available. When Royal Navy vessels ventured inshore, the forts opened up, showing that their gunners were merely awaiting good targets. Bad weather, starting on 20 February, prevented British operations until 25 February. When operations resumed, two battalions of the Royal Marine Light Infantry (RMLI) began shore operations but found that even the fire of the fifteen-inch guns had made little impact on the forts at

[4] Andrew Syk, *The Military Papers of Lieutenant General Frederick Stanley Maude, 1914–17* (Stroud, UK: History Press for the Army Records Society, 2012); Charles Townshend, *When God Made Hell: The British Invasion of Mesopotamia and the Creation of Iraq, 1914–1921* (London: Faber & Faber, 2010); and K. C. Ulrichsen, *Logistics and Politics of the British Campaigns in the Middle East, 1914–22* (Basingstoke, UK: Palgrave Macmillan, 2011).

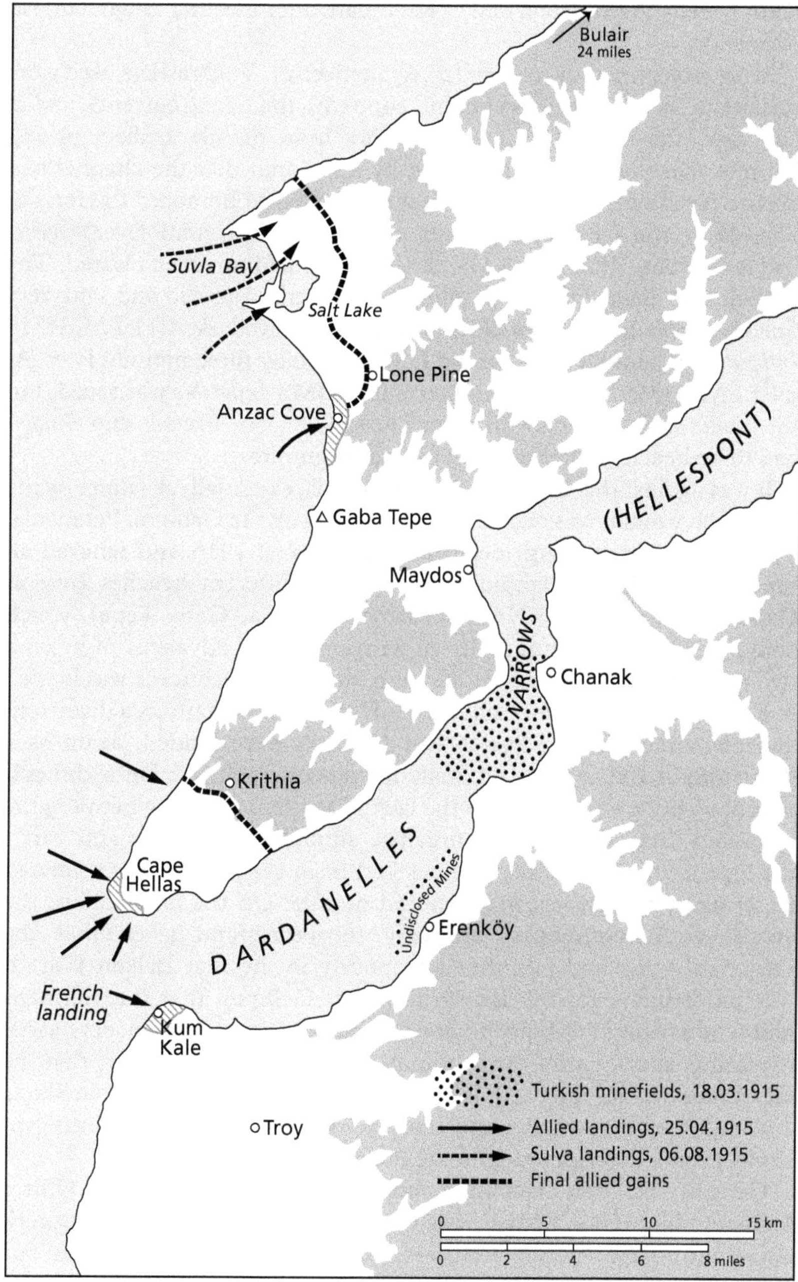

Map 17 Gallipoli, 1915–1916

Kum Kale, and they soon had to re-embark after meeting tough Turkish resistance.

Mine sweeping proved to be largely ineffective. The trawlers used were unsuitable as their engines couldn't cope with the strong currents, and in any case, they quickly came under fire from mobile artillery pieces. Despite these problems, it was felt by 18 March that the channel had been cleared of mines, and the fleet proceeded to bombard the forts at Kilid Bahr and Chanak. However, the tiny Turkish mine layer *Nousret* had laid twenty mines on 8 March, and these had not been cleared. The French ship *Bouvet* first hit a mine at 2 PM and capsized and sank very quickly – only twenty-one of her 700 crew survived. At 4:11 PM, HMS *Inflexible* hit another mine, as did HMS *Irresistible* three minutes later. At 6:05 PM, HMS *Ocean* hit another mine. HMS *Inflexible* was saved, but the others sank, though with a small loss of life. The French ship *Gaulois* had to be beached after being damaged by gunfire.

It was against this background of what was, essentially, a failure by the Royal Navy that it was decided to land troops on the Gallipoli Peninsula. The first major landings occurred on 25 April 1915 and ignored all sensible doctrine by landing forces at six different beaches (five at Cape Helles and the ANAZCs further North at Gaba Tepe), which could not have been mutually supporting unless advances of around two miles had been made. At the same time, a French force was landed at Kum Kale on the other side of the Dardanelles Straits as a diversion, and elements of the Royal Naval Division were landed, again as a diversion, at Bulair. The rationale for this operational plan is difficult to follow, but partly it reflects the lack of any real planning between the navy and army over how to organise amphibious assaults and partly it suggests that the Turkish forces had been seriously underestimated in terms of manpower, materiel and morale. On the latter point, the views of contemporaries are easy to understand given that the Ottoman Army had performed so poorly in the first Balkan War. It was unfortunate for the British forces at Gallipoli that the Germans had sent a team of military advisers, experts in coastal defence, to assist the Turks shortly after the Ottoman Empire entered the war, that the Ottomans had recently acquired batteries of high-quality, mobile Skoda 150-millimetre howitzers and that the Turkish defenders themselves showed such determination in the defence of their homeland.

General Sir Ian Hamilton appointed as the General Officer Commanding (GOC) MEF, was deemed to be one of the most experienced and competent senior officers in the British Army. He had been one of the members of the British military mission which had observed the Russo- Japanese War and, as a result of this, was thought to be well suited to deal with the challenges of modern industrialised warfare. Yet his command of the Gallipoli campaign was little short of a disaster. Certainly, Hamilton was dealt a bad hand: British intelligence on the Turkish Army was practically non-existent and maps of the Gallipoli Peninsula poor. In addition, he had to make do with a staff formed from scratch, and bar the 29th Division, his troops were drawn from the Territorial Force (TF) and New Armies. Hamilton was also somewhat in awe of Lord Kitchener and refused to deal with him as he probably would have with a civilian Secretary of State for War, believing that an argument with such a senior soldier over military resources would be futile. As a result, Hamilton launched his attack with insufficient troop numbers, insufficient preparation and insufficient artillery support. Hamilton also presided over the planning process which led to the decision to disperse forces during the landings. Tim Travers identifies what he terms the 'umpiring system' which evolved as a major problem in the command and control of the operation. While Hamilton was best placed to see how the landings were unfolding, operational command of the Cape Helles landings was given to Major General Aylmer Hunter Weston, one of the most controversial British commanders of the First World War, and Hamilton failed to intervene when it was obvious to him, but not to Hunter Weston, what was happening on the five separate beaches.

The landings at Cape Helles on 25 April 1915 were conducted by units of the 29th Division, landing just after 6:00 AM. This division was a priceless asset, one of the last regular divisions of the British Army, constructed on the outbreak of war from long-service regular troops who were on garrison duty in India. Troops landing on the beaches had very different experiences. At V beach, the situation was desperate. There three battalions, the 2nd Hampshire Regiment, 1st Royal Dublin Fusiliers and 1st Royal Munster Fusiliers, were landed, and a converted collier, the SS *River Clyde*, was used as a landing craft to bring in half the attacking force, the rest being rowed ashore in ships boats. The concept of using the SS *River Clyde* was a good one, and it is hard to criticise the man who came up with the idea of converting this collier, Commander Edward Unwin, as he won the Victoria Cross for his actions on 25 April 1915. Unwin's idea had been that once the River Clyde beached, then an attached steam hopper and three lighters would come into position to provide a bridge for the troops between the ship and the beach. For reasons which remain unclear, the engines of the hopper were either stopped or reversed when the *River Clyde* beached, but in this moment of crisis, Unwin himself, along with Able Seaman Williams, dived into the water and dragged two lighters into position, forming a bridge allowing troops to disembark. However, the men leaving the ship soon came under heavy fire from machine guns, rifles and two pompom guns; Captain Geddes of the 1st Royal Munster Fusiliers, who was the first officer of his regiment to leave the ship, was later told that of the forty-eight men who immediately followed him, all were killed or wounded before reaching the beach. By dusk, British forces were just holding on at V beach, and Captain Geddes, with a bullet through his shoulder, was in command of what was left of 1st Royal Munster Fusiliers, all senior officers having been killed or wounded. The 1st Royal Munster Fusiliers had lost seventeen officers killed or seriously wounded, and the 1st Royal Dublin Fusiliers twenty-four, with over 50 per cent casualties among the rank and file in both units. By contrast, S beach saw the easiest landing with just thirty-six casualties. The small force, three companies of the 2nd South Wales Borderers and one company of Royal Engineers, received excellent support from Royal Navy gunfire and were opposed by just one Turkish platoon.

The Australian and New Zealand Army Corps (ANZAC) fared little better than the British troops at Cape Helles. There was little precision about where the ANZAC should be landed, with many orders merely mentioning anywhere between Gaba Tepe and Fisherman's Hut, a distance of three miles, which has led to allegations by some historians that the Royal Navy landed the troops on the 'wrong' beach, too far to the North. This lack of precision in staff work was worrying it itself but also meant that individual commanders did not have a clear understanding of the terrain they would face or their immediate objectives. The other problem was Turkish resistance; this was present from the outset (indeed, some boats came under fire from a machine gun located near Fisherman's Hut while landing troops), especially from well-concealed snipers, and the situation deteriorated further for the ANZAC when Lieutenant Colonel Mustafa Kemal (later famous as Ataturk) arrived with the 57th Infantry Regiment and told his outnumbered command, 'I do not expect you to attack; I order you to die. In the time which passes until we die, other troops and commanders can come forward and take our places.' Against such determined resistance, the inexperienced ANZAC troops did well to establish a beach head at all.

Attritional warfare over the following months allowed the beach heads at Cape Helles and ANZAC Cove to be expanded slightly. In August, Hamilton decided to begin offensive operations in the Suvla Bay area; a landing there was planned to link up with the ANZAC forces and cut Turkish communications to Cape Helles, forcing a Turkish retreat from the peninsula. The initial landings of two divisions, the 10th (Irish) and 11th (Northern), were carried out on 6 and

7 August 1915 against minimal opposition, and the British beach head was very quickly consolidated. Unfortunately, the commander of IX Corps at Suvla Bay, Lieutenant-General Sir Frederick Stopford, brought little sense of urgency to his mission. Again, General Sir Ian Hamilton had been dealt a bad hand: while he had wanted either Lieutenant-General Sir Julian Byng or Lieutenant-General Sir Henry Rawlinson to command the newly formed IX Corps, Kitchener had refused to release either of them from the Western Front. The seniority of Lieutenant-General Sir Bryan Mahon, GOC 10th (Irish) Division, meant that a very senior officer was required to outrank him in the new corps structure, as while Hamilton did not want to see Mahon promoted he thought he should be allowed to remain in command of the division which he had raised on the outbreak of war. This accounts for Stopford's selection despite the fact that he had been retired for five years and was Governor of the Tower of London when selected for the new command. Stopford had never commanded large bodies of troops in the field and was in poor health, which made him a disastrous choice. Stopford, obsessed with consolidating his position at Suvla Bay, ordered his troops to dig in when the obvious objective should have been to capture the high ground at Kiretch Tape to the north, especially when it appears that IX Corps was initially opposed by no more than 1,500 Turkish troops. Far from breaking the stalemate on the Gallipoli Peninsula, Suvla Bay was another isolated beach head.

In the aftermath of the Suvla Bay landings, General Sir Ian Hamilton asked for 95,000 additional men. But on 20 August, the Dardanelles Committee decided that only 25,000 troops could be sent to Hamilton. In October, Hamilton was asked to estimate how many men he would lose in carrying out an evacuation of the peninsula and replied estimating 50 per cent losses. On 15 October, due to this pessimism, Hamilton was replaced as GOC MEF by General Sir Charles Monro, who proved an effective army commander on the Western Front and was later to become General Officer Commanding-in-Chief (GOC in C), India. Kitchener himself was to visit Gallipoli in early November 1915, and the Cabinet decided on 7 December 1915 to evacuate Suvla Bay and ANZAC Cove, and they were evacuated on 18–19 December. On the 23 December it was similarly decided to evacuate Helles, and this occurred on 8–9 January 1916. Ironically, the best handled operation in the whole Gallipoli campaign was the evacuation and well-organised withdrawal, which left the Turks confused and meant that not one British soldier was left behind, although large amounts of military supplies, horses and rations were captured by the Turks.[5]

When Gallipoli was evacuated in January 1916, the troops were initially sent to Egypt. The newly appointed GOC of the Egyptian Expeditionary Force (EEF), General Archibald Murray, reorganised and re-equipped these forces, which meant that between March and June 1916, ten divisions were sent to France and one to Mesopotamia, leaving four TF divisions of the British Army in Egypt itself. Murray quickly came to the conclusion that the best way to defend Egypt was to advance across the Sinai Peninsula to the town of El Arish, where the EEF would be in a position to take the offensive against Turkish forces in southern Palestine. Murray built up extensive logistical support, including a water pipeline and railway system, to support this advance, all too aware of the logistical failings in Mesopotamia. However, Murray's progress can be characterised as plodding, and when his forces attempted to push into Palestine, they were defeated at the first two battles of Gaza in March and April 1917. General Sir Edmund Allenby arrived in Egypt on 27 June 1917 to take command of the EEF and to restore some vigour to the offensive. Allenby moved his HQ to Khan Yunis just behind the front line and undertook a series of visits to front-line troops to restore morale. Allenby's first battle as GOC EEF was the third Battle of Gaza, which occurred in October 1917 with the objective of capturing Jerusalem. Allenby's arrival had also seen a serious reinforcement of the EEF, which by October 1917 was a force of seven infantry and three cavalry divisions well supported with artillery and aircraft. Allenby adopted a plan which had been worked out by Murray's staff which focused on the capture of Beersheba, allowing Turkish defences to be outflanked from the east. This plan was successful, but the cavalry of the EEF could not carry out a proper pursuit of Turkish forces due to lack of water. Jerusalem was finally captured in December 1917 when two NCOs from the 60th (London) Division, out on patrol, encountered the Mayor of Jerusalem, who was looking for someone to surrender the city to and presented them with the keys.

Allenby seems to have considered any further major operations beyond Jerusalem impossible without significant troop reinforcements, and in early 1918, Robertson as Chief of the Imperial General Staff (CIGS)

[5] E. J. Erickson, *Ordered to Die: A History of the Ottoman Army in the First World War* (London: Greenwood Press, 2001), 78–92; Nigel Steel and Peter Hart, *Defeat at Gallipoli* (London: Macmillan, 1995); Robin Prior, *Gallipoli: The End of the Myth* (New Haven, CT: Yale University Press, 2009); Tim Travers, *Gallipoli 1915* (Stroud, UK: Tempus, 2001); and Tim Travers, 'Command and Leadership Styles in the British Army: The 1915 Gallipoli Model', *Journal of Contemporary History* 29(3) (1994), 403–42.

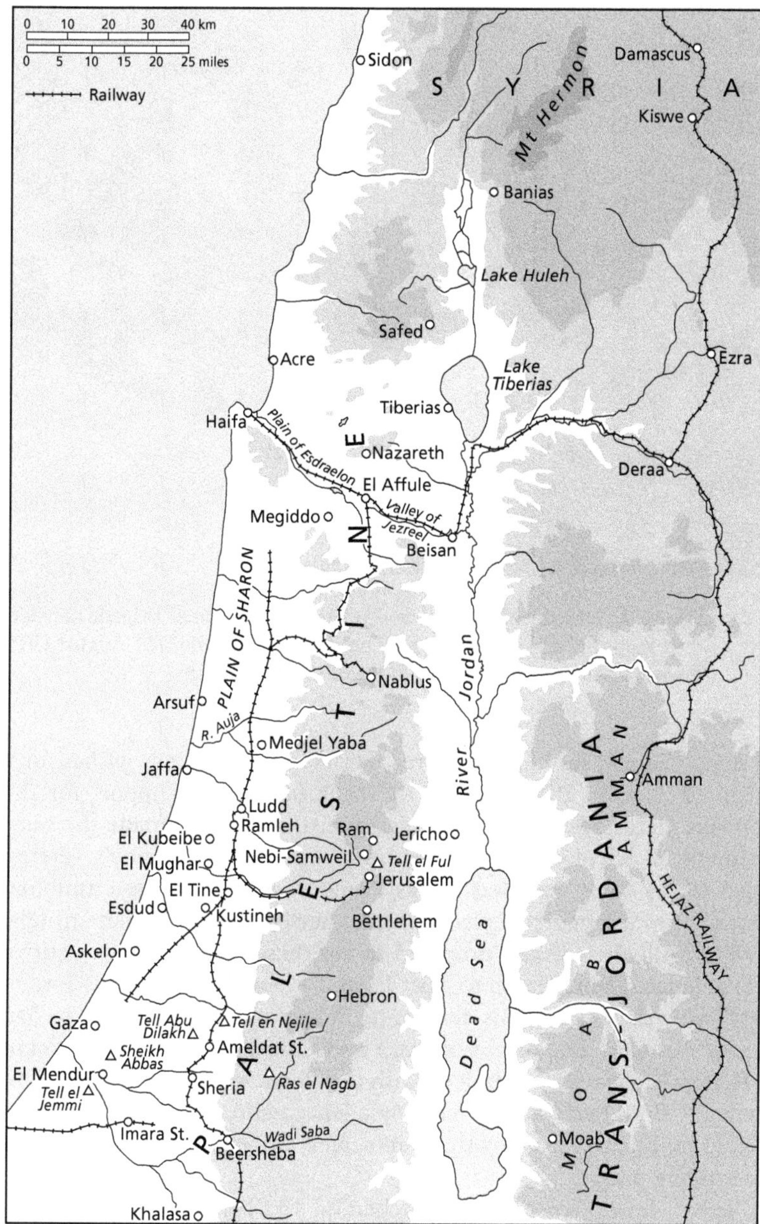

Map 18 Allenby's last campaign

Figure 9. Officers of the 2nd South Midland Mounted Brigade consult their maps prior to an attack on Chocolate Hill, Gallipoli, 21 August 1915
Source: Courtesy of Soldiers of Oxfordshire Museum

had none to spare for him, whatever David Lloyd George's wishes for a further advance in Palestine, on the back of popular support for the campaign there. The German spring offensives of 1918 made the reinforcement of Allenby absolutely impossible; indeed, Allenby's veteran British forces were denuded to rush reinforcements to the crumbling Western Front, being replaced with newly raised Indian troops. However, Allenby was not prepared to use these constraints to justify a static defence. From March to May 1918, he launched two trans-Jordan 'raids' with the bulk of his remaining forces across the River Jordan towards Amman. The object of these raids appears to have been to cut the Hedjaz Railway and to link up with the allied Arab forces under T. E. Lawrence. Both raids were essentially unsuccessful, seeing sharp defeats inflicted on British forces by the Turks, who among much else captured nine artillery pieces.

Allenby's final offensive was launched on 19 September 1918, the so-called Megiddo campaign, named after an ancient settlement. Allenby made very effective use of this cavalry forces in this campaign, which routed and destroyed three Turkish armies and put the entire Levant region under British control. An armistice was signed with Turkish forces at Mudros on 30 October 1918.[6]

The politics of the entente saw British troops deployed in two other theatres, Salonika and Italy. As discussed in Chapter 5, the Salonika operation, initially designed to bring Greece into the war and assist Serbia, was persevered with by the British government due to French interests. Anglo-French forces, the British contingent initially consisting of the 10th (Irish) Division, withdrawn from Suvla Bay in Gallipoli, began landing at Salonika on 5 October 1915. While the conditions for success in the campaign began to close very quickly, with the Greek government becoming more determined to enforce its neutrality and Bulgarian forces acting aggressively, both to cut off the Serbian Army's retreat and to surround Salonika, British troops were reinforced. At its height, from late 1916 to early 1917, the British Salonika Force, then under the command of Lieutenant General George Milne, consisted of XII and XVI Corps, containing six divisions. British forces were in trench stalemate, facing Bulgarians for most of their time in Salonika; offensives were launched against Doiran on 24–25 April and 8–9 May 1917 and successfully on 18–19 September 1918. The campaign concluded with the surrender of Bulgaria on 30 September 1918. The number of British casualties in Salonika was already high for a 'side show', with 9,668 killed and 16,837 wounded, but it appears that most of the troops who served there were infected with malaria.[7]

Recent studies of the Italian front have sought to minimise the role of British troops, describing the battle of Vittorio Veneto as an 'Italian battle'.[8] By contrast, the British Official History of the First World War devoted an entire 450-page volume to the role of British forces in the Italian campaign.[9] At the height of British involvement in Italy, in

[6] Matthew Hughes, *Allenby and British Strategy in the Middle East 1917–19* (London: Frank Cass, 1999); Matthew Hughes (ed.), *Allenby in Palestine: The Middle East Correspondence of Field Marshal Viscount Allenby* (Stroud, UK: Sutton Publishing for the Army Records Society, 2004); J. E. Kitchen, *The British Imperial Army in the Middle East: Morale and Military Identity in the Sinai and Palestine Campaigns, 1916–18* (London: Bloomsbury, 2014); and Ulrichsen, *Logistics and Politics of the British Campaigns in the Middle East, 1914–22.*

[7] Alan Wakefield and Simon Moody, *Under the Devil's Eye: Britain's Forgotten Army at Salonika 1915–1918* (Stroud, UK: Sutton Publishing, 2004); *General Annual Reports of the British Army, 1913–1919*, Cmd. 1193 (1921); Mark Harrison, *The Medical War: British Military Medicine in the First World War* (Oxford University Press, 2010), 230–9.

[8] Nicola Labanca, 'The Italian Front', in Jay Winter (ed.), *The Cambridge History of the First World War*, Vol. I: *Global War* (Cambridge University Press, 2014), 290–1; and Mark Thompson, *The White War: Life and Death on the Italian Front, 1915–1919* (London: Faber & Faber, 2008), 356–61.

[9] J. E. Edmonds and H. R. Davies, *Military Operations, Italy 1915–1919* (London: HMSO, 1949).

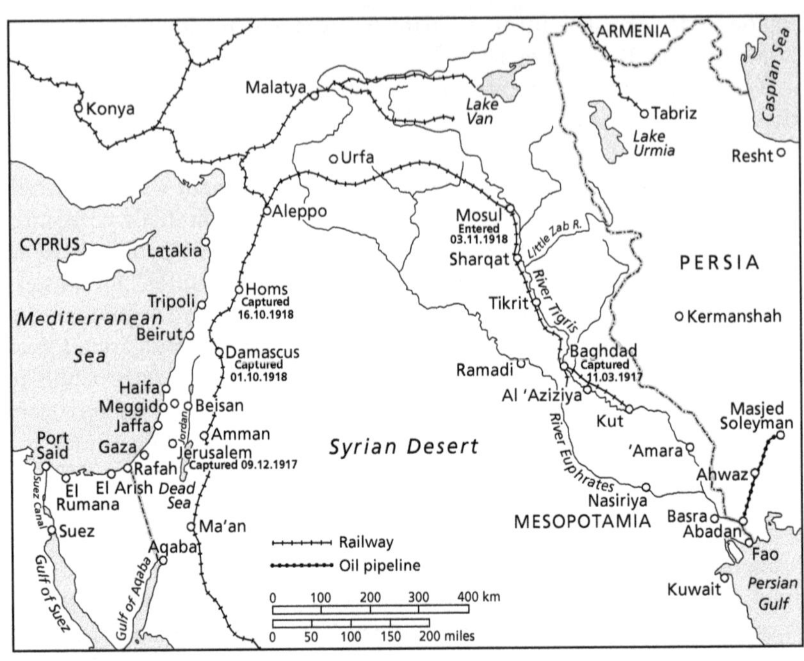

Map 19 Turkish Collapse, 1917–1918

December 1917, after the disaster at Caporetto, there were four British divisions in the theatre under the command of General Plumer. The casualty lists of 2,071 men killed and 4,689 wounded are also not negligible, even if they seem small by First World War standards. However, the fact that the Italians managed to stabilise their own lines meant that British troops were not involved in major offensive operations through most of 1918, merely holding sections of the front line and conducting some trench raids. In mid-February 1918, two of the British divisions in Italy were recalled to France as General Foch, now President of the Executive War Board, was concerned that reserves in France were too low compared to those in Italy. Offensive action by the remaining two British divisions in Italy took place in October 1918 as part of the Vittorio Veneto campaign. General Lord Cavan was in command of the Italian 10th Army, which consisted of two British and two Italian divisions. British forces started their offensive by capturing the Papadopoli Islands on the 23 October. Supported by effective artillery fire, British troops were able to advance across the River Piave against Austro-Hungarian positions with the use of a series of pontoon bridges. British troops headed the advance, against light opposition. On 31 October, the 23rd Division liberated Sacile as the Austro-Hungarian Army collapsed. The role of British troops was not decisive at Vittorio Veneto, but they performed well in the amphibious landing role, always a difficult operation which had defeated a number of British expeditions earlier in the war.

Among these various overseas campaigns, the British Army had also to deal with a domestic rebellion in Dublin on Easter 1916. Shortly after the outbreak of the First World War, John Redmond's support of the British war effort had led to a fracture in the Irish National Volunteer movement. Around 160,000 men remained loyal to the Irish Parliamentary Party and Redmond's leadership. But around 10,000 took the name 'Irish Volunteers' and elected Eoin MacNeill, a Professor of History at University College Dublin, as their leader. A section of the Irish Volunteers, largely in the Dublin area, came under the influence of the extreme republican movement, the Irish Republican Brotherhood. It was, in Roy Foster's memorable phrase, this 'minority of a minority' which staged the uprising in Dublin on Easter Monday, 24 April 1916, supported by the smaller, socialist Irish Citizens' Army.

In all, rebel forces mustered something like 1,000 men, most armed with German rifles landed at Howth shortly before the outbreak of war. The rebel strategy seems to have been based on an old Fenian plan of 1867 to seize key buildings in the centre of Dublin, notably the General Post Office in what is now O'Connell Street. The rising in Dublin was then to be the signal for a nationwide rebellion, with German military support expected to arrive. James Connolly, leader of the Irish Citizens' Army, appears to have believed that the British government would not use artillery against rebel positions in Dublin because of the damage this would cause to private property. Rather than following the example of the Boers and staging a guerrilla war, which was to prove so successful in Southern Ireland between 1919 and 1921, the rebels occupied a widely dispersed collection of buildings, which offered little mutual support. The ineptitude of rebel strategy is shown by the decision to dig trenches in St. Stephen's Green, which were overlooked by buildings on four sides, and the failure to capture Trinity College Dublin, which straddled rebel communications, and, at least initially, was defended by nothing more than a scratch force drawn from the University of Dublin Officer Training Corps (OTC).

It is, of course, something of an indictment of the British Army, and particularly its command and intelligence structures, that a rebellion broke out in Ireland at all in 1916. However, Augustine Birrell, the Chief Secretary for Ireland, brought little dynamism to civilian government in Ireland, and both G Division of the Dublin Metropolitan Police and the Special Branch of the Royal Irish Constabulary, both specifically

Figure 10. Officers of 1/1st Buckinghamshire Battalion and 1/4th Oxfordshire and Buckinghamshire Light Infantry in St. Mark's Square, Venice, 1918
Source: Courtesy of Soldiers of Oxfordshire Museum

responsible for the detection of 'political crime', failed to provide any clear warning about the rising. Major Ivon Price, the head of British military intelligence in Ireland, atoned for his intelligence failings by his almost single-handed defence of Dublin Castle, the seat of British power, against an attack by the Irish Citizens' Army. Among all this ineptitude, only the Royal Naval intelligence system emerges with any credit. A German merchant ship, the *Aud*, disguised as a Norwegian steamer and carrying 20,000 captured Russian rifles and 1 million rounds of ammunition, was forced to scuttle when intercepted by a Royal Navy patrol off the coast of Cork on Good Friday, 21 April 1916.

However, once the rising actually commenced, British forces concentrated swiftly against the rebels. This was impressive, given that key personnel including the GOC Major-General Sir Lovick Friend, were on leave over the Easter holidays and that while the British garrison in Dublin numbered around 2,400 troops, only 400 were immediately available to act against the rebellion. Indeed, it is often forgotten that it was the reserve battalions of Irish regiments based in Dublin, notably the 3rd Royal Irish Regiment, the 3rd Royal Irish Rifles and the 10th Royal Dublin Fusiliers, which initially contained the rising despite the fact that most of their personnel consisted of raw recruits, many of whom had not undertaken any musketry training. British reinforcements reached Dublin quickly; by 5:30 PM on Easter Monday, 1,600 troops had already arrived from the Curragh Camp in County Kildare, and on the following day, elements of the 59th Division, a second-line territorial division which had been quartered in the Luton area to counter any German naval landing in the United Kingdom, started to arrive in Ireland. The newly appointed GOC, Lieutenant General Sir John Maxwell, arrived in the early hours of Friday 28 April, in time to impose an unconditional surrender on the rebel commander, Patrick Pearse, who formally surrendered at 3:45 PM on Saturday 29 April, ordering other rebel outposts to surrendered later that afternoon. By this stage there were close to 20,000 British troops in Dublin. In strictly military terms, it was an achievement for the British forces to have forced the rebels to capitulate in under a week. British Army losses amounted to 116 dead and 368 wounded, mostly men of the 59th Division, who had been caught in sniper fire at Mount Street Bridge while marching from Kingston Port to the centre of Dublin. Rebel and civilian losses amounted to 318 dead and 2,217 wounded. Artillery had devastated the centre of Dublin, and estimated damage amounted to over £1 million in terms of property and £750,000 in terms of stock in O'Connell Street alone.

However, Major General Sir John Maxwell handled the aftermath of the rising poorly. Martial law was declared, and a number of rebels were tried hastily by court-martial. Fifteen men were executed before the government intervened to halt any further executions, and these men quickly came to be seen as martyrs. Around 1,600 suspects from throughout Ireland were imprisoned or interned under Regulation 14 or 14B of the Defence of the Realm Act following the rising. Many of these were moderate nationalists who were radicalised by their experience of internment in Frongoch Camp through the remainder of 1916. Maxwell, supposedly appointed because of his experience in dealing with civil–military relations in Egypt, did enormous damage in undermining support for the Irish Parliamentary Party and encouraging many Irish nationalists to support Sinn Fein, which was to triumph in the general election of 1918.[10]

There is a danger, when reviewing the British Army's experience in some of the campaigns beyond the Western Front, in subscribing to the 'great man' view of history and coming to the conclusion that Allenby's appointment brought success to the Palestine campaign or Maude's to Mesopotamia. Both were effective commanders, but with regard to Allenby, it should be remembered that he was deemed to have failed as a commander at Arras when commanding an army of the BEF, so his appointment to the EEF was essentially an example of 'Stellenbosching'. His experience in command saw defeat as well as victory, and at least initially, Allenby was implementing plans drawn up by his predecessor. One of the major criticisms of the British Army during the First World War is that fixated on its colonial experience, it could not easily adapt to the demands of a modern European war. However, the experience of some of the more obviously 'colonial' campaigns of the Great War, notably that against German East Africa and Mesopotamia, suggests that fundamental principles of colonial warfare, learned slowly and painfully through various Victorian campaigns, especially those concerning logistics, had been too easily forgotten in the aftermath of the South African War.

[10] M. T. Foy and Brian Barton, *The Easter Rising* (Stroud, UK: History Press, 2011); Fearghal McGarry, *The Rising: Ireland: Easter 1916* (Oxford University Press, 2010); and Charles Townshend, *Easter 1916: The Irish Rebellion* (London: Allen Lane, 2005).

Conclusion

Pre-war there had been confusion over what the British Army actually existed to do. The Haldane reforms of 1906–8, which created both the British Expeditionary Force (BEF) and the Territorial Force (TF), were carried out within a very tight financial ceiling and in many cases simply served to rebrand existing military forces. Indeed, the existing regimental structure and its concept of linked battalions were a continuation of the Cardwell-Childers reforms of 1868–81. The role of the British regular army remained very much that of an imperial police force, and the elements of the regular army which were left in the United Kingdom, after the requirements of overseas garrisons, largely in India, had been met, remained under-strength and poorly trained. Indeed, it is often forgotten that the original BEF relied heavily on army reservists to bring its units up to strength on mobilisation, and this makes the performance of the BEF in the retreat from Mons all the more remarkable.

The TF, which was formed from the old Rifle Volunteer and Yeomanry regiments as part of the Haldane reforms, initially promised much. Unlike its predecessors, the TF was designed as a self-contained second-line army with its own artillery, medical and logistics units. However, despite initial enthusiasm, by the outbreak of war in 1914, the TF was suffering from the same problems of poor training, outdated equipment and falling recruiting, which had dogged its predecessors. The fact that the TF had enlisted purely for home defence meant that it was of limited use in fulfilling Britain's military needs in August 1914, which explains Kitchener's decision to form his New Armies. All pre-war planning concerning the TF had assumed that following mobilisation, units would be allowed six months' full-time training before being considered for overseas service. The military needs of 1914 meant that the first TF unit, the 1/14th London (Scottish) Regiment, to see action took part in the action at Messines at the end of October 1914. Similarly, the Officer Training Corps (OTC) established as part of the TF looked like a spectacular failure by the end of June 1914. While many school pupils, willingly or unwillingly and normally at elite public schools, served in the junior division and a high percentage of university students served in the senior division of the OTC, pitifully few had taken up commissions in either the regular army, Special Reserve or TF before the outbreak of war. Nevertheless, when war came, it was OTC products, with scant training mostly provided by schoolmasters and university lecturers, who provided a high proportion of officers for both the expansion of the TF and the formation of the New Armies.

The British General Staff, a fairly recent pre-war creation, had carried out limited planning concerning the role of the British Army in a major European war. The fragmentation of the General Staff on the outbreak of war produced a critical situation when British strategy passed into the hands of enthusiastic amateurs, who received virtually no advice from professional soldiers, until Lieutenant-General William Robertson was appointed Chief of the Imperial General Staff (CIGS) in late 1915. Confusion over the number of troops required for home defence and over-planning for the Gallipoli expedition served to show just how poor inter-service cooperation with the Royal Navy had been pre-war. Nevertheless, even a perfectly functioning General Staff with great strategic vision would have struggled to envisage the challenges which confronted the British Army between 1914 and 1918. The rapid Belgian collapse and French retreat on the Western Front, combined with the crushing Russian defeat at Tannenberg, meant that the British Army had to develop as a major continental army. Kitchener, whatever his many faults, fully appreciated this necessity from the outbreak of war, and while his New Armies performed inconsistently throughout 1915 and 1916 on both the Western Front and at Gallipoli, incurring appalling casualties, nevertheless their formation remained an impressive feat of improvisation. Elsewhere, the British Army found itself in a number of campaigns in Africa and the Middle East which had many of the hallmarks of the classic Victorian small wars. Some of these campaigns were mismanaged, notably those in Mesopotamia in 1914–16 and in East Africa throughout the war, and one would have expected more professionalism from officers who had learned their trade in colonial warfare. However, poor performance had much to do with the fact that the most able officers had been sent to the Western Front and that Britain's colonial forces in Africa, the West African Frontier Force and King's African Rifles, were lightly armed and contained many officers on short-term appointments, who had little knowledge of the native languages. The British Army also found itself having to confront a domestic rebellion in Dublin on Easter 1916, and British Army units essentially carried out policing roles in Ireland for the rest of the war and, indeed, into 1919–21 when dealing with a full-blown Irish Republican Army (IRA) insurgency campaign.

Reserve battalions of the Royal Irish Regiment, Royal Irish Rifles and Royal Dublin Fusiliers played a crucial role in containing the Easter rising in its opening hours, and domestic tension in Ireland did not translate into disciplinary problems in the Irish regiments. It is not surprising, that the British Army did not perform well in some of these campaigns given the limited pre-war planning for such scenarios and the small cadre on which the British Army had to expand.

The First World War confronted the British Army with an incredibly difficult task in terms of its manpower requirements. The small pre-war BEF of just six infantry and one cavalry divisions mobilised efficiently and incurred heavy losses in the retreat from Mons. The difficulty for Lord Kitchener was in trying to allocate his slender military resources between reinforcing units already in France and Belgium and providing a cadre for the massively expanded TF and New Armies. The fact that some units were sent to France with poor training and obsolete equipment and that some of the retired officers posted to train New Army units were simply not up to the task should not prove a surprise. The expansion of the British Army and the need to replace losses were originally accomplished through voluntary recruitment as thousands of men eagerly volunteered through the late summer and autumn of 1914. Britain was the only major power in Europe not to have conscription before the war, and conscription proper was only introduced in early 1916 as a result of declining numbers of volunteers. The later creation of the Ministry of National Service was a reflection of the fact that, in total war, many men were better serving their country in their civilian jobs, notably in war industries, shipbuilding, mining and agriculture, than they would have as soldiers. This meant that the British Army was a declining asset in the last two years of the war, and its manpower ceiling was reached in the autumn of 1917 when each infantry brigade was reduced from four to three battalions. In the aftermath of the German spring offensives of 1918, many of the reinforcements sent to France were men in low medical categories who prior to this crisis had been regarded as unfit for overseas service. The age and medical categories of conscripts were increased throughout the war and only in Ireland, where it was clear that massive civil unrest would greet any attempt to enforce conscription, did the voluntary system continue.

Officer supply remained problematic throughout the war, especially as the British Army had the largest expansion of its officer corps of any European army during the Great War. The introduction of conscription brought in a systematic approach to officer training with the creation of the Officer Cadet Battalions. Prior to this (and arguably throughout the war), the 'old school tie' and establishment family connections proved important in obtaining a commission. It was the case that by the end of the war, about half the officers serving in the British Army had served in the ranks, but this bald statement disguises the fact that a disproportionately large number had started their careers in so-called swank regiments like the Artists' Rifles or Inns of Court Regiment in the TF, the various Public Schools Battalions in the New Armies or in socially exclusive Yeomanry regiments. One of the more curious aspects of the commissioning process during the war was that the work of the Royal Military Academy and Royal Military College carried on with minor changes, taking, by 1918, eighteen months to train a regular officer, whereas temporary commissions were handed out in a very haphazard manner at the start of the war, and the Officer Cadet Battalions introduced a curriculum which lasted around twelve weeks. Trying to work out the processes behind promotion and demotion among officers during the First World War is almost impossible, given the destruction of the Military Secretary's records in the Second World War. However, it seems that as with the pre-war system, the old British tradition of 'buggin's turn' remained important, and even when it was clear that officers were incompetent, there was a tendency to 'Stellenbosch' them into some sort of administrative or training job back in the United Kingdom rather than to dismiss them from the service. Promotion at the very highest ranks could be dizzyingly fast: Hubert Gough, who started the war as a brigadier-general in charge of 3rd Cavalry Brigade, was, by 1917, Commander of Fifth Army. Finding men to officer the new, or greatly expanded, technical corps, like the Royal Flying Corps (RFC), Machine Gun Corps (MGC) and Tank Corps led to some surprising appointments and promotions. Before the war, the Staff Colleges at Camberley and Quetta turned out a tiny number of graduates each year (fewer than 100 in 1913), and with the outbreak of war, they were effectively closed. This meant that many staff posts were filled by unqualified officers from the start of the war, and this naturally was not a problem which eased as the army expanded. The army seems to have had some success in placing officers with relevant pre-war civilian experience, notably in logistics, into senior staff positions. Otherwise, these staff posts were filled with regular officers whose only qualification, in some instances, was that they had been too badly injured to return to front-line service. Various staff courses were improvised in France from 1916, but these were of a very short duration and relied heavily on apprenticing trainee staff officers to staff officers in the field, which rather assumed that the incumbents were competent and effective teachers.

Clearly, during the First World War, the British Army did undergo some sort of a learning process. In every war in history this has been the case, particularly for victorious armies. It can, indeed, be argued that the BEF was the most effective army in Europe by November 1918. However, it should be noted that this is to measure the British Army against a fairly low metric given the appalling losses which the French and Germans had suffered, even compared to the shocking British losses, and much was still wrong with the British Army. While doctrine was developed and codified, it was not always widely disseminated, and it is telling that when the storm broke in March 1918 with the German spring offensives, no doctrine pamphlet had been produced concerning the role of units in the defensive. The British Army also retained a very strict hierarchical structure, with too much directive command, which prevented most divisional commanders from developing effective operational art. The corps structure in the British Army proper (as opposed to its function with the Australian and New Zealand Army Corps (ANZAC) and the Canadian Expeditionary Force (CEF) formations) remained underdeveloped and was largely an administrative structure. This all served to stifle initiative and innovation among the high command. Having noted all this, Douglas Haig, on whom the burden of command of the BEF rested for most of the war, was clearly an effective theatre commander, and it is hard to imagine that any of the other senior British officers of the period could have performed any better. It was not Haig's fault that pre-war he had limited command experience with large bodies of troops or that he was leading a hastily improvised army.

Of course, what the British Army on the Western Front was struggling to learn through the lengthy Somme campaign of 1916 was, arguably, the lessons that the French had learned in the Battles of Artois in 1915.[1] Similarly, there was a lack of cooperation between the British and French over the development, use and doctrine of tank warfare, which hindered the effective use of this arm. Nevertheless, the British Army did manage to develop as a technological army throughout the war, effectively developing its capabilities with machine guns, aircraft, tanks, poison gas and trench mortars. Indeed, some of the combined arms warfare practised by the BEF in the last hundred days of the war serves as a precursor to the so-called blitzkrieg tactics practised by the German Army in 1940.

How the British Army (and, indeed, the other combatant armies) managed to maintain its morale and discipline during the Great War is an enduring debate. It should, of course, be recognised that while the French, German, Austro-Hungarian and Russian Armies endured heavy losses in the first three months of the war, the expansion of the British

[1] Jonathan Krause, *Early Trench Tactics in the French Army: The Second Battle of Artois, May-June 1915* (Farnham: Ashgate, 2013)

Army meant that similar losses were not seen in the BEF until July 1916 at the battle of the Somme. There is an argument that the sustained attritional warfare which saw the actual collapse of the Russian Army and near collapse of the French Army in 1917 would not have been witnessed by the BEF unless the war had continued into late 1919. Beyond this, many of the morale-boosting measures used in the BEF were similar to those used in other armies; the British regimental system was, effectively, an attempt to copy the German system, focusing on localised recruitment and trench newspapers were common throughout the British, French and German Armies. The centrally planned 'patriotic instruction' measures used in the Austro-Hungarian and German Armies were not fully introduced into the British Army before the end of the war. However, there does seem to be a convincing argument that officer–man relations were rather better in the British Army than most others, and the British Army, certainly in France and Belgium, prided itself on its excellent logistics, which ensured both that men were comparatively well fed and that letters and parcels posted in the UK generally arrived two days later with the troops. Some elements of British popular culture, notably sport and music hall type entertainments, quickly found their way into the army, though pre-war, sport had already been seen as an important morale boosting activity in the British Army. There is a convincing argument that this exportation of British popular culture to the Western Front, combined with generally good relations with Belgian and French civilians, did much to boost the morale of British soldiers.

The emotive subject of executions has tended to dominate the work on discipline in the British Army during the Great War. A public campaign to secure pardons for those executed tended to portray all those 'shot at dawn' as victims of shell shock and entirely ignored the variety of cases involved or how the contemporary civil courts functioned. The lack of surviving paperwork on court-martial cases prevented any sensible discussion of why some men were executed and others were not, and in 2006, the then-Labour government simply decided to pardon all those executed during the First World War, with the exception of murderers. Such emotion has tended to cloud the fact that only 346 men (or 0.006 per cent) were executed serving in the British Army during the First World War. If this was a harsher disciplinary framework than that of the Germans and Belgians, it was rather more lenient than that of the French and Italians. The point must also be made that purely in terms of military discipline, at least in some cases, the execution of men 'for the sake of example' was effective. Crime rates, notably of drunkenness and absence without leave, which had been poor in the 107th Brigade, fell noticeably after the execution of three soldiers in February 1916.[2]

In the immediate aftermath of the First World War, the size of the British Army was drastically cut to pre-war levels, with conscription phased out in 1919. In November 1918, the army stood at a strength of 3,779,825; by November 1919, it was already just 888,952 strong; and by November 1922, in the wake of the so-called Geddes axe which disbanded or amalgamated a number of regular regiments, was down to just 217,986. This occurred at a time when Britain's global responsibilities had increased with League of Nations mandates in Iraq and Palestine and with the Army of Occupation in Germany on top of the pre-war colonial garrisons. The Territorial Army was established in 1920 as a result of considerable parliamentary pressure and at a time when no one could envisage the military situation which would make it of much use. It was considerably smaller than the pre-war TF but still, in 1921, numbered 137,032 all ranks.[3]

[2] Timothy Bowman, *Irish Regiments in the Great War: Discipline and Morale* (Manchester University Press, 2003), pp. 113–117.

[3] Brian Bond, *British Military Policy between the Two World Wars* (Oxford: Clarendon Press, 1980), pp. 10–35, Peter Dennis, *The Territorial Army 1907–1940* (London: Royal Historical Society and the Boydell Press, 1987), pp. 38–181, Keith Jeffery, 'The Post-war Army' in Beckett and Simpson, *A Nation in Arms*, pp. 211–34.

Bibliography

Archival Sources

Queen's University, Belfast, Archives

QUB/B/1/2/4–6, Senate minutes (including Military Education Committee reports), 1914–19.

Duke of Cornwall's Light Infantry Museum, Bodmin

'Record of Service of Officers, 1st Duke of Cornwall's Light Infantry', c.1890–1914.

Honourable Artillery Company Archives, London

'HAC Act Papers, 1907–08'.
Court minutes.

Imperial War Museum, London

Department of Documents

PP/MCR/11, Memoirs of Major General S. C. M. Archibald.
PP/MCR/136, Memoirs of Brigadier G. S. Brunskill.
76/51/1, W. T. Colyer, 'War Impressions of a Temporary Soldier'.
87/41/1, Major General L. A. Hawes, 'The Memories and Dreams of an Ordinary Soldier' (unpublished manuscript).
03/21/1, G. L. Boys-Stones papers.
J. H. Stewart-Moore, 'Random Recollections' (unpublished manuscript).

Sound Archive

46, Interview with J. M. L. Grover.
188/7, Interview with E. G. White.
212/4, Interview with T. H. Painting.
314/12, Interview with Percy Snelling.

4935/5, Interview with E. S. Humphries.
9959, Interview with W. H. Wood.
10699, Interview with J. M. Rymer-Jones.
11962, Interview with Roger Powell.

University of Leeds Archives

University Committees Minute Book, 11 and 12, Military Education Committee minutes, 1914–18.

Liddle Hart Centre for Military Archives, King's College London (LHCMA)

Lieutenant General Sir Ian Hamilton papers.
Lieutenant General Sir Neville Lyttleton papers.

London Metropolitan Archives

A/TA/1 Minutes of County of London Territorial Force Association.
Records of Inns of Court Regiment (transferred from Guildhall Library and un-catalogued at time of writing).

National Library of Ireland

Ms. 10,561, Colonel Maurice Moore papers.

National Library of Wales

B23, Welsh Army Corps papers.

Public Record Office of Northern Ireland (PRONI)

D. 618, Records relating to 4th Leinster Regiment.
D. 1889, Colonel R. W. Wallace papers.
D.3835, Farren Connell papers: personal papers of Lieutenant General Sir Oliver Nugent.

Royal Military Academy Sandhurst

WO151/6, Royal Military College Cadet Register, 1903–7.
WO151/8, Royal Military College Cadet Register, 1910–14.
WO152/73 and 74, Royal Military College correspondence, 1903–9.

Various Royal Military College correspondence, 1909–18 (un-catalogued at time of writing).

Staffordshire Record Office

D.5528, Records relating to Staffordshire Territorial Brigade.

Staffordshire Regimental Museum

Records of North Staffordshire Regiment, 1902–18.
Records of South Staffordshire Regiment, 1902–18.

Tameside Record Office

Manchester Regiment collection.

The National Archives, London (PRO)

WO32, Miscellaneous War Office files.
WO76, Records of officers service.
WO163, Minutes of the Army Council.
WO339, Officers' personal files.
WO374, Officers' personal files.

University of London Special Collections

ME/1/1/1 and 2, Reports of Military Education Committee, 1908–19.

Primary Published Material

Army List, 1902–1918.
Hart's Army List, 1902–1918.
London Gazette.
Anon, *The Subaltern's Handbook of Useful Information* (Aldershot: Gale & Polden, 1918).
Baden-Powell, Robert, *Quick Training for War: A Few Practical Suggestions* (London, Jenkins, 1914).
Beach, Jim (ed.), *The Military Papers of Lieutenant Colonel Sir Cuthbert Headlam, 1910–1942* (Stroud: History Press for the Army Records Society, 2010).
Beckett, Ian F. W. (ed.), *The Army and the Curragh Incident, 1914* (London: Bodley Head for the Army Records Society, 1986).
The Judgement of History: Sir Horace Smith-Dorrien, Lord French and 1914 (London: Tom Donovan, 1993).

Blake, Robert (ed.), *The Private Papers of Douglas Haig, 1914–19* (London: Eyre & Spottiswoode, 1952).

Boraston, J. H. (ed.), *Sir Douglas Haig's Despatches* (London: Dent, 1919).

Brock, Michael and Brock, Eleanor (eds.), *H. H. Asquith: Letters to Venetia Stanley* (Oxford University Press, 1982).

Campbell, D. H. (ed.), *Forward the Rifles: The War Diary of an Irish Soldier, 1914–18: Captain David Campbell, M.C.* (Dublin: Nonsuch Publishing, 2009).

Deane, H. F. W. and Bulkeley Evans, W. A. (eds.), *The Public Schools Yearbook: The Official Book of Reference of the Headmasters' Conference* (London: Year Book Press, 1916).

Hamilton, Ian, *Compulsory Service: A Study of the Question in the Light of Experience* (London: John Murray, 1910).

Hughes, Matthew (ed.), *Allenby in Palestine: The Middle East Correspondence of Field Marshal Viscount Allenby* (Stroud: Sutton Publishing for the Army Records Society, 2004).

Martin, F. X. (ed.), *The Irish Volunteers, 1913–1915* (Dublin: James Duffy, 1963).

Morris, A. J. A. (ed.), *The Letters of Lieutenant-Colonel Charles à Court Repington CMG, Military Correspondent of the Times, 1903–1918* (Stroud: Sutton Publishing for the Army Records Society, 1999).

Norwich, J. J. (ed.), *The Duff Cooper Diaries, 1915–1951* (London: Weidenfeld & Nicolson, 2005).

Perry, Nicholas (ed.), *Major General Oliver Nugent and the Command of the 36th (Ulster) Division 1915–1918* (Stroud: Sutton Publishing for the Army Records Society, 2007).

Robbins, Simon (ed.), *The First World War Letters of General Lord Horne* (Stroud: History Press for the Army Records Society, 2009).

Roberts, F. S., *Fallacies and Facts: An Answer to 'Compulsory Service'* (London: John Murray, 1911).

Sheffield, Gary and Bourne, John (eds.), *Douglas Haig: War Diaries and Letters 1914–1918* (London: Weidenfeld, 2005).

Syk, Andrew (ed.), *The Military Papers of Lieutenant-General Frederick Stanley Maude, 1914–17* (Stroud: History Press for the Army Records Society, 2012).

Winterton, Earl of, *Orders of the Day: Memories of Nearly Fifty Years in the House of Commons* (London: Cassell, 1953).

Woodward, David (ed.), *The Military Correspondence of Field Marshal Sir William Robertson, Chief of the Imperial General Staff, December 1915–February 1918* (London: Bodley Head for the Army Records Society, 1989).

Parliamentary Papers

1902 (Cd. 982), *Report of the Committee Appointed to Consider the Education and Training of Officers of the Army* (Akers-Douglas Report).

1904 (Cd. 1903), *Return Showing the Establishment of Each Unit of Militia in the United Kingdom and the Numbers Present, Absent and Wanting to Compete at the Training of 1906.*

1907 (Cd. 3367), *The Annual Return of the Volunteer Corps of Great Britain for the Year 1906.*

1907 (Cd. 3513), *Report of the War Office Committee Appointed to Discuss Certain Militia Questions with Representative Officers of Militia.*

1908 (Cd. 3801), *The Annual Return of the Volunteer Corps of Great Britain for the Year 1907.*

1908 (Cd. 3798), *The General Annual Report on the British Army for the Year Ending 30th September 1907.*

1908 (Cd. 3932), *Return Showing the Establishment of Each Unit of Militia in the United Kingdom and the Numbers Present, Absent and Wanting to Compete at the Training of 1907.*

1908 (Cd. 4933), *Army Medical Department Report.*

1912 (Cd. 7201), *Report on the Health of the Army.*

1912–13 (Cd. 6065), *The General Annual Report on the British Army for the Year Ending 30th September 1911, with Which Is Incorporated the Annual Report on Recruiting.*

1914 (Cd. 7252), *The General Annual Report on the British Army for the Year Ending 30th September 1913.*

1914 (Cd. 7254), *The Annual Return of the Territorial Force for the Year 1913.*

GENERAL Annual Reports of the British Army for the Period 1 October 1913 to 30 September 1919 (cited in Beckett and Simpson as an HMSO Publication 1921 but surely a Cmd).

Newspapers

Daily Express
Daily Mail
Illustrated London News
Manchester Guardian
Morning Post
Observer
Pall Mall Gazette
The Times
Westminster Gazette

Official History

Edmonds, J. E., *Military Operations France and Belgium, 1914*, Vol. 2 (London: Macmillan, 1925).

Edmonds, J. E. and Wynne, G. C., *Military Operations France and Belgium, 1915*, Vol. 1 (London: Macmillan, 1927).

Edmonds, J. E., *Military Operations France and Belgium, 1915*, Vol. 2 (London: Macmillan, 1928).

Edmonds, J. E., *Military Operations France and Belgium 1916*, Vol. 1 (London: Macmillan, 1932).

Miles, W., *Military Operations France and Belgium 1916*, Vol. 2 (London: Macmillan, 1938).

Falls, C., *Military Operations France and Belgium 1917*, Vol. 1 (London: HMSO, 1940).

Edmonds, J. E., *Military Operations France and Belgium 1917*, Vol. 2 (London: HMSO, 1948).

Miles, W., *Military Operations France and Belgium 1917*, Vol. 3 (London: HMSO, 1948).

Edmonds, J. E., *Military Operations France and Belgium, 1918*, Vol. 1 (London: Macmillan, 1935).

Edmonds, J. E., *Military Operations France and Belgium, 1918*, Vol. 2 (London: Macmillan, 1937).

Edmonds, J. E., *Military Operations France and Belgium, 1918*, Vol. 3 (London: Macmillan, 1939).

Edmonds, J. E., *Military Operations France and Belgium, 1918*, Vol. 4 (London: HMSO, 1947).

Edmonds, J. E., *Military Operations France and Belgium, 1918*, Vol. 5 (London: HMSO, 1947).

Official History of the Great War: Medical Services: Hygiene of the War, 2 vols. (London: HMSO, 1923).

Official History of the Great War: Medical Services: Casualties and Medical Statistics (London: HMSO, 1931).

Statistics of the Military Effort of the British Empire in the Great War (London: HMSO, 1922).

Central Statistical Office, *Fighting with Figures: A Statistical Digest of the Second World War* (London: CSO, 1995).

Regimental and Formation History

Anon., *University of London Officer Training Corps, Roll of War Service 1914–1919* (London: Military Education Committee of the University of London, 1921).

Anon., *The Regimental Roll of Honour and War Record of the Artists Rifles (1/28th, 2/28th and 3/28th Battalions, The London Regiment, T.F.)*, 3rd edn. (London: Howlett, 1922).

Atkinson, C. T., *A History of the South Wales Borderers, 1914–18* (London: Medici Society, 1931).

Moyse-Bartlett, H., *The King's African Rifles: A Study in the Military History of East and Central Africa, 1890–1945* (Aldershot: Gale & Polden, 1956).

Clarke, F. A. S., *The History of the Royal West African Frontier Force* (Aldershot: Gale & Polden, 1964).

Dublin, *University of, Trinity College War List* (Dublin: Hodges, Figgis, 1922).

Falls, Cyril, *The History of the First Seven Battalions, Royal Irish Rifles (Now the Royal Ulster Rifles) in the Great War* (Aldershot: Gale & Polden, 1925).

Goold Walker, G, *The Honourable Artillery Company 1537–1987*, rev. edn. (London: Honourable Artillery Company, 1986).

Hamilton, A. S., *The City of London Yeomanry (Roughriders)* (London: Hamilton Press, 1936).

Haig-Brown, A. R., *The O.T.C. and the Great War* (London: Country Life, 1915).

Hanna, Henry, *The Pals at Suvla Bay: Being a Record of 'D' Company of the 7th Royal Dublin Fusiliers* (Dublin: E. Ponsonby, 1916).

Hutchinson, G. S., *Machine Guns: Their History and Tactical Employment (Being Also a History of the Machine Gun Corps, 1916 to 1922)* (London: Macmillan, 1938).

King, E. J., *History of the 7th Battalion Middlesex Regiment* (London: Harrison & Son, 1927).

Lindsay, J. H., *The London Scottish in the Great War* (London: Regimental HQ, 1925).

Marden, T.O., *A Short History of the Sixth Division, August 1914–March 1919* (London: Hugh Rees, 1920).

May, H. A. R., *Memories of the Artists' Rifles* (London: Howlett, 1929).

Moody, R. S. H., *Historical Records of the Buffs, East Kent Regiment 1914–1918* (London: Medici Society, 1922).

Moyse-Bartlett, H, *The King's African Rifles: A Study in the Military History of East and Central Africa, 1890–1945*, Vol. I (Aldershot: Gale & Polden, 1956).

Nichols (Quex), G. H. F, *The 18th Division in the Great War* (Edinburgh: William Blackwood and Sons, 1922).

Pease, Howard, *The History of the Northumberland (Hussars) Yeomanry 1819–1919 with Supplement to 1923* (London: Constable, 1924).

Regimental Publications Committee, *The Fifth Battalion, The Cameronians (Scottish Rifles) 1914–1919* (Glasgow: Jackson and Son, 1936).

A. P. I. S[amuels] and D. G. S., *With the Ulster Division in France: A Story of the 11th Battalion Royal Irish Rifles (South Antrim Volunteers) from Bordon to Thiepval* (Dublin: privately published, 1916).

Scott, Major-General Sir Arthur B. P. and Brumwell Middleton (eds.), *The History of the 12th (Eastern) Division in the Great War, 1914–1918* (London: Nisbit, 1923).

Stewart, J. and Buchan, John, *The Fifteenth (Scottish) Division 1914–1919* (Edinburgh: William Blackwood, 1926).

Williams-Ellis, Clough and A., *The Tank Corps* (London: Country Life, 1919).

Wylly, H. C., *History of the Manchester Regiment (Late the 63rd and 96th Foot)* (London: Forster Groom, 1925).

Walker, G. Goold, *The Honourable Artillery Company, 1537–1987* (London: Honourable Artillery Company, 1987).

Published Secondary Sources

Memoirs and Biographies

Amery, Leo, *My Political Life*, 3 vols. (London: Hutchinson, 1953–5).

Baynes, John, *Far From a Donkey: The Life of General Sir Ivor Maxse* (London: Brasseys, 1995).

Baynes, John, *The Forgotten Victor: The Life of General Sir Richard O'Connor* (London: Brasseys, 1989).

Beckett, Ian F. W., *Johnnie Gough VC: A Biography of Brigadier-General Sir John Edmund Gough* (London: Tom Donovan, 1989).

Beckett, Ian F. W., *The Memoirs of Sir James Edmonds* (Brighton: Tom Donovan. 2013).

Boyle, Andrew, *Trenchard: Man of Vision* (London: Collins, 1962).

Buckmaster, Viscount, *Roundabout* (London: H.F. & G. Witherby, 1969).

Callwell, C. E., *Field Marshal Sir Henry Wilson: His Life and Diaries*, 2 vols. (London: Cassell, 1927).

Baker-Carr, C. D., *From Chaffeur to Brigadier* (London: Ernest Benn, 1930).

Carrington, Charles, *Soldier from the War Returning* (London: Hutchinson, 1965).

Cassar, George, *Kitchener: Architect of Victory* (London: William Kimber, 1977).

Childs, Major General Sir Wyndham, *Episodes and Reflections* (London: Cassell, 1930).

Churchill, Randolph S., *Lord Derby: King of Lancashire* (London: Heinemann, 1959).

Crozier, F. P., *Brass Hat in No Man's Land* (London, Jonathan Cape, 1930).

Crozier, F. P., *Impressions and Recollections* (London: T. Werner Laurie, 1930).

De Groot, Gerard J., *Douglas Haig 1861–1928* (London: Unwin Hyman, 1988).

De Lisle, Beauvoir, *Reminiscences of Sport and War* (London: Eyre & Spottiswoode, 1939).

Dunn, J. C. (ed.), *The War the Infantry Knew, 1914–19*, 2nd edn. (London: Jane's, 1987).

Eden, Anthony, *Another World 1897–1917* (New York: Doubleday, 1977).

Edmonds [sc. Carrington], Charles, *A Subaltern's War* (London: Peter Davies, 1929).

Farr, Don, *The Silent General: Horne of the First Army* (Solihull: Helion, 2007).

French, Field Marshal Viscount, *1914* (London: Constable, 1919).

Gilbert, Martin, *Winston S. Churchill*, Vol. III: *1914–1916* (London: Hinemann, 1971).

Gough, Hubert, *Soldiering On* (London: Arthur Barker, 1954).
Grey, Lord, *Twenty Five Years, 1892–1916*, 2 vols. (London: Hodder & Stoughton, 1925).
Harris, J. P., *Douglas Haig and the First World War* (Cambridge University Press, 2008).
Hitchcock, F. C., *'Stand To': A Diary of the Trenches, 1915–1918* (London: Hurst & Blackett, 1937).
Holmes, Richard, *The Little Field Marshal: A Life of Sir John French* (London: Weidenfeld & Nicolson, 2004).
Horrocks, Brian, *A Full Life* (London: Collins, 1960).
Jeffery, Keith, *Field Marshal Sir Henry Wilson: A Political Soldier* (Oxford University Press, 2006).
Kirkpatrick, Ivonc, *The Inner Circle* (London: Macmillan, 1959).
Law, Francis, *A Man at Arms: Memoirs of Two World Wars* (London: Collins, 1983).
Lucy, John, *There's a Devil in the Drum* (London: Faber & Faber, 1938).
Lynch-Robinson, Christopher, *The Last of the Irish R.M.s* (London: Hutchinson, 1951).
McCudden, James, *Five Years in the RFC* (London: Aeroplane and General Publishing Company, 1918).
Montgomery, B. L., *The Memoirs of Field Marshal Montgomery* (London: Collins, 1958).
Morgan, Frederick, *Peace and War: A Soldier's Life* (London: Hodder & Stoughton, 1961).
Pile, Frederick, *Ack-Ack: Britain's Defence against Air Attack during the Second World War* (London: George G. Harrao, 1949).
Richards, Frank, *Old Soldiers Never Die* (London: Faber & Faber, 1964).
Robbins, Simon, *British Generalship during the Great War: The Military Career of Sir Henry Horne* (Farnham: Ashgate, 2010).
Robertson, N., *Crowned Harp: Memories of the Last Years of the Crown in Ireland* (Dublin: Allen Figgis, 1960).
Rogerson, Sidney, *Twelve Days* (London: Arthur Barker, 1933).
Sheffield, G. D., *The Chief: Douglas Haig and the British Army* (London: Aurum Press, 2011).
Smith-Dorrien, Horace, *Memories of Forty-Eight Years' Service* (London: John Murray, 1925).
Smyth, John, *Milestones: A Memoir* (London: Sidgwick & Jackson, 1979).
Senior, Michael, *Haking: A Dutiful Soldier – Lt. General Sir Richard Haking, XI Corps Commander, 1915–18 – A Study in Corps Command* (Barnsley: Pen & Sword, 2012).
Snow, Dan and Pottle, Mark (eds.), *The Confusion of Command: The War Memoirs of Lieutenant General Sir Thomas D'Oyly Snow, 1914–15* (London: Frontline Books, 2011).
Spears, Edward, *Prelude to Victory* (London: Jonathan Cape, 1939).
Spiers, E. M., *Haldane: An Army Reformer* (Edinburgh University Press, 1980).

Stirling, W. F., *Safety Last* (London: Hollis & Carter, 1953).
Tredrey, F. D., *Pioneer Pilot: The Great Smith Barry Who Taught the World How to Fly* (London: Peter Davies, 1976).
Terraine, John, *Douglas Haig: The Educated Soldier* (London: Hutchinson, 1963).
Vasili, Phil, *Walter Tull (1888–1918): Officer, Footballer* (London: Raw Press, 2009).
Wyndham, Horace, *Following the Drum* (London: Andrew Melrose, 1912).
Young, Desmond, *Try Anything Twice* (London: Hamish Hamilton, 1963).

Monographs

Adams, R. J. Q. and Poirier, Philip, *The Conscription Controversy in Britain, 1900–18* (Basingstoke: Macmillan, 1987).
Anderson, Julie, *War, Disability and Rehabilitation in Britain: Soul of a Nation* (Manchester University Press, 2011).
Anderson, Ross, *The Forgotten Front 1914–18: The East African campaign* (Stroud: Tempus, 2007).
Andreopoulos, George and Selesky, Harold (eds.), *The Aftermath of Defeat: Societies, Armed Forces, and the Challenge of Recovery* (New Haven, CT: Yale University Press, 1994).
Ashworth, Tony, *Trench Warfare 1914–1918: The Live and Let Live System* (Basingstoke: Macmillan, 1980).
Babington, Anthony, *For the Sake of Example* (London: Leo Cooper, 1983).
Badsey, Stephen, *Doctrine and Reform in the British Cavalry, 1880–1918* (Aldershot: Ashgate, 2008).
Badsey, Stephen, *The British Army in Battle and Its Image, 1914–18* (London: Continuum, 2009).
Bailey, Jonathan, *The First World War and the Birth of the Modern Style of Warfare* (London: HMSO and Strategic and Combat Studies Institute, 1996).
Banham, Peter, *Forgotten Lunatics of the Great War* (New Haven, CT: Yale University Press, 2004).
Barr, Niall, *The Lion and the Poppy: British Veterans, Politics and Society, 1921–1939* (Westport, CT: Praeger, 2005).
Bartlett, Thomas and Jeffery, Keith (eds.), *A Military History of Ireland* (Cambridge University Press, 1998).
Beach, James, *Haig's Intelligence: GHQ and the German Army, 1916–1918* (Cambridge University Press, 2013).
Becker, Jean-Jacques and Audoin-Rouzeau, Stéphane (eds.), *Les sociétés européennes et la guerre de 1914–1918* (Nanterre, France: Université Paris-X Nanterre, 1990).
Beckett, Ian F. W. and Gooch, John, (eds.), *Politicians and Defence: Studies in the Formulation of British Defence Policy, 1845–1970* (Manchester University Press, 1981).

Beckett, Ian F. W., *Riflemen Form: A Study of the Rifle Volunteer Movement 1859–1908* (Aldershot: Ogilby Trust, 1982).

Beckett, Ian F. W. and Simpson, Keith (eds.), *A Nation in Arms: A Social Study of the British Army in the First World War* (Manchester University Press, 1985).

Beckett, Ian F W, *The Amateur Military Tradition, 1558–1945* (Manchester University Press, 1991).

Beckett, Ian F. W., *Ypres: The First Battle, 1914* (Harlow: Longman/Pearson, 2004).

Beckett, Ian F. W. and Corvi, Steven J., (eds.), *Haig's Generals* (Barnsley: Pen & Sword, 2006).

Beckett, Ian F. W., *Home Front, 1914–18: How Britain Survived the Great War* (London: National Archives, 2006).

Beckett, Ian F. W., *The Great War, 1914–18*, 2nd edn. (Harlow: Longman/Pearson, 2007).

Beckett, Ian F. W. (ed.), *1917: Beyond the Western Front* (Leiden, the Netherlands: Brill, 2009).

Beckett, Ian F. W. *The Making of the First World War* (New Haven, CT: Yale University Press, 2012).

Bidwell, Shelford and Graham, Dominick, *Firepower: British Army Weapons and Theories of War, 1904–1945* (London: Allen & Unwin, 1982).

Boff, Jonathan, *Winning and Losing on the Western Front: The British Third Army and the Defeat of Germany in 1918* (Cambridge University Press, 2012).

Bond, Brian, *The Victorian Army and the Staff College, 1854–1914* (London: Eyre Methuen, 1972).

Bond, Brian and Roy, Ian, (eds.), *War and Society: A Yearbook of Military History* (London: Croom Helm, 1975).

Bond, Brian (ed.), *The First World War and British Military History* (Oxford: Clarendon Press, 1991).

Bond, Brian, *British Military Policy Between the Two World Wars* (Oxford: Clarendon Press, 1980).

Bond, Brian and Cave, Nigel (eds.), *Haig: A Reappraisal 70 Years On* (Barnsley: Pen & Sword, 1999).

Bond, Brian (ed.), *'Look to Your Front': Studies in the First World War* (Staplehurst: Spellmount, 1999).

Bond, Brian, *The Unquiet Western Front: Britain's Role in Literature and History* (Cambridge University Press, 2002).

Bourke, Joanna, *Dismembering the Male: Men's Bodies, Britain and the Great War* (London: Reaktion, 1996).

Bourne, John, *Britain and the Great War* (London: Edward Arnold, 1989).

Bowman, Timothy, *Irish Regiments in the Great War: Discipline and Morale* (Manchester University Press, 2003).

Bowman, Timothy, *Carson's Army: The Ulster Volunteer Force, 1910–22* (Manchester University Press, 2007).

Bowman, Timothy and Connelly, Mark, *The Edwardian Army: Recruiting, Training and Deploying the British Army, 1902–1914* (Oxford University Press, 2012).

Bragg, Sir Lawrence, Dowson, A. H., and Hemming, H. H. (eds.), *Artillery Survey in the First World War* (London: Field Survey Association, 1971).

Braybon, Gail (ed.), *Evidence, History and the Great War: Historians and the Impact of 1914–18* (Oxford: Berghahn Books, 2003).

Brose, Eric Dorn, *The Kaiser's Army: The Politics of Military Technology in Germany during the Machine Age, 1870–1914* (Oxford University Press, 2001).

Brown, Ian Malcolm, *British Logistics on the Western Front, 1914–1919* (Westport, CT: Praeger, 1998).

Brown, J. M. and Louis, W. R. (eds.), *The Oxford History of the British Empire: The Twentieth Century* (Oxford University Press, 1999).

Brown, Malcolm and Seaton, Shirley, *Christmas Truce: The Western Front December 1914* (London: Leo Cooper, 1984).

Burk, Kathleen (ed.), *War and the State: The Transformation of British Government, 1914–18* (London: Allen & Unwin, 1982).

Calder, Kenneth, *Britain and the Origins of the New Europe, 1914–18* (Cambridge University Press, 1976).

Canini, Gerard (ed.), *Les Fronts Invisibles: Actes du Colloque International sur La Logistique des Armées au Combat pendant la Première Guerre Mondiale* (Presses universitaires de Nancy, 1984).

Cecil, Hugh and Liddle, Peter (eds.), *Facing Armageddon: The First World War Experienced* (London: Leo Cooper, 1996).

Chandler, David and Beckett, Ian (eds.), *The Oxford History of the British Army* (Oxford University Press, 1994).

Chasseaud, Peter, *Artillery's Astrologers: A History of British Survey and Mapping on the Western Front, 1914–18* (Lewes: Mapbooks, 1999).

Clayton, Anthony, *Paths of Glory: The French Army, 1914–1918* (London: Phoenix, 2005).

Coetzee, Frans and Shevin-Coetzee, Marilyn (eds.), *Authority, Identity and the Social History of the Great War* (Providence, RI: Berghahn Books, 1995).

Cohen, Deborah, *The War Come Home: Disabled Veterans in Britain and Germany, 1914–39* (Berkeley: University of California Press, 2001).

Connelly, Mark, *Steady the Buffs! A Regiment, a Region and the Great War* (Oxford University Press, 2006).

Constantine, Stephen (ed.), *Emigrants and Empire* (Manchester University Press, 1990).

Constantine, Stephen, Kirby, Maurice and Rose, Mary (eds.), *The First World War in British History* (London: Arnold, 1995).

Cook, Tim, *No Place to Run: The Canadian Corps and Gas Warfare in the First World War* (Vancouver: University of British Columbia Press, 1999).

Cooke, Miriam and Woollacott, Angela, *Gendering War Talk* (Princeton, NJ: Princeton University Press, 1993).
Cooper, Malcolm, *The Birth of Independent Air Power: British Policy in World War I* (London: Allen & Unwin, 1986).
Corns, Cathryn and Hughes-Wilson, John, *Blindfold and Alone: British Military Executions in the Great War* (London: Cassell, 2001).
Crang, Jeremy, *The British People and the People's War 1939–1945* (Manchester University Press, 2000).
Cunningham, Hugh, *The Volunteer Force: A Social and Political History* (Hamden: Archon Books, 1975).
Dahrendorf, Ralf, *A History of the London School of Economics and Political Science 1895 to 1995* (Oxford University Press, 1995).
Davidoff, Leonore and Westover, Belinda (eds.), *Our Work, Our Lives, Our Words* (Totowa, NJ: Barnes & Noble, 1986).
Davis, Paul K., *Ends and Means: The British Mesopotamian Campaign and Commission* (Cranbury, NJ: Farleigh Dickinson University Press, 1994).
De Cecco, Marcello, *Money and Empire: The International Gold Standard, 1890–1914* (Oxford: Blackwell, 1974).
DeGroot, Gerard, *Blighty: British Society in the Era of the Great War* (Harlow: Longman, 1996).
Denman, Terence, *Ireland's Unknown Soldiers: The 16th (Irish Division) in the Great War* (Dublin: Irish Academic Press, 1992).
Dennis, Peter, *The Territorial Army 1907–1940* (London: Royal Historical Society and Boydell Press, 1987).
Dennis, Peter and Grey, Jeffrey, *Defining Victory, 1918* (Canberra, Australia: Army History Unit, Department of Defence, 1999).
Dennis, Peter and Grey, Jeffrey (eds.), *1917. Tactics, Training and Technology* (Canberra, Australia: Army History Unit, Department of Defence, 2007).
Dockrill, Michael and French, David (eds.), *Strategy and Intelligence: British Policy during the First World War* (London: Hambledon, 1996).
Doughty, Robert, *Pyrrhic Victory: French Strategy and Operations in the Great War* (Cambridge, MA: Belknap/Harvard University Press, 2005).
Douglas, R. M., *Feminist Freikorps: The British Voluntary Women's Police, 1914–40* (Westport, CT: Praeger, 1999).
Driver, Hugh, *The Birth of Military Aviation: Britain, 1903 to 1914* (Woodbridge: Royal Historical Society and Boydell Press, 1997).
Duffett, Rachel, *The Stomach for Fighting: Food and the Soldiers of the Great War* (Manchester University Press, 2012).
Dutton, David, *The Politics of Diplomacy: Britain and France in the Balkans in the First World War* (London: I.B. Tauris, 1998).
Erickson, E. J., *Ordered to Die: A History of the Ottoman Army in the First World War* (London: Greenwood Press, 2001).
Falls, Cyril, *The First World War* (London: Longman, 1960).

Farrar-Hockley, Anthony, *The Death of an Army* (London: Arthur Baker, 1967).

Fedorowich, Kent, *Unfit for Heroes: Reconstruction and Soldier Settlement in the Empire between the Wars* (Manchester University Press, 1995).

Ferguson, Niall, *The Pity of War: Explaining World War I* (London: Allen Lane, 1998).

Fitzpatrick, David (ed.), *Revolution? Ireland, 1917–23* (Dublin: Trinity History Workshop, 1999).

Foley, Robert T., *German Strategy and the Path to Verdun: Erich von Falkenhayn and the Development of Attrition, 1870–1916* (Cambridge University Press, 2005).

Foy, M. T. and Barton, Brian, *The Easter Rising* (Stroud: History Press, 2011).

Fraser, Murray, *John Bull's Other Homes: State Housing and British Policy in Ireland, 1883–1922* (Liverpool University Press, 1996).

Freedman, Lawrence, Hayes, Paul and O'Neill, Robert (eds.), *War, Strategy and International Politics: Essays in Honour of Sir Michael Howard* (Oxford: Clarendon Press, 1992).

French, David, *British Economic and Strategic Planning, 1905–15* (London: Allen & Unwin, 1982).

French, David, *British Strategy and War Aims, 1914–1916* (London: Allen & Unwin, 1986).

French, David, *The Strategy of the Lloyd George Coalition, 1916–1918* (Oxford University Press, 1995).

French, David, *Raising Churchill's Army: The British Army and the War against Germany, 1919–45* (Oxford University Press, 2000).

French, David and Holden Reid, Brian (eds.), *The British General Staff: Reform and Innovation, 1890–1939* (London: Frank Cass, 2002).

French, David, *Military Identities: The Regimental System, the British Army and the British People, c.1870–2000* (Oxford University Press, 2005).

Friedberg, Aaron, *The Weary Titan: Britain and the Experience of Relative Decline, 1895–1905* (Princeton, NJ: Princeton University Press, 1988).

Fuller, John, *Troop Morale and Popular Culture in the British and Dominion Armies, 1914–18* (Oxford: Clarendon Press, 1990).

Gardner, Nikolas, *Trial by Fire: Command and the British Expeditionary Force in 1914* (Westport, CT: Praeger/Greenwood, 2003).

Gibson, Craig, *Behind the Front: British Soldiers and French Civilians, 1914–18* (Cambridge University Press, 2014).

Gill, D. and Dallas, G., *The Unknown Army: Mutinies in the British Army in World War One* (London: Verso, 1985).

Gliddon, Gerald (ed.), *Norfolk and Suffolk in the Great War* (Norwich: Gliddon Books, 1988).

Gooch, John, *The Plans of War: The General Staff and British Military Strategy, c.1900–1916* (London: Routledge/Kegan Paul, 1974).

Gooch, John, *The Prospect of War: Studies in British Defence Policy, 1847–1942* (London: Frank Cass, 1981).

Gorges, E. H., *The Great War in West Africa* (London: Hutchinson, 1930).

Green, Andrew, *Writing the Great War: Sir James Edmonds and the Official Histories, 1915–1948* (London: Routledge, 2004).

Greenhalgh, Elizabeth, *Victory through Coalition: Britain and France during the First World War* (Cambridge University Press, 2005).

Gregory, Adrian and Pašeta, Sonia (eds.), *Ireland and the Great War: A War to Unite Us All* (Manchester University Press, 2002).

Gregory, Adrian, *The Last Great War: British Society and the First World War* (Cambridge University Press, 2008).

Grieves, Keith, *The Politics of Manpower, 1914–1918* (Manchester University Press, 1988).

Griffith, Paddy, *Battle Tactics on the Western Front: The British Army and the Art of Attack, 1916–1918* (New Haven, CT: Yale University Press, 1994).

Griffith, Paddy (ed.), *British Fighting Methods in the Great War* (London: Frank Cass, 1996).

Gudmundsson, Bruce I., *Stormtroop Tactics: Innovation in the German Army 1914–1918* (New York: Praeger, 1989).

Guinn, Paul, *British Strategy and Politics, 1914–18* (Oxford: Clarendon Press, 1965).

Guoqi, Xu, *Strangers on the Western Front: Chinese Workers in the Great War* (Cambridge, MA: Harvard University Press, 2011).

Haber, L. F., *The Poisonous Cloud: Chemical Warfare in the First World War* (Oxford University Press, 1986).

Hamilton, Richard and Herwig, Holger (eds.), *War Planning, 1914* (Cambridge University Press, 2010).

Hammond, Bryn *Cambrai, 1917: The Myth of the First Great Tank Battle* (London: Weidenfeld & Nicolson, 2008).

Harding, B., *Keeping the Faith: The History of the Royal British Legion* (Barnsley: Pen & Sword, 2001).

Harris, Jose (ed.), *Civil Society in British History: Ideas, Identities, Institutions* (Oxford University Press, 2003).

Harris, J. Paul, *Men, Ideas and Tanks: British Military Thought and Armoured Forces, 1903–19* (Manchester University Press, 1995).

Harris, J. Paul and Barr, Niall, *Amiens to the Armistice. The BEF in the Hundred Days' Campaign, 8 August–11 November 1918* (London: Brassey's, 1998).

Harris, J. Paul, *Douglas Haig and the First World War* (Cambridge University Press, 2008).

Harrison, Mark, *The Medical War: British Military Medicine in the First World War* (Oxford University Press, 2010).

Hayes, D., *Conscription Conflict* (London: Shepherd Press, 1949).

Hazlehurst, Cameron, *Politicians at War, July 1914 to May 1915: A Prologue to the Triumph of Lloyd George* (London: Jonathan Cape, 1971).

Herwig, Holger H., *The First World War: Germany and Austria-Hungary, 1914–1918* (London: Arnold, 1997).

Higonnet, Margaret, Jenson, Jane, Michel, Sonya and Collins, Margaret (eds.), *Behind the Lines: Gender and the Two World Wars* (New Haven, CT: Yale University Press, 1987).

Hirst, Francis W., *The Consequences of the War to Great Britain* (Oxford University Press, 1934).

Hodges, Geoffrey, *The Carrier Corps: Military Labour in the East African Campaign, 1914–18* (Westport, CT: Greenwood, 1986).

Horne, John (ed.), *State, Society and Mobilisation in Europe during the First World War* (Cambridge University Press, 1997).

Howard, Michael, *Studies in War and Peace* (London: Temple Smith, 1970).

Howard, Michael, *The Continental Commitment: The Dilemma of British Defence Policy in the Era of Two World Wars* (Harmondsworth: Penguin, 1974).

Howe, Glenford, *Race, War and Nationalism: A Social History of West Indians in the First World War* (Oxford University Press, 2002).

Hughes, Matthew, *Allenby and British Strategy in the Middle East* (London: Frank Cass, 1999).

Hughes, Matthew and Seligmann, Matthew (eds.), *Leadership in Conflict, 1914–18* (Barnsley: Leo Cooper, 2000).

Hunt, Barry and Preston, Adrian (eds.), *War Aims and Strategic Policy in the Great War* (London: Croom Helm, 1977).

Jaumain, Serge, Amara, Michaël, Majerus, Benoît and Vrints, Antoon (eds.), *Une Guerre Totale? La Belgique dans la Première Guerre Mondiale* (Brussels: Archives générales du Royaume, 2005).

Jeffery, Keith, *The British Army and the Crisis of Empire, 1918–22* (Manchester University Press, 1984).

Jeffery, Keith, *Ireland and the Great War* (Cambridge University Press, 2000).

Johnson, Matthew, *Militarism and the British Left 1902–1914* (Basingstoke: Palgrave Macmillan, 2013).

Jones, Heather, *Violence against Prisoners of War in the First World War: Britain, France and Germany, 1914–20* (Cambridge University Press, 2011).

Jones, Spencer, *From Boer War to World War: Tactical Reform of the British Army, 1902–14* (Norman: Oklahoma University Press, 2012).

Jones, Spencer (ed.), *Stemming the Tide: Officers and Leadership in the British Expeditionary Force, 1914* (Solihull: Helion, 2013).

Keegan, John, *The Face of Battle* (Harmondsworth: Penguin, 1978).

Keegan, John, *The First World War* (London: Hutchinson, 1998).

Kennedy, Greg and Neilson, Keith (eds.), *Far Flung Lines: Essays on Imperial Defence in Honour of Donald Mackenzie Schurman* (London: Frank Cass, 1997).

Kennedy, T. C., *The Hound of Conscience: A History of the No Conscription Fellowship, 1914–19* (Fayetteville: University of Arkansas Press, 1981).

Kenyon, David, *Horsemen in No Man's Land. British Cavalry and Trench Warfare, 1914–1918* (Barnsley: Pen & Sword, 2011).

Kettle, Michael, *Russia and the Allies, 1917–20: The Road to Intervention, March to November 1918* (London: Routledge, 1988).

King, Alex, *Memorials of the Great War in Britain: The Symbolism and Politics of Remembrance* (Oxford: Berg, 1998).

Kitchen, James, *The British Imperial Army in the Middle East: Morale and Military Identity in the Sinai and Palestine Campaigns, 1916–18* (London: Bloomsbury, 2014).

Kitchen, Martin, *The German Offensives of 1918* (Stroud: Tempus, 2005).

Knight, Jill, *The Civil Service Rifles in the Great War: 'All Bloody Gentlemen'* (Barnsley: Pen & Sword, 2005).

Lambert, Nicholas A., *Planning Armageddon: British Economic Warfare and the First World War* (Cambridge, MA: Harvard University Press, 2012).

Lee, Janet, *War Girls: The First Aid Nursing Yeomanry in the Great War* (Manchester University Press, 2005).

Leed, E. J., *No Man's Land: Combat and Identity in World War I* (Cambridge University Press, 1979).

Leese, Peter, *Shell Shock: Traumatic Neurosis and the British Soldier of the First World War* (Basingstoke: Macmillan, 2002).

Leneman, Leah, *Fit for Heroes: Land Settlement in Scotland after World War I* (Aberdeen University Press, 1989).

Liddell Hart, B. H., *The Real War* (London: Hutchinson, 1934).

Liddell Hart, B. H., *A History of the First World War* (London: Cassell, 1970).

Liddle, Peter (ed.), *Home Fires and Foreign Fields: British Social and Military Experience in the First World War* (London: Brassey's, 1985).

Liddle, Peter (ed.), *Passchendaele in Perspective: The Third Battle of Ypres* (London: Leo Cooper, 1997).

Lloyd, Nicholas, *Loos, 1915* (Stroud: Tempus, 2006).

Locicero, Michael, Mahoney, Ross and Mitchell, Stuart (eds.), *A Military Transformed? Adaptation and Innovation in the British Military, 1792–1945* (Solihull: Helion, 2014).

Lotz, Rainer and Pegg, Ian (eds.), *Under the Imperial Carpet: Essays in Black History, 1780–1950* (Crawley: Rabbit Press, 1986).

Lowe, Peter, *Great Britain and Japan, 1911–15* (London: Macmillan, 1969).

Lupfer, Timothy T., *The Dynamics of Doctrine: The Changes in German Tactical Doctrine during the First World War* (Fort Leavenworth, KS: US Army Command and General Staff College, 1981).

Macdonald, Catriona and McFarland, Elaine W. (eds.), *Scotland and the Great War* (East Linton: Tuckwell Press, 1999).

Macdonald, Lyn, *The Roses of No Man's Land* (London: Michael Joseph, 1980).

Mackenzie, S. P., *Politics and Military Morale: Current Affairs and Citizenship Education in the British Army, 1914–50* (Oxford: Clarendon Press, 1990).

Macleod, Jenny (ed.), *Gallipoli: Making History* (London: Frank Cass, 2004).

Macleod, Jenny and Purseigle, Pierre (eds.), *Uncovered Fields: Perspectives in First World War Studies* (Leiden, the Netherlands: Brill, 2004).

Madigan, Edward, *Faith under Fire: Anglican Army Chaplains and the Great War* (Basingstoke: Palgrave Macmillan, 2011).

Marble, Sanders, *British Artillery on the Western Front in the First World War* (Farnham: Ashgate, 2013).

Marble, Sandars (ed.), *Scraping the Barrel: The Military Use of Substandard Manpower, 1860–1969* (New York: Fordham University Press, 2012).

McCartney, Helen, *Citizen Soldiers: The Liverpool Territorials in the First World War* (Cambridge University Press, 2005).

McDermott, James, *British Military Service Tribunals, 1916–18: 'A Very Much Abused Body of Men'* (Manchester University Press, 2011).

McGarry, Fearghal, *The Rising: Ireland: Easter 1916* (Oxford University Press, 2010).

Maurice-Jones, K. W., *The Shop Story 1900–1939* (Woolwich: Royal Artillery Institution, 1954).

Messenger, Charles, *Broken Sword: The Tumultuous Life of General Frank Crozier, 1879–1937* (Barnsley: Praetorian Press, 2013).

Meyer, Jessica, *Men of War: Masculinity and the First World War in Britain* (Basingstoke: Palgrave-Macmillan, 2012).

Meyer, Jessica (ed.), *British Popular Culture and the First World War* (Leiden, the Netherlands: Brill, 2008).

Middlebrook, Martin, *The Kaiser's Battle, 21 March 1918: The First Day of the German Spring Offensive* (London: Penguin, Allen Lane, 1978).

Middlebrook, Martin, *Your Country Needs You: The Expansion of the British Army Infantry Divisions 1914–1918* (Barnsley: Leo Cooper, 2000).

Millman, Brock, *Pessimism and British War Policy, 1916–1918* (London: Frank Cass, 2001).

Mitchinson, K. W., *Gentlemen and Officers: The Impact and Experience of War on a Territorial Regiment 1914–18* (London: Imperial War Museum, 1995).

Mitchinson, K. W., *Defending Albion: Britain's Home Army, 1908–19* (Basingstoke: Palgrave, 2005).

Mitchinson, K. W., *England's Last Hope: The Territorial Force, 1908–14* (Basingstoke: Palgrave, 2008).

Moody, Simon and Wakefield, Alan, *Under the Devil's Eye. Britain's Forgotten Army in Salonika, 1915–1918* (Thrupp: Sutton, 2004).

Moore-Blick, Christopher, *Playing the Game: The British Junior Infantry Officer on the Western Front, 1914–18* (Solihull: Helion, 2011).

Moran, Lord, *The Anatomy of Courage* (London: Constable, 1945).

Morris, A. J. A., *The Scaremongers: The Advocacy of War and Rearmament 1896–1914* (London: Routledge/Kegan Paul, 1984).

Morton-Jack, George, *The Indian Army on the Western Front: India's Expeditionary Force to France and Belgium in the First World War* (Cambridge University Press, 2014).

Neilson, Keith, *Strategy and Supply: The Anglo-Russian Alliance, 1914–17* (London: Allen & Unwin, 1984).

Nelson, Robert, *German Soldier Newspapers of the First World War* (Cambridge University Press, 2011).

Noakes, Lucy, *Women in the British Army: War and Gentle Sex, 1907–48* (London: Routledge, 2006).

Oakes, John, *Kitchener's Lost Boys: From the Playing Fields to the Killing Fields* (Stroud: History Press, 2009).

Occleshaw, Michael, *Armour against Fate: British Military Intelligence in the First World War* (London: Columbus Books, 1989).

Omissi, David, *Indian Voices of the Great War: Soldiers' Letters, 1914–18* (Basingstoke: Palgrave Macmillan, 1999).

Oram, Gerald, *Death Sentences Passed by Military Courts of the British Army, 1914–1924* (London: Francis Boutle, 1998).

Oram, Gerald, *Worthless Men: Race, Eugenics and the Death Penalty in the British Army during the First World War* (London: Francis Boutle, 1998).

Osborne, J. M., *The Voluntary Recruiting Movement in Britain, 1914–16* (New York: Garland, 1982).

Palazzo, Albert, *Seeking Victory on the Western Front: The British Army and Chemical Warfare in World War I* (Lincoln: University of Nebraska Press, 2000).

Panayi, Panikos (ed.), *Racial Violence in Britain, 1840–1950* (Leicester University Press, 1993).

Passingham, Ian, *The Battle of Messines Ridge, June 1917* (Thrupp: Alan Sutton, 1998).

Pearce, Cyril, *Comrades in Conscience: The Story of an English Community's Opposition to the Great War* (London: Francis Boutle, 2001).

Pennell, Catriona, *A Kingdom United: Popular Responses to the Outbreak of the First World War in Britain and Ireland* (Oxford University Press, 2012).

Perry, F. W., *The Commonwealth Armies: Manpower and Organisation in Two Worlds Wars* (Manchester University Press, 1988).

Philpott, William, *Anglo-French Relations and Strategy on the Western Front, 1914–1918* (Basingstoke: Macmillan, 1996).

Philpott, William, *Bloody Victory: The Sacrifice on the Somme and the Making of the Twentieth Century* (London: Little, Brown, 2009).

Playne, Caroline, *The Pre-War Mind in Britain: An Historical Review* (London: Allen & Unwin, 1928).

Prior, Robin and Wilson, Trevor, *Command on the Western Front: The Military Career of Sir Henry Rawlinson, 1914–18* (Oxford: Blackwell, 1992).

Prior, Robin and Wilson, Trevor, *Passchendaele, The Untold Story* (New Haven, CT: Yale University Press, 1996).

Prior, Robin and Wilson, Trevor, *Somme* (New Haven, CT: Yale University Press, 2005).

Putkowski, Julian and Sykes, Julian, *Shot at Dawn* (Barnsley: Pen & Sword, 1989).

Rae, John, *Conscience and Politics: The British Government and the Conscientious Objector to Military Service, 1916–19* (Oxford University Press, 1970).

Reese, Peter, *Homecoming Heroes* (Barnsley: Pen & Sword, 1991).

Reid, Fiona, *Broken Men: Shellshock, Treatment and Recovery in Britain 1914–1930* (London: Continuum, 2011).

Reznick, Jeffrey, *Healing the Nation: Soldiers and the Culture of Caregiving in Britain during the Great War* (Manchester University Press, 2004).

Richter, Donald, *Chemical Soldiers* (London: Leo Cooper, 1972)

Robb, George, *British Culture and the First World War* (Basingstoke: Palgrave, 2002).

Robbins, Simon, *British Generalship on the Western Front 1914–1918: Defeat into Victory* (Abingdon: Routledge, 2005).

Rothstein, Andrew, *The Soldiers' Strikes of 1919* (London: Macmillan, 1980).

Rothwell, V. H., *British War Aims and Peace Diplomacy* (Oxford: Clarendon Press, 1971).

Samuels, Martin, *Doctrine and Dogma: German and British Infantry Tactics in the First World War* (Westport, CT: Greenwood, 1992).

Samuels, Martin, *Command or Control? Command, Training and Tactics in the British Armies, 1888–1918* (London: Frank Cass, 1995).

Sandford, Stephen, *Neither Unionist nor Nationalist: The 10th (Irish) Division in the Great War* (Sallins, Ireland: Irish Academic Press, 2015).

Schreiber, Shane B., *Shock Army of the British Empire: The Canadian Corps in the Last 100 Days of the Great War* (Westport, CT: Praeger, 2005).

Schweitzer, Richard, *The Cross and the Trenches: Religious Faith and Doubt among British and American Great War Soldiers* (Westport, CT: Praeger, 2003).

Scott, Peter T., *Dishonoured: The Colonels' Surrender at St. Quentin, the Retreat from Mons, August 1914* (London: Tom Donovan, 1994).

Seldon, Anthony and Walsh, David, *Public Schools and the Great War: The Generation Lost* (Barnsley: Pen & Sword, 2013).

Sheffield, Gary (ed.), *Leadership and Command: The Anglo-American Experience since 1861* (London: Brasseys, 1997).

Sheffield, Gary, *Leadership in the Trenches: Officer-Man Relations, Morale and Discipline in the British Army in the Era of the First World War* (Basingstoke: Macmillan, 2000).

Sheffield, Gary, *Forgotten Victory: The First World War Myths and Realities* (London: Headline, 2001).

Sheffield, Gary, *The Somme* (London: Cassell, 2003).

Sheffield, Gary and Todman, Dan (eds.), *Command and Control on the Western Front: The British Army's Experience 1914–18* (Staplehurst: Spellmount, 2004).

Shukman, Harold, *War or Revolution: Russian Jews and Conscription in Britain, 1917* (Edgware: Valentine Mitchell, 2006).

Silbey, David, *The British Working Class and Enthusiasm for War, 1914–16* (London: Frank Cass, 2005).

Simkins, Peter, *Kitchener's Army: The Raising of the New Armies, 1914–1916* (Manchester University Press, 1988).

Simkins, Peter, *From the Somme to Victory: The British Army's Experience on the Western Front, 1916–18* (Barnsley: Pen & Sword, 2014).

Simmonds, Alan G. V., *Britain and World War One* (Abingdon: Routledge, 2012).

Simpson, Andy, *Directing Operations: British Corps Command on the Western Front 1914–1918* (Stroud: Spellmount, 2006).

Simpson, Keith, *The Old Contemptibles: A Photographic History of the British Expeditionary Force, August-December 1914* (London: Allen & Unwin, 1981).

Sims, Charles, *The Royal Air Force: The First Fifty Years* (London: Adam and Charles Black, 1968).

Smith, Angela, *Discourses Surrounding British Widows of the First World War* (London: Bloomsbury, 2012).

Smith, Paul (ed.), *Government and Armed Forces in Britain, 1856–1990* (London: Hambledon Press, 1996).

Smith, Richard, *Jamaica and the Great War: Race, Masculinity and the Development of National Consciousness* (Manchester University Press, 2004).

Snape, Michael, *God and the British Soldier: Religion and the British Army in the First and Second World Wars* (London: Routledge, 2005).

Spiers, Edward, *Chemical Warfare* (London: Macmillan, 1986).

Spiers, E. M., *The Late Victorian Army 1868–1902* (Manchester University Press, 1992).

Steel, Nigel and Hart, Peter, *Defeat at Gallipoli* (London: Macmillan, 1995).

Steel, Nigel and Hart, Peter, *Passchendaele, the Sacrificial Ground* (London: Cassell, 2000).

Stevenson, David, *1914–1918: The History of the First World War* (London: Penguin, 2005).

Stevenson, David, *With Our Backs to the Wall: Victory and Defeat in 1918* (London: Allen Lane, 2011).

Strachan, Hew, *History of the Cambridge University Officer Training Corps* (Tunbridge Wells, UK: Midas Books, 1976).

Strachan, Hew, *The First World War*, Vol. I: *To Arms* (Oxford University Press, 2001).

Strachan, Hew, *The First World War: A New Illustrated History* (London: Simon & Schuster, 2003).

Summers, Julie, *Remembering Fromelles: A New Cemetery for a New Century* (Maidenhead: Commonwealth War Graves Commission, 2010).

Summerskill, Michael, *China on the Western Front: Britain's Chinese Work Force in the First World War* (London: privately published, 1982).

Taithe, Bertrand and Thornton, Tim (eds.), *Propaganda: Political Rhetoric and Identity, 1300–2000* (Stroud: Sutton, 1999).

Teagarden, Ernest M., *Haldane at the War Office* (New York: Gordon Press, 1976).

Terraine, John, *Mons: Retreat to Victory* (London: Batsford, 1960).

Terraine, John, *The Road to Passchendaele: The Flanders Offensive of 1917 – A Study in Inevitability* (London, Leo Cooper, 1977).

Terraine, John, *To Win a War, 1918: The Year of Victory* (London: Sidgwick & Jackson, 1978).

Terraine, John, *White Heat: The New Warfare 1914–1918* (London: Sidgwick & Jackson, 1982).

Terraine, John, *The First World War, 1914–1918* (London: Macmillan, 1965 and 1983 (Hutchinson) editions).

Thomas, H. S., *The Story of Sandhurst* (London: Hutchinson, 1961).

Thompson, Mark, *The White War: Life and Death on the Italian Front, 1915–1919* (London: Faber & Faber, 2008).

Todman, Dan, *The Great War: Myth and Memory* (London: Hambledon & London, 2005).

Townshend, Charles, *Easter 1916: The Irish Rebellion* (London: Allen Lane, 2005).

Townshend, Charles, *When God Made Hell: The British Invasion of Mesopotamia and the Creation of Iraq, 1914–1921* (London: Faber & Faber, 2010).

Travers, Tim, *The Killing Ground: The British Army, the Western Front and the Emergence of Modern Warfare* (London: Unwin, Hyman, 1987).

Travers, Tim, *How the War Was Won: Command and Technology in the British Army on the Western Front, 1917–1918* (London: Routledge, 1992).

Travers, Tim, *Gallipoli 1915* (Stroud: Tempus, 2001).

Turner, John (ed.), *Britain and the First World War* (London: Unwin Hyman, 1988).

Tynan, Jane, *British Army Uniform and the First World War: Men in Khaki* (Basingstoke: Palgrave Macmillan, 2013).

Turner, John, *British Politics and the Great War: Coalition and Conflict, 1915–18* (New Haven, CT: Yale University Press, 1992).

Ugolini, Laura, *Civvies: Middle-Class Men on the English Home Front, 1914–18* (Manchester University Press, 2013).

Ulrichsen, K. C., *Logistics and Politics of the British Campaigns in the Middle East, 1914–22* (Basingstoke: Palgrave Macmillan, 2011).

Van Emden, Richard, *Boy Soldiers of the Great War*, 2nd edn. (London: Bloomsbury, 2012).

Van Pul, Paul, *In Flanders Flooded Fields* (Barnsley: Pen & Sword, 2006).

Wakefield, Alan and Moody, Simon, *Under the Devil's Eye: Britain's Forgotten Army at Salonika 1915–1918* (Stroud: Sutton, 2004).

Ward, Stephen R. (ed.), *The War Generation* (Port Washington, NY: Kennikat Press, 1975).

Warwick, Peter and Spies, S. B. (eds.), *The South African War* (London: Longman, 1980).

Watson, Alex, *Enduring the Great War: Combat, Morale and Collapse in the German and British Armies, 1914–18* (Cambridge University Press, 2008).

Watson, Janet, *Fighting Different Wars: Experience, Memory and the First World War in Britain* (Cambridge University Press, 2004).

Watts, Martin, *The Jewish Legion and the First World War* (Basingstoke: Palgrave, 2004).

Whitehead, I. R., *Doctors in the Great War* (Barnsley: Leo Cooper, 1999).

Williams, Rhodri, *Defending the Empire: The Conservative Party and British Defence Policy 1899–1915* (London: Yale University Press, 1991).

Williamson, Samuel, *The Politics of Grand Strategy: Britain and France Prepare for War, 1904–14*, 2nd edn. (London: Ashfield Press, 1990).

Wilson, Trevor, *Myriad Faces of War: Britain and the Great War, 1914–18* (Cambridge: Polity Press, 1986).

Winter, Denis, *Death's Men: Soldiers of the Great War* (London: Penguin Allen Lane, 1978).

Winter, Jay, *The Great War and the British People* (Basingstoke: Macmillan, 1986).

Wohl, Robert, *The Generation of 1914* (Cambridge, MA: Harvard University Press, 1980).

Woodward, David, *Lloyd George and the Generals* (East Brunswick, NJ: Associated University Presses, 1983).

Wootton, Graham, *The Politics of Influence* (Cambridge, MA: Harvard University Press, 1963).

Wynne, Captain G. C., *If Germany Attacks: The Battle in Depth in the West* (London: Faber & Faber, 1940).

Yates, Nigel (ed.), *Kent in the Twentieth Century* (Woodbridge: Boydell & Brewer, 2001).

Zuber, Terence, *The Mons Myth: A Reassessment of the Battle* (Stroud: History Press, 2010).

Chapters and Journal Articles

Aalen, F. H. A., 'Homes for Irish Heroes: Housing under the Irish Land (Provision for Sailors and Soldiers) Act, 1919 and the Irish Soldiers' and Sailors' Land Trust', *Town Planning Review* 59 (1988), 305–23.

Adams, R. J. Q., 'Asquith's Choice: The May Coalition and the Coming of Conscription, 1915–16', *Journal of British Studies* 25 (1986), 243–63.

Ashley-Smith, Peter, 'Kineton and the Military Tribunals, 1915–1918', *Warwickshire History* 13 (2005), 15–24.

Ashworth, Tony, 'The Sociology of Trench Warfare, 1914–18', *British Journal of Sociology* 19 (1968), 407–23.

Auerbach, Sasha, 'Negotiating Nationalism: Jewish Conscription and Russian Repatriation in London's East End, 1916–18', *Journal of British Studies* 46 (2007), 594–207.

Bailey, Jonathan, 'British Artillery in the Great War', in Griffith (ed.), *British Fighting Methods*, 23–49.

Niall Barr, 'Command in Transition from Mobile to Static Warfare, August 1914 to March 1915', in Sheffield and Todman (eds.), *Command and Control*, 13–38.

Barr, Niall and Sheffield, Gary, 'Douglas Haig, the Common Soldier and the British Legion', in Bond and Cave (eds.), *Haig: A Reappraisal*, 223–39.

Barr, Niall, 'The British Legion after the Great War: Its Identity and Character', in Taithe and Thornton (eds.), *War*, 213–33.

Beach, Jim, 'Issued by the General Staff: Doctrine writing at British GHQ, 1917–18', *War in History* 19(4) (2012), 464–91.

Beckett, Ian F. W., 'The Local Community and the Great War: Aspects of Military Participation', *Records of Buckinghamshire* 20 (1978), 503–15.

Beckett, Ian F. W., 'The Singapore Mutiny of February 1915', *Journal of the Society for Army Historical Research* 62 (1984), 132–53.

Beckett, Ian F. W., 'The Stanhope Memorandum of 1888: A Reinterpretation', *Bulletin of the Institute of Historical Research* 57 (1984), 240–47.

Beckett, Ian F. W., 'Aspects of a Nation in Arms: Britain's Volunteer Training Corps in the Great War', *Revue Internationale d'Histoire Militaire* 63 (1985), 27–39.

Beckett, Ian F. W., 'The Real Unknown Army: British Conscripts, 1916–19', *The Great War* 2 (1989), 4–13.

Beckett, Ian F. W., 'The Nation in Arms, 1914–18', in Beckett and Simpson (eds.), *A Nation in Arms*, 1–36.

Beckett, Ian F. W., 'The Territorial Force', in Beckett and Simpson (eds.), *Nation in Arms*, 127–64.

Beckett, Ian F. W., 'The Plans and the Conduct of the Battle', in Liddle (ed.), *Passchendaele in Perspective*, 102–16.

Beckett, Ian F. W., 'The Territorial Force in the Great War', in Liddle (ed.), *Home Fires and Foreign Fields*, 21–38.

Beckett, Ian F. W., 'The British Army: The Illusion of Change', in Turner (ed.), *Britain and the First World War*, 99–116.

Beckett, Ian F. W., 'Hubert Gough, Neill Malcolm and Command on the Western Front', in Bon (ed.), *Look to Your Front*, 1–12.

Beckett, Ian F. W.,' King George V and His Generals', in Hughes and Seligmann (eds.), *Leadership in Conflict*, 247–64.

Beckett, Ian F. W., 'Going to War: Southampton and Military Embarkation', in Miles Taylor (ed.), *Southampton: Gateway to the British Empire* (London: I.B. Tauris, 2007), 133–48.

Beckett, Ian F. W., 'Henry Rawlinson', in Beckett and Corvi (eds.), *Haig's Generals*, 164–82.

Bessel, Richard and Englander, David, 'Up from the Trenches: Some Recent Writing on the Soldiers of the Great War', *European Studies Review* 11 (1981), 387–95.

Blanch, Michael, 'British Society and the War', in Warwick and Spies (eds.), *The South African War*, 210–38.

Boff, Jonathan, 'Combined Arms during the Hundred Days Campaign, August-November 1918', *War in History* 17 (2010), 459–78.

Bogacz, Ted, 'War Neurosis and Cultural Change in England, 1914–22: The Work of the War Office Committee of Enquiry into "Shell-Shock"', *Journal of Contemporary History* 24 (1989), 227–56.

Bourne, John, 'British Generals in the First World War', in Sheffield (ed.), *Leadership and Command*, 93–116.

Bourne, John, 'Major General Sir Archibald Murray', in Jones (ed.), *Stemming the Tide*, 51–69.

Bourne, John, 'Charles Monro', in Beckett and Corvi (eds.), *Haig's Generals*, 122–40.

Bourne, John, 'British Divisional Generals during the Great War: First Thoughts', *Gun Fire* 29 (1987), 22–31.

Bourne, John, 'British General Officers and the Somme: Some Career Aspects', *Gun Fire* 39 (1997), 12–25.

Bourne, John,' The BEF's Generals on 29 September 1918: An Empirical Portrait with British and Australian Comparisons', in Dennis and Grey (eds.), *1918*, 96–113.

Bourne, John, 'Major General W. C. G. Heneker: A Divisional Commander of the Great War', in Hughes and Seligmann (eds.), *Leadership in Conflict*, 54–67.

Bowman, Timothy, 'The Irish Recruiting and Anti-recruiting Campaigns, 1914–18', in Taithe and Thornton (eds.), *Propaganda*, 223–38.

Bowman, Timothy, 'The Ulster Volunteer Force and the Formation of the 36th (Ulster) Division', *Irish Historical Studies* 32 (2001), 498–518.

Bowman, Timothy, 'Officering Kitchener's Armies: A Case-Study of the 36th (Ulster) Division', *War in History*, 16 (2009), 2.

Brown, Ian M., '"Not Glamorous, But Effective": The Canadian Corps and the Set-Piece Attack, 1917–1918', *Journal of Military History* 58 (1994), 421–44.

Buckley, Suzann, 'The Failure to Resolve the Problem of Venereal Disease among the Troops in Britain during World War One', in Bond and Roy (eds.), *War and Society*, 65–85.

Bush, Julia, 'East London Jews and the First World War', *London Journal* 6 (1980), 147–61.

Cameron, Ewen and Robertson, Iain, 'Fighting and Bleeding for the Land: The Scottish Highlands and the Great War', in Macdonald and McFarland (eds.), *Scotland and the Great War*, 81–100.

Cohen, S. A., 'The Genesis of the British Campaign in Mesopotamia, 1914', *Middle Eastern Studies* 12 (1976), 119–30.

Collins, Tony, 'English Rugby Union and the First World War', *Historical Journal* 45 (2002), 797–818.

Connelly, Mark, 'Lieutenant General Sir James Grierson', in Jones (ed.), *Stemming the Tide*, 133–50.

Coogan, John W. and Coogan, Peter F., 'The British Cabinet and the Anglo-French Staff Talks, 1905–15: Who Knew What and When Did He Know It?', *Journal of British Studies* 24 (1985), 110–31.

Cook, Tim, 'The Politics of Surrender: Canadian Soldiers and the Killing of Prisoners in the Great War', *Journal of Military History* 70 (2006), 637–66.

Cook, Tim, 'Fighting Words: Canadian Soldiers' Slang and Swearing in the Great War', *War in History* 20 (2013), 323–44.

Cook, Tim, 'Storm Troops: Combat Effectiveness in the Canadian Corps in 1917', in Dennis and Grey (eds.), *1917*, 43–61.

Corvi, Steven, 'Horace Smith-Dorrien', in Beckett and Corvi (eds.), *Haig's Generals*, 183–207.

Dalley, Stuart, 'The Response in Cornwall to the Outbreak of the First World War', *Cornish Studies* 11 (2003), 85–109.

Denman, Terence, 'Sir Lawrence Parsons and the Raising of the 16th (Irish) Division', *Irish Sword* 17 (1987–8), 90–103.

Denman, Terence, 'The Red Livery of Shame: The Campaign against Army Recruitment in Ireland, 1899–1914', *Irish Historical Studies*, XXIX(114) (1994).

Dewey, P. E., 'Military Recruiting and the British Labour Force during the First World War', *Historical Journal* 27 (1984), 199–224.

Donner, Henriette, 'Under the Cross – Why VADs Performed the Filthiest Tasks in the Dirtiest War: Red Cross Women Volunteers, 1914–18', *Journal of Social History* 30 (1997), 687–704.

Dony, J. G., 'The 1919 Peace Riots in Luton', *Bedfordshire Historical Record Society* 57 (1978), 205–33.

Douglas, Roy, 'Voluntary Enlistment in the First World War and the Work of the Parliamentary Recruiting Committee', *Journal of Modern History* 42 (1970), 564–85.

Doyle, Peter and Bennett, M., 'Geology and Warfare on the Western Front', *Stand To* 49 (1997), 34–8.

Duder, C. J. D., 'Beadoc: The British East Africa Disabled Officers' Colony and the White Frontier in Kenya', *Agricultural History Review* 40 (1992), 142–50.

Duder, C. J. D., '"Men of the Officer Class": The Participants in the 1919 Soldier Settlement Scheme in Kenya', *African Affairs* 92 (1993), 69–87.

Duffett, Rachel, 'A War Unimagined: Food and the Rank and File Soldier of the First World War', in Meyer (ed.), *British Popular Culture*, 47–70.

Dutton, David, 'The Calais Conference of December 1915', *Historical Journal* 21 (1978), 143–56.

Dutton, David, 'The "Robertson Dictatorship" and the Balkan Campaign in 1916', *Journal of Strategic Studies* 9 (1986), 64–78.

Egan, David, 'The Swansea Conference of the British Council of Soldiers' and Workers' Delegates, July 1917', *Llafur* 1 (1975), 162–87.

Elkins, W. F., 'A Source of Black Nationalism in the Caribbean: The Revolt of the British West Indies Regiment at Taranto, Italy in 1918', *Science and Society* (1970), 99–103.

Englander, David and Osborne, James, 'Jack, Tommy and Henry Dubb: The Armed Forces and the Working Class', *Historical Journal* 21 (1978), 593–62.

Englander, David, 'Die Demobilmachung in Grossbritannien nach dem Ersten Weltkrieg', *Geschichte und Gesellschaft* 9 (1983), 195–210.

Englander, David, 'Mutiny and Myopia', *Bulletin of the Society for the Study of Labour History* 52 (1987), 5–7.

Englander, David, 'Military Intelligence and the Defence of the Realm: The Surveillance of Soldiers and Civilians in Britain during the First World War', *Bulletin of the Society for the Study of Labour History* 52 (1987), 24–32.

Englander, David, 'Troops and Trade Unions, 1919', *History Today* 37, 3 (1987), 8–13.

Englander, David, 'People at War: France, Britain and Germany, 1914–18 and 1939–45', *European History Quarterly* 18 (1988), 229–38.

Englander, David, 'The National Union of Ex-Servicemen and the Labour Movement, 1918–20', *History* 76 (1991), 24–42.

Englander, David, 'Soldiering and Identity: Reflections on the Great War', *War and History* 1 (1994), 300–18.

Englander, David, 'Discipline and Morale in the British Army, 1917–18', in Horne (ed.), *State, Society and Mobilisation*, 132–6.

Englander, David, 'Manpower in the British Army', in Canini (ed.), *Les Fronts Invisibles*, 93–102.

Evans, N., 'The Deaths of Qualified Staff Officers, 1914–18', *Journal of the Society for Army Historical Research* 78 (2000), 29–37.

Farr, Martin, 'A Compelling Case for Voluntarism: Britain's Alternative Strategy, 1915–16', *War in History* 9 (2002), 279–306.

Federowich, Kent, '"Society Pets and Morning Coated Farmers": Australian Soldier Settlement and the Participation of British Ex-servicemen, 1915–29', *War & Society* 8 (1990), 38–56.

Ferguson, Niall, 'Prisoner Taking and Prisoner Killing in the Age of Total War: Towards a Political Economy of Military Defeat', *War in History* 11 (2004), 148–92.

Ferris, John, 'The British Army and Signals Intelligence in the Field during the First World War', *Intelligence and National security* 3–4 (1988), 23–48.

Finn, Michael, 'Local Heroes: War News and the Construction of Community in Britain, 1914–18', *Historical Research* 83 (2010), 520–38.

Fitzpatrick, David, 'The Logic of Collective Sacrifice: Ireland and the British Army, 1914–18', *Historical Journal* 38 (1995), 1017–30.

Foley, Robert T. 'The Other Side of the Wire: The German Army in 1917', in Dennis and Grey (eds.), *1917*, 155–78.

Fox-Godden, Aimée, '"Hopeless Inefficiency"? The Transformation and Operational Performance of Brigade Staff, 1916–18', in Michael Locicero, Ross Mahoney and Stuart Mitchell (eds.), *A Military Transformed? Adaptation and Innovation in the British Military, 1792–1945* (Solihull: Helion, 2014), 139–56.

Fowler, Simon, 'War Charity Begins at Home', *History Today* 49 (1999), 17–23.

Fox-Golden, Aimée, 'Hopeless Inefficiency? The Transformation and Operational Performance of Brigade Staffs, 1916–18', in Locicero, Mahoney and Mitchell (eds.), *A Military Transformed*, 139–56.

Fraser, Peter, 'The British "Shells Scandal" of 1915', *Canadian Journal of History*, 28 (1983), 69–86.

French, David, 'Spy Fever in Britain, 1900–15', *Historical Journal* 21 (1978), 355–70.

French, David, 'The Military Background to the "Shell Crisis" of May 1915', *Journal of Strategic Studies* 2 (1979), 192–205.

French, David, 'The Origins of the Dardanelles Campaign Reconsidered', *History* 68 (1983), 210–24.

French, David, 'Sir John French's Secret Service on the Western Front, 1914–15', *Journal of Strategic Studies* 7 (1984), 423–40.

French, David, 'The Dardanelles, Mecca and Kut: Prestige as a Factor in British Eastern Strategy, 1914–16', *War & Society* 5 (1987), 45–61.

French, David, 'The Meaning of Attrition, 1914–16', *English Historical Review* 103 (1988), 385–405.

French, David, 'Watching the Allies: British Intelligence and the French Mutinies of 1917', *Intelligence and National Security* 6 (1991), 573–92.

French, David, '"A One-Man Show?" Civil-Military Relations in Britain during the First World War', in Smith (ed.), *Government and the Armed Forces in Britain*, 75–107.

French, David, 'Allies, Rivals, Enemies: British Strategy and War Aims during the First World War', in Turner (ed.), *Britain and the First World War*, 22–35.

Gardner, Nikolas, 'Command in Crisis: The BEF and the Forest of Mormal, August 1914', *War & Society* 16 (1998), 13–32.

Gibson, Craig, 'My Chief Source of Worry: An Assistant Provost Marshal's View of Relations between 2nd Canadian Division and Local Inhabitants on the Western Front, 1915–17', *War in History* 7 (2000), 413–41.

Gibson, Craig, 'Sex and Soldiering in France and Flanders: The BEF along the Western Front, 1914–19', *International History Review* 23 (2001), 535–79.

Gibson, Craig, 'The British Army, French Farmers and the War on the Western Front, 1914–18', *Past & Present* 180 (2002), 175–240.

Gilbert, Sandra M., 'A Soldier's Heart: Literary Men, Literary Women and the Great War', in Higonnet, Jenson, Michel and Collins (eds.), *Behind the Lines*, 197–226.

Gill, D., and Dallas, G., 'Mutiny at Etaples Base, 1917', *Past & Present* 69 (1975), 88–112.

Gooch, John, 'The Maurice Case', *Journal of Contemporary History* 3 (1968), 211–28.

Gooch, John, 'Soldiers, Strategy and War Aims in Britain, 1914–18', in Gooch (ed.), *Prospect of War*, 124–45.

Gooch, John, 'Haldane and the "National Army"', in Beckett and Gooch (eds.), *Politicians and Defence*, 69–86.

Grant, Peter, 'Edward Ward, Halford Mackinder and the Army Administration Course at the London School of Economics, 1907–14', in Michael Locicero, Ross Mahoney and Stuart Mitchell (eds.), *A Military Transformed? Adaption and Innovation in the British Military, 1792–1945* (Solihull: Hellion, 2014).

Graubard, S. R., 'Military Demobilisation in Great Britain Following the First World War', *Journal of Modern History* 19 (1947), 297–311.

Grayzel, Susan, 'The Outward and Visible Sign of Her Patriotism: Women, Uniform and National Service during the First World War', *Twentieth Century British History* 8 (1997), 145–64.

Greenhalgh, Elizabeth, 'Why the British Were on the Somme in 1916', *War in History* 6 (1999), 147–73.

Greenhalgh, Elizabeth, 'Parade-Ground Soldiers: French Army Assessments of the British on the Somme', *Journal of Military History* 63 (1999), 283–312.

Greenhalgh, Elizabeth, 'Flames over the Somme: A Retort to William Philpott', *War in History* 10 (2003), 335–42.

Greenhalgh, Elizabeth, '"Myth and Memory": Sir Douglas Haig and the Imposition of Allied Unified Command in March 1918', *Journal of Military History* 68 (2004), 771–820.

Greenwood, M., 'British Loss of Life in the Wars of 1794–1815 and 1914–18', *Journal of the Royal Statistical Society* 105 (1942), 1–16.

Gregory, Gregory, 'British War Enthusiasm in 1914: A Reassessment', in Braybon (ed.), *Evidence, History and the Great War*, 67–85.

Gregory, Adrian, '"You Might as Well Recruit Germans": British Public Opinion and the Decision to Conscript the Irish in 1918', in Gregory and Pašeta (eds.), *Ireland and the Great War*, 113–32.

Gregory, Adrian, 'Military Service Tribunals: Civil Society in Action, 1916–18', in Harris (ed.), *Civil Society*, 177–90.

Grieves, Keith, 'Military Tribunal Papers: The Case of Leek Tribunal in the First World War', *Archives* 16 (1983), 145–50.

Grieves, Keith, 'Total War: The Quest for a British Manpower Policy, 1917–18', *Journal of Strategic Studies* 9 (1986), 79–95.

Grieves. Keith, 'Mobilising Manpower: Audenshaw Tribunal in the First World War', *Manchester Region History Review* 3 (1989–90), 21–29.

Grieves, Keith, 'Making Sense of the Great War: Regimental Histories, 1918–23', *Journal of the Society for Army Historical Research* 69 (1991), 6–15.

Grieves, Keith, 'Lowther's Lambs: Rural Paternalism and Voluntary Recruitment in the First World War', *Rural History* 4 (1993), 55–75.

Grieves, Keith, 'Remembering an Ill-Fated Venture: The 4th Battalion, Royal Sussex Regiment at Suvla Bay and its Legacy, 1915–39', in Macleod (ed.), *Gallipoli*, 110–24.

Griffith, Paddy, 'The Tactical Problem: Infantry, Artillery and the Salient', in Liddle (ed.), *Passchendaele in Perspective*, 61–72.

Griffith, Paddy, 'The Lewis Gun Made Easy: The Development of Automatic Rifles in the Great War', *The Great War* 3 (1991), 108–15.

Gullace, Nicoletta, 'White Feathers and Wounded Men: Female Patriotism and the Memory of the Great War', *Journal of British Studies* 36 (1997), 178–206.

Harris, J. Paul and Marble, Sanders, 'The Step-by-Step Approach: British Military Thought and Operational Method on the Western Front, 1915–17', *War in History* 15 (2008), 17–42.

Harrison, Mark, 'The British Army and the Problem of Venereal Disease in France and Egypt during the First World War', *Medical History* 39 (1995), 133–58.

Hartigan, John, 'Volunteering in the First World War: The Birmingham Experience, August 1914 to May 1915', *Midland History* 24 (1999), 167–86.

Hiley, Nicholas, '"Kitchener Wants You", and "Daddy, What Did You Do in the War": The Myth of British Recruiting Posters', *Imperial War Museum Review* 11 (1997), 40–58.

Hodges, Paul, 'The Plight of Belgium and the British Soldier', in Serge Jaumain, Michaël Amara, Benoît Majerus and Antoon Vrints (eds.), *Une Guerre Totale? La Belgique dans la Première Guerre Mondiale* (Brussels: Archives générales du Royaume, 2005), 367–76.

Hodgkinson, Peter, 'The Infantry Battalion Commanding Officers of the BEF', in Jones (ed.), *Stemming the Tide*, 293–313.

Holland, Robert, 'The British Empire and the Great War', in Brown and Louis (eds.), *The Oxford History of the British Empire*, 114–37.

Hopkins, John, 'The Asylum War Hospitals Scheme: Crises and Solutions in the Treatment of Great War Casualties', *Stand To* 75 (2006), 19–25.

Housden, Christine, 'Kingston's Military Tribunal, 1916–18', *Occasional Papers in Local History* (Kingston University: Centre for Local History Studies, 2004).

Howard, Michael, 'Empire, Race and War in Pre-1914 Britain', *History Today* 31(12) (1981), 4–11.

Howie, David and Howie, Josephine, 'Irish Recruiting and the Home Rule Crisis of August-September 1914', in Dockrill and French (eds.), *Strategy and Intelligence*, 1–22.

Hughes, Clive, 'The New Armies', in Beckett and Simpson (eds.), *Nation in Arms*, 99–126.

Hussey, John, 'The Deaths of Qualified Staff Officers in the Great War: A Generation Missing?' *Journal of the Society for Army Historical Research* 75 (1997), 246–59.

Hussey, John, 'A Hard Day at First Ypres: The Allied Generals and their Problems, 31 October 1914', *British Army Review* 107 (1994), 70–89.

Hussey, John, 'Haig's Ride Up the Menin Road at First Ypres on 31 October 1914: Did He Invent the Whole Story?' *Bulletin of the Military Historical Society* 46 (1995), 1–29.

Jackson, Jacqueline, 'The 1919 Riots', in Panayi (ed.), *Racial Violence in Britain*, 92–111.

Jeffery, Keith 'The Post-War Army', in Beckett and Simpson (eds.), *Nation in Arms*, 212–234.

Jenkinson, Jacqueline, '"All in the Same Uniform": The Participation of Black Colonial Residents in the British Armed Forces in the First World War', *Journal of Imperial and Commonwealth History* 40 (2012), 207–50.

Johnson, Matthew, 'The Liberal War Committee and the Liberal Advocacy of Conscription in Britain, 1914–16', *Historical Journal* 51 (2008), 399–420.

Jones, Heather, 'The Final Logic of Sacrifice? Violence in German Prisoner of War Labour Companies in 1918', *The Historian* 68 (2006), 770–91.

Jones, Simon, 'Under a Green Sea: The British Response to Gas Warfare', *The Great War* 1 (1989), 126–32; 2 (1992), 14–21.

Jones, Simon, 'Gas Warfare: The British Defensive Measures – The Second Battle of Ypres', *Stand To* 14 (1985), 15–23.

Jones, Spencer, 'The Thin Khaki Line: The Evolution of Infantry Attack Formations in the British Army, 1899–1902', in Locicero, Mahoney and Mitchell (eds.), *A Military Transformed*, 83–96.

Jones, Spencer and Corvi, Steven J., '"A Commander of Rare and Unusual Coolness": Lieutenant General Sir Horace Lockwood Smith-Dorrien', in Jones (ed.), *Stemming the Tide*, 151–70.

Jones, Spencer, '"The Demon": Brigadier General Charles Fitzclarence, VC', in Jones (ed.), *Stemming the Tide*, 240–62.

Joseph, C. L., 'The British West Indies Regiment, 1914–18', *Journal of Caribbean History* 2 (1971), 94–124.

Justice, Simon, 'Vanishing Battalions: The Nature, Impact and Implications of British Infantry Reorganisation Prior to the German Spring Offensives of 1918', in Locicero, Mahoney and Mitchell (eds.), *A Military Transformed*, 157–73.

Kennedy, Paul, 'Strategy versus Finance in Twentieth Century Britain', *International History Review* 3 (1981), 44–61.

Killingray, David, 'All the King's Men: Blacks in the British Army in the First World War, 1914–18', in Lotz and Pegg (eds.), *Under the Imperial Carpet*, 164–81.

Kosmin, Barry A., Waterman, Stanley, and Grizzard, Nigel, 'The Jewish Dead in the Great War as an Indicator for the Location, Size and Social Structure of Anglo-Jewry in 1914', *Immigrants and Minorities* 5 (1986), 181–92.

Lammers, C. J., 'Strikes and Mutinies: A Comparative Study of Organisational Conflicts between Rulers and Ruled', *Administrative Science Quarterly* 14 (1969), 558–72.

Lawrence, Jon, 'Forging a Peaceable Kingdom: War, Violence and the Fear of Brutalisation in Post-First World War Britain', *Journal of Modern History* 75 (2003), 557–89.

Lee, John, 'Some Lessons of the Somme: The British Infantry in 1917', in Bond (ed.), *Look to Your Front*, 79–88.

Lee, John, 'The British Divisions at Third Ypres', in Liddle (ed.), *Passchendaele in Perspective*, 215–27.

Leed, E. J., 'Class and Disillusionment in World War I', *Journal of Modern History* 50 (1978), 680–99.

Leeson, David, 'The Scum of London's Underworld? British Recruits for the Royal Irish Constabulary, 1920–21', *Contemporary British History* 17 (2003), 1–38.

Leonard, Jane, '"Getting Them at Last": The IRA and Ex-Servicemen', in David Fitzpatrick (ed.), *Revolution? Ireland, 1917–23* (Dublin: Trinity History Workshop, 1999), 118–29.

Levine, Philippa, '"Walking the Streets in a Way No Decent Woman Should": Women Police in World War I', *Journal of Modern History* 66 (1994), 34–78.

Lloyd, Anne, 'Between Integration and Separation: Jews and Military Service in World War I', *Jewish Culture and History* 12 (2010), 41–60.

Locicero, Michael, '"A Tower of Strength": Brigadier General Edward Bulfin', in Jones (ed.), *Stemming the Tide*, 211–39.

Lockwood, Carol A., 'From Soldier to Peasant? The Land Settlement Scheme in East Sussex, 1919–39', *Albion* 30 (1998), 439–62.

Macleod, Rory, 'Sight and Sound on the Western Front: Surveyors, Scientists and the Battlefield Laboratory, 1915–18', *War & Society* 18 (2000), 23–46.

Mackenzie, S. P., 'Morale and the Cause: The Campaign to Shape the Outlook of Soldiers of the BEF, 1914–18', *Canadian Journal of History* 25 (1990), 215–31.

Mackenzie, S. P., 'The Ethics of Escape: British Officer POWs in the First World War', *War in History* 15 (2008), 1–16.

Mackinder, H. J., 'The Geographical Pivot of History', *Geographical Journal* 23 (1904), 421–44.

Madigan, Edward, '"Sticking to a Hateful Task": Resilience, Humour and British Understandings of Combatant Courage, 1914–18', *War in History* 20 (2013), 76–98.

Mansfield, Nicholas, 'Volunteering and Recruiting', in Gliddon (ed.), *Norfolk and Suffolk in the Great War*, 18–31.

Mathew, William, 'Wartime Contingency and the Balfour Declaration of 1917: An Improbable Regression', *Journal of Palestine Studies* 40 (2011), 26–42.

McCarthy, Chris, 'Queen of the Battlefield: The Development of Command Organisation and Tactics in the British Infantry Battalion during the Great War', in Sheffield and Todman (eds.), *Command and Control*, 173–94.

McCartney, Helen, 'Interpreting Unit Histories: Gallipoli and After', in Macleod (ed.), *Gallipoli*, 125–35.

McConel, James, 'Recruiting Sergeants for John Bull? Irish Nationalist MPs and Enlistment during the Early Months of the Great War', *War in History* 14 (2007), 408–38.

McDermott, James, 'Conscience and the Military Service Tribunals in the First World War: Experiences in Northamptonshire', *War in History* 17 (2010), 60–85.

McDermott, John, 'The Revolution in British Military Thinking from the Boer War to the Moroccan Crisis', *Canadian Journal of History* 9 (1974), 159–78.

Miller, Caroline, and Roche, Michael, 'New Zealand's New Order: Town Planning and Soldier Settlement after the First World War', *War & Society* 21 (2003), 63–82.

Millman, Brock, '"A Counsel of Despair": British Strategy and War Aims, 1917–18', *Journal of Contemporary History* 36 (2001), 241–70.

Mitchinson, K. W., 'The Reconstitution of 169 Brigade, July to October 1916', *Stand To* 29 (1990), 8–11.

Mitchinson, K. W., 'The Transfer Controversy: Parliament and the London Regiment', *Stand To* 33 (1991), 29–32.

Monger, David, 'No Mere Silent Commander? Henry Horne and the Mentality of Command during the First World War', *Historical Research* 82 (2009), pp. 340–59.

Morris, A. J. A., 'Haldane's Army Reforms, 1906–08: The Deception of the Radicals', *History*, 56 (1971), 181.

Neilson, Keith, 'Kitchener: A Reputation Refurbished?' *Canadian Journal of History* 15 (1980), 207–27.

Neilson, Keith, 'Great Exaggerated: The Myth of the Decline of Great Britain before 1914', *International History Review* 13 (1991), 695–725.

Nelson, Robert, 'Soldier Newspapers: A Useful Source in the Social and Cultural History of the First World War and Beyond', *War in History* 17 (2010), 167–91.

O'Connor, Damian, 'The Lion and the Swallow: The Somalialand Field Force, 1901–1920', *Royal United Services Institution Journal*, 151(5) (2006), 68–73.

Oram, Gerald, '"The Administration of Discipline by the English Is Very Rigid": British Military Law and the Death Penalty, 1858–1918', *Crime, History and Societies* 5 (2001), 93–110.

Oram, Gerald, 'Pious Perjury: Discipline and Morale in the British Forces in Italy, 1917–18', *War in History* 9 (2002), 412–30.

Osborne, John M., 'Defining their Own Patriotism: British Volunteer Training Corps in the First World War', *Journal of Contemporary History* 23 (1988), 59–75.

Ouditt, Sharon, 'Tommy's Sisters: The Representation of Working Women's Experience', in Cecil and Liddle (eds.), *Facing Armageddon*, 736–51.

Palazzo, Albert P., 'The British Army's Counter Battery Staff Office and Control of the Enemy in World War I', *Journal of Military History* 63 (1999), 55–74.

Payne, Emily, 'The Battle against Venereal Disease in Wartime Britain', *Stand To* 76 (2006), 9–12.

Perry, Nicholas, 'Nationality in the Irish Infantry Regiments in the First World War', *War & Society* 12 (1994), 65–95.

Perry, Nicholas, 'Maintaining Regimental Identity in the Great War: The Case of the Irish Infantry Regiments', *Stand To* 54 (1998), 5–11.

Petter, Martin, '"Temporary Gentlemen" in the Aftermath of the Great War: Rank, Status and the Ex-Officer Problem', *Historical Journal*, XXXVII(1) (1994).

Phillips, Gervase, 'Dai Bach Y Soldiwr: Welsh Soldiers in the British Army, 1914–18', *Llafur* 6 (1993), 94–105.

Philpott, William, 'The Strategic Ideas of Sir John French', *Journal of Strategic Studies* 12 (1989), 455–78.

Philpott, William, 'Kitchener and the 29th Division: A Study in Anglo-French Strategic Relations, 1914–15', *Journal of Strategic Studies* 16 (1993), 375–407.

Philpott, William, 'Britain and France Go to War: Anglo-French Relations on the Western Front, 1914–18', *War in History* 23 (1995), 43–64.

Philpott, William, 'Why the British Were Really on the Somme: A Reply to Elizabeth Greenhalgh, *War in History*, 9 (2002), 446–71.

Pollins, Harold, 'Jews in the British Army in the First World War', *Jewish Journal of Sociology* 37 (1995), 100–11.

Powell, J. M., 'Soldier Settlement in New Zealand, 1915–23', *Australian Geographical Studies* 9 (1971), 144–60.

Powell, J. M., 'The Debt of Honour: Soldier Settlement in the Dominions, 1915–40', *Journal of Australian Studies* 5 (1980), 64–87.

Poynter, Denise, '"Regeneration" Revisited: W. H. R. Rivers and Shell Shock during the Great War', in Hughes and Seligmann (eds.), *Leadership in Conflict*, 227–44.

Prete, Roy A., 'French Strategic Planning and the Deployment of the BEF in France in 1914', *Canadian Journal of History* 24 (1989), 42–62.

Purseigle, Pierre, 'Beyond and Below the Nations: Towards a Comparative History of Local Communities at War', in Macleod and Purseigle (eds.), *Uncovered Fields*, 95–123.

Prete, Roy A., 'Joffre and the Origins of the Somme: A Study in Allied Military Planning', *Journal of Military History* 73 (2009), 417–48.

Putkowski, Julian, 'Toplis, Etaples and the "Monocled Mutineer"', *Stand To* 18 (1986), 6–11.

Rawcliffe, Michael, 'Population', in Yates (ed.), *Kent in the Twentieth Century*, 1–26.

Reid, Fiona, 'Playing the Game to the Army: The RAMC, Shellshock and the Great War', *War & Society* 23 (2005), 61–86.

Reuther, John, 'Freemasonry and the Great War', *Ars Quatuor Coronatorum* 111(199) (1998), 188–95.

Robert, Krisztina, 'Gender, Class and Patriotism: Women's Paramilitary Units in First World War Britain', *International History Review* 19 (1997), 52–65.

Robert, Krisztina, 'Constructions of "Home", "Front", and Women's Military Employment in First World War Britain: A Spatial Interpretation', *History and Theory* 52 (2013), 319–43.

Ryan, W. Michael, 'The invasion controversy of 1906–8: Lieutenant-Colonel Charles à Court Repington and British Perceptions of the German Menace', *Military Affairs*, 44(1) (1980).

Schneider, Eric F., 'The British Red Cross Wounded and Missing Enquiry Bureau: A Case of Truth-Telling in the Great War', *War in History* 4 (1997), 296–315.

Schultz, J. A., 'Finding Homes fit for Heroes: The Great War and Empire Settlement', *Canadian Journal of History* 18 (1983), 99–110.

Schweitzer, Richard, 'The Cross and the Trenches: Religious Faith and Doubt among some British Soldiers on the Western Front', *War & Society* 16 (1998), 33–58.

Scott, Peter, 'Captive Labour: The German Companies of the BEF, 1916–20', *Army Quarterly and Defence Journal* 110 (1980), 319–31.

Scott, Peter, 'The Staff of the BEF', *Stand To!* 15 (1985), 44–61.

Scott, Peter, 'Mr Stokes and His Educated Drainpipe', *The Great War* 2 (1990), 80–95.

Senior, Michael, 'The Price of Fags', *Stand To* 78 (2007), 30–1.

Shaw, Diana, 'The Forgotten Army of Women: The Overseas Service of Queen Mary's Army Auxiliary Corps with the British Forces, 1917–21', in Cecil and Liddle (eds.), *Facing Armageddon*, 365–79.

Sheffield, Gary, 'The Effect of The Great War on Class Relations in Britain: The Career of Major Christopher Stone', *War & Society* 7 (1989), 87–105.

Sheffield, Gary, 'British Military Police and their Battlefield Role, 1914–18', *Sandhurst Journal of Military Studies* 1 (1990), 33–46.

Sheffield, Gary, 'An Army Commander on the Somme: Hubert Gough', in Sheffield and Todman (eds.), *Command and Control*, 71–98.

Sheffield, Gary, 'Haig and the British Expeditionary Force in 1917', in Dennis and Grey (eds.), *1917*.

Simkins, Peter, 'Co-Stars or Supporting Cast? British Divisions in "The Hundred Days", 1918', in Griffith (ed.), *British Fighting Methods*, 50–69.

Simkins, Peter, '"Building Blocks": Aspects of Command and Control at Brigade Level in the BEF's Operations, 1916–1918', in Sheffield and Todman (eds.), *Command and Control*, 141–72.

Simkins, Peter, 'Soldiers and Civilians: Billeting in Britain and France', in Beckett and Simpson (eds.), *Nation in Arms*, 165–92.

Simkins, 'Haig and the Army Commanders', in Bond and Cave (eds.), *Haig*, 78–97.

Simkins, Peter, '"Each One a Pocket Hercules": The Bantam Experiment and the Case of the 35th Division', in Marble (ed.), *Scraping the Barrel*, 79–104.

Simpson, Andy, 'British Corps Command on the Western Front, 1914–1918', in Sheffield and Todman (eds.), *Command and Control*, 97–118.

Simpson, Keith, 'Dr. Dunn and Battle Stress: The Experiences of a Regimental Medical Officer of 2nd Royal Welch Fusiliers, 1915–18', *The Great War* 3 (1991), 76–86.

Simpson, Keith, 'Dr. James Dunn and Shell-Shock', in Cecil and Liddle (eds.), *Facing Armageddon*, 502–22.

Simpson, Keith, 'The British Soldier on the Western Front', in Liddle (ed.), *Home Fires and Foreign Fields*, 135–58.

Simpson, Keith, 'The Officers', in Beckett and Simpson (eds.), *Nation in Arms*, 63–98.

Slocombe, Ivor, 'Recruitment into the Armed Forces during the First World War: The Work of Military Tribunals in Wiltshire', *Local Historian* 30 (2000), 105–23.

Sneddon, John Mason Sneddon, 'The Company Commanders', in Jones (ed.), *Stemming the Tide*, 314–31.

Spencer, John, '"The Big Brain in the Army": Sir William Robertson as Quartermaster General', in Jones (ed.), *Stemming the Tide*, 89–108.

Spiers, E. M., 'The Late Victorian Army 1868–1914', in Chandler and Beckett (eds.), *Oxford History of the British Army*, 187–212.

Spiers, E. M., 'The Regular Army', in Beckett and Simpson (eds.), *Nation in Arms*, 37–61.

Spiers, E. M., 'The Scottish Soldier at War', in Cecil and Liddle (eds.), *Facing Armageddon*, 314–35.

Spiers, E. M. 'University Officers Training Corps and the First World War', COMEC Occassional Paper No. 4, Reading, 2014.

Spinks, Peter, 'The War Courts: The Stratford-upon-Avon Borough Tribunal, 1916–18', *Local Historian* 32 (2002), 377–92.

Spoerer, Mark, 'The Mortality of Allied Prisoners of War and Belgian Civilian Deportees in German Custody during the First World War: A Reappraisal of the Effects of Forced Labour', *Population Studies* 60 (2006), 121–36.

Springhall, J. O., 'The Boy Scouts, Class and Militarism in Relation to British Youth Movements, 1908–30', *International Review of Social History* 16 (1971), 125–58.

Strachan, Hew, 'The Battle of the Somme and British Strategy', *Journal of Strategic Studies* 21 (1998), 79–95.

Strachan, Hew, 'Liberalism and Conscription, 1789–1919', in Hew Strachan (ed.), *The British Army: Manpower and Society into the Twenty-First Century* (London: Frank Cass, 2000).

Strachan, Hew, 'The British Army, its General Staff and the Continental Commitment, 1904–14', in French and Holden Reid (eds.), *British General Staff*, 75–94.

Taylor, Justine, 'Preserving Property and Privilege: The formation of the Territorial Army and the HAC Act of 1908', *Honourable Artillery Company Journal*, 85 (2008), 474.

Teagarden, E. M., 'Lord Haldane and the Origins of the Officer Training Corps', *Journal of the Society for Army Historical Research*, XLV(182) (1967).

Todman, Dan, 'The Grand Lamasery Revisited: General Headquarters on the Western Front 1914–1918', in Sheffield and Todman (eds.), *Command and Control*, 39–70.

Towle, Philip, 'The Russo-Japanese War and British Military Thought', *Journal of the Royal United Services Institute for Defence Studies* 116 (1971), 64–8.

Travers, Tim, 'The Offensive and the Problem of Innovation in British Military Thought, 1870–1915', *Journal of Contemporary History* 13 (1978), 531–53.

Travers, Tim, 'The Hidden Army: Structural Problems in the British Officer Corps, 1900–18', *Journal of Contemporary History* 17 (1982), 523–44.

Travers, Tim, 'Learning and Decision-Making on the Western Front, 1915–16: The British Example', *Canadian Journal of History* 18 (1983), 87–97.

Travers, Tim, 'A Particular Style of Command: Haig and GHQ, 1916–18', *Journal of Strategic Studies* 10 (1987), 363–76.

Travers, Tim, 'The Evolution of British Strategy and Tactics on the Western Front in 1981: GHQ, Manpower and Technology', *Journal of Military History* 54 (1990), 173–200.

Travers, Tim, 'Could the Tanks of 1918 Have Been War-Winners for the British Expeditionary Force?' *Journal of Contemporary History* 27 (1992), 389–406.

Travers, Tim, 'Command and Leadership Styles in the British Army: The 1915 Gallipoli Model', *Journal of Contemporary History* 29 (1994), 403–42.

Tucker, A., 'The issue of army reform in the Unionist government, 1903–5', *Historical Journal* 9(1) (1966).

Turner, John, 'Lloyd George, the War Cabinet, and High Politics', in Liddle (ed.), *Passchendaele in Perspective*, 14–30.

Ulrichsen, Kristian, 'The British Occupation of Mesopotamia, 1914–22', *Journal of Strategic Studies* 30 (2007), 349–77.

Vandiver, Frank E., 'Field Marshal Sir Douglas Haig and the Generals', in Liddle (ed.), *Passchendaele in Perspective*, 30–44.

Veitch, Colin, '"Play Up! Play Up! And Win the War": Football, the Nation and the First World War, 1914–15', *Journal of Contemporary History* 20 (1985), 363–78.

Ward, A. J., 'David Lloyd George and the Irish Conscription Crisis', *Historical Journal* 17 (1974), 107–29.

Ward, Stephen R, 'The British Veterans' Ticket of 1918', *Journal of British Studies* 8 (1968), 155–69.

Ward, Stephen R., 'Intelligence Surveillance of British Ex-servicemen, 1918–20', *Historical Journal* 16 (1973), 179–88.

Ward, Stephen R., 'Great Britain: Land Fit for Heroes Lost', in Ward (ed.), *War Generation*, 10–37.

Watson, Alex and Porter, Patrick, 'Bereaved and Aggrieved: Combat Motivation and the Ideology of Sacrifice in the First World War', *Historical Research* 83 (2010), 146–64.

Watson, Janet, 'Khaki Girls, VADs and Tommy's Sisters: Gender and Class in First World War Britain', *International History Review* 19 (1997), 32–51.

White, Bonnie, 'Volunteerism and Early Recruitment Efforts in Devonshire, August 1914 to December 1915', *Historical Journal* 52 (2009), 641–66.

Whitmarsh, Andrew, 'The Development of Infantry Tactics in the British 12th (Eastern) Division, 1915–1918', *Stand To* 48 (January 1997), 28–32.

Wilson, Janet, 'Wars in the Wards: The Social Construction of Medical Work in First World War Britain', *Journal of British Studies* 41 (2002), 484–510.

Wilson, Keith, 'The Anglo-Japanese Alliance of August 1905 and the Defending of India', *Journal of Imperial and Commonwealth History* 21 (1993), 314–56.

Winter, Jay, 'Britain's Lost Generation of the First World War', *Population Studies* 31 (1977), 449–66.

Winter, Jay, 'Some Aspects of the Demographic Consequences of the First World War in Britain', *Population Studies* 30 (1976), 539–62.

Winter, Jay, 'Military Fitness and Civilian Health in Britain during the First World War', *Journal of Contemporary History* 15 (1980), 211–44.

Winter, Jay, 'Army and Society: The Demographic Context', in Beckett and Simpson (eds.), *Nation in Arms*, 193–210.

Winter, Jay, 'Oxford and the First World War' in Brian Harrison (ed.), *The History of Oxford*, Vol. VIII: *The Twentieth Century* (Oxford: Clarendon Press, 1994).

Wood, Evelyn, *The Citizen Soldier* (London: privately printed, 1939).

Woodeson, Alison, 'The First Women's Police: A Force for Equality or Infringement?' *Women's History Review* 2 (1993), 217–32.

Woodward, David, 'The Origins and Intent of Lloyd George's January 5th War Aims Speech', *Historian* 34 (1971–2), 222–39.

Woodward, David, 'Britain in a Continental War: The Civil-Military Debate over the Strategic Direction of the War of 1914–18', *Albion* 12 (1980), 37–65.

Woodward, David, 'Did Lloyd George Starve the British Army of Men Prior to the German Offensive of 21 March 1918?' *Historical Journal* 27 (1984), 241–52.

Woollacott, Angela, 'Sisters and Brothers in Arms: Family, Class and Gendering in World War I Britain', in Cooke and Woollacott (eds.), *Gendering War Talk*, 128–47.

Worthington, Ian, 'Socialization, Militarization and Officer Recruiting: The Development of the Officers Training Corps', *Military Affairs*, 43(2) (1979).

Unpublished Theses

Blanch, M. D., 'Nation, Empire and the Birmingham Working Class, 1899–1914', unpublished PhD thesis, University of Birmingham, 1975.

Gale, Andy, 'The West Country and the First World War: Recruits and Identities', unpublished PhD thesis, University of Lancaster, 2010.

Good, Kit, 'England Goes to War, 1914–15', unpublished PhD thesis, University of Liverpool, 2002.

Hallifax, Stuart, 'Citizens at War: The Experience of the Great War in Essex, 1914–18', unpublished DPhil thesis, University of Oxford, 2010.

Hay, G. M., 'The British Yeomanry Cavalry, 1794–1920', unpublished PhD thesis, University of Kent, 2011.

Hodgkinson, P. E., 'British Infantry Battalion Commanders in the First World War', unpublished PhD thesis, University of Birmingham, 2013.

Hughes, Clive, 'Army Recruiting in Gwynedd, 1914–16', unpublished MA thesis, University of Wales, 1983.

Lynch, P. J., 'The Exploitation of Courage: Psychiatric Care in the British Army, 1914–18', unpublished MPhil thesis, University of London, 1977.

Mack, A. R., 'Conscription and Conscientious Objection in Leeds and York during the First World War', unpublished MPhil thesis, University of York, 1983.

Moon, Howard, 'The Invasion of the United Kingdom: Public Controversy and Official Planning, 1888–1918', unpublished PhD thesis, University of London, 1968.

Morris, Patricia, 'Leeds and the Amateur Military Tradition: The Leeds Rifles and Their Antecedents, 1859–1918', unpublished PhD thesis, University of Leeds, 1983.

Saunders, Anthony. 'A Muse of Fire: British Trench Warfare Munitions, Their Invention, Manufacture and Tactical Employment on the Western Front, 1914–18', unpublished PhD thesis, University of Exeter, 2008.

Townley, Helen, 'The First World War and Voluntary Recruitment: A Form for Regional Identity? An Analysis of the Nature, Expression and Significance of Regional Identity in Hull, 1900–16', unpublished PhD thesis, University of Sussex, 2007.

Wilson, J. Brent, 'The Morale and Discipline of the BEF, 1914–18', unpublished MA thesis, University of New Brunswick, 1978.

Young, Derek Rutherford, 'Voluntary Recruitment in Scotland, 1914–16', unpublished PhD thesis, University of Glasgow, 2001.

Index

For EU product safety concerns, contact us at Calle de José Abascal, 56–1°,
28003 Madrid, Spain or eugpsr@cambridge.org.

www.ingramcontent.com/pod-product-compliance
Ingram Content Group UK Ltd.
Pitfield, Milton Keynes, MK11 3LW, UK
UKHW020404140625
459647UK00020B/2635

* 9 7 8 0 5 2 1 1 8 3 7 4 1 *